Transformations

IMMIGRATION, FAMILY LIFE, AND ACHIEVEMENT MOTIVATION AMONG LATINO ADOLESCENTS

D1300793

TRANS-

Carola and Marcelo Suárez-Orozco

FORMATIONS

Immigration, Family Life, and
Achievement Motivation Among
Latino Adolescents

Stanford University Press
Stanford, California
1995

Stanford University Press
Stanford, California

© 1995 by the Board of Trustees of the
Leland Stanford Junior University

Printed in the United States of America

CIP data are at the end of the book

Stanford University Press publications are
distributed exclusively by Stanford University
Press within the United States, Canada, Mexico,
and Central America; they are distributed
exclusively by Cambridge University Press
throughout the rest of the world.

For Marisa and Lucas

and all children of immigrants

Acknowledgments

We conceived this book during a series of conversations in the old colonial towns of Guanajuato in the heart of the Mexican republic. Walking past colorful bougainvillea and aromatic market stalls, we began to articulate the position that the field of immigration was in urgent need of comparative, interdisciplinary, and transnational research. In those early conversations, Carola noted that no important psychosocial studies had yet compared the characteristics and experiences of potential Mexican emigrants who ultimately leave in search of opportunities "up north" with those of their compatriots who stay behind. How might emigrants differ, if at all, from nonemigrants? We thought that by examining the lives of those who *might* emigrate, and how their experiences differ from those who *do*, we might be able to say something interesting about the vicissitudes of immigration—a topic that has come to capture with some fury many of the paradoxes and contradictions of the postindustrial era.

Those early casual conversations slowly came into sharper focus. One result—and there will be others—is this book. Many individuals in Mexico, the United States, and Europe were highly instrumental in the making of this project. It is a privilege to thank these individuals, institutions, and agencies.

In Mexico, the Maxwell family, especially "Lucha" and Roberto, helped open important doors for us. During early conversations about our emerging ideas for a research project comparing the experiences of adolescents in Mexico with the experiences of immigrant and Mexican American adolescents in California, Señora Lucha wanted to know whether this project would help Mexicans in the

United States. Señora Lucha, along with many other Mexicans who helped us during the Mexico-based phase of our research, saw helping us as an indirect way of helping Mexican immigrants making their way to the United States. Keenly aware of the limitations of our own influence, we stressed that although we hoped our research could be useful to those working with Mexican immigrants—particularly in schools—we could not guarantee any direct results. In spite of this, Señora Lucha put considerable energy into helping us get the project off the ground. The symbolic meaning of Lucha's name should not be overlooked. "Lucha," meaning "struggle" in Spanish, is also the term Mexican immigrants often use to refer to their journey north— *"hacer la lucha."*

Through Señora Lucha, we met the principals of various schools until we found the school most appropriate to house our research. The principal, Señor Leonardi, confirmed that over the years many of his students had emigrated to the United States and welcomed us into his school. Through him we were led to teachers, staff, students, and parents—far too many to name individually here. A simple collective *gracias* will have to do.

In Mexico a central concern of many of those helping us was how our study might aid Mexican immigrants in the United States; in California the concern was decidedly different. One U.S. assistant superintendent was eager to have us work in some schools in his district, "but only if you are objective," he said, "and don't blame the schools for *their* problems." One of the U.S. principals we interviewed was puzzled by an unsettling phenomenon: immigrant kids arrive full of hope and a desire to learn, and with time they become "more like American kids." He did not mean this to be a compliment. Rather he was expressing frustration that the more "assimilated" kids are more difficult to manage than the new arrivals.

We wish to thank the assistant superintendent, the principals, the staff, and the teachers—particularly the staff and teachers of the English as a Second Language programs—and, of course, the students, who shared their experiences with us. *Muchas gracias y adelante.*

Our research was funded by many institutions. Generous grants from the Academic Senate Committee on Research of the University of California, San Diego, and the University of California Consortium on Mexico and the United States made the first phase of this study possible. The Mellon Foundation, the National Science Foundation, the Center for German and European Studies at the

University of California, Berkeley, and the Spencer Foundation also provided funding. We are grateful to all of them.

We completed the first draft of this book at the Center for Advanced Study in the Behavioral Sciences at Stanford in 1992–93. We thank the staff of the center, and particularly Bob Scott and Phil Converse, for making our stay there such an enjoyable intellectual experience. We are grateful for financial support from the John D. and Catherine T. MacArthur Foundation, grant number 8900078.

We were very fortunate to have had the opportunity to present many of the ideas in this book to our academic colleagues. We presented parts of Chapter 1 at two international conferences, one at U.C. San Diego's Center for U.S.-Mexican Studies in March 1992 and one at the Graduate School of Education at the University of Wisconsin, Madison, in January 1993; parts of Chapters 2, 4, and 5 at a conference on immigrant students in California schools at the Center for U.S.-Mexican Studies at the University of California, San Diego (January 1993); parts of Chapters 3, 4, and 5 at the Center for Advanced Study in the Behavioral Sciences at Stanford (April 1993), the Department of Psychology at the University of California, Santa Cruz (May 1993), the California School of Professional Psychology in San Diego (May 1993), the Department of Social Psychology at the University of Barcelona (October 1993), and the Department of Human Development at Harvard University (March 1994); and parts of Chapter 3 at an international conference jointly sponsored by the Centre National de la Rechèrche Scientifique (Paris) and the Fundación "la Caixa" held in Barcelona (October 1993).

The collaboration and support of many others was crucial to us as well. We are eternally grateful to all of you:

Our research assistants, C. R. Hibbs, Yolanda James, Sandy McMullen, Julie Nemiroff, and Martina Will, all did an excellent job. Without them this project would have taken years longer to complete.

Cathy Asciutto, Leslie Becker, Ben Lungen, and Erin Stanford were efficient and cheerful in conducting what was doubtless a tedious but essential task: systematically rating some of the psychological data.

Leo Chavez, Wayne Cornelius, Ron Gallimore, Jeff Passel, Alejandro Portes, Gene Roosens, and Dan Wolf kindly shared with us drafts of some of their own research findings in the field of immigration.

William Fals-Stewart, Lynn Gale, and Lincoln Moses provided crucial consultation for the statistical analyses.

Celia Falicov's wealth of clinical experience and culturally sensitive insight provided a seed of inspiration for this project. Richard Baker, Placida Gallegos, and Thomas McGee generously gave of their time and contributed many refinements. Bob and Sarah LeVine tactfully alerted us to a problem with an earlier version of the manuscript—its title!

We are most grateful for the support and inspiration that we received from Bob and Barbara Nemiroff, who first introduced us to lovely Guanajuato. George De Vos, Suzanne Lake De Vos, and Henry Trueba were—as usual—most generous with their time and wisdom and offered their enthusiastic support from the very beginning. Donald Hansen, Vicky Johnson, and Marcela and George Nazzari gave us crucial emotional *apoyo*, as they have done throughout our years of friendship.

And to the most significant products of our collaboration—our children, Marisa and Lucas, who generously shared so much time with this undertaking—thank you. *Los amamos*. We dedicate this book to you.

Contents

Tables

Foreword

HENRY T. TRUEBA

Carola and Marcelo Suárez-Orozco present us with a book that is not only unique and timely but totally out of the ordinary. It urges reflection in a powerful and eloquent way, and it does so not only about Latino population issues, which are its focus, but also about transcendental and universal matters: the nature of human solidarity, the type of American society in which we want to live, and our deepest personal and social values on race, ethnicity, education, and culture. This book is an authoritative, ambitious, cohesive, and far-reaching statement in the face of epistemological, ideological, and existential challenges confronted by humanity.

I have followed the work of Marcelo Suárez-Orozco for at least a decade. A young, creative, and brilliant scholar has gradually become a "maestro," a mature and distinguished scholar with a rare depth of knowledge and wisdom. This book shows the art of his scholarship, now matched by the fresh and imaginative approaches of Carola. Carola and Marcelo make an extraordinary team: Marcelo, a cultural anthropologist recognized as one of the most eminent in the field of psychological anthropology, and Carola, an insightful and expert clinician who understands the complexities of cross-cultural psychological research.

Their subject is none other than the very fabric of American democracy, which is changing under the impact of immigration during difficult times of social unrest and cultural confusion. Focusing on the process of ethnic identification and the achievement motivation of adolescents, the study compares adolescents with a Mexican cultural background (from native Mexicans in Mexico to

second-generation Mexican Americans) to white American mainstream adolescents. The study is placed within broad sociopolitical,
theoretical, and ethnohistorical and demographic contexts that help
the reader understand Latino adolescents. The sociopolitical context
is a global malaise over immigration, the theoretical context a disciplinary malaise over social science research. The ethnohistorical and
demographic context offers a rich and detailed description of Latino
populations in the United States.

The authors are well qualified to discuss immigration from a global
perspective because of their international experience and their familiarity with European immigration currents, especially in Belgium,
France, Germany, and Spain. Their knowledge about personality
structure and cultural ecological factors affecting academic achievement by immigrant and low-income students helps them explore
difficult issues involving Latino students in the United States: their
changing responses to American pressure for conformity in the face
of racism, exploitation, and rejection by mainstream society. The
authors examine American fears and dilemmas, providing flashing
insights and analytical comments extrapolated from the larger international context that help the readers understand the interpretation
of similar phenomena across cultures.

The authors start by pointing out the public malaise over immigration and the fears of mainstream Americans in the face of ethnic di-
versification. They compare the public paranoia of the 1880s, which
resulted in stereotyping and scapegoating, with that of the 1990s,
when we see similar effects. Under the "postindustrial paradox,"
nations in Europe and North America seek cheap foreign labor to
make their economies more internationally competitive, while rejecting laborers and their families socially and preventing them from
becoming part of the nation on the ground that the long-term presence of foreigners (especially people of color) puts ethnic and cultural purity at risk. Undocumented immigrants in America, most of
them brown, are clearly perceived as the cause of major economic
problems, and their substantial economic, social, and cultural contributions are trivialized or ignored. The Suárez-Orozcos call this
phenomenon, which is also occurring in Belgium, France, Germany,
and Spain, nativism, xenophobia, and even hysteria. This hysteria
is responsible for many random violent acts and crimes committed
by individuals driven by irrational fears and hatred, including white
youngsters, border patrol agents, and others who have not been prosecuted. Other kinds of less conspicuous violence and exploitation are
suffered in jobs demanding nine to twelve hours a day, seven days a
week, with inadequate pay. Politicians, argue the authors, have prof-

ited from public hatred, anxiety, and exploitation of immigrants. In California the anti-immigrant hysteria exists despite the fact that according to some studies undocumented workers pay more in federal taxes than they receive in government services. The authors argue that California is the victim not of undocumented workers but of unfair distribution of federal tax revenues.

The theoretical context in psychology and anthropology is a disciplinary malaise that questions the basic value and even the possibility of doing social science research. The authors strongly endorse the use of a variety of methodological research approaches: clinical and phenomenological, ethnographic, qualitative, quantitative, historical, theoretical-explanatory, and cross-cultural. Current debates by postmodernists single out anthropology and cross-cultural psychology as lacking objectivity and validity. Their criticisms of ethnography clearly ignore a century of substantial empirical research and longitudinal historical data and the legitimacy of ethnographic inquiry.

Understanding the limitations of research methodology allowed the authors to proceed with a careful design for data collection grounded on historical records, the use of various instruments, and clear analysis of the pursuit of comparative measures across cultures. The authors describe Latino populations in the United States in detail, including their demographic, social, economic, and cultural characteristics, as well as their socioeconomic diversity, adaptive strategies, hopes, efforts, and often disillusionment.

The study design is clear. There are four groups of adolescents: Mexican-born of Mexican parents, residing in Mexico; Mexican-born of Mexican parents, residing in the United States; second-generation Mexican American, born and raised in the United States of Mexican immigrant parents; and North American "mainstream" youth, white non-Hispanics born in and residing in the United States. The 189 adolescents who participated, ages 13–18 (mean age 15.7), 96 females and 93 males, were attending public schools at the middle or high school level. The study compares adolescents belonging to two baseline cultures (Anglo American and Mexican) and focuses on the impact of immigration on the Mexicans and Mexican Americans and their self-identity. The issues examined include level of familism, adherence to home culture and community culture, and concerns about poverty, school achievement, and conflict. Via psychological instruments (including the Thematic Apperception Test, the Problem Situation Test, the Sentence Completion Test, and others), the authors measured familism and family conflict and configured student profiles for purposes of cross-cultural comparisons. The psychological assessment of relationships with family, peers, and friends was done comparatively among the four groups of students.

All three groups of Mexican origin showed a similar level of familism, and a higher level than that of white Americans. Familism, which is contrasted with individualism, is related to enduring psychological features of the Latino population. In the stories narrated from TAT cards, family conflict was much less frequent among the Mexicans than among the white Americans. Also, the stories told by members of the Mexican and immigrant groups tended to resolve family conflicts, whereas those told by the Mexican Americans and white Americans tended to reach solutions independent of family. Mexican and immigrant students perceived greater emotional and material support from—and hence greater interdependence with—the family than did the other two groups. The immigrant students also had a sense of obligation to act as "cultural translators" for their parents. Family conflict was no higher for Mexican Americans than for the other Latino groups.

Among white American adolescents the authors found greater ambivalence toward and frustration with authority and schooling, greater concern with autonomy and independence, higher levels of family conflict, more of a peer group orientation, and less achievement motivation than among Mexican students in Mexico. Mexican adolescents showed more commitment to achieve and to help others, and a clear understanding of the relationship between hard work and success. Mexican immigrants were deeply committed to helping the family by achieving through hard work. Second-generation Mexican American students are truly transitional and live in two worlds. They revealed a strong family orientation and less family conflict than white students, but they felt ambivalent about authority and school, were less committed to achievement, and had less confidence in their ability to succeed.

The authors found that the Mexican and immigrant groups placed greater importance on education and academic achievement than did the white and Mexican American groups. For the Mexicans, achieving academically and working hard were means to show concern for parents. Latino adolescents in the United States were highly motivated, but their expectations for success were colored by experiences of societal hostility and discrimination. Therefore, they had problems cooperating with the educational institution. The authors point out that marginalization continues to grow among the second-generation Mexican Americans who develop "defensive" or "oppositional" identities and the feeling that minorities don't belong in the university. They analyze the case of Richard Rodriguez, who, in spite of his fame and successful career, still suffered from "a sense of shame, marginality, and alienation." He felt compelled to reject his culture, language, parents, and community in order to belong to mainstream American society, only to discover in the end that he was never accepted as American. He confesses that he found himself angry and retaliated by intentionally hurting his parents and Mexican friends.

In brief, immigrants bring talents and energy to their new homeland. Mexican immigrants want to learn and work hard to achieve their dreams, while maintaining a separate sense of identity. However, the violence, discrimination, and obstacles faced by immigrants affect their identity and commitment to learn, and exploitation and hostility affect their own sense of esteem.

This book makes many important contributions. Among other things, it:

- Points out the global malaise over immigration, race, ethnicity, and cultural differences and its particular form within the United States
- Presents a cross-cultural comparison that permits us to see in detail the differential personality configuration and intrapsychological structuring of adolescents' values changing over time as a function of this malaise
- Telescopes in a clever research design several generations of immigrants from the point of origin in Mexico until the final destiny in the United States
- Clearly shows the cumulative impact of racism and discrimination in American society
- Offers fine detail of differential attitudinal responses to various psychological tests and scales
- Shows further the erosion of traditional cultural values such as the cohesiveness and paramount importance of the family as the center of gravity for all social activities, as a source of motivation to achieve, and as the principal source of emotional support in times of crisis
- Gives an abrupt wake-up call to Americans to reassess their position on immigrants and reexamine their views on cultural values and the impact of exploitation and oppression
- Reaffirms the enormous resiliency of immigrants and their capacity to make lasting contributions to American democracy

Thus, this book opens the door for what George and Louise Spindler call "cultural therapy" and for what Paulo Freire calls the "pedagogy of hope." Freire states:

I cannot understand human existence and the necessary struggle to improve it, without hopes and dreams. Hope is an ontological need. As a
program [for action], lack of hope paralyses us and makes us fall into fatalism where it is impossible to muster the necessary strength in order to
fight for recreation of the world. I am not hopeful out of stubbornness,
but because of the existential and historical imperative. . . . Hope alone
cannot win a struggle, but without hope we will be weak and hesitate
in the struggle. We need critical hope, in the same way that a fish needs
clean water. (Freire 1993: 10)

Cultural therapy, as understood by the Spindlers, deals with a fundamental comprehension of the relationship between culture and politics, between education and ethnicity, between politics and learning
abilities. It also gets into the issues of cultural hegemony and the
need to recognize and respect our ethnic, linguistic, and cultural
identity, as well as our membership in a single human species. It recognizes the solidarity of humankind while respecting the diversity
of ethnic, cultural, religious, and historical backgrounds across and
within nations. George Spindler's *enduring self*, grounded to the key
values and norms learned in the early developmental years of life,
adjusts to change via the *situated self*, the new self-identification in
a given new environment that carries new cultural demands and behaviors. When the contrast and relationships between the enduring
self and the situated self become conflictive and confused, cultural
therapy can be of great help. Cultural therapy is a means of exploring
inner structural changes in the construction of the self-identity as an
adaptive individual response to psychological and cultural environmental changes and as a social response to oppressive forces focused
on ethnic, racial, or socioeconomic groups. The work of George and
Louise Spindler is truly complementary to this volume and provides
a logical follow-up.

Awareness of our psychological, ethnic, racial, and cultural
makeup resulting from cultural therapy needs to be taken to its
ultimate consequences. This is done via critical pedagogy, which is
intended to create a new ideology and a vigorous political movement
that links popular culture to educational reflective actions intended
to empower all individuals.

As McLaren states:

A critical pedagogy situates itself in the intersection of language, culture
and history—the nexus in which the students' subjectivities are formed,
contested, and played out. The struggle is one that involves their history,
their language, and their culture, and the pedagogical implications are
such that students are given access to a critical discourse or are condi-

tioned to accept the familiar as the inevitable. Worse still, they are denied a voice with which to be present in the world; they are made invisible to history and rendered powerless to shape it. (McLaren 1989: 233)

We must conceptualize a new social reality, but first we must become aware, as the authors have stressed in this volume, that the oppression and violence existing within the hegemonic relationships of dominant groups to some immigrant and minority groups have profoundly destructive consequences. Critical pedagogy is based on the principle that consciousness of oppression leads to awareness of a basic human right to one's own cultural rights, which should be respected and defended by all. The contributions of Carola and Marcelo to this end are indeed significant. They have made us aware of the need to construct a new social reality in the United States and in the entire world.

Transformations

IMMIGRATION, FAMILY LIFE, AND ACHIEVEMENT MOTIVATION AMONG LATINO ADOLESCENTS

Introduction

In virtually all major postindustrial societies, including the United States, Germany, France, and Belgium, few topics are as potentially explosive as legal and undocumented immigration, the growing number of asylum seekers, and the adaptation problems of the children of immigrants.[1] In the "age of diminished expectations" (Krugman 1994) many are asking: just how many new arrivals can a country accept? In the United States, an increasing number of Americans seem to find the answer in the categorical words of Dan Stein of the restrictionist Federation for American Immigration Reform, "We cannot accommodate even a fraction of the people who want to move here" (Weiner 1993: 1).

On both sides of the Atlantic, there is a widespread feeling that some countries of the world are sinking and that the islands of wealth in Europe and North America simply cannot rescue all those who need rescuing. The language of the new immigration is the apocalyptic language of deluge: ever-growing waves of immigrants from developing countries are said to be flooding the shores of the more developed world. In the United States this feeling feeds metaphorically on the seemingly routine reports of boats and rickety rafts carrying Chinese, Cuban, and Haitian asylum seekers toward the coasts of New York, Florida, and California.

A striking feature of the new immigration is the similarity of issues facing a number of countries—most of those in western Europe, the United States, and even Japan (Cornelius, Martin, and Hollifield 1994). Countries that in the recent past welcomed, indeed actively recruited, immigrant laborers, such as Belgium and France, are now swept by the hateful winds of xenophobia. Countries that until recently generously granted refuge, such as Germany, are now turning away asylum seekers.

A major new concern of immigration authorities throughout western Europe and in the United States is distinguishing bona fide asylum seekers—those motivated by a "well founded fear of persecution"—from those categorized as economic refugees who are escaping hunger and misery in search of a better life in the developed world.

During the cold war era, the matter of asylum was somewhat simpler: refugee policy was often used to embarrass and harass one's enemies (Conover 1993: 56–78). In the United States, for example, those fleeing communist regimes, such as Cuba's, clearly benefited from superpower tensions. On the other hand, those escaping brutal regimes closely allied with the United States, such as those of Guatemala and El Salvador, were much less likely to receive formal asylum (Suárez-Orozco 1989). With the cold war over, there is no longer such a clear, if morally dubious, formula.

There is another important dimension to the debate over the new arrivals: the significant shift in the demographic profile of those seeking refuge. It was one thing to grant refuge to a few high-profile ballerinas, sports stars, and professionals from the former Soviet bloc. It is quite another to grant refuge to large and increasing numbers of people of color seeking shelter from all sorts of terrors, including political, religious, and ethnic persecution. Numbers may speak louder than words: during the late 1960s and early 1970s the average number of asylum applications received by the United States was 200 per year. As we write in 1995, there is a backlog of 300,000 applications.

There is increasing evidence that in the United States and most of western Europe public opinion has turned decisively against all forms of immigration (Morganthau 1993; Caldwell 1993; Weiner 1993, 1994). Everywhere, a new kind of "stranger anxiety" seems to be on the rise. In the San Ysidro sector of the California/Mexico border, where every day the U.S. border patrol apprehends on average 1,400 undocumented migrants (and it is estimated that only half of those crossing the border are apprehended—see Caldwell 1993: 4), there are periodic "light up the border" events in which anti-immigrant groups gather with the high beams of their cars pointed toward the Mexican side of the border to protest "the invasion" of undocumented Mexicans and other Latin Americans.

Who are the new arrivals? What do they want? How are they adapting? Unfortunately, the anxieties about immigration are the source of a great deal of prejudice, ignorance, and confusion about these questions.

This study considers some of the typical concerns of Mexican adolescents who have not migrated, both those who are still in Mexico and those whose parents left Mexico but who themselves were born in the United States. We then ask: How does immigration to the United States affect Mexican-origin adolescents, and how do their concerns differ over time and space? How are the experiences of second-generation (the first generation of U.S.-born) Mexican American youths like and unlike those of their counterparts in Mexico? And how are the experiences of Mexican and Mexican-origin youths similar to (and different from) those of non-Hispanic white adolescents identified with "mainstream" American culture?

Latinos, also known as Hispanics, are the second-largest and the fastest-growing minority group in the United States. By early in the twenty-first century, it is projected that Latinos will outnumber African Americans as a result of both high fertility rates and continuing immigration. The most recent Bureau of the Census report (1990) calculates that during the 1980s the population of Hispanic origin grew "at a rate substantially higher than the population as a whole." Indeed, the report concludes that the Latino population grew "at a rate more than triple that of the entire population" (Hollman 1990: 3, 9). By the year 2025, the United States will have the second-largest population of Spanish speakers in the world.

Recent studies estimate that there are around 22.3 million Latinos living in the United States (Portes and Zhou 1993: 5). This figure does not, however, include the estimated 2 to 4 million "undocumented aliens," the great majority of whom are thought to be of Latino origin. In all, it is certain that there are more than 25 million Latinos residing permanently in the United States.

Demographers have projected that the Latino population in the United States will continue to grow at a fast pace (see Day 1992). There are two immediate reasons for this. First, Latinos are younger than the general population: according to 1988 census data the median age of non-Hispanic whites was 33.2, while the median age of Latinos was 25.8. Thus, Latinos tend to be at or nearing the prime child-bearing years. Latinos also make up the core of the "new" (post–1965 Immigration Act) immigrants (Portes and Zhou 1993). Indeed, "immigration from Latin America, the Caribbean and Asia, a trickle in 1965, has steadily widened so that it now comprises about 90 percent of the total" (Morganthau 1993: 22).

Another feature of the new immigration—found also in northwestern Europe—is the marked concentration of immigrants in certain geographic areas. In 1991, over 50 percent of all new immigrants to the United States settled in just three states: California (40 percent), Texas (12 percent), and Arizona (2 percent). Mexican immigrants make up the great majority of the new arrivals: in 1991, 86 percent of all legal immigrants into Arizona, 80 percent of all legal immigrants into Texas, and 69 percent of all legal immigrants into California were Mexicans.

There is a tendency, certainly by the media but also by some scholars, to collapse Latinos into a monolithic category. Although they share some characteristics, Latinos are a diverse demographic and sociocultural population. Some Latinos lived in what is today the American Southwest before the territories were taken from Mexico. Instead of their coming to the United States, the United States came to them.

The majority of Latinos are of more recent immigrant origin. Latinos come from many different countries and from different socioeconomic, educational, and professional backgrounds. Their experiences vary considerably depending on whether they enter the United States as documented or undocumented immigrants, whether they immigrate voluntarily or because of political persecution, whether they are seasonal migrants planning to return home or "settlers" who intend to reside in the United States more or less permanently, and whether they come to the United States as a family unit or as individuals. The number of generations in this country and their level of acculturation are also important influences on the Latino experience in the United States.

Immigrants from Mexico and U.S.-born Mexican Americans make up the largest group of Latinos in the United States. Over 60 percent of all Latinos are of Mexican ancestry (Portes and Zhou 1993: 5). This book focuses on their experiences. Our aim is to develop a theoretical framework for exploring some central psychosocial features of Latino immigration.

Immigration is a complex, multifaceted process involving economic, political, psychological, and other cultural factors. In this book we are particularly interested in analyzing two aspects of the immigrant's journey, an effort that we hope will inform the current debate over immigration. We explore some pivotal features of immigration and family life and immigration and the motivational dynamics of youths.

This study is the first attempt to systematically compare significant aspects of family life and motivational dynamics among Mexicans in Mexico, Mexican immigrants in California, first-generation U.S.-born Mexican Americans, and a comparable group of white adolescents representing the dominant American culture.

A common charge in the current immigration debate is that the new arrivals, unlike previous waves of immigrants from Europe, refuse to learn the English language. Some analysts construe the immigrants' wish to maintain their cultural traditions, including their language, mores, and other "habits of the heart," as a refusal to learn English and to adapt to American life. Another incendiary charge is that many, if not most, new arrivals are motivated primarily by a desire to gain access to public services without paying their fair share.

Contrary to these charges, our research suggests that even though immigrant youths must cope with the losses and stresses of immigration, "culture shock," and a wide array of difficulties and hostilities in conflict-ridden inner-city schools, they nevertheless desperately try, seemingly against all odds, to learn the language and to use the educational system, not the welfare system, to "become somebody."

Teachers working with Latino immigrant students reported to us, almost unanimously, that the new arrivals are simply the best students they have ever had: appreciative, well behaved, and above all desperate to learn. As a classroom veteran put it to us, "The immigrant students are just great. I would rather teach ESL [English as a second language] anytime. They are so eager to learn. . . . These students have a discipline that you just don't see anymore in American students. They have a respect and a desire to learn that is fantastic. They behave the way our kids [American-born students] used to behave 30 years ago. And they love the teacher. It is a great feeling!"

Another teacher with ample experience said, "The newcomers are very respectful and desperate to learn. You see it in the way they pay attention, the way they sit down at their desks. They are all ears, all ready to learn. They hang on to every word you say. . . . It is most gratifying to see the respect they have for us. And the great enjoyment they get from learning."

The fact that immigrants and their children may wish to maintain their cultural traditions does not mean that they refuse to learn English or to adapt to American life. Empirical studies, in fact, suggest otherwise. For example, Portes and Zhou found that among the children of new immigrants English reigns supreme: almost 90 percent of the children of immigrants spoke English "very well" or "well." And 47.7 percent were found to speak "only English" (Portes and Zhou 1992: 34; see also Sharp 1993; Sontag 1993b). Furthermore, some data suggest that the better immigrant students know their own culture and their own language, the better they tend to adapt to American schooling (Matute-Bianchi 1991).

We are interested in exploring the differences between newly arrived immigrants and more acculturated, U.S.-born Latinos. One area of interest is how minority status in the U.S.-born first generation shapes the patterning of family life and achievement motivation.

Although a number of studies have looked at the psychosocial aspects of immigration, no study to date has systematically compared the experiences of likely emigrants in Mexico with those of Mexican immigrants in the United States, second-generation Mexican Americans, and non-Hispanic white nonimmigrants. Hence it is not possible to tell from the existing studies how Mexican immigrants in the United States differ from Mexicans in Mexico, and how these groups, in turn, differ from second-generation Mexican Americans and "mainstream" Americans. We explore how these groups differ in certain important dimensions and provide a theoretical framework for understanding their differences. Specifically, we investigate how family orientation—including what psychologists and others have called "familism" and family conflict—and achievement orientation differ among these groups.

In addition, we address a central paradox in the Latino experience: whereas new immigrants are widely reported to be extremely motivated to learn English and use the educational system to improve their lot, more acculturated Latinos drop out of schools at alarmingly high rates. The same teachers who reported "loving" to teach newly arrived immigrant students were at a loss to explain the problems of more acculturated Latino students.

A perceptive teacher with long experience in conflict-ridden schools noted a grave paradox: "As the Latino students become more American, they lose interest in their school work. . . . They become like the others, their attitudes change." As someone else said, "The more Americanized [Latinos] are different. You see a change of attitudes over time. The family remains the most important factor in their lives, but you see differences. They become more disrespectful as time goes by. They are more rebellious as they become more American." Another teacher said, "Immigrant students when they first come have a great smile, and a great attitude." She added that acculturated Latinos tend to be "more confrontational, they make more trouble, become more antagonistic. . . . They go from wearing great smiles to wearing their [gang] colors."

Yet another teacher, himself a Latino, said, "They begin by testing you. They push the limits, they want to test the limits. Anglo kids do this so the Latino kids see it and they learn. At first they are very polite and do as they are told. Then they see the Anglo kids, the way they behave in school, and they start acting like them. Many Anglo kids don't even bring books to school. They don't want to be seen with books, it is not 'cool.' So the Latino kids see this. Then they test you to see what they can get away with. If you don't put limits, they'll walk all over you."

How do we account for this paradox? Why is it that newly arrived students who have been in the United States a few years display such eagerness to do well in school and those who have been here longer—including U.S.-born Latinos—display more ambivalence about school and school authorities?

This book reports the findings of a three-year interdisciplinary (anthropological, psychological, and educational) research project carried out by a research anthropologist (Marcelo M. Suárez-Orozco) and a research psychologist (Carola Suárez-Orozco) in an area of emigration in central Mexico and in an immigrant-receiving area of southern California. Using a sample of 189 informants, we report data on school dynamics, peer and family life, and achievement concerns gathered using structured interviews, "objective" and "projective" tests, ethnographic observations, and other methods.

We address some normative patterns in cultural psychology among two groups of nonimmigrants (Mexicans in Mexico and white Americans in the United States) and then systematically compare them with immigrants and U.S.-born Mexican Americans.

We ask the following questions: How is achievement motivation patterned in Mexican family life? What are the special issues facing recently arrived immigrant youths? How does the peer group influence school life? What are the stresses facing U.S.-born Mexican American adolescents? How are the concerns of white American adolescents different from those of adolescents from the other groups studied? Is the turmoil and turning away of adolescence reported in the mainstream American experience found in the other groups?

With this book we hope to chart a course through the sometimes rough waters where psychological anthropology and cross-cultural psychology meet. In the course of conducting our research we have come to believe that neither anthropology nor psychology can, by itself, do justice to the complexities involved. Current anthropology, in a moment of disciplinary introspection (some would say malaise), finds itself doubting some of its once-sacred ideas. Some sectors of psychology are now struggling to lift the methodological choke-hold of experimental psychology that has almost strangled that field. We attempt to marry psychological anthropology and cultural psychology in the name of understanding a complex and urgent psychosocial problem.

By necessity, then, we explore some of the issues currently raging in anthropological and psychological scholarship. How can we know the inner experience of a culturally different "Other"? How can research psychology negotiate the apparent tensions between "methodological rigor" and "fairness" to culturally different minority populations? These are some of the topics considered in this book.

In Chapter 1 we frame the current American discourse on immigration in the context of a broader "postindustrial paradox." Most, if not all, advanced postindustrial societies, which until recently relied on immigrant labor, now face an "immigrant problem." In Europe immigration has become an explosive topic. Europeans are concerned about issues that are in some ways similar to current U.S. themes: (1) the growing number of undocumented workers and asylum seekers during a period of severe economic challenges; (2) the non-European, nonwhite origin of the new arrivals (in Europe there is great concern about the influx of Muslims from North Africa and elsewhere); (3) the problems facing the children of immigrants in schools and in the streets; and (4) the rise of xenophobic violence targeted at immigrants and asylum seekers. A comparative view of the issues makes it possible to explore the contexts, processes, and outcomes contributing to the near-hysteria over the new immigrants on both sides of the Atlantic.

In Chapter 2 we offer an overview of some of the recent debates in the field of Latino immigration, with special reference to family dynamics, achievement motivation, and schooling. We examine some competing paradigms for exploring the problem of minority status and schooling in plural societies.

In Chapter 3 we explore current theoretical concerns and methodological challenges facing psychological anthropology and cross-cultural psychology in the postmodern moment. We reject the more radical assertions of postmodern anthropology as to the impossibility of approaching a culturally different "Other." We make a plea for a fair but rigorous approach to the inner experience of culturally distinct groups. No knowledge is ever complete, and cross-cultural knowledge is no exception. However partial cross-cultural knowledge may be, we must not surrender to the nihilistic view that all such attempts are futile at best and politically and morally dangerous at worst. We have only partial answers to offer. But we take comfort in the thought that they are partial answers to some of the most troubling questions facing the fin de siècle.

In Chapter 3 we also provide a general outline of our study methods, including a description of our informants and the instruments used to conduct our research. We make a plea for an interdisciplinary and methodologically flexible strategy for psychocultural research. We hope to strike a balance between the methodological rigor of traditional psychological research—which includes concerns about sampling, validity, and reliability—and the anthropological commitment to "cultural fairness" in exploring other worlds.

In Chapter 4 we present our findings on family dynamics in the four groups. Although we had anticipated some themes, we were surprised by many of the concerns that surfaced. The level of family conflict related by the white American adolescents was certainly unexpected. In this chapter, we also explore the relative salience of peers and the psychosocial differences in peer group dynamics across the four groups. Adolescence is about identity. The peer group is an essential aspect of the adolescent experience. We shall explore important psychosocial differences in peer group dynamics across the four groups.

In Chapter 5 we turn to the topic of achievement motivation and attitudes toward school. Again we were surprised by the data. Contrary to widespread notions about Mexican achievement motivation, our data suggest that Mexican students in Mexico, as well as Mexican immigrant students in California, display comparatively high concerns about achievement. Indeed, Mexican and immigrant students related more concerns about their achievement in school than either white American students or U.S.-born Mexican American students. We also found revealing differences in attitudes toward authorities—including parents, teachers, and principals.

Chapter 6 briefly reviews the prevailing worldwide debate over immigration and offers some general conclusions suggested by our data.

The Epilogue examines some of the issues involved in the movement that led to the November 1994 passage in California of the ballot measure Proposition 187, which would deny all government-funded social services to undocumented immigrants. We also point out some of the proposition's possible consequences if the law is upheld by the courts.

CHAPTER I

Civilization's New Discontent

IMMIGRANTS AND REFUGEES IN A
POST-UTOPIAN MOMENT

We think of the United States as the archetypal country of immigrants.[1] Many nostalgically celebrate the great accomplishments of the transatlantic European immigrants and their descendants. Indeed, the immigrant past is an essential aspect of the exceptionalism that, according to the *ur*-American myth, makes the country unlike any other: the United States took in millions of humble foreigners and made them into successful and loyal Americans; America is utopia realized.

The successful insertion of European immigrants and their children into the mainstream institutions of America represents, in the hearts of many, the very embodiment of the "American dream." Never mind the terrible losses the immigrants endured, the discrimination they faced, and the hardships they overcame—they eventually became proud Americans. These romantic notions are mostly about the experiences of immigrants from Europe. The experiences—and accomplishments—of immigrants from Asia, Latin America, and elsewhere have not been as well documented or discussed as those of the European immigrants (Takaki 1993). The American romance with immigration has been decisively Eurocentric.

Although the immigrant past is romanticized, the immigrant present is another story. Facing economic hardships and social upheaval at home, many Americans are increasingly fearful of a seemingly uncontrollable invasion by a new kind of immigrant: brown-skinned, low-skilled workers and asylum seekers from Latin America and Asia. By the early 1990s many had come to believe that, in the words of the director of the Immigration and Naturalization Service (INS) office in New York City, William S. Slattery, "the aliens have taken control" (Weiner 1993).

Immigration has created rapid demographic changes in many traditional immigrant destinations. In California, where the immigration uproar is arguably loudest, demographic changes have been swift. Demographers say that in California ethnic minorities are rapidly becoming the absolute majority of the population.

The growth of the Latino population illustrates the California pattern: "In 1940, barely 5.6 percent of the population was Latino. By 1980, it had grown to 19.2 percent. Fueled by high fertility and immigration, the Latino population appears to be a major component of the population of the future" (Hayes-Bautista, Schink, and Chapa 1988: 17). In the 1990s Latinos make up 25 percent of the population. And what might the future population of California look like? Hayes-Bautista, Schink, and Chapa project "a steady growth, with Latinos constituting 35.5 percent of the state's population by the year 2030" (ibid.: 29).

Such rapid and profound changes are unsettling to many—whites and others—who wonder how the culture of California will be affected by the "browning" of the state. Frustrated by economic and sociodemographic upheaval, many are singling out the new immigrants as prime suspects in the creation of California's woes: the economic crisis, the budget crisis, the health care crisis, chaotic schools, and crime, to mention a few.

It is imperative, we argue, to establish whether the new immigrants are a central cause of these serious problems. If they are guilty as charged—of ruining the state's economy, of busting city and county budgets, of committing much of the serious crime—then the current anxiety may be perfectly rational. If, on the other hand, it turns out that the case against immigrants is less than convincing, we must turn our analytic equipment to the possible irrational foundations of the new anti-immigrant sentiment. In that case, we must examine what the relevant literature on irrational fears, frustration, endangerment, and aggression tells us about the psychodynamic processes that might help us understand—and possibly assuage—the current anxieties (see Dollard et al. 1939; Freud 1930; Fromm 1973; Kohut 1972; Mitchell 1993; Nemiroff n.d.).

There are many fruitful ways to examine the raging debate over the new immigration. For example, current sentiment is not unlike that created by new arrivals at the turn of the century, when, between 1880 and 1930, some 28 million immigrants entered the United

States from southern, central, and eastern Europe. There was also at that time much talk (and action) about the perils of immigration.

The idea that the past is not what it used to be is relevant to shifting discourses on immigration. The great achievements of peasants from the European periphery and their descendants have been recorded in the mythical space reserved for quasi-sacred narratives describing how the country came to be in its present form. Frequently overlooked is the fact that just seventy years ago virulent anti-immigrant racism, then dressed in the pseudoscientific frock of eugenics, led to the Immigration Act of 1924, which in no uncertain terms discriminated against southern, central, and eastern Europeans.

These fin de siècle historical, demographic, and social changes led people to distinguish between "good" and "bad" immigrants, as many are doing in the 1990s. At the turn of the century, the "good" immigrants were said to be the earlier settlers from western and northern Europe and Great Britain.[2] The "bad" immigrants were the poor, "disease-infected" peasants arriving from southern, central, and eastern Europe and Ireland (Kraut 1994). The people's anxiety then was fed, in part, by ethnically inspired fears about "criminal" Mediterranean peasants and "intellectually inferior" eastern and central Europeans. These groups were thought to be unassimilable into American culture (see Morgan 1987: 197–228).

A *New York Times* editorial written in 1880 could have been written a hundred years later with only small changes—just replace "Italians" and "Irish" with "Latinos":

> There is a limit to our powers of assimilation and when it is exceeded our country suffers from something very much like indigestion. We are willing to receive immigrants just as fast as we can make them over into good American citizens . . . [but] we are not in need of any more aliens at present. Foreigners who come here and herd together like sheep remain foreigners all their lives. We know how stubbornly conservative of his dirt and his ignorance is the average immigrant who settles in New York, particularly if he is of a clannish race like the Italians. Born in squalor, raised in filth and misery and kept at work almost from infancy, these wretched beings change their abode, but not their habits in coming to New York. . . . A bad Irish-American boy is about as unwholesome a product as ever reared in any body politic. (Quoted in Chavez 1992: 14)

Important contemporary events may also help us dissect the current anti-immigrant sentiment. Much of Europe today, including Belgium, France, Germany, and even Italy and Spain, is saturated with talk about "the immigrant problem"—in this case, new arrivals from North Africa and eastern Europe. We are interested in what can be learned about our current predicament by examining the relevant features of this latest European debate.

In this chapter we address the fact that in labor-importing post-industrial democracies as different as the United States, Belgium, France, and Germany immigration has become an urgent concern.[3] Indeed, the issue is no longer solely Euro-American. Japan, long proud of its lack of need of foreign workers ("one people, one nation"), today has an emerging problem of undocumented immigrants from Thailand, Korea, the Philippines, and elsewhere in Asia (Cornelius 1994). Furthermore, the reasons for concern sound very similar. In Europe and the United States the new immigrants are said to have become a burden on the economy—they are putting overwhelming pressures on the welfare state, they are not assimilating, and they are committing crimes. And in all of these settings anti-immigrant sentiment has grown strong.[4] We hope to demonstrate that it is hardly a uniquely American phenomenon. It seems to be created by certain specific tensions, contradictions, and paradoxes of the advanced postindustrial world.

In recent years, the debate over immigration and ethnicity has taken a decidedly post-utopian twist. Long-held notions that labor-importing democracies could absorb and live in multiethnic harmony with immigrants have been overwhelmed by extreme nativistic discourse. In France, for example, the once popular notion that French culture could absorb all immigrant groups has been guillotined. By 1994, the French minister of the interior was working on plans to send "boatloads and trainloads" of new immigrants and asylum seekers back home to North Africa and eastern Europe (*New York Times* 1994a).

After identifying some of the key symptoms of ethnic angst in Europe, we turn our attention to the current charges against the new immigrants in the United States. In this context we consider some of the most relevant recent materials examining the complex relationships between the new immigrants and the economy and the new immigrants and crime. We then propose a psychosocial model for exploring why immigrants and asylum seekers have become such powerful symbols of economic decline and sociodemographic upheaval.

Needed but Not Wanted: A Postindustrial Paradox

Although, to paraphrase Tolstoy, each nation is unhappy in its own way, in the field of immigration countries as diverse as Belgium, Germany, Italy, Spain, and the United States have similar complaints. Let us look first at western Europe.

In western Europe today few topics are as heated as that of immigration. All major European countries are debating and exploring ways to gain control of increasing waves of undocumented immigrants and asylum seekers (Cornelius, Martin, and Hollifield 1994). Even countries that have traditionally considered themselves to be sources of emigrants and not destinations of immigrants are now struggling to control their borders. Italy and Spain, countries of emigration par excellence, are now having to jealously guard their borders against unwanted new arrivals.[5] And anti-immigrant sentiment is steadily growing in both countries. In southern Spain, now said to be the California of Europe (making the Mediterranean Europe's Rio Grande), there is anxiety about a new "Moorish" invasion from North Africa. In the 1990s Italy and Spain became the most important European entry points for undocumented immigrants and asylum seekers from North Africa, Latin America, and Asia (Cornelius 1994; Calavita 1993). Facing economic stagnation, unemployment twice the U.S. level, and pressure from the European Community (EC) to stop the flow of undocumented immigrants, Italy and Spain are trying to control their borders even as they continue to think of themselves as countries of emigrants, which should now welcome immigrants.

Unlike Italy and Spain, Germany has a history of immigration (Martin 1993). After World War II, the pressures of having to rebuild the country and a shortage of workers led German authorities to recruit "guest workers" from the Mediterranean nations (Hollifield 1992). According to some immigration scholars, those workers, from Turkey and elsewhere, helped fuel what became the great postwar German economic boom (Castles 1984; Castles and Kosack 1973; Cohn-Bendit 1992; Fassmann and Münz 1992; Hollifield 1992).

Other northern European countries, such as Belgium, also recruited foreign laborers (principally from southern Italy, Spain, Turkey, and Morocco) after the war (Aubert 1985; Castles 1984; Castles and Kosack 1973; Commission of the European Communities 1992; Foblets 1988; Hammar 1983; Leman 1987; Morin 1984; Nayer and Nys 1992; Roosens 1988, 1989a, n.d.; Wander 1990). The economic crisis of the early 1970s effectively ended the formal—or legal—immigration into most western European countries. Thereafter the new immigrants came in through various "family reunification" programs (for the families of the guest workers to join relatives) or without formal papers (as undocumented aliens or asylum seekers).

After World War II, many western European countries, including

Germany, implemented liberal asylum policies, which are responsible for at least one of the serious immigration issues facing Germany today: the large and increasing number of asylum seekers (in
1993 there were 630,000 unresolved cases pending in Germany; see
Kamm 1993). In addition, xenophobia in Germany has recently taken
a vicious turn as neo-Nazis have attacked, and sometimes killed, immigrants and asylum seekers (Schmidt 1993). The violence has been
aimed principally at immigrant Turks and at asylum seekers from
eastern Europe, Africa, and Asia. Some estimate that there are over
50,000 active German neo-Nazis attempting to rid Germany of the
foreigners (Leman 1993).[6]

Most major western European countries have similar xenophobic,
anti-immigrant groups. In France it is the Front National, led by Jean-
Marie Le Pen; in Belgium the Vlaams Blok (Flemish bloc), which
is an important political force in Flanders, Belgium's most powerful
region economically (it won 25 percent of the vote in the 1994 elections). What is common to these parties is their uncompromising
anti-immigrant stance.

Europe's citizens increasingly fear that the continent will be overwhelmed by people seeking asylum from wars, starvation, and natural disasters.[7] Many are keeping an anxious eye on developments
in the former Soviet bloc, the former Yugoslavia, and North Africa. In
the words of Charles Pasqua, the French interior minister, who is in
charge of immigration: "Instability in the former Soviet bloc could
result in an influx of immigrants, while high birthrates and unemployment rates are feeding an exodus from North Africa. By the year
2000, 60 million of the 130 million people in Algeria, Tunisia, and
Morocco will be under the age of 20 and without a future" (quoted
in *New York Times* 1994a).

Since the parliamentary election of March 1993, the French have
established tighter immigration controls.[8] In addition to making it
more difficult for foreigners to acquire residency papers and asylum,
the new laws provide that French-born children of foreigners no
longer become French citizens automatically at age eighteen (Hollifield 1993; Hoffmann 1994).[9]

Asylum policy has become a central focus in the current debate.
About 3 million asylum applications were submitted to western
European countries in the 1980s and early 1990s—a tenfold rise over
the decade. Newly organized Moscow- and Hong Kong–based rings
of "people smugglers" are bringing large numbers of refugees (mostly
from Iraq, the former Yugoslavia, China, and Somalia) into northern
Europe (Kamm 1993).[10] The enormous costs associated with housing,

feeding, and processing asylum applicants (a reported $8.3 billion in western Europe in 1992) contribute to a widespread feeling that the developed world simply cannot rescue all those who need rescuing.

Some observers note that the low acceptance rate of asylum applications (about 5 percent in western Europe) confirms what right-wing politicians have been saying all along: that the great majority of asylum seekers are really "economic refugees" in search of a better life. Similar arguments have been made in the United States. Many Europeans say that these economic refugees abuse the asylum system by gaining entry into the country and then "disappearing" before their cases are resolved. At the same time, human rights and refugee rights groups are alarmed by what they see as the erosion of international asylum rights agreements. In the words of David Petrasek, Amnesty International's London refugee specialist, "We don't think the vast majority of people coming to Europe are bogus" (quoted in Kamm 1993).

An important factor in the asylum equation in northwestern Europe is that many of the asylum laws and policies were guided by the European experience with Nazism and communism, and they are perhaps ill-designed to deal with large numbers of brown and black non-Europeans—mostly Muslims. Some observers are asking unsettling questions: Can these non-European populations, which are so different in culture and religion from earlier waves of refugees and immigrants from within Europe, truly be assimilated? Can there be a modern, European Islam? (See Dassetto and Bastenier 1988.)

After World War II, and in the context of the ensuing cold war, people from some (communist) countries could apply for asylum more easily than those from others. But the liberal asylum laws of the cold war era were never fully tested because of the strict control of population movement by the former Eastern bloc countries. Since the fall of the Iron Curtain and the onset of crises in the former Yugoslavia and elsewhere, populations are again moving freely, and European governments are urgently formulating new laws and strategies to cope.

Most countries have developed formal and informal strategies and policies for dealing with the sharp increase in asylum applications. In June of 1993 Germany enacted a more restrictive asylum policy. Belgium, Germany, and others have adopted the controversial "safe country" formula. When in a given year 5 percent of all applications for asylum come from a single country and fewer than 5 percent of those applications are approved, then the country becomes a "safe country," from which all future applications are more easily rejected.

The "safe country" list in Belgium currently includes Ghana, Pakistan, India, Poland, and Rumania. Applicants from Zaire and China still may be admitted (Belgium has a tradition of offering asylum to the opposition in Zaire). Human rights organizations have argued that some of these so-called safe countries have been recently accused of systematic human rights violations (Foblets 1993; see also Kamm 1993). Legal-defense groups in western Europe have challenged the safe-country rule, noting that reference to the percentage of rejected applications from the previous year is not necessarily relevant because political climates can change rapidly and that the rule is not flexible enough.

Some countries have adopted what we call "nonpolicy policies" to deal with new arrivals from the former Yugoslavia. France, for example, gives asylum seekers from Bosnia who waive their right to petition for formal refugee status a limited right to stay. They agree to go back home once the danger is over. Applicants for asylum who retract their applications gain the provisionary right to stay and work until peace makes it possible for them to return home.[11]

Throughout the continent there seems to be a general retreat from previous mechanisms that generously provided for the permanent settlement of asylum seekers.[12] Governments are concerned that as wars and conflicts break out elsewhere, others will rush to northwestern Europe claiming the same rights as those granted to the Bosnians. In Belgium, government actions in the case of Bosnia appear to be expedient and purposely vague: the objective is to control, as effectively as possible, legal entry into the country.[13]

According to some European researchers, the asylum principle that a well-founded fear of persecution should guarantee shelter has been undermined by politics. The fear that new conflicts may produce an unmanageable number of asylum seekers has contributed to a more "instrumental" and "realistic" approach. For example, in an effort to make the asylum-seeking process more difficult and less open, many European governments require asylum seekers to present valid passports and even visas. Many asylum seekers do not have such documents. Another strategy is to turn part of the "policing" function over to airline personnel; airlines that transport passengers without proper documents are fined. One effect of this policy is that would-be asylum seekers are weeded out by airline personnel in the country of origin, before they enter the country in which they intend to seek asylum. Those who do make it into an international airport find that some governments, among them the French and Dutch, have "declared areas of their main airports 'international territory.'

This permits them to circumvent obligations under international conventions to give applicants an asylum hearing when they arrive 'in the country' " (Kamm 1993).[14] Lawyers working on behalf of asylum seekers argue that many if not all of these strategies may violate the fair hearing aspects of the Geneva convention.

In January 1994 the French government announced new plans to step up the deportation of undocumented foreigners to discourage further immigration from eastern Europe and North Africa. According to French interior minister Charles Pasqua, "When we have sent home several planeloads, even boatloads and trainloads, the world will get the message. We will close our frontiers" (quoted in *New York Times* 1994a).

In northwestern Europe undocumented immigrants find work in limited sectors of the economy—women typically work as maids, as baby-sitters, or caring for the elderly, and men work in construction, petrochemical industries, and agriculture (Leman 1993). In Brussels, the maids of choice are undocumented Colombians, Filipinas, Peruvians, and Poles (Van Broeck 1993). Undocumented Polish workers are routinely bused into the wealthier neighborhoods of Brussels and Leuven, where they wait on corners to be picked up for daily work cleaning houses (Roosens 1993). This scene is almost identical to that facing undocumented workers from Mexico and Central America all over California.

An undocumented housekeeper in Brussels is paid about half what a legal worker would be paid.[15] By hiring undocumented "black workers," employers avoid making payments into the social security system. The opposite side of the coin is that an undocumented worker from Poland (where in certain rural regions the average monthly wage is about $200) can earn about $6 an hour cleaning houses in Brussels or Leuven. The wage differentials that drive immigrants from the peripheries are enormous.[16]

Many employers today believe that without a reliable source of "disposable" undocumented workers, paid substandard wages, they simply could not compete in the global marketplace (Kilborn 1993). In Belgium, agricultural producers have argued that without undocumented workers to pick vegetables and fruits, they could not sell produce at affordable prices (Leman 1993). In the clothing industry, the employment of "black workers" has made it possible for Belgians to purchase designer clothes at a fraction of the price they would cost if made by Belgian workers at official rates (Timmerman 1993). Some employers mention that it is simply impossible for them to compete with low-wage operations in Southeast Asia (see Cohen 1993b).

Many undocumented workers in Europe work in substandard conditions. Willing to do things local workers cannot or will not do —such as working with dangerous pesticides and chemicals—undocumented workers are the most vulnerable of all workers in northwestern Europe.[17]

In addition to these hardships, Belgian psychologists report that children of undocumented workers worry constantly that their parents will be caught and sent back to their home countries (Van Broeck 1993). Some even wish their parents *would* be caught and sent back to put an end to their terror. They then feel guilt.

A Common Dilemma

There is an emerging consensus among researchers that the problem of undocumented immigration goes well beyond country boundaries (Cornelius, Martin, and Hollifield 1994). In western Europe, now that border controls within the community have been removed, an immigrant who gains entry into one member state has gained entry into all of them.[18]

Although EC citizens may move and work freely within the community, this right is not extended to non-EC immigrants (Foblets 1993). A Moroccan immigrant legally residing in Paris cannot, without authorization, enter another EC country for longer than three months; immigrants who intend to stay more permanently must register with the authorities. An estimated 9 million non-EC legal immigrants in western Europe are affected by this policy. Yet immigration researchers predict that without border controls the policy will be difficult to enforce. Once an immigrant has gained (legal or illegal) entry into western Europe, monitoring population movements and enforcing the laws will be extremely difficult.

Control of Europe's external borders therefore becomes more important. Northwestern Europeans worry that their southern neighbors (particularly Spain and Italy) are not able to control entry effectively (Cornelius, Martin, and Hollifield 1994). Once workers from Africa and Latin America gain entry into Spain, they have free access to the rest of the EC. Current policy makes each country of entry responsible for controlling the subsequent movement of immigrants and allows asylum seekers to apply to only one EC country at a time.

In France and Belgium immigrants tend to concentrate in certain areas, making themselves even more visible to the majority population. Some natives are offended by the immigrants' non-European dress and codes of behavior and resent the high rate of immigrant unemployment (twice the rate of native worker unemployment in some settings), the crimes committed by immigrants, and the immigrants' use—and abuse—of the social security system.

Still, some sectors of the economy need foreign workers. According to some estimates, France will need to recruit between 150,000 and 350,000 foreign workers before the end of the century. In fact, Charles Pasqua, the French cabinet minister who has threatened to send home "several planeloads, even boatloads and trainloads" of immigrants, more recently cautiously announced that "100,000 foreign workers a year will be needed to fill jobs which French workers are either unqualified or unwilling to fill" (New York Times 1994a; Droziak 1994).

In Germany there is a similar contradiction between xenophobic sentiment and the economic need for foreign laborers. "German politicians also acknowledge that non-German contributions to pension and welfare programs are necessary. A spokesman for the Social Democrats reports that the 2 million foreign workers in Germany contribute 10 percent of the national [economic] output, and pay an even greater proportion of taxes and pension fund contributions" (Droziak 1994). Likewise, Belgium will likely continue to rely on foreign labor in labor-intensive manufacturing (e.g., of leather goods and clothing) as well as agriculture and construction (Leman 1993). And "black workers" from Pakistan, India, Morocco, and the Philippines are routinely employed by the food industry in Belgium's Limburg province.[19]

Until recently many mainstream western European politicians were reluctant to address the issue of immigration. Their silence left a vacuum that was filled by extremists. Although most politicians pay lip service to the notion that undocumented immigration cannot be tolerated, their political will to enforce regulations seems weak, resulting in what we have called nonpolicy as policy.

Nativistic Responses

In Belgium the Vlaams Blok continues to gain power, particularly in Flanders. The party, with its historic ties to Nazism, is one of the most articulate architects of the right-wing extremism revisiting Europe. Mainstream politicians were flabbergasted by the Vlaams Blok's successes in the 1991 and 1994 elections.[20]

Although many Belgians abhor the more extreme views of the Vlaams Blok leadership, public opinion polls suggest that a majority of the population supports some watered-down version of their anti-immigrant agenda. A recent survey indicated that up to 70 percent of the Flemish population would like to see the immigrants go home, but not by any forced means (Billiet, Carton, and Huys 1990).[21]

In western Europe, anti-immigrant sentiment is at the intersection of a number of distinct issues. There is general public anxiety about the budget crisis, unemployment, and continued waves of undocumented immigrants and asylum seekers. More specific concerns include the adaptation problems of previous waves of legal immigrants and their children, the high unemployment rates among non-EC documented immigrants, and their reliance on the generous European social security system. Others have noted the high failure rates of non-EC immigrant children and high delinquency rates among the Moroccans and Turks (see Alaluf 1982; Alamdar-Niemann, Bergs-Winkels, and Merkens 1991; Boos-Nünning and Hohmann 1989; *Cahiers Marxistes* 1988; Cammaert 1986a, 1986b; Costa-Lascoux 1989, 1992; Eldering 1989; Eldering and Kloprogge 1989; Extra and Vallen 1989; Hermans 1993; Leman 1991; Payet 1992; Riding 1993c; Roosens 1988, 1989a, 1989b, 1993; Stromqvist 1989; Suárez-Orozco 1991; Tomlinson 1989, 1991; Vasquez 1992).

In Belgium, where a national Belgian identity is not relevant, and where there is a history of ethnic tensions between the Flemish and the Walloons, culture and language seem to be increasingly important. Many see immigrants as a threat to ancient cultural traditions. There are cultural anxieties about preserving language and local traditions in the face of ongoing waves of new arrivals. Some Europeans see the local concentrations of immigrants publicly displaying their differences in language, dress, and conduct as sending the message: here we are, we are different, we are not going to change, we will remain outsiders.[22]

A great deal of the European debate over immigration policy is also about the costs associated with immigration. As Marie-Claire Foblets, an immigration law researcher at the Universities of Leuven and Paris, put it:

> The [European] population is in general anti-immigrant. The right wing parties do not want to see immigrants sustained by public funding. The public prefers not to have them dependent on public funding. Illegals also have rights to some minimal social security (in Belgium there is a basic food and lodging allowance for the truly indigent of 11,000 B.F. a month [$355]). This is now being furiously debated. There is a movement to cut all aid to the illegals. (Foblets 1993)

Other observers have noted that immigrants contributed, substantially, to the European economic boom of the postwar era (see Calavita 1993; Fassmann and Münz 1992; Hollifield 1992). Mr. P. Flynn, a former Irish justice minister and current EC commissioner for social policy and immigration, recently stated, "Immigration to Europe has been a positive development with substantial economic and social benefits" (quoted in *Wall Street Journal* 1994).[23]

We have outlined some key concerns regarding immigration in western Europe. We have examined some of the tensions that have emerged from conflicting interests. These include a concern with securing international borders versus an enduring dependency in certain sectors of the economy on foreign workers—a more "plastic," globally competitive labor force. There are also contradictions between demographically based labor shortages and native xenophobia. In addition, there are anxieties over the future of European cultures in the context of large numbers of non-European Muslim immigrants, which clash with longstanding legal stances regarding asylum and freedom of movement.

The concerns voiced in Europe include (1) the growing number of undocumented immigrants and asylum seekers; (2) their cultural and ethnic distinctiveness from the majority population; (3) their nonassimilation; and (4) their exploitation of limited economic resources.

Closing The Golden Gate

By the early 1990s there was a near panic that the U.S. southern border had "fallen." In the words of Demetrios Papademetriou, former director of immigration policy at the Labor Department and current head of the Carnegie Endowment's Immigration Policy Program, the feeling in the general public is that "immigration is out of control; our borders have fallen" (Weiner 1993: 1). There were loud cries to further militarize the U.S.-Mexico border to stop the estimated 1.2 million people entering the United States without proper documentation each year.[24] In response, in Texas, the border patrol of the Immigration and Naturalization Service thoroughly "sealed" a section of the border for a couple of days in October 1993. Though extremely costly (a large number of border patrol personnel were stationed, day and night, in a small but heavily trafficked area of the border), this action was hailed by politicians and others as an experimental success. It was reported that undocumented crossings were virtually stopped for the duration of the program. There was immediate talk of trying a similar intense patrolling program in the most trafficked area of the U.S.-Mexico border, the San Ysidro section in San Diego County, California (see Stern 1993b).

The "fear of strangers" generated by the new immigration has blurred the vision of many (Allen 1993). Talk about immigration now routinely collapses distinct phenomena such as "legal" and "undocumented" immigration, crime, the budget crisis, and the issue of asylum seekers into a single powerful concern: that "the aliens have taken control."

The issues that once dominated the discourse about immigration and ethnicity, such as the wisdom of bilingual education and multilingual ballot materials, have been replaced with rantings about the invasion of illegals, alien crime, and alien welfare abuse. In 1993, leading California politicians, including Governor Pete Wilson and U.S. Representatives A. Beilenson (a Democrat) and P. Gallegly (a Republican), called for proposals to amend the constitution to deny citizenship to the U.S.-born children of undocumented aliens and social services to all undocumented immigrants. In this post-utopian moment the focus has clearly shifted away from seeking integration to building walls.

What caused this shift? The economic recession, which hit parts of the United States particularly hard—especially traditional immigrant destinations such as California—combined with the increase in numbers of new immigrants and asylum seekers in a volatile mix. Another element is the ethnic makeup of the new arrivals: whereas in 1940, 70 percent of all immigrants came from Europe, in 1992, 81 percent of all immigrants came from Latin America and Asia (44 percent from Latin America, 37 percent from Asia).

According to a recent *Time*/CNN poll, 30 percent of respondents said they felt "least favorably" about Latin American and Caribbean immigrants; only 2 percent reported feeling least favorably about recent immigrants from eastern Europe (Nelan 1993: 10–11).

In 1991 during the presidential primaries, Pat Buchanan—then challenging President Bush for the Republican nomination—began a nationwide debate when he said that U.S. borders were being overwhelmed by "illegals" from Latin America and that "Zulus" did not fit into American culture as well as Anglo-Saxon Europeans. Many interpreted these remarks as racist, implying that some immigrants, such as those of Anglo-Saxon European stock, "fit in" more naturally than the "Zulus," a code word for the new immigrants of color.

In early 1993, President Clinton's first nominee for the office of attorney general, Zoë Baird, removed herself from consideration when it was revealed that she had hired two undocumented domestic workers from Peru. The flap raised awareness about the 2 million undocumented workers currently residing in the United States.[25]

In mid-1993, the scandal was about the alleged participation of some undocumented immigrants and asylum seekers from the Middle East in a terrorist bombing of Manhattan's World Trade Center. There was also the case of a Pakistani refugee charged in the killings of two CIA employees just outside the agency's headquarters. The resulting media accounts began asking direct questions about the loopholes in asylum laws and procedures: How did these alleged terrorists get into the country? How were they able to get work permits and purchase weapons? And how many other terrorists and criminals are slipping through?

The alleged participation of illegal immigrants and refugees in these terrorist acts injected another dose of anxiety into the public debate. To many, these dark men speaking with thick accents seemed to symbolize everything that had gone wrong with immigration policies. The World Trade Center came to embody America's collective fears about the new immigrants, much as Ellis Island represents a "safer" immigrant past.

After the New York bombing there was a widespread feeling, evident in media coverage, that the noble practice of granting refuge had been taken advantage of by opportunists, criminals, and even terrorists (see McDowell 1993). According to one report, "The wholesale abuse of asylum law must be stopped. Immigrants with no legitimate claim to resettlement in the United States routinely request political asylum knowing that they will likely be released pending INS interviews a year or so hence. Many disappear and are never apprehended" (Caldwell 1993: 4).

In the days after the arrests of the suspects accused of the World Trade Center bombing, news cameras flocked to major airports to report on what were portrayed as lax immigration policies. Some reporters noted, erroneously, that just about anyone can get past immigration officials by simply claiming political asylum. Other reports emphasized that because of the lack of space at detention facilities, asylum seekers who are detained are routinely released, pending a future INS hearing (Conover 1993: 58).[26]

In early June 1993, the wreck off the shore of New York of a smuggler's ship carrying Chinese passengers created another wave of distress: "Americans, pinched and worried, say asylum seekers are a burden," read the headline in the *New York Times* (Weiner 1993; see also DePalma 1993a, 1993b).

In mid-July 1993, the *New York Times* reported, "More than 650 undocumented Chinese men and women remained crammed aboard three rusty tramp steamers about 60 miles west of Mexico's Pacific coast today as the Clinton Administration tried to figure out what to do with the aliens without either abandoning its own new get-tough immigration policy or antagonizing the Mexican Government" (DePalma 1993; see also Gross 1993). Eventually, the Mexican government, reportedly under pressure from U.S. officials, escorted the crippled steamer to the port of Ensenada in Baja California and immediately flew the U.S.-bound passengers back to China (DePalma 1993). In a kafkaesque twist, Mexican authorities agreed, in what was believed to be a quid pro quo deal relating to some sticky points in the North American Free Trade Agreement, to handle the problem of the undocumented Chinese sailing for United States shores. On the same day that Mexican officials had the asylum seekers flown back to China, additional ships carrying Chinese asylum seekers to the United States were spotted off the coast of Hawaii.[27]

By then many Americans seemed to agree with Ira Mehlman, a spokesman for the restrictionist Federation for American Immigration Reform, who said, "Enough is enough" (Mydans 1993). Indeed, on July 27, 1993, President Bill Clinton presented a plan to crack down on undocumented immigration. Arguing that "our borders leak like a sieve," President Clinton proposed a $172.5 million plan, which included adding up to 600 border patrol agents along the U.S.-Mexico border. A priority in the Clinton plan was to curb "political asylum abuses."[28] Soon thereafter, a commentator noted, "Political conditions in Congress have never been better for tightening immigration laws. Polls reflect strong concern among voters over the economy and immigration. Now both parties see potential political capital in clamping down on immigration abuses" (Stern 1993a).

Questions of the kind that some find unsettling in a society with pluralistic and multicultural pretensions began to be raised: How many low-skilled and unskilled immigrants and asylum seekers from Latin America and Asia can be let in? Who will guard the borders of the United States against the feared "southern invasion"? Since employer sanctions (sanctions making it illegal to hire undocumented workers) have largely failed to stop the flows of new arrivals, should workers be required to carry identity cards to prove they are here legally?[29]

Broadly speaking, there are five distinct but related areas of concern in the debate over the new immigrants. The first is the notion that too many immigrants and asylum seekers are coming in and that immigration controls—including employer sanctions—have failed to contain undocumented immigration. By the end of June 1994, it was estimated that over five thousand Haitians were seeking asylum each week in the United States. The influx led to the reopening of a center for claims processing at the U.S. base in Guantanamo, Cuba, and to talk of a U.S. invasion of Haiti. In addition, demographers report that the new immigrants tend to be in their prime childbearing years and to have fertility rates higher than those of nonimmigrant whites (Williams 1986).

The second concern is that the new immigrants and asylum seekers are culturally and ethnically unlike their predecessors from Europe. Most are low-skilled and unskilled Latin Americans and Asians. In the words of Larry Eig of the Library of Congress, "People . . . [in the United States] are culturally scared as well as economically scared" (Weiner 1993: 1). In California, recent immigration has significantly altered the state's ethnic mix: in the 1970s Latinos constituted 12 percent of the population of 19.9 million; in the 1990s they are 25 percent of the population of 30.8 million. As an observer in San Diego County put it:

> It's not just the [economic recession]. It is the fact that this county has to come to terms with the reality that by the end of this decade, every group is going to be a minority group here. The "browning" of the county, which is most visible in North County . . . is scaring the hell out of people. The combination of these two things [the recession and racial hostilities] is making the immigration debate so intemperate that I'm not sure where some rationality can be injected into it. (Quoted in Eisenstadt and Thorup 1994: 52–53)

The third concern is the fear of many that the new immigrants and their children do not seem to "assimilate" into the institutions of mainstream society in the way previous waves of European immigrants did. For example, the INS says that fewer of the new immigrants, particularly those from Latin America, seek citizenship. Indeed, applications for naturalization from immigrants dropped from 67 percent of all eligible legal immigrants in 1943 to only 37 percent in 1992 (Sontag 1993a).

Fourth, there is concern that the new immigrants have become a drag on the economy (Borjas 1994: 76–84). According to one observer, "At today's massive levels, immigration has major negative consequences—economic, social and demographic—that overwhelm its advantages" (quoted in Chavez 1992: 16). Julian Simon reports that "47 percent of Americans felt most immigrants wind up on welfare" (1989: 105). Others noted that new immigrants also use more than their share of precious and shrinking public resources: health services, schools, and the judicial system. The Los Angeles County Board of Supervisors responded to public concerns about immigrants' costs to the county by conducting a study (Los Angeles County 1992). We shall return to the findings of this highly debated report shortly.

Fifth is the explosive charge that immigrants contribute significantly to the problem of crime in America. A recent survey shows that fully 59 percent of Americans believe the new immigrants "add to the crime problem" (Nelan 1993: 11).

All of these concerns are intertwined with ideas about race, society, and culture. Concern number one—that there are too many immigrants—is based on several facts and beliefs: immigration is in fact at its highest level in a hundred years, and an estimated 1.2 million people annually enter the country without documentation.[30] And many believe that the ratio of new arrivals to the native-born population is at historic highs, but is it? Simon writes: "Near the turn of the century, immigration substantially topped the million mark in many years. And the burden of absorbing immigrants was much greater in those times relative to the population size. For instance, immigrants who arrived between 1901 and 1910 constituted 9.6 percent of the population; those who arrived between 1961 and 1970 constituted only 1.6 percent, and between 1971 and 1980 only 2.0 percent" (Simon 1989: 338).

The second concern is the dramatic shift in country of origin of the new arrivals: in 1940, 70 percent of all immigrants came from Europe; in 1992 only 15 percent of all immigrants came from Europe, and more than 80 percent came from Latin America and Asia. Fully 22 percent of all immigrants came from a single country, Mexico.

We examine aspects of the third concern—that immigrants and their children do not seem to assimilate well—in Chapters 2, 3, and 4 when we consider the Latino case. As we shall see, this concern is greatly exaggerated. For example, among the children of Latino immigrants English, not Spanish, is by far the dominant language (see Portes and Zhou 1992). In Chapters 4 and 5 we examine how in a variety of areas—from achievement motivation to attitudes toward authority—U.S.-born children of immigrants in fact share much with their white American peers.

But let us first explore concerns four and five, the more controversial charges that the new immigrants are an overall socioeconomic burden and dangerously crime-prone in a state that is almost synonymous with immigration: California.

A Case of Hysteria

California, once again, is at the cutting edge of a controversial issue. In the early 1990s, each year some 200,000 legal immigrants and an estimated 100,000 undocumented aliens settled in the state as it remained in economic recession. The California response to immigration has led to the formation of some unlikely political alliances; liberal Democrats and conservative Republicans now share a common cause:

> Calls for a crackdown on illegal immigration are coming from liberals and conservatives alike. California's moderately liberal Democratic Sen. Dianne Feinstein and very liberal Rep. Anthony Beilenson are joining with such conservative activists as San Diego's Rep. Duncan Hunter in supporting funding for an additional 600 Border Patrol agents. Feinstein and Beilenson are also joining the drive to close the gaping loopholes that permit gross abuses of the law granting asylum to political refugees. (Caldwell 1993)

At the same time, California has witnessed an out-migration of large companies and skilled and low-skilled white workers in search of jobs and better living conditions in other states (Holmes 1994; McGuire and Murr 1993). Some observers have noted that the twin pressures of ongoing economic recession (and the departure of good jobs and taxpaying workers) plus the increasing numbers of low-skilled and unskilled immigrants have created an atmosphere in which the "inevitable result is a monumental uproar over immigration itself" (McGuire and Murr 1993: 25; see also Denton 1993; Murr 1993).[31]

In some important ways California reflects the national mood writ large.[32] Many believe that the new immigrants overuse shrinking public resources. A *New York Times* survey reports the words of a respondent that capture how many Americans seem to feel: "A 33-year-old postal worker . . . said her opinions had been shaped by the way she had seen immigrants treated in her hometown. 'I saw the amount of aid that went out to them and the way that was abused. . . . I feel that our economy is in a bad state and we should take care of our own'" (Mydans 1993). People's image of industrious immigrants pulling themselves up by their bootstraps has been replaced with the image of parasitic aliens abusing public aid.

Much of the public debate in California has been over the public costs associated with the new immigration (see Alvord 1993; Cornelius 1993a, 1993b, 1994; Huddle 1993; Miller 1993; Passel 1994; Rothman and Espenshade 1992). Media accounts repeatedly point out how expensive immigrants are—for example, that they "consume more than their share of tax-supported services like welfare, health care, and public education" and that "the immigrant population costs [the California] government $5 billion a year" (McGuire and Murr 1993: 25). By mid-1993, Republican governor Pete Wilson was arguing that "the federal government should either regain control of the U.S.-Mexico border, and reduce legal immigration as well, or pay the state in full for the estimated $4 billion-plus in annual costs for health care, education, social services, and law enforcement for immigrants and their dependents" (Caldwell 1993).[33]

Others reported that "some 400,000 illegal aliens are eligible for the state's publicly funded health-care system, and public schools all across southern California are bulging at the seams" (McGuire and Murr 1993: 25). In a hearing of the Joint Committee on Refugee Resettlement, International Migration, and Cooperative Development of the California Legislature (held in the U.S.-Mexico border town of San Ysidro on June 22, 1990), a member of the Alliance for Border Control presented the following testimony: "Illegal aliens cost the taxpayers over a *BILLION DOLLARS A YEAR* in Medical care at the present time," and "*the total cost of illegal alien education in California probably reaches the Trillions*" (California Legislature 1990: 10–14, emphasis in the original). Such exaggerated numbers revive xenophobia and fuel the collective anger across the political spectrum.

What, then, of the charges that immigrants are bankrupting the state? Are they parasites living off the generosity of taxpaying citizens? Are they "stealing" jobs from nonimmigrant workers? Are they depressing the wages, and hence the standard of living, of native-born workers?

These are important questions. If indeed the new immigrants are a burden on the economy, then the current anxiety can be framed in rational cost and benefit terms: if immigrants are causing economic and other troubles, stop immigration and the troubles will stop too. If, however, it can be shown that the new immigrants pay their fair share and indeed contribute to the well-being of the communities in which they settle, then we must search for other reasons for society's fears and for other solutions.

Los Angeles County made an ambitious attempt to determine the impact of new arrivals on costs, revenues, and services. The resulting study concluded that the new arrivals (those who arrived after 1980) cost the county in 1991–92 approximately $946,705,000. They received Department of Health services (worth about $365 million), Justice-related services (about $351 million), Department of Public Social Services assistance (about $102 million), and Department of Mental Health services (about $5.5 million). In addition, the study estimated that the immigrant-related costs to school districts in Los

Angeles County were about $1.5 billion. All told, new immigrants cost the county of Los Angeles roughly $2.5 billion in 1991–92.

This is a very large figure. How much did these new arrivals contribute to the government coffers through taxation? The Los Angeles study estimated that the new arrivals contributed a total of $4.3 billion to the county, state, and federal governments. In short, the new immigrants paid about $1.85 billion more in taxes than they used in services (see Los Angeles County 1992: 11). Even undocumented immigrants paid more in taxes than they took out in county services— note that undocumented workers are ineligible for almost all public benefits, including food stamps, Aid to Families with Dependent Children (AFDC), Medicaid and Medi-Cal, public housing, unemployment, and social security, though they often pay into these programs through taxes and payroll deductions (see Heer 1990: 166–67). The study estimated that while the net county cost of undocumented immigrants and their children was about $400 million, they generated over $900 million in county, state, and federal taxes (see Los Angeles County 1992: 6, 11).

This study agrees with the findings of Heer, who concluded that undocumented persons and legal immigrants receive entitlements— including food stamps, AFDC, unemployment insurance, Medicaid and Medi-Cal, and public subsidized housing—at lower rates than native-born citizens (Heer 1990: 156–66).[34] Finally, we must note that Jeffrey Passel, director of the Program for Research on Immigration Policy at the Urban Institute, estimates that California immigrants in general—including undocumented workers—pay $12 billion more in taxes than they "cost" (Passel 1994).

In short, the most ambitious study to date, by L.A. County, suggests that immigrants, as Simon had concluded, "tend to have especially desirable characteristics from the economic point of view" (1989: 339; for other views on the impact of immigrants on the U.S. economy, see Borjas 1990; Glazer 1990; Huddle 1993; Piore 1971).[35] And more recently, in a major overview of studies of immigrants and taxes, Jeffrey Passel concludes, "Most national studies encompassing all levels of government suggest that immigrants do not fiscally burden the native population" (1994: 1). Likewise, George Borjas, hardly an advocate of open borders, concludes that at "the national level, therefore, it would not be far-fetched to conclude that immigration is near a washout" (Borjas 1994: 78).

What, then, motivated the Los Angeles hysteria that prompted the study? A careful examination of the report reveals that although the immigrants generated a great deal of revenue through taxation, the county of Los Angeles kept only a small percentage of it ($139 million of the total $4.3 billion). Most of the immigrant-generated revenue went to the federal government.

Some scholars have argued that a fundamental but typically over-looked problem contributing to anxiety about the economics of im-migration is the *allocation of the funds generated by immigrants.* Wayne Cornelius, for example, has noted, "California suffers from an unfair distribution of the tax revenues contributed by immigrants themselves, with the federal government keeping the lion's share and returning to heavily impacted states and localities considerably less than is needed to provide basic human services to the immigrants they are absorbing" (1993a).[36]

Other, tangible benefits of immigration are also overlooked, such as the fact that many immigrants work where native workers will not (in strenuous, dangerous, and poorly paid agricultural, manu-facturing, and service jobs; Cornelius 1993a). Younger immigrant workers pay into the social security system, which will be critical in supporting nonimmigrant retirees in the near future. Demogra-phers predict that in California, where whites have fertility rates below replacement, the Latino population, mostly immigrants and children of immigrants, will be increasingly important in the work-place: "The Anglo Baby Boomers will retire in the early part of the twenty-first century, and our work force will become far more depen-dent on the skills and productivity of Latinos and other minorities" (Hayes-Bautista, Schink, and Chapa 1988: viii).[37]

Those who grant that immigrants may fill needs in certain sectors of the economy charge nevertheless that their overall social impact is negative because they depress the wages of nonimmigrant workers. Recent studies suggest that this is not true. An Urban Institute study concluded that "places that got immigrants during the 1980's did generally better in terms of wage growth than places that didn't." In fact, it has been suggested that immigrants "help expand the demand for labor and increase the number of jobs, which tends to outweigh any negative effects they may have" (Rohter 1993).

What about the common charge that immigrants take away jobs from nonimmigrant citizens? Immigration expert Demetrios Papa-demetriou has noted that "the overall impact of immigrant workers on U.S. workers is small" (1994: 1). In fact, a number of leading immi-gration researchers have pointed out that the assumption that new immigrants are "stealing" jobs from native-born workers is simply not true:

In the midst of a recession, particularly one that has hit California the hardest, it is easy to argue that current levels of immigration are excessive. There are fewer jobs available and more people chasing them. But this ignores a critical fact: Native-born workers and immigrants cannot easily be substituted for one another. Skilled workers who are laid off will seek retraining or move to a market where their skills can be employed; they will not seek work as housecleaners or gardeners. (Cornelius 1993a)

Other empirical research suggests that immigrants may *create* jobs for nonimmigrants: "The question always seems to be phrased in terms of immigrants taking jobs from Americans, when lots of Americans have jobs because of the impact of immigrants in the economy. . . . Immigrant restaurants and businesses pay taxes, and their workers buy clothes and food and homes in neighborhoods that were formerly dead. There is a multiplier effect" (quoted in Rohter 1993).

Between 1982 and 1987, Latino businesses grew by 81 percent. These businesses generated significant tax revenues and hired many workers—including native citizens. Fierman writes, "Compelling evidence even shows that immigrants boost overall employment on balance. . . . [F]or every one-hundred-person increase in the population of adult immigrants, the number of new jobs rose by forty-six. By contrast, for every one hundred new native-born Americans, the number of jobs rose by just twenty-five" (Fierman 1994: 70). Although immigration creates some short-term costs, research suggests that the longer immigrants are in the country, the greater is their contribution to the American economy (Rohter 1993; Simon 1989).

The arguments over health care costs and immigration are good illustrations of current public opinion about all immigration-related issues. People fear that the health care system is being overwhelmed by fraudulent freeloaders, and their outrage is aimed at immigrants and foreigners. In early 1994, television's "60 Minutes" reported that large numbers of Mexican women illegally cross into the United States to have their babies in San Diego. Why? Because it is free, and the babies automatically become U.S. citizens. The majority of the mothers, it was reported, then go on welfare. But researchers say the health care costs of illegal immigrants are inflated:

A series of articles in the *San Diego Union-Tribune* estimated that Medi-Cal fraud cost San Diego and Imperial counties approximately $6.8 million in 1991. Most of the fraud resulted from foreign nationals claiming fake U.S. residences in order to receive free medical care. According to these accounts, there is strong evidence that "Medi-Cal has been used as a health plan for northwest Mexico and beyond, with citizens of many nations being drawn to California for care." The series indicated that much of the abuse stemmed from laws to ensure that undocumented immigrants received needed emergency and prenatal care. (Eisenstadt and Thorup 1994: 60)

What of the charge that undocumented workers are bankrupting Medi-Cal? It is of course true that immigrants, surely including undocumented immigrants, do use the public health care system, particularly emergency room service. It is also true that even a few upper-status Mexican nationals have fraudulently received publicly funded health treatment in the United States (see Eisenstadt and Thorup 1994: 59). However, Eisenstadt and Thorup conclude that in San Diego, "The majority of undocumented Mexican immigrants do not use public health services, despite the fact that they cannot afford private care providers." They note that many undocumented immigrants "try home remedies, or seek medical attention in Tijuana" (ibid.: 69, 60).

And outside the San Diego region, studies show that Latinos —most of whom are immigrants and the children of immigrants —underutilize the publicly financed health care system (Hayes-Bautista 1993). The great irony is that in all probability Latinos pay more into the health system than they take out of it. This fact does not excuse fraud, but it should be a cautionary note to those who would blame immigrants for the high cost of health care.

What about the California governor's charge (quoted in Rohter 1993) that the new immigrants are "drawn by the giant magnet of Federal incentives"? Anyone who has worked with new arrivals knows that, in the words of Wayne Cornelius:

> the vast majority of Mexican migrants—regardless of legal status—are motivated by the availability of jobs here that are far better-paid and more secure than the alternatives available to them in their home country. The second most frequently cited reason for migration is family reunification: to join relatives already settled in California. . . . In sum it is highly misleading to suggest that a large proportion of the new immigrants arriving in California today, especially from Mexico, are coming to "tap into the system." (Cornelius 1993a)

Upon arrival the new immigrants do use the resources available to them, but there is no evidence that they come specifically to take advantage of the U.S. welfare system. It is one of the ironies of late postindustrial capitalism that new immigrants are recruited to perform the dangerous or poorly paid work that native-born workers will not, and that, in the process, their use of some of the services of the advanced welfare state creates a lot of resentment (Hollifield 1992).

In sum, there is enough evidence to cast doubt on the argument that immigrants take more than they contribute: "Immigrants are successfully absorbed into the U.S. labor market. . . . The overall economic contributions of immigration exceed its economic liabilities" (Papademetriou 1994: 1).[38]

Paranoid Vigilance and the "Criminal Alien"

We turn now to arguably the most unsettling of all charges against the new arrivals: that they contribute disproportionately to the crime problem. An important feature of the anxiety generated by the new immigration is the failure to distinguish between legal and illegal immigrants. A 1993 *New York Times* survey reported that fully 64 percent of respondents erroneously believed that the majority of the new immigrants are in the United States illegally (Mydans 1993).

Similarly, people's association of the terms "illegal," "criminal," and "immigrant" feeds the common belief that not only are most new immigrants "illegals," but they are here with the purpose of committing crimes. A recent study found that 59 percent of those surveyed agreed with the statement that "immigrants add to the crime problem" (Nelan 1993: 11).

Talk of immigrant crime is even more charged than talk of crime in general. In the more primitive versions of this charged talk, crime is something that "aliens" bring into our world: "The new criminals are undocumented aliens from Mexico, some of whom live here but many of whom sleep in their native land and cross daily into the United States to commit their crimes. At the end of their workday, they go back into Mexico with a few dollars to show for their efforts" (quoted in Chavez 1992: 16). There is an everydayness implied in such talk: sleep, get up, cross the border, commit crimes, go back to Mexico. Simply, all aliens crossing the border are criminals.

The following assertion captures the exaggeration in much of the talk on immigrant crime. Audrey W. Bergner of the Alliance for Border Control testified to a committee of the California legislature that "98% of all aliens caught and held for return to Mexico at El Centro have criminal backgrounds" (California Legislature 1990: 3). In any other climate it would go without saying that it is not true that 98 percent of all undocumented aliens detained for deportation "have criminal backgrounds." In fact, according to INS estimates, only 11 to 15 percent "of the [San Diego County prison] population is deportable, and this number includes some legal residents as well as the undocumented" (Eisenstadt and Thorup 1994: 53).[39]

Much of the new talk deploys Hobbesian images of chaotic disorder and lack of control in which growing waves of criminal aliens threaten to destroy our way of life. Consider the angst reflected in the words of a former director of the INS in San Diego: "One only need go down to this border just a short distance south of us to see how wildly out of control it is. And when we speak of out of control, we're not just talking about a few folks wanting to come in to get a job, we're talking about a torrent of people flooding here, bringing all kinds of criminal elements and terrorists and all the rest with them" (Wolf 1988: 2). This is a description of a country under siege. As someone else said, "Every night I can see the campfires those [immigrant] men make. I know what they are doing out there. I know they are just waiting for the right time to rob us, or worse. I just want you to know that every night I go to bed with a pistol under my pillow to protect myself from them" (quoted in Chavez 1992: 18). The fear of the "terrorist" men waiting for the right moment to strike has led to renewed cries to further militarize the border region. In December 1993, the San Diego Police Department began turning over to the INS all undocumented immigrants they apprehend (Thornton 1993). And in February 1994, Attorney General Janet Reno announced a plan to add another 1,010 front-line agents to the border.[40]

Although some immigrants do commit crimes, their involvement in crime is exaggerated. For example, Simon concluded that, though there are few reliable studies on this topic, "the rate of all crime has been less among immigrants than among natives" (1989: 304). In the words of Eisenstadt and Thorup, the "incidence of such crime has been exaggerated or misrepresented by those opposed to immigration" (1994: 52). The appropriate question is, how exaggerated is the involvement of immigrant workers in crime?

Daniel Wolf, who has conducted the most systematic study of undocumented immigration and crime in southern California, has concluded that in San Diego County, an area heavily populated by undocumented immigrants, on average some 12 percent of those arrested—not convicted—for felonies are undocumented aliens (Wolf 1988). Although this figure is not small, we would make three important points. First, undocumented aliens tend to be arrested (again, not convicted) at rates higher than the general population (Wolf 1988). Second, there is reason to suspect that a significant number of the crimes reported as "undocumented alien crimes" are not committed by immigrant *workers* but by professional Mexican "border bandits" and drug smugglers, who are nevertheless counted as undocumented aliens when apprehended on the U.S. side of the international border (see Lamm and Imhoff 1985; Wambaugh 1984). Third, immigrant workers tend to be the *victims* of much of the crime committed by professional border bandits. Wolf writes, "There exists substantial unanimity among police that, as a group, migrant workers do not appear to be responsible for much serious crime. Most migrant workers are honest and hardworking" (Wolf 1988: 23).[41]

If migrant workers are, according to police accounts, not responsible for much serious crime, where does the fear of immigrant crime come from? We have already considered how the criminal acts of some highly visible immigrants and asylum seekers, such as those involved in the World Trade Center bombing, tend to make suspects of all immigrants. In addition, there may be two other important sources: the kernel-of-truth hypothesis, which says that all irrational fears are elaborations based on some fact, however small and insignificant, and our own model of psychological exploitation and ethnic disparagement. Let us first consider the kernel-of-truth hypothesis (see also Allport 1979).

According to Daniel Wolf, much of the concern about immigrant crime in southern California probably grows out of the work of border bandits, also called the "rob and return bunch." These are professional robbers who are not immigrant workers but who operate on both sides of the international border. According to this view, the kernel of truth is that both immigrant workers and border bandits are foreigners, and because the public is unable or unwilling to differentiate between the two groups, the sins of one are also attributed to the other. Ironically, Wolf found that immigrant workers are much more likely than native-born U.S. citizens to be the victims of border-bandit crime: "The 'border bandits' who commit robbery, rape, and murder perpetrate almost all their crimes in the dark of night *against* undocumented migrants crossing the border. (Some bandits 'work' the migrant camps further north.) *The undocumented alien worker, preyed upon by these violent criminals, is far more likely to be a victim of serious crime than a perpetrator of it*" (Wolf 1988: 23, emphasis added).

Our own view is that the fear of immigrant crime can be best described as irrationally out of proportion and even paranoid. Paranoia works, partly, on spectacular elaborations on kernels of truth (Shapiro 1965: 54–107). It is irrational to assume that because foreign border bandits and drug smugglers are known to commit crimes, all immigrant workers are criminals.

At this point we might well ask: Are the new immigrants really one of our most serious problems? Or are we using the new arrivals to deal, via the psychological mechanisms of projection and displacement, with shared, overwhelming anxieties? For example, in the United States since 1960 violent crime has increased 500 percent, and in 1990 alone 6 million violent crimes were committed (Wootton 1993: 12). Immigrants make easy scapegoats. Blaming them distracts everyone from looking seriously at the real causes of our growing problems, including widespread illiteracy, the breakdown of family and community, and the increased competition from foreign workers, be they in Japan or Los Angeles.

Much of the current fear of immigrants is irrational and paranoid in nature. We call it "paranoid fear" when group fear is laced with paranoid content. A person or group is singled out as the cause of another group's unbearable tensions (see Shapiro 1965: 73) and accused of possessing unacceptable traits (such as savagery, primitiveness, or aggression). The disparaged group that is singled out as the cause of unbearable anxieties then becomes a target of further self-righteous hatred and aggression.

Projecting its own hatred and desire to destroy onto the scapegoated group, the paranoid group is ever vigilant, certain that the disparaged "Other" is a constant threat. In paranoia, the more severe one's inner tension, the more the "Other" becomes "the bad object," in psychodynamic terms (Klein and Riviere 1964); the more intense the hatred toward the Other is; and the more intense is the certainty that the Other is dangerous. The paranoid "loses a sense of proportion" (Shapiro 1965: 65).[42] Thus paranoia leads to persecution.

The fear of immigrant crime, like all intense fears, has a deeply irrational component that is out of proportion with actual estimates of immigrant involvement in crime. People's anxiety, for example, extends well beyond the border region. In announcing his plan to add up to 600 agents to the U.S. Border Patrol along the U.S.-Mexico frontier, President Clinton said: "The simple fact is that we must not and we will not surrender our borders to those who wish to *exploit* our history of compassion and justice. We cannot tolerate those who traffic in human cargo, nor can we allow our people to be endangered by those who would enter our country to *terrorize* Americans" (quoted in Stern 1993, emphasis added).

In order to explore a second possible explanation of the irrational fear of aliens, we might profitably turn President Clinton's point around. Let us ask who, in fact, is terrorizing and exploiting whom.[43] Are the new immigrants terrorizing and exploiting U.S. citizens? Or are they the victims of terror and exploitation? The World Trade Center bombing aside, there is reason to suspect that the new immigrants in general—and particularly the more defenseless undocumented immigrants—are themselves targets of systematic terror and exploitation (see Lamm and Imhoff 1985; Lewis 1979; Wambaugh 1984).

As noted by Wolf (1988), undocumented immigrant workers are the targets of the great majority of crimes committed by border bandits. And what are their experiences once they settle in the new land? Leo Chavez reports, "Undocumented immigrants are the victims of random crimes committed by individuals with an irrational hatred or fear of them. For example, in November 1988 two teenagers in the community of Escondido, motivated by their dislike for Mexicans, used an AK-47 assault rifle to gun down two Mexican workers walking along a field of avocado trees" (1992: 60). In July 1993, two youths in Rancho Peñasquitos, San Diego County, shot a Mexican immigrant several times as he was sleeping in a canyon (*Rancho Peñasquitos News* 1993).

Are these the random acts of disturbed and angry teenagers, or is violence against immigrant workers more systematic? In the words of Senator Art Torres, chairman of the California Legislature Joint Committee on Refugee Resettlement, International Migration, and Cooperative Development:

> 1979, gang shoots, injures migrant workers in a camp; 1980, in Escondido, reports of assaults on migrant workers by law enforcement and gangs; 1981, Del Mar, Mexican man beaten to death; 1982, Escondido, migrant worker beaten severely by gang in a truck; 1983, Oceanside, Pablo Martinez Toledo and Raul Mejia Garcia shot and killed by three white youths; 16-year-old migrant worker shot and wounded in park; 1984, Fallbrook, California, six U.S. Marines conduct, quote, "beaner raids," unquote, armed attacks on Mexican migrant workers in their caves; 1985, Fallbrook, California, sniper shoots and wounds 17-year-old migrant in back, paralyzing him from the waist down; 1986, November, Encenitas, California, three 17-year-old white youths arrested in sniper shootings of migrant workers; San Ysidro, November of 1986, seven undocumented people shot by unidentified assailants on the freeway; 1987, north San Diego County, unidentified bodies of migrant workers—victims of violence—begin to appear throughout north county; 1988, Del Mar, California, killing of two migrant workers by two self-proclaimed white supremacists—victims: Hilario Salgado Castaneda and Matilde de La Sancha; October, 1989, Poway, California, gangs of white teens attack and shoot 14 mi-

grant workers with guns and paint bullets; Encenitas, October of '89, California, two border patrol agents shoot at, detain, and beat migrant worker; 1990 in Carlsbad, two store owners beat, handcuff, and kidnap migrant; 12-year-old Emilio Jimenez shot and killed by unidentified assailants; Carlsbad, California, robberies continue on migrant workers; Chula Vista, California, 1990 Border Patrol Agent shoots into a van filled with Salvadorians, wounding two; Vista, California, 1990, Sergio Mendez, farm worker, shot in the face by paint pellet fired in drive-by-shooting. (California Legislature 1990: 24)

Government employees, too, have mistreated immigrants. According to the human rights monitoring organization Americas Watch, border patrol supervisors "encourage the punitive beatings of suspects who run away from agents. The agents termed the practice, 'Thump 'em if they run'" (Americas Watch 1993). And "the remarks of one Border Patrol supervisor to his agents—remarks made in front of a visiting *Los Angeles Times* reporter—are illustrative: 'Catch as many tonks as you guys can. Safely. An alien is not worth busting a leg.' ('Tonk' is the word used to refer to an undocumented immigrant and refers to the sound of an agent's flashlight striking an immigrant's head)" (Americas Watch 1993: 11). According to another report by Americas Watch:

U.S. Border Patrol agents have committed many serious abuses against Mexican nationals. . . . In 1989, the American Friends Service Committee's U.S./Mexico Border program documented the cases of five Mexicans who were killed and seven others who were wounded by Border Patrol agents in five separate shooting incidents in the Tijuana area. Some of the incidents involved only border control agents. Others involved the Border Crime Prevention Unit, a joint venture of the Border Patrol and the San Diego police. One of those killed was fourteen-year-old Luis Eduardo Hernández who was run over and killed by a Border Patrol vehicle on August 20, 1989. The following week fifteen-year-old Pedro García Sánchez was shot in the back and wounded while trying to run back into Mexico. In December, officers of the Border Crime Prevention Unit shot and wounded another minor, Manuel Martín Flores. . . . Flores is now paralyzed from the waist down. On May 25, 1990, a U.S. Border Patrol agent fired three bullets from his service revolver . . . a sixteen-year-old Mexican boy was hit in the neck and seriously injured, and a woman was hit in the arm by the gun fire. According to Roberto Martínez of the American Friends Service Committee in San Diego, "No Border Patrol agent has been prosecuted for any unjustified killing of an alien in the past five years." . . .

In addition to violent acts of this type by the Border Patrol and police officials, citizens along the border have waged a campaign of intimidation against Mexicans and other aliens trying to cross the border without authorization. Organized under the slogan "Light Up the Border," citizens in the San Diego area hold monthly rallies during which they drive their cars to the U.S. border and turn their headlights onto Mexicans and other aliens waiting to cross. Participants in the campaign blame undocumented immigrants for a variety of social ills, including the influx of drugs into their community.

A more serious menace is posed by gangs of white supremacist youths in the San Diego area who dress in combat fatigues, carry knives, bows and arrows, and high powered rifles, and have been responsible for assaults and killings of Mexican immigrants. (Americas Watch 1990: 86–87)

In a follow-up report Americas Watch concluded that "serious abuses by U.S. immigration law enforcement agents continue and that current mechanisms intended to curtail abuses and discipline officers are woefully inadequate." The report states that even "after heightened scrutiny from legislators, human rights groups, community activists, and the press concerning the conduct of their agents . . . the agencies (INS, Border Patrol and Customs) have failed to introduce measures needed to curtail agent misconduct or to hold abusive agents accountable." The report established that "beatings and other forms of mistreatment are still common during the arrest and detention of undocumented immigrants, U.S. citizens and legal residents (of Latino origin). While less frequent than beatings and mistreatment, unjustified shootings and sexual assaults also occur" (Americas Watch 1993: 1–2).

Likewise, a 1992 American Friends Service Committee report said:

Significant and serious abuses continue to occur in the enforcement of immigration law along the U.S.-Mexico border . . . [including] psychological and verbal abuse (use of racial or ethnic insults, rude or abusive language, threats or coercion, and prolonged or aggressive interrogation techniques); physical abuse (shootings, beatings, sexual assault, injury by vehicles and high-speed chases), at least seven of which resulted in death; illegal or inappropriate searches (including questioning based solely on ethnic appearance, entry without warrant or consent, overzealous execution of search warrants, strip searching without proper motive, and illegal law-enforcement raids); violation of due process (failure to advise persons of their legal rights or eligibility for statutory benefit, denial of access to counsel, and fabrication of evidence); illegal or inappropriate seizures of persons (unlawful temporary detention, false arrest, and illegal deportations); seizure or destruction of property; violations of the rights of Native Americans to cross the border freely. (American Friends Service Committee 1992: 3)

And a three-part *Los Angeles Times* story recorded "persistent reports of abusive behavior by agents, improper shootings and crimes including drug smuggling, sexual assault and theft" (Rotella and McDonnell 1993). As long as INS officers feel under siege, and as long as they operate with impunity at the border, human rights violations of immigrants will likely continue.

According to our perspective, there is an unmistakably "projective" and paranoid quality to the fear and hatred of immigrants. Nowhere is this projective quality more evident than in imputing criminal motivations to undocumented immigrants. Undocumented immigrants are, after all, among the most vulnerable of all workers (Chavez 1992; Walsh 1993; Lewis 1979).

If they are not attacked by organized bands of nativists "hunting Mexicans" on the U.S. side of the international border (Americas Watch 1990: 87) and are able to get past the border zone and find work, they are arguably the most exploited of all workers. Before "employer sanctions" were in place (the law making it illegal for employers to hire undocumented workers), some employers turned workers in to the INS for deportation rather than pay them what they were owed (Conover 1987).

In the exclusive north county area of San Diego, we collected dozens of reports of undocumented domestic workers who were underpaid or never paid for their work. Without any legal recourse, most simply left their places of work, without collecting their earnings, in search of better luck and some compassion elsewhere. A lawsuit filed in September 1993 in the Sonoma County Superior Court illustrates what often happens to immigrants:

> When Adam Zuniga came to the United States at age 14, he didn't enroll in school. He went to work. A rancher hired him as a stable boy, Zuniga said, and housed him in a [discarded horse] trailer, with no heat and no running water, charging him $200 a month rent. . . . Zuniga, now 24, charged that he regularly worked 9–12 hour days, sometimes seven days a week, for James Stembridge and Sandra Harper, co-owners of James Stembridge Stables. Zuniga said he spent most of his teen-age years in service to Stembridge and Harper for a promised salary of $125 a week, which he claims, he often did not receive. . . . Immigrant rights lawyers say Zuniga's case is important because of what it says about the treatment of newcomers who do jobs U.S. citizens won't take, and the treatment of immigrant children. . . . [His lawyer] hopes his story will encourage tough prosecution of employers who ignore the minimum wage and overtime laws as they exploit immigrant workers. [The lawyer hopes] the case will bring public understanding that "there's a whole hidden economy in this state that depends upon the exploitation of immigrant laborers. . . . Our neighborhoods and businesses are full of immigrants being treated like slaves or animals, or worse." (Marinucci 1993)

For other such reports see Lamm and Imhoff 1985; Lewis 1979; and Wambaugh 1984. The reality that immigrant workers are routinely exploited is changed, through the psychological mechanism of projection, into a paranoia that they are here to exploit us. This defense mechanism justifies the initial exploitative treatment: we should not feel guilty for exploiting people who are exploiting us (stealing, taking our resources, using our services, and the like).

Particularly when a dominant group feels threatened, it tends to use those in a subordinate position as receptacles for their unacceptable anxieties (see Kristeva 1991). In addition, different ethnic groups elicit different conscious and unconscious fantasies from the dominant culture. Disparaged groups—usually those who look, sound, and indeed "are" most unlike ourselves—are those with whom empathic linkage is most difficult to achieve.

In the post-utopian moment, the more pathetic, helpless, and exploited the new arrivals seem, the greater our repulsion and empathic flight. It is as if we are afraid that the drowning will—through the principle of "contagion"—drown us all. The fear of being engulfed by their misery reflects our own anxieties about such things as crime, the economy, and natural disasters.[44]

Racists typically single out a group or groups onto which they project their own anxieties (Kristeva 1991). A disparaged group may be thought of as crime-prone, or dirty, or parasitic, or hypersexual, or hyperaggressive, or obscenely preoccupied with money, or even prone to drink infant blood (see Dundes 1991).

Today, those who are least like the dominant population—the new immigrants—have been singled out for such projection. Psychological theorists of varied perspectives have argued that frustration, injury, endangerment, and upheaval often lead to aggression (see Dollard et al. 1939, Freud 1930, Fromm 1973, Kohut 1972, Kristeva 1991, and Mitchell 1993). This model explains the current U.S. condition as well as developments in Europe.

Consider the words of Daniel Cohn-Bendit, director of multicultural affairs for the city of Frankfurt, Germany:

> Over the last several years, we have witnessed the emergence of a new xenophobia in Europe. This ostensible fear of foreigners is as much a product of anxiety about change in society as it is an actual fear of foreigners themselves. Western societies are passing through a difficult stage in the process of modernization. Many people simply cannot handle all the changes. Family relations are changing, jobs are being lost, and people find their social status shifting. Many people developed a vision of personal consumption that is very difficult to realize in today's economic

environment. All these uncertainties about individual identity have produced a new assertiveness about national identity. People again feel a need
to belong to a secure and well defined group.

The presence of new immigrants accentuates those fears. To live with
foreigners is always something new and uncertain—a challenge. (Cohn-
Bendit 1992: 62)

And Stanley Hoffmann writes of the French malaise:

French discontent seemed particularly strong during 1993. . . . The new
disillusionment results from a series of blows to French pride and hopes,
and from the sense that virtually all of the possible political formulas for
dealing with the "twenty-year crisis" that began in 1973 have been tried
in vain. . . .

Unemployment has been the worst of the shocks inflicted on French
self-esteem. . . . With more than three million people officially out of
work—12 percent of the active population—the situation is unprece-
dented since World War II. . . .

Indeed, during much of 1992 and 1993, what was most striking about
French political life was its regression into a kind of shrill, defensive,
and protectionist nationalism which recalled previous episodes of French
chauvinism in French history. (Hoffmann 1994: 10–11)

Hoffmann concludes that things in France are not as bad as the
French think they are. He uses the astonishing argument that today
there is no "war of French against French" in assigning blame for the
"twenty-year crisis":

It is not only the cheap goods produced by overpopulated poor countries that threaten France, it is also their miserable masses attracted by
Europe's wealth. As the Gaullist interior minister keeps insisting, the
door must be closed to them as well. . . . [But] large numbers of these
foreign invaders are already within the wall; hence the government has
shown a new vigor in defending the traditional model of an integrated
French nation, and in fostering the already widespread view that multiculturalism *à l'américaine* would balkanize and dismantle the Republic.
(Ibid.: 13)

In the United States, as in Europe, anti-immigrant fever has
reached such dangerous proportions that almost any frustration leads
to violence. The devastation left by the Los Angeles earthquake of
January 1994 led to another wave of immigrant bashing. When President Clinton proposed $8.6 billion in disaster relief to the earthquake
victims, a number of California politicians, including Rep. Anthony
Beilenson and Sen. Dianne Feinstein (both Democrats) and Rep. Ron
Packard (a Republican), moved quickly to introduce provisions that

would prevent federal relief aid from going to undocumented immigrants.

In the words of Rep. Packard, "When it comes to the spending of taxpayers' dollars, I cannot turn my head and treat undocumented aliens like citizens. They just keep coming across the border" (quoted in Mydans 1994). Likewise, Rep. Beilenson said, "I don't think the taxpayers of this country should be asked to pay for two months or more of rent, or to replace the costs of furniture and clothing that may have been lost by . . . [undocumented immigrants]" (quoted in Reeves 1994). They ignored the fact that undocumented aliens in Los Angeles County generated well over $900 million in tax revenues during the 1991–92 fiscal year (see Los Angeles County 1992: 6).

That such statements are more about benefiting from the politics of hatred than about promoting sound fiscal management is revealed by the fact that even the conservative Republican mayor of Los Angeles, Richard Riordan, came out against the proposed amendments because they would create a "bureaucratic nightmare" (quoted in Mydans 1994) that would end up costing even more of the taxpayers' money. The same is true of Proposition 187, the California initiative approved by voters in November 1994, which would make undocumented immigrants ineligible for public services such as public education and nonemergency health care. If fully implemented, the new law—according to California's independent legislative analyst—would put at risk "billions of dollars annually" provided by the federal government (see Epilogue).

There is a feedback of sorts between the violence in "psychological exploitation" (blaming immigrants for problems not of their making and lashing out at them) and the violence in "instrumental exploitation" (exploitation of a subordinate group for cheap labor, for example). Indeed, psychological exploitation feeds instrumental exploitation: because members of the subordinate group are "bad" (they take our tax money, commit crimes, etc.), we must treat them harshly. The result is that exploitation is frequently defended as what those being exploited deserve.

Many of the new immigrants—particularly those from Latin America—are victims of extraordinary violence—at the hands of border bandits, corrupt Mexican officials, the U.S. Border Patrol, and self-appointed paramilitary groups. And once inside the United States, they face racist violence. In addition, psychological violence is inflicted on the new immigrants when they are blamed for problems such as crime and the economic downturn. In fact, the overwhelming majority of new immigrants, documented and undocumented, are decent, hard-working, taxpaying people, driven by the dream of providing their loved ones a better life.

In this chapter we have reviewed some of the problems—real and perceived—associated with immigration in the United States and Europe.

As we have seen, many labor-importing European democracies are facing dilemmas not unlike those heatedly debated in the American public arena. Facing the pressures of a general economic downturn (including high unemployment rates) and ongoing waves of undocumented immigrants and asylum seekers, public opinion on both continents has turned against the new immigrants and asylum seekers.

In the United States there is worry about uncontrollable waves of poor, brown-skinned, low-skilled immigrants from Latin America; Europeans worry about waves of Africans, an influx of Islamic fundamentalists, and the refugees escaping civil war in the former Yugoslavia. On both sides of the Atlantic there is concern about the cultural adaptation of the new immigrants, the problem of crime, and the costs associated with immigration.

At the same time, studies in both Europe and the United States suggest that more immigrant laborers will be needed in the future, and that immigrants in general contribute more than their fair share to the economies of their new countries. Because so many of the fears about immigrants seem unfounded, we believe the psychosocial aspects of "immigrant anxiety" need to be kept in mind.

CHAPTER 2

Uncertain Journeys

LATINOS IN THE UNITED STATES

In Chapter 1 we examined some of the salient features of people's anxiety about immigration. We established that immigration and asylum are among the most controversial topics in a number of advanced postindustrial societies, including the United States. We specifically addressed two of the most heated charges in the current debate: that immigrants are, overall, an economic burden and that immigrants are responsible for a large portion of crime.

A review of the relevant data and studies suggests that there is a great deal of misunderstanding and uncertainty about the new immigration. Some surveys indicate that for many Americans the distinction between legal and illegal immigrants has been blurred. In fact, some studies have found that a majority now think, incorrectly, that most new immigrants are in the country illegally.

Many observers casually collapse legal immigrants, illegal immigrants, asylum seekers, and refugees into a single category. But the experiences of legal immigrants are typically quite different from those of undocumented immigrants and refugees. And as we shall see, there are important differences among the various Latino subgroups (e.g., Mexican immigrants, Mexican Americans, Cubans, mainland Puerto Ricans, and Central and South Americans). In the shadowy world of undocumented immigration, figures and statistics are particularly unreliable. Quite simply, no one knows with any certainty even very fundamental facts such as how many undocumented immigrants now reside in the United States. This lack of certainty has become fertile ground for outrageous claims about their number, their crime activities, their cost to the state, and so forth. Some politicians have used these statistics to further their own agendas.

Lost in the resulting heated debate are the new arrivals themselves. Who are the new immigrants? What do they want? Why are they here? How do they experience their uncertain journey north?

In this chapter we turn to a discussion of some central themes in the cultural psychology of Latino immigrants and their children. We explore various aspects of the Latino experience, considering first- and second-generation (U.S.-born) individual, family, and group dynamics. We examine some of the most important findings in the research on Mexican immigrants, U.S.-born Mexican Americans, and recent immigrants and refugees from war-torn Central America. We also point out some relevant findings of researchers working with Cuban Americans and mainland Puerto Ricans.

We consider how certain enduring psychocultural features of the immigrant experience are central to understanding the psychosocial (and particularly the educational) condition of the various Latino subgroups. Later in the book we place the findings of our own empirical research in the context of the wider body of research considered in this chapter.

A significant weakness in the relevant literature, a problem we set out to overcome in developing our own research agenda, is that no study had systematically compared the experiences of Latinos before they immigrated with those of newly arrived immigrants, second-generation Latinos, and non-Latino, nonimmigrant whites. We have done so, using the experiences of a sample of youths in the state of Guanajuato, an immigrant-sending area of Mexico. In addition, we provide a psychocultural theoretical framework for understanding their different experiences.

The Latino Tapestry

Just as the Latino condition is not a monolithic phenomenon, neither are Latinos a single people. Although they share a number of characteristics, Mexican immigrants, Mexican Americans, Cuban Americans, mainland Puerto Ricans, and immigrants and refugees from Central and South America are distinct populations. These groups share various degrees of familiarity with the Spanish language and such cultural traits as the importance of the extended family ("familism"), an emphasis on spiritual and interpersonal relationships, respect for authority, and a focus on the "here and now" (rather than on the future, which is the orientation of the dominant American culture).

Yet it is important to emphasize that Latinos in the United States are a diverse demographic and sociocultural population. Latinos come from many countries and from different socioeconomic, educational, and professional backgrounds. Cuban Americans (1 million in 1990), for example, tend to attain higher educational levels than all other Latino groups and have higher incomes as well (Portes and Bach 1985).

On average, Cuban Americans are older than other Latinos (according to 1990 census figures their median age was 39.1), have lower unemployment rates (5.8 percent in 1990), a lower percentage of out-of-wedlock births (16.1 percent), and a lower percentage of families living in poverty (12.5 percent). Although some of the more recent Cuban immigrants have been poorer and less well educated than their predecessors (for example, the estimated 129,000 Cuban refugees who arrived over the course of a few weeks in 1980), many of the earlier refugees were professionals who left for political reasons after Fidel Castro's ascent to power in 1959.

Some have argued that their professional backgrounds and refugee status gave the earlier Cuban immigrants "a sense of specialness which may have facilitated their adaptation to new environments and may be connected to their relative success [in the United States]" (Bernal 1982: 197). In addition, U.S. refugee policy during the cold war favored refugees fleeing Cuba over those fleeing genocidal—but anticommunist—regimes in Guatemala and El Salvador.

Conversely, Puerto Ricans (about 2.5 million of whom live on the U.S. mainland, according to 1990 figures) tend to have the lowest levels of education and the poorest economic conditions of all Latino groups (Rodriguez 1991). In 1990 the median age of Puerto Ricans living on the mainland was 27. Puerto Ricans tend to have higher unemployment rates than other Latinos (8.6 percent). They also have the highest percentage of out-of-wedlock births (53 percent)[1] and the highest percentage of families living in poverty (30.4 percent). Linda Chavez summarizes:

> [Mainland] Puerto Ricans are not simply the poorest of all Hispanic groups; they experience the highest degree of social dysfunction of any Hispanic group and exceed that of blacks on some indicators. Thirty-nine percent of all Puerto Rican families are headed by single women; 53 percent of all Puerto Rican children are born out of wedlock; the proportion of men in the labor force is lower among Puerto Ricans than in any other

group, including blacks; Puerto Ricans have the highest welfare participation rate of any group in New York, where nearly half of all Puerto Ricans in the United States live. (Chavez 1991: 140)

Although Puerto Ricans have U.S. citizenship, the quasi-colonial nature of the relationship between the United States and Puerto Rico has created some enduring problems in the mainland Puerto Rican community (Ogbu 1978). Their experiences in New York, where large numbers went to work in low-skilled garment industry jobs in the 1940s and 1950s, strongly influenced Puerto Ricans' lives on the mainland. By the 1950s and 1960s, when New York lost almost 40 percent of its jobs in manufacturing, "Puerto Rican families chose to stay, and many ended up on welfare." Indeed, by the "1960s half of all Puerto Rican families [in New York] were already receiving some public assistance" (Chavez 1991: 142).

Chavez speculates that welfare dependency was in part encouraged by certain cultural patterns: the marriage rate is lower among Puerto Ricans than among other Latinos, and the large percentage of female-headed households not only encouraged welfare dependency but also hindered their socioeconomic mobility (ibid.: 139–59). She fails to discuss, however, the role racism and discrimination may have played in the Puerto Rican experience on the U.S. mainland (see Rodriguez 1991). A significant number of Puerto Ricans are phenotypically black. Hence their experiences may have been significantly different from those of "mestizos" or phenotypically "whiter" Latinos.

Latinos of Mexican origin (some 13.3 million according to the 1990 census) and immigrants and refugees from Central and South America (2.8 million in 1990)[2] tend to fall somewhere between Cubans and mainland Puerto Ricans in educational attainment and income level. According to the most recent census data, Mexican-origin Latinos (both U.S.-born Mexican Americans and foreign-born Mexican immigrants) are the youngest of all Latino subgroups: their median age in 1990 was 24.1 (it was 33.5 for the non-Hispanic population; see Bureau of the Census 1993).

Mexican-origin Latinos have the highest unemployment rate of all subgroups (9.0 percent) and the second-lowest (second to Cubans) percentage of out-of-wedlock births (28.9 percent). In 1990 some 25.7 percent of all Mexican-origin families lived in poverty. Mexican-origin Latinos are themselves a highly heterogeneous population that includes new arrivals from various regions of Mexico as well as the descendants of residents of the formerly Mexican territories of the U.S. Southwest (see Alvarez 1987; Grebler, Moore, and Guzman 1970; Madsen 1964; Meier and Rivera 1993; Stoddard 1973; Wagner and Haug 1971).

According to 1990 census figures, Latinos of Central and South American origin had a median age of 28 and an unemployment rate of 6.6 percent. Their percentage of out-of-wedlock births was 37.1, and some 16.8 percent of their families lived in poverty. Latinos of Central and South American origin are an extremely diverse group: they include recently arrived asylum seekers from rural Central America as well as earlier waves of professionals from Argentina, Brazil, Chile, and other countries.

The immigrant experience of newer arrivals from Mexico and Central and South America varies tremendously, depending on whether they entered the United States as documented or undocumented immigrants (see Chavez 1992); whether they came voluntarily or because of political persecution; whether they came as seasonal migrants or with plans to stay permanently; and whether they came to the United States as a family unit or as individuals.

Latino immigration to the United States is an extremely complex phenomenon. Although analytically we advocate differentiating the issues facing the immigrants from those facing the U.S.-born first generation, many individuals may not fit either category well. For example, there are those who are born on the U.S. side of the border but who over the years spend significant amounts of time in Mexico or Central America and then return to settle permanently in the United States. There are those who are born in the United States who maintain a cultural identity as Mexicans or Salvadorans and not Mexican Americans or even Latinos; they may be called "intergenerational" Latinos. Within the same family there may be legal residents as well as undocumented immigrants. And there are those who were in the Southwest territories before they became part of the United States, where they are now the largest "minority" group;[3] and they cannot of course be considered immigrants. In our model, in considering such cases, we are less interested in where a person was actually born than we are in their own self-identification (e.g., as Mexican, Chicano, Latino, or Salvadoreño).

All of the factors we have discussed greatly influence Latino opportunities and experience. However, one common denominator in the experience of most immigrant Latinos is that they come from relatively impoverished developing countries, and typically from the lower socioeconomic strata, into a more affluent society.

Immigration and Its Discontents

By far the majority of Latinos in the United States are immigrants or the children of immigrants. Therefore any serious consideration of the Latino condition must provide an understanding of how the immigration background shapes experience.

In our view, immigration is an open-ended process that differentially affects the experiences of the generations (the immigrants themselves, the first generation, and the second generation). Hence we are critical of theories of immigrant assimilation and acculturation that make "closed" statements (e.g., "by the second generation group X was fully assimilated") about what is, in our estimation, a dynamic intergenerational process.[4]

Among immigrants, tales of past generations are handed down to children and grandchildren. For many second- and third-generation Latinos the immigrant past may also *be* the present.[5] The autobiography of Ruben Navarrette, a high-achieving, self-described Harvard Chicano, makes this point well. He writes of leaving his sleepy town in the San Joaquin valley, a popular immigrant destination in rural California, for a life of privilege at Harvard: "I stared out the window and into the peach trees that rushed by the roadside in the blur of speed. Months earlier, Mexican farm workers had been in those fields at six in the morning, standing on wooden ladders and picking fruit in one hundred degree heat for minimum wage. *Boys my age, living my grandfather's life*" (Navarrette 1993: 34, emphasis added).

Among Latinos the past is not only kept alive through family narratives but unfolds in front of our very eyes as recent arrivals endure anew the cycle of deprivation, hardship, and discrimination that is characteristic of first-generation immigrant life.[6]

Immigrants often arrive in a new land as pioneers with a dream of making a better life for themselves and their children. The priorities of the immigrant generation are relatively clear: get a job, earn money, learn a new language, educate the children. Many new immigrants, in fact, hope eventually to return home once financial considerations allow it.

The obvious difficulties that most immigrants face include language inadequacies, a general unfamiliarity with the customs and expectations of the new country (what anthropologists refer to as "cultural discontinuities"), limited economic opportunities, poor housing conditions, discrimination, and what psychologists term the "stresses of acculturation" (Rogler, Cortes, and Malgady 1991; see also Arevalo 1987; Cervantes, Salgado de Snyder, and Padilla 1989; Kantor 1969; Malzberg 1969; Padilla 1993; Padilla, Alvarez, and Lindholm 1986; Rodriguez 1989; Rogler, Malgady, and Rodriguez 1989; Salgado de Snyder 1990; Sluzki 1979).

Despite these obstacles, in many cases immigrants feel better off than they did in their country of origin, although they may still seem poor and disadvantaged by the standards of their host country. Because the home country remains their point of reference, many may fail to internalize the negative attitudes of the host country toward them (Roosens 1989a: 132–34). Immigrants commonly view and experience their circumstances in terms not of the ideals and expectations of the majority society but of those of the "old culture" (De Vos 1973).

This is part of an interesting orientation that can be called "the immigrant's dual frame of reference" (Suárez-Orozco and Suárez-Orozco 1992). Immigrants constantly compare and contrast their current lot in the host society with their previous lives (see also Leman 1987). During the earliest phases of immigration, the new arrivals may idealize the new country as a land of unlimited opportunities:

> Here [in the United States] there are more opportunities to find a good job. There [in Guatemala] we have no national funds, the national bank of Guatemala is empty. It is a big robbery. The different presidents come in saying that they want to help the country, and all they really do is take care of themselves. The people stay poor without anything. Now here you can study, you can better yourself. There are many opportunities here. I learned English here. Few people in Guatemala can learn another language. Here you can express yourself, you can complain out loud. There is no persecution like in Guatemala. There everything depends on who you know.[7]

Many new arrivals may at the same time concentrate on the negative aspects of life in the land left behind. A new arrival from El Salvador illustrated this principle when he noted:

> Life in my country is very backward. There we live in a humble way. You are remote from everything. The people are ignorant. You can't do anything there, you can't travel, you can't learn another language. Here people are open and there is freedom. Here there are people from all over the world. This is a liberal country. This is the most modern country in the world. There kids grow up in the shadows of their mothers' skirts. They train you to be obedient. Here I don't see that. . . . Here you have the freedom to do whatever pleases you. Here there are opportunities we do not have [in El Salvador].

These sentiments are also found among other Latino immigrants, including many from Mexico.[8] Rogler, Cortes, and Malgady explore the psychosocial consequences of an important generational discontinuity between the Mexico-born parents and their California-born children that relates to the immigrant's dual frame of reference. They write, "The selectivity of the migration stream from Mexico to California tends to create a psychologically robust first-generation immigrant population who feels less deprived because migration has increased their standard of living; in contrast, the Mexican Americans born in the United States feel more deprivation because of their much higher but unrealized aspirations" (1991: 589).

We concur with this observation. The children of immigrants evaluate their experiences in the new country differently from the immigrant generation. In part, this is because the U.S.-born children of immigrants did not experience the limitations and hardships of life in the old country. In fact, the children of immigrants may even romanticize and idealize the old country.

It is important to note that immigrants may increase both their own standard of living and (perhaps more important) the standard of living of the family members left behind. Latino immigrants send billions of dollars every year to their relatives in Mexico and Central and South America. Parker and Rea estimate that the annual remittances of undocumented immigrants in San Diego County alone are over $220 million (1993: x).[9]

"Maria," a new arrival from Mexico, illustrates how for many Latinos an important aspect of immigration is improving the lives of those left behind.[10] Maria came to the United States in the early 1990s when she was twenty-nine years old. Her husband's sudden death from cancer had made their already precarious economic situation unbearably difficult. In order to feed her four children, she said, the family decided Maria should go to the United States in search of work. Two of her sisters, as well as many other friends from her *rancho* (village) in Mexico, had already come to the United States to escape the Mexican economic crisis of the 1980s. They sent word that Maria could find employment in the service sector and earn between $100 and $150 a week. After a harrowing journey, which included *"hacer la lucha"* (battling) corrupt Mexican officials, dangerous border bandits, abusive "coyotes" (professionals who for a fee of $100 to $300 dollars per person help undocumented migrants cross the border; see Conover 1987), and the feared *migra* (INS), she made it to the United States.

As a live-in maid in a middle-class southern California suburb,

Maria eventually earned enough to send home between $200 and $300 every month. This sum, Maria said, was more than double the wage she was making in Mexico before she left.[11] The money Maria sends back goes to feed and dress her children, whom she left in the care of her parents. Now they can even buy an occasional toy, even a bicycle. Maria's remittances are also critical for purchasing fertilizer, animal feed, and the agricultural equipment used by her father and brothers. Whenever possible, she also sends home clothes, toys, and other goods she is able to purchase at bargain prices at the local flea market. Maria's dream now is to obtain her "papers" (immigrant documents) so that she may bring her children to the United States to be with her. Like many other undocumented immigrants, if she is not able to obtain her papers, Maria said she would want to go back to her *rancho* as soon as she had saved enough money (see Ross 1993).

A single immigrant is thus responsible for ameliorating the standard of living of many others. The psychological losses Maria suffered in leaving her family behind are alleviated by her realization that by being away she can best help those she loves. Many immigrants experience similar losses, marginality, and deprivation but know that they are making a tremendous difference in the lives of those left behind.

The children of immigrants typically do not share their parents' dual frame of reference. Not being immigrants themselves, they cannot frame their current experiences in terms of the old country's ideals, standards, and expectations. The U.S.-born generation is less likely to send money to the relatives in the old country. Rather than seeing themselves as better off, they more clearly see their deprivation and marginality in relation to the majority culture (Horowitz 1983). Thus the second generation often faces the same discriminations and economic difficulties that its parents faced, but *does not* perceive the benefits as they did.

Ongoing discrimination and ethnic tension can have an erosive effect on the vulnerable children of immigrants. José Villareal insightfully describes the phenomenon:

> Their bitterness and hostile attitude towards "whites" was not merely a lark. They had learned hate through actual experience with everything the word implied. They had not been as lucky as he and had the scars to prove it. . . . [Their experiences, however,] were due more to the character of a handful of men than to the wide, almost organized attitude of a society, for just as zootsuiters were blamed *en masse* for the actions of a few, they, in turn, blamed the other side for the very same reason. (Villareal 1959: 150–51)

Villareal's description is timeless. It was written in 1959 but could just as well have been written in 1969, 1979, 1989, or 1994. Anthropologists George De Vos and John Ogbu have argued that the specific problems facing the children of immigrants and other minority groups must be seen in the context of the distinct psychosocial experiences of each group as it enters a dominant society (see De Vos 1973, 1980, 1983, n.d.; Ogbu 1974, 1978, 1981, 1982, 1983, 1991a, 1991b; Ogbu and Matute-Bianchi 1986; Gibson and Ogbu 1991; Fordham and Ogbu 1986; see also Jacob and Jordan 1987 and 1993; for a critique of Ogbu see Pieke 1991). Ogbu (1991a) describes the special problems facing minority groups that were initially incorporated into a dominant society against their will—such as African Americans through slavery or Native Americans and the original Mexican Americans through conquest.

In addition to their original subordination, these groups have been subjected to what Ogbu calls a job ceiling. They were assigned the most undesirable menial jobs in the opportunity structure and could not rise above these positions regardless of effort, talent, motivation, or achievement.

We pointed out in Chapter 1 that minorities may be subject to both "instrumental exploitation" for economic purposes and "psychological exploitation" (such as negative stereotyping). Economic exploitation and psychological exploitation are, in a sense, two sides of the same coin: psychological exploitation and disparagement justify the dominant society's economic treatment of these groups.[12]

Psychological and instrumental exploitation deeply affect the children of immigrants. How do they respond to such assaults on their identity? Some immigrant and second-generation youths struggle to synthesize aspects of the two traditions. Among those who "make it" (in the idiom of the dominant society), guilt and the need to make reparation often become important. In many such cases, one's success in the context of the deprivation and suffering of loved ones may create intense feelings of guilt. Guilt is often assuaged by helping less fortunate members of one's group. Others, who leave their own ethnic group and attempt to join the dominant group, often later suffer shame and doubt about their decision, for which they may overcompensate. Yet others may resolutely reject the society that rejects them and turn to those who share their predicament—their peers. From this third situation typically emerge countercultural groups or gangs who reject aspects of the dominant society—including schools—and affirm their own ethnic identity. Much of

the anger and violence in gang life is a reaction to the ethnic injuries and assaults endured by the members, their families, and their
friends.

Gates to the Dream: Latinos in Schools

Among Latinos, poor achievement in school continues to be a serious problem (Suárez-Orozco 1989). According to 1993 census data,
only 51.3 percent of all Hispanics age twenty-five and older have
completed high school (the figure is 79.9 percent for whites), and
only 9.7 percent of all Hispanics age twenty-five and older have
completed four years of college or more (22 percent of whites have;
Bureau of the Census 1993). There are also important differences in
educational experience among the Latino subgroups (see Appendix,
Table A.1).

The reasons for the poor performance of Latinos in schools are
complex. Vigil (1988a) attributes it to the fact that many Latino immigrant parents have not had much education themselves and yet
have attained a modest degree of prosperity. Hence some parents
may be sending the message to the children, "We made it without
formal schooling, so you can too." But research shows that Latino
parents typically *want* their children to have the formal education they themselves could not have (Goldenberg, Reese, and Gallimore 1992; Reese, Gallimore, Balzano, and Goldenberg 1991; Suárez-
Orozco 1989). Others have observed that Latino families encourage
youths to get jobs, marry, and have children early, activities that may
divert them from formal education (see Navarrete 1993).

A number of theoretical models have attempted to explain poor
Latino school performance. During the 1960s proponents of the culture of poverty model (also called the cultural deprivation model)
rejected the notion that poor Latino performance was due to innately
inferior intelligence (see Suárez-Orozco 1989). According to cultural
deprivation theorists, the problem was in large part due to cultural
influences. They argued that certain cultures failed to provide their
children with the basic tools required for successful school functioning. For example, Bloom, Davis, and Hess wrote that the roots of
cultural deprivation "can be traced to . . . experiences in the home
which do not transmit the cultural patterns necessary for the types
of learning characteristics of the schools and the larger society"
(1965: 4).

In discussing the specific problems facing Latino children in

American schools, Heller wrote, "The kind of socialization Mexican American children receive is not conducive to the development of capacities needed for advancement in a dynamic society. This type of upbringing creates stumbling blocks to future advancement by stressing values that hinder mobility—family ties, honor, masculinity, and living in the present—and by neglecting the values that are conducive to it—achievement, independence, and deferred gratification" (Heller 1966: 34–35).

By the 1970s, leading researchers began to turn away from such explanatory models, noting serious flaws in the main tenets of the cultural deprivation model (see Ogbu 1978; Trueba 1987). First, the assortment of a more or less arbitrary list of traits hardly constitutes a culture in the standard anthropological use of the term. Second, as Trueba (1987) and others perceptively pointed out, "the cultural deprivation rationale coheres beautifully to the American brand of ethnocentrism: Minority problems are caused by *their* peculiar form of culture" (Carter and Segura 1979: 77; emphasis in original). In addition, these models seemed to use middle-class majority-culture traits as the yardstick for normality, making ethnic and minority deviations from this arbitrary standard pathological. Other researchers suggested that, far from being the causes of school failure and poverty, some minority traits were the consequences of powerlessness and discrimination over generations. From the viewpoint of the 1990s, another obvious flaw in these earlier models is that they are mechanistic and do not take account of human agency, group variability, and change.

Our data, as we shall see, strongly suggest that Mexican youngsters in Mexico are highly achievement oriented and hence cast doubt on the generalization that Mexican socialization "is not conducive to the development of the capacities needed for advancement in a dynamic society" (Heller 1966: 34). From our viewpoint, the problems facing Latinos in U.S. schools have less to do with their cultural background per se than with the process of immigration, resettlement, and resulting minority status.

By the 1970s and 1980s researchers began to carefully examine the processes leading to failure in school. Henry Trueba and his colleagues and others approached the problems facing Latino youths in American schools by exploring majority-minority "cultural discontinuities" (in language, cognition, value orientation, and the like). According to these scholars, the root of the problem is that schools fail to provide culturally appropriate educational experiences to their minority students (see Trueba 1989a, 1989b; Delgado-Gaitan and

Trueba 1991; Trueba, Rodriguez, Zou, and Cintrón 1993). Much of this important work was influenced by theoretical breakthroughs in the field of sociolinguistics by John Gumperz and his associates (Gumperz 1981; Gumperz and Hymes 1972; Mehan 1978). A series of careful ethnographic studies documented the language and other discontinuities between Latino students and the English-speaking middle-class school system (see Carter and Segura 1979; Suárez-Orozco 1986, 1987; Trueba 1989a, 1989b, 1993).

In Gumperz's model, communication is a complex phenomenon that includes verbal utterances (words), situated meanings (speakers' intentions), and context (speakers' perceptions of social situations; see Gumperz 1981: 3–23). In order for communication to take place, persons must also share an understanding of common meta-communication cues such as intonation, code switching, stress, syntax, and loudness. These are culturally constructed cues. Face-to-face interactions in small settings, such as schools, often capture and re-create the class and ethnic inequalities that permeate the larger sociocultural environment. In brief, the classroom is a microscopic version of the larger socioeconomic power structure, where teachers from the dominant majority culture and minority students miscommunicate and interact in an environment of social inequality. Ogbu summarizes the strengths and weaknesses of this approach:

> The significance of these and other theories based on classroom studies is their elucidation of the processes or mechanisms by which school failure and school success are achieved. This knowledge is very useful in developing programs (e.g., for preparation of teachers) and in encouraging cautious interpretations of quantitative studies of children's academic performance.
>
> However, these theories cannot claim to provide general explanations of minority children's school failure or failure to learn to read. This is partly because the theories are based on research on one type of minority, *caste-like minorities* [involuntary minorities]. They have yet to be applied to other minorities (e.g., immigrants) who are more successful in schools, although they have cultural and communicative backgrounds different from those of their public school teachers. (Ogbu 1982: 280)

We concur with Ogbu on the overall usefulness of concentrating on the communicative basis of school failure. Even though cultural discontinuities are significant and must be taken into account, they cannot by themselves account for the variability in minority school failure and success. How is it that Punjabi Sikh students, for example, have done so well in California public schools (Gibson 1988)? Are their communicative skills closer to those of the dominant

American culture than those of U.S.-born Latinos? That could hardly be the case.

Ogbu has approached the problem of poor Latino performance in school from a related perspective (Ogbu 1974). He says that there is a perception based on experience, particularly among exploited minorities—African Americans, Native Americans, Mexican Americans, mainland Puerto Ricans—that educational achievement does not bring the same rewards to them that it brings to the majority population. Hence, according to Ogbu, some minority youths do not invest in school because they do not think it will benefit them in the job market. Ogbu argues that because the rewards in the post-educational opportunity structure continue to be differentially patterned for some minority groups than for the majority population, many minority students simply learn to put less effort into their school work.

The latest census data on educational attainment and income seem to support Ogbu's contentions (see Hollman 1990). For Latinos, years of schooling completed translate into significantly less income earned than for the majority population. In the 1990s, the income inequality between Latinos and whites with the same amount of schooling remains striking. The mean 1990 annual income by educational attainment for white male high school graduates was $22,521, while for Hispanics it was $14,644.

And what does a college education do to the gap between whites and Latinos? How do the incomes of Latinos who completed four years of college compare with those of their white classmates? The mean 1990 income for white males who completed four years of college was $40,636, and for Hispanics it was $25,911. The sad truth is that for Latinos more education means more inequality.[13]

In addition, school personnel are typically indifferent or hostile to the linguistic and other cultural needs of Latino families (Suárez-Orozco 1989). Latino students reported to us that they are the targets of the racial prejudice of their white classmates, teachers, and other school personnel. Even highly motivated newly arrived immigrant students are affected by such hostilities and pressures. Sensitive teachers who noted the positive attitude toward schooling and learning among newly arrived immigrant students from Mexico were puzzled by the more ambivalent attitudes of the more acculturated Latino students. One teacher said that after only a few years in the United States, Latino students become increasingly ambivalent about school and school authorities. As a perplexed teacher said,

"The more Americanized they become, the worse is their attitude in school."

In short, sociolinguistic and socioeconomic factors, coupled with the economic pressures of providing for a large family, may lead many Latino students to develop ambivalence about school and education. In addition, there are problems of nonlearning, when success in an institution of the dominant culture—such as school—comes to be experienced by minority students as an act of ethnic betrayal, or as signifying a wish to "be white" (see Fordham and Ogbu 1986). Consequently, a high dropout rate from school continues to be a severe problem in the Latino community (Horowitz 1983; Suárez-Orozco 1989; Vigil 1988a).

Between Worlds

Stonequist beautifully described the experience of social dislocation as when an "individual who through migration, education, marriage, or some other influence leaves one social group or culture without making a satisfactory adjustment to another, find[ing] himself on the margin of each but a member of neither." He said that "wherever there are cultural transitions and cultural conflicts there are marginal personalities" (Stonequist 1937: 4). These cultural differences create more difficulty where there are sharp ethnic contrasts and hostile social attitudes. The result may be "acute personal difficulties and mental tension" for individuals identified with aspects of both groups (ibid.). Stonequist maintained that the common traits of what he termed the "marginal man" evolved from the *conflict* of two cultures rather than from "the specific content of any culture" (ibid.: 9). We agree with this observation.

In the best-case scenario, Stonequist argues, certain individuals with the right potential can overcome such adverse circumstances and "return as creative agents . . . to contribute to the solution of the conflict of races and cultures" (ibid.: 15). Although this is undoubtedly true, such marginal status comes at considerable psychological cost.

This brings us to the psychological toll paid for immigrating to another country. Although immigration may improve the immigrant's economic circumstances, it also ruptures the immigrant's "supportive interpersonal bonds," well recognized to be crucial for psychological well-being (Rogler, Malgady, and Rodriguez 1989: 25). In addition, immigration often results in multiple losses, the effects of which are not always immediately apparent (Garza-Guerrero 1974; Grinberg and Grinberg 1989). Rogler, Cortes, and Malgady summarize their recent overview of the literature on acculturation and mental health status among Cuban Americans, mainland Puerto Ricans, and Mexican Americans:

> Migration is likely to disrupt attachments to supportive networks in the society of origin and to impose on the migrant the difficult task of incorporation into the primary groups of the host society. The migrant is also faced with problems of economic survival and social mobility in an unfamiliar socioeconomic system. These uprooting experiences are accompanied by problems of acculturation into a new cultural system, of acquiring the language, the behavioral norms and values characteristic of the host society. (Rogler, Cortes, and Malgady 1991: 585)

For individuals who possess sufficient psychological resources to withstand the trauma and who have adequate available social support, the immigration experience can result in personal enrichment and psychological growth. For many, however, the losses exacerbate psychological problems (Garza-Guerrero 1974). A study of mainland Puerto Ricans reports that (not surprisingly) "[those] with fewest psychological resources for coping with the new environment reported the worst stress outcomes" (Rogler, Cortes, and Malgady 1991: 593).

Grinberg and Grinberg (1989) describe three typical patterns of psychological problems that may occur after immigration. These include problems with "persecutory anxiety" (whereby the host environment, which once was idealized, is experienced as hostile and persecutory), "depressive anxiety" (when the individual is preoccupied with losses due to the migration), and "disorienting anxiety" (which results from attempting to adjust to new customs and circumstances).

Persecutory anxieties may be manifested in the form of irrational fears about life in the host society. During the first days of the Persian Gulf war, a rumor spread among Latino immigrants in southern California that all undocumented persons captured by the border patrol would be sent to fight on the front lines. The undocumented immigrants' well-grounded fear of persecution by the border patrol metamorphosed into an irrational fear of being sent to a far-away war. The more hostile the receiving environment is, the more likely it is that immigrants will experience such persecutorial anxieties.

Immigrants may also feel "let down" when their initial idealization of life in the new land does not come true. This may occur when they realize that life will indeed be difficult in the new country. A recently arrived Latino immigrant said:

> I am so disappointed. I had so many ideas [about life in the United States]. When I was young, I remember the way people that went back [home] from the United States would bring so much money with them! And they would tell us that life here was so different, so easy to make money in the United States. Really, it is a big lie. These are the kind of people that work like slaves here, work, work, work, all day, and save all their money to use . . . when they go back . . . to show it off back there. They don't use any of their money here. So when I came in, I encountered all these problems here too.

At this point many disappointed Latino immigrants choose to return home. As a man returning to his native Mexico put it, "The American dream is not true. It didn't happen. I have no more dreams, no way to pay the rent" (quoted in Ross: 1993).

Grinberg and Grinberg (1989) argue that depressive anxiety is characterized by the immigrant's preoccupation with psychological losses. The Mexican Nobel laureate Octavio Paz described his own feelings when in Los Angeles: "Yes, we withdraw into ourselves, we deepen and aggravate our awareness of everything that separates or isolates or differentiates us. And we increase our solitude by refusing to seek out our compatriots, perhaps because we fear we will see ourselves in them, perhaps because of a painful, defensive unwillingness to share our intimate feelings. . . . We live closed within ourselves" (Paz 1961: 19).

A young Latino immigrant speaks of the tremendous sense of solitude many feel in the new land:

> Here I have no family, I have no home. If I had my family and a home here I would be more optimistic. Now I feel tired. I am sure that if I had a home here, my mother would be waiting for me with my food ready. Now I come back home, and I have to make my own food. I get up in the morning to go to school, and I am all by myself. I make my own coffee, iron my clothes, do everything alone. I come back from work at night and I am all alone. I feel very low. I sit in bed all alone, and I lose morale. I think about my future and about being all alone. This depresses me a lot; I feel desperate.

Note the poignant longing for maternal nurturing suggested by the wish that his mother would be there waiting for him with his food ready. Mother's food—that is, the food of the motherland—is typically laden with symbolic and expressive significance in the lives of immigrants (see Gamio 1971: 140–47). It is as if by eating their own ethnic foods, immigrants attempt to re-establish a link with the lost motherland.

Homesickness, which immigrants sometimes suppress by focusing on their improved economic circumstances, sometimes takes center stage. The following immigrant song is entitled "The Farm Where I Was Born":

> I don't care to dance in the halls
> That you have here;
> What I want is an earth floor
> Like on the farm where I was born.
>
> I don't care for your automatic pistols
> That you have here;
> What I want is a black rifle
> Like on the farm where I was born.
>
> I don't care for your silk shirts
> That you have here;
> What I want is a suit of blue jumpers
> Like on the farm where I was born.
>
> I don't care for your automobiles
> That you have here;
> What I want is a cart with oxen
> Like on the farm where I was born.
>
> I don't like your wide trousers
> That you have here;
> I like them close to the skin
> Like on the farm where I was born.
>
> (Gamio 1971: 88–89)

We return later to the problem of loss and mourning as a key feature of immigration.

The sense of anxious disorientation described by Grinberg and Grinberg (1989) is related to what anthropologists have termed the "culture shock" one typically experiences entering a substantially different way of life. As a new arrival from Mexico stated, "Immigration was like being born again—I had to learn to speak, I had to learn to eat and I had to learn to dress." Another Latin American immigrant elaborated on this point:

When we come here, we are afraid. We are even afraid of talking to people with the little English we speak. . . . At first I was so timid. I could not even engage in a conversation. I was afraid people would laugh at my English. We are afraid of this so we shut ourselves in our little universe.

When I came here, I noticed how different people are [from Latinos].

Here they dress differently, they talk differently, they act differently. I did not know how to act here, I did not know how to speak English, I did not know what to do or what to say. So the first thing I did was try to dress like everybody else. I did not want to stand out. Because people here notice if you are dressed very differently. They may not say anything directly to you, but they do notice. I did not want to look like a stranger, I did not want to stand out. The next thing I did was to pay attention to what people here did, how they spoke and how they acted. I tried to learn how and why they acted in a certain way because I didn't know.

The children of Latino immigrants become the repositories of the parents' anxieties, ambitions, dreams, and conflicts. They are frequently vested with responsibilities (such as translating and caring for siblings) beyond what is culturally expected for children at their stage of psychosocial development. Because they speak little English, many Latino immigrant parents are unable to help their children with their schoolwork. This may bring about further anxieties and a sense of inadequacy and shame. Although the parents may feel ashamed of such shortcomings, at the same time, they typically over-restrict the activities of the children and attempt to minimize the host country's influence.

Latino immigrant youths, particularly young women residing in crime-ridden inner cities, told us that they had much less freedom in the United States than they did back home. Some Latino immigrant parents eventually decide to return to their home countries to prevent the "Americanization" of their children. Others return after sensing that the elusive American dream has escaped them. Yet others return to escape inner-city crime. For example, Ms. Pacheco, a long-term immigrant from Colima, Mexico, finally decided to go back: "I don't want to send her to school here," she said, referring to her ten-year-old daughter. "As soon as you start junior high, it's gangsters, guns, and drugs. I don't have nothing against Americans. It's just the city itself, how it's going" (Ross 1993: 22).

The children of immigrants may also suffer shame and doubt, which compromise and undermine their self-confidence and development (see Paz 1961: 9–28). Feelings of inadequacy and inferiority may lead a child to doubt his or her ability to succeed in the new setting (Grinberg and Grinberg 1989). A range of choices seems to emerge: at one end of this psychological spectrum some youths choose dropping out of school and giving up on education as the route toward status mobility; at the other end, some become over-achievers. We return to a discussion of these choices later, when we examine the cases of Richard Rodriguez, Ruben Navarrette, and other high-achieving Latino youngsters.

Ethnic Identities

Grinberg and Grinberg (1989) and Vigil (1988a and 1988b) maintain that perhaps the most critical task facing the children of immigrants is developing a positive sense of identity. According to Erickson (1963), forging a sense of self-identity is the key to development during adolescence. Generally, there must be a certain amount of complementarity between the individual's sense of self and the social milieu. If there is too much cultural dissonance or role confusion, an adolescent will find it difficult to develop a strong sense of identity.

Children of Latino immigrants may suffer from what Vigil (1988a) calls "multiple marginalities," which in some cases compromise the development of a positive sense of identity. Vigil and others have noted that such children are likely to experience intense culture conflict on both an individual and a group level. For many second-generation Latino youths:

> Language inconsistency at home and school, a perceived gap in the status of their parents and the quality of their environment and those of the larger society, and the dangers and attractions of *barrio* streets create an ambiguity in their ethnic identity. Parents and older siblings are often unable to effectively guide youngsters in ways to reconcile the contrasting cultural worlds, and this results in an uneven adoption of acculturative strategies. (Vigil 1988a: 41)

In some cases, second-generation youths attempt to resolve identity issues by embracing total assimilation and a wholesale identification with dominant American values. They may actively reject the use of Spanish. Others may create a new ethnic identity for themselves, incorporating selected aspects of both the Latino and the dominant American culture (frequently achieving bilingual fluency in the process). For still others, the adaptation is not as smooth, and a "subculture of cultural transitionals" emerges (Vigil 1988a: 39). Vigil calls these "transitional" youths *cholos*. Within the same family each child may adopt his or her own way; the result may be that each occupies a different spot on the spectrum—from *cholo* to "anglicized," and from bilingual to "Spanglish" speaking to English-only speaking (Vigil 1988a).

Villareal articulates the effects of cultural marginality and discrimination on the children of Mexican migrant workers. In this passage, Villareal's protagonist eloquently describes how racism and disparagement affect second-generation cultural identity issues:

> They had a burning contempt for people of different ancestry, whom they called Americans, and a marked hauteur towards Mexico and toward their

parents for their old-country ways. The former feeling came from a sense of inferiority that is a prominent characteristic in any Mexican reared in southern California; and the latter was an inexplicable compensation for that feeling. They needed to feel superior to something, which is a natural thing. The result was that they attempted to segregate themselves from both their cultures, and became truly a lost race. . . . In spite of their behavior, which was sensational at times and violent at others, they were simply a portion of confused humanity, employing their self-segregation as a means of expression. (Villareal 1959: 149–50)

Forced to "oscillate between two irreducible worlds—the North American and the Mexican" (Paz 1961: 18), many second-generation Latino youths reject some of the institutions—including schools—of the society that violently rejects them, and they seek refuge with their peers. It is such choices that lead many second-generation Latino youths to join gangs. We agree with Alejandro Portes that "as second generation youth find their aspirations for wealth and social status blocked . . . they may join native minorities in the inner-city, adopting an adversarial stance toward middle-class white society, and adding to the present urban pathologies" (Portes 1993: 2).

Vigil contends that gangs are largely a phenomenon of the second (U.S.-born) generation. In his perceptive studies, Vigil traces the historical pattern of Latino gang formation in urban areas since the beginning of large-scale Mexican immigration to the United States at the turn of the century. He says several key factors account for the development of Latino gangs. These include: low socioeconomic status, urban poverty, and limited economic mobility; ethnic minority status and discrimination; lack of training, education, and other constructive opportunities; and a breakdown in the social institutions of school and family. Vigil also points out major causal factors in "a first- and second-generation conflict within each ethnic group, which creates loyalty discord and identity confusion; and a noted predisposition among youths to gravitate toward street peers for sources of social associations and personal fulfillment" (Vigil 1988a: 4).

These factors hold particularly true for many U.S.-born Latino youths. In addition, the continuous migration from Latin America has kept the cycle of "marginality" going and prolonged the lives of *cholo* gangs (see Vigil 1988a).

We concur with Vigil's observations. Latino youths join gangs in search of refuge and belonging. Gangs are most attractive to youths who receive the least parental and familial attention. A teacher told us: "The gangs are in their community, in their own barrios. They see the gangs all around them. Their parents are often gone all day at work. So these kids are alone with no supervision. The parents are not there. The gangs offer company, it gives them protection. It is kind of a family. It is cool and exciting for them to belong to a gang." Yet another teacher said: "These Latino kids are in a desert. The gangs offer them company and protection. There is a pressure to join. Many kids, that is all they have, their gangs. If they don't join they are left without friends. They are alone, social outcasts. These kids are alone a lot of the time. Their parents are away during the day. So they get into gangs." When parents and other adults are occupied with work and other demands, adolescent youths who find themselves in a hostile environment turn to their peers and frequently join gangs.

On the positive side, gangs provide a "mechanism of adaptation for many youths who need a source of identification and human support." The gang provides a "reforging of Mexican and American patterns . . . creating a culture [and language] of mixed and blended elements." Vigil maintains that "although *cholos* are Americanized, either by accident or design, they refuse or are unable to be totally assimilated" (Vigil 1988: 6, 7).

As Paz noted of the *pachuco* (the historical predecessor but the structural equivalent, in this context, of Vigil's *cholo*), he "does not want to become a Mexican again; at the same time he does not want to blend into the life of North America" (1961: 14). *Cholos* and *pachucos* retain certain Mexican values, sometimes in exaggerated form, such as a strong sense of peer (gang) group as family, male bravado or machismo, and honor (see Paz 1961: 9–28; Horowitz 1983; Vigil 1988a and 1988b).

At the same time, second-generation youths in gangs may not feel "Mexican" and in some cases may actually display considerable antipathy toward Mexican immigrants (Dayley 1991) and themselves disparage them (see Vigil 1988a). Some feel that they are in competition for scarce resources (such as jobs, education, housing, and so forth) with the newer arrivals. The second generation may view the new arrivals as embodying aspects of themselves that they wish to disclaim. In the November 1994 elections, some 30 percent of all Latino voters are said to have voted for Proposition 187, the controversial California initiative that would ban all undocumented immigrants (mostly Mexicans) from receiving public education and other services.

Gamio has written: "The attitude of Mexicans who are American citizens toward the immigrants is a curious one. Sometimes they speak slightingly of the immigrants (possibly because the immigrants are their competitors in wages and jobs), and say that the immigrants should stay in Mexico. . . . The immigrant, on his part, considers the American of Mexican origin as a man without a country. He reminds him frequently of the inferior position to which he is relegated by the white American" (Gamio 1971: 129).

Both Vigil (1988a) and Horowitz (1983) have found that the individuals that are most heavily involved in gangs come from the most troubled families: with absent parents and a history of alcohol or drug addiction, child neglect, and/or abuse. Vigil estimates that 70 to 80 percent of the heavily involved Latino gang members in southern California come from such families.[14] For such youths, gang membership becomes incorporated into their sense of identity. Gangs offer their members a sense of belonging, solidarity, support, discipline, and warmth. Gangs also structure the rage *cholos* feel toward the society that rejected their parents and themselves. Although many less conflicted second-generation and immigrant youths may look to gangs for cues about dress, language, and attitude, most remain on the periphery and eventually outgrow the gang mystique after working through the challenges of adolescence. The gang ethos provides a sense of identity and cohesion for marginal youths during a turbulent stage of development.

Cultural dissonance, then, may lead to what we term "defensive identity" (see also De Vos and Suárez-Orozco 1990). Joining a gang or developing a *cholo* persona is but one of the forms this defensive identity may take. In a much more sublimated manner, achievement-oriented Ruben Navarrette, Jr., describes his first days at Harvard:

> It begins appropriately, as it does with students of all color, with a distinct element of self-doubt. For generations, bright young adults have wandered through Harvard Square in the first few weeks feeling like frauds. We are convinced that the admissions officer must have made some dreadful mistake. This is Harvard, we tell ourselves. . . . What are we doing here?
>
> For Latinos, and other minority students who may see themselves— indeed, have been encouraged by hometown insults to see themselves— as the winners of the dubious affirmative action lottery, the question of unworthiness endures like a stale odor. You begin to believe old critics, assuming that you have come to this bizarre place not by your own merit but by the grace of a government handout. (Navarrette 1993: 60)

This light-skinned young man who until Harvard entered his life never "felt" like a minority, is now caught by—and must defend against—feelings of shame and doubt: "The insane irony behind the cultural riddle stuffed in the fortune cookie of affirmative action was that the light-skinned, English-proficient grandson who was acceptable to Harvard because he was most American and least Mexican was then oddly expected to be less American and more Mexican" (ibid.: 84).

He senses an "implied expectation that I serve as a cultural ambassador to sheltered white people" and goes on to describe his process of becoming "ethnically aware," though he remembers that "up to that point—five months before my classmates' affirmative tantrums—I did not even really consider myself Mexican American. . . . Above all, I was preoccupied with what I considered the extraordinary significance of being Latino at an elite, predominantly white school" (ibid.: 83, 76, 85). In the process he develops what he calls "a new sense of illegitimacy. I worried about our ability, indeed about the ability of all Mexican Americans on campus to honor our obligation [to educate the ethnically unaware]. I felt that I was being asked to produce something that, at the time, I barely myself understood" (ibid.: 83).

He begins to question his ability to transmit a culture that he had only just recently embraced and was "not my culture, really, but my Mexican grandfather's" (ibid.: 83). He admits to knowing firsthand more about hamburgers, Bruce Springsteen, CNN, and Little League than about *mole*, Vincente Fernandez, *Univisión*, and soccer. Although it makes him feel like a double fraud, he responds with the following strategy: "My guilt mandated action. If I did not have culture then I would manufacture it. If I did not have a truly ethnic persona, then I would create one. I exaggerated my ethnicity" (ibid.: 69). He discovers the student organization La RAZA, tequila, Mexican beer, and serapes: "My connection with RAZA members was instant. . . . We were family. . . . My relationship with RAZA was bathed in intimacy, and I would learn only later, vulnerability" (ibid.: 78). He develops a "defiant strut like the one I remembered little cholos using" and intermixes "Spanish and English as if to obscure my proficiency in one and my deficiency in the other. . . . Resisting assimilation, I wanted to be noticed, seen as different. I wore my ethnicity as a badge. No, a shield. Like a Halloween costume" (ibid.: 85).

He becomes perplexed by his finding that only approximately one-fifth of Harvard's Latino students belong to RAZA and, indeed, to similar organizations on other elite campuses. Protecting his status anxieties—does he belong at Harvard?—with his newly erected ethnic shield, he worries about the other students:

> The omission of Chicano students from the ranks of groups intended to serve them prompted, for those brave enough to address it, an embarrass-

ing set of questions. . . . Why do the vast majority of Mexican American students on college campuses choose not to participate in ethnic organizations that were created in their name to address . . . issues of concern to them? . . . And should the membership breakdown be blamed, if blame is called for, on individual students or on the organizations themselves?

I remembered meeting these other Mexican Americans. I disliked them without knowing them. I resented the ease with which they passed from one world to another. They seemed to trivialize ethnic differences. . . . They were not like me, these coconuts. White on the inside. Though now, years later, I realized that I may have confused dislike with envy. They seemed not to be troubled by the insecurities that were growing stronger in me each day. (Ibid.: 79)

Through this process, Navarrette becomes alienated from nonminority students, from nonethnically aware Latino students, from his hometown peers, and in time, from members of the RAZA organization. In the end, who is really like him?

Labyrinths of Solitude: Instrumental Mobility and Expressive Affiliation

In joining gangs and developing a defensive identity, many secondgeneration youths reject the society that rejects them and seek refuge in others who share their predicament. At the same time, secondgeneration Latinos who choose to join the dominant American culture may continue to suffer from a marginal status:

Individuals who choose to measure their competency in terms of the wider society rather than in terms of local identity risk a loss of emotional support from peers and kin. Trusting and close relationships must be developed with new people and on different terms. The movement away from the traditional sources of support and the traditional basis of social relationships can create feelings of acute loneliness. Little within the Chicano community prepares them for the competitive, individualistic Anglo world of social relationships in which they must face lack of acceptance and some degree of discrimination. They become caught between two worlds. (Horowitz 1983: 200–1)

Those who choose to move "away from the traditional sources of support" become immigrants of another sort. Richard Rodriguez's autobiographical account of his experiences growing up in Sacramento, California, is a rich illustration of his attempts to integrate himself into the dominant society by actively rejecting his native tongue, familial networks, and culture. It captures with poignancy how shame and doubt may become interwoven with ethnic mobility.

Rodriguez is successful by almost anyone's standards, and certainly by those of the dominant society. As a Stanford, Columbia, and Berkeley graduate he has come a long way from the humble Sacramento of his youth. However, a close reading of his controversial autobiography shows that Rodriguez suffered from the same sense of shame, marginality, and alienation that other immigrants and second-generation youth do.

Rodriguez's mother, stymied in her own attempts to get ahead, "willed her ambition to her children. 'Get all the education you can. With an education you can do anything,' " she told them (Rodriguez 1982: 54–55). The local nuns told his mother to stop using the "private" language (Spanish) and to start using the more instrumental "public" language (English) at home. Rodriguez admits that he was angry at his parents for encouraging him to use English. He retaliated by intentionally hurting his parents, correcting them when they made mistakes in English. "But gradually this anger was exhausted, replaced by guilt as school grew more and more attractive to me" (ibid.: 50).

The more Rodriguez was propelled into the public world of school and the dominant culture, the more alienated he became from his private world: family, ethnicity, and culture. His embarrassment about his parents' accent and their inability to help him even with his second-grade homework fueled his shame. When his teachers said, "Your parents must be proud of you, . . . shyly I would smile, never betraying my sense of irony: I was not proud of my mother and father" (ibid.: 52).

Unable to identify with his humble, silent, Mexican father, Rodriguez turned to his teachers, who were powerful in his eyes. "I wanted to be like my teachers, to possess their knowledge, to assume their authority, their confidence, even to assume a teacher's persona" (ibid.: 55). One senses that the only identification he was able to make with his father was with his silence.

With the acquisition of English and an education, Rodriguez gained the capacity to enter the public arena he valued and to command the attention of powerful members of the dominant culture. But he lost his feeling of belonging to his family. With the transition to English, his family was "no longer so close; no longer bound tight by the pleasing and troubling knowledge of our public separateness." He lost the easy intimacy and open communication natural among family members. "The family's quiet was partly due to the fact that, as we children learned more and more English, we shared fewer and fewer words" (ibid.: 23). He also lost interest in the affective nuances of language and became more concerned with content: "Conversation became content-full. Transparent. Hearing someone's tone of voice—angry or questioning or sarcastic or happy—I didn't distinguish it from the words it expressed" (ibid.: 22). Rodriguez developed a sense of anomic withdrawal from his family. A numbness engulfed him, separating him further from his parents. He became deeply depressed. The child of Mexican immigrants, he himself becomes an immigrant, leaving his family behind on his journey to "success."

Rodriguez made a choice then, between instrumental mobility and expressive affiliation. He found himself profoundly alone—alienated from his family and from his peers, knowing no one able or willing to take his path. He became a vocal opponent of both bilingual education and affirmative action: because he "made it" by renouncing his ethnicity, so should others.[15]

In reading Rodriguez, one feels pity for both him and his parents. One senses that he was so alone that he sought intimacy with his readers: "encouraged by physical isolation to reveal what is most personal; determined at the same time to have my words seen by strangers" (ibid.: 187). His parents lose their favorite son. His mother's attempts at intimacy and involvement are consistently rebuffed. The gulf between them seems interminable and irreparable.

Rodriguez's controversial condemnation of bilingual education deserves further comment. Certainly users of non-mainstream English (Spanglish, black English, lower-class English) are at a disadvantage in a society that evaluates people on the basis of their ability to communicate appropriately and effectively. However, we question whether it is necessary to give up one's native language, one's affective language, in order to succeed. One should not have to choose one or the other. An analogy here is that one does not have to forget how to play the piano before learning to play the violin.[16]

Rodriguez's devastating account goes directly to the symbolic and affective aspects of language. To see language as a mere instrumental tool for communication is to miss its deep affective roots. Giving up Spanish to acquire English is a symbolic act of ethnic renunciation: it is giving up the mother tongue for the instrumental tongue of the dominant group.

We contend that in such contexts, when learning the language and culture of a dominant group is symbolically equated with giving up one's own ethnic identity, learning becomes a problem. Ruben Navarrette, an ambitious and achievement-oriented Mexican American student, recalls the taunts from his less successful peers: "They will call me 'Brain' as I walk through hallways in the junior high school. Mimicking adults, some of them will even practice ethnic division. They will accuse me, by virtue of my academic success, of 'trying to be white'" (Navarrette 1993: 260). When learning comes to be equated with ethnic betrayal, many ethnic minority youths find it even more difficult to succeed in school (see Fordham and Ogbu 1986).

The Flemish-speaking people in Belgium can speak English at no emotional cost. In contrast, historically the Flemish have found it difficult to learn French—the language of the once dominant and oppressive Walloons. An understanding of the affective aspects of language and learning also helps to explain why minority ethnic-rights movements often pick up language as a symbolic banner of "belonging" (e.g., the Basques in Spain, supporters of bilingual education in the United States, and defenders of black English.)

Guilt and Repair

If Rodriguez's autobiography illustrates how issues of shame and doubt may be related to achievement orientation and ethnic status mobility, the autobiography of Ruben Navarrette, Jr. (1993), illustrates how guilt and reparation are intimately related to Latino patterns of achievement motivation.

Navarrette's complex journey (migration, really) from rural California to Harvard Square is a study of the paradoxes, contradictions, and chagrin of a society struggling to deal with its multicultural pretensions. A hard-working overachiever, Navarrette, a second-generation Mexican American, was justifiably enraged when he sensed that, as far as his white peers and teachers were concerned, he got into Harvard only because of some quota system.

He found these allegations particularly insulting because he is a light-skinned, middle-class, and self-described "fully acculturated" hyphenated American. Navarrette was so acculturated that, as he himself was fully aware, his attempts at Harvard to pass as "a real Mexican" by speaking Spanish were hilarious.[17] Navarrette responded to the assaults by his white peers and teachers with a bravado that betrayed his Latino origins. His journey through Harvard can be read as an exercise in showing them, and himself, that he can conquer that most exclusive institution of the WASP establishment. Yet one cannot escape the feeling that his chutzpah and narcissistic arrogance were a deep cover for unsettling feelings of doubt and guilt about the nature of his success.

As he dealt with his own wounds, the insults reactivated the indignities and abuses endured by previous generations, including his proud Mexican grandparents, parents, uncles, and their friends. One day he received a call from a woman: " 'You don't understand,' she said. 'What you have done [going to Harvard] . . . you don't know what it means, what it means to all of us, here in this town.' Suddenly there is a sniffle. 'You don't know'—by the time she finishes her sentence, she is in tears—'how they treated us back then' " (Navarrette 1993: xv). He journeyed off to Cambridge carrying not only his own fresh wounds and hopes but the ancestral wounds and expectations of generations of immigrants that came before him.

At the university, Navarrette developed a serious case of status fever, but his robust narcissism was constantly undermined by Harvard's indifference. His description of his battles, disappointments, and triumphs reveals a bright young man driven to prove that he could do what Rodriguez said could not be done: succeed without becoming alienated from his family and ethnic group.[18]

During several trips between Harvard and California (interrupted by a guilt-induced term at Fresno State University, where he hoped to see what kind of education "real Chicanos" receive), he sensed that his experiment might fail and began to fear that Rodriguez's prediction was coming true: that the gulf between himself and his family was widening. After all, he had started reading the editorial page of the *New York Times* every day, while his father continued to rely on the *Fresno Bee*.

Finally, though, guilt bridged the distance between the *New York Times* and the *Fresno Bee*. After graduating from Harvard—although he failed to get into Harvard Law School—Navarrette was courted by some of the most interesting graduate programs in his second field of choice, education. The "conspicuous, bend-over-backward" efforts of professors and deans not about to let this Harvard Chicano star get away now embarrass him. Eventually, he enrolled at UCLA. By the time he started his studies there, the grandiose shell that protected this San Joaquin Valley kid in Cambridge had begun to peel off. A depressive, guilt-ridden self made an entrance. It is worth quoting the poignant revelation at length:

> Even with the discomfort over the fawning that introduced me to my doctoral program, I did not expect that, in that program, I would learn the single most important and most painful lesson of my academic career. What I learned would be so personal and so disturbing that, consumed with the force of revelation, I would be unable to complete the power journey. Overwhelmed with guilt, I would eventually find relief only in the complete surrendering of ambition and with the dramatic, and what some consider self-destructive, renunciation of academic privilege.
>
> The defining lesson comes to me in memory, a childhood memory

prompted in large part by the curriculum of my graduate program; specifically, a series of classroom lectures, class discussions, and assigned readings about the educational practice known as ability-grouping, or "tracking."

Memory takes me back to Madison Elementary School, an inconspicuous assortment of gray buildings in my brown and white hometown. The place where, during recess, I first played with my Mexican American friends. The place where, in the classroom, I was first set apart from them. . . .

One fateful day, in the second grade, my teacher decided to teach her class more efficiently by dividing it into six groups of five students each. Each group was assigned a geometric symbol to differentiate it from the others. There were the Circles. There were the Squares. There were the Triangles and Rectangles. I remember being a Hexagon. . . .

The Hexagons were the smartest kids in the class. These distinctions are not lost on a child of seven. . . .

As Hexagons, we would wait for her to call to us, then answer by hurrying to her with books and pencils in hand. We sat around a table in our "reading group," chattering excitedly to one another and basking in the intoxication of positive learning. We did not notice, did not care to notice, over our shoulders, the frustrated looks on the faces of Circles and Squares and Triangles who sat quietly at their desks, doodling on scratch paper or mumbling to one another. Obediently, they waited their turn at the reading table, anticipating their few minutes of attention. Occasionally, the teacher would look up from our lesson and command to the rest of the class, *"Could I have all my Circles be quiet . . ."*

We knew also that, along with our geometric shapes, our books were different and that each group had different amounts of work to do. . . . The Circles had the easiest books and were assigned to read only a few pages at a time. The Triangles had books that were a little more difficult than those of the Circles, and they were expected to read a few more pages in them. Not surprisingly, the Hexagons had the most difficult books of all, those with the biggest words and the fewest pictures, and we were expected to read the most pages.

The result of all of this education by separation was exactly what the teacher had imagined that it would be: Students could, and did, learn at their own pace without being encumbered by one another. Some, I realized only as a doctoral student at a pristine university, did not learn at all.

What I had been exposed to, and in truth had benefited from, in that dusty elementary school was the educational practice of ability grouping, or tracking. . . .

So, in truth, it was tracking, along with the support of my family and my own effort, that had ultimately carried me from a small town to the most prestigious university in the country. And now, it was tracking that was responsible for the new assortment of "goodies"—the doctoral program, the administrative policy exceptions, and, of course, the excessive fellowship that filled my bank account. . . .

I see myself as a little boy. I am in the second grade. I am lucky. I am a Hexagon. I will be cared for. I call out the right answer. My teacher smiles her approval and I smile back. I do not notice the others, the Circles and Squares and Triangles daydreaming in their boredom. I do not notice something else—a curious observation that will ultimately define the character of my life. I am an oddity.

I am a Hexagon. I am also the only Mexican American Hexagon. In a classroom, in a school, and in a town where over half the population was Mexican American, I was the only one. The lucky one. (Navarrette 1993: 255–59)

Overwhelmed by guilt, Navarrette quit graduate school to reach out to the Circles, Squares, and Triangles left behind in dusty rural schools. He began visiting those rural schools to convince Latino youths that they too could make it and became an aggressive recruiter of Latino students for his beloved Harvard.

Navarrette's guilt is laced with cultural meanings that are shared by other highly motivated Latino students (Suárez-Orozco 1989). He was devastated when he felt that his success was possible only because others, his Latino friends in the second grade, suffered and failed. In a psychosocial world of "limited goods"—where wealth, prestige, and success are said to exist in limited amounts—his gain could come only at somebody else's expense.[19] Hexagon success *requires* the failure of Circles, Squares, and Triangles.[20]

Navarrette's guilt was based, in part, on an inner belief that he made it because his childhood friends failed: "I was allowed to excel in the American educational system by virtue of the same form of ability-grouping [tracking] that had undermined the educational progress of so many other Mexican American students like me" (Navarrette 1993: 261). The guilt of having benefited from the harm done to his friends led him to devote himself to repairing and undoing the injustices suffered by other Latino students.

Navarrette then turned to help those who had been sacrificed on his behalf: he was able to accept his achievements only after leaving the individualistic "power journey" and becoming an advocate for the education of all Latinos. Ruben Navarrette, Jr., is to ethnic guilt what Richard Rodriguez is to ethnic shame.

In examining the less glamorous achievement patterns of recent arrivals from Central America we identified a related concern with achievement motivation, "trying to become a somebody," coupled with a wish to turn toward family and loved ones, to help alleviate their ongoing hardships. In this case, guilt also emerged as a powerful factor in the motivational dynamics of Latino students.

Asylum-seeking youngsters felt a strong sense of responsibility toward those who had sacrificed to send them to safety, many of whom continued to live in collective terror and scarcity. This fact has created unique interpersonal and intrapsychic concerns in this cohort of Latino youths. They all continued to be affected in one way or another by the uncertain fate of the less fortunate folk at home. Indeed, an intense sense of duty to less fortunate relatives is prominent in the psychosocial profile of many new arrivals. Guilt about surviving, coupled with opportunities in the new land not shared by those left behind, nourished their hope for a better tomorrow, for themselves and, most important, for their families.

Among many new arrivals, particularly those with close relatives remaining behind in war-torn regions, something akin to "survivor guilt" appeared (Bettelheim 1980: 274–314). The syndrome experienced by many arrivals from Central America is similar in some respects to the guilt felt by survivors of the Nazi concentration camps. Bettelheim described the belief of many survivors that their lives were spared because someone else had died or suffered. To some degree, our Central American informants thought similarly about their survival and the often inexplicable death and suffering of others.

We believe that the guilt of these new arrivals is a function of a specific interpersonal morality. A person's system of morality is rooted in an awareness that action and thought may have positive or negative consequences on others. As they mature, human beings become increasingly aware of their capacity to hurt or help others by doing or failing to do something (Piaget 1930).

In a normally adjusted person, an awareness that one's circumstances or behavior may cause pain in others makes one prone to feelings of guilt. Navarrette's guilt was based on his inner belief that he was allowed to succeed because his second-grade peers were made to fail. Likewise, a proneness to guilt among new Central American immigrants derives from insight that (1) loved ones sacrificed much for them in securing their well-being, (2) they have been selected over others, often siblings, to escape to the United States, and (3) they enjoy relative security and opportunities while loved ones continue to face terror and scarcity (Suárez-Orozco 1989; see also Ready 1991).

Such awareness creates a ready propensity to intense guilt when they fail or become derelict in their social duties. These feelings can be assuaged only by a reparatory reapplication to the task at hand.

Among achievement-oriented Central American youths we found feelings of desperation giving way to a determination to seize upon any opportunity in the affluent society. Working to ease familial and ethnic hardships is intimately related to this psychosocial syndrome of proneness to guilt about one's selective survival and opportunity to succeed.

Ruben Navarrette felt guilty because his success seemed to have required the failure of his friends. Similarly, many Central Americans felt guilty because their escape provided them with new opportunities while the circumstances of those left behind were as difficult as ever (see Suárez-Orozco 1989).

In the next three chapters we analyze the results of our empirical study of family dynamics, achievement motivation, and other interpersonal concerns among adolescents in four groups: Mexican youths in the immigrant-sending state of Guanajuato, Mexican immigrant youths in southern California, second-generation Mexican American youths, and a comparable sample of non-Hispanic white American youths. The study investigates what these youths have in common as well as what makes them different from each other.

By starting our journey deep in the heart of Mexico, we hope to illuminate those aspects of the Latino experience that are related to specific cultural and societal patterns and those that relate to the migratory journey. This is the first psychosocial study to interview a sample of possible immigrants from an emigration center in Mexico. Indeed, the vast majority of studies of Mexicans in the United States start out with immigrant samples. A problem inherent in all such studies is the impossibility of separating the experiences rooted in the stresses of immigration from those that are rooted in the Mexican culture.

Turning to first-generation U.S.-born youths of Mexican parents, we explore whether their attitudes are more similar to the experiences of Mexicans in Mexico, of immigrants, or of nonimmigrant, non-Latino, American youths. Of theoretical relevance to models of ethnicity and acculturation are our discussions of the different patterns leading to "immigrant identity" and "ethnic minority identity."

We hope to illustrate the important effects of immigration and minority status by comparing the attitudes and behaviors of those youths with those of nonimmigrant, nonminority youths. The non-Hispanic white sample allows us to explore cross-cultural differences as well as the vicissitudes of minority acculturation to mainstream norms.

A central paradox this study explores is the fact that new arrivals from Mexico, indeed from Latin America in general, display an eagerness to do well in school; yet the longer they are in the United States, the less interested and motivated they become (see Suárez-Orozco and Suárez-Orozco 1992). Contrary to widespread belief, our data show that Mexican youths in Mexico by and large display patterns of self-motivated achievement orientation that seem ideally suited for schoolwork in the U.S. setting. Immigrant youths arrive in American schools with a tremendous desire to learn the language, please teachers, and succeed. In our interviews, recently arrived Latino youths told us of their dreams of using the educational system to better themselves and finding a career that would allow them to earn enough money to help their relatives.

Likewise, teachers working with immigrant students in conflict-ridden inner-city schools largely reported that recently arrived Mexican immigrant students display a positive energy and drive to learn. These same teachers reported that the longer these immigrant kids are in school, the more they become "like American students" ("disrespectful," "unmotivated," and even "cynical"). Teachers also told us that many U.S.-born Latino students are not as respectful and eager to learn as their immigrant peers are.

Given the stresses of immigration described in this chapter—including the psychological losses, culture shock, language and other cultural discontinuities, discrimination, and economic pressures—it is not surprising that second- and third-generation Latino youths tend to complete school at higher rates than new immigrants (Chapa 1988; Bean et al. 1991). Indeed it would be surprising if it were otherwise.

We must emphasize, however, that the Latino experience subverts the predictions of "assimilation" models that each new generation will tend to do substantially better than the previous one, eventually reaching parity with the mainstream population (see Chavez 1991). Even second- and third-generation Latinos lag far behind whites and blacks in educational achievement and occupational status:

> As [Latino] immigrants and their offspring become more aware of the obstacles they face in further socioeconomic advancement, the second generation may not put as much emphasis on the further educational attainment of their children. . . . [That] the educational gap between third generation Mexicans and non-Hispanic white natives is not narrowing provides discouraging news concerning the prospects for future assimilation. . . . The proportions of second and third generation Mexican American males who have completed less than twelve years of school-

ing are similar to one another, and both are much higher than those for non-Hispanic whites. (Bean et al. 1991: 17)

Likewise, Chapa writes:

The average educational level of [third-generation] Mexican Americans is 10.4 years—substantially lower than the 12.5 years for third generation Anglos. It is also lower than the level attained by third generation Blacks. . . . A large part of the Mexican American population is not being assimilated. By this I mean that a substantial portion of third generation Mexican Americans have educational levels that have shown no indication of converging with Anglo levels, and their earnings and occupational status have decreased compared to those of Anglos. (Chapa 1988: 3, 6)

Too many first-, second-, and third-generation Mexican American youths are giving up on schools. How are we to account for this paradox?

CHAPTER 3

Between Paradoxes

Anthropology and psychology find themselves (for very different reasons) in a moment of disciplinary turmoil. In recent years, anthropology has been turning inward. Leading anthropologists are not only heatedly debating the discipline's epistemological raison d'être, but many seem to be less interested in exotic, faraway places, which once were the source of their bread and butter. Instead, they are turning their attention to sociocultural problems in the developed world.

In contrast, over the past few years many research psychologists have turned outward, leaving the walls of the sanctuary of the experimental laboratory in pursuit of new research methodologies and interdisciplinary dialogue. A number of leading psychologists are increasingly questioning whether the rigorous methodological agenda of experimental psychology can do justice to the complexities of the fin de siècle (see, e.g., Cowan et al. 1993; Bruner 1990).

A tension in research psychology seems to be between its experimental tradition and the growing interest, particularly among younger psychologists, in understanding our increasingly diverse population. Can the measures devised and carefully normed for studying "mainstream" white Americans fairly and respectfully assess the differences in language, cognition, emotion, attitudes, values, and worldviews in our culturally diverse society?

In this chapter, we explore some of the debates in psychological anthropology and cross-cultural psychology that are relevant to the empirical findings we present in the next two chapters. First, we consider key arguments within anthropology about conducting cross-cultural research. We take up an area of concern of immediate relevance to our own research interests: can we systematically approach the inner experience of members of a culturally different group?

Then, we consider some of the most important concerns voiced by psychologists about the problems inherent in systematic cross-cultural research. Research psychologists have been particularly concerned about articulating explicit criteria for conducting methodologically sound but culturally sensitive research. In the process they have made some sobering arguments about the conclusions that can—and cannot—be drawn from such research attempts. As we shall see, leading cross-cultural psychologists and cultural anthropologists—from different epistemological stances and theoretical perspectives—have pointed out the serious problems and limitations facing those interested in meaningful cross-cultural research.

In the final section of the chapter, we explain how we navigated these troubled methodological and epistemological currents in developing our own research design and examining family dynamics and achievement motivation.

From Method to Anxiety in the Behavioral Sciences: Psychological Anthropology and Postmodernism

Just as anthropologists have begun to question the epistemological foundations of their discipline, their methods have been enthusiastically adopted in a variety of related disciplines. Ethnographic perspectives, for example, have gained increasing importance in educational research in recent years. Ethnographers of education are interested in topics such as the reproduction of social inequality in school settings, cultural discontinuities and the sociolinguistics of intercultural (mis)communication in ethnically plural schools, and the performance of minority groups in school settings (see Jacob and Jordan 1993, 1987; Ogbu 1991a; Spindler and Spindler 1987; Suárez-Orozco 1989). The increasing number of first-rate monographs on ethnographic approaches to these and other theoretical problems make it clear that, putting aside the concerns of the more "quantitative" researchers, ethnography has achieved a place of importance in educational research.

Ethnography established itself, in part, by successfully addressing modernist challenges to its claims. The *modernist* critique of ethnography concentrated on its alleged lack of scientific rigor and problems with sampling, representativeness, reliability, and reproduction of findings. An important task of the first generation of ethnographers was to systematically address the substance of such critiques (see Spindler and Spindler 1987).

Just as ethnographers of education—and of other fields, including law and medicine—began achieving credibility, there appeared new, *postmodernist* critiques of their methods. Here we examine the nature of these postmodernist critiques of anthropology. We consider some key epistemological and political debates in anthropology as they relate to the status of research in the field. How, for example, can we make claims about the inner experience of youths in four different groups at a time when many mainstream anthropologists argue that the discipline cannot bridge the alleged epistemic gulf between researcher and "other"?

Anthropology finds itself in a moment of disciplinary malaise.[1] The field is going through its own version of the identity crisis affecting all the social sciences (Bauman 1991; Crook 1991; Hammersley 1992). Ideas that once were held sacred are being challenged or dismissed. The idea of the "four fields" (archeology, physical anthropology, linguistic anthropology, and cultural anthropology) appears increasingly irrelevant.[2]

The fundamental anthropological *grande idée* that we can study, understand, and explain other cultures is now rejected by many in anthropology. Melford Spiro has noted that some contemporary anthropologists have rejected this vision as "arrogant, misguided, or futile, if not all three. Arrogant, because it is an expression of Western, hegemonic, phallocentric, patriarchal discourse; misguided because it is a manifestation of scientism, positivism, and reductionism; futile because non-Western cultures and peoples are 'Other,' opaque in principle to Western investigators, however well-informed, fair-minded, or empathic they might be" (Spiro 1992: ix).

It follows, then, that comparison, a key tenet in cultural anthropology until very recently, is also suspect among many contemporary anthropologists. Even the ethnographic fieldwork approach that triumphantly defeated the armchair anthropology of yesteryear is under assault as futile on epistemological grounds or immoral on political grounds.[3]

Renato Rosaldo, for example, incriminates the "old ethnography" as having offered the necessary fictional ideologies for the creation of colonialism and imperialism. He contends that ethnographic writings replicate an order of violence by artificially enforcing sharp borders between "us" (objective, detached anthropologists) and "them" (the rigidly uniform, eternally static "natives").[4] Rosaldo writes, "Although depictions of traditional societies where people slavishly follow strict rules have a certain charming formality, alternative accounts of the same societies lead [Jerome] Bruner to a harsh conclusion, not unlike my own. He regards the once-dominant ethnographic portrait of the timeless traditional society as a fiction used to aid in composition and to legitimate the subjugation of human populations" (Rosaldo 1989: 43).[5]

New postmodern critiques of anthropology pay increasing attention to issues of power (and empowerment), domination, resistance, and "cultural construction." There is increasing interest in the making of ethnographic texts, experimenting with "multivocalities," and exploring how the "anthropological gaze" may reproduce (Western) discourses of domination, albeit in another idiom (Clifford and Marcus 1986). Some in contemporary anthropology, as we shall explore below, have taken the relativistic stance of anthropology to the extreme of suggesting that there is no way of knowing a culturally different "Other."

Many adherents of the new approaches particularly scorn psychological anthropology. Dorothy Holland speaks for many when she rejects the usefulness of this field by constructing a question she well knows the answer to: "How many of us will choose an anthropology—cultural or psychological—that begins by virtually dismissing the importance of power, struggle and dissent to the stories we can tell?" (Holland 1992: 747–48). As Nancy Scheper-Hughes (1994) has noted, psychological anthropology has been seen as retrograde or, in today's argot, definitely not politically correct.

Criticism of psychological anthropology in particular has a long history (see Spindler 1994). The love-hate relationship between psychological anthropology and mainstream anthropology continues. Let us turn to one of the most controversial debates in anthropology: the place of objectivity and subjectivity in the creation of knowledge.[6]

The problem of objectivity goes right to the heart of how we apprehend the world. Jean Piaget (1930), particularly in his early work, describes in detail how the child moves from the "realism of perception" to increasingly more objective understandings of the world and its workings. Early on, according to Piaget, the child "misapprehends" the world through perceptual and emotional distortions (creating a "realism of perception"). Piaget illustrates these distortions with the classic example that the child thinks that as she walks, the moon or sun "follows" her. Eventually, through psychological differentiation, the child gains more objective understandings of the world around her. The child, according to Piaget, eventually comprehends that the sun follows its own path. She trades the misperception that it follows her for the more detached observation that the sun is so high up it just seems to follow her.

This early human tendency to engage in egocentric thinking leaves some powerful residue in the human psyche.[7] According to Piaget, a prerequisite for the emergence of objectivity is the ability to separate out what is part of the self and what is part of the outer world. In its earliest phases, human thought is laced with "magical" qualities: thoughts are "omnipotent" and "charged with efficacy," causing things to happen in the world. The child—and here Piaget and Freud agree, albeit using rather different theoretical frameworks—must learn to separate what is part of the self (her subjective experience) and what is part of the outer or other world. And here is perhaps one of the earliest human disappointments: the world, the child learns, is governed by certain principles *on which her own wishes and thoughts have no influence.*[8]

Yet according to postmodern critics in contemporary anthropology, there is no mind independent of the world (culture). Mind, they say, is exclusively the product of cultural construction (the world). As Rosaldo writes, "Even those so-called realms of pure freedom, our fantasy and our 'innermost thoughts,' are produced and limited by our own local culture" (Rosaldo 1989: 25). Note the categorical nature of Rosaldo's announcement: thoughts and fantasies are "produced and limited" (not just shaped or molded) by local culture.[9] Indeed, as Spiro has noted, "radical cognitive relativism," fashionable in contemporary postmodern anthropology, has concluded that "our thought processes, our emotions, our beliefs, and our motives are virtually wholly determined . . . by culture" (Spiro 1992: x).

The idea that mind emerges from the interactions of certain biologically based maturational capacities and psychic structures that are independent of culture, widely shared by developmental and cognitive psychologists, is either ignored or rejected by many contemporary postmodern anthropological critics committed to a radical cultural constructivism. Most influential developmental and cognitive psychologists, Piaget, Vygotsky, and their followers among them, have rejected the "empty box," tabula rasa model implied in the thinking of contemporary cognitive relativists.[10]

There is, of course, a history to the radical cognitive relativism found in contemporary postmodern anthropology. The tabula rasa was the twin sister of the idea of cultural determinism. According to the British empiricists (Locke, especially), human beings were born a tabula rasa onto which experience imprinted itself through social institutions (see Spiro 1978). In their battle against racism and biological reductionism, the early modern anthropologists found comfort in this idea: the human being is born a blank slate onto which culture writes infinitely varied scripts. A major intellectual task of the second generation of psychological anthropologists was to replace the empty-box model with a model for understanding human experience and behavior as patterned by culture through the mediating and structuring functions of personality (see Suárez-Orozco, Spindler, and Spindler 1994). And unlike American behaviorism, most personality models originating in European thought simply rejected the empty-box model.[11]

Given that many postmodern radical cognitive constructivists continue to assert that mind is wholly created by culture, it follows that the idea of objectivity would be seen as futile at best, ethnocentric and politically dangerous at worst.

The *modern* anthropological ideal that through ethnography we must strive to achieve an objective understanding of a culture—or even an objective understanding of how members of another culture understand their world—widely shared throughout most of this century, has come under heavy *postmodern* fire. The new critiques of objectivity in contemporary anthropology are different from the earlier work in psychological anthropology on the important problem of what happens *"within the observer"* who is emotionally involved with a human "subject" he or she wishes to understand (La Barre 1967: ix).

Since Einstein and Heisenberg, scientists have had to reckon with *"the position of the observer* in a relativistic universe [Einstein] . . . [and Heisenberg] has shown us the indeterminability . . . of some intra-atomic events *without, in the process of observing, changing the events themselves"* (La Barre 1967: vii). In all observation, the observer and the observed are brought together in the creation of a moment whose very existence transforms them. In the behavioral sciences, the problems of observation increase exponentially as, in attempting to study fellow humans, the behavioral scientist is seriously, but not fatally, caught by his or her *own psychological and cultural position in a social field.*

In his classic contribution to the problem of method in the behavioral sciences, psychoanalytic anthropologist George Devereux noted that "behavioral science data arouses anxieties" (1967: xvii) because of our inevitable emotional involvement with the human beings we attempt to understand. Devereux argues that behavioral scientists typically ward off these anxieties by shielding themselves with rigorous "pseudo-methodology . . . [which] is responsible for nearly all defects of behavioral science" (ibid.).[12]

According to Devereux, the ethnographer must not, in the name

of a facile objectivism, disregard the subjective nature of the interactions between observer and observed (1960, 1967, 1969, 1978; see
also Kracke 1994; Crapanzano 1994). On the contrary, the ethnographer must mine his or her subjective "countertransference" (see
Suárez-Orozco 1994) as "the royal road to an authentic, rather than
fictitious, objectivity" (Devereux 1967: xvii). Our greater emotional
involvement with human beings (than, say, with atoms or stars)
accounts for the special problems of objectivity in the behavioral
sciences.

To recapitulate, according to earlier work in (psychological) anthropology, objectivity is the relative awareness of our own subjectivity. It logically follows that within this theoretical framework
the behavioral scientist must systematically use introspection as a
compass for exploring the world of the Other he or she attempts to
understand.

As Weston La Barre put it: "The un-selfexamined anthropologist
henceforth has no right or business anthropologizing" (1967: ix).[13]
For example, we had to examine some of our own experiences as
immigrants when we were reminded of them by the issues we chose
to examine in our research: loss, rage, guilt, reparation, shame, and
so forth.[14] Once these and other memories were reawakened, they
naturally insinuated themselves into the research paths we chose. In
the process, we learned a great deal, about our own losses, and more
important, about these issues in general.

Because we are so close to the subject, we wanted to put some
distance between us and it in the form of methodological rigor.
Although our inner compass might have helped chart our course,
we wanted not to draw ourselves into the inner sea of our own subjectivities but to be able to generalize beyond our own experiences.
Although it would have been much easier, and certainly more *à la
dernière*, to write a more subjective study of our own experiences as
immigrants, it would be of limited value as a general statement on
the vicissitudes of immigration.

The new critics of objectivity have by and large ignored these
psychological problems. Instead they have concentrated on the *political* aspects of objectivity in the social sciences. Some have claimed
that the mantle of objectivity is worn to hide political privileges
and to avoid taking (political) sides in the conflicts that accompany
the making of society and social analysis. Objectivity, the postmodern critics of ethnography claim, rarefies the Other as it hides the
power relationships of domination and subordination it reproduces.[15]
We disagree with this position. Indeed, one of our aims is to be as

"objective" as we can about the consequences of domination and disparagement.

Other postmodern critics of ethnography argue that objective knowledge of another culture is impossible on *epistemological* grounds. These critics note that because of the radically different, indeed incommensurate, epistemologies separating the ethnographer (armed with his or her typically Western discourse) and the (typically native) Other, objective knowledge can never be created. The very strategic demarcation of the "Other" (with a capital O, currently à la mode) underscores an allegedly unbridgeable epistemic gulf.

According to this line of thought, there are no universal continuities or shared human potentials, only culturally constructed, radically discontinuous, and mutually incomprehensible systems of meaning. As Melford Spiro has observed, "Contemporary [postmodern] anthropology argues that cultural diversity is of a magnitude that renders every culture incommensurable with any other" (Spiro 1992: x). Hence in today's literature we have "Others," not "brothers."

Some critics have argued that objectivity, far from being a universal maturational potential, is itself a Western social construct or "ethnoscience."[16] The idea of objectivity is further questioned when it is framed as a social construct that is part of a hegemonic discourse, a "gaze" that glosses over the exercise of (Western) power and domination in the mystifying language of science, neutrality, and impartiality.[17] The misuses of science (for example, from craniometry through the IQ debate) are often invoked as examples of how the idea of objectivity and its offspring science have been corrupted and put in the service of shameful projects of human exploitation.[18]

Given that objectivity itself is questioned, it is no coincidence that an important component of the contemporary postmodernist approaches to anthropology is celebrating the anthropologist's subjective responses in the encounter with the Other. Logically, since the Other is ultimately unknowable, all there is to work with is anthropologists' responses to the alien Otherness. Hence we return, full circle, to the kingdom of subjectivity.[19]

Another frequent postmodern criticism is that psychological anthropology has been blind to the workings of power in culture (Holland 1992: 747–48). Although some psychological anthropologists have indeed neglected the study of power, it would be a gross simplification to conclude that the whole discipline is wanting in this critical area of scholarship. Indeed, in recent years a number of psychological anthropologists have made important theoretical contributions to the study of power in culture (see, for example, De Vos and Suárez-Orozco 1990; De Vos 1992; Ogbu 1991a; Scheper-Hughes 1994). One of our objectives has been to forge a language for the psychosocial study of domination in multicultural settings (see, for example, Suárez-Orozco 1989, 1994; Suárez-Orozco and Suárez-Orozco 1992; De Vos and Suárez-Orozco 1990).

In our own work we have insisted that insight into the etic structures of exploitation must be complemented with attempts to understand the *experience* of inequality and disparagement in situations of rigid class, ethnic, gender, or age exploitation. And any such attempt necessitates a theoretical framework for exploring the self as an experiential frame of reference. Indeed, the most exciting theoretical work in psychological anthropology continues to try to synthesize two approaches that many social scientists *still* consider antithetical—social and personality aspects of the human condition.

We believe that many of the issues raised by postmodernism are very important—such as the question of subjectivity and objectivity in fieldwork, authority and authorship in the construction of ethnographic texts, and power in culture. However, we disagree with many of the conclusions flowing from the postmodern critique.[20]

In the next two chapters we claim, in a positivistic light, that we have gained some insight into the inner experiences of four groups of adolescents. Our approximations are tentative, partial, and far from complete, but it is possible to achieve difficult, cross-cultural communication—and empathic linkages. The epistemic gulf imagined by postmodern anthropology is, in our cross-cultural experience, narrower than is now fashionable to envision.

Out of the Lab and into the Woods? Cross-Cultural Research Challenges in Psychology

Cross-cultural research presents different kinds of challenges to psychologists than to anthropologists (see, for example, Abel 1973; Berry 1992; Berry and Dasen 1974; Cole and Means 1981; Cowan et al. 1993; De Vos 1973; Lindzey 1961; Lonner and Berry 1986; Price-Williams 1975; Retschitzki, Bossel-Lagos, and Dasen 1989; Rogoff and Morelli 1989; Stevenson and Shin-Ying 1990; Stevenson, Azuma, and Hakuta 1986; Tharp and Gallimore 1988). Social scientists in general have been struggling for decades with how best to conduct this type of research. Psychologists conducting cross-cultural research have used a variety of techniques, including projective and objective psychological tests, experiments, case studies, surveys, observation, and interviews. No method has avoided attack for its limitations.

Research psychologists have been specifically concerned with the fact that preexisting groups of individuals (such as Mexicans in Mexico and Mexican immigrants in the United States) encompassing a multitude of characteristics and experiences do not lend themselves to the rigors of the ideal case scenario found in experimental design—the pillar supporting a "scientific psychology." Cole and Means have noted that "the comparative study does not meet even the most basic assumption of experimental design" (1981: 13). In experimental research, the subject population is held constant while a treatment variable is manipulated. In a comparative study, the opposite occurs—the task or characteristic under consideration is held constant while the subject population varies, so that researchers may determine how the characteristic or performance of each group differs. Hence, random assignment, the sine qua non of experimental design crucial to guaranteeing internal validity, is violated. Cole and Means have rightly observed that it is impossible to be certain that groups formed by nature (immigrants and nonimmigrants, for example) rather than by random assignment are equivalent and hence to attribute the cause of group differences to the variable under consideration (ibid.: 32). They point out that groups "will differ on not one but on a multitude of dimensions. Hence, we will have difficulty in proving that any one particular difference between our groups is the source of observed difference in performance" (ibid.: 35).

In order to avoid misattributing performance to one factor while ignoring other potentially significant factors, Cole and Means suggest the strategy of matching along potential relevant characteristics "that are not under study . . . but that could also produce the predicted effect" (ibid.: 39). However, there is a limitation to the solution of matching because "we can never be sure it is carried far enough" (ibid.). In other words, there may always be a variable that has been overlooked or that has not been matched because of logistical obstacles (such as expense or lack of availability of subjects with the desired characteristics).

Many leading psychologists, including Cole and Means (1981), Price-Williams (1975), Abel (1973), and Lindzey (1961), have pointed out some of the limitations of assessment instruments that have been used in cross-cultural studies. The ideal requirement is not just "*some* meaningfulness and familiarity of the materials for all groups tested, but . . . *equality* in terms of familiarity, meaningfulness and any other stimulus characteristic relevant to performance" (Cole and

Means 1981: 44). Unfortunately, this requirement can seldom if ever be met.

All of these factors may lead some to the conclusion that cross-cultural comparisons in psychology should not be attempted because they will be hopelessly limited. We agree with Cole and Means that comparative studies cannot justify assertions of causal relationships in the way that experimental research can. In this type of research we must forgo causal interpretations and "[treat] results as we do the findings between two subject characteristics, that is, as an indication that two qualities tend to covary without any implication that one of them causes the other" (ibid.: 60). Hence, when we argue that immigrant adolescents tend to be more preoccupied with psychological losses than Mexican adolescents in Mexico, we cannot say that immigration, per se, causes an increased preoccupation with losses. All we can say is that immigration and preoccupation with losses covary.

Although we are aware of the limitations inherent in cross-cultural research, we must also note that a great deal of research in psychology has been overly obliging to the almost tyrannical requirements of experimental design. After an exhaustive review of the cross-cultural family research conducted over the past few decades, Berkeley psychologists Cowan, Field, Hansen, Skolnick, and Swanson urge psychologists not to allow research to become "static, a-contextual and method-bound" (Cowan et al. 1993: 465). They express concern that much psychological research in this area loses sight of the forest for the trees:

> We must work to move beyond the period of methodological imperialism that has dominated family research in the greater part of this century. No single method can be allowed to delimit the meaning and reality of our knowledge about families. It is necessary to consider how information from clinical and phenomenological studies, ethnographic qualitative studies, theoretical-explanatory quantitative studies, historical analyses, cross-cultural comparisons and case studies can be articulated and integrated. (Cowan et al. 1993: 465–66)

In conducting comparative cross-cultural research in psychology we must therefore: (1) clearly understand its limitations, (2) proceed carefully in design and implementation, and (3) never claim that links are causal. Cross-cultural comparisons in psychological research are at best descriptive rather than explanatory. In order to be on firm ground, comparative cross-cultural psychologists must stay close to the data, acknowledge the limitations of their findings, and make interpretations and recommendations carefully.

This study hopes to navigate these difficult currents in psychological anthropology and cross-cultural psychology. It is an experimental project incorporating the strengths—and weaknesses—of research strategies in both fields. The study is guided by the assumption that, though extremely challenging, it is nevertheless possible to systematically approximate aspects of the inner world and interpersonal concerns of culturally different populations.

We share with research psychologists a belief that certain methodologies are necessary in order to move beyond subjective impressions into the realm of replicable generalizations. In our study, however, we depart from the "methodological imperialism" that has characterized most research in psychology over the past few decades (Cowan et al. 1993). We examine behavior and experience using the approach of modern anthropology: hence, we collected data using ethnographic interviews, naturalistic observations, projective and objective tests, and various other tasks.[21]

Studying Family Dynamics and Achievement Motivation in Four Groups: Some Hypotheses

Given our theoretical interest in immigration and ethnicity and the complexities of conducting comparative research, we decided to focus specifically on family life and achievement motivation. In the next two chapters we address the following specific research question: how do familism, family conflict, and achievement orientation differ among Mexican, immigrant Mexican, second-generation Mexican American, and white American "mainstream" youth?

We first compare Mexican and white non-Hispanic adolescents because these groups represent a "baseline" for the two cultures. Then we look at how immigration affects youths who have a Mexican identity and have immigrated to the United States. Last, we consider the similarities and differences between Mexican American youths who are "between cultures" and the other three groups.

On the basis of our previous research experience and our reading of the relevant literature, we developed several hypotheses:

1. We expected adolescents from each of the three Latino groups to demonstrate higher levels of familism than white American adolescents.

2. We expected adolescents residing in Mexico to demonstrate the highest level of familism.

3. We expected Mexican and Mexican immigrant youths to be more oriented toward achievement with a motivation to help others than

either white American or second-generation Mexican American youths.

4. We expected Mexican and Mexican immigrant adolescents to express more concern about poverty and about succeeding in school in order to overcome poverty than either white American adolescents or second-generation Mexican American youths.

5. Because of the high dropout rate of second-generation Mexican Americans, we expected these adolescents to display the greatest tendency to avoid challenging tasks.

6. We expected Mexican immigrants and second-generation Mexican Americans to demonstrate higher levels of family conflict than Mexicans in Mexico or white American adolescents.

7. We expected second-generation Mexican American youths to be more oriented toward their peers than members of the other three groups.

Not surprisingly, our findings bore out some of our hypotheses but not others; and we made some unanticipated findings. Our specific findings are discussed in Chapters 4 and 5.

We turn now to an outline of the methodologies we employed to address these research questions. This study was decidedly eclectic in its methodology, using the methods of psychological anthropology, research psychology, and cross-cultural psychology. As we have discussed, cross-cultural research is unusually complex, challenging, and fraught with controversy; however, we believe that the pressing social issues of our time require that questions be addressed on something other than an ad hoc basis.

DESIGN

Our study, then, used static group comparison with one independent variable. Every informant participating in this study fell into one of the following groups:

Group 1: Mexicans (born of Mexican parents and residing in Mexico)

Group 2: Mexican immigrants/settlers (born of Mexican parents in Mexico and residing in the United States)

Group 3: Second-generation Mexican Americans (born and raised in the United States of Mexican immigrant parents)

Group 4: White Americans (born and raised in the United States of white, non-Hispanic, U.S.-born parents)

Our informants were 189 adolescents (96 female and 93 male) currently attending public middle school and high school.[22] Participation was entirely voluntary. Participation was restricted to adolescents between the ages of 13 and 18; the mean age for the entire sample was 15.7.[23]

We obtained our Mexican sample of forty-seven students from a public middle school in a town of approximately 50,000 inhabitants in the state of Guanajuato.[24] We chose Guanajuato because it is one of the three Mexican states—along with Jalisco and Michoacan—that send the great majority of emigrants to the United States (Cornelius 1990). Indeed many of our informants had relatives and friends who had made the journey north. Although it is difficult to predict which of our informants, if any, would themselves eventually emigrate (see Massey et al. 1987), it is reasonable to expect a number of them to follow the path of friends and relatives.

Given the historic tradition of emigration and the tourist appeal of this region of Mexico, many of these youths had been exposed to outsiders. They felt comfortable discussing international topics such as Argentine soccer, U.S. foreign policy in Latin America, and changes in the former Soviet Union. Our informants came from the middle range of the Mexican socioeconomic classes; they were neither wealthy nor poverty stricken. Their parents included shopkeepers, service sector workers, artisans, and a few professionals. Overall, members of this group came from a slightly lower socioeconomic class than the adolescents in the white American sample, but from a higher class than the immigrants and second-generation Mexican Americans (see Table A.4 for the specifics of their economic distribution).

We chose to work with youngsters attending a public middle school because many of them are forced by economic pressures to leave school before entering the *preparatoria* (precollege high school), and they are representative of those who later might emigrate. Thus, in order to avoid biasing the Mexican sample by concentrating on the more selective *preparatoria*, we chose to focus on the more representative middle school. Our remaining informants were students in a middle school and a high school in a rapidly growing immigrant-receiving area in southern California. The immigrant group consisted of forty-eight adolescents born in Mexico of Mexican parents; they had lived at least the first five years of their lives in Mexico, spoke Spanish fluently, and had immigrated to the United States no less than one year before participating in our research.

All the adolescents in this group said they were Mexican, not Chicano, not Mexican American. We excluded from our study immigrant adolescents who spent longer than three months per year

in Mexico—we did not want to distort our findings by working
with students exposed to the upheavals of frequent migrations. Our
sample of immigrants were very recent arrivals whose mean number of years in the United States was 4.04.[25] As we noted above, we
have reason to suspect that more acculturated Latino immigrants
(say, those who have been in the United States longer than ten years)
may have achievement motivations and attitudes toward school that
are unlike those of very recent arrivals. The adolescents in our immigrant sample had the lowest socioeconomic status of the four
groups.

Forty-seven adolescents made up the second-generation Mexican
American group. All of these youths were born and raised in the
United States; their parents were born in Mexico and emigrated before their birth. These adolescents had the second-lowest socioeconomic status of the four groups.

The last sample consisted of forty-seven adolescents who self-
identified as "white American."[26] Both they and their parents were
born in the United States and did not identify themselves as members of an ethnic minority (such as African American, Asian American, Native American, or Latino). The adolescents in this group were
highest in socioeconomic status.

It is important to emphasize that the four groups are not equal
in socioeconomic status. *However, our samples are representative
of the populations from which they were drawn.* The Mexican and
white American adolescents came from a representative range of
socioeconomic status in their respective countries and are roughly
comparable to one another. In other words, we did not compare
upper-middle-class white American adolescents with lower-class
Mexicans in Mexico. In selecting our immigrant and Mexican American informants, we recognized that these groups in the United States
are generally of lower socioeconomic status (see Bean et al. 1991;
Chapa 1988). We could have made all the groups comparable in socioeconomic status by drawing our Mexican immigrant and Mexican
American informants from higher-status private schools in the San
Diego suburbs, but they would not have been representative of the
vast majority of Mexican immigrants and Mexican Americans living
in the United States.

The "white American" comparison group was made up of adolescents who identified themselves as being of Anglo-Saxon, European
origin. They felt themselves to be "nonethnic" and "mainstream."
The members of this group constitute what George and Louise
Spindler call the "referent ethniclass" of the United States (1990: 33).

These are individuals of Anglo-Saxon, northern European, protestant origin *or who subscribe to "mainstream" cultural characteristics.*

The Spindlers say that this group represents the "American cultural mainstream" for several reasons. Historically, "the referent ethniclass in America has its beginnings in colonial America, where about 60 per cent of the colonists were Anglo-Saxon," and they continue to make up more than half of the American population. They are the " 'reference' by which people have measured their success, achievement and essentially, their 'mainstreamness'. This referent ethniclass is that population in the United States of America that has disproportionately furnished the personnel for positions of power and influence in our society" (ibid.: 34).

In this study we had three dependent variables: family conflict, achievement orientation, and familism. In addition, for each informant we calculated a cumulative familism score (made up of the three separate scores on the items listed under "familism" below).

FAMILY CONFLICT

1. Verbal
2. Physical
3. Family ambiance/covert tension

ACHIEVEMENT ORIENTATION

1. Independent achievement: achievement in a self-initiated manner—without the help of others
2. Affiliative achievement: achievement with the help of others and/or to help others
3. Compensatory achievement: achievement in compensation for previous relative deprivation or poverty
4. Engaging in or avoiding a challenging task

FAMILISM

1. Perceived emotional and/or material support *from* the family
2. Perceived obligation to provide emotional and/or material support *to* the family
3. Relatives as behavioral and attitudinal referents

We also compared *peers* as behavioral and attitudinal referents.

Using Campbell and Stanley's (1963) framework, this study meets the criteria of a static group design. It is a preexperimental design because informants are not assigned to the groups under study. A nonequivalent control group design generally controls for the following sources of internal invalidity: history, testing, instrumentation, and regression. However, in this study, the Mexican data were collected a year before the rest, so history is not entirely controlled for.

A primary limitation of the nonequivalent control group design is that findings cannot be generalized beyond the sampled group. Another major weakness is that it is impossible to be certain that the groups are equivalent in all ways other than for the independent variable under consideration. Cole and Means point out that groups "will differ on not one but on a multitude of dimensions. Hence, we will have difficulty in proving that any one particular difference between our groups is the source of observed difference in performance" (1981: 35).

In order to maximize the probability that the groups were made up of roughly comparable subjects, we evaluated the following *control variables*:

1. *Socioeconomic status:* Using the Hollingshead (1975) Four Factor Index of Social Position (which is based on education and occupation of the parents, sex, and marital status), we determined the socioeconomic range of the informants. This measure, though normed in the United States, has been used in cross-cultural research (Erinosho and Ayonrinde 1981; Maziade 1984; Mennen 1988). We checked for significance of socioeconomic status using analysis of variance. As this variable reached significance, it was used as a covariant in analyses of covariance.[27]

2. *Age:* Participation was restricted to youths between the ages of thirteen and eighteen (see Table A.3).

3. *Gender:* Groups were equated for gender. Analyses of differences between groups by gender were made (see Table A.2).[28]

4. *Participation in psychotherapy:* Informants currently in individual or family therapy were excluded from this study. We made this decision primarily because we wished to generalize findings to "normal adolescents" rather than to patients. Furthermore, we thought that students in psychotherapy might have higher levels of family conflict, be more likely to avoid achievement tasks, and so forth, than others.

We gathered a variety of ethnographic and psychological data using the Problem Situation Test, a sentence completion test, and other formal tasks.[29] For example, we gathered data on our informants' living arrangements and classified each one as: (1) living in an intact family, (2) living with mother after divorce or separation, (3) living with father after divorce or separation, (4) living with an adult sibling, (5) living with a nonnuclear family member (e.g., a grandparent, uncle, aunt, or godparent), (6) living in a multiple-generation family (e.g., with parents and grandparents), or (7) living with an adult non–family member.

There were significant differences in living arrangements. For example, while 74 percent of the adolescents in our Mexican sample lived in intact families, only 40 percent of the white American adolescents did so. Immigrants and Mexican Americans fell in between these two groups. Given that divorce rates are lower in Mexico than in California, our samples seem representative on this dimension of the populations from which we drew.

PROCEDURES

We gathered the data in Mexico one year before we gathered the data in California. As is common when conducting research in Latin America, we first established contact with school authorities through friends. After visiting several schools we decided on a middle-school site as most appropriate. The school administrators were advised that the purpose of the research was to establish a baseline measurement of educational procedures, classroom styles, and student attitudes toward schooling, achievement, family, and peers in order to compare their experiences with those of comparable students in the United States.

The doors of the school were opened to us at once. The principal was eager to participate. He noted that over the years he had seen many of his students emigrate to the United States and had always wondered how they had fared in the new land. The principal also said that he wanted to help out in any study that might be of help to Mexican immigrant students in the United States.

After observing classroom activities for several weeks, a research assistant began to conduct ethnographic interviews and administer tests and questionnaires. The bilingual research assistant was trained in interviewing, test administration, and classroom observation.[30]

In the United States we contacted school authorities in two school districts in southern California, both of which had a heavy concentration of immigrant and Mexican American students. We chose one of the school districts in which to conduct our research and collected the data with five bilingual research assistants trained in classroom observation, interviewing, and test administration.[31]

We interviewed two principals in the local middle school and high school. Like their Mexican counterpart, they were eager to participate in the study and instructed their staffs to help us conduct our research. The principal of the middle school was eager to learn more about the special issues facing immigrant students in her school, and the high school principal was particularly interested in why immigrant students seem to lose their enthusiasm about school the longer they are here.

We obtained names of possible informants from school records and made announcements in the classrooms calling for participants. We asked interested potential participants to complete short questionnaires to help us determine whether they were members of any of the groups under investigation. We interviewed those whose responses were not clear. We gave those who qualified a consent form (in English or Spanish) for their and their parents' or guardians' signatures.

Both schools provided us with a quiet space where we could work with the students with minimal distraction. As we had done in Mexico, we observed the students and chatted with them informally in a variety of school settings. The students who wished to participate more formally were interviewed individually. The formal ethnographic interviews and testing were conducted either in English or in Spanish, according to the student's preference and proficiency. Some of the immigrant and Mexican American informants switched back and forth between languages (see Table A.6). After we had established some rapport, we asked each student a set of questions to elicit demographic, life history, and migration-related information. Eventually we addressed issues relating to their experiences at school and with their families and peers.

We administered the Thematic Apperception Test (TAT) to all the students. Following Murray's (1943) suggestion, we told our informants that the TAT was a creative task (rather than a personality test). We asked each student to look at the pictures on eight TAT cards (cards 1, 2, 3BM, 4, 6BM, 7BM, 8BM, and 8GF) and tell a story with a beginning, a middle, and an end about what they saw on the cards. We also asked them to describe what the protagonists in the story were thinking and feeling.

In order to maintain uniform TAT administration we decided to make as few inquiries as possible. When necessary, we encouraged the students to tell longer TAT narratives (if theirs were too brief) and reminded them that the task was to tell a story, not to describe the card.

We then administered the sentence completion test (borrowed from De Vos 1973), the familism scale (Sabogal et al. 1987), and the Problem Situation Test.[32]

PSYCHOLOGICAL MEASURES

We used the following psychological measurement tools to gather our data: a familism scale (Sabogal et al. 1987), a family conflict scale (Beavers, Hampson, and Hulgus 1985), the Thematic Apperception Test (Murray 1943), a version of the Problem Situation Test (De Vos 1973), and a sentence completion test (ibid.).

We used the familism scale adapted by Sabogal et al. (1987) to measure self-reported familism. This scale has been used with 452 Hispanics and 227 non-Hispanic whites and has been found to distinguish between the Hispanics and non-Hispanics. The fourteen questions in the scale relating to familism were arranged along a Likert scale. The questions were subjected to a factor analysis with a varimax rotation. The three conceptually clear factors (with eigenvalues of more than 1.0) that emerged, accounting for 48.4 percent of the variance, are: (1) family obligations, (2) perceived support from the family, and (3) family members as referents. These are conceptually equivalent to the familism-related factors we measured using the TAT rating scale. We evaluated each of the three familism scores as well as a cumulative familism score.

We measured evidence of family conflict using questions from the family conflict scale of the self-report family questionnaire designed by Beavers et al. (1985). This instrument demonstrated respectable reliability (Cronbach's alpha of .85). The instrument also has fair concurrent validity, correlating with clinical ratings (.62) as well as with well-established family rating scales. The family conflict subscale consists of twelve questions and was evaluated separately from the familism scales.

The twenty-six-question familism/family conflict questionnaire was translated into Spanish for the Mexican informants and for the immigrants who preferred to work with us in Spanish (see Table A.6).

Henry Murray and his associates at the Harvard Clinic developed the Thematic Apperception Test (TAT) in the 1930s (Murray 1943). It consists of thirty pictures, ten to twenty of which are presented sequentially to subjects. Murray specified which cards were appropriate for male and female adults and which for boys and girls. Today these original guidelines are not always observed.[33]

Murray's instructions are to show the cards to the informants one at a time and ask them to make up a story with a past, a present, and a future based on what they see in the pictures. Each informant is to be asked: What are the characters in the pictures doing? What are they thinking and feeling? What happened earlier, and how does the story end?[34]

The TAT rests on the logic that informants, when presented with ambiguous stimuli, such as the pictures on the cards, will reveal much about their own attitudes and concerns (Lindzey 1961; Bellak 1986). The narratives they create will to a certain extent reflect their wishes, fantasies, fears, dreams, and worries.

The test can be used for individual assessment or, when given to well-defined populations, to postulate normative patterns for a group as a whole. We chose to use the TAT because of its widespread use in cross-cultural research.

It has been argued that the TAT serves as a powerful complement to interviews and other data to systematically elicit key, typical concerns or the interpersonal "atmospheric condition" of a group (De Vos 1973). A variety of interpersonal characteristics and behaviors such as patterns of achievement motivation (Vaughn 1988) and suicide (De Vos 1973) in Japan, changing attitudes in Korea toward traditional family roles (De Vos 1983), changing attitudes among kibbutz-niks toward their venture (Rabkin 1987), machismo among Mexican American male youths (Urrabazo 1985), the fatalism of southern Italians (Banfield 1958), attitudes of the rural Irish about sexuality (Scheper-Hughes 1979), and "survivor guilt" among Central American refugees (Suárez-Orozco 1989) have been explored using the TAT as a measure. (For a review of these and other studies using the TAT, see Abel 1973; and Lindzey 1961; and Suárez-Orozco 1989.)

The TAT, though widely used in cross-cultural research, is not without its critics. Mainstream cultural anthropologists have by and large been skeptical of its usefulness in ethnographic research (see Suárez-Orozco 1990). In part this can be related to Richard Shweder's point that cultural anthropologists in general are quite "psycho-phobic" (Shweder 1992; see also Spindler 1994). Systematic analysis of psychological processes is simply not the forte of most cultural anthropologists (see Suárez-Orozco 1994).

A second factor accounting for the general skepticism of the TAT— and projective techniques in general—in anthropology has to do with the fact that many cultural anthropologists believe that the test, because it was developed in a Euro-American setting, simply could not "work" among culturally different peoples. Also key in the anthropological critique of the TAT is the fact that, with precious few exceptions, it simply has not been used properly within anthropology.

Gardner Lindzey (1961) carefully considered a number of cross-cultural studies conducted using projective instruments. He found that many cross-cultural studies using the TAT were seriously flawed methodologically. Among his principal concerns were that researchers (largely anthropologists) were using the test without having been trained in its administration and loosely interpreting the stories without using any standardized scoring system, that the sample sizes used to make cross-cultural generalizations were too small, and that many cross-cultural studies were conducted without explicit hypotheses. Furthermore, Lindzey expressed concern that use of the TAT in a nonclinical ethnographic context could impose a language of clinical psychopathology on the anthropologists' informants.

For the purpose of our study, the focus is not the TAT's *clinical, psychodiagnostic* use but how the TAT reflects *shared, patterned, thematic clusters* when given to a specific population. In addition, the TAT has been extremely useful in eliciting key affect-laden concerns about sexuality (see Scheper-Hughes 1979), family obligations (see De Vos 1983), and guilt (see Suárez-Orozco 1989), which are typically difficult to elicit by other means (such as direct questioning and interviews). In our study we standardized administration and established a strict scoring method (see below). Last, we obtained an adequate sample size (189 subjects) and articulated explicit hypotheses.

Abel (1973) pointed out that many have criticized the TAT's "culture-bound" drawings, which could conceivably make it difficult for subjects from other cultures to find "sufficient content with which to identify" (1973: 94). Responding to this criticism, a number of researchers have taken Murray's standard set and adapted it to the group under study. Some have simply redrawn the characters on the cards, giving them the racial characteristics of the group under study (De Vos 1973), and others have created their own altogether different cards with characters and content thought to be more culturally familiar to the test takers.

An example of an adaptation of the TAT is Temas (themes), a projective storytelling test developed for Hispanics and blacks. Researchers have argued that minority children were more verbally fluent on the Temas than on the TAT and that the Temas accurately classified into the appropriate group (clinical and nonclinical, black and Puerto Rican children) 89 percent of the subjects of their study (Constantino and Malgady 1983; Constantino et al. 1988; Rogler and Tsui 1988). However, no studies have compared the two tests' accuracy of classification, so no conclusions can be drawn about the superiority of one instrument over another.

George De Vos (1973) developed a version of the TAT using characters who looked Japanese. In comparing the responses to the standard Murray set and the Japanese version, he found virtually no differences.

Abel (1973), in reviewing studies comparing different versions of the TAT, found that some researchers simply counted the number of words in responses as a way of measuring how different cultures responded to the cards. She rightly questioned whether number of words per se is meaningful and noted that number of words did not necessarily affect the content of the stories. Many comparisons showed that informants did not necessarily empathize more with the adapted cards (Abel 1973: 106). It seems then, as Abel concludes, that the verdict is still out on whether locally adapted cards are more appropriate than the standard Murray set. When working with nonliterate, non-Western informants, an adaptation may be appropriate.[35] However, because the participants in our study were literate and had been exposed to media representations of American culture, we chose to use a selection of cards from the standard TAT set.

Research psychologists have also pointed out some of the problems of working with the TAT. Vane describes the TAT as "a clinician's delight and a statistician's nightmare" (1981: 319). For many clinicians, the TAT has remained an "impressionistic instrument" for which there is no standardized scoring method (ibid.: 321).

The many methods of administering and scoring the test make it difficult to evaluate its overall validity and reliability and to replicate studies. Furthermore, because estimates of reliability and validity are designed more to evaluate objective psychometric instruments than they are projective ones, it is not surprising that the TAT is controversial.

The TAT has been administered to individuals (with the test administrator writing down the responses verbatim and/or recording them) and to groups (with the test takers writing out their stories by hand). The quality of the responses in a group format is affected by the simple presence of the group, by the test takers' writing skills, and by the fact that the test administrator does not ask or prompt for more elaboration.

Lundy conducted a meta-analysis of 317 studies and demonstrated that "the conditions under which the TAT is administered to subjects are closely associated with quality of research results" (Lundy 1988: 310). He found that when the TAT was presented as a test, when the administrator was viewed as an authority, and when the TAT was given in a classroom, the findings were "less successful than average" (ibid.). Lundy administered the TAT to 199 adolescents using four different assessment situations: (1) neutral; (2) after a personality test; (3) emphasizing the TAT as a personality test; and (4) in a nonthreatening but structured setting. Lundy assumed, as Murray had recommended, that in order to obtain meaningful results, the "subject's attention should be diverted from his or her psychic processes" (ibid.: 310). He found that the stories told after neutral instructions were valid predictors of his three outcome measures (need for achievement, affiliation, and power), while the stories told in the other three assessment situations yielded "nonsignificant and sometimes negative validities" (ibid.: 309). He concluded that neutral instructions were crucial to increasing the validity of the TAT. He recommended (a) that the TAT be administered in a "relaxed, friendly, and approving manner"; (b) that the TAT never follow an objective or cognitive test; and (c) that the TAT not be identified as a personality test (ibid.: 318). In our study, we followed Lundy's recommendations closely.

Because the TAT elicits unconscious motivations, it is difficult to find other measures that will help to establish its concurrent validity. Instruments used to elicit behavior or self-reported attitudes may have little in common with the TAT, which elicits unconscious motivations (Vane 1981; Winter 1973). For example, Winter found only a modest correlation (.34) between his subjects' "Need for Power" scores on the TAT and the California Personality Inventory's scale "Capacity for Status" (Winter 1973). However, McClelland (1961) and Winter (1973) both found significant relationships between the need-for-power scores and power-related actions, pointing to the TAT's construct validity.

The reliability of the TAT has also been questioned. Traditionally it has had low test-retest correlation coefficients (Lundy 1985; McClelland 1961; Winter 1973). This is not surprising because, over time, subjects' motivations and concerns may change (Winter 1973)—that is, the TAT may tap into "states" as well as "traits." Winter (1973), like Lundy (1988), pointed to the fact that TAT responses are significantly influenced by situational and contextual cues, so variations in testing situations can affect test-retest scores. Lundy (1985) also pointed out that the standard instruction to tell a "creative" story may adversely affect test-retest correlations if the test taker infers that telling the same story again is not creative.

Lundy (1985) challenged Entwisle's (1972) critique of the TAT based upon its low internal consistency (Cronbach's alpha coefficients in the range of .30–.40). Lundy states:

The psychometrics of classical internal reliability assume that any particular measure is composed of a random sample of items from a hypothetical domain of items. . . . [However], the model implicitly followed by the TAT is that of multiple regression. . . . The researcher attempts to select those predictor variables (in this case scoring themes or pictures) which will maximize the set of predictors' (the test's) correlation with criteria. For decades, psychometric theory has dictated that inter-item correlations among a relatively small set of predictors should be high, usually measured by coefficient alpha. In striking contrast, under the multiple regression model an ideal set of predictors will have inter-item correlations of zero. (Lundy 1985: 141)

Lundy conducted a test-retest study (with a one-year interval between administrations), with explicit instructions not prohibiting a replication of the previously given story. The test-retest correlations for "Need for Affiliation" and "Need for Intimacy" were .48 and .56, respectively (approximately equal to the test-retest correlations for the Minnesota Multiphasic Personality Inventory and the California Personality Inventory). Lundy's findings demonstrate a respectable test-retest correlation over a long period of time. The alpha coefficient considerably underestimated reliability, bringing into question whether assumptions of classical psychometrics should be applied to the TAT.

A final area of some controversy relates to how the TAT narratives should be scored. Many clinicians use the TAT intuitively, never bothering to formally score the stories in order to analyze them. Vane (1981) reviewed a wide variety of scoring systems developed for the TAT and pointed to their many flaws. These include the cumbersomeness of many of the systems and the difficulty many of them have meeting rigorous psychometric standards.

Some of the best-known systems developed to score TAT materials are quite expansive (see De Vos 1973; Murray 1943), while others are rather specific (see McClelland 1961; Winter 1973). Some scoring systems concern themselves with formal characteristics of the story structure ("adequacy of accomplishing the storytelling task," such as judgment, modulation of affect, inappropriate comments, and the like). Other systems consider content, such as the "specific themes that reflect the unique concerns of the storyteller" (McDrew and Teglasi 1990: 641).

The scoring system selected should depend in large part on the reason for administering the TAT. Some systems are better suited for distinguishing normal subjects from emotionally disturbed subjects (see, e.g., McDrew and Teglasi 1990). Other systems are better suited for comparing cultural groups (De Vos 1973) or for answering specific research questions such as the need for achievement, affiliation, and power (McClelland 1961; Winter 1973) or spousal, parental, and nonspousal affect (Thomas and Dudek 1985).

For the purposes of clinical consideration, a scoring system that systematically measures a wide variety of concerns would be most useful (see, e.g., Bellak 1986; Murray 1943). In the context of research, however, scoring systems tailored to a specific purpose have been most successful (Thomas and Dudek 1985).

Basing their work on the more ambitious scoring method of De Vos (1973), Thomas and Dudek (1985) developed a scoring system that is easy to use and interpret and that consequently achieved high interrater reliability (.93 to .97). The Thomas and Dudek system used a five-point scale from +2 for strong positive content through −2 for strong negative content, with 0 indicating absence of the theme. They specifically considered themes relating to spousal, parental, and nonspousal concerns. Their scoring of the TAT correlated highly with the Dydactic Adjustment Scale, indicating concurrent validity.

We chose a scoring system tailored to the research questions at hand. We found Thomas and Dudek's (1985) model the most promising for its elegant simplicity and its reliability and validity. Furthermore, because this system yields score data rather than category data, it lends itself well to more sophisticated statistical analyses.

We therefore adapted the Thomas and Dudek system to analyze our data. We used essentially the same quantitative rating formula (extending the range of +2 to −2 used by Thomas and Dudek to a range of +3 to −3 in order to increase its sensitivity).

We first conducted a pilot study of the scoring system using three independent raters. All of the raters were graduate students in clinical psychology and had been carefully trained in the use of the scoring system using five sample TAT stories.[36] The three raters were asked to score twenty stories from youths of different ethnic backgrounds. We asked the raters for feedback about the rating system, and their suggestions were incorporated into revisions of the scoring system. Finally, we verified the interrater reliability for the TAT scoring system ultimately used in this study.[37]

Once all the stories had been gathered, translated, transcribed, and coded, a random sample of 25 percent of the stories was scored by three raters. The raters were "blind" to the group membership, gender, and age of the storytellers. Interobserver reliability was then established using the Kappa statistic.[38] Because the interrater reliability was high, the remaining 75 percent of the stories were scored by only one rater.

During the course of this study, we discovered some problems with the TAT scales (though they met acceptable criteria for interrater reliability and construct validity). The seven-point Likert scale used the middle point of 4 to indicate that there was no reference to the theme under consideration in the story (e.g., no reference to achievement). A cumulative TAT score was used for all the analyses (i.e., the independent achievement cumulative TAT score consisted of adding the independent achievement scores for cards 1, 2, 4, 6BM, and 7BM together). In retrospect, this was a strategic mistake because all cards do not elicit stories about all themes (e.g., achievement stories are rarely told in response to card 4). Hence, many stories received a score of 0 (which was a score of 4 for computer analysis) on a number of the scales. Further, few stories were rated in the negative direction (i.e., when the informant tells a story of an attempt to achieve followed by failure). The stories with negative outcomes were scored from -3 to -1 on the scale (1 to 3 for computer analysis).

The result was that many stories received scores of 4, and very few stories received scores of 1 through 3 or 7 (which was assigned only to stories with extremely positive outcomes). The actual scores assigned tended to be between $+1$ and $+2$ (5 and 6 for computer analysis), resulting in a restricted range. These scales therefore may not have reached significance (and when significance was reached the size of the effect tended to be quite small). Should a similar scale be used in future studies, we recommend that the scale be extended (to perhaps eleven points) or that the scale simply score for presence or absence of a given theme.

In addition, in regard to the achievement scales, the results may have been distorted by the fact that in order to be scored a story needed to incorporate two separate concepts. For compensatory achievement, the storyteller had to refer to poverty and to efforts to achieve motivated by a desire to overcome poverty; for affiliative achievement, the storyteller had to refer to efforts to achieve and to helping or receiving help from others. The appearance of both factors did not occur frequently enough to reach statistical significance. Significant group differences were found when the stories were scored using simpler categories (such as the presence or absence of key themes) rather than Likert scales and mixed categories (involving more than one concept).

Although the a priori hypotheses under consideration were our primary interest, during our analyses we began to notice some unexpected themes emerging in the TAT stories, such as boredom, sadness, and conflict. In order to analyze these themes methodologically, all of the stories were grouped by card and by group (i.e., Mexican, Mexican immigrant, Mexican American, and white American). All the narratives for each group were read separately.

The TAT responses to cards 1, 2, and 6BM showed that different themes were prominent in each group (e.g., conflict among white Americans, sadness among immigrants, school achievement in order to help parents among the Mexican born). Instead of ignoring these concerns, which had not been explicitly predicted in the a priori hypotheses, we chose to analyze them.

We compiled a list of themes that appeared to recur. All of the stories for cards 1, 2, and 6BM were then placed together randomly and read, analyzed, and discussed by two raters who were blind to the group membership of the storyteller. Each narrative was rated for the presence or absence of each of the themes under consideration. The incidence of each theme was tallied for each group. Chi-square analyses were then conducted to check for significant differences between groups.[39] As we discuss in Chapters 4 and 5, there were indeed significant differences.

STATISTICAL DESIGN

Before analysis, all variables were examined for accuracy of data entry, missing values, and fit between their distributions and the assumptions of the linear analyses. The objective measurement tools (the familism and family conflict scales) were used with the Mexican group not during the initial research period but approximately one year later. Because only twenty-four (50 percent) of the original informants could be located (many had entered a *preparatoria* in a faraway city), a significant amount of objective data was not available for the Mexican group. Because the missing data could have adversely affected the results, we estimated the data using regression substitution.

Pearson correlations between the TAT familism score and the self-reported familism questionnaire were calculated to consider concurrent and convergent validity. Interrater reliability was calculated using the Kappa statistic.

The research questions we examined involved one independent variable, the status of the respondent (Mexican, Mexican immigrant, Mexican American, and white American), and three groups of dependent variables (familism, family conflict, and achievement orientation). The dependent variables were all measured using score data.

We tested our hypotheses with omnibus analyses of variance followed by multiple pairwise comparisons using Protected F tests (Gorsuch 1991). In addition, we conducted analyses of covariance using socioeconomic status as a covariant.

We conducted an orthogonal factor analysis in order to determine whether one or more overlapping constructs were responsible for the four group differences on one or more of the objective familism variables (Gorsuch 1983). After the variables were orthogonalized, they remained different. Hence, these variables are measuring independent constructs. Analyses of variance (ANOVAS) were conducted using the orthogonalized factor scores to check whether the four groups were different on these factors. The results were virtually identical to the results reported in the objective ANOVA section. Variable overlap, then, did not create the significant results.

We conducted a discriminant function analysis using the four objective familism variables as predictors of membership in the four groups. Predictor variables were family obligation, support from the family, family as attitudinal referent, and family conflict. These objective familism predictors were able to discriminate between groups.[40]

We conducted supplementary analyses using a category format. We tested for significance in between-group differences using chi-square analyses.

In this chapter we presented some of the problems inherent in cross-cultural research; we explained many of the controversies within psychological anthropology and cross-cultural psychology; and we concluded that is it very difficult, though not impossible, to make meaningful cross-cultural comparisons. Then we described the methodological strategies we used to conduct our research.

In the next two chapters, we discuss the relevant findings of our comparative study of family and achievement dynamics in the four groups.

CHAPTER 4

Family and Peers

There is a significant body of literature on the features of the Latino family. It is not our purpose here to offer a systematic overview of that research. Rather, in the next section we review those findings that directly relate to the importance of the extended family (what we call familism) and to conflict in Latino families. Both are central to our understanding of the Latino immigrant experience.

One of our findings is that there are differences in familism and conflict among the groups under consideration. For example, contrary to the findings of previous clinical studies, our nonclinical data do not suggest that immigration is associated with greater levels of family conflict.[1]

In addition to examining differences and similarities in interfamilial relationships in the three Latino groups (Mexicans, immigrants, and Mexican Americans), we compare them with our sample of white American adolescents. A significant (and unexpected) finding of our study is the comparatively high level of family conflict evidenced in the interpersonal preoccupations of our white American informants. We also briefly examine some relevant findings about the importance of the peer group among the adolescents in our study.

Latino Families

There have been a number of important studies of Latino families in the United States and Latin America. For example, Oscar Lewis studied family life and what he called the "culture of poverty." His most influential ethnographic studies examined family patterns in

Mexico and among Puerto Ricans in New York (see Lewis 1959a, 1959b; Hayner 1954). Lewis was interested in relating the causes of poverty to family patterns, in particular the fatalistic, rigidly patriarchal, and authoritarian features of lower-status Latino families.

Lewis's culture-of-poverty model eventually came under heavy criticism. Some scholars noted that, far from being the main causes of poverty, fatalism, familism, and authoritarianism are likely the consequences of historically patterned socioeconomic inequality. Other scholars, such as Staples and Mirandé, have argued that these early studies presented a "pejorative view of the Mexican American family" that did not adequately consider the positive aspects of family life (1980: 892).

Some psychological researchers have highlighted patterns of rigidity in Latino families. For example, Vega et al. (1986), using the Family Adaptability and Cohesion Evaluation Scales-II (normed in the United States), found that "low-acculturated" Latino respondents were more likely to score outside of the "balanced region" on adaptability. Perhaps this is not surprising given that "adaptability" was defined by mainstream American standards.

A number of other studies have examined the more positive aspects of life in Latino families. Montiel (1973), for example, argued that among Latinos the family is a nurturing and protecting unit that is more important than any of its individual members. Becerra (1988) maintained that the extended, multigenerational Latino family was highly adapted to the socioeconomic needs of agrarian and craft economies in Mexico and Latin America (see also Reese et al. 1991). Although the Mexican American family "has been modified by the social and economic pressures of American life" (Becerra 1988: 156; see also Williams 1990), the ongoing influx of Mexican immigrants serves to maintain certain enduring Mexican familial values. Becerra argues that Latino families provide "mutual support, sustenance and interaction," which are key emotional and material aids in times of stress (Becerra 1988: 156).

Likewise, Murillo (1971) concluded that Latino families provide a sense of belonging and of well-being in a cooperative environment. According to these and other authors, the family is a central institution in shaping the Latino experience. We note that much of this work is based on clinical and sociological observations rather than on methodologically rigorous research.

Other studies have examined the relationship between family systems and "acculturation." For example, Rueschenberg and Buriel, using a sociodemographic scale and the Family Environment Scale, investigated forty-five husband and wife pairs with at least one child; they were evenly distributed among three groups: unacculturated, moderately acculturated, and acculturated. They found that "as families of Mexican descent acculturate, they become increasingly involved with social systems outside the family while the basic internal family system remains essentially unchanged" (Rueschenberg and Buriel 1989: 232). Significantly, their study led them to conclude that Latino families "did not become increasingly mainstream in their patterns of family interaction" (ibid.: 241).

These and other studies portray the Latino family as a matrix providing emotional as well as material support. Many researchers have argued that the Latino family acts as a buffer against external stressors relating to immigration and upheaval (Chavez 1992; Keefe, Padilla, and Carlos 1979; Szalay et al. 1978; Vernon and Roberts 1985; Williams 1990).

Others have attempted to compare aspects of Latino family life to those of other ethnic groups. Investigating family relationships in various ethnic groups, Raymond, Rhoads, and Raymond found that Latinos attributed significantly more importance to family relationships than the other groups. In addition, they found that for Latinos both family and social relationships (those not involving family members) were highly correlated with psychological well-being. Family satisfaction, however, was more predictive of well-being and positive affect than it was of social satisfaction (Raymond, Rhoads, and Raymond 1980: 557).

Holtzman, Diaz-Guerrero, and Swartz embarked on a comparative study of Mexicans in Mexico City and white, English-speaking Americans in Austin, Texas. Employing an overlapping longitudinal design, they compared 417 American students ranging in age from 6.7 to 12.7 years with 443 Mexican students in the same age range. They conducted extensive interviews and administered numerous psychological tests (including the Holtzman Inkblot Technique, subtests of the Weschler Intelligence Scale for Children, the Embedded Figures Test, the Conceptual Styles Test, the Object Sorting Test, the Word Association Test, achievement tests, and more). They concluded that Mexicans tend to be "more family centered" than Americans (Holtzman, Diaz-Guerrero, and Swartz 1975: 385).

A number of studies have argued more specifically that familism is a dominant feature of Latino families. Triandis and his colleagues, for example, identified what they call "attitudinal familism" as central to the Latino experience (Triandis et al. 1982). Sabogal and his colleagues defined familism as "a strong identification and attachment of individuals with their families (nuclear and extended), and strong feelings of loyalty, reciprocity, and solidarity among members of the same family" (Sabogal et al. 1987: 398). Investigating whether dimensions of familism would change as a result of urbanization, acculturation, and migration, they found that familism remains an enduring trait of Latinos in the United States. Sabogal and his colleagues compared 452 Latinos residing in the United States with 227 non-Hispanics. Participants in their study were asked to complete an extensive questionnaire relating to issues of familism, "behavioral acculturation," and demographics. Despite differences in the national origin of the Latinos in their sample, they found that Mexican Americans, Central Americans, and Cuban Americans all reported similar attitudes toward the family. Familism, they concluded, is a core attitude in all major Latino groups in the United States.

In the Sabogal et al. study some fifteen questions relating to familism were factor analyzed, with three separate factors emerging: (a) family obligations, (b) perceived support from the family, and (c) family as referents. Family obligation was defined as "the respondents' perceived obligation to provide material and emotional support to the members of the extended family" (ibid.: 401). Perceived support from the family was defined as "the perception of family members as reliable providers of help and support to solve problems" (ibid.). Family as referents meant that relatives were seen as "behavioral and attitudinal referents" (ibid.: 402).

They found that although the perception of the family as a referent and the sense of family obligation tended to diminish with increasing acculturation, the perception of family support did not change among Latinos. They argue that the attitudes of even highly acculturated Latinos tend to be more "familistic" than those of white Americans.

The familism found among Latinos seems to stand in contrast to the "individualism" lying "at the very core of American culture" (Bellah et al. 1985: 143). Bellah et al. quote Alexis de Tocqueville, who wrote in 1835 that Americans "form the habit of thinking of themselves in isolation and imagine that their whole destiny is in their hands" (ibid.: 37). According to Bellah and his associates, this cultural style is prevalent in classic American literature (e.g., *Moby Dick*, *The Deerslayer*) and stories about mythical heroes (such as the Lone Ranger). The belief system of individualists consists of the notion that each individual is alone on the voyage of life, owing little to ancestors or to progeny. In this cultural context, success is the "major outcome of the operation of individual achievement" (ibid.: 148). (We return to the relationships between achievement motivation and individualism in Chapter 5.)

In summary, although many studies have considered aspects of Latino families, no study to date has systematically compared key aspects of family life among Mexicans in Mexico, Mexican immigrants, second-generation Mexican Americans, and white Americans. If we want to examine the impact of immigration and minority status on family life, we must first explore how immigrants and nonimmigrants differ.

Family Concerns in Four Groups of Adolescents

Our comparative data confirm that among Latinos the family is a central institution. Interview and other evidence collected for our study suggests that Latinos see the family as the single most important aspect of their lives. We asked all our informants identical questions; and we presented all of them with the same series of statements, with which we asked them to agree or disagree—for example, "In life, family is the most important thing." Whereas fully 92 percent of Mexicans and immigrants and 86 percent of second-generation Latino youths responded "yes," only 74 percent of white American adolescents agreed with that statement.[2] There were no significant gender differences in our data on familism, family conflict, and achievement. In a variety of tasks, Mexican girls tended to respond more like Mexican boys than like members of their own gender in the white American group.

Our interview data confirm previous research findings that the Latino family is an important source of support to its members. Mexican and immigrant adolescents are more likely than white American and second-generation youths to turn to family members in search of advice when they have a problem. We asked our informants: "When you have a problem, whom do you go to for advice?" We received very different responses for each group (see Appendix, Table A.15). The great majority of the Latino youths report turning to a family member for advice. In contrast, fully 45 percent of the white American youths say they turn to friends.

Other data collected in our study suggest that Latinos have more positive attitudes toward their parents than white American youths do. In a sentence completion task we asked all our informants to complete the following sentence: "When I think about my mother, I think _____." Thirty percent of the white American adolescents wrote negative statements such as "mother should be there for me more often," "mother is a nag," and "mother is disappointing." Only 4 percent of the Mexican and 6 percent of the immigrant youths completed the sentence negatively. The responses of the second-generation youths came closer to those of the white Americans; in 20 percent of the cases they responded with negative statements such as "mother needs to be around more," "mother is sad," and "mother is too Mexican."

There is a similar pattern of differences in attitudes toward the father. We asked our informants to complete the following sentence: "When I am with my father, I feel _____." Twenty-two percent of the white American adolescents completed the sentence with negative affect. Their responses included "angry," "mad," and "out of place." In contrast, only 6 percent of the Mexican and 8 percent of the immigrant youths completed the sentence with negative affect. The responses of the second-generation youths were again closer to the white American norm: fully 26 percent of them completed the sentence with negative affect.

Comparative Aspects of Familism

We also collected data to examine the nature of familism in the four groups. We used an objective "familism scale" that had been used in a large U.S. study of Latinos and white Americans (see Sabogal et al. 1987). We calculated a cumulative familism score as well as scores for the Family Conflict Scale and three familism subscales: (1) family support (emotional and material support provided by the family), (2) family obligation (sense of obligation to provide support to the family), and (3) family as attitudinal referent.[3]

One important question we wished to consider was whether familism differed for each of the groups under consideration. We had predicted that each of the three Latino groups would demonstrate more familism than white American adolescents. This would be determined by their scores on the objective familism scale (Sabogal et al. 1987) and the TAT familism subscales that we developed for this study. We had also predicted that Mexican immigrants would demonstrate the highest level of familism of all groups under consideration. We based this prediction on the studies, discussed above, that showed that immigrants frequently turn to the family for support and comfort.

The results of the cumulative familism scale (the Sabogal et al. objective scale) confirmed our first hypothesis. White American adolescents scored lowest of all the groups (see Appendix, Table A.9). This finding clearly confirms the general observation that Latinos tend to be more oriented to the family than white Americans (Falicov 1982; Rueschenberg and Buriel 1989; Sabogal et al. 1987). However, we found no significant differences between any of the groups of Mexican origin, and so our second hypothesis was not confirmed; in this sample, the Mexican immigrant adolescents did not demonstrate a higher level of familism than the other Mexican-origin informants. These results confirm our position that it is important to compare immigrants and nonimmigrants in order to discover which characteristics might be related to immigration and which might be related to other factors, including culture. Our findings suggest that familism is related to enduring psychocultural features of the Latino population. Immigration, per se, may not be as central to familism as has been previously argued.

The cumulative familism scale was made up of its three subscales: family support, family obligation, and family as attitudinal referent. Analysis of the scores on the family support scale revealed that the Mexican and immigrant informants perceived greater emotional and material support from the family than either the Mexican American or the white American adolescents (see Appendix, Table A.10). This finding reaffirms the centrality of the family among Mexican and immigrant adolescents.

Analysis of the scores on the family obligation scale revealed that the white American informants felt less obligation to provide emotional or material support to the family than did youths from any of the Latino groups (see Appendix, Table A.11). This finding again confirms other researchers' observations that family interdependence is important in Latino cultures. We also found a Latino preoccupation with giving help to and searching for help from family members in our supplementary analyses of the projective materials. In their telling of the stories elicited by the TAT, Latino adolescents revealed a greater willingness than white American youths to provide material and emotional support to family members.

It appears, then, that Mexican adolescents feel a sense of obligation toward the family. Our data indicate further that this sense of obligation is maintained among immigrant and second-generation Mexican American youths who have been exposed to the dominant American culture. Several factors may account for this continuity.

Immigrant and second-generation youths share an important characteristic: both have immigrant parents. The process of immigration typically entails great emotional and material sacrifices by the parents. Immigrant parents often rationalize their material sacrifices and affective losses by anticipating a better future in the new land; this future is, of course, primarily to be enjoyed by the children. Because many children of immigrant parents understand the hardships endured by their parents as sacrifices made for the children's benefit, it is possible that there is an immigrant aspect to the children's sense of obligation to the parents.

Another feature of the immigrant experience that may sustain the sense of obligation to the family is the children's ability to act as translators for their parents. Because the children of immigrants generally speak the language of the host culture and may have a better understanding of its customs, immigrant parents often turn to their children to be their "cultural translators" (Falicov 1982; Landau 1982). Children often open bank accounts, intervene in emergencies, and assist in dealing with the non-Spanish-speaking world in general. The children, aware of their parents' difficulties, may develop a special sense of responsibility for them.

None of the scores on the TAT scales related to familism that were developed for this study reached significance (see Appendix, Tables A.9, A.10, and A.11). Therefore, had these scales been the only measures of familism used in this study, our hypotheses could not have been confirmed. We believe that our results had more to do with flaws in the scoring criteria for these scales than with the characteristics we were attempting to measure. It is fortunate, therefore, that we addressed these hypotheses by other means as well.

We also gathered data to evaluate the hypothesis that conflict in Latino families would be higher among immigrant families than among nonimmigrant families, as clinical observations had indicated (Szapocznik and Rio 1989; Szapocznik and Truss 1978). The fact that the Mexican American group did not score higher, on either the objective or the TAT family conflict subscale, fails to support this hypothesis (see Appendix, text following Table A.11). We note that we developed this hypothesis after reading studies based on clinical samples (see, e.g., Falicov 1982; Sluzki 1979; Vega 1990).

Those and other studies suggest that intergenerational conflict is caused by "cultural dissonance" and by a "culture gap" that arises between immigrant parents and their U.S.-born children. The sample used for this study is made up of "normal" adolescents (in high school, not involved in individual or family therapy), whereas the clinical literature is based upon information gathered from the patients seen by clinicians. Thus is illustrated the danger of making generalizations from clinical populations.

Family Narratives

We turn now to some of our findings from the administration of the Thematic Apperception Test materials. In addition to using the rich TAT narratives to test our hypotheses, we conducted supplementary comparative analyses of themes (see Chapter 3). In this section, we review some of the dominant themes emerging from TAT cards that typically elicit family concerns.

Card 2 of the TAT depicts a farm scene. Murray writes, "In the foreground is a young woman with books in her hand; in the background a man is working in the fields and an older woman is looking on" (Murray 1943: 18). According to Henry (1956), card 2 typically elicits stories dealing with continuity and change in family life.

In many narratives told about the scene on this card, the young woman leaves the farm to pursue an education and become a professional, usually in a distant urban setting. An interesting ensuing dilemma is whether she chooses to return home to help her parents or to stay in the city enjoying her success. The stories dealing with continuity may focus on harmony and the discharge of assigned roles. Narratives told by informants in all groups confirm Henry's observation that some card 2 stories "portray a focus upon the family status quo" (ibid.: 242). In many such stories, everyone is depicted as behaving in accordance with traditional roles: the father works the fields, the mother tends to the domestic tasks, and the young woman studies. A sense of contentment with the daily routine of work characterizes many of these stories (see Table 1).

TABLE I
Responses to TAT Card 2

Theme	Whites		Mexicans		Mexican immigrants		Mexican Americans		Chi-square probability
	N	%	N	%	N	%	N	%	
Pursuit of education	16	32	28	56	26	52	18	36	.039*
Dilemma of pursuing education or work	10	20	6	12	13	26	11	22	.327
Wanting to help others	7	14	14	28	19	38	12	24	.049*
Parent-child conflict	10	20	2	4	0	0	4	8	.001*
Romantic concerns	11	22	2	4	2	4	8	16	.007*
Feeling bad or sad	10	20	3	6	17	34	12	24	.005*
Financial deprivation	10	20	13	26	6	12	4	8	.201
Wealth	5	10	0	0	0	0	3	6	.023*

*$p < .05$.

RESPONSES OF WHITE AMERICAN ADOLESCENTS

As expected, the narratives told by the white American adolescents include reference to the pursuit of education. In 32 percent of the stories, the main character is concerned with achieving success through education. Note, however, that this theme emerges among the white American adolescents significantly less than among Mexicans in Mexico (56 percent) and immigrant youths (52 percent).

In these narratives, the young woman decides to leave the farm to better herself through education. A common feature of many such narratives is using education to gain independence from the family. Here is a representative narrative:

> She is living on a farm, and she hates living there. She wants to live somewhere where there are people within 200 miles. Her parents are working really hard. She decides to move by herself. She goes away to school, gets an education, and then gets a job. Then she goes back to visit her parents. Finally, she feels that she's doing something with her life. So she keeps visiting her parents but stays at her job away from the farm. [Informant #910.30.78]

Informants in all of the groups told narratives that mention the family tensions created by the choice between pursuing education and staying at home to work on the farm. In the white American stories, 20 percent of the narratives refer to the conflict between pursuing education and staying on the farm.

> She was in a poor family with a farm. She went to school to make something of herself. She had to decide between school and family but is stopped with indecision, and she feels bad. They work hard to put her in school, but now she wants to finish school and her family wants her to work. She goes to school, becomes a scientist, and buys a big house, and her family doesn't have to work anymore. [Informant #622.30.75]

Although stories presenting a dilemma between an internal wish to pursue education and external pressure to go to work are found in all groups, in many of the white American narratives the outcome is a serious conflict between parent and child. Indeed, in 20 percent of the stories told by this group there is reference to conflict between parent and child. This contrasts sharply with the immigrant group, which told no stories involving parent-child conflict. Likewise only 4 percent of the Mexican adolescents and 8 percent of the Mexican American adolescents told narratives involving parent-child conflict.

In many of the stories involving conflict, the relationship to parental authority is ambivalent. Consider the following two narratives:

Once there lived a family on the plains in Missouri; a mother, father, son, and daughter. They had horses and lots of fields. They planted corn. The mother and father were very traditional and wanted her to help on the farm, milking the cows and doing the kind of work that women farmers do. She said: "No! I am going to school." She wanted to become a scientist. They disowned her. She left and went to the city and lived alone. She was sad leaving her family. She got a job but was lonely without her family. She finished school and became a famous scientist and went back to visit her family. While she was there, she met another farm boy and they got married. So it was the famous scientist and the farmer. They lived happily ever after. They lived on the farm together and she went to the city to do her work. And her parents approved because she married a farmer. [Informant #123.30.75]

Once there was a girl who lived on a farm. She was very poor. She wanted to go to school, but her mother and father forbade her because they needed help on the farm. But she didn't want that so she would go off on her own and study at her own time. She became really smart. She goes to college and is happy. In the picture, she feels mad at her parents because they are making her stay on the farm. If she goes to school, she can get an education and get a better job and help the family. [Informant #112.30.77]

A theme found in the last two stories is not found in the Mexican narratives. In these stories the young woman pursues her own wishes in direct contradiction to the wishes of her parents, showing an independence and a desire to be the architect of her own destiny that we think of as characteristically American.

White American responses to card 2 also differ significantly from the responses of the other groups—particularly the Mexican and immigrant groups—in their inclusion of a romantic theme. Twenty-two percent of the white American adolescents told stories with themes of love and sexuality, while only 4 percent of the Mexican and immigrant youths included such themes.

Once there was a young girl who lived on a farm. On her twentieth birthday, she was daydreaming about a man that she was going to fall in love with. He was a man on a white horse and he was everything she imagined he could be. One day, he appeared in front of her in real life, and she fell in love with him and they lived happily ever after. At the beginning, she feels that there is going to be nobody there to love her. When she meets him, she is happy because he is everything she imagined, and when she first sees him, she knows that she will spend the rest of her life with him. [Informant #316.30.75]

In other stories with romantic themes, there is conflict between the young woman and her parents. In these stories, typically, the parents forbid her to see the man she loves:

The girl is really in love with the farm worker, but her mother doesn't like him. She sends her daughter off to school so she can stay out of the way of the farmer. She feels resentment toward her mother for not allowing her the chance to fall in love with this guy. She has to do what her mother says anyway. She goes to school and sneaks off with him at night behind her mother's back. [Informant #111.30.75]

The main character is on a farm. Her family owns the farm, and they are very rich and above everyone else. This is her mom over here. I think that she is in love with the farm boy and they don't want her to be with him because he is poor. She is kind of confused and upset because she can't be with the guy she likes. She gets a bunch of money from her parents, and they take off to get their own farm. [Informant #429.30.74]

There is a beautiful woman and she lives in the South. While walking to school, she begins to like this boy, except she can't like him because he is a slave. After thinking about this for a long while, she tells her parents that she is in love with him. When she tells her parents, they become furious and demand that she never look at him again. But she does keep seeing him. After a while of seeing this boy, she tells her parents that she is going to marry him. Her parents become very mad and demand that the slave boy be taken out of the estate. Before he gets taken out, they elope. The parents discover this and they disown their daughter. No more can she live at the house. She and the boy go and live in a cottage by a river. At the cottage, she writes letters to her parents, asking for-giveness. Her parents finally forgive her and tell her that they can't rule her life. What she chooses to do is her life. They can give her advice but she doesn't have to take it. Everyone lived happily ever after. [Informant #510.30.78]

In the first two stories, the conflict between the young woman and her parents seems to be irreconcilable. The moral of the last story is to live and let live; the conflict is resolved when the parents realize that they can't rule her life. The tensions between internal needs and parental pressure again surface as a primary concern in the stories told by these youths. This dynamic, as we shall see, is also present in the narratives told in response to card 1 of the TAT.

Other stories that include romantic themes involve a romantic triangle. For example:

The girl was coming home and saw this guy—a guy that she used to like. He is with another woman and she is pregnant. She is really sad and de-pressed and hangs her head down low. She knows that there is no way that she can get him because she is pregnant. Maybe she is his wife. She goes on with her life. Maybe she finds someone else in her life who she likes and can be with. She feels depressed and sad because she really loved him. She feels like she failed again with a guy. [Informant #310.30.74]

The young lady is going to school, and she is in love with the guy that is holding the horse. But he already has someone—it is the girl that is pregnant. The two of them have something meaningful and all she feels that she has is her school. She is jealous even though she knows that her parents would probably not approve of her being with him because he is a farm boy and she is a little rich girl. She is envious and jealous because she doesn't get what she wants, and so she runs back to daddy. Then she tries to steal the boy away from the pregnant girl, but it doesn't work because they love each other too much. In the end, she feels sad because she doesn't have what the other woman has. [Informant #116.30.77]

We do not have to stretch far to see the Oedipal triangle in this last story. When the young woman tries to steal the man from the pregnant mother-figure but fails, only "daddy" can console her.

To recapitulate, white American youths told a variety of stories in their responses to card 2 of the TAT. Some of the themes found in previous studies with the TAT were well represented in these stories, such as pursuing an education and gaining independence from the parents. However, a number of unexpected themes also surfaced, including parent-child conflict and romance. These themes are all the more striking because of their relative absence from the stories told by the other groups.

RESPONSES OF MEXICAN ADOLESCENTS

Mexican youths articulated various themes in their responses to card 2. The single most important thematic cluster found in the Mexican youths' stories is pursuing an education (in 56 percent of the stories). As revealed by their TAT narratives, we conclude that this sample of Mexican adolescents is indeed a highly achievement-oriented group (see Chapter 5). Other themes include wanting to help others (in 28 percent of the stories) and financial deprivation and poverty (in 26 percent of the stories).

It is important to highlight that in only 4 percent of the stories told by the Mexican youths (as opposed to 20 percent of the stories told by the white American group) is there outright conflict between parents and child. In the Mexican stories in which there is conflict, it tends to be less severe than the conflict found in the narratives told by the white American adolescents. Compromise is frequently reached in the Mexican stories, whereas in the narratives told by white American youngsters, running away and rebellion are frequent outcomes.

Likewise, romantic themes occur in only 4 percent of the stories told by the Mexican sample (as opposed to 22 percent of the stories told by Americans). Let us turn to some representative illustrations:

These people are the parents of this girl. They come from a poor family. This woman is very interested in having her daughter get a good education so that she won't have the same life that they did because they had to work a lot for a long time. They work and they work and they earn a lot of money. Before we see this picture, they were in the house talking to her about how important the work is. They were supporting her and encouraging her. Then she goes onto school, and on her way she watches them work the earth. She is very motivated to go to school. [Informant #304.40.79]

This girl studies, and her parents work hard so that she can study. They are proud of her. Her mother supports her in everything, and she does everything to get ahead. She is worried that in the countryside she will not be able to continue with her studies. She thinks she will have to go to another place in order to continue with her studies. Her parents tell her that they do not have enough money to help her study away from home. She works herself to earn enough money to continue with her studies so that she can obtain her goal. [Informant #439.40.78]

This girl is going to school to help her parents buy machinery to seed the fields more easily. The father works hard to give the daughter the opportunity to go to school. She completes her studies with the help of her family. She becomes a professional, and she in turn helps her parents. [Informant #417.40.78]

This is a girl who is thinking that because she studies she will be able to help her parents. She is looking at the countryside and is a little sad. But in her imagination, she thinks about studying and preparing herself and that she can become an important person. She will be able to help her parents become the owners of the land around them. The mother is thinking of her daughter and she is happy because she is able to go to school. She is thinking ahead, of when she will be older and how lucky she will be to become somebody important. The man is working the earth trying to feed his wife and children. When she grows up she will be very happy about all that she is able to do for them. [Informant #913.40.77]

In these stories, the pursuit of education is framed in the context of overcoming financial deprivation and the hardships endured by parents. In many Mexican stories the parents are depicted as sacrificing themselves so the protagonist can "become somebody." In the Mexican context the motivation to achieve appears to be inspired by family: the point of achieving an education is to take care of the parents. This contrasts sharply with many of the white American stories in which pursuit of education is often seen as a way of leaving the family: education is the means for independence from the family—particularly from parental authority. In Mexico the family is a centripetal force; in the United States it is a centrifugal force.

Another remarkable feature of the Mexican stories told in response to card 2 is how often the parental figures are depicted as nurturing and supportive. Rather than rebelling against her parents, the young woman in the Mexican stories feels supported and encouraged by them. Overcoming poverty also appears as a significant theme. The pursuit of education is seen as allowing status mobility. In these stories, schooling is the way to escape poverty and the hardships of farm life.

In a few Mexican stories (12 percent) there is a dilemma between pursuing education and working on the farm. The typical tension is between cultural pressure on the young woman to stay home and help her parents (particularly her mother) and her inner desire to go away to study. In such stories, however, the climax is almost never open confrontation (as it was in the stories told by white Americans) but a compromise between the parties. The compromise may be for the daughter to study while fulfilling her culturally dictated filial obligations (i.e., she helps her parents on the farm while studying hard to achieve her dream). In other stories the compromise means giving up the wish to go to a better school far away and settling for a modest school nearby. In some stories the girl simply gives up her dream of an education and devotes herself exclusively to helping her parents on the farm. Here are examples of such stories:

In the country there was a girl who very much wanted to study. But she had to work to help her parents. Her mother did not want her to go to school because she believed that women should not study. Her mother thought that women should stay at home to learn to cook and do what needs to be done around the house. But the young woman overcomes the impossible. Working hard she eventually becomes a teacher. [Informant #320.40.77]

This is a girl who goes to school while her parents work. She won't be able to continue going because she needs to help at home. They do not agree with her going off to study because they want her to help. They want her to stay nearby and study whatever she can study in the local school. [Informant #416.40.79]

The girl wants to study, but at her house they need her to work and help her parents on the ranch. The mother needs her more than ever now that she is pregnant again. The girl has to choose between helping her family and staying on the ranch or going off to pursue the studies she wants to do. She decides to sacrifice, and she does not do what she wants to do but remains with the family to help. [Informant #119.40.76]

Such stories are fraught with the gender conflicts that face many young women in society.

The narratives told by immigrant youths include a variety of themes also found in those told by the other groups. However, what is striking is the *relative* presence and absence of certain themes in the stories told by immigrant adolescents.

By far the most important topic included in the narratives told by immigrant youths is pursuing education. In 52 percent of the immigrants' stories (in 56 percent of stories told by Mexican youths in Mexico), we find reference to achieving through the pursuit of schooling. Only 32 percent of the stories told by the white American adolescents included school achievement as a theme. This finding is in keeping with the comments made to us by teachers working with immigrant students: immigrant students seem to be highly motivated to use the educational system for status mobility.

The second most important theme found in the immigrants' narratives is wanting to help others. In fully 38 percent there is reference to helping others. Notably, none of the stories told by the immigrant youths refer to parent-child conflict (whereas 20 percent of the stories told by white American youths did). The immigrant youths also seem less concerned about poverty and financial deprivation than the Mexican adolescents in Mexico. Here are some representative stories:

> This is a peasant family. The young woman goes to school. Her mother it seems to me is pregnant. The young woman says that she wants to study. She wants to get ahead in life. She doesn't want to have children right now. She one day becomes a doctor. She studies to become a professional and with all the money she makes is able to one day help her mother and family. [Informant #829.10.74]

> This is a family in a town. They have a daughter. She wants to study. She has to help her parents, but she really wants to study. She goes to a school near her village and she studies. She is thinking that she has to help her parents. Her parents are very proud of her. She helps them. She feels very satisfied that she is able to study and she is able to help her parents. She is going to make it. She is going to study and help her parents. She will change everything for them. [Informant #101.10.73]

> These parents are working the fields, pursuing as much as they can from the earth. This seems to be his wife, and she is pregnant. I think the girl is going to school to receive an education. They continue cultivating the earth and the girl goes to school to get an education to help her parents. I say that she gets an education, and when she gets a good job they are all going to leave the countryside and go to live with her. She is going to give them a house to help them. [Informant #413.10.74]

Among the immigrants, the ethos in which achievement motivation flourishes reveals a continuity with the concerns articulated by the Mexican adolescents in Mexico. In these narratives achievement motivation is not framed as an individualistic enterprise; rather, it is the product of social interdependence. Reciprocity is the unifying principle in many of these stories. The parents are depicted as working hard. The protagonist pursues schooling in order to help her sacrificing parents. The point of achievement is not independence from the family or individualistic material gains but reciprocal nurturing.

The tension between pursuing an education and the need to work and help the parents is also present in this group (in 26 percent of the stories), though it never results in open conflict. In these stories a tough choice has to be made:

> One day she is going to school, and she sees that her mother is leaning against the tree. She sees that her mother is very tired, and she stays to help her clean the house. Her brother is helping by taking care of the animals in the field. She stops going to school so that she can help her mother. She feels very sad because she realizes that life is not easy. [Informant #304.10.78]

> This girl is going to school and her parents are poor. She isn't able to finish studying because her parents want her to work. She feels really bad. [Informant #423.10.75]

> Her parents want her to work, but she wants to study. Her mom wants her to help at home, but she would rather study. She talks with them about what she wants to study and explains that in the long run she can find a better job if she studies. They agree and let her study. She does well and gets a good job and helps them buy a house. She feels happy. [Informant #570.10.78]

In these stories there are twin pressures: studying to achieve a better way of life in the long run and meeting the immediate economic and domestic needs of the family. In some cases the tension is resolved by the protagonist's giving up school to help her parents. In other stories, she must explain that if she studies she will eventually be able to earn money for the family. These concerns are identical to the pressures facing many immigrant students in their own daily lives.

A very significant theme found in the narratives told in response to card 2 by immigrants is sadness. While only 6 percent of the Mexican adolescents and 20 percent of the white American adolescents made reference to sadness, 34 percent of the Mexican immigrant adolescents told narratives that were permeated by sadness. As we shall see in Chapter 5, this theme also emerged in the stories told by

immigrants in response to card 1 of the TAT. Here are some examples
of some of the ways sadness is expressed:

> The girl doesn't want to go to school. She wants to stay with her parents
> and help them at home because she is afraid to go. But her mom made her
> go, and so she got showered and dressed and got her books and left. But
> she still feels sad and doesn't want to go. She ends up going to school, and
> she eventually starts to like it. She loses her fear of what it would be like.
> [Informant #324.10.77]

> This girl is going to school and her parents are poor, and she isn't able to
> finish studying because her parents want her to work. She feels really sad.
> [Informant #423.10.75]

> She feels sad because she is bored and embarrassed and ashamed because
> her parents are working so hard and she is only going to school. Her par-
> ents are working so hard while she is going to school so that she can learn
> and one day help them. In the end she learns how to write and read and
> gets a good job and helps her parents, and they do not have to work ever
> again. [Informant #721.10.77]

Sadness in the stories above appears in the context of having to go
to (a foreign?) school (in the first story), having to give up a dream
in order to help parents (in the second story), and sorrow that the
parents must work so hard (in the third story).

We relate this sadness to the vicissitudes of the immigrant journey. In the first story we get a glimpse of the "sense of disorienting
anxiety" described by Grinberg and Grinberg (1989) in their work
with immigrants. The other two stories are about the losses immigrants endure and the hardships they must overcome.

RESPONSES OF MEXICAN AMERICAN ADOLESCENTS

In their responses to TAT card 2, second-generation Mexican American youths reveal many preoccupations that are similar to those
of the other groups. Some of the concerns of Mexican Americans
are similar to those of their white American peers. For example,
36 percent of the youths in this group told stories about pursuing
education; 32 percent in the white American group did so. These
percentages are significantly lower than those in the stories told by
either of the Mexican-born groups. This finding agrees with the observations of many teachers that more acculturated Latino students
seem to be less eager to do school work than the more recent arrivals
(see Chapters 2 and 5).

In other respects, the stories told by the second-generation youths
reveal a thematic similarity to the narratives told to us by the

Mexican-born adolescents. Many of the achievement-oriented stories express a wish to help parents and others (24 percent of the stories). In some of these narratives the protagonist sees how hard her parents must work to offer her the opportunity of an education and hence a better tomorrow. She makes up her mind to take advantage of the opportunity to study. Achievement is not framed in individualistic terms: She works hard in school so that she will be able to help her parents. For example:

> This girl is on her way to school. She sees how they are out in the fields working. She sees how hard he has to work to put her through school. She feels grateful. She sees her mom, and she is pregnant. She is grateful her parents are working to get her ahead in life. That is why she is going to school: so she can better herself and help out her parents. When she is better educated, she'll be able to make more money. She goes to school and helps them out in the end. [Informant #410.20.74]

> I see a woman and her parents. They live on a farm. She wants to succeed. She does not want to work hard on the farm. She goes to school to succeed. She makes her parents proud of her. Her dad is working so hard. The dad tells her not to stop studying. Not to waste her opportunities. She is interested in what he says. She takes her study seriously and she makes progress. She listens to her dad. [Informant #729.20.73]

In other narratives the protagonist feels conflicting pressures to pursue an education and to help at home (in 22 percent of the stories). In some of these stories the pressures facing the protagonist seem all-consuming:

> This is a poor family. She wants to go to school but she has to help her family with the farm. She feels sad and confused. She doesn't know if she should go to school to get an education or if she should stay and help her family. She decides to go to school, and every day she looks back on her family and thinks about getting a job to help her family. She goes to school, gets an education, gets a good job, and makes money to help the farm and her family. [Informant #415.20.77]

> This is a girl, and she is watching her parents working so hard. She is trying to study, and she doesn't know what to do to help her parents. She feels like they have a big problem. She tries to help her parents, but she also has to study. In the end she just tries to help them. [Informant #204.20.76]

> This girl is coming home from school. She sees them working very hard, and she feels bad because she is going to school and they are working so hard. Then, she thinks she has to go to school and she feels like a traitor—she is not home helping. She helps them after she goes to school. [Informant #816.20.76]

She is the oldest daughter of this family. She is faced with a problem of helping her family or getting an education. She wants to help her family, but she also wants to help herself. She goes to school and gets an education and helps her family out that way. [Informant #214.20.73]

This girl is going to school. Her parents are working. It looks like she would rather help her parents and stay and work at home. Her mom is pregnant and she needs her to help. The girl is thinking she needs to help her because she [her mom] can't work much. She feels bad because she also has work to do at school. She ends up going to school because she really wants to learn. Her parents are working hard. Maybe tomorrow she'll stay home and help them and not go to school. [Informant #121.20.77]

In only a few cases does the protagonist choose to study and not help.

This is a girl who wanted to study because she didn't want to work in the fields and be like the pregnant woman who was standing there in the fields. So she started studying all the time and she went to school. She then went to college, and she became important and she was happy that she had followed her dreams. She felt happy that she didn't listen to what everyone else had wanted her to do. [Informant #513.20.78]

To summarize, the narratives told in response to TAT card 2 elicited a number of revealing themes. An important feature of the TAT is its ability to elicit themes of salience across groups as well as highlight differences, thereby revealing similarities and differences in the interpersonal preoccupations of the groups under consideration.

The most striking feature of the stories told by white Americans is the low level of concern with achievement. They also showed a comparative overrepresentation of parent-child conflict. Last, many included romantic themes—some that led to parent-child conflict; this theme was much less well represented in the stories told by Mexican-born groups.

We interpret these findings in relation to two factors. First, our TAT card 2 data confirm the observation that (white American) adolescence in the United States is a period of conflict and upheaval (Erikson 1963). In addition, during adolescence white American youths are more likely than adolescents from other groups to turn to their peers for emotional support or for romance.

In the Latino groups, we found less evidence of parent-child conflict and romantic pursuits. The great majority of the Latino stories revealed concerns with achievement—very often to overcome poverty and, most important, to help others. Immigrant adolescents especially revealed feelings of sadness. Their narratives also told of the difficult gendered choice for young women between pursuing schooling and working to help the family. We relate these concerns to some central features of the immigrant experience: the feelings of sadness are related to the losses endured by immigrants, the desire for an education is related to the immigrant dream of a better tomorrow, and the choice between school and work is related to the economic struggle to make ends meet in the new land.

Mexican American adolescents were also likely to tell stories about the choice between going to school and working to help others. Perhaps it is not surprising that Mexican American students in our sample should tell such stories. After all, these students were more likely than students in all other groups to work—and to work longer hours. In addition, the Mexican American students who worked most often reported working "to help out my family." On the other hand, the white American students who worked said they did so to have their own money or to buy "special things" for themselves.

On Mothers and Sons

Whereas card 2 frequently elicits daughter-parent themes, card 6BM frequently elicits son-mother themes. Murray describes the picture on card 6BM in the following way: "A short elderly woman stands with her back turned to a tall young man. The latter is looking downward with a perplexed expression" (1943: 19). According to Henry (1956), card 6BM typically elicits stories dealing with leaving home and the delivery of sad or bad news.

In most stories told in response to this card the protagonists are said to be mother and son. In some cases, one of them is delivering shocking news, such as that the father or a brother has died, usually unexpectedly, such as in an accident. In other stories the young man is saying good-bye to his aging mother. The stories dealing with the young man's leaving home sometimes mention the tension caused by his decision; others refer to his eventual return (i.e., he leaves for a job but comes back to take care of his mother); and others make no reference at all to his return (see Table 2).

RESPONSES OF WHITE AMERICAN ADOLESCENTS

Informants in all groups told narratives confirming Henry's observation that themes of bad or sad news and leaving home are common in response to card 6BM of the TAT. Of interest in the context of our study are differences in the relative presence and absence of such concerns across groups. How are the tensions about leaving home

TABLE 2
Responses to TAT Card 6BM

Theme	Whites		Mexicans		Mexican immigrants		Mexican Americans		Chi-square probability
	N	%	N	%	N	%	N	%	
Bad news	17	34	3	6	4	8	10	20	.0001 *
Leaving	11	22	14	28	11	22	7	14	.379
Conflict	12	24	8	16	9	18	8	16	.970
Illicit/criminal behavior	10	20	2	4	2	4	10	20	.006 *
Asking advice	2	4	7	14	10	20	4	8	.071
Asking forgiveness	0	0	7	14	6	12	1	2	.003 *
Sadness	9	18	12	24	18	36	10	20	.171
Anger	5	10	5	10	3	6	7	14	.329
Scolding	0	0	4	8	2	4	1	2	.157

*$p < .05$.

constructed in different groups? Is the departure full of conflict, or is it more positive? Do different groups tell a similar number of "bad news narratives"?

Indeed, there are important differences in the kinds of stories the groups included in this study related. For example, 34 percent of the white American adolescents told stories about the delivery of bad news; only 6 percent of the Mexicans and 8 percent of the immigrants told such stories. This pattern confirms the findings of Fromm and Maccoby's study of social character in a rural Mexican village: "It is interesting to note that in the United States, Card 6BM frequently suggests the theme of a young man bringing bad news about the death of the woman's husband or son. . . . In the [Mexican] village, stories hardly ever refer to anyone else but the mother and son" (Fromm and Maccoby 1970: 290).

Our white American informants told stories with a variety of expected and some unexpected themes. The greatest percentage of stories told by these youngsters, not surprisingly, were about the delivery of bad or sad news (34 percent). Some representative examples:

> These two people have just been told something bad has happened. They are very worried and shocked. Right now they are just worried; they are not really thinking because they are just shocked because the man's father has died. They all go out to the funeral and the man will still be very sad for the death of his father, but he will get over it. [Informant #122.30.74]

> Once upon a time there was a little old lady named Josephine. She had three sons and they were all in the army. The eldest son, Timothy, finally came home after the war, but he was all by himself. Josephine asked where her other sons were, and he regretfully said that they had died. For days she was very mournful, and she felt very alone. But she realized that she

still had one son left, and he could stay by her side. In the picture, he feels really sad about his brothers' death and sorry for what his mother is going through. [Informant #132.30.77]

This guy is her son and he's here to tell her that last night his brother got into a serious car accident and has passed away. She is not taking it so well. They feel sad and depressed. They don't know why or what happened. They have a funeral and bury the body. Everybody misses the son. [Informant #101.30.77]

Viewed through a psychoanalytic lens, these stories certainly reveal Oedipal themes.

The issue of leaving home surfaced in 22 percent of the narratives told by this group. Examples include:

"It's time, mother." He knows he must leave his mother and start his own life and family. His mother sits and looks back upon all of the things she's done, what she is going to do without him, all of the worrying she's gone through and will go through about him. And all he can do is think about how it's going to be out in the free world, exploring new things, new possibilities. He feels happy, glad, a sense of responsibility, as she's scared and stressed about her son's leaving. He is moving away to go to another city. [Informant #411.30.74]

A guy is talking to his mom. It is in the 1930s and he is telling her he plans to get married. He wants to move someplace far away from his mom. His mom is upset because she is getting old and she wants him to help out. She is angry at his fiancee; she feels her son is being taken away from her. But he is going to go away. He'll move far away and leave his mom for his wife. The mom probably will not talk to him anymore. He'll end up moving away and they probably won't talk anymore. [Informant #220.30.76]

Note that in the above narratives the mother-son separation is conflictful. In the first story, gaining independence from the mother is framed as joining the "free world." In the second narrative, the separation seems to be final: there is to be no further contact between the man and his mother.

In 24 percent of the stories told by this group we find outright conflict between the mother and the son. In many of these stories the people are arguing or fighting. Typically there is a battle of wills. Some examples:

They are mother and son. He is telling her that he's getting married to someone she doesn't approve of. She's really upset, so she is looking out the window. And he is really upset because his mom's upset, because he has always been close to his mom. The mom was probably angry and criticizing the girl. He doesn't want to disappoint her, but he loves this girl that he's going to marry, and he's going to do it. He's not going to change just because of his mom. And he hopes that she understands. After they're married and they have a little baby boy, she understands and deals with it. She and her son's wife become really close. [Informant #310.30.74]

Since he was a little boy, his mom ruled over him, always telling him what to do, where to go, which friends to have, and who he is. He grows up and becomes a successful lawyer. He tells his mom he is getting married to a girl. She wants him to marry a Mormon. But he marries her anyway. When she says something, he just walks away and never talks to her again. She dies of old age. He resents his wife for making him lose his mother. But he loves his wife and never goes to see his mother. They live happily ever after together. They have two kids. [Informant #622.30.75]

The guy asked his mom about a girl he wants to see. But his mom doesn't like her. She is upset and she told him. But he really wants to marry the girl and he loves her. So he does it anyway. The mother disagrees with this, but she probably gets used to it and likes her [his wife] after a while. [Informant #240.30.78]

These stories are about separation from the world of the mother and entry into adulthood. The tension created by conflicting "wills" depicted in these narratives is identical to the tension found in the responses to card 1, which we examine in the next chapter. In some of the stories related to card 6BM the dilemma is: Will he marry the girl he likes or will he follow his mother's will? In these cases there is a tension between individual will and the will of the (m)other. Just as American individualism is deeply rooted in history and the psyche, among these adolescents the experience of self seems to be construed as being "against" rather than "embedded in" social others.

An unexpected cluster of themes that emerged in the narratives told in response to this card relate to illicit and criminal behavior. In 20 percent of the stories told by the white American youths, the young man is depicted as having gotten into trouble with the law. For example:

His mother sees something she doesn't like. He is in on it, but he cannot tell her. If he tells her that he was involved in this thing, she will be disappointed in him. She wants him to call the police and confess, but he doesn't want to. He doesn't tell her that he is involved. He is hiding. He says it isn't any of her business. They leave the situation, and she never finds out that he was involved in this thing. [Informant #660.30.76]

The mother and son are fighting about his work. He doesn't work in the family business. He is in gangs. He is in trouble. His mom doesn't like it. They are arguing about it. It ends up that he will not change or go into the family business. He leaves his parents and says good-bye. He is angry and confused because he isn't sure if he should go into the family business and make his mom happy or do what he wants. So he decides to do what he wants. He leaves her. His mom is sad. [Informant #413.30.78]

A guy kills someone and his grandma feels sad about him killing a person. The guy is trying to talk about it, but she will not listen and instead she just looks out the window. The guy keeps telling her how sorry he is and she says finally that she understands him. She forgives him and in the end they both feel pretty happy. [Informant #817.30.78]

To recapitulate, white American youths told a variety of stories in their responses to card 6BM of the TAT. Some of the themes found in previous studies with the TAT were well represented in the stories in our sample. They include the delivery of bad news and leaving home. Two unexpected themes also surfaced in a number of stories. These include family conflict and illicit criminal behavior. In the white American ethos, conflict tends to take the form of a battle of individual wills.

An interesting recurring theme in the stories told by this sample is the conflict inherent in "triangular" relationships between a mother, a son, and his girlfriend. In some stories, the mother doesn't approve of his relationship, and she is depicted as pressuring him to marry someone else (see responses to card 1 in Chapter 5). He must choose between following his feelings and pleasing his mother. A typical resolution is for the young man to follow his will, and, if necessary, stop seeing his mother altogether. In other cases the young man follows his will and the mother eventually learns to like her rival.

A battle of wills with the parents—most often the mother—and the youth's wish to choose his own path appears to be a fundamental concern among white American adolescents. Individualism is, in part, framed as resisting the will of others and following one's own path.

RESPONSES OF MEXICAN ADOLESCENTS

Mexican youths included a variety of themes in the stories they told in response to card 6BM. As noted above, only 6 percent of the narratives told by the Mexican adolescents are about the delivery of bad news. The most significant theme in the Mexican stories is departure.

In many of these stories the young man must leave, often to pursue a career. He is saying good-bye to his mother. The mother is typically depicted as sad. In many cases, he leaves for another town to work *but will eventually return to take care of his loving mother.*

The nature of the tension in these Mexican stories is quite different from what we encountered in the narratives told by white Americans. The tension in this case is caused by the son's desire to leave without hurting the mother. If hurting his mother is inevitable, the issue in many of these stories becomes explaining to the mother why he must go. Let us consider some representative illustrations:

> The son is telling his mother that he needs to go make his own life. He tells his mother that he will always be with her even though he will not be living with her anymore. He tells her that he is not going forever, that he's just going for a time to try to get good work and to make a good life for them. The mother begs him not to go because she is going to feel very alone and sad. The son tells her that he will come back to visit her often, and again she asks him not to go. The son tries to help his mother understand why he needs to go. He says that he doesn't want to be a useless son, that he wants to be hardworking and helpful, and he decides to go anyway even though the mother is sad about it. [Informant #119.40.76]

> This young man left town in order to find work. He didn't realize his parents were having economic problems when he left his home. When he returns, he finds his parents were having economic problems after he left home. When he returns he finds out, and he begs forgiveness of his mother. He explains to her that he had gone looking for work in order to help them so that they would never have any needs in their old age. Now that he has returned, he helps them. [Informant #417.40.78]

> The man is with his mother. He returned from a trip and he wants to go again. The mother is very sad because she doesn't want her son to go again. The son decides that he must go after all so that he can work and help his mother. [Informant #318.40.78]

In these stories, leaving is framed as a necessity. Yet separation from the mother is not seen as final: in the Mexican stories the young man most often returns to take care of his mother, or he regularly visits her. In some stories, the young man goes away, finds a good job, and then sends for his mother. In the Mexican stories, leaving is framed not as an individualistic end but as a means to an end: the money that he earns will allow him to take care of the (m)other.

As we found in the responses to card 2, social action in this context is family centered: achieving in school and working make it possible for the youth to take care of others—most often parents. This is in direct contrast to many of the stories told by white Americans, in which education, work, and leaving home are framed as means of gaining independence from the family. Again, in Mexico the family seems to be a centripetal force; in the United States it is a centrifugal force.

Another interesting feature of the stories told by Mexicans in response to card 6BM is the frequency with which the protagonist is depicted as approaching the mother to ask for forgiveness or advice (in 14 percent of the stories in each case). White American adolescents in our sample did not relate a single narrative in which the hero of the story asks for forgiveness, and only 4 percent of the stories told by white American youngsters were about asking for advice. Here are some representative stories:

> This is a son who's having a problem with his mother. He said something to her, and now he has returned and is asking her forgiveness. He feels bad, and his mother is very sad because her son did something terrible and she can't forgive him. But he is her son, and in the end she does forgive him. [Informant #416.40.79]

> There was a young man and his mother. They were having a discussion about a problem that he had with his friends. He was asking her advice. She gives him advice. They are just talking about it, trying to come up with a solution to the problem. Then he left the house to find his friends. They begin talking about the problem and they come up with a solution. They decided to do what was best for all of them. So then he went back to his house, and he talked with his mother about the solution they had come up with. She is telling him that she is very pleased and that he did well. [Informant #917.40.78]

> This is a man with his mother. He is asking her advice about a problem that he has. His mother helps him to resolve the problem. [Informant #215.40.77]

Another theme of the stories told by the Mexican sample (and not found in the stories told by white Americans) is that of the mother scolding the son. In these stories the young man is depicted as being involved in questionable activities. The mother is punishing him. In these cases the discharge of parental authority (in the form of scolding) is framed as a legitimate and fair act. For example:

> Here is the mother. She is mad at him because he made her believe he was studying, but he was actually going out and fooling around doing things that he shouldn't be doing. She is reminding him about all that she has spent in order to help him get a good career. She helps him to see the wrong in what he did. He buckles down and starts studying. [Informant #543.40.78]

> The lady is scolding the young man because she wanted him to follow a different career path. [Informant #506.40.78]

> The woman is with her son. She is very embarrassed about something he did. He stole from someone, and the mother tells him that it is not O.K.

He is bowing his head in shame. The mother promises the father that her son will never do such a thing again. To punish him, she tells him that he must go and that she will never see him again. After he has gone, she feels very bad, and she is looking out the window, feeling sad. After a few months pass he returns, and she finds out he's working, that he has returned all the money he had taken, and that he wants to give her money to help her with her expenses. [Informant #503.40.78]

RESPONSES OF MEXICAN IMMIGRANT ADOLESCENTS

The narratives told by immigrant youths include themes also found in those told by the other groups. Those themes include leaving home (22 percent) and conflict (18 percent). As the Mexican youths did, immigrants related fewer stories about bad news (only 8 percent) than either the white American group (34 percent) or the Mexican American group (20 percent). Also as the Mexicans did, immigrants related fewer stories about illicit or criminal activities (4 percent) than either the white Americans (20 percent) or the Mexican Americans (20 percent).

As they did in response to card 2, a significant number of immigrant adolescents related stories about feeling sad or bad (36 percent). Only 18 percent of the stories told by white Americans referred to sadness. In some immigrant stories leaving home is framed as necessary. Leaving is a sad occasion, but the sadness disappears when the son returns home to take care of his mother and make her life easier. These stories subtly capture the immigrant choice between affective losses and instrumental gains. For example:

Here is a mother and a son. She is very sad because he went to her house and told her that he was going to leave. He also looks sad. But he wants to go and study and have a better life, so he can help her. Afterward, the mother understands him and he leaves. He returns later, and he's become someone important and helps his mother. The two of them live happily together. [Informant #118.10.75]

His mom and he both felt really bad because he was going to go away to university. His mom said it was too far. He told her that in the future he could help her more if he went away. But he felt guilty leaving her there. So he told her that he would go and visit her every weekend so that she would feel better. He does that, but he still felt very bad and didn't want to leave her alone. [Informant #507.10.78]

The boy wants to move to the city so that he can study. He wants to become a doctor. His grandmother doesn't want him to go away. She says it's better that he stays in the village so he can help her with the business she has with animals, and that in this manner he can also become a rich man. But he tells her that he has always enjoyed helping people who are sick, and that they do not need money to be happy. He would feel better being a doctor. He leaves, and she's sad. One day, after he becomes a doctor, he returns and helps the people there. She feels better. [Informant #110.10.74]

In these stories the tension over leaving is very different from that in the stories related by the white American youths. In the case of immigrants, leaving creates sadness and guilt, which are overcome when the son returns, empowered to help those he left behind. Leaving is not framed as a selfish project but as the means to an end: by leaving he can empower himself to take care of others.

Another theme in the immigrant narratives is asking advice (in 20 percent of the stories) and asking forgiveness (in 12 percent). In this regard, the stories of immigrant adolescents are more like those of the Mexicans than like those of the white Americans or Mexican Americans. Here are some representative immigrant stories about asking for advice and forgiveness:

There was once a rich family. There was only one son. He was spoiled. One day he went out with his friends and left his parents alone. They were getting old and they needed his help. He disappeared for a week. Finally he re-appeared. When he got there his mother asked why he had left them alone. At first he gets mad, but after a while he realizes what he has done. He realizes that he's done something bad, and he begs the forgiveness of his parents. They forgive him. [Informant #122.10.77]

This man wants to talk with his mother about a problem he has had. He has had a problem in school. He feels nervous. He tells his mother what happened. The mother is very understanding. He is no longer nervous. He is no longer afraid. [Informant #101.10.73]

He had a fight at the school but didn't want to tell his mom about it. His mom asked him why he didn't want to go to school today. At first he told her that it was simply because he didn't want to go to school. But she was mad at him for not going to school. So he decided he had better tell her he had a fight at school. She gave him advice. She said that it was O.K., that he needed to go back to school and face the situation but that he shouldn't fight in school. He went back and everything was fine. That is how the story ends. [Informant #570.10.78]

The stories above contain several revealing themes. In the first story, family obligations are first and foremost: the son's disappearance to be with his friends is framed as reckless disregard for his loving, dependent parents. The son sees his transgression (putting self and friends over family obligations) and begs for forgiveness. In the other two narratives, a worried young man turns to his understanding mother for advice. The mother is soothing, and her advice helps the young man resolve his problems.

RESPONSES OF MEXICAN AMERICAN ADOLESCENTS

Mexican American informants told a variety of stories in response to TAT card 6BM. In some respects their responses are closer to the responses of white American youths than to the responses of either Mexican or immigrant youths. For example, 20 percent of the narratives told by Mexican American youngsters are about bad news and are very similar to the stories told by the white American youths. Typically a relative has died and the young man finds himself in the difficult position of having to give his mother the bad news or console her. His foremost concern is to avoid hurting her. Some representative stories:

> The son is going to tell the lady bad news. Her husband died. He knows he can't tell her, and he is sad and afraid if he tells her she will die too—of sadness. He's trying to figure out how to tell her the bad news. He tells her and he tries to figure out how to help her. She gets sick and lonely from the news. She ends up living all alone in her house with no one else. [Informant #121.20.77]

> This mother and son got a phone call one day. The father has just died. They feel sad and they don't know what to do. The son feels he has to be strong to help out his mom. He goes to his dad's funeral. The son helps out his mom. They leave together. He moves in with her to help her out. She doesn't have to live by herself. [Informant #124.20.77]

Another theme of the stories told by Mexican Americans that is similar to those told by white Americans relates to gang and other illicit activities (20 percent of the stories). In these stories, the young man is "caught" participating in some illegal activities. For example:

> This is some guy with his grandma. His grandma is mad at him. He just robbed a store. He is mad because she is mad. His grandma makes him take what he stole back or she tells him he has to go to the police station. He's mad at his grandma. He ends up taking it back and staying mad. [Informant #221.20.77]

> There was a big accident. She's watching the looting in South Central L.A. She sees people running around with things in their hands: clothes, VCRs, couches. She is staring at them, shocked. He feels embarrassed because he did that too. He doesn't want her to know that he is a looter too. He is hoping she doesn't find the things he has in his room—he has a VCR in his room. He is thinking of taking them to go sell them, because he doesn't

want her to know. He gets caught and gets grounded. She is his mother. [Informant #218.20.76]

This mother is ashamed of her son because he did something wrong. She cannot forgive him for what he did. The son is angry at himself for what he did. He betrayed the family by maybe dealing drugs. His mom is mad about what became of her son. At the end she forgives him and he doesn't do it again because he knows how it feels to have another person hate him. [Informant #513.20.78]

These narratives suggest a preoccupation with illicit activities, a theme that is insignificant among Mexican and immigrant students. How are we to account for this? On this topic, Mexican American youngsters seem to have adopted the concerns of the mainstream population (20 percent of the white American narratives were about illicit and criminal behavior). Another way to phrase this is to say that without having our Mexican and immigrant samples we would have concluded that such preoccupations are typical in response to this card. Their responses may be related to the *cholo* gang scene to which many second-generation Mexican American youths are attracted (see Chapter 2; see also Vigil 1988a and 1988b). Gangs are an important reference point in the lives of these youngsters. The school they and their neighbors attended had competing, highly visible gangs. And even if most of our informants stayed out of the gang scene, as indeed most Mexican American youngsters do, the gangs nevertheless are a force to be reckoned with.

Peers and Friends

Adolescence is a phase in the life cycle when peers become an important point of reference. As adolescents carve out their own self-identities, they typically turn to peers to help them "work through" their central concerns. Peers typically navigate together the vicissitudes of first romances, future plans, and career options.

When there are family problems, or family members are absent (because of immigration or divorce, for example), the peer group may become an even more important point of reference. Adolescents turn to peers for protection or counsel, or simply to have fun. In this section we explore the peer group dynamics and relations in our four groups. The groups differ significantly in their construction of peer relations.

The peer group is an essential reference point for white American youths. In our interviews, as well as in the projective data, we found that these adolescents devote a great deal of time and energy to their peers. In their responses to the TAT cards, they revealed the highest overall tendency to turn to their peers for opinions.

We asked our informants in all groups the question: What three things make a good friend? Our informants responded to this question differently, and indeed, our data suggest that the peer group serves different functions among Latinos than among white American youths.

For white American youths the most important aspect of a good friendship is communication. According to our informants, a good friend is someone who "listens to you," someone "you can talk to," and someone "who understands you." A second significant feature of the white American notion of friendship relates to personal attributes. According to our informants, friends are "fun" and "nice" and "have good personalities." The third important component of a good friendship is "trust." As one informant summarized: "A good friend is someone who listens to you, somebody you can confide in. You can trust him with your secrets. He is nice and fun to be with."

Mexican-born youths have different expectations of their peers than do white American adolescents. According to our Mexican-born informants, the most important aspect of a friendship is mutual help. When we asked Latino youths what makes a good friend, the great majority said that friends are those who "help you." Whereas not one of the white American adolescents brought up the connection between school work and friendships, 20 percent of our Latino informants said that a good friend is someone who "helps you with your homework." The second most important characteristic of a friendship in Mexico was related; good friends, they said, "give you good advice." Good communication ("a good friend is someone you can talk to and is understanding") was the third most important characteristic of a friendship. One said, "A good friend is someone who motivates me to study, she gives me good advice and helps me with my problems. She helps me with my homework. She supports me. She understands me."

We had predicted that the Mexican American second generation and the white American youths would demonstrate a greater tendency to turn to peers as behavioral and attitudinal referents than would either the Mexican or the Mexican immigrant youths. Our analysis of the attitudinal referent subscale revealed that the white American youths demonstrated the highest overall tendency to rely on their peers for opinions about behaviors and attitudes. Contrary to prediction, however, the Mexican American group was not significantly different from the Mexican and Mexican immigrant groups on this dimension (see Appendix, Table A.12).

The Three Ps: Peers, Parents, and Problems

The Problem Situation Test offers an opportunity to systematically compare how the youngsters in each of the four groups responded spontaneously to common dilemmas and problems. In constructing the test, we created a problem in which a youngster would have to resolve conflict between parental and peer group pressures.

We presented all of the groups with the following problem: "His/ Her parents want him/her to work with the family; he/she wants to play with his/her friends."

RESPONSES OF WHITE AMERICAN ADOLESCENTS

The great majority of the white American informants resolved the problem by stating that the young man or young woman with the problem should do both: work with the family *and* play with his or her friends. Seventy-four percent said that he or she should first help the parents and then play with his or her friends. Interestingly, only 4 percent of the white American students suggested that the youngster should help the parents and not accept the peer invitation to play; and 12 percent of the white American youths said the youngster should choose friends *over* parents. (Only 4 percent of the Mexican youths chose friends over parents.)

What is most interesting is that although 74 percent said the youngster should fulfill his or her responsibilities to the family (while still making time to play), fully 40 percent indicated that the youngster would feel "pressured," "frustrated," or "angry" with the parents for presenting him or her with this dilemma. (In the Mexican group only 2 percent said the youngster would feel frustration or anger.) Also striking is that only 2 percent of the white American adolescents said that the youngster would feel "good" about deciding to work with the family. (Some 22 percent of the Mexican youths said the same thing.) The following are typical white American adolescent responses:

> He should work with his family first, then play later. He will feel resentful at his parents for it.

> She should work with the family because families are more important than friends, and she feels mad at her parents and sad because she would rather be with her friends. Then she can play.

> She should be able to do a little bit of both because the kid needs a social as well as a family life. She feels mad because she can't go with her friends and is bored to tears staying at home.

> She should try to compromise and possibly work part-time. She feels frustrated and angry that she can't always be with her friends.

> He should do both. I'd just go. He feels mad at his parents because they don't let him do what he wants.

Here are some examples of responses in which the adolescent does what he or she pleases:

> This should be her decision and she should do what she wants to do. She will feel pressured by her parents, but it's her decision.

> She should go with her friends because she always does. She feels guilty.

> He plays with his friends and he tells his parents why he would rather play. He feels uncomfortable for letting his parents down.

The tone of these responses is striking. Most of the American and Mexican youths said the youngster presented with the dilemma should help his or her parents. However, white American adolescents tended to say the youngster would be angry with the parents for placing him or her in this situation.

RESPONSES OF MEXICAN ADOLESCENTS

The most striking feature of the Mexican responses to this problem situation is that fully 88 percent said the youngster should help the parents. Half of them said the youngster should do both. Typically they said that the youngster should first help his or her parents and then play with friends. Another 44 percent said the parents should come first and that the youngster should reject or avoid peer pressure to play. Only 4 percent of the Mexican respondents said peers should be chosen over the parents.

Another interesting feature of these responses is the affect that is associated with these twin pressures. Twenty-two percent of the Mexican youngsters said the young man or young woman would feel "good" about helping the parents. Some of their responses expressed concern with what is the "right" thing to do:

> If the young man has the opportunity to help he should. If his parents are loving toward him, then by all means he should help them out.

> He should do what his father says because his father has asked him to help out economically by working with his father. Then the boy will feel better and it will also be beneficial to him. It will turn out to be a positive thing because he will help his father get ahead.

The boy must help his father and then if he has time play with his friends.

He will feel good and better about helping his father rather than playing.

Some said that the youngster would derive pleasure from helping the father:

> He should please his father but at the same time have fun, and not everything should be work. But to help his father and work with him he will feel content because he is doing something and he is cooperating with his father.

RESPONSES OF MEXICAN IMMIGRANT ADOLESCENTS

The immigrant youths responded similarly to their Mexican peers; 86 percent of the immigrant students said that the youngster should help the parents. Some 48 percent made no suggestion that the youngster do both—help and play. Thirty-eight percent said the youngster should first help the parents and only then go play with his or her friends. Not one of the Mexican immigrants said the youngster should choose friends over parents.

Ten percent said they might be angry at being forced to help out with a task. This is substantially less than in the white American adolescent sample but greater than in the Mexican sample. Only 6 percent of the immigrant youths said they would feel good about helping out, in contrast to 22 percent of the Mexican sample.

The immigrant sample stands out most in saying that they would feel sad to be faced with this dilemma. Some 16 percent of the youths in the immigrant sample stated that they would feel sad or bad, while only 2 percent of the Mexican sample and 2 percent of the American sample made reference to feeling sad or bad. This is in keeping with the sadness found in responses of the immigrant sample:

> The father should talk to the son and tell the son to help him. He is very tired. Dad is very tired and needs his help. The son feels bad because he doesn't want to work and he would rather play, but he does what he needs to do.

> He has to work with family because it is a good thing for them all to get along. He feels sad because he can't go to play.

> You work with your father but you will feel bad. But it is better to work and study than play with your friends.

> She feels upset but will go to work because friends don't bring you anything good.

RESPONSES OF MEXICAN AMERICAN ADOLESCENTS

In the second-generation sample we find themes that show similarities to the Mexican and the immigrant groups on the one hand and to the white American group on the other. Like the white American youths, the second-generation youths decide it is best to both help parents and play with friends (in 80 percent of the stories). Only 10 percent of these youths said the youngster should choose peers and playing over parents and work. In 36 percent of the responses the general affect associated with the dilemma is anger. Notably, no second-generation students said the youngster would feel good about helping out the parents. To them, doing both—working, then playing—is the ideal compromise. The anger associated with having to help out the parents is comparable to that found in the white American responses. Here are some representative solutions:

> He should work with the family because his parents raised him and he should do what they tell him.
>
> He is mad in general, but he helps.
>
> She should work with the family and then go to play with her friends.
>
> She feels mad because she wants to play and her parents won't let her.
>
> She should attend to her family and then go and play.
>
> She feels as if she has been stepped on. She feels obligated.
>
> She should do both—work and then go out for a while. It's important to be with your family. Family should come first.
>
> She feels ignorant and foolish because she is going to be with her parents.
>
> It depends on if he is too young. If he is he can't work, but if he is 17 or so he should get a job and help out his parents. At first he will be wishing that he could be with his friends, but then he will get used to working. He will still have time to be with his friends after working.

We also presented the following dilemma to all four groups: "His/Her best friend is involved in a gang. If he/she tells his/her parents, they can help the friend, but they will be very mad at him/her."

RESPONSES OF WHITE AMERICAN ADOLESCENTS

Some 60 percent of the white American youths said the youngster should tell the parents and try to get them to help. However, only 14 percent said that the parents would actually be helpful (38 percent of the Mexican youths said the parents would be helpful). In these responses the youngster approaches the parents and tells them, but the parents are not helpful. Thirty-five percent said it is up to the youngster to help the friend.

Fourteen percent said that the parents reject or become angry with the youngster for his or her gang connections. Eighteen percent of the white American youths said that the youngster should not tell his or her parents about the problem. An additional 14 percent said that the youngster should not get involved in the problem at all. Likewise, 18 percent said the youngster feels confused and does not know what to do. This group was far more likely then the Mexican-born groups to state that parents should not be told or it is best not to get involved. Here are some representative solutions:

> He should try to help him by himself, should not tell his parents because it is not his problem. He feels sorry for his friend.

> [He should] talk to friends and get a counselor of some kind to talk to him, not parents.

> He should try to get his friend out of the gang. He feels confused and upset at the situation. He should tell his parents, but they can't really help.

> It wouldn't be right to tell the parents. It is not my responsibility to watch over him. I would just tell him to handle it. I wouldn't feel anything about it.

> He should tell his parents because if it helps him that's what matters. His friend will thank him later. He feels confused and torn between what he wants and what is best.

> Just because she is in a gang it doesn't mean she needs help. She should talk to her friend first and not the parents. She feels bad about hurting her friend by telling others she is in a gang. But she may be hurting more if she doesn't tell.

RESPONSES OF MEXICAN ADOLESCENTS

The most common solution to this problem situation articulated by the Mexican youths is to tell the parents. In 68 percent of the responses the informants have the youngster turn to the parents for advice and help in dealing with the friend. What will the parents do? In 38 percent of those responses the parents are in fact helpful, articulate, and resourceful in solving the problem. In only 6 percent do the parents get angry with the youngster or reject him or her. In only 4 percent of the responses is the youth confused or unsure about what to do. Here are some representative solutions to this problem situation:

I would tell. Maybe they can help.

The adult couple can give him good advice, but if he continues in the gang they should not allow their son to be his friend.

They [parents] should give him direction and give him as much love as possible so he won't go into a depression.

They should try to get him out of the gang, talk to his parents, even if they become upset. They should all try to help him.

They will not be mad because they will see that their son trusts them and they will correct the situation.

RESPONSES OF MEXICAN IMMIGRANT ADOLESCENTS

The immigrant adolescents were the most likely to say that the youngster should tell the parents about the problem (76 percent). Immigrant adolescents perceived the parents to be more helpful than the white American adolescents did, and they were less likely to state that the youngster should not get involved in the friend's life. As in their responses to other problems, the immigrant adolescents were the most likely to state that the youngster felt sad or bad when faced with the situation. Here are some examples of immigrant responses to this question:

He feels sad because he will lose his friend's confidence. He should tell his parents because they can help.

It is better to tell the parents because they could help her friend avoid many problems, and she cares for her friend. She feels sad for having deceived her friend by telling her parents.

He should tell his parents so they can help, but he feels bad that he has to do this.

He should tell the parents because he feels sad and upset about his friend. His future will be worse.

She talks with her friend and she tells her not to be in the gang. She tells the parents not to get mad at them. They can talk to the friend. She feels bad about the whole situation. They help her.

RESPONSES OF MEXICAN AMERICAN ADOLESCENTS

Second-generation Mexican American youths were the least likely of all the groups to say the youngster should tell his or her parents about the problem (54 percent). They were also the least likely to report that the parents could help with the situation (6 percent).

The second-generation youths were as likely as the white American youths to state that the youngsters should not tell their parents about this problem. They were the most likely of all the groups to refer to confusion (26 percent). Here are some examples of responses made by the second generation:

> He would feel confused. Most people don't talk to their parents. He should tell, though, because parents may get mad but it's not because they hate you; it's because they care. I would tell them. I would feel trapped and confused and then explain to the friend how she needed to be understood.

> She should talk to a counselor and let them resolve it so they will not know she said it. She feels confused about whether to tell the friend's parents or the counselor. Once she tells the counselor she is relieved.

> He shouldn't tell the parents. He tries to talk to his friend, who tells him to get out of it or just stay away because they will try to drag him into it. He feels confused.

> She feels confused and doesn't know what to do. She should tell the parents so they can help her.

We could speculate that this confusion and lack of willingness to turn to the parents for help are related to the view of the second generation that their parents are not likely to be effective in dealing with such problems in the host society. It is possible that they experience increased levels of confusion as they try to cope alone with a situation that is beyond their developmental capabilities.

Our third problem situation again raises the possibility of conflict between parental expectations and peer group dynamics: "A group of friends comes by to pick him/her up to go play in the park. Her/his parents do not let him/her go until he/she finishes his/her homework."

RESPONSES OF WHITE AMERICAN ADOLESCENTS

Many of the responses of this group to this problem situation contain themes similar to those found in their responses to the TAT cards. The most striking feature of the white American student responses is the number of times the youngster is said to be mad or angry at the parents for making him or her do homework before going out to play. In 36 percent of the responses there is reference to being mad or angry at the parents or to being forced by the parents to do something.

The second largest number recognize the youngster's responsibility to do homework before going out to play. Thirty-two percent say that the young man or young woman should follow parental advice without getting angry or mad. In some responses there is a process of negotiation, as the youngster tries to convince the parents of the importance of peers and playing. When that doesn't work some say that the youngster sneaks out to play or defies the parents outright. Here are some representative responses:

> He should tell his parents he'll do the homework later, negotiate and negotiate. He feels that if he can't go with his friends then they will think he isn't cool.

> She should stay and finish her homework because that's what her parents want. It will save her from getting into trouble and getting a bad grade. She may feel angry at her mom.

> She feels embarrassed, upset, and dumb. She will quickly do her homework, put down any old answers, and tell her parents that she is done and then go out and redo the homework later.

> He feels embarrassed and stupid that he has to stay and finish his homework when he made plans with his friends. So he sneaks out and gets busted.

> I'd be mad because I'm missing the fun with my friends. Then what I'd do is hurry up and finish my homework, then ask if I can go out. He is mad at his parents because he couldn't do what he wanted to do.

> She would feel as if her parents were making her decisions for her again. She would tell her friends that she needs to finish the homework and then she will meet her friends later.

RESPONSES OF MEXICAN ADOLESCENTS

The majority of the Mexican youth (80 percent) recognized parental authority and said the youngster was responsible for doing homework before going out to play. In the majority of the Mexican responses accepting responsibility is taken as a matter of fact, and there is little fighting off parental authority on this topic. Parental authority is depicted as legitimate and appropriate. In only 14 percent of the responses of the Mexican youth is there reference to the youngster's being mad at the parents for making him or her do the homework before playing. Here are some representative responses:

> He should do his homework so he can be somebody in life, because his friends could be smoking, doing drugs, or he can get into a car accident with them. He feels better afterward, and he will understand that it was better that they didn't let him go out because they were protecting him. The parents were protecting the one they love.

> He should do his homework and tell his friends to go ahead, and when he is done with his homework he will join them. At the moment he will be angry with his parents, but later he'll know it was for his own good.

She must finish her homework because her parents want her to be a good student and better off than they were when she is older. She feels sad but shouldn't be sad because her parents do only what is best for her.

Do the homework and then go out and have fun. First priority is school. The parents should enforce what is important first and leave having fun for later.

Yes, this is good. It is good that they do not let him go out until he does his homework, because if he goes out first, when he returns he won't feel like doing any of his homework. This way he'll feel more responsible.

RESPONSES OF MEXICAN IMMIGRANT ADOLESCENTS

The immigrants were the most likely of all the groups to say that the youngster should complete his or her homework before playing with friends (86 percent). They were significantly less likely to refer to anger toward the parents than either the white American or second-generation youths. Consistent with our other findings, they were most likely to express sadness or bad feeling in response to this problem. Following are some examples of immigrant responses to this question:

She feels sad because she can't go play right away but also has the obligation to finish her homework. The best thing is to finish the homework and play later.

He does his homework and goes to play. School is the most important thing. He feels okay because he knows his mom is right.

You do your homework when you are supposed to so you can be free to go out. He feels bad that he can't go and for not using his time in the right way.

There is a time for everything. She could have done her homework before. Now she has to do it. She feels sad that she can't go out with her friends.

He should obey his parents because they are his parents and they are older than he is. He feels sad that he can't go out but good about obeying his parents.

RESPONSES OF MEXICAN AMERICAN ADOLESCENTS

In the group of second-generation Mexican Americans, 68 percent responded that it was important to be responsible and do the homework first (comparable to the Mexican sample and significantly more than the white American sample). However, a large percentage of these respondents said that the adolescents were angry at their parents for pointing out their responsibility to them (40 percent), just as the white Americans do. Again, the second generation's stories contain some of the themes found in the stories of the Mexican youths and others found in the stories of the white Americans. Here are some examples of second-generation responses:

> He would finish his homework and then go to the park. He feels mad because he wants to be with friends and he wants to have a choice about what to do.

> She should finish the homework. If she's done, then she should go to the park. She's angry because her parents won't let her go.

> He should do what he wants. I would go if I wanted to. I'd feel happy. I'd tell my parents that I did my homework at the park. If I felt that what they were telling me was important, then I would do what they said.

> He feels angry. He should finish his homework, then have his parents take him to the park.

> She tells friends that she'll meet them later after finishing her homework. She feels that she is in a hurry to do the stuff and maybe a little angry at her parents because they didn't let her go.

We have summed up the main findings of the Problem Situation Test as they relate to the dynamics of peer group and family interactions. As with the TAT, we found interesting differences and similarities across groups. The immigrant students seem to believe that work and parental authority are more important than play or peer group fun. The peer group seems to be less significant among the immigrants than among any of the other groups.

In both the non-Hispanic group and the second-generation Mexican American group, we see increasing tensions between parental authority and peer group pressures. Although many of these youths recognize and will submit to parental authority, they do so grudgingly. They express anger and frustration at the parents for making them do work before they have fun.

The data presented in this section call into question the notion that, typically, adolescence is a time of peer orientation and of pushing away the family. Although this may be true for white American and Mexican American adolescents, it may not be true in other cultures and for other nationalities.

Our findings on the importance of the peer group among white Americans are consistent with Geoffrey Gorer's observations in his classic study of American culture. Gorer discussed the American tradition of a "moral rejection of authority," which has long been present in the social and political structure of American society (Gorer 1963: 53). Gorer argued that in America the parent is rejected "as a guide and model" and the peers take on a central role in affirming self-esteem, "with a feeling of far greater psychological urgency than is usual in other countries" (ibid: 27, 108). Our data suggest that for Mexican-born adolescents, the family remains the key institution and peers do not necessarily achieve the powerful influence that they do in the lives of white American adolescents.

CHAPTER 5

Achievement Motivation and Attitudes Toward School

In Chapter 4, we examined family and peer dynamics across groups. We now turn to the issue of achievement motivation and attitudes toward school. This is a very important area of inquiry as Latinos continue to be overrepresented in school underachievement, failure, and dropout rates.

As we discussed in Chapter 2, a number of theoretical models have been advanced to make sense of this phenomenon. A problem of special theoretical interest is that Latinos do not seem to fit the predictions of assimilation theories: even in the third generation the gap between Latinos and whites in educational achievement and income attainment remains substantial (see Kantrowitz and Rosaldo 1991; Bean et al. 1991; Chapa 1988).

A number of theorists have specifically singled out the Latino family—indeed, the culture in general—as primarily responsible for the problem of low achievement among Latino youths. Some scholars have argued that Latino families do not value education and do not foster independence and individualism—which are framed as prerequisites for achievement. For example, Heller writes that Latino families hinder mobility "by stressing . . . [such values as] family ties, honor, masculinity . . . and by neglecting values that are conducive to it, achievement, *independence*, and deferred gratification" (Heller 1966: 35, emphasis added). But do Latino families indeed neglect the values that are said to be conducive to achievement? Is it required, as some claim, that in order to achieve, Latinos need to reduce their dependence on family? Or can family ties be a key ingredient of achievement orientation?

Most researchers who have considered the *psychocultural* patterning of achievement motivation among Latinos have explored these issues only with immigrants and the second generation. To do so, however, confuses issues of Latino family structure and values with such factors as immigration and minority status. As we saw in Chapter 2, many issues—loss, culture shock, disorientation, discrimination, and economic pressures to work—associated with immigration and minority status surely influence achievement patterns and attitudes toward school.

In order to assess Latino achievement motivation *independently of immigration and minority status*, we compared Mexican youth in Mexico, immigrant youth, second-generation youth, and white American youth. How do the motivational dynamics and attitudes toward school of Mexicans in Mexico differ, if at all, from those of immigrant and second-generation students? How do they differ from those of white Americans? It is only by addressing these differences that we might be able to distinguish the achievement motivation and attitudes toward school that are culturally influenced from those that may be a result of immigrant and minority status.

Given the current anti-immigrant sentiment, it is urgent to establish whether students born in Mexico—and who immigrate—arrive in the United States with motivational ambivalence about schools and learning. If it can be shown that Mexican-born students are not typically ambivalent about schooling, then we must consider whether their development of ambivalence is caused by other factors—including minority status.

Achievement Motivation and Individualism

David McClelland and his associates conducted pioneer research on achievement motivation among white Americans. They defined achievement motivation as "competition with a standard of excellence" (McClelland et al. 1953: 161). They argued that achievement motivation flourishes within a specific interpersonal climate that trains youngsters to become independent from others, including family. They attempted to document achievement concerns in experimental conditions through the use of projective tests, including the Thematic Apperception Test (TAT).

McClelland and his associates found that in their American middle-class samples, TAT narratives told by achievement-oriented individuals related achievement to gaining independence from the family. They found achievement motivation and independence to

be highly correlated. The relationship between achievement motivation and individualism was then examined in the narratives of other
cultures (see McClelland 1961)—Greek mythology, North American Indian folktales, and Pakistani children's books. According to
McClelland, "need Achievement" in various settings flourishes in
an atmosphere of rugged individualism. Children who are taught to
solve problems at an early age *by themselves*, and who are encouraged to think of themselves as independent of their caretakers, are
said to have higher levels of achievement motivation as adults (ibid.:
301–36; for a critique of McClelland's cross-cultural model see De
Vos 1973; see also Suárez-Orozco 1989).

Some have suggested that, among Latinos, a culture that orients
individuals strongly to the family is responsible for crippling their
achievement motivation. Carter and Segura (1979) reviewed a number of studies that argued that because Latino children are not suf-
ficiently trained in "independence" patterns, they remain caught in
a family web of counterproductive values that hinder achievement
motivation. Such thinking is based on the erroneous supposition that
independence training is a prerequisite for achievement motivation
and that Latino family traditions of interdependence, cooperation,
and mutual nurturance are impediments to the growth of achievement motivation. Although McClelland's model may correctly address achievement motivation themes among white middle-class
Americans, his conclusions about the relationship between achievement and individualism do not agree with the subtle motivational
dynamics encountered among other ethnic groups, including the
Japanese (see De Vos 1973) and Central American immigrants and
refugees (see Suárez-Orozco 1989).

For example, in an earlier study of fifty recent arrivals from war-
torn Central America (twenty females and thirty males, ages fourteen to nineteen), 56 percent of the narratives told in response to
card 2 of the TAT were about achievement motivation (working hard
to "become somebody") and nurturing (returning home to help support the parents; Suárez-Orozco 1989). Whereas the more independent and individualistic North Americans commonly told stories
in which the protagonist leaves the parents permanently to pursue
schooling or a career (De Vos 1983), in the stories told by the Central American immigrants the protagonist commonly *returns* home
after earning a degree or learning a profession to take care of the
poor parents. In this respect the narratives told by Central Americans are similar to those told by Mexicans in response to TAT card 2
(see Chapter 4).

Marcelo Suárez-Orozco concluded that among the Central American immigrants a pattern of "compensatory achievement" was related to feelings of responsibility based on guilt about parental sacrifice (Suárez-Orozco 1989). They viewed "becoming somebody" as a reparative act that would alleviate parental hardships. Indeed, rather than a preoccupation with achievement via independence, the interpersonal concerns of most of the Central American immigrants involved a strong wish to achieve to be able to nurture their parents, relatives, and others left in Central America.

In the Central American sample, most of the immigrant youth were keenly aware of the cultural chain of mutual nurturance and affiliation. Many reported that their parents had worked hard at a young age to help their own parents and siblings make ends meet. Rather than viewing their parents as aloof and distant, the new arrivals portrayed them as warm and caring. They perceived that their parents had sacrificed tremendously to settle them in the safety of the United States (Suárez-Orozco 1989).

Hence, the Central American data do not fit the white American paradigm of achievement motivation. The most motivated of these Latino immigrants are not individualists searching for self-advancement and independence. Our research with Central Americans captured other facets of this achievement-nurturance phenomenon: the older, more experienced youth systematically turned to the younger or more recent arrivals to help them find work, to tutor them, and to otherwise aid them in their first steps in the new land. In addition, the Central American youths who worked while attending school full time (about 68 percent in a sample of fifty informants) all reported sending money back home on a regular basis (Suárez-Orozco 1989).

In the case of Central American immigrants, rather than a pattern of rugged individualism and independence, we identified a worldview that calls for orienting the self to others. It seems, then, that McClelland's theoretical model does not apply cross-culturally. Whether the findings for Central Americans would hold true for other Latino immigrant groups is a theoretical question of some interest. Is achievement to benefit the family a motivator for other Latino groups?

As we shall see, our psychosocial and other data strongly suggest that Mexican adolescents in Mexico and Mexican immigrant youths in the United States are comparatively highly achievement oriented. Furthermore, our data suggest that among these youths, self-initiative is the most common achievement mode. Our data revealed important differences between the achievement dynamics and attitudes of the Mexican-born youths and those of both second-generation and white American youths. As they did in response to the problem situations designed to elicit information about family dynamics, Mexican-born girls discussing achievement motivation tended to use terms more similar to those of Mexican-born boys than to those of white American girls.

In the next sections of this chapter, we examine our findings on attitudes toward school and achievement motivation. We also offer a critical evaluation of the relevant literature on achievement motivation as it relates to individualism among white Americans and among Latinos.

Attitudes Toward School

Informants in all groups told us that school is a very important part of their lives. We engaged them in a variety of conversations and tasks designed to reveal their school habits, attitudes, and behaviors. Our interview data suggest that students in all groups share a conviction that school is the key to a good life and a good future.

The great majority of informants in all groups saw doing well in school as a requirement for getting a good job. Here are some of their responses to the question "How do you get ahead [in California/in Mexico]?" According to white Americans, "You get ahead by doing good in school," "Go to college," "Get a good education"; according to Mexicans, "Studying, putting a lot of effort into studying," "Studying until you finish a career," "Studying a lot. My parents are supporting us to study," "By being serious, putting a lot of effort, having self-confidence, studying hard"; according to Mexican immigrants, "Studying a lot in school and putting effort into college," "Speaking English well, studying a lot, getting good grades," "Doing well in school is most important"; and according to second-generation Mexican Americans, "Studying hard is the key to get ahead," "Studying hard, learning, getting along with others," "Good grades is the most important thing, also motivation, and hard work."

Some idiosyncratic themes emerged in these conversations. For example, Mexican immigrants tended to point out the importance of learning English as a key to getting ahead. Indeed our interview data strongly suggest that the new immigrants are aware of the importance of learning English, and they spontaneously reported wanting to do well in school.

Although, as we shall see, there were group differences in attitudes toward school, the majority of our informants in all groups believed that in general their own schools prepared them to get ahead in life. We did not find any significant differences in the amount of time students spent doing their homework (an average of 6.8 hours per week for the three groups of adolescents in the United States and a bit more—7.6 hours per week—for the group in Mexico).

In addition to interviews and observations, we also formulated a number of school-related sentence completion tests, problem situation tests, and other tasks. Finally, we asked all our informants to respond to TAT cards known to "pull" for achievement themes (including cards 1 and 2). Let us turn to this evidence.

Even though school is important to the great majority of students in our samples, the data suggest that there are indeed significant differences across groups.

Students differed in what they thought was important about school. We asked all students to complete the following sentence: "The most important thing about school is _____." Forty-four percent of the white American youths completed the sentence with words such as "learning," "studying," and "getting a good education." A significantly higher percentage of Mexican and Mexican immigrant students (74 percent in each group) and 62 percent of the Mexican American students completed the sentence with similar terms. In other words, white American students placed less emphasis on learning. Interestingly, many of the white American students said the most important thing about school was simply "getting the diploma."

We also asked all of our informants to respond "yes" or "no" to the following statement:

"To me school is the most important thing."

	Whites	Mexicans	Mexican immigrants	Mexican Americans
Yes	40%	75%	84%	55%
No	60%	25%	16%	45%

Chi-square * p < .001.

It is important to highlight that of all students the immigrant youths saw schooling as most important. We also asked all students to respond to the following statement:

"Doing my homework is more important than helping my friends."

	Whites	Mexicans	Mexican immigrants	Mexican Americans
Yes	20%	34%	68%	36%
No	80%	66%	32%	64%

Chi-square * p $<$ .001.

The differences in responses were again significant. Again, the immigrant youths were more likely to say school tasks should come before peers. These responses are in keeping with our general findings that newly arrived immigrants tend to see schooling as a very important institution in their lives. For immigrant students, school is the key to a better tomorrow. Finally, there were significant differences in how students responded to the following question:

"I always finish what I set out to do."

	Whites	Mexicans	Mexican immigrants	Mexican Americans
Yes	66%	90%	88%	76%
No	34%	10%	12%	24%

Chi-square * p $<$ .005.

We also asked all of our informants some less specific questions about what is important to them. Here again, there were revealing differences across groups. For example, we asked them to complete the following sentence: "In life the most important thing is _____." Among white American youths the most common response was "success" (20 percent); 48 percent of Mexican youths said "success"; 50 percent of Mexican immigrant youths said "success"; and only 20 percent of Mexican American youths said "success." It is striking to note that the two Mexican-born groups view success—very often combined with hard work—as key. White American and second-generation Mexican American students were comparatively less preoccupied with hard work and success. These two groups both spoke of "happiness" as an important aspect of life.

It is one thing for students to be convinced that working hard in school is a key to their future success. It is quite another thing for them to actually like school. White American students were more likely to say they did not like school (18 percent); only 2 percent of the Mexican students and 8 percent of Mexican American students said the same thing; and not a single immigrant student said he or she did not like school.

We investigated student attitudes toward school in a variety of ways. For example, we asked all our informants to complete the following sentence: "My school is _____." For analytical purposes we divided student responses into three categories: positive, neutral, and negative.

Again, there were significant group differences. White American students were more likely to complete the sentence with negative responses—fully 42 percent of their responses were negative. These included "boring," "the worst," "junky," "stupid," "terrible," and "hell." Only 20 percent of the white American youths completed the sentence with positive terms (including "cool," "fun," and "pretty nice"). The rest completed the sentence with neutral terms (such as "a place to go on a daily basis").

Mexican youngsters completed the sentence quite differently. Fully 84 percent of them used positive words, including "a great place with great teachers," "a happy place," and "the key to my success." Not a single Mexican student completed the sentence with a negative term. Sixteen percent of these students responded in neutral terms (such as "home of education," "regular," and "an institution where rules must be followed").

The responses of immigrant students were similar to those of the group in Mexico. Eighty-eight percent of the immigrant students completed the sentence with a positive term. Only one student included a negative term. The rest were neutral. Here are some typical immigrant responses: My school is "the greatest thing I ever had," "pretty. I can study a lot here," "the most beautiful school in the county," and "fabulous."

Mexican American students completed the sentence in ways that reveal similarities to both their Mexican-born and their white American peers. Sixty-six percent of them completed it positively: "great," "the best," "cool." Yet 20 percent of them responded negatively: "boring," "ugly," "cheap." Among U.S.-born students—both white Americans and second generation—boredom is a typical complaint.

We also wanted to compare how students experienced various aspects of school life. For example, we presented all informants with the following sentence completion task: "When I am with the school principal, I feel _____." Again, there were significant group differences. Only 14 percent of the white American students reported positive feelings, such as "respected," "secure," and "I have done something good." The great majority of the white American adolescents—72 percent—completed the sentence with a negative term, such as "scared," "shaken," and "what did I do now?" For all groups "fear" was the most common negative association.

In contrast, 40 percent of the Mexican adolescents completed the sentence about the principal with a positive thought: "he will give me good advice," "proud that he is our principal," "like I admire him." Among immigrant students, 30 percent completed the sentence with a positive reference such as "respect," "happy," "good," and "he is someone that gives me advice so things can go well." Among immigrants, when a negative term was used, "nervousness" was the most frequently expressed emotion.

Perhaps most striking were the responses of second-generation students: not a single one completed the sentence with a positive word or phrase. Their responses included "very nervous," "like I'm being interrogated," "not happy," "scared," "angry," "embarrassed," and "like I'm going to get in trouble."

Also revealing is how students completed the sentence "The school principal is ____." Fully 40 percent of the white American students used negative terms: "mean and dorky," "a jerk," "a mean person," "weird," "an idiot," "closed-minded," "a pain." On the other hand, only 6 percent of the Mexican students had negative responses. But even those were quite different from the disrespectful tone of the white American students. One student, for example, said "sometimes he is unfair," and another said "someone I don't like." The great majority of the Mexican associations were positive: "a very special person," "a person who has brought respect to the name of our school," "a person who has reached his goals," "a good person," "a respected person."

Among immigrant students the response pattern was similar to that of the group in Mexico. Only 10 percent of the immigrants completed the sentence with negative terms such as "hard" and "ugly." The great majority of their responses—over 60 percent—were positive: "very friendly," "a good principal because he has done a lot to improve discipline," "a good and capable person," "an exciting person." Note that these students are referring to the same principal as the white American students!

The responses of Mexican American students tend to fall in between the white American and the Mexican-born norms. For example, 32 percent used negative terms such as "a dork," "boring," "racist," and "a big jerk off." And 32 percent had positive associations: "cool," "a good person," "fun." The rest completed the sentence with neutral terms.

We wanted to examine more closely the attitudes of the four groups toward the exercise of authority. We asked students to finish the following sentence: "When the teacher told me to do the problem, I felt _____."

There are important differences in how students completed the task. Among white American students the primary responses were embarrassment, frustration, and anger (30 percent). Only 6 percent of the students completed the sentence with a mildly positive term (such as "O.K."). The responses of Mexican students were very different. Some 24 percent of the students finished the sentence with positive phrases such as "the desire to do it," "proud," and "enthusiastic." None mentioned embarrassment, and only 4 percent of the Mexican students said they felt anger. The predominant sentiment in their responses was a positive one—with an edge of nervousness that revealed a wish to do well.

Among the immigrant students we found nervousness (20 percent), fear (16 percent), and sadness (9 percent). Only 10 percent of them completed the sentence with a positive word or phrase. In general, the predominant feeling among the immigrants was one of anxiety about completing the task.

Second-generation students' responses again fell between those of the Mexican-born and the white American students. They gave more positive responses (20 percent) than the white American students. They were also more likely than the Mexican-born students to display embarrassment and anger (18 percent).

We also presented all our informants with the following sentence completion task: "When the teacher told me to leave the room, I felt _____." The most common responses among white American students were "embarrassed" (24 percent) and "angry" (22 percent). In many of these responses, there is a feeling of injustice and a sense of embarrassment about being singled out in front of peers. Mexican students referred to sadness (28 percent) and fear (20 percent). Many of these responses mention shame about letting down the teacher. Among immigrant students the most common emotion expressed was sadness (52 percent). Among second-generation students, 18 percent referred to anger, 16 percent to embarrassment, and 16 percent to sadness.

The last sentence we asked our informants to complete was: "When I am with my teacher I feel _____." Over 50 percent of the white American students gave either neutral ("O.K.," "normal") or negative ("bored," "uncomfortable," "not so happy") responses. The Mexican responses were strikingly different: fully 70 percent were

positive, and only 4 percent were negative. Among the positive responses were "admiration," "trust," and "she is helping me become
somebody in life."

The responses of the immigrant group were quite similar to those
of the Mexican youths: 62 percent were positive, including "content," "secure," and "happy." It is interesting to note that 20 percent
of their responses revealed anxiety about being with the teacher
("nervous," "timid"). Once again, Mexican American students fell
between the Mexican-born and the white American students. Their
responses were less positive than those of the Mexican-born students (only 40 percent). And 30 percent offered negative associations
such as "mad," "weird," and "embarrassed."

We also examined what students thought was most difficult about
their school experiences. Again there were revealing differences.
We asked all students, "What is the most difficult thing about
school?" The most common response of white American students
was "homework" (24 percent). In contrast, only one Mexican student
said "homework"; 36 percent referred to a subject such as "mathematics," "chemistry," or "physics."

The responses of immigrant students were very much like those
of Mexican students. The majority referred to a specific subject.
Perhaps not surprisingly, 44 percent of all immigrant students said
learning English was the most difficult thing about school. Two immigrant students reported that racism was the most difficult thing
for them. One said, "Well, here there is racism. The Americans say
negative things about Mexicans . . . that we are lazy and stupid and
that we are always getting into fights." Another immigrant student
said, "The Americans put us down; they put Mexicans down. It is
hard. They call us names. They don't understand our culture." Only
one immigrant student said the most difficult thing about school
was the homework. Second-generation students were likely to say
homework was the most difficult thing about school (20 percent);
others referred to subjects, peer and gang pressures, and keeping up
their grades.

It is interesting to note that although there were no group differences in the amount of time students spent doing homework, there
were significant group differences in how students did their homework. White American students said they rely on parental help (46
percent) or do the work by themselves (26 percent). Sixty-four percent of Mexican students rely on parents, and 24 percent do the
work by themselves. Immigrants, on the other hand, are much less
likely to turn to parents for help (only 16 percent) and much more

likely to rely on siblings (34 percent); 34 percent said they do the work by themselves. Many of these students felt their parents, with their limited knowledge of English, simply could not help them with their homework. One informant said, "When we were in Mexico, my mom used to help. Now she can't. She doesn't speak English. Here my oldest sister helps me." Only 20 percent of second-generation Mexican American students are likely to turn to their (immigrant) parents for help; 30 percent are likely to turn to siblings; the rest do it by themselves.

We found interesting group differences in what happened to students when they received a poor grade in school. White American students reported that their parents were likely to "yell" at them and punish them. Here are some student responses: "Nothing really happens, they yell at me." "They take away my privileges. They make me study more." "I get yelled at and grounded." "I get a lecture, then I get put on restriction for a while." Mexican students were more likely than others to report that their parents discuss their grades with them, often bringing up the future: "They just advise me to study more and to take advantage of the opportunity to study, to think about my future." "Papá calls it to my attention. We talk about it. He tells me to put more effort into studying. To get ahead in the future, you need an education." "Papá scolds me. He tells me he wants me to have an education. He wants me to be a somebody." Similarly, immigrant students said, "They call it to my attention. They say that I must study, it is for my life, for my future." "They ask me why, what's going on? They try to help and have me study more." Likewise, Mexican American students report that their (immigrant) parents are likely to "have a talk" with them. Mexican American students tended to report that they might be talked to or lose privileges. Ten percent reported that their parents were relatively passive about their children's poor grades, saying, "They don't look at our report cards," "Nothing," "I can't use the phone for a day," "Little, they just tell me to study."

Most students in all groups reported wanting to go on to college. Eight percent of the white American students, 0 percent of the Mexican students, 6 percent of the immigrant students, and 6 percent of the second-generation students said they were not planning to go on to college. We asked all students, "What would you like to do when you finish school here?" The U.S.-born students—both white American and second-generation—were more likely to say they did not know (10 percent in each group) than the Mexican-born students (0 percent). Immigrant students were more likely than any other group to say they would have to work after finishing school (14 percent).

In this section, we examined a variety of attitudes toward school and found some striking similarities: the two Mexican-born groups show many commonalities in their attitudes toward school.[1] As expected, Mexican American students share many concerns and attitudes with both white American and Mexican-born students.

There is also evidence that the groups differ in their attitudes toward school and school authorities. White American students tended to display highly ambivalent attitudes toward school and, particularly, school authorities. These students are convinced they have to go to school and do well in order to have a good future, but they are more likely to say they do not like school than students from any of the other groups. They are also much more likely to have negative feelings about school and school authorities. Many seem to experience school as "boring" and school authorities as "unfair." Some just want to graduate and "get out of here," as one informant put it.

Mexican and Mexican immigrant students tended to articulate much more positive attitudes toward school and school authorities. These students were not bored and alienated but appreciative and gratified. They respect their teachers and principals and believe that they exercise authority in a legitimate and fair manner. When facing a disciplinary action, these students are more likely to feel shame and sadness at having let the teacher down. White American students report more anger and frustration. Mexican American students, truly the children of two worlds, share the attitudes of both groups.

Our study also detected some of the special issues facing newly arrived immigrants. Immigrant students are less likely to turn to parents for help with school-related tasks; they tend to rely more on siblings. They are also more likely to think about going to work full time when they finish high school. Among these students, we found a sense of obligation to help the family by working full time to earn money. This is in keeping with the "projective" Thematic Apperception Test data. The TAT data show that immigrants—and Latinos more generally—strive to achieve not for self-advancement but in order to help others (see Chapter 4).

Achievement, School, and the Future

Our study addressed questions about achievement orientation using a variety of means. In addition to observations, student interviews, and other tasks, we used the TAT to explore motivational dynamics (see Chapter 3; see also De Vos 1973; McClelland 1961; and Suárez-Orozco 1989).

As we discussed earlier, prior research with Central American adolescents (Suárez-Orozco 1989) had led us to the hypothesis that Latinos in general, and Mexicans in particular, would construct TAT narratives in which the protagonists' achievements would be inspired by social obligations and mutual interdependence. We assumed that Mexican and Mexican immigrant youths would express more concern with affiliative achievement than would white American and Mexican American youths.

The Mexican and Mexican immigrant youths did not in fact score higher on the TAT affiliative achievement subscale. After scoring the data, however, we realized that the groups expressed their affiliative concerns differently. Because this scale incorporated two separate concepts (affiliation and achievement), both had to occur in a specific manner in order to be scored. We found that the results confounded the two issues. As we describe in greater detail in the next section, the affiliative concerns of the groups did in fact differ significantly.

We postulated that Mexican American youths would express more desire to avoid challenging tasks than would any of the other three groups. The fact that the Mexican American youths scored lower than any of the other groups on the TAT engaging/avoiding task subscale confirms this hypothesis (see Appendix, Table A.14). Indeed, second-generation Mexican American youths related more narratives in which the protagonist is depicted as avoiding or giving up on the task at hand. One can interpret this finding to mean that although members of the immigrant generation typically demonstrate high expectations and an optimism that through schooling they can achieve status mobility, the second generation may develop a less enthusiastic faith in the school system.

Our finding is consistent with the observations of Ogbu (1974), Matute-Bianchi (1991), and Patthey-Chavez (1993). According to these researchers, second- and third-generation Mexican American youths may respond to ongoing patterns of discrimination and cultural alienation in schools by giving up on education:

> Latino adolescents are highly motivated, but their expectations of success are colored by experiences of hostility and discrimination from the society at large. They question whether school is working in their interest. . . . They find it difficult to cooperate in the educational enterprise. Many of them simply leave it altogether. (Patthey-Chavez 1993: 56)

Interestingly, the scores on the independent achievement scale reached significance but in a direction that was unexpected. Analysis of these scores revealed that the Mexican students demonstrated a significantly greater need for self-initiated achievement than either the Mexican American or the white American students (see Appendix, Table A.13). That white American students revealed less concern with self-initiated achievement than the Mexican youths is a finding that is not in keeping with cultural stereotypes or with expectations based on the literature. There was no significant difference in the independent achievement scores of Mexican and Mexican immigrant students.

A Tour of Violin Playing in Four Cultures

It is particularly instructive to delve into the most significant themes emerging from the responses to card 1 of the TAT. This card depicts a boy about ten years of age pensively gazing at a violin on a table before him. This card tends to elicit stories that include the themes under consideration—achievement orientation and parent-child relations (Henry 1956). The stories told in response to card 1 illustrate in rich and subtle detail many of the issues we have already discussed.

All of the stories were grouped by card and by respondent group, and all of the responses for each group were read separately. In reading through the TAT responses to card 1, we realized that different themes seemed to be prominent in the responses of each group. We compiled a list of the themes that appeared to recur and then placed all of the stories together randomly. Two raters who were blind to the group membership of the storyteller then read, analyzed, and discussed them, rating each story for the presence or absence of each of the themes under consideration. The incidence of each theme was tallied for each group. Chi-square analyses were then conducted to check for significant differences between groups (see Table 3).

RESPONSES OF WHITE AMERICAN ADOLESCENTS

The predominant theme of the stories told by white American adolescents in response to card 1 is frustration. Fully 50 percent of the white American youths—in contrast to only 2 percent of the Mexican sample—told stories in which the protagonist expressed frustration and anger about performing the task at hand. This is particularly striking when one considers the relative absence of this theme among the stories told by the other groups.

In the majority of the narratives, frustration seems to be caused by

TABLE 3
Responses to TAT Card 1

Theme	Whites		Mexicans		Mexican immigrants		Mexican Americans		Chi-square probability
	N	%	N	%	N	%	N	%	
Outside parental pressure	18	36	0	0	3	6	15	30	.001 *
Internal motivation	7	14	27	54	16	32	9	18	.001 *
Succumbing to pressure (parental and other)	7	14	3	6	2	4	4	8	.274
Avoiding pressure	8	16	1	2	5	10	8	16	.114
Hard work	5	10	17	34	5	10	8	16	.005 *
Instant gratification	3	6	2	4	2	4	1	2	.789
Success as a result of efforts of self	5	10	15	30	10	20	5	10	.026 *
Success as a result of efforts of others	3	6	3	6	5	10	3	6	.813
Success as a result of efforts of self and others	7	14	4	8	5	10	4	8	.707
Achievement motivated by desire to help self	0	0	2	4	0	0	0	0	.007 *
Achievement motivated by desire to help others	1	2	4	8	5	10	4	8	.429
Achievement motivated by desire to help self and others	0	0	2	4	0	0	0	0	.707
Concerns with adequacy	8	16	14	28	17	34	9	18	.013 *
Concerns with failure	2	4	1	2	1	2	14	28	.001 *
Boredom	3	6	1	2	1	2	7	14	.134
Frustration, resolved	17	34	0	0	3	6	3	6	.001 *
Frustration, unresolved	8	16	1	2	1	2	4	8	.016
Broken violin, purposeful	5	10	0	0	0	0	1	2	.008 *
Broken violin, accidental	4	8	0	0	7	14	4	8	.063
Anger	7	14	0	0	3	6	10	20	.004 *
Sadness	16	32	8	16	33	66	17	34	.001 *
Searching out help	2	4	6	12	13	26	6	12	.012 *
Pleasure	3	6	9	18	8	16	3	6	.115
Financial deprivation	2	4	6	12	3	6	3	6	.451
Daydreaming/imagining	2	4	16	32	5	10	1	2	.001 *
What do I want to do? (confusion)	6	12	0	0	0	0	1	2	.002 *
Parenting style, pressuring	18	36	4	8	5	10	5	10	.001 *
Parenting style, nurturing	5	10	8	16	4	8	4	8	.541
Parenting style, punitive	2	4	1	2	1	2	3	6	.644

*$p < .05$.

either the difficulties and challenges presented by the task at hand (playing the violin) or the pressures of a parental figure's imposing the task on an unwilling child (in 36 percent of the narratives). The theme running through these stories is motivational ambivalence and tension, which results from the fact that the parents are imposing the task on the child. The narratives told by the white American adolescents reflected concerns about independence and gave some indication that for these youths adolescence is a period of significant turmoil, which is particularly revealed by tension between the adolescents and their parents. Themes of individuation and independence are prominent within this group.

The theme of their stories is not "he wants to play the violin" but "they are making him play the violin." Indeed, the theme of embracing the task as a result of an internalized wish to learn to play is expressed in only 14 percent of the stories told by the white American sample. It should be noted that this finding of tension resulting from perceived parental pressure is highly consistent with findings from earlier TAT responses of white Americans collected by Banfield (1958), De Vos (1973), and Vaughn (1988).

In many of the stories told by the white Americans, the child is depicted as being pressured to play the violin and responds in a variety of ways. In some stories, the child succumbs to parental pressure and eventually achieves mastery over a demanding task. For example:

> He is thinking. His parents are forcing him to take violin lessons. He is looking at the violin, thinking that maybe it won't be so hard. He takes the lessons and turns out to like them and turns into the next Mozart. Right now, he is wondering why his parents want him to do it, and then afterwards he understands that his parents just want him to be a well-rounded person. [Informant #429.30.74]

> He is practicing the violin, and he got frustrated because he couldn't play it well. He decided to just give up. He is feeling bad because he gave up and didn't try. His mom comes and makes him play it. Then he finally gets good at playing it, and he feels really happy again. [Informant #611.30.78]

In some stories, the child succumbs to parental pressure. For example:

> His parents bought him the violin to play, but he does not want to play it. He would rather do other things, but he learns to play it anyway. He is upset because his parents bought it for him without asking him. [Informant #131.30.76]

> His parents want him to take violin lessons, and they sent him to his room to practice until he got good. He doesn't like the violin and is sitting

there looking at it, thinking that maybe he should play it to get out of his room. But he really doesn't want to. He stares at it. He has played it and doesn't like it. Eventually, his parents come up and see that he hasn't played it at all. They make him play it anyway. He feels frustrated that he can't do what he wants, but he has to do what his parents say, no matter how stupid it seems. [Informant #111.30.75]

In other stories the child simply refuses to succumb to the parental pressure. In these stories, the child angrily refuses to do what the parents want him to do and chooses instead to follow his own path. For example:

The boy is in a music class. He is at home; his parents are making him practice the violin. He doesn't want to practice. He feels angry that his parents are making him do something that he doesn't want to do. He is refusing to play. His parents end up letting him quit since he doesn't like the violin. He joins something else that he does like. [Informant #660.30.76]

There is a boy, and for his birthday he is given a violin. His parents expect him to learn to play it, but he becomes frustrated and never plays it. His mom has a party and expects him to play it there. He sits at his desk and stares at it. The day before the party, he tells his mom the truth. She understands and forgives him. He asks if he can play a different instrument and she says that she will be just as proud. In the picture he is confused and mad that he can't play it. He feels like a disappointment to his parents. [Informant #718.30.78]

In other stories, the motivational ambivalence and battle of wills with the parents leads to the child's giving up on the task altogether. In the following case, the pressured child appears to "burn out":

This boy is named Frederick and is a child prodigy violinist. He also writes music, and he has an upcoming concert tonight. He is just beginning to realize that he is just a child and that his parents are pressuring him to be older than he is. The night of the concert, he makes the decision not to go to the concert and is feeling very depressed because he let his parents down. But yet, he had to do it; he couldn't deal with the stress anymore. [Informant #211.30.76]

In the most extreme cases, the child actively resists the parents' pressures by destroying the violin. In 10 percent of the stories, the child is depicted as responding to parental pressure by purposely destroying the violin. None of the Mexican or immigrant adolescents told stories in which the violin was purposely broken, and only 2 percent of the Mexican American youths did so. For example:

Once upon a time, a boy lived in a mansion. He had very rich parents. They made him take violin lessons. And every day he had to sit down and play the violin. He hated it and really wanted to play the piano. He couldn't get this piece of music. He would sit with his head in his hands. He felt like he was letting his parents down because they had such high expectations. One day the boy went downstairs and smashed the violin on the floor. And he never had to play it again. He learned to play the piano. [Informant #123.30.75]

The boy is sad because his parents want him to play the violin. He wants to be something else. He is sitting there and is looking at the violin and is trying to think about what to say to his parents. He throws his violin and breaks it. His parents get mad, and so he tells them he wants to play baseball. He is sad and angry, and he feels forced into something. He gets mad, and they finally realize that it is his life, and they encourage him to do what he wants. [Informant #220.30.76]

To recapitulate, the most common theme in the stories of the white American informants is frustration rooted in motivational ambivalence toward the task to be accomplished. In the most positive resolution, frustration resulting from parental pressures results in the child's mastering the task and appreciating the parental pressure. In the most negative resolution, the outcome is destruction of the violin.

RESPONSES OF MEXICAN ADOLESCENTS

The most significant feature of the stories told by the Mexican adolescents is self-motivated achievement. In 54 percent of these stories—and in only 14 percent of white American students'—the protagonist is depicted as self-motivated to accomplish the task. In these stories, the boy wants to play the violin and does not refer to taking on a task imposed by his parents. For example:

Since he was very small this boy liked the violin. He believes that in the future he will be able to become a good violinist and musician, so he works hard and concentrates on achieving his goal. [Informant #121.40.78]

This is a boy who has liked the violin since he was very young. He worked hard to learn how to play it. Because he was talented he became a great violinist. [Informant #127.40.78]

Rather than entering into a battle of wills with an imposing adult, an important preoccupation of the protagonist in these stories is succeeding at the difficult but self-imposed task. The boy wants to play the violin; the question is, can he do it? And perhaps more important, will he be good at it? In 22 percent of these stories, there is an explicit concern with adequacy. How is this resolved? In 34 percent

of the Mexican stories, the boy is depicted as working very hard to
learn to play the violin. In these stories, achieving success is the
product of long hours of diligent work. For example:

> This is a young boy that is concentrating on the violin. He's thinking that
> he's not going to be able to learn the notes of the melody that he wants
> to learn to play. But with time he keeps trying, and he eventually learns
> to play the melody. It comes out really well because of all his efforts.
> And when he gets it perfect, he calls his friends to show them what he
> has learned. They listen to him, and they tell him how beautiful the
> music is. They tell him his success is due to all his hard work. [Informant
> #429.40.78]

> There was a boy that wanted to learn to play the violin, but he did not
> know how. He is sitting there thinking and contemplating the future. He's
> thinking about whether he will be able to learn to play and become a great
> violinist. Just now he is imagining that he is in a concert hall giving a
> concert. After thinking about it he tells himself that he needs to put a lot
> of effort and enthusiasm into learning so that he will be able to achieve
> his dreams in the future. [Informant #917.40.78]

In the Mexican sample, the theme of frustration does not appear
to be a major preoccupation. In only 2 percent of the stories is
frustration brought up. Likewise, not a single story in the Mexican
sample suggests that the boy feels any anger about learning to play
the violin. It is, of course, impossible to determine from these data
whether Mexican adolescents are less prone to anger and frustration
than white American youths. We can say that in our sample, Mexican youths are much less likely to voice anger toward their parents
than white American adolescents.

An interesting feature of the Mexican stories is the frequency with
which the parents are depicted as nurturing, warm, and supportive
(in 16 percent of the stories). For example:

> This boy is looking at his violin that he inherited from his father. He
> doesn't have anyone to help him learn to play the violin. He is very sad,
> and he realizes that he doesn't know how to play the violin. His mother
> is going to help him find someone to help him learn to play. His family
> doesn't have any money to get anyone to help. She manages anyway, and
> when he gets to be older he has learned how to play. He learns to play very
> well. He learned when he was 15 years old and he began working, and
> with the money that he earned he took more and more lessons in order to
> become a better musician. [Informant #503.40.78]

A related theme of the Mexican stories is searching for a competent person to help the protagonist accomplish the difficult task (in
12 percent of the stories). For example:

The boy is sad because he doesn't know how to play the violin. He thinks that if someone could help him he might be able to learn, and then he would be happy. He gets help, his parents buy him a violin, and he eventually learns to play well. He becomes a great musician. [Informant #318.40.78]

He is thinking of the instrument that he sees before him. He is thinking that he wants to play it, and he is thinking of who he knows who might teach him to play it since he doesn't know how to play it. After someone teaches him, he will become a star and will earn a lot of money and will be able to buy anything he wants. [Informant #543.40.78]

Another theme expressed in these stories is pleasure that the boy derives from the activity (in 18 percent of the Mexican stories). Although the task may be depicted as difficult and challenging, it is intrinsically pleasurable.

The boy is sad because he doesn't know how to play the violin. But he works at it until he becomes excellent at it. He learns how to play, and he gives concerts and demonstrations at schools. He helps to teach other students how to play. He gets a lot of satisfaction from the help that he gives others as well as from his success. [Informant #417.40.78]

This is a boy who very much loves music, particularly the violin. He is dreaming that one day when he grows up he will become a great violinist. He decides to practice every day so he can become the best that he can be. [Informant #527.40.77]

Another feature of the Mexican stories is the prevalence of imagination and creative daydreaming attributed to the protagonist. In 32 percent of the stories the boy is depicted as experiencing a rich inner world of imagination and fantasy. Only 4 percent of the stories related by our white American informants and 2 percent of those told by our Mexican American informants refer to imaginary scenes. Here is a Mexican story about daydreaming:

He is thinking. He is thinking that he would like to play. He has a lot of dreams. He would like to play the violin. At this moment he is imagining that he is playing in front of a group of people and that he fascinates them, and he enjoys that. Therefore he tries to play the violin. Then he imagines that next to him is an angel playing. The angel also plays the violin. He begins to play the violin and together they arrive at this marvelous place. There are beautiful flowers that he had never seen before and beautiful birds, and all the birds are quiet. The birds stop singing to listen to his beautiful music. They find a beautiful waterfall and from the waterfall come some voices. The voices accompany their songs—the piece they are playing together. When he starts coming back, all of a sudden he trips on something and he falls down, and he opens his eyes and he realizes that he has been daydreaming all along. [Informant #117.40.70]

Financial deprivation and preoccupation with money emerge as themes in 12 percent of the Mexican stories. In many of these stories, the boy wants to play the violin but lacks the financial resources to purchase the violin or to pay for the lessons he would like to take. It should be noted that financial deprivation was also a theme in TAT stories told by refugees from Central America (Suárez-Orozco 1989) and by peasants living in an impoverished area of southern Italy (Banfield 1958). Here is a representative story:

> The boy is thinking about the violin, but he doesn't know how to play it. He wants to learn, but he is very poor and doesn't have the money to go to music school. His parents want to help him, but they do not have the money to give him what he wants. He still wants to play and decides that when he is older he will do so. He works hard so that one day he is able to pay for school, and he becomes a very good violinist. [Informant #320.40.77]

In summary, in the majority of the Mexican narratives, the boy successfully accomplishes the task at hand. The stories reveal an orientation toward self-motivated achievement.

RESPONSES OF MEXICAN IMMIGRANT ADOLESCENTS

Perhaps the most striking feature of the narratives articulated by the immigrant youngsters is the sadness attributed to the protagonist of the story. Sixty-six percent of the stories depict the boy as feeling sad, feeling low, or feeling bad. It should be noted that many TAT cards, including card 1, tend to elicit such themes (Bellak 1986). What is significant is the *relative* occurrence of such themes across groups. While only 16 percent of the Mexican adolescents attributed sadness to the protagonist, and 32 and 34 percent, respectively, of the white American and Mexican American informants told stories with such themes, the percentage nearly doubles for the Mexican immigrant sample. Here are some representative narratives:

> He's very sad because he doesn't know how to play the violin. But if somebody helps him he can learn it, and he can become a great musician. No one helps him. He will try to play it until he can do it. He succeeds. [Informant #110.10.74]

> He is sad because he is not able to play the violin and he doesn't know who he can ask to help him. He is trying to figure out how he might be able to play it. His mom is sad also because she asked him if he could play and he said no. She decided that he needed to get someone to help him.

> She finds someone to help him and teach him how to play, and he learns how to play and he feels really happy about it. [Informant #708.10.78]

The pervasive sadness found in the stories told by this sample of immigrant youngsters is consistent with the general pattern of reactive depression found in other studies of recent immigrants (Antokoletz 1993; Brenner 1990; Espin 1987; Garza-Guerrero 1974; Grinberg and Grinberg 1989; Kaminsky 1993; Padilla 1993). These immigrant youths are coping with the multiple losses of immigration as well as with culture shock. Many of their parents are unavailable to them either physically (because of long work hours) or emotionally (because of their own depressions triggered by the stresses of immigration).

As the Mexican youths did, the immigrants articulate an orientation toward self-motivated achievement (in 32 percent of the stories), often laced with concerns about adequacy (in 34 percent of the stories). Again, the protagonist has internalized a desire to play the violin and wonders whether he will be able to master the task. For example:

> He is looking at it, trying to use it—what parts it has. He feels worried and preoccupied because he is still unable to use it well. He will find out how to play this. He doesn't have help. He does it alone. He feels sad and thinks that he needs someone who can help him, show him how to use it. He will be happy when he knows how to use it. [Informant # 118.10.75]

> This boy wants to learn to play the violin but he does not know how to. He is thinking about how he will learn to play. He feels very sad because he is not able to play the violin. The violin is his father's. In the end he learns how to play it and he feels good. [Informant #111.10.74]

In 26 percent of the stories the boy is able to overcome his sense of inadequacy. In only 2 percent of the stories does he fail. In 8 percent of the stories, the outcome remains unresolved.

Note, however, that many of these stories appear to be about small victories. Whereas the Mexican informants often told of important large-scale successes and fame, many stories told by immigrant adolescents reveal much smaller successes. Rather than playing in orchestras all over the world or being applauded by many, the protagonist of the immigrant stories, when he succeeds, merely learns how to play. The immigrants' expectations for success seem to be lower. For example:

> This is a boy that liked to play the violin, but he didn't know how. He is sad, but he takes classes on how to learn. After a time he learns to play and he is content. [Informant #221.10.77]

This little boy wanted to learn how to play the violin, and he feels bad because there is no one who helps him. He's thinking of what he should do to learn it. He asks his parents for help, and he learns to play. [Informant #211.10.73]

An important theme of the immigrants' stories is searching for help from others. Twenty-six percent of the immigrant stories depict the boy turning to a family member, friend, or teacher for help; that occurred in only 12 percent of the stories told by Mexican and Mexican American youths and 4 percent of those told by white American youths. For example:

He is thinking about the fact that he cannot play the violin even though he really wants to. It is because he does not know how, and he feels desperate about this. So he tells his parents that he does not know how to play the violin, and they tell him that he needs to take a class to learn how. So he goes to his teacher and the teacher helps him, and little by little he learns how to play. [Informant #507.10.78]

He feels really sad because he was practicing the violin but he can't play a song that he had heard and wanted to play. Later, he asks a friend to help. He gets help and he practices a lot and his friends help him to learn to play well. [Informant #570.10.78]

This turning to others for help is more evident in the stories told by all of the Latinos than in those told by the white Americans. That the theme occurs most often in the stories related by the immigrants may be related to the disorienting anxiety (Grinberg and Grinberg 1989) experienced by immigrants and the need for a cultural interpreter to assist them in understanding the new culture and in accomplishing difficult tasks in a new setting.

Just as the Mexicans did, the immigrants told stories in which the protagonist derives pleasure from the process of mastering the task (16 percent).

Ten percent of the stories refer to daydreaming and to the imaginary life of the protagonist. Although the immigrants' stories include these themes much less often than the Mexicans', they occur more often in the immigrant sample than in either the white American or the Mexican American sample (4 and 2 percent, respectively).

Mexican immigrants depicted the parental figures as less nurturing than did the Mexicans in Mexico. They related fewer stories, however, in which the boy feels pressure from his parents than did the white American adolescents.

In the stories in which the violin is broken (14 percent), the breakage is always the result of an accident rather than a purposeful act. At times there is also an anxious quality to these stories. For example:

> This boy was trying to play the violin, and he accidentally broke a string. He feels sad because he has to finish an assignment and now he can't. He can't finish it until his parents arrive and buy him a new string. And he won't be able to finish one of his assignments that his music teacher gave him. His parents arrive, and they scold him because he hasn't finished his homework and because he'd been playing a lot with the strings, and broke one. [Informant #403.10.73]

Overall, then, the stories told by Mexican immigrants resemble those told by the Mexicans in their focus on achievement and adequacy. However, the immigrants told more stories about actively seeking help, and their successes had more to do with basic competence than with fame and fortune. This group stands out for its telling of the most narratives imputing sadness to the protagonist.

RESPONSES OF MEXICAN AMERICAN ADOLESCENTS

In the stories told by the second-generation Mexican Americans, we encountered some themes also present in the other groups' stories. For example, like the white Americans' stories, many of the narratives articulated by the second-generation youths told of authority figures (parents, teachers, and others) pressuring the protagonist to perform the task (in 30 percent of the stories). Likewise the percentage of stories in which the predominant theme is self-motivated achievement is comparable to the white American sample (18 percent and 14 percent, respectively). The following exemplify self-motivated achievement stories told by Mexican American adolescents:

> This is a guy and he saw a violin on his dad's table. He had not seen it before this. He was trying to figure out how it worked. He got the stick and he started putting it against the violin. It makes noise, so he started playing music. He wasn't very good at first and he waited until his dad came home. His dad taught him how to play and he really liked it. So after school he took lessons and played a lot, and when he was grown up he became a popular violin player and artist. [Informant #513.20.78]

> The grandfather died; the boy missed him and remembered him when he looked at the violin. Every night before bed he would look at the violin. He started to play. Every day he played, and he got better and better. His parents put him in a class to help him with the violin. Eventually he played in concerts and knew that his grandfather would be proud. He feels sad because his grandfather can't be there with him. [Informant #415.20.77]

Note that in the above stories self-motivation leads to success in an atmosphere of social interdependence (e.g., the boy's success is due partly to the inspiration of the grandfather and is achieved with the help of a parent or with the parents' emotional support). In these stories, hard work is involved, but success is socially mediated: help or inspiration from others is crucial.

Notably, 28 percent of the second-generation narratives refer to threatened failure to achieve the task at hand. This contrasts with 2 percent among the Mexican and Mexican immigrant groups and 4 percent among white Americans. Although many of the stories told by the Mexicans and the immigrants raise concerns about adequacy, they also include a strong sense of hope and optimism for the future (i.e., the initial inadequacy is overcome through hard work, and success is finally achieved). In a number of the stories told by the second generation, however, there is a disturbing preoccupation with failure and a sense of hopelessness. In many such stories, the future looks bleak:

> The child was very interested in playing the violin in the beginning. Now he doesn't know what to do without any help. Now he is going through stages where he puts in too much effort and nothing is happening. So he is feeling depressed. He loses his interest in music and now has a mental block. He can't solve other problems. He gives up all interest in music and has a mental block. He loses confidence in solving problems. [Informant #214.20.73]

> He is trying to learn to play the violin, but he is having trouble and he is getting frustrated and is about to give up on it. He was picking it up, practicing before the picture. His mom wanted him to play the violin. It ends up with him continuing to practice, but he is never good at it so he quits. After she heard him play, his mom agreed with his decision to quit. [Informant #110.20.74]

> He probably went to try out for a music class and he didn't make it. So he is sad. He looks sad because he didn't make it. He goes home and tells his mom what happened—that he didn't get to make it. He fails. [Informant #116.20.73]

> There was this little boy who wanted to play the violin. He had the violin but no money to take classes. He got a job and worked and worked for days. Finally, he got money but he couldn't find where to go to take classes. He looked and looked and found someplace to go and learn. He took classes but couldn't learn how to play it. One day, he was playing in the park with some friends and he kicked a ball and broke a window. He went to his parents and told them and asked them to pay for the window. They said "no." He either would have to work or sell his violin, they told him. He went to his room and sat down and stared at it and thought about it. He decided to sell it. He feels sad because he was starting to learn to play it and let it go. [Informant #360.20.78]

In some of these stories the protagonist attempts to engage with the task; he tries to play the violin but eventually quits, realizing that he is not competent. In others, the protagonist cannot learn without help or tries but is unable to play adequately and is disheartened. In yet other narratives, his worry about failure is related to obstacles in the environment that prevent him from taking on the challenge. In these stories, the boy is trying to learn the violin but must give it up because of factors beyond his control. In some cases, though the protagonist struggles with the threat of failure, he eventually finds a solution by asking for help from others.

In 12 percent of the stories told by Mexican Americans in response to card 1, the protagonist seeks help from others. This figure is comparable to that in the stories told by Mexicans, significantly higher than in the stories told by Americans, and lower than in the stories told by immigrants.

A sense of frustration is found in 14 percent of the stories told by the second-generation Mexican Americans. This is higher than in the stories told by Mexicans in Mexico or by Mexican immigrants in the United States. However, it is lower than in the stories related by the white American sample (50 percent included frustration themes). A sense of anger is revealed in fully 20 percent of the stories told by the Mexican American sample. This is significantly higher than in the stories told by the Mexican or immigrant samples (0 percent and 6 percent, respectively). The theme of anger was found in 14 percent of the white Americans' stories. It is recognized that anger and frustration are conceptually related concepts; American adolescents chose the word "frustration" more frequently, while the Mexican American adolescents chose the words "mad" or "angry."

The discontinuities in the narratives told by the Mexicans in Mexico, the Mexican immigrants, and the second-generation Mexican Americans are revealing. Whereas Mexican and immigrant students seemed to believe that hard work would bring success, many of the second-generation youths told stories in which failure was the outcome. The energy and faith directed toward "making it" that are characteristic of the Mexican and immigrant students seem to have significantly diminished by the second generation.

We relate these findings to the differences facing immigrants and second-generation youngsters. Typically, immigrants endure their affective losses by concentrating on the material gains to be made by exploiting the new opportunities in a host country. Members of the second generation, on the other hand, do not measure their current state in terms of life back in Mexico. Rather, they use as their standard the ideals and expectations of the majority society (Suárez-Orozco and Suárez-Orozco 1994). Using this standard, many Mexican Americans may fall short of their aspirations. Racism, disparagement, and lack of equal opportunity may compromise the faith of at-risk youths and reduce their ability to succeed. These may well be among the reasons for the disturbingly high dropout rates among second- and third-generation Mexican American youths (Bean et al. 1991; Chapa 1988; Kantrowitz and Rosaldo 1991).

To summarize, the biggest difference between the stories told by the Mexican Americans and those told by the other samples is in the prevalence of the theme of failure. Some themes overlap with those found in the stories told by the white American sample (such as outside pressure to perform the task and the protagonist's rejection of that outside pressure). Other themes of the second generation's narratives clearly overlap with those found in the stories told by Mexican and immigrant youths (such as seeking help from others and being motivated to achieve in order to help others).

Affiliative Achievement

The responses to TAT card 1 are in keeping with the narratives told in response to TAT card 2. As we discussed in Chapter 4, Mexican and Mexican immigrant students told more achievement-oriented stories in response to card 2 than did either of the American-born groups. In addition, the achievement stories narrated by Latino youths are typically quite different from those narrated by white American students. The achievement stories told by Mexican students in response to card 2 tend to be about self-motivation—the protagonist works hard to achieve success, *but she does so with the aim of being able to help her parents.* It is interesting to note that, of all groups, it is the immigrant students who reveal the greatest concern with achieving to help others (see stories in Chapter 4). Whereas white American students articulate narratives in which achieving success is a means of gaining independence from the family, Latinos typically offer stories in which achieving success or "becoming somebody" means returning to give back to the family.

Our data suggest several important issues in reference to earlier work on achievement motivation. A key point is that Mexican youths in Mexico and Mexican immigrants displayed much higher concerns with achievement than either white Americans or second-generation Mexican Americans. In fact, we were surprised to find an achievement motivation of white American youths that is even lower than that found in earlier studies.

Many white American students approach education ambivalently; they see it as a necessary frustration that will ensure a good job and the good life. This is especially significant when we take into account that, in our sample, the white youths came from the highest socio-economic status of all our informants. Yet they displayed the least concern about achieving in school and highly ambivalent attitudes toward schooling, particularly toward school authorities.

That Mexican-born youths (both Mexicans in Mexico and Mexican immigrants) revealed more self-initiative and less ambivalence about school and school authorities than white American youths is a finding that is not in keeping with cultural stereotypes or with expectations based on the literature. Carter and Segura, for example, reviewed a number of studies that assessed U.S. teachers' views of Mexican cultural values and orientations. Traits that were frequently imputed by educators to Mexican students included fatalism, present-time orientation, low level of aspiration, and non-competitiveness (Carter and Segura 1979: 83). "Noncompetitive" can be read as meaning non–achievement oriented. As noted earlier, the classic definition of achievement orientation given by McClelland et al. is "competition with a standard of excellence" (1953: 161). McClelland's (1961) pioneering studies established that self-motivation was the predominant motivation for achievement among his white informants. The findings of our study were somewhat different: self-motivated achievement was of greater concern among Mexican-origin youths than among white American youths.

These findings are important when we take into consideration Ogbu's contention that "in general American social scientists . . . tend to assume explicitly or implicitly that the main cause of school failure lies in the background of the children" (Ogbu 1983: 3). By "background," Ogbu means genetic, linguistic, cultural, psychological, and sociocultural characteristics. The "cultural deprivation" model articulated by Bloom, Davis, and Hess asserted that school failure among minorities can be attributed to "experiences in the home which do not transmit the cultural patterns necessary for the types of learning characteristic of the schools and larger society" (1965: 4). In the case of Latinos, and more specifically Mexican-origin populations, some have argued that cultural background is somehow responsible for the relatively high levels of school failure and dropping out.

The findings of our study do not support these contentions. Our findings suggest that the Mexican cultural background does emphasize self-initiated achievement as well as the notion that hard work is critical for success, although interdependence, familism, and obtaining help from others are valued more highly than they are by white Americans (see also Delgado-Gaitan and Trueba 1991; Trueba 1989b; and Trueba et al. 1993).

The achievement-individualism cluster identified among white Americans in the classic studies of McClelland and his associates does not explain achievement motivation among Latinos (or, for that matter, other ethnic groups—see De Vos 1973). Among Latinos and other ethnic groups, achievement motivation flourishes in an atmosphere of affiliation and interdependence. Our data suggest that Latino families and Latino culture in general do indeed foster the values and behaviors that are conducive to achieving in schools. Therefore, whatever problems Latinos face in U.S. schools cannot be the consequence of so-called cultural or familial deficits.

While our data reveal that Mexican youths in Mexico and Mexican immigrants believe that school is the key to a better future, among more acculturated Latinos we found diminished expectations. The more acculturated students become, the more skeptical and ambivalent they are about schools. In many ways the concerns of Mexican American youths overlap with those of Mexican-origin and white American students.

These findings suggest that the problems in the motivational dynamics and schooling experiences of second-generation Mexican American youths cannot be attributed to cultural background per se. We must conclude, then, that a shift occurs in the psychosocial patterning of achievement motivation of Mexican-origin populations after they acquire minority status in the United States. Mexican American youths may take on the white American adolescents' ambivalence toward authority and schools. In addition, other factors such as the stresses of minority status, discrimination, alienating schools, economic hardship, and pressure to work may all contribute to the high school dropout rate in this population. Further studies will be required to carefully examine the nature of this generational discontinuity.

CHAPTER 6

Anxious Neighbors

Immigration has become an issue of global urgency. In Japan, the United States, western Europe, and elsewhere immigration is in the forefront of public debate. Today few topics are as controversial as asylum policy and undocumented immigration. Immigration captures many of the contradictions, paradoxes, and tensions of post-industrial societies.

At a time of widespread economic uncertainty among native workers there is nevertheless, in some industries, a structural dependence on migrant and immigrant workers (Cornelius, Martin, and Holli-field 1994). In the "post-wall" era in which free trade and the free circulation of goods are being reaffirmed by ambitious international agreements, there are increasingly loud cries to build new walls to keep immigrants out. In all countries facing an "immigrant problem" there is widespread fear of drowning in the floods of new arrivals. Even countries that thrive on international interdependence and that celebrate their multicultural societies are struggling with cultural anxieties about the integration of the new immigrants of color.

Although some industries could not survive without the new immigrants, immigrants have also been singled out as the cause of everything from economic recession to crime epidemics. The new arrivals are disparaged by ethnic stereotypes characterizing them as lazy, parasitic, and crime prone. In many countries there is now a widespread perception that immigrants create great public costs and generate no substantial benefits.

We have argued that such disparagement has particularly poisonous effects on the children of immigrants. During adolescence the children of immigrants must struggle to develop a sense of identity. In some cases, an outcome of such psychosocial violence is to reject the society that rejects them and adopt "countercultural" identities. They may join gangs and develop ambivalent attitudes toward the authority figures and the institutions of the dominant culture, including schools. This disparagement of the minority by the majority seems to have little to do with the culture of origin of the minority group. It occurs in the second and third generations among diverse groups in various postindustrial settings. It is happening to second-generation Moroccans in Brussels (Hermans 1993), to Turks in Germany (Kinzer 1993), to Koreans in Japan (Lee and De Vos 1981), and to Latinos in the United States.

In the preceding chapters we examined some key aspects of the experiences of Latinos as immigrants and minorities and how those experiences reflected and affected family dynamics and achievement motivation. We considered some of the challenges of conducting interdisciplinary and comparative research. In our study we experimented with various methods, borrowing freely from psychological anthropology and cross-cultural psychology. Although rewarding, such interdisciplinary enterprises, we found out, create their own unique problems. We discussed some of them in Chapter 3.

The complexity of examining aspects of the experiences of four groups in two countries caused us to proceed with methodological caution. Because we did not want to end up comparing Mexican apples with American oranges, we used a variety of techniques to elicit comparable data across the groups. Of all the tools we used, the Thematic Apperception Test (TAT) was the most costly (see also Lindzey 1961). Gathering, transcribing, translating, coding, scoring, and interpreting narratives is simply a herculean task. The TAT is, however, very good at picking up subtle group differences that may have otherwise been overlooked.

We made every effort to develop a priori TAT rating scales that would be both valid and reliable. However, after the stories were collected and read we realized that we could obtain even more information by using additional categories to analyze the data. We chose to be flexible instead of adhering rigidly to what Cowan et al. refer to as "methodological imperialism" (1993: 472). In making cross-cultural comparisons, the goal of research should be to document expected group characteristics *and* to describe and analyze actual differences and similarities between groups. Examining data through a microscope, though methodologically sound, may detect certain types of trees only to miss the forest.

Our findings both surprised us and did not surprise us. Among white American adolescents we found an ambivalence toward authority and schooling, higher levels of family conflict, a peer group orientation, and less achievement orientation than among Mexicans. One might say that individualism has its discontents or that autonomy is closely related to anomie. The data revealed that white American youths are concerned about achieving independence and are likely to become frustrated with authority figures such as parents, teachers, and principals. Our data suggest that among these youths, adolescence is a period of significant turmoil, which is particularly revealed by struggles with authority figures.

We had not expected white American adolescents to reveal so much conflict with authority. We struggled with this finding. However, considering Gorer's (1963) classic analysis of American culture, our findings are not so surprising.

Mainstream Americans consider adolescence a more highly conflictful stage of development than other cultures do. An informal sampling of the cultural expectations and values portrayed in popular films and television programs aimed at children and adolescents would also confirm our findings. The mass media portray adolescence as a period of turmoil, conflict, and intergenerational misunderstandings and frustrations. Parents and other authority figures are often depicted as buffoons who know little, do not understand their children, and cannot be relied upon. Children, on the other hand, are often depicted as precocious little people who must resolve dilemmas on their own and who can truly rely only on their peers. These portrayals are in keeping with the attitudes revealed by our own empirical research.

Among Mexican adolescents in Mexico we found evidence of less conflict with authority than is generally expected with American adolescents. Mexican youths revealed less ambivalent and more respectful attitudes toward authority figures. We also found evidence of a high family orientation and less conflictful family relations. Among Mexican adolescents there appears to be less peer group orientation than among white Americans. Our data suggest that Mexican students are highly achievement oriented, though in the context of helping others rather than themselves. The Mexican adolescents reveal a pattern of self-motivated achievement and an understanding of the connection between hard work and success that contrast sharply with the conventional stereotype of the Mexican culture held by many mainstream Americans.

Our data suggest that newly arrived Mexican immigrants maintain a healthy commitment to the family, a high achievement orientation, and a conviction that hard work and school are keys to a better future. The paradigmatic pattern of motivation among Mexican-born youths is self-initiated achievement *in order to help others*. Our data suggest that Latino culture cannot be singled out as "causing" the problem of school underachievement among U.S. Latinos.

We also found among these adolescents a preoccupation with losses and a sense of sadness related to the upheaval of immigration. This is highly consistent with previous research findings of reactive depression resulting from immigration losses and stresses (Brenner 1990; Cervantes, Salgado de Snyder, and Padilla 1989; Espin 1987; Grinberg and Grinberg 1989; Padilla 1993; Padilla, Alvarez, and Lindholm 1986). The mourning of losses endured in the context of immigration appears to be typical. Not only are immigrant youths preoccupied with their own losses, but the stresses and losses of their parents affect their psychological ability to help their children meet the challenges of adolescence and adjust to the new culture. As parents' psychological resources are consumed by their own losses, culture shock, and financial needs in the new country, they have less time and energy to help their children work through their losses and stresses. Under these conditions Latino youths are most likely to gravitate toward peers and in some cases gangs.

It seems to us that among Latino immigrant students the wish to help the family leads to different school outcomes. Some immigrant students work hard in school with the dream of achieving a future that will enable them to "become somebody" and help their families. Other students feel the need to start working as soon as possible. These students may reluctantly leave school, not because they are ambivalent about it but because they feel obligated to work full time to help the family.

Our data suggest that second-generation Mexican American youths are truly the children of two worlds. We found that Mexican American youths maintain a family orientation that is similar to that of their Mexican-born peers. We also found less family conflict among them than the clinical literature had suggested. Mexican Americans operate in two cultural realms and are preoccupied with many of the issues that concern adolescents in both cultures. Issues faced by the second generation are in some respects different from those faced by the immigrant generation; second-generation youths reveal less sadness, but frustration appears to be significant.

Mexican American youths seem to adopt some aspects of the dominant American paradigm of adolescent ambivalence toward authority and schools. When asked directly, all groups voice a conviction that schooling provides status mobility. However, when we analyzed the results of tests that measure these issues less directly (e.g., the sentence completion test, the problem situation task, and the TAT), we picked up certain motivational ambivalences among second-generation students. We believe that the decrease in achievement orientation and increase in ambivalence toward schools may be largely accounted for by two factors. First, second-generation youths are adopting the ambivalences of white American youths. Second, they are responding to the prejudices they encounter in school and in society in general and to the stresses of life in the barrio.

Some of the second-generation youths revealed less confidence in the school system as the key to status mobility. Whereas Mexican and immigrant students displayed a faith that through hard work in school success was possible, many second-generation youths focused on failure. This is in keeping with the findings of other researchers (see Gibson and Ogbu 1991).

The energy and faith directed toward "making it" that are characteristic of the Mexican and immigrant youths seem to diminish significantly among the second generation. We relate these findings to the difficulties relating to second-generation minority status. Immigrants typically endure their affective and material losses by concentrating on the material gains to be made by exploiting new opportunities in the host country. We also believe that immigrants develop a "dual frame of reference" to measure their current state against their lives in the home country.

Members of the second generation are typically unable to measure their current state against life in Mexico, and so they use as their standard the ideals and expectations of the majority society. Using this standard, many members of the second generation fall short of their aspirations. Racism, disparagement, and lack of equal opportunity may compromise their faith in their ability to succeed. A compromised sense of self-esteem seems to be a corollary of the second generation's minority status (Padilla 1993; Padilla, Alvarez, and Lindholm 1986) and may be related to the high dropout rate among second- and third-generation Mexican American youths (Bean et al. 1991; Chapa 1988). Successful Latino role models may be effective in conveying hope to second-generation youths who seem concerned with failure.

Second-generation youths must navigate between the cultural familism of Hispanics and the American mainstream cultural ideal of independence and making it on one's own. Those working with second-generation youths would be wise to look for psychosocial problems and conflicts caused by the stresses of immigration and minority status. Given that familism is an enduring trait, the family must remain a significant point of reference for understanding this population (Diebba and Montiel 1978; Falicov 1980, 1982; Falicov and Karrer 1984; Karrer 1987; Sluzki 1979; Vega 1990; Vega et al. 1986).

It is very important, we believe, to consider the different psychosocial worlds inhabited by immigrants and the second generation. Immigrants typically set out with a relatively clear set of objectives. They want to do better than they did before, actively using the host society's institutions, including the school system, as avenues for status mobility. Although they may freely cross the cultural borders between the "old" and "new" worlds, immigrants are typically firmly anchored in their identity. They have a sense of security about who they are: outsiders hoping to "move up."

The second generation, on the other hand, faces some very different issues. Perhaps even more than nonimmigrant children, the children of immigrants become the repository of their parents' expectations. But their self-identity may be less securely anchored than their parents', particularly in situations of marginality and ethnic conflict (Vigil 1988a, 1988b).

The school, perhaps more than any other social institution, is an arena in which many of the problems facing Latinos, both first and second generation, are played out. Educators exposed to Latino immigrant children are often surprised to see how vigorously the new arrivals pursue their dream of a better tomorrow through education. These same educators are puzzled and distressed to see the more acculturated second- and third-generation Latinos grow disaffected with the school system, fail to thrive in school environments, and turn to gangs or drop out (see Rumbaut and Cornelius 1995). Their expectations, raised by the eagerness of the new arrivals, are rooted in a simplistic notion of what it means to "assimilate."

Many now are asking the question: are the new immigrants good for the United States? The question asked less often is arguably as important: is the United States still good to immigrants? Our study and others confirm what many already know: immigrants bring a special energy (perhaps to compensate for all the losses that are inherent in immigration) that is positive, when well harnessed. Study after study has shown that new immigrants, whether they are Punjabi Sikhs in California (Gibson 1988), Hmong in Minnesota (McNall et al. 1994), or Japanese in Chicago (De Vos 1973), display achievement patterns that surpass those of the native-born population. Mexican immigrants fit the same pattern. Our study suggests that immigrants want to learn and to work hard to achieve the dream of a better tomorrow, while maintaining their separate sense of identity.

However, the violence, discrimination, and other obstacles immigrants encounter affect the self-identity of many youths, particularly in the second generation. Throughout American history, many ethnic groups have been the target of prejudice (Allport 1979). Previous waves of immigrants from Japan, China, and eastern and Mediterranean Europe all had to contend with discrimination and hostilities. However, some groups have been singled out for disparagement. The Japanese were believed to be sneaky and untrustworthy, but never lazy, crime prone, or intellectually inferior. The Jews were thought to be preoccupied with money and loyal only to each other, but they were also said to be industrious and clever. Latinos have had to contend with similar insidious and destructive stereotypes. Furthermore, as Latin Americans continue to arrive, the old stereotypes are sustained. They have been particularly devastating for adolescents, whose main task is to develop a positive sense of who they are. The negative images of Latinos reproduced in the media, in the teachers' lounge, and in books include references to lazy, slow-witted, crime-prone parasites who are undeservingly feeding on American wealth.

We believe that these stereotypes are the result of paranoia. As we saw in Chapter 1, immigrants from Mexico are among the most vulnerable and exploited of all groups in the United States. Anyone driving from San Diego to San Francisco will likely see thousands of Mexican workers laboring under the brutal sun for the minimum wage. Likewise, as teachers working with newly arrived immigrants attest, the great majority of the immigrant youngsters are hardworking and highly appreciative of opportunities to learn. Immigrants are seldom "the problem." The serious social problems associated with immigrants tend to be created by paranoid fear, psychosocial violence, and disparagement.

The United States will continue to be a country of interdependence and diversity, and its future will likely rest on how society deals with the inevitable tensions, paradoxes, and contradictions of ever-changing social formations.

The Need for Strangers

PROPOSITION 187 AND THE
IMMIGRATION MALAISE

In November 1994, California voters overwhelmingly approved Proposition 187, known as the Save Our State initiative. In part, the proposition claims that the people of California "have suffered and are suffering economic hardship caused by the presence of illegal aliens in this state" and "that they have suffered and are suffering personal injury and damage caused by the criminal conduct of illegal aliens in this state" (Proposition 187 1994: 91).

Proposition 187 will, among other things, exclude an estimated 300,000 undocumented immigrant children from elementary and secondary public schools. The proposition's incendiary language confirms that hysteria over immigration has become one of the principal discontents of our civilization. This phenomenon is by no means limited to California or even the United States. With well over 100 million immigrants worldwide, immigration today is a global issue (Cornelius, Martin, and Hollifield 1994).

In October 1994, voters in Flanders, Belgium, elected a member of the neo-Nazi Vlaams Blok mayor of the elegant city of Antwerp (*Economist* 1994: 68). The winning party's slogan was: "Our people first, seal our borders, send the immigrants home." Likewise in Austria the leader of the far-right Freedom Party, Joerg Haider, recently announced his intention to make immigration a key theme in the 1996 electoral campaign. In an inversion of Tolstoy's famous dictum, when it comes to immigration all the families of the postindustrial democratic world are unhappy in the same way.

A large part of today's immigration crisis in the postindustrial democracies is of their own making. Policies designed to recruit inexpensive foreign workers have spurred—via transnational labor-

recruiting networks, family reunification policies, and wage differentials—much of the recent movement of undocumented populations.[1]
Even in the midst of severe anti-immigrant sentiment, the need
for cheap foreign workers seems to remain constant (Lydia Chavez
1994). In post–Proposition 187 California, agricultural enterprises
fear labor shortages. Conservative analyst Martin Anderson—a domestic policy adviser to President Ronald Reagan and now a Fellow
at the Hoover Institution—has recently advocated that California
initiate new "guest-worker programs, under which foreign nationals
who wish to work in the United States could do so lawfully, with
dignity, with no threat of being hunted down and deported" (quoted
in del Olmo 1995: 2).[2]

Some immigration experts have argued that such guest-worker
programs offer a short-term fix that produces long-term problems.
Doris Meissner, the current Immigration and Naturalization Commissioner, has wisely noted that "the notion that a country can add
workers to its labor force and not residents to its population is fundamentally flawed" (quoted in *Migration News* 1995: 3). Furthermore,
there are data that suggest that in certain sectors of the economy
employers often prefer to hire the relatives and friends of immigrant workers they trust (see Waldinger 1994), thus generating new
cycles of undocumented migration. Quite often, as temporary migrant workers become enmeshed in life in the new setting, many
choose not to return home but rather settle permanently in the
new land.

Recent immigration has been a by-product of stunning global economic and political transformations. Liberalization of third world
economies—in much of Latin America engineered by U.S.-trained
economists—has stimulated migratory patterns. In Mexico and Central America, a fierce pattern of competitive allocation of land between land-poor agriculturists and powerful transnational interests
will continue to be a factor in immigration. Over the next two decades economic transformations caused by NAFTA (the North American Free Trade Agreement) will "push" perhaps 2 to 3 million Mexican farmers off the land.

Other transnational economic developments go hand-in-hand with
today's immigration flows—be they legal or undocumented. The
U.S. Treasury has estimated that the January 1995 devaluation by 50
percent of Mexican currency (resulting in the loss of an estimated
250,000 jobs in the first three months of 1995) could increase undocumented immigration to the United States by as much as 30 percent
(Sanger 1995). Indeed, during January and February 1995 the numbers

of undocumented immigrants apprehended at the southern border jumped by 30 percent over the previous year's levels.

Proposition 187: Politics as Catharsis

Catharsis is a discharge of emotions that does not necessarily cure the underlying pathology. Proposition 187 may have served California voters as an outlet for anger and frustration over the severe economic recession that hit California so hard in the 1990s. There are anxieties about diminishing expectations (Krugman 1994), crowded schools, and rapid demographic changes—political minorities are fast becoming California's demographic majority. In addition, the state has recently been shaken by seemingly unending cycles of deadly and expensive natural disasters, including earthquakes, urban wildfires, and floods, which have done billions of dollars' worth of damage. Then there was the rage and terror that followed the Rodney King beating and the urban upheaval precipitated by the verdict in the first trial. Whereas the underlying frustrations are varied and complex, lashing out at immigrants concentrates much anxiety and frustration on a single target.

Proposition 187 is both a beginning and an end. It is the beginning of a new kind of marginality in California. It is also the beginning of a long and costly legal battle over whether it is constitutional to bar undocumented immigrant children from schools and from other publicly funded services (Ayres 1994b: 16; Cleeland 1994).

Proposition 187 can be seen as the climax of a series of developments we outlined in Chapter 1. In the months leading to the November 1994 vote, several polls suggested that many Americans believed "immigration was now harmful" (Mills 1994: 18). Many Americans believe there are too many immigrants coming into the United States. With over 700,000 documented immigrants and an estimated 300,000 unauthorized immigrants arriving each year, a historic high, many believe that immigration must be stopped altogether.

Indeed, sensing a growing anti-immigrant sentiment in the population, President Clinton made clear that he would not let Republicans monopolize the immigration issue. As he said in his 1995 State of the Union address:

All Americans are rightly disturbed by the large numbers of illegal aliens entering our country. The jobs they hold might otherwise be held by citizens or legal immigrants; the public services they use impose burdens on our taxpayers. That's why our administration has moved aggressively to

secure our borders more by hiring a record number of new border guards,
by deporting twice as many criminal aliens as ever before, by cracking
down on illegal hiring, and by barring welfare benefits to illegal aliens.
(Clinton 1995: 8)

By thus relying on superficial but politically powerful clichés—undocumented immigrants take jobs away from citizens, burden public
services, and are criminals in need of deportation—the president did
little to inject rationality into today's increasingly angry immigration debate.[3]

Many Americans seem distressed because the great majority of
today's immigrants are culturally and ethnically unlike the great
bulk of the earlier, European-origin immigrants. Today, 81 percent of
all new arrivals are from Latin America, the Caribbean, and Asia. In
1940, in contrast, 70 percent of all immigrants came from Europe.

Some claim that the new immigrants and their children are not
"assimilating" into mainstream society as successfully as previous
waves of European immigrants. Those opposing immigration have
asserted that new arrivals share certain cultural values and attitudes
that are simply not compatible with the norms of the dominant culture and that lead to school failure and social malaise (Brimelow
1992, 1995).

Yet empirical data do not support this position. Kao and Tienda
(1995), in their study of 24,599 students, found that immigrant students tend to receive better grades, score higher on standardized
tests, and aspire to college at a greater rate than their third-generation
U.S.-born peers. Likewise, our data presented in Chapters 4 and 5
strongly suggest that Latino immigrants are highly family- and
achievement-oriented. Paradoxically, in the United States such
family and achievement values are most frequently espoused by the
very conservative political groups that are now calling for immigration restrictions.

Advocates of Proposition 187 have made the explosive charge that
the new arrivals contribute disproportionately to the problem of
crime in America. This psychologically charged indictment, as we
examined in Chapter 1, is drawn from powerful paranoid images of
the immigrant "Other" as persecutorial criminal. It is simply not
based on any serious empirical evidence. If anything, the only reasonable empirical study of undocumented immigrants and crime
suggests that they are far more likely to be the *targets* of violent
crime than its perpetrators (Wolf 1988).

Finally, advocates of Proposition 187, and others, have claimed that
new immigrants become an overwhelming drain on the economy (see

Huddle 1993).[4] As we examined in Chapter 1, such claims ignore the substantial contributions to the economy that both legal and undocumented immigrants make through taxes, immigrant businesses, and the like. In Chapter 1 we also noted that it is extremely difficult to calculate in a meaningful way the "costs" and "benefits" associated with a phenomenon as complex and multifaceted as immigration. It is even more difficult to estimate the "costs" and "benefits" associated with the problem of undocumented immigrants—the data are simply not good enough.[5]

In short, there is reason to be critical of the assertion that immigrants—both documented and undocumented—are the cause of "economic hardship," as the proponents of Proposition 187 claimed. Some of the anxiety generated by the new immigration has to do with the fact that the federal government keeps the great bulk of the taxes paid by immigrants, whereas the local governments are responsible for providing most services that immigrants use, including health care and education.[6] George Borjas, a controversial voice in the immigration debate, concludes his somewhat sensationalist essay entitled "Tired, Poor, on Welfare" with a thoroughly uncontroversial assessment: "At the national level, therefore, it would not be far-fetched to conclude that immigration is near a washout" (1994: 78). Not far-fetched at all! And Linda Chavez, the executive director of the U.S. Commission on Civil Rights during the Reagan administration—hardly an advocate of open borders—writes: "Studies in the 1980s estimated that both legal and illegal immigrants were net contributors to the California economy, paying more in taxes than they received in services and creating jobs rather than displacing American workers" (Linda Chavez 1994: 33).

There is enough evidence, therefore, to suggest that the current hysteria over immigration has little to do with "objective" measures of economic "costs" and "benefits." Indeed, we concur with Nathan Glazer's observation that "economics in general can give no large answer as to what the immigration policy of the nation should be" (1994: 42).

In addition to its superficial assumptions about immigration and the economy and immigration and crime, Proposition 187 is based on the equally problematic assertion that "California's bounty of social services is the magnet drawing illegal immigrants across the border" (Noble 1994: 11). Systematic studies suggest that it is simply not true that immigrants—documented or undocumented—are drawn by the "magnet" of the welfare state. Indeed, studies suggest that most new arrivals come in search of better employment opportunities or to reunite with family members already in the United States (Cornelius 1993a: 1). Moreover, undocumented immigrants are already banned from receiving most social services.

The Need for Strangers

If the sometimes dismal science of economics cannot explain why the debate over immigration has become so heated, a theory of psychocultural anxieties might enable us to understand its intensity. From our theoretical point of view, the construction, as in Proposition 187, of powerful landscapes of "Otherness"—discourses portraying immigrants as parasites and criminals taking our diminishing resources—is largely a projective mechanism serving primitive psychological needs in times of social upheaval and anxiety.

Heuristic models are relevant only when they can elucidate the god in the details. Why, we may ask, are these anti-immigrant landscapes of Otherness so powerful in certain parts of the world today? The California experience may be paradigmatic. In a climate of frustration over natural disasters, economic deterioration, urban crime, and rapid demographic changes, those who are least like the dominant population—the new immigrants—have been singled out as the cause of such ills.

Our contention is that Californians are dealing with unsettling contemporary problems by using the immigrant "Other" to contain overwhelming anxieties and focus their rage. A number of psychoanalytic theorists have argued that in times of upheaval and endangerment, we use Others to contain our anxieties and focus aggression.[7] We concur with Julia Kristeva's observation that "a distraught self . . . protects itself . . . [with] the image of a malevolent other into which it expels the share of destruction it cannot contain" (Kristeva 1991: 183–84).

But this is only one side of the coin. There is a price in the economy of anger. The "malevolent other," the stranger constructed to contain badness and focus anger, cannot fail to activate powerful persecutorial fantasies. Melanie Klein's analysis of the "bad object" (see Klein and Riviere 1964) is relevant here. The object constructed to contain badness becomes a powerfully charged persecutorial object. Hence we come, psychoculturally, to close the circle of fear and hatred. The immigrant Other charged with badness is now experienced as a persecutorial criminal or abusive parasite that must be expelled.

Today immigrants have become the Other of choice. The distraught and endangered self of postmodernity, unable to integrate the stunning upheavals and contradictions of the fin de siècle, defends by creating various projective landscapes of Otherness. This is not a new phenomenon. Indeed, throughout much of our history, the Western world has had its need for Others. At various times, Muslims, Africans, and Native Americans have been Europe's "outer Other." And the Jews, of course, have been its "inner Other."

More recently, following the unique atrocities of the Holocaust, Western discourses saw the Soviet Union take its place as the "Evil Empire." The Soviets, of course, played the "evil" role quite well. Indeed, during the cold war, Soviet communism was, among other things, an important container of anxiety and focus of rage. With the collapse of the Soviet system was broken the most recent container for Western anxieties, one that gave them a sharp sense of purpose. We are now looking for another container. We are, once again, in need of strangers.

Powerful envy fantasies are critical ingredients in the organization of irrational fears and Other-hating. As George Foster brilliantly noted in his famous essay, "The Anatomy of Envy," in an ethos of "limited goods" where a gain to somebody (in this case immigrants) is framed as a loss to somebody else (citizens), envy becomes a dominant interpersonal concern (Foster 1972). Constructing the debate over immigration as a simple—and simplistic—they-win, we-lose proposition becomes a building block in the construction of hatred and self-righteous lashing out.[8]

The Implementation of Proposition 187

Cormac McCarthy writes in his beautiful novel *The Crossing*: "Doomed enterprises divide lives forever into the then and the now" (1994: 129). Proposition 187 is a doomed enterprise. It is a failure to intelligently debate and envision better solutions to serious problems. It is about division, hate, and scapegoating.

As a measure intended to curb undocumented immigration, Proposition 187 is bad law. Immigration scholars predict that it is unlikely that Proposition 187—even if it is fully implemented—would be a significant deterrent to undocumented immigration (Cornelius 1995). Furthermore, it should not be overlooked that past efforts—including employer sanction—have largely failed to contain the flow of undocumented immigration.

Proposition 187 is facing several legal challenges (Ayres 1994b; Feldman and Rainey 1994; Noble 1994). It may be in violation of the

1982 Supreme Court ruling in *Plyler v. Doe*. In the majority opinion, which struck down a Texas statute denying school enrollment to undocumented immigrant children, the Supreme Court noted that "these children can neither affect their parents' conduct nor their own undocumented status" (*Plyler v. Doe* 1982: 203). Acting against children for any transgressions their parents may have committed seems to us immoral and, in the opinion of the Court, against "fundamental conceptions of justice" (ibid.: 220). In the majority opinion, the Supreme Court noted:

> Persuasive arguments support the view that a State may withhold its beneficence from those whose very presence within the United States is the product of their own unlawful conduct. These arguments do not apply with the same force to classifications imposing disabilities on the minor *children* of such illegal entrants. At the least, those who elect to enter our territory by stealth and in violation of our law should be prepared to bear the consequences, including, but not limited to, deportation. But the children of those illegal entrants are not comparably situated. . . . Even if the State found it expedient to control the conduct of adults by acting against their children, legislation directing the onus of a parent's misconduct against his children does not comport with fundamental conceptions of justice. . . .
>
> But [the Texas statute] is directed against children, and imposes its discriminatory burden on the basis of a legal characteristic over which children can have little control. It is thus difficult to conceive of a rational justification for penalizing these children for their presence within the United States. Yet that appears to be precisely the effect of [the Texas statute]. (Ibid.: 219–20)

In the Texas case, the Supreme Court noted that even if public education is not a "right" granted to individuals by the Constitution, neither is it "merely some governmental 'benefit' indistinguishable from other forms of social welfare" (ibid.: 221). Rather, "public education has a pivotal role in maintaining the fabric of our society and in sustaining our political and cultural heritage; the deprivation of education takes an inestimable toll on the social, economic, intellectual, and psychological well-being of the individual, and poses an obstacle to individual achievement" (ibid.: 203). The Court also noted that excluding undocumented children from school is not likely to make families leave the United States and return to their country of origin. Furthermore, given that—because of amnesty and other legal factors—the "illegal alien of today may well be the legal alien of tomorrow" (ibid.), denying access to public education to undocumented immigrant children "already disadvantaged as a result of poverty, lack of English-speaking ability, and undeniable racial preju-dices" will result in their being "permanently locked into the lowest socio-economic class" (ibid.).

In more general terms the Supreme Court commented that the spirit and the letter of the Texas statute raise "the specter of a perma-nent caste of undocumented resident aliens, encouraged by some to remain here as a source of cheap labor, but nevertheless denied the benefits that our society makes available to citizens and lawful resi-dents. The existence of such an underclass presents most difficult problems for a Nation that prides itself on adherence to principles of equality under the law" (ibid.: 219).

Many of the issues considered in the Supreme Court's *Plyler v. Doe* opinion are pertinent to central aspects of Proposition 187. Yet even as Proposition 187 faces a long legal battle, it is likely that other states will follow the California example and attempt to enact similar laws in the near future.

Given that there are no studies to support the assertion that im-migrants are drawn to California by the "magnet" of welfare, it is doubtful that most undocumented immigrants who have settled in the United States would return home if Proposition 187 were en-forced (as many of its proponents believe). Furthermore, many fami-lies have both legal and undocumented members because a U.S.-born child is "legal" even if the parents are undocumented, so "mass de-portation would inevitably mean splitting of hundreds of thousands of families" (McDonnell 1994a: 1).

If it is upheld by the courts, Proposition 187 would require school districts to verify the legal status of students in California. By Janu-ary 1, 1996, the schools would also have to verify the legal status of parents or guardians. It is estimated that over 300,000 students could be dismissed from California schools under the new law. Under Proposition 187, undocumented immigrants also would be ineli-gible for all public health services (including children's vaccines), except emergency medical care. State officers responsible for pro-viding health, welfare, and public education services would be re-quired to report "suspected" undocumented immigrants to the U.S. Immigration and Naturalization Service. The costs associated with implementing these programs could be quite high.

There might be additional costs associated with medical problems. Since the November vote, there have been a number of preliminary reports that undocumented immigrants have become more hesitant to seek medical care for fear of being reported to the INS (McDonnell 1994b). Indeed, some deaths that might have been prevented have already been reported (Cowley and Murr 1994). Some health authorities have noted that as undocumented immigrants fail to receive proper medical attention, including routine vaccinations, serious—and, incidentally, much more costly—medical problems are likely to develop. Viruses, unlike laws, do not discriminate: unvaccinated undocumented children will be equally contagious to citizens and immigrants alike.

Other "costs" that cannot be easily measured in dollars and cents would surely be paid. Given its vagueness, the law would turn every immigrant (whether legal or undocumented), every person with an accent, every "foreign-looking" person into a "suspect." This would likely engender even more suspicion, mistrust, and blatant racism than already are evident.

There is also the troubling issue of turning teachers, school personnel, health practitioners, and administrators into agents of the INS. If the law is fully implemented, it is not clear whether these professionals would comply with their new responsibilities to report "suspected" undocumented immigrants to the INS. If noncompliance became a serious issue, there could be substantial costs associated with prosecuting and punishing professionals who refuse to obey the law.

There is some evidence to suggest that Proposition 187 has already worsened undocumented immigrants' terror of "being caught." Furthermore, there are reports that suggest Latinos and other "foreign" individuals are now seen by some as "guilty until proven innocent." A few days after Proposition 187 was approved, a Latino cook in Los Angeles was "threatened with citizen's arrest by an Anglo customer unless he produced a green card" (Wood 1994: 2). In Palm Springs, a pharmacist refused to fill a "prescription of a regular customer because he could not produce on-the-spot evidence of citizenship" (ibid.). In the words of immigration attorney Lucas Guttentag, "The reign of terror has begun against lawful and unlawful immigrants alike" (quoted ibid.).

Other reports suggest that undocumented students not only are afraid of being deported but feel their dream of pursuing an education will be shattered. In the words of a Los Angeles student, "Proposition 187 has got to be the worst thing that's ever happened to me. . . . They'll kick me out of this school. I'm just getting ready to graduate, and now this? I can't go back to Mexico. What am I going to do out in the streets?" (quoted in Ayres 1994a). Proposition 187 will surely reactivate—and accentuate—"persecutorial anxieties" and issues of marginality and shame, particularly among vulnerable undocumented immigrant children and second- and third-generation children of immigrants (see Chapter 2).

In Chapter 1 we argued that the new immigration seems to be generating isomorphic conditions in varied settings. Although the new immigrants are needed in certain sectors of the economy, they have also been singled out with particular fury to account for all kinds of problems, from economic decline to crime epidemics. The new arrivals, furthermore, are disparaged by ethnic stereotypes characterizing them as lazy, parasitic, and crime-prone.

Such disparagement has particularly poisonous effects on the children of immigrants. During adolescence the children of immigrants must struggle with special issues in developing a sense of identity while navigating sometimes conflicting cultural currents. In some cases, a response to psychosocial violence is to reject the institutions of the society that rejects them and to create "countercultural" identities. This may take the form of identifying with gangs and developing ambivalent attitudes toward the institutions of the dominant culture, including schools and authorities.

This majority-minority dialectic seems to have little to do with the culture of origin of a given minority group. It appears to occur in the second and third generations among diverse groups in various postindustrial settings. It is happening among disparaged second-generation Moroccans in Brussels (Hermans 1993), Turks in Germany (Kinzer 1993), Koreans in Japan (Lee and De Vos 1981), and Latinos in the United States.

A number of studies confirm what many teachers already know: immigrants bring a special energy and optimism, perhaps to compensate for all the losses and mourning resulting from migration. That energy is quite positive when well harnessed. Study after study shows that recent arrivals display achievement patterns that often surpass those of their native-born peers (see, for example, De Vos 1973; Gibson 1988; Kao and Tienda 1995; McNall, Dunnigan, and Mortimer 1994).

Latino immigrants fit this pattern. The data we presented in Chapters 4 and 5 of this book suggest that immigrants want to learn and want to work hard to achieve the dream of a better tomorrow, while maintaining a separate sense of identity. However, the psychosocial violence, discrimination, and obstacles immigrants encounter eventually affect the identity and schooling strategies of many youths, particularly in the second generation. Many of these youths respond to the psychological and social violence they encounter by turning away from schools—hence the enduring high dropout rates among second- and third-generation Latino students.

The future of the world—and of the United States in it—is one of new forms of transnationalism, interdependence, and diversity. It is our challenge to creatively navigate and attempt to constructively resolve the tensions, paradoxes, and contradictions engendered by these newly emerging social formations.

Statistical Tables

TABLE A.1

Level of Schooling Completed in the United States by Hispanic Persons
25 Years and Older

(percentage)

Group	High school +	Four years of college +
Cubans	62.0%	20.5%
Central/South Americans	61.7	14.7
Mexicans	45	6
Puerto Ricans	60	8

SOURCE: Frederick Hollman, *United States Population Estimates, by Age, Sex, Race, and Hispanic Origin: 1980–1988* (Washington, D.C.: U.S. Government Printing Office, 1990).

DESCRIPTIVE STATISTICS

Tables A.2 through A.8 describe the characteristics of the groups studied.

TABLE A.2

Gender Distribution and Number of Students per Group

Group	Male	Female	Total
Mexican	28	19	47
Mexican immigrant	21	27	48
Mexican American	24	23	47
White American	20	27	47
Total	93	96	189

NOTE: There were no significant differences between these groups on the dimension of gender distribution, chi-square (3, 185, N = 189), n.s. (p = .3).

TABLE A.3
Mean Age Distribution

Group	Age
Mexican	14.47
Mexican immigrant	15.73
Mexican American	15.23
White American	15.13

NOTE: The omnibus analysis of variance (ANOVA) conducted on these data reached significance [F (3, 184) = 4.19, p < .01]. Multiple pairwise comparisons using Protected F tests (Gorsuch 1991) revealed that the students in the Mexican group were somewhat younger than the students in the other groups.

TABLE A.4
Socioeconomic Distribution Based on the Hollingshead Four-Factor Index

Group	Mean (socioeconomic status)	Standard deviation
Mexican	8.23	3.51
Mexican immigrant	4.92	3.10
Mexican American	5.45	2.39
White American	10.34	2.36

NOTE: A one-way ANOVA was calculated to analyze between-group differences in socioeconomic status. The results showed significant differences among the groups [F (3, 184) = 35.95, p < .0001]. Multiple pairwise comparisons using Protected F tests revealed that the students in the Mexican immigrant and Mexican American groups were of a significantly lower socioeconomic status than were the Mexican and white American students (p < .0001). Mexican and white American students were also significantly different from one another (p < .01).

TABLE A.5
Students' Living Arrangements

	Mexicans		Mexican immigrants		Mexican Americans		White Americans	
	N	%	N	%	N	%	N	%
Intact family	37	74	34	68	31	62	20	42.5
Divorced, living with mother	2	4	6	12	13	28	19	40.5
Divorced, living with father	1	2	1	2	1	2	8	17
Sibling	0	0	2	4	0	0	0	0
Nonnuclear family	0	0	1	2	1	2	0	0
Multigeneration family	7	14	3	6	1	2	0	0
Nonfamily	0	0	1	2	0	0	0	0

TABLE A.6
Language of Interview

Group	English	Spanish	Mixed
Mexican	0	47	0
Mexican immigrant	12	20	16
Mexican American	43	0	4
White American	47	0	0

TABLE A.7
Grade Point Average Distribution

Group	Mean	Standard deviation
Mexican immigrant	3.06	.74
Mexican American	2.85	.72
White American	3.26	.64

NOTE: Grade-point averages were not available for the Mexican sample.

A one-way ANOVA was calculated to analyze between-group differences in grade-point average. The results showed significant differences among the groups [F (3, 184) = 18.6, $p < .01$]. Multiple pairwise comparisons using Protected F tests revealed that the Mexican American students had significantly lower GPAs than did the immigrant ($p < .05$) and white American ($p < .01$) students.

TABLE A.8
Results of Discriminant Function Analysis

Variable	Eta	Chi-square	df	p	R
Family obligation	.34	63.67	3, 184	.0001 *	.38
Family as referent	.31	53.33	3, 184	.0001 *	.38
Family support	.30	51.91	3, 184	.0001 *	.38
Family conflict	.27	40.50	3, 184	.0001 *	.38

NOTE: This analysis indicates that the four variables effectively distinguish among the groups.
* = statistically significant ($p < .05$).

OBJECTIVE DATA ANALYSES OF VARIANCE

Family Variables

The data summarized in this section include Sabogal et al.'s (1987) cumulative familism score as well as the family conflict scale and the familism subscale scores derived from the factor analysis of Sabogal's familism scale: (1) family support (support provided by the family), (2) family obligation (sense of obligation to provide support to the family), and (3) family as an attitudinal referent.

These data were subjected to omnibus analyses of variance followed by multiple pairwise comparisons using Protected F tests. When significance was reached, magnitude of effect was reported using R (Gorsuch 1991). Tables A.9 through A.11 report the objective test results.

TABLE A.9
Analysis of Variance for Familism

Source	SS	df	MS	F	p	R
Between groups	541.71	3	180.57	5.50	.001 *	.24
Within groups	6004.45	183	32.81			

Group	Mean	Standard deviation
Mexican	49.73	5.26
Mexican immigrant	50.13	5.08
Mexican American	49.24	6.27
White American	45.85	6.19

NOTE: This analysis reached significance. In doing all possible multiple pairwise comparisons using Protected F tests, it became evident that Mexican ($p < .05$), Mexican immigrant ($p < .01$), and Mexican American ($p < .05$) students all scored significantly higher than white non-Hispanic American students on this dimension. Mexican immigrants demonstrated the highest level of familism.
* = statistically significant ($p < .05$).

TABLE A.10
Analysis of Variance for Family Support

Source	SS	df	MS	F	p	R
Between groups	64.86	3	21.62	4.18	.01 *	.25
Within groups	950.86	184	5.17			

Group	Mean	Standard deviation
Mexican	12.72	2.23
Mexican immigrant	11.94	1.95
Mexican American	11.21	2.47
White American	11.36	2.42

NOTE: This analysis reached significance. In doing all possible multiple pairwise comparisons using Protected F tests, it became evident that Mexican students scored significantly higher than Mexican American ($p < .01$) and white American ($p < .01$) students on this dimension.
* = statistically significant ($p < .05$).

TABLE A.11
Analysis of Variance for Family Obligation

Source	SS	df	MS	F	p	R
Between groups	155.33	3	51.78	6.21	.001	.30
Within groups	1535.20	184	8.34			

Group	Mean	Standard deviation
Mexican	22.85	2.31
Mexican immigrant	23.67	3.12
Mexican American	23.49	3.13
White American	21.36	2.89

NOTE: This analysis reached significance. In doing all possible multiple pairwise comparisons using Protected F tests, it became evident that on this dimension, white American students scored significantly lower than did students of all other groups (Mexican $p < .01$; Mexican immigrant $p < .001$; and Mexican American $p < .001$).

Family as attitudinal referent and family conflict were also analyzed but did not reach significance.

PROJECTIVE DATA ANALYSES OF VARIANCE

The data analyzed in this section include the Thematic Apperception Test subscales developed for card 1.

As with the objective test data, the projective test data were subjected to omnibus analyses of variance followed by multiple pairwise comparisons using Protected F tests. When significance was reached, magnitude of effect was reported using R (Gorsuch 1991). Tables A.12 through A.14 report these projective test results.

Peer Relations

TABLE A.12
Analysis of Variance for Peers as Attitudinal Referents

Source	SS	df	MS	F	p	R
Between groups	37.87	3	12.62	4.85	.005 *	.27
Within groups	478.87	184	2.60			

Group	Mean	Standard deviation
Mexican	20.28	1.53
Mexican immigrant	20.12	1.50
Mexican American	20.21	1.59
White American	21.23	1.82

NOTE: This analysis reached significance. In doing all possible multiple pairwise comparisons using Protected F tests, it became evident that on this dimension, white American students scored significantly higher than students in all other groups ($p < .001$ for all comparisons).
* = statistically significant ($p < .05$).

Family Relations

Analyses of variance of the TAT scales developed a priori to this study were conducted. These scales included: support provided by the family; sense of obligation to provide support to the family; relatives as behavioral and attitudinal referents; verbal family relations; physical family relations; and family ambiance. None of these scales reached significance.

Achievement Orientation

TABLE A.13
Analysis of Variance for Independent Achievement

Source	SS	df	MS	F	p	R
Between groups	42.85	3	14.28	3.53	.02 *	.23
Within groups	744.83	184	4.05			

Group	Mean	Standard deviation
Mexican	23.07	2.14
Mexican immigrant	22.56	1.76
Mexican American	21.87	2.15
White American	21.98	1.97

NOTE: This analysis reached significance. In doing all possible multiple pairwise comparisons using Protected F tests, it became evident that on this dimension, Mexican students scored significantly higher than Mexican American ($p < .01$) and white American ($p < .01$) students.
* = statistically significant ($p < .05$).

TABLE A.14
Analysis of Variance for Engaging/Avoiding Task

Source	SS	df	MS	F	p	R
Between groups	41.91	3	13.97	2.86	.04 *	.21
Within groups	897.34	184	4.88			

Group	Mean	Standard deviation
Mexican	23.46	1.96
Mexican immigrant	22.92	1.80
Mexican American	22.28	2.37
White American	22.36	2.62

NOTE: This analysis reached significance. In doing all possible multiple pairwise comparisons using Protected F tests, it became evident that on this dimension, Mexican students scored significantly higher than Mexican American ($p < .01$) and white American ($p < .02$) students.
* = statistically significant ($p < .05$).

Affiliative and Compensatory Achievement

Analyses of variance for affiliative achievement and compensatory achievement did not reach significance.

PROBLEM SITUATION TEST: SOURCES OF ADVICE

TABLE A.15
When You Have a Problem, Whom Do You Go to for Advice?

Response	Mexicans	Immigrants	Mexican Americans	White Americans	Chi-square
Parents	87%	70%	42%	43%	< .01 *
Extended family	8	16	35	12	< .05 *
Friends	4	10	18	45	< .01 *
Teacher	1	4	5	0	n.s.

* = statistically significant ($p < .05$).

Reference Matter

Notes

Introduction

1. Throughout the book we use the term "immigration" in its broadest possible sense. We use the term "immigrants" to refer to those entering a new country in order to settle there. "Refugees" and "asylum seekers" are subtypes of immigrants. However, refugees and asylum seekers differ from other immigrants in a variety of ways. First, their departure from the country of origin is typically involuntary, often due to a well-founded fear of persecution. Second, refugees and asylum seekers may plan to return home as soon as the political climate allows it. Third, refugees and asylum seekers may be more prone to develop psychosocial problems, such as "survivor guilt" (see Suárez-Orozco 1989) about leaving friends and relatives behind to suffer political repression, war, and scarcity.

Chapter 1

1. Americans are of course not alone in thinking of their country as a country of immigrants. Argentines, Australians, and others also think of their countries as archetypal countries of immigration. In Argentina and Australia, as in the United States, the aboriginal populations were rapidly defeated and marginalized by European power.

2. In the mid-1700s there was ethnic anxiety about the new arrivals from Germany. The fears then were not unlike today's: many people believed that too many immigrants were arriving and not assimilating. Benjamin Franklin wrote in 1751, "Why should the Palatine boors be suffered to swarm into our settlements, and, by herding together, establish their language and manners, to the exclusion of ours? Why should Pennsylvania, founded by the English, become a colony of aliens, who will shortly be so numerous as to Germanize us, instead of our Anglifying them?" (quoted in Chavez 1992: 14).

3. And in all of these countries, discussions of the economy—arguably the main topic on the public agenda—are riddled with references to immigration (i.e., to the adverse impact of immigrants on the economy).

4. In Germany, for example, the authorities estimate that there are between 40,000 and 50,000 active neo-Nazis who share an almost monomaniacal anti-immigrant agenda (see below). The neo-Nazis are, of course, the most extreme form of a more general anti-immigrant current.

5. Italy and Spain were the sources of great population movements to the Americas at the fin de siècle and of large postwar emigrations to Germany, Belgium, and elsewhere in northern Europe.

6. In 1992 the German Psychoanalytical Association prepared a statement on the xenophobia in Germany. It reads in part, "We must all become aware of our own xenophobia and learn to integrate psychically that which is alien, where it is in fact in unconscious terms something of our own. Hence tolerance and humanity towards foreigners call for a constant effort of civilization and culture. This is the only way to diminish the power of projections and to mitigate the conception of 'us' as a national entity which aggressively excludes others" (quoted in Volkan 1993: 64).

7. The Clinton administration's handling of the Haitian refugee crisis points to the structural similarities between the recent U.S. and western European experiences. Candidate Clinton had denounced as immoral—if not illegal—the Bush administration's practice of having the U.S. Coast Guard halt boats carrying Haitian asylum seekers in the high seas before they reached U.S. waters. President Clinton reversed himself and continued the policy of "high seas interdiction" of Haitian boats. By June 1994, it was reported that each week over 5,000 Haitians were leaving the troubled island in search of refuge.

The strategy of stopping the would-be asylum seekers outside U.S. territorial waters rests on the technicality that under the terms of the Geneva Convention on Refugees, a person has the right to a "fair hearing" for asylum once he or she reaches a safe country. A country that stops and returns potential applicants in international territory (or international waters) does not violate the letter of the law. The Clinton administration was working on proposals "to 'streamline' the asylum process, allowing immediate determination of an applicant's ability to file an asylum claim, and presenting the possibility of 'expedited exclusion'—quick deportation of many refugees" (National Network for Immigrant and Refugee Rights 1993: 2).

8. Paradoxically, demographers in a number of the countries facing a near-hysteria over immigrants and asylum seekers, including France, predict that foreign laborers will be needed in the future to compensate for shortages of native-born workers (Hollifield 1993; Cornelius, Martin, and Hollifield 1994). In addition, competition from businesses operating more cheaply in developing countries makes it necessary, according to some observers, for businesses in Europe to rely on undocumented laborers (in Europe they are often called "black workers"), who are paid only a fraction of what legal workers would be paid.

9. Similarly in the United States, California politicians, including Governor Pete Wilson and others, at various times supported a constitutional amendment to deny citizenship to U.S.-born children of undocumented parents.

10. In January 1994, the Associated Press reported that almost the entire Chinese community of northern Bavaria in Germany was rounded up and fingerprinted as part of a large-scale investigation of "people smuggling" from Hong Kong via Moscow into Europe. It was reported that gangs charge up to $25,000 to fly Chinese people to Moscow and Prague and then arrange for Czech smugglers to transfer them to Germany. Note the similarity to the U.S. concern about rings of professional smugglers (known as "snakeheads" in Chinese) smuggling Chinese workers into U.S. cities.

11. Belgium has followed a similar course but in a more tentative, less organized fashion. Bosnian asylum seekers who withdraw their formal asylum applications are given a conditional, carefully worded, temporary permit to stay. According to a legal scholar, these temporary permits do little more than prohibit the police from repatriating the holders to their countries of origin, although in a limited number of cases, they have been given a temporary right to work (Foblets 1993).

12. In retrospect, it appears that the liberal asylum laws of 1951 flourished in part because the communist regimes controlled through terror the movement of large numbers of potential exiles. Had many people from the Eastern bloc been able to escape before Soviet communism collapsed, it is likely that many western European countries would have been forced to reconsider their asylum policies sooner.

13. Some northwestern European countries have dealt with asylum by setting up quota systems: a limited number of applications are granted in a given year, and the authorities decide which groups from which countries are eligible to apply. In Belgium there is no such quota system. Another strategy is to grant asylum seekers whose applications have been formally denied the right to stay for additional but limited periods of time. But the policy leaves applicants in a kind of "twilight zone, as temporary residents at risk of being deported" (Kamm 1993; see also *Wall Street Journal* 1994). In Germany alone there are 630,000 unresolved asylum cases.

14. Another strategy is to make it difficult for asylum seekers to meet human rights and refugee rights lawyers. In many western European countries lawyers are in a struggle with the authorities for access to potential asylum seekers at airports (the bar of Brussels, for example, has lawyers at the Brussels airport to inform potential asylum applicants of their rights). Also, newly arrived asylum seekers who do not have local mailing addresses are assigned P.O. box numbers in the office of the U.N. High Commissioner for Refugees, where notices of their hearings are sent. Those unfamiliar with the system who fail to pick up the notices and miss their hearings are denied asylum.

15. Contrary to popular opinion, far from coming from the lowest socioeconomic and educational rungs of their societies, many undocumented

workers from Latin America have some education, in addition to talent and ambition. Women trained as nurses and teachers in South America take jobs as baby-sitters in the United States simply because, without papers, few people will hire them in other jobs. Likewise, in Brussels undocumented Peruvians and Colombians, high school and in some cases college graduates, work as baby-sitters and maids (Van Broeck 1993). These women bring a certain cultural capital to low-paying jobs that would be impossible to expect (at those wages) from local workers. And in Japan, Brazilian-Japanese immigrants, some with degrees in computer science, take jobs well beneath their qualifications, as factory laborers, for example (see Cornelius 1994).

16. Similarly, an undocumented Latina in the United States can make $150–$300 per week cleaning houses. Her husband can make more than that in agriculture, construction, or restaurant work. The average yearly salary in El Salvador is less than $700.

17. There are similar reports from Spain where undocumented workers from Algeria and Morocco do many of the demanding, dirty, and dangerous jobs in agriculture (see Riding 1993a).

18. Citizens of EU (European Union) countries can now freely reside and work in any of the member countries. Although specialized professionals may move from one country to another, it is not expected that large numbers of EU workers will do so. In general, then, "immigrants" almost universally refers to non-EU citizens in the community. Hence the significant numbers of Dutch nationals living on the Belgian side of the border, typically to pay lower taxes, are not seen as part of the immigration problem in contemporary Belgian society (Fassmann and Münz 1992: 474; Roosens 1993).

19. As in the United States, working-class natives and their unions argue that "black workers" take jobs and other resources from Europeans. Social security is a case in point. Belgian companies, for example, pay a specific amount into the social security system for each of their Belgian employees; so not only are black workers said to take jobs away from European workers, but companies that hire them do not pay into the social security system. Hence all legal workers lose resources. Non-EU legal immigrants also resent black workers because they call attention to the presence of the legal workers.

20. To an outside observer, their political agenda appears to be focused on a single issue: the immigrant problem. According to the Vlaams Blok leadership, Belgium's problems (unemployment, crime, the current budget crisis, etc.) will go away only when the immigrants go away. The Vlaams Blok employs an extreme version of the doctrine of cultural relativism: they argue that each culture is unique and in some respects incommensurable with other cultures. Peoples, they note, have a fundamental right to their own language and culture. Hence the Vlaams Blok supported, in principle, the right of young Moroccan girls to wear veils in school (Foblets 1993). They also argue, though, that each group can be fulfilled only in its own land, in its own culture. Just as the Flemish can be happy and fulfilled only in Flanders, so the Moroccans and Turks can be happy only in their own coun-

tries, they argue. One member said, "We respect other people's identity. . . . We don't say one people is better than another. We say that the only way to preserve people's identity is to keep them apart" (quoted in Havemann 1993).

21. In Belgium, older folk appear to be more anti-immigrant than younger folk. Catholics appear to be more conservative than non-Catholics (see Billiet, Carton, and Huys 1990).

22. Even those who do not share the extreme views of the Vlaams Blok or the Front National believe that the immigrants must adapt to the cultural norms of the dominant majority. Mr. Flynn, the EC commissioner for social policy and immigration, stated, "Immigrants should be encouraged to integrate rather than retain their original citizenship" (Droziak 1994). Some argue that in the best-case scenario, non-EU immigrants will "disappear" in the mainstream, learning the language and adopting the dress and mores of the dominant culture. But the process of immigrant "melting" will take a couple of generations: some Europeans hope that the third generation will "look" more European in language, dress, and conduct, easing the anxieties brought about by the presence of the immigrants as a whole.

23. In the 1980s some studies conducted in Belgium suggested that because legal immigrants tend to produce more than they consume, regulations regarding family unification should be liberalized. As for the undocumented immigrants, there are no data on their impact on the economy. Nevertheless, as a researcher informally noted, "Everyone knows that the illegals are productive in the sense that for some employers they are key. Most restaurants in Brussels would just go bankrupt without the illegals" (Foblets 1993).

Yet many citizens think that rather than regularize or hire undocumented workers, Europe should train and hire the unemployed legal immigrants. Given the generous European social security system (in Brussels, for example, an unemployed legal immigrant may receive up to 80 percent of his or her full salary for up to a year), many think it is simply not possible to continue to support large numbers of unemployed immigrants.

24. A side effect of the Bush administration's "war on drugs"—a war widely believed to have failed miserably (see García Márquez 1994)—is that the U.S.-Mexico border is now highly militarized. Consider the following excerpt from an American Friends Service Committee (AFSC) report:

> [During the first half of the Bush administration] INS attainment and development of sophisticated new equipment continued. The low-light level television system was expanded to additional, unspecified border sectors. . . . Further, the INS was in the process of obtaining new land-mobile infrared imaging equipment and additional airborne forward-looking infrared radar (FLIR) equipment. . . . The INS also requested an additional $8.6 million for fiscal 1991 for infrared nightscopes, portable ground sensors, and additional low-level television equipment, to enable the Border Patrol to increase its number of apprehensions of undocumented immigrants, though the equipment was also said to detect drug smugglers. Finally, the

INS obtained five new A-Star 350-B helicopters capable of carrying seven people each, which were to be used for various special operations. . . . Each of these new helicopters is equipped with a "Nite Sun" search light and forward-looking infrared radar (FLIR), that has heat sensing capacities and is especially useful in night detection and surveillance activities. (AFSC 1992: 9)

25. Two weeks later, the president's second candidate for the post also withdrew when it was revealed that she had hired an undocumented worker from Trinidad as a baby-sitter—though she had done so before the 1986 Immigration Reform Control Act made it illegal. The case, variously called in the media "Nannygate II" and "Alien II," further contributed to the debate over undocumented immigration in the United States.

26. In many reports, the implied message was that, once released, the asylum seekers de facto gain more or less permanent entry into the United States. In fact, researchers in the field of refugee and asylum law are increasingly disturbed by new formal and informal policies developed in the United States and Europe to reduce the number of asylum requests. Many countries have created policies that may violate both the spirit and the letter of international agreements on refugee and asylum rights. We shall return to this issue later.

27. These professional smugglers are reported to charge up to $40,000 per passenger. Those who make it into the United States typically "face ruthless exploitation in restaurants and sweatshops, and those who fail to pay their debts may be kidnapped, tortured, or forced into crime and prostitution. Desperate to escape poverty and deprivation in China, they often find misery and servitude in America" (Liu 1993: 23; see also Duffy 1993).

28. In February 1994, the INS disclosed plans to begin charging a $130 fee to applicants seeking political asylum. The United States would be the only nation in the world to charge an asylum application fee (see *New York Times* 1994b). INS officials argued that in 1993 there were 150,386 formal requests for asylum and only 150 asylum officers to process the claims. According to one observer, "The system in the past year and a half just collapsed under its own weight" (quoted in Weiner 1994). Human rights and refugee rights advocates noted that the new fee would simply further undermine the right to asylum. Others noted that a universal right is now for sale (see *New York Times* 1994b; Stern 1993a).

29. In July 1993 the French Senate approved a bill giving the police wide-ranging powers to make spot identity checks as part of a general crackdown on undocumented immigration, particularly from North Africa. The bill was approved despite initial objections to the police's use of race in deciding whom to check (see *New York Times* 1994a; Riding 1993b).

30. Although this is an impressive number, no one knows what percentage of those entering settle here permanently; it may be that the percentage is small. In 1992, for example, it was estimated that in California some 100,000 undocumented aliens settled in the state (less than 10 percent of the estimated 1.2 million undocumented persons who entered the country).

31. Demographers have questioned the extent of the middle-class California exodus. For example, according to William Frey, between 1985 and 1990 "California lured more college graduates from other states than it lost" (quoted in Opatrny 1993: 1) and had a "net gain of 151,921 people earning $35,000 or more a year . . . and a net loss of 112,217 of people earning less than $35,000" (ibid.).

32. A *New York Times*/cbs News poll conducted in late June 1993 found that 50 percent of the respondents said the new immigrants "cause problems" and that "a large majority of Americans surveyed said they favored a decrease in immigration. Many cited the economy as a factor in their opinion." According to the survey, there is a widespread perception in the population, not based in fact, that "most immigrants are in the United States illegally" (Mydans 1993). In California, according to another report: "There also has been an ugly side to the immigration backlash. Thinly veiled racism, nativism, even xenophobia motivate some to protest any immigration" (Caldwell 1993).

33. Both figures—$5 billion and $4-plus billion—are exaggerated. Governor Wilson's office estimated that the state of California incurs around $3.6 billion annually in unreimbursed expenses to provide services to 1.3 million undocumented immigrants. Governor Wilson asked the federal government—which keeps the greatest share of the tax-generated income from undocumented workers—to reimburse the state for its expenses or repeal the mandate that California provide education, school lunches, and prenatal and Medicaid services to undocumented workers and their children. His figures, as we shall see, fail to take into consideration the federal tax revenues generated by undocumented workers.

34. The topic of the impact of *undocumented* immigrants on the economy is far more controversial than the already heated field of *documented* immigrants and the economy. And perhaps nowhere is the "dismal science" as hopeless as in the shadowy world of the economic impact of undocumented immigrants. Although there is near universal consensus that some jobs exist only because undocumented immigrants are here, almost everything else in this field is fiercely contested. According to some economists, immigrants—including undocumented immigrants—do not strain the economy (see Simon 1989); others claim that immigrants cost the economy $42.5 billion a year (Huddle 1993; for a rebuttal of Huddle, see Passel 1994; see also Thomas and Murr 1993). But because there are no reliable data on undocumented immigrants in general, assessments of their impact on the economy are highly tentative (see Cornelius 1993b; Heer 1990). Nevertheless, Simon argues that "analysis of the economic effects of illegal immigrants is quite similar to the analysis for legal immigrants, and leads to the same mainly positive judgment with respect to the native economic welfare" (1989: 305). Others are more skeptical. For example, a controversial San Diego County study concluded that "the costs to state and local governments associated with processing undocumented immigrants through the criminal justice system [estimated at $151,220,101], and with providing health ser-

vices [estimated at $50,053,773], education [estimated at $60,021,516], and social and other public services [estimated at $42,714,695] for this population is $304,010,085. The state and local government revenues associated with tax receipts are $59,722,386. The excess of costs over revenues is equal to $244,287,699" (Parker and Rea 1993: xii). This assessment leaves the reader with the impression that for every dollar an undocumented immigrant pays into the tax structure he or she takes out approximately four dollars in services. This study was used to support the argument that undocumented immigrants are bankrupting the county and that therefore all services to undocumented immigrants—including schooling and health care—must be stopped at once.

Yet the figures presented above—indeed the entire study—are highly suspect. For example, these figures do not factor in the $162,632,543 the authors themselves estimate that undocumented workers paid in *federal* taxes in San Diego County (see Parker and Rea 1993: v). Subtracting the federal revenues from the total "bill," we shrink the alleged deficit associated with undocumented immigrants to $81,655,156—still admittedly a significant figure. However, given that this report was commissioned and paid for by the California State Senate Special Committee, with the aim of providing the California legislature with data to use in petitioning the federal government for reimbursement, the study was hardly inspired by scientific curiosity or theory building. Those who commissioned the study had much to gain by inflating the costs and deflating the benefits associated with undocumented immigration.

Wayne Cornelius, director of the University of California Center for U.S.-Mexican Studies, has made the following observations about the accuracy of the Parker and Rea report:

> First and most fundamentally, the accuracy and potential utility of this report is compromised by the way in which the total population of undocumented immigrants in San Diego County was estimated. The report's estimates of fiscal impacts are further weakened by methodological deficiencies in the collection of data from the immigrant population itself. The samples of migrant workers who were interviewed for the Rea & Parker study were not sufficiently large, nor sufficiently diverse in socioeconomic and demographic composition, to permit generalization to the entire undocumented population of San Diego. (Cornelius 1993b: 2)

Another University of California expert on the condition of undocumented immigrants in San Diego County concludes:

> The findings of Rea and Parker do not live up to the requirements of empirical accuracy. They are almost certainly exaggerated by extraordinary margins. And, though it may be impossible to know the exact ratio of costs and benefits of undocumented aliens, the ratio is almost certainly much smaller than that proposed by Rea and Parker. Therefore, whatever may be the bonafide legal, moral, and philosophical arguments for or against tolerating illegal immigrants, the financial arguments provide little basis for

settling them—and certainly are not strong enough to justify widespread alarm." (Wolf 1993: 2)

Furthermore, the authors fail to assign a dollar value to many other obvious benefits associated with the undocumented immigrant presence in San Diego County—benefits they acknowledge but do not bother to systematically consider. For example, they say, "Reduced wages to undocumented immigrants can be expected to permit some business enterprises to compete nationally and internationally and, therefore, to remain in business in the United States rather than to relocate" (Parker and Rea 1993: x). Given that an estimated 30 percent of all undocumented immigrants in their sample work in factories and shops, it is probable that if they had to rely exclusively on the more costly legal workers, many of these operations would have simply closed down and moved shop to the Mexican side of the border in search of cheaper labor. Parker and Rea also grant that "consumer prices in selected industries and services are somewhat lower than they otherwise would be because of lower wages to undocumented immigrants" (ibid.). Finally, they note, "The general economic benefits of undocumented immigration may well accrue disproportionately to upper income households and business owners. The costs, however, are borne by lower skilled, lower income workers, who must compete for jobs which are less financially rewarding and less secure" (ibid.).

In short, the Parker and Rea report fails to make a convincing case that undocumented migrants significantly burden the economy.

35. Some have argued that the Los Angeles County study considerably underestimated the contributions of immigrants to the local economy (see Miller 1993). It did not count tax revenues from immigrant businesses, and it examined the economic impact of only very recent arrivals (post-1980). There is evidence that the longer immigrants are in the country the more they contribute to the tax system (Simon 1989). Hence the likely substantial contributions of the estimated 1.1 million who entered Los Angeles County before 1980 were not taken into consideration.

36. For example, the 1994 state budget included a request for $2.3 billion in federal assistance to cover statewide costs said to be associated with undocumented immigration. Likewise, the mayors of the ten largest California cities have together appealed to federal authorities to help pay the costs associated with undocumented immigration in urban California (LaVelle 1994). They argue that the federal government should return to the states their fair share of the tax revenue generated by undocumented immigrants. Likewise, a *New York Times* report concluded, "The real problem, it would appear, is that most of the taxes immigrants pay end up in the hands of the Federal government, with little of the bonanza actually returning to the areas where immigrants live" (Rohter 1993).

37. Immigrants, refugees, and their children have produced some of the greatest scientific, medical, and industrial breakthroughs of the century. For example, "since 1901, 30 percent of the U.S. Nobel prize-winners have been immigrants" (*Time* 1993, p. 15). But previous generations also never

imagined that the children and grandchildren of immigrant peasants would revolutionize science, medicine, and industry.

38. Julian Simon estimates that immigrants, over their lifetime, pay $15,000 to $20,000 more in taxes than they receive in government benefits. Simon writes, "Compared to natives, their rate of participation in the labor force is higher, they tend to save more, they apply more effort during working hours, they have a higher propensity to start new businesses and to be self-employed. They do not have a higher propensity to commit crime or to be unemployed . . . [and] contrary to common belief, immigrants do not use more transfer payments and public services than do natives; rather they use much smaller amounts in total. . . . Natives get a windfall from immigrants through the Social Security mechanism" (Simon 1989: 339).

39. Simon notes that "illegal" immigration inevitably raises "the specter of a breakdown of order and a loss of social control" (1989: 300). Even though there is no evidence that undocumented immigrants contribute significantly to the crime rate in the United States, some have argued that their very presence may undermine respect for the law. Consider the following excerpt from the Final Report of the Select Commission on Immigration: "Most serious is the fact that illegality breeds illegality. . . . As long as undocumented migration flouts U.S. immigration law, its most devastating impact may be the disregard it breeds for other U.S. laws. . . . It is this undermining of national values that poses the greatest threat to U.S. society, not the displacement of U.S. workers or the use of social services by undocumented workers" (quoted in Simon 1989: 300).

40. Another fear associated with the loss of border control is that "dirty" criminal aliens, while terrorizing and robbing innocent citizens, including children, spread contamination and pollution. The fear of contamination was based on an isolated report of a migrant worker infecting another *migrant worker* with malaria in their migrant camp (Wolf 1988: 17). For a history of the fear of immigrant "contamination" and disease, see Kraut 1994. The image of the criminal immigrant stalking children grew out of the following incident: "[A fifteen-year-old] girl was walking past Kelly school [north county, San Diego] in mid-day, with three immigrant workers in front of her and three behind. An acquaintance across the street noticed the six men drawing closer to her and called her to cross the street, which she did" (Wolf 1988: 17). Six workers casually walking by a young girl thus became, through a paranoid prism, "huge gangs" of criminals "shaking down our children" and looking for "homes to rob." There is no evidence that the immigrant workers intended or attempted to "shake down" the girl, and none of the workers was charged with any crime or offense.

41. Wolf's findings agree with those of some earlier studies. Simon notes, "For the period around the turn of the century [studies] concluded that, by any measure the rate of serious crime has been less among immigrants than among natives, though the rate of petty crime (vagrancy, disorderly conduct, breach of the peace, drunkenness) has sometimes been greater among immigrants. When age and sex are controlled for, the rate of all crime has been less

among immigrants than natives. And one would expect petty crime among illegals to be even less than among legal immigrants because of their fear of being sent out of the country" (1989: 394).

42. Another key manifestation of paranoia is a terror of "disintegration," loss of control, pollution, and contamination (see Shapiro 1965: 54–107). In someone with an irrational fear of losing control and/or of being polluted, overwhelming anxieties of inner worthlessness, disintegration, and emptiness are projected onto an outsider. The internal battle becomes an external battle against an outer enemy. As we have seen, discussions of the "immigrant problem" are saturated with references to loss of control (of the border), crime, pollution, and contamination (see Kraut 1994).

43. We differentiate between the "instrumental" aspects of exploitation, as defined and understood within Marxist theory, and the psychological and expressive aspects of exploitation, as articulated in this chapter (see also De Vos and Suárez-Orozco 1990: 164–203). According to this line of thought, the expressive aspects of exploitation serve as powerful additional motivators for instrumental exploitation (e.g., exploitation for material gain).

44. But the socioeconomics should not be overstated. Also present is concern about the sexuality of the newcomers, evident in talk about their "high birth rates." Consider the following assertion made by John Tanton, founder of the vocal group that calls itself U.S. English:

> Will Latin American migrants bring with them the tradition of the *mordida* (bribe), [and] the lack of involvement in public affairs? Can *Homo contraceptivus* compete with *Homo progenitiva* if borders aren't controlled? Or is advice to limit one's family simply advice to move over and let someone else with greater reproductive powers occupy the space? . . . On the demographic point: perhaps this is the first instance in which those with their pants up are going to get caught by those with their pants down! (Quoted in Chavez 1991: 92)

The fear here is overtly about losing control—over the borders and over sexuality. Note also the cultural anxiety captured in the statement. As we argue in discussing the problem of immigrant crime, a terror of primitive aggression is recycled as pseudorational talk about immigrant crime.

Chapter 2

1. Chavez writes: "Civic or religious marriage has traditionally been less common among poor Puerto Ricans than among other Hispanics, on the island as well as in the United States. As late as 1950 one-quarter of all unions in Puerto Rico were consensual or common law" (1991: 142).

2. The U.S. census does not distinguish between persons of Central and South American origin.

3. Throughout this book we use the term "minority" not in a demographic or numerical sense. In fact, in parts of California and elsewhere, the so-called ethnic minorities are fast becoming numerical majorities. Rather we use

minority to refer to the group's share of total resources and representation in positions of power.

Another group often included in the Hispanic category (in census reports and surveys) are "Hispanos," as they are sometimes called, descendants of the Spanish colonizers of the Southwest. This group was also in the United States before the existence of the Union. For a discussion of the use of "Hispanic" and "Latino," see Gonzalez 1992.

4. The best-selling novel *The Joy Luck Club*, made into a beautiful film, is an insightful study of how, in the process of immigration, the past shapes and reshapes the present. *The Joy Luck Club* is about the experiences of a group of Chinese immigrant friends and their U.S.-born children now living in northern California. The story elegantly shows that we must consider the triumphs and tragedies of their parents, grandparents, and even great-grandparents in China over half a century earlier in order to make sense of the lives of very successful, vaguely neurotic, and seemingly "fully acculturated" second-generation Chinese Americans in San Francisco today.

5. The film *An American Me*, about the brutality of Latino gangs in southern California in the 1960s and 1970s, is an important study of how suppressed sorrow and rage in one generation may be acted out by the next generation. The film shows a flashback to World War II, when the mother of a particularly sadistic gang member is raped and his father is brutally beaten by Anglos in Los Angeles. The parents' unelaborated rage, their inability to mourn their losses and injuries and to receive justice in a racist society, is acted out by their children. In our view, a great deal of the destructiveness associated with gang life is fed by rage over the injuries of racism and disparagement, past and present.

6. The current anti-immigrant sentiment—directed mostly at new arrivals from Latin America—naturally is harmful to all Latinos, even the fully acculturated second, third, and fourth generations. The hysteria over the new waves of "wetbacks" (first-generation undocumented immigrants) reactivates the racist indignities earlier generations of Latino migrants endured.

7. Interviews of Central American refugees were conducted by Marcelo Suárez-Orozco between 1984 and 1986. All other interviews were conducted in 1991–92 by the authors and their bilingual research assistants. Interviews conducted in Spanish were translated by the research assistants and the authors.

8. Chavez's informants tell him: "In Mexico, if you don't work for yourself you really can't live because another person, the person you work for will take it all from you. You just can't make it. . . . I had decided to change my life because I realized that life in Mexico was too difficult. There is much poverty. The jobs are very difficult to obtain. If you had family members involved in politics, then you would have a good job. If not, and if you are not well educated, then you do not have a good job. . . . I liked it [the United States], and I stayed. I have my life here. I am married and I have children and I work, like the rest of the world" (Chavez 1992: 29).

9. The worldwide economic implications of immigration are extremely

complex (see Chapter 1). Immigrant workers are credited with helping bring about various postwar "economic miracles"—anti-immigrant sentiment notwithstanding. James Hollifield notes in his important book on immigration in Europe and the United States: "Foreign workers contributed significantly to economic growth by helping employers avoid labor shortages while keeping wages in check. Indeed, the argument has been made that the postwar miracle (Wirtschaftswunder) in Europe could not have occurred without immigration, which provided 'unlimited supplies of labor' during crucial periods of economic expansion in the 1950s and 1960s" (Hollifield 1992: 4). Immigrant workers also contribute significantly to the economic life of various third world countries via their remittances. Economists estimate that the approximately 100 million immigrants and refugees residing outside their countries of citizenship each year send some $40 billion home.

10. All names of informants have been altered to protect their identity and privacy.

11. There is a long history of wage differentials leading many to migrate from Mexico to the United States. During the first quarter of this century, Manuel Gamio estimated that a Mexican immigrant worker earned, on average, six times more than a worker in Mexico could earn for the same type of work. Indeed, Gamio concluded, "The emigration of Mexican laborers is directly caused by the low wages and unemployment in the various parts of Mexico from which they come, indirectly by the political instability, and secondarily through the desire for progress and the spirit of adventure" (Gamio 1971: 38, 171). We would only add that family reunification has also become a major factor.

12. We have become less concerned about whether a group has minority status "voluntarily" (such as new arrivals from Mexico and Central and South America) or "involuntarily" (African Americans, Native Americans, the original Mexican Americans of the Southwest). Economic exploitation and social disparagement are not reserved exclusively for involuntary minorities. Many immigrants who arrive voluntarily are nevertheless also exploited and disparaged. The subsequent economic and psychological treatment of a group is just as important as the group's initial mode of incorporation.

13. The 1990 census data on the relationships between educational attainment and income among Latinos and whites make it clear that Linda Chavez's upbeat report that "Hispanics are 'making it' on their own" is largely wishful thinking. According to 1991 census data, over a quarter of all Hispanics (28.7 percent) were living in poverty (9.2 percent in the non-Hispanic population). The income gap between the Hispanic and non-Hispanic population was likewise extraordinary: the median income of Hispanic males with year-round, full-time employment was $19,769; for non-Hispanic whites it was $31,046 (Hollman 1990). Though we do not mean to minimize the important and hard-earned progress of the Latino population, it is simply not empirically true that Latinos, as a group, have now joined the "mainstream." Chavez's 1991 book, *Out of the Barrio*, may have been better titled *It Is Morning in the Barrio*.

14. Our observations concur with the findings of Vigil (1988a) and Horowitz (1983). Teachers, counselors, and others told us repeatedly during the course of our research that Latino kids involved in gangs typically come from a variety of troubled backgrounds (alcohol and drug addictions, child abuse and neglect, absent parents, single parents, etc.). A common denominator seems to be the absence of strong figures (parents, aunts and uncles, older siblings) available to help them navigate the tensions of adolescence in the barrio. In the absence of strong support and guidance, youths turn to their peers—and to gang life—for comfort.

15. Rodriguez's relationship with his ethnicity can be best characterized as a style of approach-avoidance. An opponent of bilingual education, Rodriguez now makes a living as a public television commentator on immigrant and multicultural affairs in California. Yet still Rodriguez seems uncomfortable with his ethnicity. A deep anxiety about his "Mexican-ness" is revealed when he writes about his terror of drinking dirty Mexican water during a visit to Tijuana. A dark man, scarred by his relatives' attempts when he was a little boy to make his skin lighter with bleach, Rodriguez is understandably preoccupied with dirt. He grew up in a racist society saturated with references to dirty Mexicans. In a sense, his education achieved symbolically what the bleach could not: it gave him some mastery over his anxieties about his "dark" and "dirty" background.

16. The United States has a long tradition of "demanding" that the newly arrived abandon their languages and learn English as a sine qua non to sharing in the mythical American dream. According to this cultural logic, giving up one's language and learning American English is a key act of loyalty to the new land. There may be a connection between requiring immigrants to learn English and many Americans' resistance to learning other languages. Whereas most taxi drivers in Geneva can communicate in several languages, many students in U.S. doctoral programs have difficulty communicating in *any* foreign language.

17. Even in his published book a number of the Spanish words and phrases are misspelled or misused.

18. At Harvard he fought many battles, including a decidedly Oedipal assault on the saintly father of the Mexican farm workers, Cesar Chavez, during a presentation Chavez made at the Kennedy School of Government; and he suffered many disappointments, such as when his fellow "Harvard Chicanos" turned on him after he told Chavez that the United Farm Workers Union no longer represented the interests of migrant workers but had become a corrupt bureaucracy.

19. See Foster 1979 for a brilliant study of "the image of limited goods" among Mexicans.

20. Navarrette is correct in believing that "tracking" is particularly damaging to Latino students. Empirical research has found that Latino students who participated in an "untracking" experiment that placed them in academically rigorous college prep courses "enrolled in college in numbers

exceeding local and national averages. . . . Of the Latino students who participated in AVID [the name of the untracking program] for three years, 44 percent enrolled in four-year colleges, compared to the San Diego City Schools'
average of 25 percent and the national average of 29 percent" (Mehan and
Villanueva 1994: 1).

Chapter 3

1. For the first time in its short history, there is no reigning paradigm in
anthropology. Indeed in the 1990s, that fact is the only thing anthropologists
seem to agree on!

2. See Brown and Joffe 1992 and Givens and Skomal 1992 in the special
issue of the *Anthropology Newsletter*, the official publication of the American Anthropological Association. The lead essays are entitled "Is Fission
the Future of Anthropology?" and "The Four Fields: Myth or Reality?" The
first essay begins: "Is anthropology coming apart at the seams? Is it break-
ing down into academic specialties that are unable or unwilling to talk to
one another? Are departments organized around the traditional four-field
approach of anthropology clinging to a myth about the unity of the discipline?" (Brown and Joffe 1992: 1). The second essay begins with the words of
Clifford Geertz: "There are now more departments that don't do more than
give lip service to the four-field notion. And even where it exists, it's a little
unreal—there are just four little departments within the larger one" (Givens
and Skomal 1992: 1; see also Geertz 1991). Although many anthropologists
may insist on paying lip service to the four-field approach, strong centrifugal
forces continue to pull them apart. As a result, many in biological anthropology today share more scientific interests with molecular biologists than
they do with cultural anthropologists. The majority of graduate students in
the best departments of anthropology do not gain competence in all four
areas of scholarship.

3. It is indeed paradoxical that just as some anthropologists now reject
the ethnographic approach, other disciplines (including education, medicine, and even philosophy) have recently "discovered" ethnography and apply
it to their special intellectual problems with considerable enthusiasm. In
anthropology, without fieldwork, of course, there cannot be "holism," the
anthropological promise to explore all of the central aspects of culture (including ecology, economy, social organization, politics, religion, cosmology,
psychology, etc.).

4. The philosopher Adrian Cussins argues that the problem of objectivity
is at the heart of the representational dilemma of the "post-wall era: In
modernity, objectivity is aiming at an external target, which imposes the
wall between subject and object" (Cussins 1992: 20).

5. Others have argued that the direct impact of anthropology and anthropological writings on the making of the colonial project is less mechanistic
than Rosaldo and others would have us believe. Talal Asad, for example,

notes, "The role of anthropologists in maintaining structures of imperial domination has, despite slogans to the contrary, usually been trivial; the knowledge they produced was often too esoteric for government use, and even where it was usable it was marginal in comparison to the vast body of information routinely accumulated by merchants, missionaries, and administrators" (Asad 1991: 315).

6. For a lengthier consideration of these questions see Suárez-Orozco, Spindler, and Spindler 1994.

7. Piaget also refers to this early phase as "participation" thinking. During this phase, Piaget argues, the world (the sun, the moon, the stars, etc.) "participates" with our own thoughts and wishes (a child thinks the sun comes up in the morning so she can go out to play with friends, etc.). Events are willed and intentional; everything has a purpose; things in the world (even pebbles, for example) make efforts that participate, or coordinate, with our own wishes and thoughts.

8. Another way to approach objectivity is to frame it as a human potential, as the maturational potential to gain increasing awareness of our own subjectivities. The task becomes struggling against "the limitations of the mind" (see *Webster's New Universal Unabridged Dictionary* under "subjectivity"), toward apprehension of a world that is "independent of mind" (ibid.) and that can be checked, confirmed, and verified by others.

9. The notion that local culture "determines" mental processes is based on the old-fashioned idea that cultures are uniform. This model would argue that Bororo thought is determined by (local) Bororo culture, ergo all Bororo think alike. The important theoretical work of Swartz (1991) on cultural variation makes this position no longer tenable.

10. Piaget (1930) and his followers in cognitive and developmental psychology long ago discarded the notion that the world (culture) simply "imprints" itself in the mind of the child as if she were a tabula rasa. Piaget (1930) argued that there are biologically given maturational factors and psychic structures, or schemas, which interact with the social world as the child grows, jointly constructing the mind.

Indeed, the great majority of research psychologists now reject the once popular behaviorist idea that any child can be conditioned at any age to learn anything. Conversely, other cognitive capacities, recent research in cognitive and development psychology suggests, are present at birth (i.e., before experience). Piaget had claimed that certain cognitive structures are missing at birth and are constructed from subsequent sensory-motor schemas. Recent research strongly suggests, contra Piaget, that structuring of cognitive experience is present at birth (see Baillaergeon forthcoming; Mandler 1988). We must also note that developmental and cognitive psychologists currently influenced by computer science write of mind in terms of "hardware," "software," and "central processor."

Finally, cognitive and developmental psychologists like Vygotsky, who argue that "higher mental functions" are strongly shaped by culture, nevertheless emphasize the influence of universal, species-specific cognitive capacities for structuring experience present at birth. In short, overwhelming evidence suggests that contemporary radical cognitive relativists in anthropology are swimming against a strong current of findings in related fields.

11. When anthropologists turned to psychology to explore models of personality, they found that psychoanalysis offered the most ambitious and complex theoretical framework. Hence a central intellectual concern in psychological anthropology has been the relationship between personality, broadly conceived within a psychodynamic view (the "inchoate psychoanalytic model" described by Spindler [1994]), and culture.

12. Devereux elaborates on the problem of humans studying humans:

The scientific study of man: 1- is impeded by the anxiety arousing overlap between the subject and observer; 2- which requires an analysis of the nature and locus of the partition between the two; 3- must compensate for the *partialness* of communication between the subject and the observer on the *conscious* level; but 4- must avoid the temptation to compensate for the completeness of communication between subject and observer on the *unconscious* level; 5- which arouses anxiety and therefore also countertransference reactions; 6- distorting the perception and interpretation of the data; and 7- producing countertransference resistances masquerading as methodology, which cause further *sui generis* distortions; 8- since the existence of the observer, his observational activities and his anxieties (even in self observation) produce distortions which it is not only technically but also logically impossible to eliminate; 9- any effective behavioral science methodology must treat these disturbances as the most significant and characteristic data of behavioral science research and; 10- must use the subjectivity inherent in all observation as the royal road to an authentic, rather than fictitious, objectivity; 11- which must be defined in terms of what is really possible, rather than in terms of what "should be;" 12- when ignored, or warded off by means of countertransference resistances masquerading as methodology, these "disturbances" become sources of uncontrolled and uncontrollable error, although; 13- when treated as basic and characteristic data of behavioral science they are more valid and more productive of insight than any other type of datum. (Devereux 1967: xvii)

13. Likewise, psychologists and psychiatrists have institutionalized self-examination by requiring in most training institutes that those responsible for examining others examine themselves (i.e., undergo psychotherapy and/or supervision).

14. It is obvious that the concerns we chose to study in the first place were in part determined by our own experiences. And once our memories were reawakened by our informants, we subjectively "knew" we were on the right path: many of the concerns our informants shared with us we "felt"—subjectively—to be true.

15. Rosaldo, for example, writes:

The truth of objectivism—absolute, universal and timeless—has lost its monopoly status. It now competes, on more nearly equal terms, with the truths of case studies that are embedded in local contexts, shaped by local interests, and colored by local perceptions. The agenda for social analysis has shifted to include not only eternal verities and lawlike generalizations but also political processes, social changes, and human differences. Such terms as *objectivity, neutrality* and *impartiality* refer to subject positions once endowed with great institutional authority, but they are arguably neither more nor less valid than those of more engaged, yet equally perceptive, knowledgeable social actors. Social analysis must now grapple with the realization that its objects of analysis are also analyzing subjects who critically interrogate ethnographers—their writings, their ethics, and their politics. (Rosaldo 1989: 21)

On close scrutiny, Rosaldo seems to reduce the problem of objectivity in social analysis to the (power) "positions" of various subjects in a given field. By framing the problem as one between insiders and outsiders, he sustains the analysis with unfortunate clichés: that those promoting an "objectivist discourse" believe that only the "outside" ethnographer (armed with self-deluding fantasies about being neutral, impartial, and apolitical) can be objective. The other side of that worn coin is the equally vacuous notion that, according to "objectivists," the "inside" informant can only be hopelessly subjective.

All good fieldworkers, Rosaldo included, in fact constantly and consciously struggle to keep in touch with and learn from their own subjectivities as they process the meaning of "local knowledge" (see the essays in Suárez-Orozco, Spindler, and Spindler 1994). And we have all eventually learned that there is always an insider (typically our favorite informant) who has an uncanny *objective* insight into some social problem we have been struggling with. It took Rosaldo, for example, many years and the tragic accidental death of his first wife to understand what Ilongot headhunters had been telling him all along: that headhunting was, to a large degree, an expression of grief through rage (Rosaldo 1989: 1–21).

16. Once the idea of an objective anthropology is framed as a Western social construct or ethnoscience, it follows that it becomes "epistemologically impermissible to explain non-Western cultures, or non-Western peoples, by the explanatory schemata of these disciplines. Even granting the validity of these schemata for the understanding of Western peoples, they are not valid, they argue, for the understanding of non-Western peoples who (by definition) are 'Other'" (Spiro 1992: x).

17. The criticisms of scientific positivism in current anthropology take at least two forms. One takes what we might call a benevolently (if watchfully) tolerant stance toward science. The suspiciously tolerant argue that a scientific discourse is one of many alternative and equally valid and important ways of knowing (which may include humanistic discourses, feminist discourses, peoples-of-color-discourses, and the like). They are watchful

because they suspect that those privileging a scientific approach disdain them and have in mind a hegemonic project to do in all nonscientific ways of knowing in anthropology. Those who see science as an essentially corrupt and disguised exercise in power want, of course, to get rid of science altogether.

18. Other postmodern critics have directly related the objectivist approach in the social sciences to conservative political agendas. Rosaldo, for example, writes: "The partisan evangelical fervor of the conservative agenda's implementation during the 1980s . . . has favored explanations that deal in timeless eternal principles. Hence the 'objectivist' emphasis found most prominently in sociobiology and cognitive science, including certain areas of ecology, neurology, ethology, artificial intelligence, generative linguistics, and experimental psychology" (Rosaldo 1989: 219). But this argument is too facile: the fact that "objectivist" approaches in most, if not all, the disciplines Rosaldo names *predate by decades* the neoconservative ascent to power in the 1980s makes his ex cathedra assertion simply untenable. In addition, it should go without saying that the fact that there has been "bad" science does not necessitate the abandonment of the *idea* of science as an elegant way of knowing.

19. Following this approach, there cannot be any replication of findings in cultural anthropology because the personality of the ethnographer would significantly, if not wholly, filter perceptions of the Other.

20. Another way to state this is to say that we agree with the essence of Spiro's assessment that "what is true about post-modernism is not new and what is new about post-modernism is not true" (Spiro n.d.). Spiro argues that what is true about postmodern currents in anthropology—but, alas, not new—is that anthropologists must pay close attention to the subjectivities and meanings embedded in the dynamics of "transference" and "countertransference" in fieldwork (for a discussion of these dynamics see Suárez-Orozco 1994). Spiro argues that what is new—but not true—about postmodern claims in anthropology is an antirational stance and a flight from examining the meanings of culturally different others (see Spiro n.d.).

21. Because of limited space, we present only a small proportion of the data gathered in the course of this study, concentrating instead on the materials most closely related to our interests in this book: interpersonal concerns about family and peers and interpersonal concerns about achievement motivation in the four groups studied.

22. See Appendix, Table A.2, for the specific breakdown of subject distribution by group and gender.

23. Differences between group age means were calculated and are presented in Table A.3.

24. It is understood that just as groups labeled Latino and mainstream American are made up of individuals from a wide range of ethnic backgrounds, so is the group labeled Mexican. Some Mexicans have European ethnic backgrounds, while others have various Native American or mestizo

backgrounds. As with informants in all other subgroups, we worked only with individuals who self-identified as belonging to the specific group under consideration. Hence, individuals who self-identified as "Anglo-Mexican" or "Hungarian-Mexican" or anything other than Mexican were excluded from the study.

25. SD = 2.16.

26. In our preliminary survey, students who identified themselves as "Anglo-Saxon," "Anglo-American," "white," "WASP," or "white American" were asked to participate. Two students circled "Native American" but when questioned clearly indicated that to them native meant born in the United States, not American Indian.

27. Because the socioeconomic status of the groups under study differed, analyses of covariance (ANCOVA) were performed using these variables as covariants. The ANCOVA results were virtually identical to the ANOVA results for all the comparisons. The results remained significant, even when variance due to socioeconomic status was factored out. Hence, we could conclude that socioeconomic status did not account for the group differences on the dependent variables under consideration. Because these results were comparable, the ANOVAS are reported for conceptual clarity in the Appendix.

28. Each of the variables discussed in this section was analyzed for gender differences. Each variable was subjected to ANOVAS by group and gender. Hence, for example, family obligation was analyzed separately for each group by gender. Sixteen analyses (the eleven Thematic Apperception Test [TAT] scales and the five objective scales) were conducted for each of the four groups. Given the number of comparisons, a Bonferroni correction was made in order to protect against family wise error (Miller 1966). Once the significance level was adjusted to $p < .003$, none of the gender comparisons were significant. Hence, no differences were found in response patterns between genders.

29. We discuss only data relevant to family and peers and achievement motivation.

30. We administered the Sabogal familism/family conflict test after we had concluded the initial period of observation, interviewing, and testing.

31. Four of the research assistants were graduate students in Latin American Studies at UCSD; one was an undergraduate.

32. The data in Mexico were collected in the same sequence, with the exception of the familism scale, which was obtained last. We conducted our research in accordance with the guidelines set forth by the Committee for the Protection of Human Subjects of the American Psychological Association (1987) and the University of California, San Diego. All participants and their parents were informed that we were studying attitudes toward school and family among adolescents in Mexico and the United States. All participants and their parents signed a consent form available in both English and Spanish. Informants were told that we would ask them to tell some stories, fill out questionnaires, and answer questions. They were also informed that they could withdraw from the study at any time.

33. We administered eight TAT cards to all informants (cards 1, 2, 3BM, 4, 6BM, 7BM, 8BM, and 8GF). We selected these cards because there is a consensus that they best elicit stories about family-related concerns and achievement motivation (Bellak 1986; De Vos 1973). Bellak (1986) suggests that the cards typically elicit information about the following: card 1—relationships with parental figures; card 2—family concerns; card 4—male-female relationships; and card 6BM—mother-son relationships. In our research, 7BM frequently elicited information about father-son relationships.

Given the time-consuming nature of TAT story scoring, interpretation, and analysis, we discuss only our findings most directly related to the topics under consideration. This is a common procedure (see De Vos 1973; McClelland 1961; Thomas and Dudek 1985; and Winters 1978).

34. For this study, the instructions for the TAT were translated from Spanish back into English to ensure that the same instructions were given to all groups.

35. A major drawback to using adapted cards is that meaningful systematic comparison with samples collected in other parts of the world is not possible—unless, of course, the same adapted set is used in many different cultural settings. But this solution is no solution because the argument can be made that what is adapted to rural China would be foreign to urban Mexico.

36. Detailed information about this scoring system is available from the authors upon request.

37. We then calculated the interrater reliability of the three trained raters and one of the principal investigators. The interrater reliability of the four raters for each item ranged from .77 to .83, with an average of .80. An overall Cronbach's alpha coefficient was also calculated. The alpha coefficient was .69, representing adequate internal consistency; although there is some intended overlap in the scales, each scale represents a distinct concept. The expert's alpha was approximately equivalent to that of the other raters.

A confirmatory factor analysis was conducted. This analysis confirmed the presence of four factors (as designed), lending support to the validity of the scale. To establish construct validity, four independent raters were given each of the seven items for each of the eleven scales on separate slips of paper in random order. They were asked to "sort the 7 items into what appear to you to be the most logical order (starting with the item which appears to be the most likely to have the +3 value and ending with the item which appears to be the most likely item to have a −3 value)." Initially, there was 100 percent agreement among the raters on nine out of eleven of the scales. On two of the scales there was some confusion about two of the items. The wording of these items was clarified, and the raters were asked again to sort the items. On the second trial, there was 100 percent agreement among the raters.

Concurrent validity was investigated by administering a self-report measure of familism and family conflict (Sabogal et al. 1987). We assumed that there should be some correlation between the self-report measure and the

TAT story ratings. However, we did not expect that the correlations would be high because the TAT measures unconscious interpersonal concerns while the paper-and-pencil questionnaire is a self-report measure that taps into conscious preoccupations. Also, we are aware that the TAT and Sabogal's familism and family conflict scales may measure different aspects of familism and family conflict.

38. Sattler (1988) recommends Conger's Kappa as a means of measuring interobserver reliability (or agreement) for ordinal data when there are multiple categories (in the case of this study, eleven scales for five separate cards for a total of fifty-five observations) with three raters.

This statistic takes into consideration "both the occurrence and nonoccurrence" (Sattler 1988) of a rating, and it corrects for chance agreement between raters. The Kappas ranged from .71 to .95, with an overall Kappa of .81. Hence, the remaining stories were rated by only one rater. For those stories with three raters, the modal score for the three raters was used as the story's rating. In the few cases where there was no agreement among the raters (and hence no mode score), the mean score was used.

39. A limitation of the post hoc qualitative analysis is, of course, the potential for experimenter bias. It is possible that without meaning to, the researcher may selectively attend to or ignore certain data. Every attempt was made to avoid this, but the potential for this bias exists. By having raters blindly score the stories and then checking for statistical significance between groups, we attempted to minimize experimenter bias.

40. See Table A.8. This analysis yielded an index of discrimination of $R = .38$ ($p < .0001$).

Chapter 4

1. The clinical studies we refer to are those based on samples of those in psychotherapy or seeking any kind of psychological counseling or service.

2. Chi-square * $p < .005$.

3. These data were subjected to omnibus analyses of variance and multiple pairwise comparisons using Protected F tests. When significance was reached, magnitude of effect was reported using R (Gorsuch 1991). See Appendix for the statistical results of the objective tests.

Chapter 5

1. These data suggest that whatever SES (socioeconomic status) differences there are between the Mexican and immigrant samples (see Chapter 3), the two groups share certain core cultural attitudes toward school and work that transcend class differences.

Epilogue

1. California governor Pete Wilson, while a U.S. senator, promoted policies to bring in workers to support the needs of his state's large agricultural interests. "Policies promoted by the state's leaders in the 1980's actively encouraged illegal immigration into California, and as a result hundreds of thousands of illegal immigrants came" (Brinkley 1994: 1). Indeed, in 1986, Pete Wilson and "others from the California delegation held up passage of the Immigration Reform and Control Act until a provision was added to allow several hundred thousand immigrants into the country temporarily so that they could help harvest crops. Under the provision that eventually resulted, more than one million came to stay" (ibid.).

2. On February 6, 1995, less than three months after passage of Proposition 187, California Attorney General Dan Lungren called for a new guest-worker program to bring temporary agricultural workers to California.

3. The next U.S. presidental campaign surely will be saturated with angry anti-immigrant imagery. Patrick Buchanan, in a preview of things to come, said in his March 20, 1995, speech announcing his presidential candidacy, "What is the matter with our leaders? Every year millions of undocumented aliens break our laws, cross our borders, and demand social benefits paid for with the tax dollars of American citizens. California is being bankrupted. Texas, Florida, and Arizona are begging Washington to do its duty and defend the states as the Constitution requires. . . . Yet our leaders now, timid and fearful of being called names, do nothing" (*Boston Globe* 1995, p. 10).

4. Indeed, by late 1994 Republican legislators were proposing to bar even legal immigrants from many federal services. Some Republican legislators argued that barring legal immigrants from a number of programs—including Medicaid, food stamps, and welfare—could save over $20 billion over five years.

5. Those who see immigration as a burden maintain that the new immigrants cannot resist the seductive entitlements of the welfare state (Borjas 1994: 76–80). This school of thought holds that the new immigrants end up "costing" more in terms of the services they use than they contribute in taxes. Rice University economist Donald Huddle in a highly publicized report claimed that immigrants—legal and undocumented—"present in the United States in 1992 cost all levels of government that year more than $45 billion above and beyond the taxes they paid" (Huddle 1993: 1).

Those who see the new immigrants as contributors to the economy seem to speak another language altogether. They argue that the new arrivals—documented and undocumented—contribute far more to the economy than they use in services (Passel 1994; Fierman 1994: 67–75; Francese 1994: 85–89). Passel and his associates reexamined Huddle's figures and concluded that far from costing more than $45 billion, legal and undocumented immigrants nationwide contributed a net surplus of $28.7 billion—and a net surplus to the California economy of $12 billion (Passel 1994: 1; see also

Meissner 1992; Rothstein 1994: 48–63; Miles 1994: 132). Other observers have noted that although there are regional differences—for example, some studies suggest that African Americans in the Los Angeles service sector have been "displaced" by Mexicans and Central Americans (Waldinger 1994; see also Miles 1994)—immigrants do not on aggregate "depress" the wages of native workers (Fierman 1994: 70).

Other researchers have noted that new immigrants have played a critical role reinvigorating "abandoned" urban zones, opening ethnic businesses, and, via the "multiplier effect," creating job opportunities for the native-born. Fierman writes, "Compelling evidence even shows that immigrants boost overall employment on balance. . . . For every one-hundred-person increase in the population of adult immigrants, the number of new jobs rose by forty-six. By contrast, for every one hundred new native-born Americans, the number of jobs rose by just over twenty-five" (Fierman 1994: 70). Still others argue that immigrant workers will be increasingly critical when large numbers of baby boomers begin to retire and become "consumers" of social security and Medicare (Rothstein 1994: 55–57; Francese 1994: 89).

6. Governor Pete Wilson repeatedly asserted that a good part of his motivation to push for passage of Proposition 187 was to force Washington to "accept responsibility" for closing the southern border to undocumented immigrants or reimburse the state of California for the services it must provide.

7. We feel comfortable with work on psychoanalysis relating aggression to frustration, injury, and endangerment; we find the psychoanalytic work on "projection" (Freud), the "bad object" (Klein), and the "malevolent other" (Kristeva) useful in thinking about the unsettling discourses of Otherness plaguing our increasingly fractured world.

8. The current push to ban legal immigrants from federal and state aid programs is, likewise, saturated with envy and "limited good" imagery. Dan Stein, a member of the restrictionist Federation for American Immigration Reform (FAIR), captures well the strategic use of envy to gather anger: "When Americans are tightening their belts in every way, it's not justifiable to lavishly dole out benefits to legal immigrants" (*Boston Globe* 1995, p. 7).

Bibliography

Abel, Theodora. 1973. *Psychological Testing in Cultural Contexts*. New Haven, Conn.: College and University Press.

Abt, Lawrence, and Leopold Bellak, eds. 1950. *Projective Psychology*. New York: Grove.

Alaluf, Matéo. 1982. *The Education and Cultural Development of Migrants: Migrant Culture and Culture of Origin*. Strasbourg: Council for Cultural Cooperation, Council of Europe/Conseil de l'Europe.

Alamdar-Niemann, M., D. Bergs-Winkels, and H. Merkens. 1991. "Educational Conditions of Turkish Migrant Children in German Schools." In Marcelo M. Suárez-Orozco, ed., *Migration, Minority Status and Education: European Dilemmas and Responses in the 1990s*. Theme Issue. *Anthropology and Education Quarterly* 22, no. 2: 154–61.

Allen, D. 1993. *Fear of Strangers and Its Consequences*. New York: Bennington Books.

Allport, Gordon. 1979. *The Nature of Prejudice*. Twenty-fifth anniversary ed. Reading, Mass.: Addison Wesley.

Alvarez, Robert, Jr. 1987. *Familia: Migration and Adaptation in Baja and Alta California, 1800–1975*. Berkeley: University of California Press.

Alvord, Valerie. 1993. "County Sending Clinton Tab for Immigrants." *San Diego Union-Tribune*, Sept. 29.

American Friends Service Committee. 1992. *Sealing Our Borders: The Human Toll*. Third Report of the Immigration Law Enforcement Monitoring Project (ILEMP). A Project of the Mexico-U.S. Border Program. Philadelphia: American Friends Service Committee.

American Psychological Association. 1987. *Ethical Principles in the Conduct of Research with Human Participants*. Washington, D.C.: American Psychological Association.

Americas Watch. 1990. *Human Rights in Mexico: A Policy of Impunity.* New York: Americas Watch.

———. 1993. *United States Frontier Injustice: Human Rights Abuses Along the U.S. Border with Mexico.* New York: Americas Watch.

Antokoletz, Juana. 1993. "A Psychoanalytic View of Cross-Cultural Passages." *American Journal of Psychoanalysis* 53, no. 1: 35–54.

Arevalo, L. E. 1987. *Psychological Distress and Its Relationship to Acculturation Among Mexican Americans.* Ph.D. diss., California School of Professional Psychology, San Diego.

Asad, Talal. 1991. "Afterword: From the History of Colonial Anthropology to the Anthropology of Western Hegemony." In George W. Stocking, Jr., ed., *Colonial Situations: Essays on the Contextualization of Ethnographic Knowledge.* Madison: University of Wisconsin Press.

Aubert, Roger, ed. 1985. *L'immigration italienne en Belgique: histoire, langues, identité.* Brussels: Instituto Italiano di Cultura, Université Catholique de Louvain, Louvain-La-Neuve.

Ayres, B. Drummond. 1994a. "Curb on Aliens Dims Dreams in Hollywood." *New York Times,* Nov. 11.

———. 1994b. "Court Blocks California on Alien Rules." *New York Times,* Nov. 17.

Baillaergeon, R. Forthcoming. "The Object Concept Revisited: New Directions." In C. E. Granrud, ed., *Visual Perception and Cognition in Infancy.* Carnegie-Mellon Symposia on Cognition, vol. 23. Hillsdale, N.J.: Lawrence Erlbaum.

Banfield, E. C. 1958. *The Moral Basis of a Backward Society.* New York: Free Press.

Bauman, Z. 1991. *Intimations of Postmodernity.* London: Routledge.

Bean, Frank D., J. Chapa, R. Berg, and K. Sowards. 1991. "Educational and Sociodemographic Incorporation Among Hispanic Immigrants to the United States." Paper presented at the conference "Immigration, Ethnicity and the Integration of America's Newest Immigrants," Urban Institute, Washington, D.C., June 17–18.

Beavers, W. R., R. B. Hampson, and Y. F. Hulgus. 1985. "Commentary: The Beavers Systems Approach to Family Assessment." *Family Process* 24, no. 3: 398–405.

Becerra, R. M. 1988. "The Mexican American Family." In C. H. Mindel, R. W. Habenstein, and R. Wright, eds., *Ethnic Families in America: Patterns and Variations.* 3d ed. New York: Elsevier.

Bellah, Robert N., R. Madsen, W. M. Sullivan, A. Swidler, and S. M. Tipton. 1985. *Habits of the Heart: Individualism and Commitment in American Life.* New York: Perennial Library.

Bellak, Leopold. 1986. *The Thematic Apperception Test, the Children's Apperception Test and the Senior Apperception Technique in Cinical Use.* 4th ed. New York: Grune and Stratton.

Bernal, G. 1982. "Cuban Families." In M. McGoldrick, J. K. Pearce, and

J. Giordano, eds., *Ethnicity and Family Therapy.* New York: Guilford Press.

Berry, John. 1992. *Cross-Cultural Psychology: Research and Applications.* New York: Cambridge University Press.

Berry, John, and P. R. Dasen, eds. 1974. *Culture and Cognition: Readings in Cross-Cultural Psychology.* London: Methuen.

Bettelheim, B. 1980. *Surviving and Other Essays.* New York: Vintage Books.

Billiet, Jaak, Ann Carton, and Rik Huys. 1990. *Onbekend of onbemind? Een sociologisch onderzoek naar de houding van de Belgen tegenover migranten.* Leuven, Belgium: Sociologisch Onderzoekinstituut, K. U. Leuven.

Bloom, B. S., A. Davis, and R. Hess. 1965. *Compensatory Education for Cultural Deprivation.* New York: Holt, Rinehart and Winston.

Boos-Nünning, Ursula, and Manfred Hohmann. 1989. "The Educational Situation of Migrant Workers' Children in the Federal Republic of Germany." In Lotty Eldering and Jo Kloprogge, eds., *Different Cultures, Same School: Ethnic Minority Children in Europe.* Amsterdam: Swets and Zeitlinger.

Borjas, George. 1990. *Friends or Stangers: The Impact of Immigrants on the U.S. Economy.* New York: Basic Books.

———. 1994. "Tired, Poor, on Welfare." In N. Mills, ed., *Arguing Immigration.* New York: Simon and Schuster.

Boston Globe. 1995. "Ready to Lead a 'Cultural War,' Buchanan Opens '96 Campaign." Mar. 21.

Brenner, E. 1990. *Losses, Acculturation and Depression in Mexican Immigrants.* Ph.D. diss., California School of Professional Psychology, San Diego.

Brimelow, Peter. 1992. "Time to Rethink Immigration?" *National Review,* June 22.

———. 1995. *Alien Nation: Common Sense About America's Immigration Disaster.* New York: Random House.

Brinkley, Joel. 1994. "California's Woes on Aliens Appear Largely Self-Inflicted." *New York Times,* Oct. 15.

Brown, P., and N. Joffe. 1992. "Is Fission the Future of Anthropology?" *Anthropology Newsletter* 33, no. 7: 1–21.

Brownstein, Ronald. 1994. "Wilson Proposes U.S. Version of Prop. 187." *Los Angeles Times,* Nov. 19.

Bruner, Jerome. 1990. *Acts of Meaning.* Cambridge, Mass.: Harvard University Press.

Bureau of the Census. 1993. *Statistical Abstract of the United States: 1993.* Washington, D.C.: U.S. Government Printing Office.

Cahiers Marxistes. 1988. "Les jeunes." *Issus de l'immigration* 164 (Dec.): 1–13.

Calavita, Kitty. 1993. "Immigration in Italy." Paper presented at the workshop "Controlling Illegal Immigration in Global Perspective." Center for U.S.-Mexican Studies, University of California, San Diego, Mar. 18–20.

Caldwell, Robert. 1993. "To Save Sensible Immigration, Curb Current Abuses." *San Diego Union-Tribune*, July 25.

California Legislature. 1990. *Joint Interim Hearing on International Migration and Border Violence*. San Ysidro, Calif., June 22.

Cammaert, Marie-France. 1986a. "The Long Road from Nador to Brussels." *International Migration* 24, no. 3: 635–50.

———. 1986b. "Cultural and Shifting Identity: Berber Immigrants from Nador (N.E. Morocco) in Brussels." *Journal of the Anthropological Society of Oxford* 27, no. 1: 27–45.

Campbell, D. T., and J. C. Stanley. 1963. *Experimental and Quasi-experimental Designs for Research*. Chicago: Rand McNally College.

Carter, T. P., and R. D. Segura. 1979. *Mexican Americans in School: A Decade of Change*. New York: College Entrance Examination Board.

Castles, Stephen. 1984. *Here for Good: Western Europe's New Ethnic Minorities*. London: Pluto Press.

Castles, Stephen, and Godula Kosack. 1973. *Immigrant Workers and Class Structure in Western Europe*. Oxford: Oxford University Press.

Cervantes, R. C., V. N. Salgado de Snyder, and A. M. Padilla. 1989. "Post-traumatic Stress in Immigrants from Central America and Mexico." *Hospital and Community Psychiatry* 40, no. 6: 615–19.

Chapa, Jorge. 1988. "The Question of Mexican American Assimilation: Socioeconomic Parity or Underclass Formation?" In *Public Affairs Comment*. Austin: Lyndon B. Johnson School of Public Affairs, University of Texas at Austin.

Chavez, Leo R. 1992. *Shadowed Lives: Undocumented Immigrants in American Society*. Fort Worth, Tex.: Harcourt Brace.

Chavez, Linda. 1991. *Out of the Barrio: Toward a New Politics of Hispanic Assimilation*. New York: Basic Books.

———. 1994. "Immigration Politics." In N. Mills, ed., *Arguing Immigration*. New York: Simon and Schuster.

Chavez, Lydia. 1994. "More Mexicans, More Profits." *New York Times*, Dec. 9.

Cleeland, Nancy. 1994. "Judge Puts Hold on Most of Prop. 187." *San Diego Union-Tribune*, Nov. 17.

Clifford, J., and G. E. Marcus. 1986. *Writing Culture: The Poetics and Politics of Ethnography*. Berkeley: University of California Press.

Clinton, Bill. 1995. "State of the Union Address." *Boston Globe*, Jan. 25.

Cohen, Roger. 1993a. "Price of European Unity Is Reckoned in Lost Jobs." *New York Times*, Jan. 10.

———. 1993b. "Europeans Fear Unemployment Will Not Fade with Recession: Companies Shifting Jobs to Low-Wage Countries." *New York Times*, June 13.

Cohn-Bendit, D. 1992. "Immigration in Europe." *World Link* (Geneva) Mar./Apr.: 60–64.

Cole, Michael, and B. Means. 1981. *Comparative Studies of How People Think*. Cambridge, Mass.: Harvard University Press.

Commission of the European Communities. 1992. *Immigration Policies in the Member States: Between the Need for Control and the Desire for Integration.* Working Document. Brussels: Directorate General, Employment, Industrial Relations, and Social Affairs.

Conover, Ted. 1987. *Coyotes: A Journey Through the Secret World of America's Illegal Aliens.* New York: Vintage Books.

———. 1993. "The United States of Asylum." *New York Times Magazine,* Sept. 19, pp. 56–78.

Constantino, G., and R. Malgady. 1983. "Verbal Fluency of Hispanic, Black and White Children on TAT and TEMAS, a New Thematic Apperception Test." *Hispanic Journal of Behavioral Sciences* 5, no. 4: 199–207.

Constantino, G., R. G. Malgady, L. H. Rogler, and E. C. Tsui. 1988. "Discriminant Function Analysis of Clinical Outpatients and Public School Children by TEMAS: A Thematic Apperception Test for Blacks and Hispanics." *Journal of Personality Assessment* 52, no. 4: 670–78.

Cornelius, Wayne. 1990. "Los migrantes de la crisis: el nuevo perfil de la migración de mano de obra Mexicana a California en los años ochenta." In Gail Mummert, ed., *Población y trabajo en contextos regionales.* Zamora, Michoacán: El Colegio de Michoacán.

———. 1993a. "Neo-Nativists Feed on Myopic Fears." *Los Angeles Times,* July 12.

———. 1993b. Letter to the Honorable Richard A. Polanco, chair, Select Committee on California-Mexico Affairs Hearing on Immigrants, Immigration, and the California Economy. Sacramento: California State Assembly, Feb. 19.

———. 1994. *The New Immigration and the Politics of Cultural Diversity in the U.S. and Japan.* La Jolla, Calif.: Center for U.S.-Mexican Studies, University of California, San Diego.

———. 1995. "Their Bags Are Packed in Tlacuitapa." *Los Angeles Times,* Feb. 20.

Cornelius, Wayne, Philip L. Martin, and James F. Hollifield. 1994. *Controlling Immigration: A Global Perspective.* Stanford, Calif.: Stanford University Press.

Costa-Lascoux, Jacqueline. 1989. "Immigrant Children in French Schools: Equality or Discrimination." In Lotty Eldering and Jo Kloprogge, eds., *Different Cultures, Same School: Ethnic Minority Children in Europe.* Amsterdam: Swets and Zeitlinger.

———. 1992. "L'enfant, citoyen á l'école." *Revue française de pédagogie* 13: 71–78.

Cowan, P. A., D. Field, D. A. Hansen, A. Skolnick, and G. E. Swanson. 1993. *Family, Self, and Society: Toward a New Agenda for Family Research.* Hillsdale, N.J.: Lawrence Erlbaum.

Cowley, Geoffrey, and Andrew Murr. 1994. "Good Politics, Bad Medicine." *Newsweek,* Dec. 5.

Crapanzano, Vincent. 1994. "Rethinking Psychological Anthropology: A Critical View." In M. M. Suárez-Orozco and G. and L. Spindler, eds., *The*

Making of Psychological Anthropology II. Fort Worth, Tex.: Harcourt Brace.

Crook, S. 1991. *Modernist Radicalism and Its Aftermath: Foundations and Anti-Foundations in Radical Social Theory*. London: Routledge.

Cussins, Adrian. 1992. "Constructing a World in a Painting: Representation in the Post-Wall Era." In A. Cussins, B. Latour, and B. Smith, eds., *Registration Marks*. London: Pomeroy Purdy Gallery.

Dassetto, Felice, and Albert Bastenier. 1988. *Europa: Nuova Frontiera dell'Islam*. Rome: Edizioni Lavoro.

Day, J. 1992. *Population Projections of the United States by Age, Sex, Race and Hispanic Origin: 1992 to 2050*. U.S. Bureau of the Census, Current Population Reports. Washington, D.C.: U.S. Government Printing Office.

Dayley, J. 1991. "One Big Happy Family." *Reader* 20, no. 17: 5–8.

Delgado-Gaitan, Concha, and Henry T. Trueba. 1991. *Crossing Cultural Borders: Education for Immigrant Families in America*. London: Falmer Press.

Del Olmo, Frank. 1995. "Perspective on Immigration." *Los Angeles Times*, Jan. 31.

Denton, Nicholas. 1993. "Illegal Immigrant Crackdown Agreed." *New York Times*, Feb. 17.

DePalma, Anthony. 1993a. "Three Ships of Smuggled Aliens Adrift in Diplomatic Limbo." *New York Times*, July 11.

———. 1993b. "Refugees Are Sent Back to China Hours After They Dock in Mexico." *New York Times*, July 18.

Devereux, George. 1960. *Mohave Ethnopsychiatry and Suicide*. Bureau of American Ethnology Bulletin No. 175. Washington, D.C.: U.S. Government Printing Office.

———. 1967. *From Anxiety to Method in the Behavioral Sciences*. The Hague: Mouton.

———. 1969. *Reality and Dream: Psychotherapy of a Plains Indian*. New York: Anchor Books.

———. 1978. *Ethnopsychoanalysis: Psychoanalysis and Anthropology as Complementary Frames of Reference*. Berkeley: University of California Press.

De Vos, George. 1973. *Socialization for Achievement: Essays on the Cultural Psychology of the Japanese*. Berkeley: University of California Press.

———. 1980. "Ethnic Adaptation and Minority Status." *Journal of Cross-Cultural Psychology* 11, no. 1: 101–25.

———. 1983. "Achievement Motivation and Intra-Family Attitudes in Immigrant Koreans." *Journal of Psychoanalytic Anthropology* 6, no. 1: 25–71.

———. 1992. *Social Cohesion and Alienation: Minorities in the United States and Japan*. Boulder, Colo.: Westview Press.

———. N.d. "Differential Minority Achievement in Cross-Cultural Perspective: The Case of Koreans in Japan and the United States." Department of Anthropology, University of California, Berkeley. Photocopy.

De Vos, G. A., and M. Suárez-Orozco. 1990. *Status Inequality: The Self in Culture.* Newbury Park, Calif.: Sage.

Diebba, I., and M. Montiel. 1978. "Hispanic Families: An Exploration." In M. Montiel, ed., *Hispanic Families: Critical Issues for Policy Programs in Human Services.* Washington, D.C.: National Coalition of Hispanic Mental Health and Human Service Organizations.

Dollard, J., L. W. Doob, N. E. Miller, O. H. Mower, and R. R. Sears. 1939. *Frustration and Aggression.* New Haven, Conn.: Yale University Press.

Droziak, W. 1994. "Europe's 'Birth Dearth' Spawns Reappraisal of Immigration." *Washington Post,* Jan. 19.

Duffy, Brian. 1993. "Coming to America: An Endless Tide of Illegal Aliens Leaves Many Living as Virtual Slaves in the Promised Land." *U.S. News & World Report,* June 21, pp. 26–31.

Dundes, Alan, ed. 1991. *The Blood Libel Legend: A Casebook in Anti-Semitic Folklore.* Madison: University of Wisconsin Press.

Economist. 1994. "Western Europe's Nationalists: The Rise of the Outside Right." Oct. 15.

Eisenstadt, T. A., and C. L. Thorup. 1994. *Caring Capacity vs. Carrying Capacity: Community Responses to Mexican Immigration in San Diego's North County.* La Jolla, Calif.: Center for U.S.-Mexican Relations, University of California, San Diego.

Eldering, Lotty. 1989. "Ethnic Minority Children in Dutch Schools: Underachievement and Its Explanations." In Lotty Eldering and Jo Kloprogge, eds., *Different Cultures, Same School: Ethnic Minority Children in Europe.* Amsterdam: Swets and Zeitlinger.

Eldering, Lotty, and Jo Kloprogge, eds. 1989. *Different Cultures, Same School: Ethnic Minority Children in Europe.* Amsterdam: Swets and Zeitlinger.

Entwisle, D. 1972. "To Dispel Fantasies About Fantasy-Based Measures of Achievement Motivation." *Psychological Bulletin* 77, no. 4: 377–91.

Erickson, E. 1963. *Childhood and Society.* New York: W. W. Norton.

Erinosho, O., and A. Ayonrinde. 1981. "A Cross-National Comparison of Patterns of Utilization and Psychiatric Care." *International Journal of Social Psychiatry* 27, no. 4: 289–96.

Espin, O. M. 1987. "Psychological Impact of Migration on Latinas: Implications for Psychotherapeutic Practice." *Psychology of Women Quarterly* 11, no. 4: 489–503.

Extra, Guus, and Ton Vallen. 1989. "Second Language Acquisition in Elementary School: A Crossnational Perspective on the Netherlands, Flanders and the Federal Republic of Germany." In Lotty Eldering and Jo Kloprogge, eds., *Different Cultures, Same School: Ethnic Minority Children in Europe.* Amsterdam: Swets and Zeitlinger.

Falicov, Celia J. 1980. "Cultural Variations in the Family Life Cycle: The Mexican American Family." In M. McGoldrick, ed., *The Family Life Cycle: A Framework for Family Therapy.* New York: Gardner Press.

———. 1982. "Mexican Families." In M. McGoldrick, J. K. Pearce, and

J. Giordano, eds., *Ethnicity and Family Therapy*. New York: Guilford Press.

———. 1988. "Learning to Think Culturally." In D. Breulin and D. Schwartz, eds., *Handbook of Family Therapy Training and Supervision*. New York: Guilford Press.

Falicov, Celia J., and B. M. Karrer. 1984. "Therapeutic Strategies for Mexican American Families." *International Journal of Family Therapy* 6, no. 1: 18–30.

Fassmann, Heinz, and Rainer Münz. 1992. "Patterns and Trends of International Migration in Western Europe." *Population and Development Review* 18, no. 3: 457–80.

Feldman, Paul, and Rick McDonnell. 1994. "Prop. 187 Sponsors Swept Up in National Whirlwind." *Los Angeles Times*, Nov. 14.

Feldman, Paul, and James Rainey. 1994. "Parts of Prop. 187 Blocked by Judge." *Los Angeles Times*, Nov. 17.

Fierman, Jaclyn. 1994. "Is Immigration Hurting the U.S.?" In N. Mills, ed., *Arguing Immigration*. New York: Simon and Schuster.

Foblets, Marie-Claire. 1988. "Migration to Europe Today: International Private Law and the New Challenge of Legal Pluralism." Paper read at the "Symposium on Legal Pluralism in Industrial Societies," Zagreb, Yugoslavia, July 26.

———. 1993. Interview with Marcelo M. Suárez-Orozco. Catholic University of Leuven, Belgium. January.

Fordham, Signithia, and J. U. Ogbu. 1986. "Black Students' School Success: Coping with the Burden of 'Acting White.'" *Urban Review* 18, no. 3: 176–206.

Foster, George. 1972. "The Anatomy of Envy: A Study in Symbolic Behavior." *Current Anthropology* 13, no. 2: 165–202.

———. 1979. *Tzintzuntan: Mexican Peasants in a Changing World*. New York: Elsevier.

Francese, Peter. 1994. "Aging America Needs Foreign Blood." In N. Mills, ed., *Arguing Immigration*. New York: Simon and Schuster.

Freire, Paulo. 1993. *Pedagogia da Esperanca: Um Reencontro Com a Pedagogio Do Oprimido*. Sao Paulo: Editora Paz e Terra.

Freud, Sigmund. 1930. *Civilization and Its Discontents*. Translated and edited by James Strachey. New York: W. W. Norton.

Fromm, Erich. 1973. *The Anatomy of Human Destructiveness*. New York: Henry Holt.

Fromm, Erich, and Michael Maccoby. 1970. *Social Character in a Mexican Village: A Sociopsychoanalytic Study*. Englewood Cliffs, N.J.: Prentice-Hall.

Gamio, Manuel. 1971. *Mexican Immigration to the United States: A Study of Human Migration and Adjustment*. New York: Dover.

García Márquez, Gabriel. 1994. "The Useless War." *New York Times Book Review*, Feb. 27.

Garza-Guerrero, A. 1974. "Culture Shock: Its Mourning and Vicissitudes of Identity." *Journal of the Psychoanalytic Association* 22, no. 1: 408–29.

Geertz, Clifford. 1991. "Interview with Clifford Geertz." *Current Anthropology* (Dec.): 1–11.

Gibson, Margaret A. 1988. *Accommodation Without Assimilation: Sikh Immigrants in an American High School.* Ithaca, N.Y.: Cornell University Press.

Gibson, Margaret, and J. U. Ogbu, eds. 1991. *Minority Status and Schooling: A Comparative Study of Immigrant and Involuntary Minorities.* New York: Garland.

Givens, D., and S. Skomal. 1992. "The Four Fields: Myth or Reality?" *Anthropology Newsletter* 33, no. 7: 1–17.

Glazer, Nathan. 1990. "Keep the Borders Open." *New York Times Book Review,* Jan. 14.

———. 1994. "The Closing Door." In N. Mills, ed., *Arguing Immigration.* New York: Simon and Schuster.

Golden, Tim. 1992. "Mexico Is Now Acting to Protect Border Migrants from Robbery and Abuse." *New York Times,* June 28.

Goldenberg, Claude, Leslie Reese, and Ronald Gallimore. 1992. "Effects of Literacy Materials from School on Latino Children's Home Experiences and Early Reading Achievement." *American Journal of Education* 100, no. 4: 497–536.

Gonzalez, David. 1992. "What's the Problem with 'Hispanic'? Just Ask a Latino." *New York Times,* Nov. 15.

Gorer, Geoffrey. 1963. *The American People: A Study in National Character.* Rev. ed. New York: W. W. Norton.

Gorsuch, R. 1983. *Factor Analysis.* 2d ed. Hillsdale, N.J.: Lawrence Erlbaum.

———. 1991. *UniMult.* Altadena, Calif.: UniMult.

Grebler, Leo, Joan Moore, and Ralph Guzman. 1970. *The Mexican American People: The Nation's Second Largest Minority.* New York: Free Press.

Grinberg, León, and Rebeca Grinberg. 1989. *Psychoanalytic Perspectives on Migration and Exile.* New Haven, Conn.: Yale University Press.

Gross, Gregory. 1993. "Migrant Ships Limp to Port." *San Diego Union-Tribune,* July 17.

Gumperz, John. 1981. "Conversational Inferences and Classroom Learning." In J. L. Green and C. Wallet, eds., *Ethnography and Language in Educational Settings.* Norwood, N.J.: Ablex.

Gumperz, John, and Dell Hymes. 1972. *Directions in Socio-Linguistics: The Ethnography of Communication.* New York: Holt, Rinehart and Winston.

Hammar, Tomas, ed. 1983. *European Immigration Policy: A Comparative Study.* Cambridge, Eng.: Cambridge University Press.

Hammersley, M. 1992. *What's Wrong with Ethnography?* London: Routledge.

Havemann, Joel. 1993. "A Dark Side of Europe's Cultural Hub." *Los Angeles Times,* Apr. 9.

Hayes-Bautista, David. 1993. "How Mexicans Are Changing Southern

California." In Abraham F. Lowenthal and Katrina Burgess, eds., *The California-Mexico Connection*. Stanford, Calif.: Stanford University Press.

Hayes-Bautista, David, W. O. Schink, and J. Chapa. 1988. *The Burden of Support: Young Latinos in an Aging Society*. Stanford, Calif.: Stanford University Press.

Hayner, N. S. 1954. "The Family in Mexico." *Marriage and Family Living* 11, no.1: 369–73.

Heer, David. 1990. *Undocumented Mexicans in the United States*. Cambridge, Eng.: Cambridge University Press.

Heller, C. 1966. *Mexican American Youth: The Forgotten Youth at the Crossroads*. New York: Random House.

Henry, William. 1956. *The Analysis of Fantasy*. New York: J. Wiley and Sons.

Hermans, Philip. 1993. "The Experience of Racism by Moroccan Adolescents in Brussels." In E. Roosens, ed., *The Insertion of Allochthonous Youngsters in Belgian Society*. Special Book Issue. *Migration* 15: 51–76.

Hoffmann, S. 1994. "France: Keeping the Demons at Bay." *New York Review of Books* 16, no. 5: 10–16.

Holland, Dorothy. 1992. "Review of *Thinking Through Culture: Expeditions in Cultural Psychology* by Richard Shweder." *American Anthropologist* 94, no. 3: 747–48.

Hollifield, James. 1992. *Immigrants, Markets, and States: The Political Economy of Postwar Europe*. Cambridge, Mass.: Harvard University Press.

————. 1993. "Immigration in France." Paper presented at the workshop "Controlling Illegal Immigration in Global Perspective." Center for U.S.-Mexican Studies, University of California, San Diego, Mar. 18–20.

Hollingshead, A. B. 1975. "Four Factor Index of Social Status." Working paper. Yale University, New Haven, Conn. Photocopy.

Hollman, Frederick. 1990. *United States Population Estimates, by Age, Sex, Race and Hispanic Origin: 1980–1988*. Washington, D.C.: U.S. Government Printing Office.

Holmes, Steven. 1994. "Now Home Is Where the Job Is." *New York Times*, Jan. 2.

Holtzman, W. H., R. Diaz-Guerrero, and J. D. Swartz. 1975. *Personality Development in Two Cultures: A Cross-cultural Longitudinal Study of School Children in Mexico and the United States*. Austin: University of Texas Press.

Horowitz, R. 1983. *Honor and the American Dream: Culture and Identity in a Chicano Community*. New Brunswick, N.J.: Rutgers University Press.

Huberty, N., and M. Morris. 1989. "Multivariate Analysis Versus Multiple Univariate Analyses." *Psychological Bulletin* 105, no. 2: 302–8.

Huddle, Donald. 1993. "The Costs of Immigration." Released by Carrying Capacity Network, July.

Hymes, Dell. 1980. *Language in Education: Ethnolinguistic Essays*. Arlington, Va.: Center for Applied Linguistics.

Jacob, E., and Cathy Jordan. 1987. "Explaining the School Performance of

Minority Students." *Anthropology and Education Quarterly* 18, no. 4 (Special Issue).

———, eds. 1993. *Minority Education: Anthropological Perspectives*. Norwood, N.J.: Ablex.

Kaminsky, Mark. 1993. "On the Site of Loss: A Response to Antokeletz's Paper on Cross-Cultural Transformation." *American Journal of Psychoanalysis* 52, no. 3: 103–8.

Kamm, Henry. 1993." 'People Smugglers' Send New Tide of Refugees onto Nordic Shores." *New York Times*, Feb. 15.

Kantor, M. B. 1969. "Internal Migration and Mental Illness." In Stanley Plog and Robert Edgerton, eds., *Changing Perspectives in Mental Illness*. New York: Holt, Rinehart and Winston.

Kantrowitz, B., and L. Rosaldo. 1991. "Falling Further Behind." *Newsweek*, Aug. 19, p. 60.

Kao, Grace, and Marta Tienda. 1995. "Optimism and Achievement: The Educational Performance of Immigrant Youth." *Social Science Quarterly* 76, no. 1: 1–19.

Karrer, B. M. 1987. "Families of Mexican Descent: A Contextual Approach." In R. B. Birrer, ed., *Urban Family Medicine*. New York: Springer-Verlag.

Keefe, S. E., A. M. Padilla, and Manuel Carlos. 1979. "The Mexican American Extended Family as an Emotional Support System." *Human Organization* 38, no. 2: 144–52.

Kilborn, Peter. 1993. "New Jobs Lack the Old Security in Time of 'Disposable Workers.' " *New York Times*, Mar. 15.

Kinzer, Stephen. 1993. "Germany's Young Turks Say 'Enough' to the Bias." *New York Times*, June 6.

Klein, Melanie, and Joan Riviere. 1964. *Love, Hate, and Reparation*. New York: Norton.

Kleinfield, N. 1993. "Immigrant Dream of Heaven Perishes in Journey of Misery." *New York Times*, June 8.

Kohut, Heinz. 1972. "Thoughts on Narcissism and Narcissistic Rage." *Psychoanalytic Study of the Child* 27, no. 1: 360–400.

Kracke, Waud. 1994. "Reflections on the Savage Self: Introspection, Empathy and Anthropology." In M. M. Suárez-Orozco and G. and L. Spindler, eds., *The Making of Psychological Anthropology II*. Fort Worth, Tex.: Harcourt Brace.

Kraut, Alan M. 1994. *Silent Travelers: Germs, Genes, and the "Immigrant Menace."* New York: Basic Books.

Kristeva, Julia. 1991. *Strangers to Ourselves*. New York: Columbia University Press.

Krugman, Paul. 1994. *The Age of Diminished Expectations*. Cambridge, Mass.: MIT Press.

La Barre, W. 1967. "Preface." In *George Devereux, from Anxiety to Method in the Behavioral Sciences*. The Hague: Mouton.

Lamm, Richard, and Gary Imhoff. 1985. *The Immigration Time Bomb*. New York: Truman Talley Books.

Landau, J. 1982. "Therapy with Families in Cultural Transition." In M. McGoldrick, J. K. Pearce, and J. Giordano, eds., *Ethnicity and Family Therapy*. New York: Guilford Press.

LaVelle, P. 1994. "Mayors Cite Urban Crisis in Appeal for Federal Help. Seek Funds to Help Pay for Costs of Immigrants." *San Diego Union-Tribune*. Feb. 5.

Lee, Changsoo, and George A. De Vos. 1981. *Koreans in Japan: Ethnic Conflict and Accommodation*. Berkeley: University of California Press.

Leman, Johan. 1987. *From Challenging Culture to Challenged Culture: The Sicilian Cultural Code and the Socio-Cultural Praxis of Sicilian Immigrants in Belgium*. Leuven, Belgium: Leuven University Press.

——. 1991. "The Education of Immigrant Children in Belgium." In Marcelo M. Suárez-Orozco, ed., *Migration, Minority Status and Education: European Dilemmas and Responses in the 1990s*. Theme Issue. *Anthropology and Education Quarterly* 22, no. 2: 140–54.

——. 1993. Interview with Marcelo M. Suárez-Orozco. Ministry for Immigrant Affairs, Brussels, Belgium. January.

Lewis, Oscar. 1959a. "Family Dynamics in a Mexican Village." *Marriage and Family Living* 8, no. 2: 218–26.

——. 1959b. *Five Families*. New York: Basic Books.

Lewis, Sasha. 1979. *Slave Trade Today: American Exploitation of Illegal Aliens*. Boston: Beacon Press.

Lindzey, Gardner. 1961. *Projective Techniques and Cross-cultural Research*. New York: Appleton-Century-Crofts.

Liu, Melinda. 1993. "How to Play the Asylum Game: Immigration, the Chinese Have Figured It Out." *Newsweek*, Aug. 2, p. 23.

Lonner, Walter, and J. W. Berry. 1986. *Field Methods in Cross-Cultural Research*. Newbury Park, Calif.: Sage.

Los Angeles County. 1992. *Impact of Undocumented Persons and Other Immigrants on Costs, Revenues and Services in Los Angeles County*. Los Angeles: Los Angeles County.

Lundy, A. 1985. "The Reliability of the Thematic Apperception Test." *Journal of Personality Assessment* 49, no. 2: 141–45.

——. 1988. "Instructional Set and Thematic Apperception Test Validity." *Journal of Personality Assessment* 52, no. 2: 309–20.

McCarthy, Cormac. 1994. *The Crossing*. New York: Knopf.

McClelland, D. 1961. *The Achieving Society*. Princeton, N.J.: Van Nostrand.

McClelland, D. J., J. W. Atkinson, R. H. Clark, and E. L. Lowell. 1953. *The Achievement Motive*. New York: Appleton-Century-Crofts.

McDonnell, Patrick. 1994a. "Complex Family Ties Tangle Simple Premise of Prop. 187." *Los Angeles Times*, Nov. 20.

——. 1994b. "Health Clinics Report Declines After Prop. 187." *Los Angeles Times*, Nov. 26.

McDowell, Edwin. 1993. "Airport Securities Facing Terrorism's New Threat." *New York Times*, July 11.

McDrew, M. W., and H. Teglasi. 1990. "Formal Characteristics of Thematic

Apperception Test Stories as Indices of Emotional Disturbance in Children." *Journal of Personality Assessment* 54, nos. 3 and 4: 639–55.

McGoldrick, M., ed. 1982. *The Family Life Cycle: A Framework for Family Therapy*. New York: Gardner Press.

McGuire, L., and A. Murr. 1993. "California in the Rearview Mirror." *Newsweek*, July 19, p. 25.

McLaren, Peter. 1989. *Life in Schools*. New York: Longman.

McNall, Miles, Timothy Dunnigan, and Jeylan T. Mortimer. 1996. "The Educational Achievement of St. Paul Hmong." *Anthropology and Education Quarterly* 25, no. 1: 44–65.

Madsen, William. 1964. *The Mexican Americans of South Texas*. New York: Holt, Rinehart and Winston.

MALDEF (Mexican American Legal Defense and Educational Fund). 1994. "Temporary Restraining Order Granted Against Proposition 187." News Release, Nov. 16.

Malzberg, B. 1969. "Are Immigrants Psychologically Disturbed?" In Stanley Plog and Robert Edgerton, eds., *Changing Perspectives in Mental Illness*. New York: Holt, Rinehart and Winston.

Mandler, J. 1988. "How to Build a Baby: On the Development of an Accessible Representational System." *Cognitive Development* 3: 113–36.

Marinucci, Carla. 1993. "Treated Like an Animal for Years: Immigrant Laborer Charges Abuse Against Employer." *San Francisco Examiner*, Sept. 26.

Martin, Philip. 1993. "Immigration in Germany." Paper presented at the workshop "Controlling Illegal Immigration in Global Perspective." Center for U.S.-Mexican Studies, University of California, San Diego, Mar. 18–20.

Massey, Douglas, Rafael Alarcón, Jorge Durand, and Humberto González. 1987. *Return to Aztlan: The Social Process of International Migration from Western Mexico*. Berkeley, Calif.: University of California Press.

Matute-Bianchi, M. E. 1991. "Situational Ethnicity and Patterns of School Performance Among Immigrant and Nonimmigrant Mexican-Descent Students." In Margaret A. Gibson and John U. Ogbu, eds., *Minority Status and Schooling: A Comparative Study of Immigrant and Involuntary Minorities*. New York: Garland.

Maziade, M. 1984. "Infant Temperament: SES and Gender Differences and Reliability of Measurement in a Large Quebec Sample." *Merrill-Palmer Quarterly* 30, no. 2: 213–26.

Mehan, Hugh. 1978. "Structuring School Structure." *Harvard Educational Review* 45, no. 1: 31–38.

Mehan, Hugh, and Irene Villanueva. 1994. "Tracking Untracking: The Consequences of Placing Low-Achievement Students in High Track Classes." *University of California Linguistic Minority Institute* 3, no. 3: 1.

Meier, Matt, and Feliciano Rivera. 1993. *Mexican Americans/American Mexicans: From Conquistadors to Chicanos*. New York: Farrar, Straus and Giroux.

Meissner, Doris. 1992. "Managing Migrations." *Foreign Policy* 86, no. 4: 66–83.

Mennen, F. E. 1988. "The Relationship of Race, Socioeconomic Status and Marital Status to Kin Networks." *Journal of Sociology and Social Welfare* 15, no. 4: 77–93.

Migration News. 1995. "Calls for Guest Workers Mount." 2, no. 3: 3–7. Department of Agricultural Economics, University of California, Davis.

Miles, Jack. 1994. "Blacks vs. Browns." In N. Mills, ed., *Arguing Immigration.* New York: Simon and Schuster.

Miller, G. 1993. "Immigrant Costs Overstated, Study Finds." *Los Angeles Times*, Sept. 3.

Miller, R. G. 1966. *Simultaneous Statistical Inference.* New York: McGraw-Hill.

Mills, Nicolaus. 1994. "Introduction." In N. Mills, ed., *Arguing Immigration.* New York: Simon and Schuster.

Mitchell, Stephen A. 1993. "Aggression and the Endangered Self." *Psychoanalytic Quarterly* 62, no. 2: 351–82.

Montiel, M. 1973. "The Chicano Family: A Review of Research." *Social Work* 18, no. 3: 22–31.

Morgan, S. 1987. "Regressivism in the Progressive Era: Immigrants, Eugenists, and Ethnic Displacement." In Scott Morgan and Elizabeth Colson, eds., *People in Upheaval.* New York: Center for Migration Studies.

Morganthau, Tom. 1993. "America: Still a Melting Pot?" *Newsweek*, Aug. 9, pp. 16–21.

Morin, Maria Elena. 1984. *Impact of Family Life and Cultural Identity on Educational Integration: A Study of Second Generation Spanish Immigrants.* Ph.D. diss., Faculty of Psychology and Pedagogy, Catholic University of Leuven, Belgium.

Murillo, N. 1971. "The Mexican American Family." In N. Wagner and M. Haug, eds., *Chicanos: Social and Psychological Perspectives.* St. Louis, Mo.: C. V. Mosby.

Murr, Andrew. 1993. "A Nasty Turn on Immigrants: Wilson Declares the State Under Siege." *Newsweek*, Aug. 23, p. 23.

Murray, Henry A. 1943. *Thematic Apperception Test.* Cambridge, Mass.: Harvard University Press.

Mydans, Seth. 1993. "A New Tide of Immigration Brings Hostility to the Surface, Poll Finds." *New York Times*, June 27.

———. 1994. "Los Angeles Debates Quake Aid for Illegal Aliens." *New York Times*, Feb. 6.

National Network for Immigrant and Refugee Rights. 1993. *Anti-Immigrant Scapegoating in the 1990s.* Oakland, Calif.: National Network for Immigrant and Refugee Rights.

Navarrette, Ruben, Jr. 1993. *A Darker Shade of Crimson: Odyssey of a Harvard Chicano.* New York: Bantam.

Nayer, André, and M. Nys. 1992. *Les migrations vers l'Europe occidentale: politique migratoire et politique d'intégration de la Belgique.* Brussels: Fondation Roi Baudouin.

Nelan, B. 1993. "Not Quite So Welcome Anymore." *Time*, Sept. 21, pp. 10–12.

Nemiroff, R. N.d. "Updating the Psychoanalytic Theories of Aggression." Department of Psychiatry, School of Medicine, University of California, San Diego. Photocopy.

Newsweek. 1993. "Marriages of Convenience?" Feb. 22, p. 3.

New York Times. 1994a. "France Gets Tougher on Immigration." Jan. 7.

———. 1994b. "Immigration Woes: Your Tired, Your Poor, Your $135 Application Fee." Feb. 20.

Noble, Kenneth. 1994. "California Immigration Measure Faces Rocky Legal Path." *New York Times*, Nov. 11.

Ogbu, John U. 1974. *The Next Generation: An Ethnography of Education in an Urban Neighborhood.* New York: Academic Press.

———. 1978. *Minority Education and Caste: The American System in Cross-Cultural Perspective.* New York: Academic Press.

———. 1981. "Origins of Human Competence: A Cultural Ecological Perspective." *Child Development* 52, no. 4: 413–29.

———. 1982. "Anthropology and Education." In *International Encyclopedia of Education: Research and Studies.* Oxford: Oxford University Press.

———. 1983. "Indigenous and Immigrant Minority Education: A Comparative Perspective." Paper read at the 82d Annual Meeting of the American Anthropological Association, Chicago, Nov. 16–20.

———. 1991a. "Minority Coping Responses and School Experience." In Marcelo M. Suárez-Orozco, ed., *Belonging and Alienation: Essays in Honor of George De Vos.* Special Issue. *Journal of Psychohistory* 18, no. 4: 433–56.

———. 1991b. "Immigrant and Involuntary Minorities in Comparative Perspective." In Margaret Gibson and J. U. Ogbu, eds., *Minority Status and Schooling: A Comparative Study of Immigrant and Involuntary Minorities.* New York: Garland.

Ogbu, John U., and Maria Eugenia Matute-Bianchi. 1986. "Understanding Sociocultural Factors: Knowledge, Identity, and School Adjustment." In *Beyond Language: Social and Cultural Factors in Schooling Language Minority Students.* Sacramento, Calif.: Bilingual Education Office, California State Department of Education.

Opatrny, Dennis. 1993. "Brain Drain Hitting State? Think Again." *San Diego Union-Tribune*, Dec. 17.

Padilla, Amado. 1993. "The Psychological Dimensions in Understanding Immigrant Students: The Missing Link." Paper presented at the conference "Immigrant Students in California Schools: Empirical Research," Center for U.S.-Mexican Studies, University of California, San Diego, Jan. 22–23.

Padilla, A. M., M. Alvarez, and K. J. Lindholm. 1986. "Generational Status and Personality Factors as Predictors of Stress in Students." *Hispanic Journal of Behavioral Sciences* 8, no. 3: 275–88.

Papademetriou, D. 1994. "Immigration's Effects on the U.S." *Interpreter Releases* 71, no. 1: 1–5.

Parker, Richard A., and Louis M. Rea. 1993. *Illegal Immigration in San Diego County: An Analysis of Costs and Revenues.* Sacramento, Calif.: Report to the California State Senate Special Committee on Border Issues.

Passel, Jeffrey. 1994. *Immigrants and Taxes: A Reappraisal of Huddle's "The Cost of Immigrants"*. Washington, D.C.: Urban Institute.

Patthey-Chavez, G. 1993. "High School as an Arena for Cultural Conflict and Acculturation for Latino Angelinos." *Anthropology and Education Quarterly* 24, no. 1: 33–60.

Payet, Jean-Paul. 1992. "Civilités et ethnicité dans les collèges de banlieue: enjeux, résistances et dérives d'une action scolaire territorialisée." *Revue française de pédagogie* 101, no. 4: 59–69.

Paz, Octavio. 1961. *The Labyrinth of Solitude*. New York: Grove.

Pear, Robert. 1994. "Deciding Who Gets What in America." *New York Times*, Nov. 27.

Piaget, Jean. 1930. *The Child's Conception of Physical Causality*. London: Kegan Paul.

Pieke, Frank. 1991. "Educational Achievement and 'Folk Theories of Success.'" In Marcelo M. Suárez-Orozco, ed., *Migration, Minority Status and Education: European Dilemmas and Responses in the 1990s*. Theme Issue. *Anthropology and Education Quarterly* 22, no. 2: 162–80.

Plyler v. Doe. 1982. 457 U.S. 202.

Piore, Michael J. 1971. *Birds of Passage: Migrant Labor and Industrial Societies*. New York: Cambridge University Press.

Portes, Alejandro. 1993. "The 'New Immigration.'" Press Release, School of International Relations, Johns Hopkins University, Baltimore, Md., June 3.

Portes, Alejandro, and R. L. Bach. 1985. *Latin Journey: Cuban and Mexican Immigrants in the United States*. Berkeley: University of California Press.

Portes, Alejandro, and M. Zhou. 1992. "The New Second Generation: Segmented Assimilation and Its Variants Among Post-1965 Immigrant Youth." Department of Sociology, Johns Hopkins University, Baltimore, Md.

Price-Williams, Douglass. 1975. *Explorations in Cross-Cultural Psychology*. San Francisco, Calif.: Chandler and Sharp.

Proposition 187. 1994. "Illegal Aliens. Ineligibility for Public Services. Verification and Reporting." Initiative Statute. Sacramento: State of California.

Rabkin, L. 1987. "Changing Kibbutzniks' Attitudes." Paper presented at the Institute of Personality Assessment and Research, University of California, Berkeley, Sept. 21.

Rancho Peñasquitos News. 1993. "Youths Shoot Immigrant Worker." July 20.

Raymond, J. S., D. L. Rhoads, and R. I. Raymond. 1980. "The Relative Impact of Family and Social Involvement on Chicano Mental Health." *American Journal of Community Psychology* 8, no. 5: 557–69.

Ready, Thomas. 1991. *Latino Immigrant Youth: Passages from Adolescence to Adulthood*. New York: Garland.

Reese, L., R. Gallimore, S. Balzano, and C. Goldenberg. 1991. "The Concept of *Educación*: Latino Family Values and American Schooling." Paper presented to the Annual Meeting of the American Anthropological Association, November.

Reeves, Richard. 1994. "Looking for Illegals in the Rubble." *San Diego Union-Tribune*, Feb. 5.

Retschitzki, J., M. Bossel-Lagos, and P. Dasen. 1989. *La recherche intercul-turelle*. Paris: L'Harmattan.

Riding, Alan. 1993a. "Welcome or No, Foreigners Do Spain's Dirty Work." *New York Times*, Feb. 16.

————. 1993b. "French Crack Down on Immigration—Identity Checks OKed." *San Francisco Chronicle*, June 12.

————. 1993c. "France Reversing Course, Fights Immigrants' Refusal to Be French." *New York Times*, Dec. 5.

Rodriguez, Clara. 1991. *Puerto Ricans: Born in the U.S.A.* Boulder, Colo.: Westview Press.

Rodriguez, Lori. 1994. "View of Reaction to Proposition 187." *Houston Chronicle*, Dec. 3.

Rodriguez, R. E. 1989. *Psychological Distress Among Mexican American Women as a Reaction to the New Immigration Law*. Ph.D. diss., Loyola University, Chicago.

Rodriguez, Richard. 1982. *Hunger of Memory: The Education of Richard Rodriguez*. New York: Bantam Books.

Rogler, L., D. Cortes, and R. Malgady. 1991. "Acculturation and Mental Health Status Among Hispanics." *American Psychologist* 46, no. 6: 585–97.

Rogler, L. H., R. G. Malgady, and O. Rodriguez. 1989. *Hispanics and Mental Health: A Framework for Research*. Malabar, Fla.: Robert E. Krieger.

Rogoff, Barbara, and Gilda Morelli. 1989. "Perspectives on Children's Development from Cultural Psychology." *American Psychologist* 44, no. 2: 343–48.

Rohter, Larry. 1993. "Revisiting Immigration and the Open-Door Policy." *New York Times*, Sept. 19.

Roosens, Eugeen. 1988. "Migration and Caste Formation in Europe: The Belgian Case." *Ethnic and Racial Studies* 11, no. 2: 207–17.

————. 1989a. *Creating Ethnicity: The Process of Ethnogenesis*. Newbury Park, Calif.: Sage.

————. 1989b. "Cultural Ecology and Achievement Motivation: Ethnic Minority Youngsters in the Belgian System." In Lotty Eldering and Jo Klop-rogge, eds., *Different Cultures, Same School: Ethnic Minority Children in Europe*. Amsterdam: Swets and Zeitlinger.

————. 1993a. Interview with Marcelo M. Suárez-Orozco. Catholic University of Leuven, Belgium. January.

————, ed. 1993b. *The Insertion of Allochthonous Youngsters in Belgian Society*. Special Book Issue. *Migration* 15, no. 3: 5–117.

————. N.d. "The Multicultural Nature of Belgian Society Today." Catholic University of Leuven, Belgium. Photocopy.

Rosaldo, Renato. 1989. *Culture and Truth: The Remaking of Social Analysis*. Boston: Beacon Press.

Ross, John. 1993. "Back to the Rancho: Fear and Anti-Immigrant Hostility Driving Some Mexicans Home." *Bay Guardian*, Aug. 25.

Rotella, Sebastien, and Patrick McDonnell. 1993. "The Troubled Border Patrol." *Los Angeles Times*, Apr. 22.

Rothman, Eric, and Thomas J. Espenshade. 1992. "Fiscal Impacts of Immigration to the United States." *Population Index* 58, no. 3: 381–415.

Rothstein, Richard. 1994. "Immigration Dilemmas." In N. Mills, ed., *Arguing Immigration*. New York: Simon and Schuster.

Rueschenberg, E., and R. Buriel. 1989. "Mexican American Family Functioning and Acculturation: A Family Systems Perspective." *Hispanic Journal of Behavioral Sciences* 11, no. 3: 232–44.

Rumbaut, Rubén, and Wayne A. Cornelius, eds. 1995. *California's Immigrant Children: Theory, Research, and Implications for Educational Policy.* La Jolla, Calif.: Center for U.S.-Mexican Studies.

Sabogal, F., G. Marín, R. Otero-Sabogal, B. V. Marín, and P. Perez-Stable. 1987. "Hispanic Familism and Acculturation: What Changes and What Doesn't?" *Hispanic Journal of Behavioral Sciences* 9, no. 4: 397–412.

Salgado de Snyder, V. N. 1990. "Gender and Ethnic Differences in Psychosocial Stress and Generalized Distress Among Hispanics." *Sex Roles* 22, nos. 7–8: 111–453.

Sanger, David. 1995. "Mexico Crisis Seen Spurring Flow of Aliens." *New York Times*, Jan. 18.

Sattler, Jerome M. 1988. *Assessment of Children.* 3d ed. San Diego: Jerome M. Sattler.

Scheper-Hughes, Nancy. 1979. *Saints, Scholars, and Schizophrenics: Mental Illness in Rural Ireland.* Berkeley: University of California Press.

———. 1994. "The Violence of Everyday Life: In Search of a Critical and Politically Engaged Psychological Anthropology." In M. M. Suárez-Orozco and G. and L. Spindler, eds., *The Making of Psychological Anthropology II.* Fort Worth, Tex.: Harcourt Brace.

Schmidt, Michael. 1993. *The New Reich: Violent Extremism in Unified Germany and Beyond.* Trans. Daniel Horch. New York: Pantheon.

Shapiro, David. 1965. *Neurotic Styles.* New York: Basic Books.

Sharp, Deborah. 1993. "English Is Kids' Language of Choice: Immigrants' Children Are Abandoning Native Tongues." *USA Today*, July 7.

Sherwood, Ben. 1994. "California Leads the Way, Alas." *New York Times*, Nov. 27.

Shweder, Richard. 1992. *Thinking Through Culture: Expeditions in Cultural Psychology.* Cambridge, Mass.: Harvard University Press.

Simon, Julian. 1989. *The Economic Consequenses of Immigration.* Oxford: Basil Blackwell.

Sluzki, Carlos. 1979. "Migration and Family Conflict." *Family Process* 18, no. 4: 379–90.

Sontag, Deborah. 1992. "Calls to Restrict Immigration Come from Many Quarters." *New York Times*, Dec. 13.

———. 1993a. "Immigrants Forgoing Citizenship While Pursuing American Dream." *New York Times*, July 25.

———. 1993b. "English Is Precious; Classes Are Few." *New York Times,* Aug. 29.

Spindler, George. 1994. "Introduction to Part I in *The Making of Psychological Anthropology, 1978.*" In M. M. Suárez-Orozco and G. and L. Spindler, eds., *The Making of Psychological Anthropology II.* Fort Worth, Tex.: Harcourt Brace.

Spindler, G., and L. Spindler, eds. 1987. *Interpretive Ethnography of Education at Home and Abroad.* Hillsdale, N.J.: Lawrence Erlbaum.

———. 1990. *The American Cultural Dialogue and Its Transmission.* New York: Falmer Press.

Spiro, Melford E. 1978. "Culture and Human Nature." In George Spindler, ed., *The Making of Psychological Anthropology.* Berkeley: University of California Press.

———. 1992. *Anthropological Other or Burmese Brother? Studies in Cultural Analysis.* New Brunswick, N.J.: Transaction.

———. N.d. "What Is New About Post-Modern Subjectivity?" Department of Anthropology, University of California, San Diego. Photocopy.

Staples, R., and A. Mirandé. 1980. "Racial and Cultural Variations Among American Families: A Decennial Review of the Literature on Minority Families." *Journal of Marriage and the Family* 11, no. 4: 887–93.

Stern, Marcus. 1993a. "Clinton Plan for Leaky Borders." *San Diego Union-Tribune,* July 28.

———. 1993b. "Border Blockade Might Come to San Diego." *San Diego Union-Tribune,* Sept. 29.

Stevenson, Harold, H. Azuma, and K. Hakuta, eds. 1986. *Child Development and Education in Japan.* New York: Freeman.

Stevenson, Harold, and L. Shin-Ying. 1990. *Contexts of Achievement: A Study of American, Chinese, and Japanese Children.* Chicago: University of Chicago Press.

Stoddard, Ellwyn. 1973. *Mexican Americans.* New York: Random House.

Stonequist, E. V. 1937. *The Marginal Man: A Study in Personality and Culture Conflict.* New York: Scribner's.

Stromqvist, Sven. 1989. "Perspectives on Second Language Acquisition in Scandinavia." In Lotty Eldering and Jo Kloprogge, eds., *Different Cultures, Same School: Ethnic Minority Children in Europe.* Amsterdam: Swets and Zeitlinger.

Suárez-Orozco, Carola, and Marcelo Suárez-Orozco. 1994. "The Cultural Psychology of Hispanic Immigrants." In T. Weaver, ed., *The Handbook of Hispanic Cultures in the United States: Anthropology.* Houston, Tex.: Arte Publico Press.

Suárez-Orozco, Marcelo. 1986. "Spaanse Amerikanen: Vergelijkende Beschouwingen en Onderwijsproblemen. Tweede Generatie Immigrantenjongeren." *Cultuur en migratie* (Brussels) 2, no. 1: 1–49.

———. 1987. "Towards a Psychosocial Understanding of Hispanic Adaptation to American Schooling." In Henry T. Trueba, ed., *Success or Failure?*

Learning and the Language Minority Student. Cambridge, Mass.: Newbury House.

———. 1989. *Central American Refugees and U.S. High Schools: A Psychosocial Study of Motivation and Achievement.* Stanford, Calif.: Stanford University Press.

———. 1990. "Speaking of the Unspeakable: Towards a Psychosocial Understanding of Responses to Political Terror." *Ethos* 18, no. 3: 353–83.

———, ed. 1991. *Migration, Minority Status and Education: European Dilemmas and Responses in the 1990s.* Theme Issue. *Anthropology and Education Quarterly* 22, no. 2: 99–199.

———. 1994. "Remaking Psychological Anthropology." In M. M. Suárez-Orozco and G. and L. Spindler, eds., *The Making of Psychological Anthropology II.* Fort Worth, Tex.: Harcourt Brace.

Suárez-Orozco, Marcelo, and Howard F. Stein. N.d. "The Don Juan Motif." Department of Anthropology, University of California, San Diego. Photocopy.

Suárez-Orozco, Marcelo, and Carola Suárez-Orozco. 1992. "La psychologie culturelle des immigrants hispaniques aux Etats-Unis: implications pour la recherche en éducation." *Revue française de pédagogie* 101, no. 1: 27–44.

Suárez-Orozco, M. M., and G. and L. Spindler, eds. 1994. *The Making of Psychological Anthropology II.* Fort Worth, Tex.: Harcourt Brace.

Swartz, Marc. 1991. *The Way the World Is.* Berkeley: University of California Press.

Szalay, L., R. Ruiz, J. Strohl, R. Lopez, and L. Turbiville. 1978. *The Hispanic Cultural Frame of Reference.* Washington, D.C.: ISSCS.

Szapocznik, J., and A. Rio. 1989. "Brief Strategic Family Therapy for Hispanic Problem Youth." In L. Beutler, ed., *Programs in Psychotherapy Research.* Washington, D.C.: American Psychological Association.

Szapocznik, J., and C. Truss. 1978. "Intergenerational Sources of Role Conflict in Cuban Mothers." In M. Montiel, ed., *Hispanic Families: Critical Issues For Policy Programs in Human Services.* Washington, D.C.: National Coalition of Hispanic Mental Health and Human Service Organizations.

Tabachnick, B. G., and L. S. Fidell. 1983. *Using Multivariate Statistics.* New York: Harper and Row.

Takaki, Ronald. 1993. *A Different Mirror: A History of Multi-Cultural America.* New York: Little Brown.

Tharp, Roland, and Ronald Gallimore. 1988. *Rousing Minds to Life.* New York: Cambridge University Press.

Thomas, A. D., and S. Z. Dudek. 1985. "Interpersonal Affect in Thematic Apperception Test Responses: A Scoring System." *Journal of Personality Assessment* 49, no. 1: 30–36.

Thomas, Rich, and Andrew Murr. 1993. "The Economic Cost of Immigration." *Newsweek,* Aug. 9, pp. 18–19.

Thornton, Kelly. 1993. "New Policy Clears SD Cops to Summon Border Patrol." *San Diego Union-Tribune,* Dec. 17.

Time. 1993. *The New Face of America: How Immigrants Are Shaping the World's First Multicultural Society.* Special Fall Issue.

Timmerman, Chris. 1993. Interview with Marcelo M. Suárez-Orozco. Catholic University, Leuven, Belgium. January.

Tomlinson, Sally. 1989. "Ethnicity and Educational Achievement in Britain." In Lotty Eldering and Jo Kloprogge, eds., *Different Cultures, Same School: Ethnic Minority Children in Europe.* Amsterdam: Swets and Zeitlinger.

———. 1991. "Ethnicity and Educational Attainment in England: An Overview." In Marcelo M. Suárez-Orozco, ed., *Migration, Minority Status and Education: European Dilemmas and Responses in the 1990s.* Theme Issue. *Anthropology and Education Quarterly* 22, no. 2: 121–39.

Triandis, H. C., G. Marín, H. Betancourt, J. Lisansky, and B. Chang. 1982. *Dimensions of Familism Among Hispanic and Mainstream Navy Recruits.* Champaign: University of Illinois.

Trueba, Henry T., ed. 1987. *Success or Failure? Learning and the Language Minority Student.* Cambridge, Mass.: Newbury House.

———. 1989a. *Raising Silent Voices: Educating the Linguistic Minorities for the 21st Century.* Cambridge, Mass.: Newbury House.

———. 1989b. Rethinking Dropouts: Culture and Literacy for Minority Empowerment. In Henry T. Trueba, G. Spindler, and Louise Spindler, eds., *What Do Anthropologists Have to Say About Dropouts?* London: Falmer Press.

———. 1993. "Race and Ethnicity: The Role of Universities in Healing Multicultural America." *Educational Theory* 43, no. 1: 41–54.

Trueba, Henry T., Cirenio Rodriguez, Yali Zou, and José Cintrón. 1993. *Healing Multicultural America: Mexican Immigrants Rise to Power in Rural California.* London: Falmer Press.

Urrabazo, R. 1985. *Machismo: Mexican American Male Self Concept.* Ph.D. diss., Graduate Theological Union, Berkeley, Calif.

Van Broeck, M. 1993. Interview with Marcelo M. Suárez-Orozco. Catholic University of Leuven, Belgium. January.

Vane, J. R. 1981. "The Thematic Apperception Test: A Review." *Clinical Psychology Review* 1, no. 1: 319–36.

Vasquez, Ana. 1992. "Etudes ethnographiques des enfants d'étrangers à l'école française." *Revue française de pédagogie* 101, no. 1: 45–58.

Vaughn, C. 1988. *Cognitive Independence, Social Independence, and Achievement Orientation: A Comparison of Japanese and U.S. Students.* Ph.D. diss., Graduate School of Education, University of California, Berkeley.

Vega, W. A. 1990. "Hispanic Families in the 1980's: A Decade of Research." *Journal of Marriage and the Family* 52, no. 11: 1015–24.

Vega, W. A., T. Patterson, J. Sallis, P. Nader, C. Atkins, and I. Abramson. 1986. "Cohesion and Adaptability in Mexican American and Anglo Families." *Journal of Marriage and the Family* 48, no. 11: 857–67.

Vernon, S. W., and R. E. Roberts. 1985. "A Comparison of Mexicans and Americans on Selected Measures of Social Support." *Hispanic Journal of Behavioral Sciences* 7, no. 3: 381–99.

Vigil, James D. 1988a. *Barrio Gangs: Street Life and Identity in Southern California*. Austin: University of Texas Press.

———. 1988b. "Group Processes and Street Identity: Adolescent Chicano Gang Members." *Ethos* 16, no. 4: 421–45.

Villareal, José A. 1959. *Pocho*. New York: Anchor Books.

Volkan, V. 1993. "Immigrants and Refugees: A Psychodynamic Perspective." *Mind and Human Interaction* 4, no. 1: 63–69.

Wagner, Nathaniel, and Marsha Haug. 1971. *Chicanos: Social and Psychological Perspectives*. St. Louis, Mo.: C. V. Mosby.

Waldinger, Roger. 1994. "Black/Immigrant Competition Reassessed. New Evidence from Los Angleles." Department of Sociology, University of California, Los Angeles. Photocopy.

Wall Street Journal. 1994. "European Union Readies Immigration Policy." Jan. 28.

Walsh, Michael. 1993. "In the Shadow of the Law." *Time* 142, no. 21 (Sept.): 16–17.

Wambaugh, Joseph. 1984. *Lines and Shadows*. New York: William Morrow.

Wander, Hilde. 1990. "Federal Republic of Germany." In William J. Serow, C. B. Nam, D. F. Sly, and R. H. Weller, eds., *Handbook on International Migration*. New York: Greenwood Press.

Weiner, Tim. 1993. "On These Shores Immigrants Find a New Wave of Hostility." *New York Times*, June 13.

———. 1994. "Immigration Woes." *New York Times*, Feb. 20.

Whitney, Graig. 1993. "Western Europe's Dreams Turn into Nightmares: Recession, Refugees and Violence Dash Hopes of a Golden Era." *New York Times*, Aug. 8.

Williams, Jennifer. 1986. *Selected Demographic Characteristics of the U.S. Hispanic Population and of Hispanic Subgroups*. Washington, D.C.: Congressional Research Service of the Library of Congress.

Williams, Norma. 1990. *The Mexican American Family: Tradition and Change*. New York: General Hall.

Winter, D. G. 1973. *The Power Motive*. New York: Free Press.

Wolf, Daniel H. 1988. *Undocumented Aliens and Crime: The Case of San Diego County*. La Jolla, Calif.: Center for U.S.-Mexican Studies, University of California, San Diego.

———. 1993. "The Rea and Parker Study of Undocumented Alien Fiscal Impact: How Accurate?" Testimony to the Immigration Hearing and Public Forum of Bill Morrow, assemblyman, seventy-third district. Oceanside City Hall, Oceanside, Calif. Dec. 9.

Wood, Daniel. 1994. "California's Prop. 187 Puts Illegal Immigrants on Edge." *Christian Science Monitor*, Nov. 22.

Wootton, James. 1993. "Lessons of Pop Jordan's Death." *Newsweek*, Sept. 13, p. 9.

Index

In this index an "f" after a number indicates a separate reference on the next page, and an "ff" indicates separate references on the next two pages. A continuous discussion over two or more pages is indicated by a span of page numbers, e.g., "57–59." *Passim* is used for a cluster of references in close but not consecutive sequence.

Winter, D. G., 105
Wolf, Daniel, 36–37, 39, 222n41
Word Association Test, 113
World Trade Center, bombing of, 25, 37, 39

Xenophobia, xiv, 2, 8, 16, 21, 23, 30, 43–44, 214n6, 219n32

Zhou, M., 6

Library of Congress Cataloging-in-Publication Data

Suárez-Orozco, Carola.
   Transformations : immigration, family life, and achievement
motivation among Latino adolescents /Carola and Marcelo Suárez-Orozco.
      p.   cm.
   Includes bibliographical references and index.
   ISBN 0-8047-2550-0 (cloth). ISBN 0-8047-2551-9
(paperback)
   1. Mexican American teenagers—California.   2. Mexican American
teenagers.   3. Achievement motivation in youth—California.
4. Teenagers—Mexico.   5. Achievement motivation in youth—Mexico.
6. Teenage immigrants—California.   7. Teenage immigrants—United
States.   8. Mexico—Emigration and immigration.   I. Suárez-Orozco,
Marcelo M.   II. Title.
F870.M5S83   1995
305.23'5'0972—dc20   95-16448   CIP

⊗ This book is printed on acid-free, recycled paper.

Original printing 1995

Last figure below indicates year of this printing:

04 03 02 01 00 99 98 97 96 95

THE POLITICS
OF SHOPPING

INTERNATIONAL INSTITUTE FOR QUALITATIVE METHODOLOGY SERIES

The International Institute for Qualitative Methodology, under the auspices of the Faculty of Nursing at the University of Alberta, was founded in 1998 to facilitate the development of qualitative research methods across a wide variety of academic disciplines through research, publications, conferences, and workshops. The series consists of volumes that have received the Dissertation Award of the Institute, then were revised for publication.

Irena Madjar, *Giving Comfort and Inflicting Pain*
Ian William Sewall, *The Folkloral Voice*
Karen Martin, *When a Baby Dies of SIDS: The Parents' Grief and Search for Reason*
Claudia Malacrida, *Mourning the Dreams: How Parents Create Meaning from Miscarriage, Stillbirth, and Early Infant Death*
Hedy Bach, *A Visual Narrative Concerning Curriculum, Girls, Photography, Etc.*
Rodney Evans, *The Pedagogic Principal*
Colleen Reid, *The Wounds of Exclusion: Poverty, Women's Health, and Social Justice*
Lynne Wiltse, *Cultural Diversity and Discourse Practices in Grade Nine*
Hazel K. Platzer, *Positioning Identities: Lesbians' and Gays' Experiences with Mental Health Care*
Helen Vallianatos, *Poor and Pregnant in New Delhi, India*
Linde Zingaro, *Speaking Out: Storytelling for Social Change*
Sheri Leafgren, *Reuben's Fall: A Rhizomatic Analysis of Disobedience in Kindergarten*
Kaela Jubas, *The Politics of Shopping: What Consumers Learn about Identity, Globalization, and Social Change*

THE POLITICS
OF SHOPPING

WHAT CONSUMERS LEARN ABOUT IDENTITY, GLOBALIZATION, AND SOCIAL CHANGE

Kaela Jubas

Walnut Creek, California

LEFT COAST PRESS, INC.
1630 North Main Street, #400
Walnut Creek, CA 94596
http://www.LCoastPress.com

ISBN 978-1-59874-666-2 hardcover

Library of Congress Cataloging-in-Publication Data:

Jubas, Kaela. The politics of shopping : what consumers learn about identity, globalization, and social change / Kaela Jubas.
    p. cm.—(International Institute for Qualitative Methodology series)
    Includes bibliographical references and index.
    ISBN 978-1-59874-666-2 (hardcover: alk. paper)
1. Shopping—Political aspects. 2. Shopping—Social aspects. 3. Shopping—Psychological aspects. 4. Consumption (Economics)—Political aspects.
5. Globalization—Economic aspects. 6. Globalization and culture.
7. Shopping in literature. I. Title.
    TX335.J83 2010
    339.4'8—dc22
                2010030799

Printed in the United States of America

♾™The paper used in this publication meets the minimum requirements of American National Standard for Information Sciences—Permanence of Paper for Printed Library Materials, ANSI/NISO Z39.48–1992.

CONTENTS

LIST OF ILLUSTRATIONS

Culture is ordinary: that is the first fact. Every human society has its own shape, its purposes, its own meanings. Every human society expresses these, in institutions, and in arts and learning. The making of a society is the finding of common meanings and directions, and its growth is an active debate and amendment, under the pressures of experience, contact, and discovery, writing themselves into the land. The growing society is there, yet it is also made and remade in every individual mind. The making of a mind is, first, the slow learning of shapes, purposes, and meanings, so that work, observation and communication are possible. Then, second, but equal in importance, is the testing of these in experience, the making of new observations, comparisons, and meanings. A culture has two aspects: the known meanings and directions, which its members are trained to; the new observations and meanings, which are offered and tested. These are the ordinary processes of human societies and human minds, and we see through them the nature of a culture: that it is always both traditional and creative; that it is both the most ordinary common meanings and the finest individual meanings. We use the word culture in these two senses: to mean a whole way of life—the common meanings; to mean the arts and learning—the special processes of discovery and creative effort.   —Raymond Williams (1993), "Culture Is Ordinary," p. 90

While I am sympathetic to attempts to restore dignity to the everyday practices that, in the past, have been equated with false consciousness by elite academics, I am reluctant to elevate these activities to guerrilla warfare in a new politics of consumption. At a time when even the Left has embraced the celebration of consumption as a form of resistance by the subordinated, it seems appropriate to explore the popular pleasures of consumption as a serious arena of critical feminist analysis.   —Dawn Currie (1999), *Girl Talk: Adolescent Magazines and Their Readers*, p. 6

ACKNOWLEDGMENTS

The cover of this book creates an illusion. It indicates that this book and the dissertation that it is based on were written entirely by me. But that is not true.

There are two individuals who have been central to this project from day one. First in my life and, therefore, in these acknowledgments is my partner, Karen Caithness. While I was still completing my MEd, it was Karen who, when I floated the idea of applying for a PhD, immediately said, "I think you've found your niche." Despite the chance that I would become her financial dependent for a while, Karen's support was wholehearted and immediate. It also never wavered. Karen eagerly agreed to act as a sort of one-person shadow committee. She carefully read drafts of presentations, papers, and chapters and reviewed the tools that I developed for my study. After I started to clip media materials, it didn't take long for Karen to join in. Some days I would arrive home and find a fabulous addition for my collection on my desk. We tried to save time for play and travel and waterfront strolls, but our conversations often revolved around a concept that I was struggling with or the latest story related to shopping. I count Karen among the very few non-academics I know who can and *will* talk to me about globalization and Gramsci. I know that no student can complete a PhD program without the love and support of others, but I'm not sure that I could have done that without the particular and special love and support you offered me, Karen. I dedicate this book to you.

Shauna Butterwick has worked with me since 2003, when I was completing my MEd, and she hired me as her Research Assistant. Four and a half years later, my employment with her ended, but we were still working together, since she had become my PhD supervisor. As a supervisor, Shauna has three unique gifts that she shares with all students: patience, curiosity, and generosity of time. It was during one of our many after-hours talks about nothing-in-particular when Shauna recognized the potential for me to study shopping as a site of learning. Shauna has opened doors for me, mentored me, and, even in my moments of frustration and confusion, greeted me with encouragement. As important as the role of supervisor is, Shauna has been much more than that: She invited me to travel the world with her and to collaborate on articles and presentations. From health food shops to duty-free stores, we have even shopped together. No student can complete a PhD without a supervisor, but I'm not sure that I would have wanted to do this without your particular and special support, Shauna. Even after I completed my PhD, Shauna continued to support me and my work, encouraging me to apply for the International Institute for Qualitative Methodology Dissertation Award, which I was fortunate to receive.

Thanks, then, are also due IIQM for honouring me with its award, which has led to the revision of my dissertation into this book. I would also like to thank my other two doctoral committee members. I invited Sunera Thobani onto my committee because of her expertise in feminist critical race studies. I am grateful for her commitment to me and my project, which was made all the more interesting and insightful because of her intellectual challenges and steady contributions. I invited Jennifer Sandlin onto my committee, because she is one of the few people in the field of adult education researching shopping. From the day we met at an Adult Education Research Conference session, she has been excited about my work. Her own work in this area has been invaluable, and her upbeat energy hugely appreciated.

My thanks also go to the remaining members of my examination committee. The careful reading of my dissertation by the external examiners, Pierre Walter and Theresa Rogers from UBC and Christine Jarvis from the University of Huddersfield, and their probing questions and feedback helped me put the finishing touches on this work. In chairing my examination, Thomas Kemple balanced attention to formalities, intellectual engagement, and good humour.

Of course, I thank the participants for their time and thoughtful reflection. Tangibly, I was able to offer them only a cup of coffee and a snack during interviews and focus groups. Many of them thanked me for an opportunity to talk about the serious along with the fun side of shopping. I'm glad that I could give them a chance to explore and share their own interests, concerns, and opinions, although it seems to me that I got much more than I gave in our exchanges.

Over the four years that I spent in my PhD program, I shared good food, good wine, good coffee, and questionable accordion playing—but always delivered with gusto and love. I thank friends and family for helping me keep my life as close to balanced as possible and for humouring me when I quizzed them about shopping. Special thanks go to my parents, Donny, who died shortly after I graduated from the PhD program, and Gilda, for happily agreeing to have their experiences included in this text. The encouragement of my Aunt Gilda Freeman in Toronto, who has been an unabashed, lifelong cheerleader for me, magically continued to reach me all the way in Vancouver.

Finally, I thank others who worked with me at UBC, who work with me now at the University of Calgary, and who have attended my presentations or reviewed my manuscripts over the years. Constructive feedback always reminded me to approach questions with an open mind and a critical eye. In particular, I thank Thomas Sork, the first person I met in Educational Studies. Throughout my six years there, Tom helped me take the next step, be that in studies, publishing, or employment. I remember one conversation that we had: I was concerned about lacking a single area of specialization. What I saw as a deficit Tom reframed as the asset of versatility. He, along with so many others, has helped me develop my capacity and my confidence as a student, a researcher, and a teacher.

INTERLUDE I

Images of Promise
and Desire

Tomato Man(ifesto), Trout Lake Farmers' Market, Vancouver, Canada, October 2006

Syn Bar & Grill, Victoria BC, Canada, March 2006 (now closed)

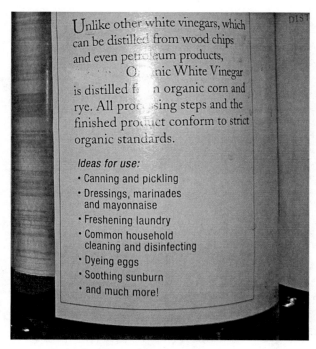

Unlike other white vinegars, which can be distilled from wood chips and even petroleum products, Organic White Vinegar is distilled from organic corn and rye. All processing steps and the finished product conform to strict organic standards.

Ideas for use:
- Canning and pickling
- Dressings, marinades and mayonnaise
- Freshening laundry
- Common household cleaning and disinfecting
- Dyeing eggs
- Soothing sunburn
- and much more!

A vinegar for all occasions, shopping trip, April 2007

1

In the Beginning . . .

Shopping is an important part of my life. Thinking back on when and how it became so integral to my identity, I see in my mind's eye the first material thing that I remember wanting *desperately*. Perhaps six or seven years old at the time, I convinced my mother that I *had* to have an apricot-coloured lacy dress with a sash tied in a bow around the back to wear to my cousin's *bar mitzvah*, the first formal event to which I'd been invited. Never a "girly girl," and not remotely interested in fashion until my early adult years, I still wonder at my insistence on that particular item.

Fast forwarding to my own *bat mitzvah* several years later, I now recognize that day as pivotal in bringing consumption together with citizenship in my own life. According to Jewish culture, the *bar/bat mitzvah* marks the transition from childhood to adulthood, the point at which responsibilities are assumed and rights are accorded—the very hallmarks of citizenship. Post-Second World War British sociologist T. H. Marshall defines citizenship as

> a status bestowed on those who are full members of a community. All who possess the status are equal with respect to the rights and duties with which the status is endowed. There is no universal principle that determines what those rights and duties shall be, but societies in which citizenship is a developing institution create an image of an ideal citizenship against which achievement can be measured and towards which aspiration can be directed. (1992, p. 18)

Feminist, postcolonial and other critical scholars note that citizenship is a much trickier concept than Marshall suggests, complicated by social divisions and competing interests. The "'vocabularies of citizenship' and their meanings vary according to social, political and cultural context and reflect historical legacies" (Lister, 2003, p. 3), and citizenship becomes an "essentially contested concept" (p. 14). Despite the importance of local and temporal context, certain types of relations seem amazingly, persistently important in differentiating and categorizing groups of citizens.

Within Judaism, the person becoming *bar/bat mitzvah* carries out certain rituals for the first time, becoming a full participant in the congregation. In the Conservative synagogue where I celebrated my *bat mitzvah*, girls were allowed to conduct these rituals only on that day; in this way, we girls were unlike boys, who could return to synagogue and continue to engage in those rituals. This is an example of how gender is evident in the structuring of social relations, within and beyond Jewish communities, and how it distinguishes some citizens from others as established rules and practices continue to favour boys and men over girls and women.

In my European Jewish-Canadian community, part of the acknowledgement of the *bar/bat mitzvah* comes through presents. For people who choose to give a monetary gift, there is even a practice to help determine the amount: Cheques are often made out in multiples of $18, representing the numerical equivalent of the word *chai*, Hebrew for "life." Not surprisingly, the wealthier the family and the family's acquaintances, the larger the cheques and the more valuable the other gifts tend to be. Class is another way in which relations are structured so that citizens are differentiated. Even Marshall (1992) recognizes the extent to which capitalism is accompanied by class-based barriers to equality in societies in which everyone has the "right" to almost everything—from food to housing to transit to toothpaste—as long as she or he has the means to pay for it. Still other characteristics that are defined in order to divide citizens might have been less obvious to me on the day of my *bat mitzvah* but are persistently evident across societies and cultures; they include race, ethnicity, (dis)ability, and sexuality. As these divisions are manifest, struggles ensue. ☼ (This icon signals illustrative text or images.)

Whether by design or by accident, on the day of my *bat mitzvah*, shopping and consumption came together with citizenship in my social identity. On the day that I became *bat mitzvah*, for the first time in my life, I had enough money to make what were, to a twelve-year-old girl

---

☼ [W]omen are not given any formal role in the construction of the state; they are instead seen as keeper and cultivators of it. This implies a certain responsibility which is placed upon women to reproduce and cultivate in democratic subjects those dominant cultural values that are endorsed by those who dominate the political machinery (and indeed political memory) of the state. This "reproductive" process leads to a cultural privileging that exalts not only the state's position on national identity but also women's position within it. In so doing, nationalist rhetoric not only privileges the dominance of male super-ordinance in state hierarchies but also represses, both epistemically and politically, the many cultural and national understandings that reside on the margins of the state. This legitimised practice of privileging also means that women who oppose or resist the dominant view of culture and nationhood are viewed as "non-persons" or "non-citizens". The non-citizen ultimately comes to signify difference.   —Jo-Anne Dillabough and Madeleine Arnot (2000), "Feminist Political Frameworks," p. 29

The urge forward along the path thus plotted is an urge towards a fuller measure of equality, an enrichment of the stuff of which the status is made and an increase in the number of those on whom the status is bestowed. Social class, on the other hand, is a system of inequality. And it, too, like citizenship, can be based on a set of ideals, beliefs and values. It is therefore reasonable to expect that the impact of citizenship on social class should take the form of a conflict between opposing principles.   —T. H. Marshall (1992), "Citizenship and Social Class," p. 18

Whiteness carries privileges; non-whiteness carries disadvantages. Despite differences in culture and history, all people of colour share one thing—they are racialised on the basis of skin colour, devalued as persons, and their histories and cultures are distorted and stigmatized.   —Vanaja Dhruvarajan (2000), "People of Colour and National Identity in Canada," p. 157

from an aspiring-to-middle-class family, significant material decisions. With the funds in my bank account, I made my own consumer decisions. (Today, I understand my choice of a stereo, but my choice of an orange vinyl bean bag chair mystifies me only slightly less than the apricot dress.) Becoming a full-fledged citizen was tied to becoming a full-fledged consumer.

As Sharon Zukin notes, across the Global North, one of the first ways that young people assert their own identities, separate from their parents', is through shopping and consumption:

> In our society, teenagers begin to break free to their parents when they start to shop for themselves. . . . Chatting with friends, handling both goods and money, dealing with the outside world without parents to run interference: teenagers' shopping experiences are both exhilarating and scary, centered only on themselves, their friends, and the few stores where they can afford to go. . . . We learn to be adults by learning to shop. (2005, p. 30)

Now as frequently conflated as the ideologies of consumerism and neoliberalism, consumption and citizenship are portrayed as interchangeable sets of rights and responsibilities. As I trace in the following chapters, consumption and citizenship have a long and intertwined history in Western societies; however, they seem to have become especially fused and confused over the past two decades. Following 9/11, the comments of President Bush and Mayor Giuliani linking the Stock

Exchange to City Hall, Disney World to the American way of life, had what Antonio Gramsci (1971) refers to as an obvious, "common sense" resonance with American consumer-citizens. ☼ Moreover, consumption has increasingly become a way of talking about shopping and purchasing, rather than retaining its older meanings of eating and using.

Having grown up in a kosher household, I learned from an early age to think about what was in the food that I ate, about what I consumed in that most literal sense. Back then, I read labels to check for lard, beef tallow, gelatine, rennet, whey powder, and other potentially problematic ingredients. Today, I still read food labels, but now I am more likely to look for fair trade and certified organic logos, locally grown designations, or ingredients that do not include hydrogenated fats. I also read manufacturers' labels on clothes and electronics and household furnishings and toiletries and . . . my traditional Jewish upbringing taught me to be mindful of consumption; somewhere along the line, I learned that there is more to consumption than the centuries-old guidelines of *kashrut* address.

In large part, changes in my personal shopping and consumption practices have been accompanied by larger social, economic, and political changes, and changes in my own affiliations by which I am identified. From my birth and early years in Canada's post-Second World War social democracy of the 1960s and early 1970s, to the increasingly

---

☼ When they struck, they wanted to create an atmosphere of fear. And one of the great goals of this nation's war is to restore public confidence in the airline industry. It's to tell the traveling public: Get on board. Do your business around the country. Fly and enjoy America's great destination spots. Get down to Disney World in Florida. Take your families and enjoy life, the way we want it to be enjoyed.
—Statement made by President George W. Bush in "At O'Hare, President Says 'Get on Board,'" September 27, 2001

We cannot let our way of life be compromised by acts of terrorism. I encourage you to take advantage of all the things that make our City the Capital of the World. New York's restaurants, theaters, stores, and museums are all open for business, and there's never been a better time to participate in the cultural and economic life of our City. And if you are traveling, take a plane with the confidence that our skies are safe.

If you have friends or family who were planning on coming to New York City in the near future, tell them to come now. Not only will they have a great time at our world-renowned restaurants, shops, museums, ballparks, and theaters, but they will be making an important statement that terrorists cannot stop us from being the land of the free and the home of the brave.   —Statement made by Mayor Rudolph Giuliani in "Moving Forward with Courage," October 10, 2001

neoliberal democracy of contemporary globalization, consumption and citizenship have been tied together in constant yet changing, ways. The function of government policies—including war—as economic drivers can be juxtaposed with "a kinder but not always more efficient means of increasing demands for goods [that] has transferred the responsibility from government's hands to those of consumers" (Zukin, 2005, p. 15), evident in the closing decades of the twentieth century. This has occurred in the Global North, alongside an enforced spread of capitalism across developing and previously communist states (see, for example, Bello, 2002; Bocock, 1993; Kiely, 2005). The claims that this structural shift threatens the viability of small-scale producers and the environmental sustainability and that it is especially devastating for producers and consumers in developing countries (Bocock, 1993; Shiva, 2005) ring true to me, as I notice local stores close and amid battles over Walmart®.

These observations and understandings have led me toward the inquiry detailed in this text. In it, I explore multiple, often contradictory, discourses and practices of shopping, consumption, and consumerism, in an attempt to learn more about how people who are concerned about globalization and consumption learn about these issues through their shopping and act on that learning in an attempt to change the status quo. This is a deeply personal inquiry, because I am one of those people. I have come to share something important with people who are anxious about their local communities or regions. Sometimes, these are people whom I have never met; sometimes we live in entirely different parts of the world. Nonetheless their thoughts resonate with me and my experiences. I find them in all kinds of places, from media reports to documentary films to online forums.

I also take note of Vandana Shiva's (2005) and Maria Mies's (1986) point that, because much of women's work has been conducted in what patriarchal, academic, and social systems have categorized as the "private" sphere of the home and unpaid, low-paid or casual labour within and outside the home, women—and poor women in particular—bear much of the brunt of globalization. I recognize that I am experiencing globalization within the context of my gender, race, class, ethnicity, religion, and nationality. At the same time, globalization's large-scale social and economic forces alter the meaning of gender, race, class, ethnicity, religion, and nationality, and the particular trajectory of my life options and considerations.

For over twenty years, my academic, paid, and voluntary work has engaged me in women's, community service, and environmental organizations and advocacy movements. I try to surround myself with people who hold progressive social outlooks. I try to shop in areas of the city and stores in those areas that seem consistent with the person I see myself as, in terms of substance as well as style. The problem is that corporate mergers and social complexities make it difficult to figure out "who" a store or a product is and which progressive practices have primacy over others. When I go grocery shopping, should I go to the nearby Choices™, part of a locally owned chain that often offers little locally grown or produced inventory? Should I go to Capers™, now part of America's largest conglomerate of health food stores, which has fostered strong relationships with local growers? Or should I drive across town to the locally owned and controlled food co-operative and health food stores on Commercial Drive? At what point do my concerns and considerations about shopping pull me into the contorted position of trying to solve problems of global magnitude through my consumption—turning me into a new kind of "silly shopper" (Bowlby, 2001, p. 133)? How do I learn to make sense of all this and begin to answer these questions? ☼

☼ In the 1980s a striking new political rhetoric gave the consumer a new place a long way from the sales or the supermarket. No longer a silly shopper, he or she acquired a grand new exemplary stature as the very type of rational modern citizenship. This consumer-citizen was an individual of no particular sex, with interests and rights and choices. Yet in the light of this character, personally seeking the best deal for himself or herself in every department of life, some other features of the . . . consumer ideal are revealed. It involves ideas of collective responsibility (as well as feminine culpability), and includes a concern for social welfare (as well as anational interests).   —Rachel Bowlby (2002), *Carried Away*, p. 133

Breaking into the Ivory Tower

Although adult education scholars and practitioners speak often about the everyday as an occasion for learning, at the outset of this inquiry I saw few examples of empirical research within the adult education field that attempts to explore what that means. Starting out in my doctoral program, I was centrally interested in globalization, which I conceptualize formally in Chapter 2, and in how adults learn to understand and respond critically to it. Finding it difficult to pinpoint a way to talk to people about a phenomenon such as globalization, which can seem abstract and overwhelming, I began to see shopping and consumption as processes through which each and every one of us comes to experience and know globalization in a very intimate way. Shopping became an example of how the mundane is not necessarily simple, of how taken-for-granted habits can be occasions for learning, of how the personal really is political.

It seems that my decision to undertake this inquiry coincided with a virtual explosion in public interest in and concern about shopping, consumption, and consumerism across and well beyond Canada. The word *shopping* is routinely applied to a growing number of settings and processes. Not long ago, the word referred to what people did in markets or stores. Individuals now talk about shopping for people, places, and things—from doctors or life partners, to vacation destinations or homes, to the stuff of everyday life. For those with access to technology and credit, commercial websites have, to some extent, eliminated the physical boundaries of the store. Even before the widespread popularization of technology, transitions from community markets and neighbourhood shops to speciality shopping areas and stores, to the department store, and, finally, to the big box store have been accompanied by shifts in relationships between producers, vendors, marketers, and shoppers. In this account, I outline how shopping has evolved in the context of historical and social developments. Because the focus of my empirical research is the Canadian city of Vancouver, British Columbia, my consideration of shopping is confined to its evolution in Western societies and, often, more specifically to middle-class practices in urban areas.

Of course, even before I fell upon an interest in shopping, there were voices speaking out about these issues. Kalle Lasn, founder of the magazine *AdBusters* and the annual Buy Nothing Day, has gained widespread attention with his sustained critique of consumerism. ☼ Edgy feminist cultural publications have explored how gender, race, and class come together in shopping and consumption and how social politics seem so easily "bought out" by apparently progressive corporations in the name of profit. ☼ Community activists and activist-journalists have been so busy at their investigations of relevant issues that, in recent years, nonfiction writing and documentary films have become regular fixtures on best-seller lists and mainstream theatre releases. Canadian contributions include Naomi Klein's international blockbuster, *No Logo* (2000 ☼), and Mark Achbar and Joel Bakan's film released in 2004, *The Corporation*, both of which continue to circulate in their original forms as well as through slick websites (see www.naomiklein.org and www.thecorporation.com).

☼ Plenitude is American culture's perverse burden. . . . More than anything else, it is our mediated, consumption-driven culture that's making us sick.   —Kalle Lasn (1999), *Culture Jam*, p. 11

☼ Clearly, the strong, self-actualized woman is an image that sells. . . . It strikes me as hypocritical, though, to push this limited, you-can-do-anything vision of feminism on women when even Vogue admits that part of the reason why women have self-esteem low enough to need to hear that we can do anything is that this same industry goes around telling us we're too fat/too dark/too loud/too aggressive in the first place, and thus need retail therapy to make ourselves feel validated again. . . . Furthermore, this sort of pro-woman schlock isn't even about feminism at all. It's not like we're all supposed to get together and think about the ways gender roles have created artificial barriers between people, or how sexism keeps us from reaching our goals. Oh, no—we're supposed to race out to the mall and buy things. Yeah, that's going to help women secure their rights to choose.   —Rita Hao (2006), "And Now a Word from Our Sponsors: Feminism for Sale," p. 113

☼ This book is not, however, another account of the power of the select group of corporate Goliaths that have gathered to form our de facto global government. Rather, the book is an attempt to analyze and document the forces opposing corporate rule, and to lay out the particular set of cultural and economic conditions that made the emergence of that opposition inevitable.   —Naomi Klein (2000), *No Logo: Taking Aim at the Brand Bullies*, p. xxi

    After I began to read about shopping and consumption earnestly in 2005, I found that, indeed, I was far from alone in my interest. There were news stories about toxins in goods for sale and the impact of travel on global climate change, as well as the possibility of buying ethically produced and marketed items. The alternative online newspaper, *The Tyee,* offered a platform for J. B. MacKinnon and Alisa Smith as they developed their now well-known "100-Mile Diet" (see www.the-tyee.ca/Series/2005/06/28/100Mile/). One of my favourite radio shows, the Canadian Broadcasting Corporation's (CBC) current affairs show *The Current*, has aired segments on global climate change, genetically modified food, organics, and fair trade, among other relevant topics. In 2006, Al Gore came to the attention of millions of people, not in his role as an American politician but as the spokesperson in and for the documentary *An Inconvenient Truth* (see www.climatecrisis.net). On a more local level, California Governor Arnold "The Governator" Schwarzenegger visited Premier Gordon Campbell in June 2007. The two politicians discussed the idea of building a "hydrogen highway" that would stretch along the Pacific Coast and support the development and use of environmentally friendly hydrogen-fuelled vehicles. And, although they preceded the start of my study, the public education and advocacy efforts of Building Better Neighbourhoods to keep Walmart®

out of the City of Vancouver in 2002 left their mark on consumer politics in this city.

As I was writing sections of this text, I became curious about the extent to which these popular concerns had been identified as legitimate academic interests. On January 21, 2008, I searched the ProQuest database for doctoral dissertations that contained the keyword "shopping." Granted I narrowed my search to dissertations written in English within the past five years; still, I was surprised to find a total of only sixty-seven titles. Except for two dissertations, one completed at The University of British Columbia and the other at McMaster University, my search returned titles of dissertations written at American universities. Of these sixty-seven documents, the vast majority were produced by students in the subject areas of marketing, finance, and business; smaller numbers were produced by students in subject areas such as home economics, geography, architecture, and history. The titles of thirty-one of these dissertations indicated a central concern with online shopping. The only study that was overtly interested in education investigated consumer education from a business management perspective. Clearly, few doctoral students across North America are studying shopping from a critical perspective, and even fewer are looking at shopping itself as a process of ongoing, informal learning.

The result of this quick search of North American doctoral dissertations both belies the fact that there has been a great deal of recent critical interest in shopping in Canada and many other countries and confirms the limited extent to which it is being taken up in the academy as a site of learning and academics' research. The work that most directly deals with consumer education does not tend to approach these topics critically. Although this situation is beginning to change, as some marketing faculty are engaging critically with the ideology of consumerism, traditionally consumer education has focused on helping consumers find information and make rational consumption decisions (Paterson, 2006; Pollay, 1986; Sandlin, 2004, 2005a).

Although shopping and learning have been connected in academic scholarship, little work focuses on shopping as a site and process of learning and on shoppers as learners. Robert Bocock recognizes that "[t]here is nothing natural about modern consumption; it is something which is acquired, learned; something which people are socialized into doing" (1993, p. 54). In his discussion of the "knowing consumer" (2006, p. 141), Mark Paterson distinguishes between ignorant "suckers" who are manipulated by marketing and structural forces (p. 142), good consumers whose skill is in "continually finding the best bargains" (p. 152), and sophisticated, "savvy" consumers (p. 152). ☼ Roberta Sassatelli warns that unless shopping is explored in the full

---

☼ Being a "savvy" consumer is not about continually finding the best bargains, although that is a useful skill. Being a savvy consumer is to be aware of the contradictions between the marketing and advertising imposed on us, but still consuming items in intended and unintended ways in order to articulate something else—a sense of self-identity, of difference, or to express a social identity, that sense of belonging to a group based on shared tastes and values. Often the sense of belonging to a group is defined in terms of resistance, as Stuart Hall argues, this being a pervasive or even seductive attitude. Using a notion from Antonio Gramsci concerning the contested "terrain of culture", wherein ideological struggles take place, Hall continues:

> The people versus the power-bloc: this, rather than "class-against-class", is the central line of contradiction around which the terrain of culture is polarized. Popular culture, especially, is organized around the contradiction: the popular forces versus the power-bloc. (1981: 238)

—Mark Paterson (2006), *Consumption and Everyday Life*, p. 152

---

array of its purposes and meanings—economic, cultural, social, political, and personal—"we prepare the ground for a normative rather than a critical analysis" (2006, p. 224). This suggests one reason why it is important to involve participants in research related to shopping as a site of learning. As I explore in later chapters, participants in this study articulated the reality that shopping can become a site of reflexivity, as well as intellectual, emotional, spiritual, and sensual learning. ☼ My inquiry places shopping and shoppers in the foreground of an exploration of what I conceptualize, in the next chapter, as "holistic learning." In this way, it complements American adult educator Jennifer Sandlin's (2000, 2004, 2005a, 2005b, 2007) work on consumer education, which connects consumer-citizenship to adult learning. Like Sandlin's most recent work (2007), my inquiry makes a unique contribution to this growing but still-small body of work in the field of adult education, shifting from a question of how consumers can be educated to how shopping can be educational.

This inquiry extends the abstract analyses and historical accounts of consumer-citizenship that constitute much of the existing academic scholarship. My empirical research contributes to contemporary studies of and writing on these topics that are emerging among sociologists and anthropologists (see, for example, Bhachu, 2004; Bocock, 1993; Grewal, 2005; Hilton, 2003; Mies, 1986; Ong, 2004); historians (see, for example, Rappaport, 2000); and literary and cultural studies scholars (see, for example, Baudrillard, 1998; Bowlby, 2002; Nava, 1999; Paterson, 2006). I touch on some of that scholarship especially in Chapter 2, where I develop

☼

NICOLE: [*pause*] Uh, I would think I'm a good shopper for myself because I'm aware
of, I feel like I need to be aware of why I'm buying things. So, um, I don't
necessarily go out and spend my money, uh, because I feel like that's what
is, um, expected of me, I feel like when I go shopping I, uh, question what
I'm doing. And, uh, and I know when I buy stuff, say, such as, like, you know,
clothing or, um, material [items], it makes me feel good and I know that I do it
because it makes me feel good. But at the same time, when I'm doing that, uh,
when I go out and shop, and I, and I say to myself, am I doing this just because
I know that I, that I will feel better about myself? Uh, I might stop and say, No,
I can't. And I won't spend that money. Or I won't necessarily buy that product.
It's not about spending money, I think money is, it's about whether or not I
need that material item. Because I don't, I don't, I try not to find value in those
material items, such as, you know, um, emotional value. Because emotional
value is not a, it's not, there is no emotional value, those materials cannot
give you what you need. So I try to find those elsewhere. Eh, I'm not sure if
I'm a great shopper when it comes to the advertising. Because I'm part of
the loophole, or I would hope that I'm part of the, of the, um, of the whole
of their marketing scheme where I'm, I don't want to be those people in the
advertisements.

KAELA: Right, right.

NICOLE: I don't want to bind myself in that specific model that, like, stressing this
lifestyle that looks really good, uh, because I know what they're getting
at, you know, and it, it's a . . . sort of emptiness. . . . And that's a very scary
thing because a lot of people are drawn into that. . . . So we've created
these categories. You know, even the person that does wear second-hand
clothing and tries their best to, like, you know, avoid the system is still
part of the system- and they're just creating a specific, there is a specific
style to that and a specific lifestyle to that. . . .   —Interview excerpt,
February 17, 2007

a conceptualization of consumer-citizenship. My particular focus on an
activity of everyday life also takes up the feminist interest in lived experience. Perhaps most importantly for an inquiry in the field of adult education, this study clearly positions adult learning alongside consumption and
citizenship as a central and relevant concern. Even sociologists and cultural studies scholars recognize the link between shopping or consumption
and learning, in one case describing them "as situated learning practices
which are co-productive of consumers desires and objectives" (Sassatelli,
2006, p. 223). Finally, it begins to fill a void in Canadian scholarship on
these topics. In the remainder of this section, I offer an overview of some
of the recent research about contemporary shopping and consumption,
often from disciplines and fields outside adult education, which has helped
inform the development of my own thinking and research.

Sharon Zukin's (2005) study of shoppers and shopping, primarily in Zukin's own home city of New York, combines historical, sociological, anthropological, and geographic questions and approaches. Zukin's title, *Point of Purchase*, is a play on words, suggesting a focus on both shopping places as points-of-purchase and the meaning of shopping or the point of (the) purchase. Her book traces the development of marketing and retail trends in the United States from the rise of department stores and mass marketing to their replacement by "big box" discount stores, segmented or niche marketing, and the importance of branding, and it is unique in its purpose of explaining contemporary American shopping and shoppers. A sociologist, she draws on the work of Pierre Bourdieu in talking about shopping and consumption, and their importance in the development of cultural capital and social status. In the context of my inquiry, Zukin's book is also important for its overall emphasis on adult shoppers.

Although at times Zukin pinpoints some of the profound tensions and paradoxes of shopping and consumerism, at other times her reflections are limited to observations such as that American men prefer shopping online, whereas women continue to prefer in-person shopping (2005, p. 228). She notes that racialized youth experience discrimination during their shopping, recounting the experiences of one black teenager who goes to Tiffany & Co.'s™ Manhattan flagship store, and that lower-class citizens have been and remain restricted in their shopping and consumption options. ☼ Contemporary consumerism holds out the illusion of equality, but clearly "five-and-dimes, supermarkets, and superstores don't want to eliminate social classes [or other social divisions]. They just want all of us to keep shopping, every day" (p. 88).

At the same time as all shoppers are confronted with rhetoric of shopping and consumption as pathways to equality and the pressure to shop ceaselessly, some develop a critical stance about shopping, consumption, and consumerism. Among these shoppers, some people put this knowledge to use primarily in changing their own practices and becoming healthier, more ethical individuals. Zukin (2005) feels good about shopping at the Greenmarket—the local farmers' market in Union Square, Manhattan—where only locally grown and produced food items can be sold, and I feel similarly good when I go to one of the local farmers' markets. But what about Vandana Shiva's (2005) and Maria Mies's (1986) more radical questions about capitalism, patriarchy, racism, and imperialism? How do concerns about gene and species patenting or privatization of the commons enter into the picture of what I see at the farmers' market or how agricultural production and consumption are practised by other farmers and shoppers? What about shoppers who cannot find the money or the time to shop at farmers' markets? Do I celebrate or protest Walmart's® intention to introduce organically grown produce

☼ J [*an aspiring rap performer*] looks serious, and I notice that none of the rather quiet clothes he's wearing today—a dark blue turtleneck, blue jeans, and boots— is sporting a logo.

He points to the turtleneck. "Armani," he says. He points to the jeans. "Guess." Finally he nods toward his feet. "Timberland."

Not a logo in sight. J settles back in his chair and gives me an appraising glance to see whether I appreciate his taste, now that he has pointed it out to me.

"We rebel," he says, in answer to my question. "But we're socialized."

—Sharon Zukin (2005), *Point of Purchase: How Shopping Changed American Culture*, p. 142

[M]any of us can't afford to buy the things we would like to have. Through magazines, television, and books, we gain cultural capital by vicarious consumption. Looking at goods in stores or on the Internet, reading reviews, and talking about them train us . . . to appreciate their subtle differences. And once we have developed a fine eye for differences among the goods, we can make distinctions among the people who use them. This is a different approach to shopping from the early years of mass consumption, when most mass market products were homogeneous and most people didn't spend so much time thinking about them.   —Sharon Zukin (2005), *Point of Purchase: How Shopping Changed American Culture*, pp. 41–42

into its stores? Even as it might spread the option of organic food consumption across classes, is it another example of how the ideologies of consumerism and neoliberalism, at work under the structure of capitalism, enable the appropriation of resistance by big business? What does it mean for a critical consumer-citizen to both "rebel" and be "socialized" (Zukin, 2005, p. 142) through consumption? These sorts of questions, which imply the limitations to consumer-citizenship and begin to connect shopping to broader social critique and engagement, are largely lacking in Zukin's (2005) work; they are central in my inquiry.

There has been some research that has taken a more overtly critical perspective and connected adults' shopping to globalization and resistance. Much of this research has focused on the environmental impacts of globalization. John Connelly and Andrea Prothero examine "how green consumers engage with environmental issues at an everyday level" (2008, p. 117). Their study centred on the assumptions that individuals are engaged in political or resistant movements and discourses, such as environmentalism, on a daily basis, and that shopping and consumption are processes with deep cultural, as well as material, meanings and impacts. It is noteworthy, because it attempts to fill "a gap [that] remains as to how environmental concerns are tied up with the emergence of an apparently more individualized and globalized society" (pp. 120–121). They draw heavily on the theoretical work of Anthony Giddens and Ulrich Beck on globalization, individualization, risk, and self-identity in their exploration of the practices adopted by environmentally conscious consumer-citizens in Dublin, Ireland. As they explain, the reflexivity that is accompanying globalization means that "green" shoppers are continually reflecting on both the effects that consumption can have on them as well as the effects that their consumption can have on the world. They outline an environmentalist discourse that features the idea of "co-responsibility" (Connelly & Prothero, 2008) of consumers and producers for these effects. That idea is both useful to my inquiry, because it bridges the distance traditionally established between production and consumption, and problematic, because it echoes a mainstream or "hegemonic" (Gramsci, 1971) discourse of neoliberalism as the individual is viewed as holding powerful decision-making power.

Connelly and Prothero's study involved a relatively small number of participants (seven people), all of whom self-identified as environmentally conscious or "green" consumers. They were recruited from environmental organizations and through participant referrals (that is, "snowballing"). The researchers conducted two sets of interviews with participants and gathered biographical details from them. They note that participants had relatively high degrees of education, identified as middle or working class, and attended to food shopping and consumption in particular as part of their environmental commitment.

Although this was a small study, it offers some useful insights for me. Connelly and Prothero approach shopping and consumption as processes "fundamentally embedded in social relations" (2008, p. 125). Environmental consciousness is only one factor that determines shopping and consumption habits, and a common identity as a green consumer is only one dimension of potentially diverse and complicated identities. They make the following point:

> One of the difficulties with this is that if people now believe they are central to environmental solutions through their own individual consumption, invariably particular practices and material goods will become identified as bad, yet these very same practices and material goods may be central (meaningfully) in social relations. Much environmental writing has not helped in this regard. (p. 128)

This reality creates tensions for shoppers who want to develop certain practices and habits. One participant in their study, Anne, who struggles to balance her opposition to the fast food and high status brands with pressure from her children to shop for and consume these items. As they note, "Green beliefs and attempts at greening specific practices co-exist alongside a more ambivalent attitude towards consuming. . . . In this study, we found a range of inconsistencies, ambivalence and dilemmas in relation to a variety of consumer practices" (pp. 126–127). Although participants in their study might have felt guilty about some of the shopping and consumption decisions that they made, such as buying a car, they also accepted "that compromise was inevitable" (p. 127).

In their article, Connelly and Prothero argue that a discourse of environmentally friendly shopping and consumption has combined with an ideology of individualization and a constant reflexivity during contemporary globalization, at least for middle-class consumer-citizens living in an urbanized Western setting. Green shoppers interpret this discourse and ideology and fit them both into their lives, according to their own material and cultural circumstances. Connelly and Prothero conclude that "feelings and thoughts (of personal responsibility) are *real* for people" (p. 142, emphasis added), rather than external impositions. Although they take issue with the argument offered by other scholars that these thoughts and feelings distract conscientious, politically minded shoppers from the consideration of power relations and structural issues (see, for example, Smith, 1998 in Connelly & Prothero, 2008, p. 141), I believe that these two positions are actually compatible: Feeling and thoughts can be real and meaningful in the construction of identity, as well as a distraction from other important elements of social life. An ideology of individualization, developed by scholars such as Beck (1992), might advise that shoppers are reflexive, choice-making individuals, but shoppers are also always embedded in social structures.

Although they are not centrally concerned with shopping, Deborah Barndt's (1999, 2002) accounts of her "Tomasita Project" have also been very helpful to me in this inquiry. That project explored globalization—food production largely in the Global South, and consumption largely in the Global North—and popular education. Barndt explains that she

> traced the journey of a tomato from the Mexican field to a Canadian fast-food restaurant. . . . I chose the tomato as a code for globalization and as a device for exploring the shifting role of women (as both producers and consumers) in this long and twisting journey, and called her Tomasita. Using a Spanish name and a female character emphasizes the fact that the continental food system similarly exploits Mexicans, women workers and the environment. In other words, the continental food system deepens inequalities between North and South as well as

between men and women (with class and race complicating the picture);
at the same time, it perpetuates human domination of the environment.
(1999, pp. 14–15)

Working from a feminist historical materialist perspective, which
puts forward the position that knowledge is built over time from experiences of complex material relations, Barndt employs the tomato as
a metaphor and a pedagogical tool. This approach resembles my use of
shopping in this inquiry. She follows the path of this basic food item
and its construction as a global agricultural commodity from seed to
field to store. The story that she tells helps "demystify globalization,
revealing the role of corporations in creating and maintaining a global
food system dependent on genetically modified seeds, pesticide packages,
expropriated Indigenous land, cheap peasant labor, and environmental
racism" (2002, p. 2). In framing her research, Barndt draws on the work
of Gramsci-inspired adult educator dian marino (1997) and marino's
attempt to discern "cracks in consent," the everyday expressions of resistance that arise in response to the always-present inconsistencies and
problems with the status quo. Barndt's research account attempts to
"weave examples of 'cracks in consent' into the stories of women workers following the tomato's trail" (2002, p. 231). I discuss some of the
educational and activist projects outlined in one of the books that came
out of the Tomasita Project, *Women Working the NAFTA Food Chain*
(Barndt, 1999), in Chapter 2.

Barndt outlines "four levels of resistance: individual responses,
local/global education, organized collective actions, and transnational
coalitional initiatives" (2002, p. 231). As I outline in Chapters 4, 5,
6, and 7, which detail my analyses, individual responses and local/
global education are especially relevant to my inquiry; references to
the final two levels noted by Barndt are also present in the data that
I analyze, but to a lesser extent. Overall, it is Barndt's epistemological and methodological assumptions that are most helpful to me in
this inquiry. Like me, she adopts a feminist historical materialist perspective in her attempt to explore how people learn about and experience the complex phenomenon of globalization. Often expressed
in abstract, technical terms, globalization can seem overwhelming;
however, by focusing on the everyday moments and processes that
make globalization's presence in people's lives evident, researchers
and adult educators can advance a critical analysis of and response to
it. I conceptualize globalization more fully in the following chapter,
but, like Barndt, I understand it as a phenomenon that links people
and places around the globe in chains of production and consumption,
even as the local and national manifestations of economic, gendered,

and racial structures maintain rifts between the Global North and the Global South and between classes or groups of people within a society. Her adoption of a feminist understanding of the role of emotions and the senses, as well as intellect, in learning is similarly consistent with the conceptualization of informal adult learning that I develop in the next chapter.

Within the field of adult education, much of the relevant research and theoretical writing centres on the environmental and other social movements as sites of learning, which I discuss in Chapter 7, or on media consumption, which I discuss in Chapter 4. An important exception is Sandlin's (2004, 2005a, 2005b) work, which more directly relates to shopping. Working from a critical cultural studies perspective, she explores formal and informal adult learning, shopping, media consumption, and "culture jamming" or the "remixing of advertisements in an attempt to unmask (rather than ornament) corporate evils" (Haiven, 2007, p. 85). As Sandlin surmises, "The focus of traditional consumer education for adults has been on teaching technical skills that create savvy and knowledgeable consumers able to navigate a complex consumer marketplace" (2005a, p. 166). Although this is true of much of the traditional consumer research based in marketing departments (Pollay, 1986), some of current writing within marketing or business schools is beginning to treat consumerism and consumption more critically (see Connelly & Prothero, 2008; Shaw, 2007). Sandlin frames consumption as an inherently political, rather than simply utilitarian, process. She then reconceptualizes consumer education "to include a variety of informal sites of learning including those focusing on curbing consumption, fighting consumer capitalism, and 'jamming' corporate-sponsored consumer culture" (2005a, p. 166).

In a more recent article, Sandlin reviews the educational potential of culture jamming. She presents culture jamming as a form of "critical public pedagogy" (2007, p. 77) through which activists "reject the passive consumption of consumer culture and seek to be active creators who live authentically." She further outlines several educational functions of culture jamming, including its ability to create "transitional spaces through cultural production" (p. 77) for new discourses; inspire communities for learning and resistance; encourage affective and sensual, as well as intellectual, learning and expression; construct an impromptu forum for the enactment of politics and values; and as a forum for transformational learning on individual, cultural, and social levels. These points appear in Chapters 4 and 7, in which I discuss, first, cultural forms and narratives and, then, learning to make change.

Aside from Sandlin's adult education work, much of the research that links shopping and learning has been conducted by sociologists of education and has concerned children and youth, rather than adults. Lydia Martens summarizes the extent to which such scholarship "heralds the idea of the market as a primary pedagogue" (2005, p. 345). Through their shopping for and consumption of both cultural and explicitly educational products, people learn about the rules and processes of economic and of social organization in their societies. Again, because my focus is on shopping as a site of informal adult learning, rather than on the more commonly explored questions of how young people learn to shop and identify as shoppers or on the corporatization of the school, I include here a summary of two books that focus on ties between schooling or formal education and shopping or consumption but raise points relevant to my inquiry.

Educational sociologists Jane Kenway and Elizabeth Bullen (2001) discuss their research completed over the last decade of the twentieth century in Australia, the United Kingdom, the United States, and Canada. Their book summarizes three projects that cumulatively involved a policy and documentary analysis of materials referring to the marketization of education; an archiving of technologically based educational projects and materials; and school-based interviews and in-class observations with children and staff at several schools in Victoria, Australia. They discuss the role of "consumer-media culture" that blends consumption with information and communication media and that has infiltrated children's and parents' lives entirely, both through schools and at home.

At least two paradoxical trends are discussed in their book: one trend toward the (re)construction of children and youth as consumers with a certain amount of power and the other toward the commercialization and commodification of schools and schooling. This is manifest in a range of ways: curriculum materials developed by for-profit corporations; corporate sponsorship of sports teams; funding for computer equipment or athletic and cultural events; corporate-sponsored schools and institutes (often tied to summer and part-time jobs for older students); and parents' (and typically mothers') fundraising for miscellaneous items. Ironically, even though the lives and the work of the children, parents, and teachers are all infused with consumer-media culture, a wedge is driven between adults, who attempt to distance themselves from that culture and retain a sense of serious purpose, and the young people who are captivated by and enjoy that culture. Kenway and Bullen conclude that

> the students are informed and agential in this context, partly because they draw on the consumption skills learned outside schools. They know how to put on *best face*, they know what the education market values and that it does not value difference (particularly social class difference) and genuine student agency. They know it is two-faced.

They know what they have to sell and give away in exchange for the image and reputation necessary for school success; they know how to *comply with illusion*. However, they learn as they go up through school and become more sophisticated, disenchanted and cynical that more things are lost than gained in this schizophrenic process. (2001, pp. 148–149, emphasis in original)

Looking for the possibility of critical responses among teachers and parents, Kenway and Bullen suggest that schools incorporate the techniques and tools of consumer-media culture in a purposeful, critical, even subversive manner. Schools can, for example, engage students in critical study of what they find attractive and fun, for example, the culture of "cool." Or, they can facilitate the development of children as *cyberflâneurs*, "spectators at the corporate bazaar, both real and virtual, but they are spectators of the 'watchdog' variety—they look back, not in wonder but with a sceptical and quizzical eye. Their object of inquiry is consumer-media culture" (2001, p. 178). They can also encourage young people to use and respond to media creatively and critically, through online publications or, as Sandlin (2007) discusses, culture jamming.

Kenway and Bullen (2001) contribute greatly to the research-based scholarship on shopping, consumption, learning, and education, especially as these topics relate to young people; however, there are also critiques of some of their analytical conclusions. Martens (2005) makes a point with which I agree: Although they generally work from a critical feminist perspective, Kenway and Bullen occasionally seem to lose sight of the social diversity of children, and teachers and the diverse ways in which social groups, as well as individuals, can consume and make sense of media and material culture. As Martens explains,

As consumers, parents and their children are treated as generalised and uniform groups, rather than as materially positioned individuals belonging to differentiated social groupings and communities in which consumption patterns vary. The corollary is that children are conceptualised as framed and integrated in consumer culture in the same way. . . . This book does not address the possibility that parents may value consumer culture in different ways (and that not all of them are necessarily critical of the efforts of commerce in relation to their children), neither do we get a sense that domestic consumer cultures may vary. (2005, p. 350)

Beyond the work already outlined, I also draw on Canadian sociologist Dawn Currie's (1999) book, which focuses on media consumption rather than shopping and details her study of Canadian adolescent girls' magazine-reading. Like Barndt (1999, 2002), Currie works from a feminist historical materialist perspective that is consistent with a Gramscian approach. She also incorporates some of the insights of post-structuralism about the importance of language, text, and the production of culture. Her study used an intertextual methodology to juxtapose the texts of magazines, transcripts of interviews with teenage girls, and previously published research accounts. In her conclusions, Currie notes that "girls' lived experiences of adolescent femininity exceed the categories of its textual representation" (1999, p. 302). This conclusion is consistent with Currie's insistence that there are differences between the cultural and the social. Currie further finds it problematic that mainstream magazines tend to neglect accounts of girls' social lives, by constructing a cultural accounting of problems as personal experiences with individualized solutions. ✿

Currie's methodological approach is especially helpful and relevant in my inquiry, since I am similarly interested in intertextuality. Her analysis of cultural products in conjunction with social relations exemplifies the cultural materialist perspective consistent with Gramsci's (1971) writing and my own approach. In particular, I juxtapose texts comprising transcripts, academic and popular scholarship, and novels in the analyses presented in this study. I also suggest how these texts can be linked to other available texts, including online conversations, or "blogs" (web logs), media reports, political speeches and commentaries, as well as images available through advertising, political cartoons, and protest graffiti. These texts and images are inserted throughout this dissertation, and, although some are analyzed more fully and formally than others, they all suggest the preponderance of possible data sources related to my central topic of shopping as a site of informal adult learning about the politics of consumption, citizenship, globalization, and identity.

✿ As noted in this chapter, while proponents of ideology begin from the study of social texts, their power is seen to lie outside, or beyond, the text itself. Specifically, power is located in social formations which are deemed the beneficiaries of the social order that these texts purportedly reproduce. To thus view women's magazines as ideological is an important move because it contextualizes cultural representations by placing them, analytically, within the social world which produced them. Such a move exposes cultural naturalizations as historical and political, questioning the interests served by representations of women as homemakers and sexual objects [and shoppers].   —Dawn Currie (1999), *Girl Talk: Adolescent Magazines and Their Readers*, p. 88

Throughout the chapters that follow, I continue to cite and draw on scholarship that explores, to some degree or another, the topics of shopping, consumption, and informal adult learning, as well as globalization and social identity. Most of the scholarship that I have summarized here relates to recent empirical studies; however, much of the work that I incorporate in later sections focuses on conceptual development, philosophical argumentation, or historical cases. This additional scholarship, as I assert in the next chapter, has been crucial to this inquiry, because it indicates the complexity of my research purpose and questions and locates them in diverse but—I contend—related scholarly traditions.

Research Purpose and Questions

Seeking to build understanding of how people—including me—experience, interpret, and navigate a complicated social life, this inquiry illuminates how everyday, mundane activities can become opportunities for informal adult learning. I was interested in investigating shopping for its potential as a site and process of learning about the links between consumption, citizenship, globalization, and resistance, and I am especially interested in how the impetus for societal justice and change surfaces as part of that learning. Drawing on various strands of critical scholarship, including feminist, postcolonial, critical race, cultural studies, and adult education (both academic and popular), I explore my own life and the lives of other participants who constitute Canadian society. Borrowing from the techniques of cultural studies scholars, I also incorporate other sources of information and evidence, including fiction, online blogs, public notices and graffiti, and political rhetoric. The inclusion of such materials is consistent with the central argument of this inquiry that learning occurs informally, as well as formally, and that evidence of social phenomena can be found in unexpected times and places that are often ignored.

This exploration focuses on one corner of Canada: Vancouver, British Columbia. Like any research environ, Vancouver is both similar to and different from other parts of this country, as well as places in other countries. Vancouver shares a certain urban culture and sensibility with other cities. A service such as public transit disrupts—if only for a short time—the anonymity and invisibility of urban life by bringing strangers together, and then reinforces those qualities as people go their separate ways. Like other cities in this period of globalization, Vancouver and its surrounding area have a growing population and changing ethno-racial composition. In a time when choice is summoned as an intrinsic value of both liberalism and consumerism, and operates to join these two ideologies, the preponderance of stores and the variety of goods available in those stores help that rhetoric to resonate in a particular way. Vancouver also has typical big-city problems, such as traffic congestion, a disparity between rich and poor, and crime. To some extent, then, Vancouver resembles other contemporary urban settings within and beyond Canada.

However, as a North American West Coast city, Vancouver is decidedly different from other places. Having grown up in Toronto, I have encountered differences between the two cities, some of which I had not imagined before I moved here. I knew that I was coming to a place where the relative ease of year-round outdoors activities was important to the city's image and culture. Like many others who are drawn to Vancouver, I admired the vista of mountains and sea. In contrast to Vancouver, which rejected the idea of building a highway through the city, Toronto has faced decades of criticism for cutting off its bit of waterfront from the rest of the city by building the raised Gardiner Expressway. What I did not anticipate was the degree to which history has left its mark here, as it has in Toronto. As a relatively new city, even by Canadian standards, Vancouver has never been one of Canada's corporate centres; from its early days as the site of the British Fort York, Toronto evolved to become a major arts and culture centre and home to the headquarters of several large corporations. Vancouver, by contrast, grew out of the logging industry and the gold rush, and the forest, the sea, and natural resources continue to exert strong cultural and economic influences.

Finally, in some ways, Vancouver is a microcosm of contemporary social life in the Global North. Like other parts of the Global North that were colonized, colonization seems to be more or less a permanent state. The fact that this has become home for the colonizers and, for a much longer time, has been home to the First Nations peoples, has created cultural, social, and material tensions and struggles. In recent decades, Vancouver has experienced a strong and steady influx of people from Asian countries such as China/Hong Kong/Taiwan, India, Korea, and Japan. Vancouver's neighbour, the City of Richmond, has an especially high level of Asian residents. Unlike people who came to Canada from Japan or China during earlier waves of migration, many of these more recent immigrants are relatively well off. Richmond's Aberdeen Centre and Yaohan Mall are two large, glitzy malls catering to Asian consumers. The economic success of Vancouver and the province of British Columbia more generally is often used to mask the depth of the poverty that is being exacerbated here by policies of neoliberal globalization. Vancouver is a city with some of the costliest real estate and one of the poorest postal districts in the country.

The ethno-racial and material diversity in this city means that there is no one way in which people understand and practise shopping. In this inquiry, shopping represents the complexities and tensions in daily life that can become opportunities for learning, including a form of learning that can help instigate societal change. Numerous tensions are apparent between the material and the cultural, the rational and the emotional, the collective and the solitary, notions of the familiar and the Other, ideals of consumer and democratic choice, messages to consume and conserve, and the myth of the "free" market and the reality of class constraints. These tensions are present in everybody's life, but they look different depending on local contexts and individuals' particular circumstances. The best that I can do here is to present a sense of how those global tensions are experienced by some individuals in this local setting.

Understood as a process of looking for and deliberating options, acquiring goods, services and experiences, and, sometimes, deciding to forego a purchase, shopping for me typically involves going into a store. One exception is when I go to a seasonal farmers' market or a craft sale. On occasion, I go to garage or yard sales or speciality fairs. I have purchased books, airline tickets, and vacation accommodations online. Having worked for some fifteen years in the not-for-profit community service sector, often in revenue development, I have come to enjoy fundraising events and have a collection of items that I bought at various auctions. Although I imagined that my conversations with participants would revolve centrally around shopping in stores, I was open to talking about these other types of shopping settings and experiences. Still other things that participants or other people mentioned to me during my inquiry include bartering, swaps, the free-cycle movement, and even organized theft.

Because this is a critical inquiry, it also challenges dominant portrayals of globalization and focuses on questions of how shopping, consumption, citizenship, and learning can be understood and experienced as examples of resistance in the name of societal change. The following questions have guided this inquiry:

- How do individuals understand and manifest the idea of "learning" and the potential to learn both instrumentally and critically in the course of daily life?
- How do individuals learn to find and respond to complicated, obscured consumer information? How is this learning, and shopping and consumption practices more generally, integrated into other parts of their lives?
- How do individuals living in Canadian society, in which a postmodern sensibility of partial, fractured identity and the phenomenon of globalization converge, understand and articulate the

implications of their "location" (within cultural milieus, social structures, and geographic places) for their shopping options, constraints, and preferences? ☼ And, relating to studies of the relationships between consumption and citizenship in earlier eras, how do individuals relate this learning and their consumption to citizenship in the nation-state and "global" citizenship? ☼

- How do individuals concerned about the status quo develop and demonstrate their resistance through activities of daily living such as shopping? Where does the notion of radicalism fit into shopping-based resistance?

As I have learned throughout this inquiry, responses to these questions can in turn be framed by three questions that maintain a steady focus on informal adult learning, in this case the learning possible and evident in the process of shopping: What do people learn to do? Who do people learn to be? How do people learn to make change?

☼ Localized global citizens asserting their voices through identity-coded products, they [i.e., British Asian clothing designers and marketers] are at the same time reinscribing the nation. Whether using a diasporic inheritance of improvisation, or newly negotiating migrant status, they are working to constitute a dynamic sense of self in their British contexts. In so doing, they create new signifiers which are about negotiating migrant status, they create new signifiers which are about negotiating a new nation, new forms of Britishness, new ways of being European.   —Parminder Bhachu (2004), *Dangerous Designs*, p. 170

Masses of young people dissatisfied by U.S. imperialism, unemployment, lack of economic opportunity, afflicted by the postmodern malaise of alienation, no sense of grounding, no redemptive identity, can be manipulated by cultural strategies that offer Otherness as appeasement, particularly through commodification.
—bell hooks (2001), "Eating the Other: Desire and Resistance," p. 427

☼ The proximity of feminist, commercial, and illicit spaces on London's West End meant that there had long been a confusion about how to identify shoppers, prostitutes, and feminist activists. Though many observers worried about how to separate one type of public woman from another, this proved to be an impossible task. Instead of lamenting this problem, however, the Suffragettes delighted in and used the ambiguities of metropolitan life. . . . The militants' protest highlights how the political West End also abutted the commercial realm. . . . The point, then, is not that political public spaces became commercial or vice versa. Rather, these two meanings were both present and necessary to each other.   —Erika Diane Rappaport (2000), *Shopping for Pleasure*, p. 218

As I moved through the research process, another topical area became apparent. It concerns methodology. In dealing with it, I consider the implications and lessons of doing critical adult education research on and during contemporary globalization. What new meaning might arise for case study methodology, which typically contains a study within a community setting or a specific site, in light of a phenomenon that claims to unbind social and economic relations within and across nation-states? In an era that emphasizes multiple levels of experience—the individual, the local, the national, the regional, and the global—and gives rise to terms such as "glocalization" and "global citizenship," where and how is evidence to be found? How can critical research respond to postmodernism's dismantling of groups and categories? These are additional questions that I have pondered during the research process and address later.

Metaphorically Speaking

Before I delve into my research account, I make one more point about me and my project: I learn metaphorically. Research is, first and foremost, a learning process, and I found metaphors helpful in working my way through and in talking about this project. Such metaphors clarify and explain the questions that I am asking and the answers that I am developing. They help me, as a writer, focus or extend a point in my narrative. This introductory chapter, for example, focuses largely on my cultural and religious background. Its title, the opening words of the Jewish Bible, brings forward the importance of my own social location and history as I begin to write about my research project. Titles of several of the remaining chapters also make such metaphorical references.

These metaphors also function to bolster epistemological and methodological claims that I make, notably in Chapter 3. The metaphors that I use here, including the icon (☼), juxtapose existing texts and images with the text that I am creating, offering a reminder that this is an interdisciplinary work that does not stand alone but that has emerged from varied traditions. The back-and-forth reading that they elicit illustrates my understanding of research as conversation—between this text and other texts, this study and other studies, one discipline and another, researcher and participants. They challenge the line between what (or who) is inside and what (or who) is outside a culture, a community, or a text. My references to content, technologies, and structures of literature, visual art, media (both new and old), and science suggest the extent to which my central concerns surround me and the extent to which educational research is a creative undertaking that can utilize diverse forms and sources of data. It is scientific, as well as artful and crafted. These metaphors are evidence of the internal conversations that I have had and of the ways that I have come to understand my inquiry *as* I wrote it (see Richardson, 2000).

These metaphors also reinforce the analytical arguments that I go on to make throughout this text. By interspersing personal reflections, visual images, and textual excerpts with the body of my text, I aim to represent of the tensions inherent in consumption, citizenship, globalization, learning, and research. My personal reflections, which I call "Interludes," are like the commercials during a television show or advertisements in a magazine, which both interrupt a program or an article and reiterate its cultural messages. As I have written, I have thought about the ideas in the foreground and the background of my analysis, and I remember how slippery these distinctions can be. In asking you, the reader, to interrupt your reading, to consider both images and words and to reflect on this text both literally and metaphorically, I am inviting you to think about and experience these tensions with me.

Choreography, Improvisation, and Stars of the Show: Research Steps and Participants

In my research proposal, I asked a series of questions that seemed relevant to my purpose and methodology: How will I step through a process of case study without clearly apparent boundaries? Given my focus on shoppers, rather than one shop or consumer organization, whom will I invite onto the stage of my study? How will I capture the complex patterns of shopping-as-learning, given that it has both solitary and social qualities and is both purposeful and "incidental" (Foley, 1999, 2001)? In responding to these questions, I incorporated multiple sources of data. Consistent with bricolage, these (re)sources and my analysis of them worked their way into the study in different ways.

Working from the premise that qualitative research in adult education can combine the (social) sciences and the humanities, I propose two artistic metaphors to characterize my process through this study: choreography and improvisation. I am not alone in thinking about research in terms of dance. I came across a chapter written by Valerie Janesick (2000), in which she explains the value to qualitative research of metaphor in general, and the usefulness of the metaphor of choreography in particular. ☼ I also note that this metaphor allows me to talk about taking steps without implying a straight-line progression; instead, steps can be understood as movements.

> ☼ Metaphor in general creeps up on you, surprises you. It defies the one-size-fits-all approach to a topic. . . . Choreography is about the art of making dances. Because dance and choreography are about lived experience, choreography seems to me the perfect metaphor for discussing qualitative research design. Because the qualitative researcher is the research instrument, the metaphor is even more apropos for this discussion, as the body is the instrument of dance.
>
> The qualitative researcher is remarkably like a choreographer at various stages in the design process, in terms of situating and recontextualizing the research project within the shared experience of the researcher and the participants in the study.   —Valerie Janesick (2000), "The Choreography of Qualitative Research Design," p. 380

Although all my methods—or, borrowing from the metaphor of dance, techniques— were choreographed, some were planned according to rules and forms, while others were more spontaneous and improvised. In addition to the completion of a standard ethics application and approval, more rule-bound methods include interviews, focus groups, and what I called modified participant observations—or accompanied shopping trips. Participants in the study were asked to choose between completing an interview or a shopping trip, and I invited them to attend a follow-up focus group. Improvised methods include an intertextual analysis of fiction, as well as incorporation of what I think of as the "found objects"—graffiti, blog entries, graphic images, news reports, and documentaries—to bolster the case that I make through formal analysis of other data.

Wanting a diverse set of participants, in terms of gender, race, class, and neighbourhoods, I selected three neighbourhoods in the City of Vancouver to focus my recruitment efforts. Despite their differences, these communities are characterized by stores marketing themselves and their goods as socially and environmentally responsible. For example, each of these areas has at least one organic grocery store. During the 1960s, Kitsilano was home to Vancouver's hippies, and, despite its upscale location, it maintains a reputation as a socially progressive area. Its West 4th Avenue is lined with a combination of locally owned stores and trendy outlets of retail chains, which sell everything from clothing and jewellery to home furnishings and accessories, from books to outdoor and fitness gear. Main Street/Mount Pleasant is known for its locally owned stores, including fashion designer studio shops, hip second hand stores, and antique shops. With the exception of a few coffee shops and the BC Liquor Store, shops on The Drive are locally owned and operated. Italian and Portuguese bakeries and cafés line the street, along with small art galleries, book stores, and clothing shops. Within a four-block stretch on The Drive, there are two organic grocery stores and the only co-operative grocery store in the city, several second-hand stores (including one operated as a social venture), and a housewares store specializing in such items as organic linens. Although many of these stores appeal predominantly to middle-class or wealthier shoppers, based on their prices and their speciality products, at least some of them might also attract lower-income and working-class shoppers. ☼

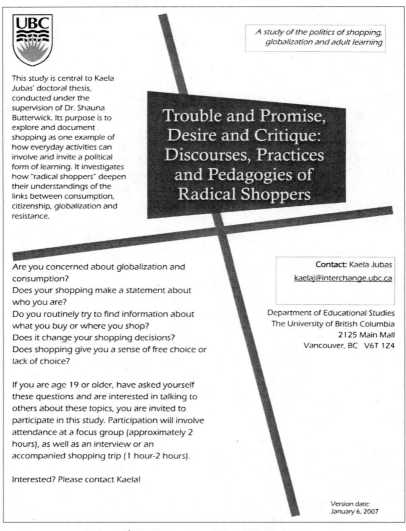

☼ Participant recruitment flyer

I developed a series of recruitment tools: a full-page flyer, a post-card, and a smaller double-sided leaflet. Ultimately, it was the listservs and word of mouth that yielded the greatest number of participants. Of the thirty-two participants in the study (not including me), six were students or faculty members in the Department of Educational Studies where I was a student, six responded to a message sent out to subscribers on the listserv of an organization focused on local, sustainable food production and distribution, and three heard about the study through the listserv of a community development program at another postsecondary institutions. Only two participants responded to my leaflets in shops or cafés; one person came forward after picking up my leaflet at the documentary screening; and one participant responded to my posting on Craig's List. An additional twelve participants learned about the study by word of mouth, either from other participants or from my own personal acquaintances. These recruitment tactics resemble those described by Connelly and Prothero (2008) in their study of green consumers.

There were additional resemblances between my study and Connelly and Prothero's study, notably in relation to how participants characterized themselves socially. Although participants ranged widely in age and, to a lesser extent, ethno-cultural identification, most identified racially as white or Caucasian. Overall, participants had a relatively high level of formal education, having completed at least some postsecondary education. Participants also tended to characterize themselves as middle class or on their way to joining the middle class as they completed their university degrees; however, some expressed uncertainty about this matter. These people had grown up in a working-class family and wondered about the impact of their postsecondary education on their social status, or saw their economic constraints as a temporary state while they were full-time students. Having grown up with one parent from an upper-middle-class, highly educated family and one parent from a working-class family, I have a class confusion that seemed rather unique.

In accordance with ethics protocol to maximize anonymity, participants were assigned pseudonyms. Many qualitative researchers choose pseudonyms for their participants, often selecting names that begin with the same letter as participants' real names and reflect their ethnic backgrounds. I was interested in finding ways to share as much control as possible within the inquiry. To this end, I offered participants the opportunity to name themselves. Seven participants chose their own pseudonyms; for the remaining participants, I used the convention of assigning pseudonyms starting with the same letter as their real names. All participants' names are pseudonyms.

Participants chose between completing a semistructured interview and a shopping trip. Interview questions were forwarded to the eighteen participants who chose this option before their interviews. Questions encouraged participants to think about how they learned about shopping and had come to understand a "good" shopper, what sorts and sources of information they valued and trusted, what kinds of messages about shopping they saw and heard around them, and how they attached shopping and consumption to other aspects of their lives, including social activism. Interviews usually lasted between sixty and ninety minutes and were often held in conveniently located coffee shops. Participants were given an opportunity to review their interview transcripts before they were treated as final.

The shopping trips were meant to provide me with a fuller understanding of how participants approached, carried out, and understood their shopping. Interview participants share what they are aware of in that moment; shopping trips helped participants (and me) to be aware of particular and concrete things. Fifteen participants chose to do a shopping trip, and these trips were very conversational. Occasionally, other shoppers or store staff overhead our conversations and joined our conversations briefly. I brought a notepad and a small digital camera with me, although I frequently found it challenging to keep up with participants as I jotted notes and took pictures of items that we were discussing. From the time participants and I met until we left the store, shopping trips varied in duration from forty-five minutes to two and a half hours. Data from both interviews and shopping trips were analyzed using an open source qualitative data analysis software package called Weft QDA (a consumption choice that I noted earlier).

In addition to completing an interview or a shopping trip, most participants were also invited to a focus group to extend our conversation. Two groups were held, and seven people participated in a follow-up discussion. The focus groups included two exercises. During the first exercise, I asked participants to talk about an item that they had brought with them to the session. I asked them to bring that they had bought and to say a few words about why they had purchased the item, what they knew about it, and what they thought it said about them. This exercise is similar to a pedagogical experiment used by Ira Shor in his adult education classroom. Shor would ask students to go through a three-step process of rational analysis of something ordinary—a classroom chair or a hamburger, for instance. The process began with students' careful observation and description of the object, then moved to "diagnosis" through a contextual examination of its purpose, development, and use, and then ended with a "reconstruction of its problematic nature" through "creative imagination" (1980, p. 157). ☼

☼ I bought a hamburger and took it to class. What better way to extraordinarily re-experience the ordinary? The burger is the nexus of so many daily realities. It's not only the kind of fast foods, the lunch/snack/dinner quickie meal, but it's also the source of wages for many students who work in the burger chains. In addition, the spread of fast food franchises is tied into the suburban dispersal of the American city. . . . With the hamburger as the problem-theme of our inquiry, we developed in a number of directions. For the Reconstruction, one class wanted to act on our distinction between "junk food" and "health food." A class organizing committee emerged to cooperatize the college cafeteria, and have it offer a nutritious, fixed-price lunch. In other classes, we began evolving an extended conceptual paradigm to represent the total analysis of the burger. I had asked one class to recreate the entire production and distribution process which delivered a burger to a consumer. This recreation unveiled the largely invisible relations of commodity culture.   —Ira Shor (1980), *Critical Teaching and Everyday Life*, pp. 162–163

For the second focus group exercise, I asked participants to choose from among a series of newspaper articles, cartoons, advertisements, and marketing materials. I asked participants to talk about what they saw in the pieces they chose: Who (or what) was represented and how were they portrayed? Who was the intended audience? What messages about shopping, consumption, and consumerism, as well as social relations and citizenship, were conveyed? In the language of methodology, I asked participants to engage in an informal, small-scale semiotic analysis. According to Gemma Penn, conducting a semiotic analysis in a focus group setting helps to overcome some of the limitations of semiology, notably the highly subjective nature of semiotic analysis, "by reinstating the lay reader" (2000, p. 242) or viewer. ☼ Because the object of this exercise was to elicit conversation about shopping, consumption, and the ideological messages encountered by consumer-citizens rather than to analyze specific visual images per se, I have not gone to the considerable, and likely futile, effort of seeking permission to reproduce the images here. When I discuss this exercise and the materials chosen by participants, I describe them in what I think is sufficient detail, although I remove any reference to corporate or brand names.

☼ Semiology provides the analyst with a conceptual toolkit for approaching sign systems systematically in order to discover how they produce meaning. . . . Semiology grew out of the discipline of structural linguistics that originated in the work of the Swiss linguist Ferdinand de Saussure (1857–1913). The structural approach sees language as a system and attempts to discover "all the rules that hold it together" (Hawkes, 1977:19).   —Gemma Penn (2000), "Semiotic Analysis of Still Images," p. 227

Focus groups were a helpful addition to my methods, because they continued to uncover the complexities and nuances of shopping and shoppers. I hoped that meeting with participants twice over a period of several weeks would encourage them to consider and talk about their own experiences of shopping-as-learning, because learning often occurs or becomes apparent over time. Although even the most critical, conscientious shopping is not the same as the collective action that Foley (1999, 2001) discusses, it is a process that can straddle the division between the hegemonic and the resistant, as well as the solitary and the social. The participants in this study, like many people who live in today's global cities, experience shopping as a solitary process at least some of the time; however, sometimes shopping can be an activity shared with a partner or a planned social activity. Often, solitary shopping becomes social, as shoppers come into contact with staff and other shoppers in the store, sometimes meeting people they know. Even when individuals shop alone, they often talk about their shopping experiences with others.

Because of time constraints, I completed only partial transcriptions of the focus group conversations. I also did not use the Weft QDA software to code them. In their well-known publication on focus group research, Jean Schensul and Margaret LeCompte advise that

> a formal coding system should be developed and applied to the data if one or more of the following three circumstances prevail: if the number of interviews is large enough (more than 20 group interviews); if the interviews are long enough to warrant full-scale computerized coding (more than 15 pages); or if the research team decides that focused group interviews will continue, thus expanding the sample over time. In general, a database of more than 20 interviews, or more than 100 pages of text, warrants the creation of a coding system. (1999, p. 107)

Given the small number of participants who attended a focus group, I was comfortable listening to the focus group recordings and transcribing the sections that seemed most interesting and useful. I was interested in listening carefully to the recordings and pulling from them both similarities to and differences from the coded interview data. This is consistent with the approach described by Anssi Peräkylä:

> In many cases, qualitative researchers who use written texts as their materials do not try to follow any predefined protocol in executing their analysis. By reading and rereading their empirical materials, they try to pin down their key themes and, thereby, to draw a picture of the presuppositions and meanings that constitute the cultural world of which the textual material is a specimen. (2006, p. 870)

I appreciate Saukko's (2003) point that divergence in perspectives can be apparent between two people and even, for that matter, within one individual's narrative; however, the nature of focus groups increases the likelihood that divergent, possibly clashing, experiences, opinions, and feelings will be expressed.

Just as talking to individuals and writing about my conversations with them was an integral part of my analytical process, so, too, did reading help me uncover and make sense of multiple, often clashing, narratives and discourses about shopping and consumption. Equally important to the academic and popular scholarship that I read was fiction, because it, too, provided important conceptual, historical, and sociological information about shopping, consumption, and consumerism. Fiction is an interesting source of narrative data for several reasons. First, a careful reading of fiction helps uncover ideology and ideologically based common sense (per Gramsci, 1971) circulating in civil society. Second, in its presentation of multiple characters, a novel is able to present a variety of ideological stances and material circumstances to its readers. Third, readers always read a work of fiction in relation to other works of fiction and cultural images. The methodology of intertextual analysis interprets a text or image "in relation to the wider cultural and social panorama, consisting of other texts" (Saukko, 2003, p. 104). To the extent that engaged readers read one text against the backdrop of previously read texts and other cultural influences, at some level readers are conducting a perpetual intertextual analysis; thus, reading becomes a source of inquiry and incidental learning. Moreover, as Christine Jarvis notes,

> reading is also a form of consumption, constructed by desire and aspiration. As such it is a space in which to practice "distinction" (Bourdieu, 1984) as part of the construction of identity and identification. As Beckett and Morris (2001) demonstrated, lifelong learning is an ontological process; learners are engaged in becoming as much as in knowing. (2003, p. 262)

Finally, there are data that have been included in this inquiry to reiterate or illustrate conceptual and analytical points being made, even though they are not formally analyzed. These include my personal reflections, notably the Interludes that bridge several chapters, as well as many of the images and words scattered throughout this text. These insertions serve methodological and analytical purposes. They are self-conscious reminders of my presence in the study and my impact on the generation of conversational data (see Fine, 1998; Naples, 2003; Richardson, 2000). The incorporation of such personal reflections into my inquiry, which is commonly referred to as researcher reflexivity, responds to

Laurel Richardson's explanation that "our Self is always present" (2000, p. 930) in our research and Michelle Fine's (1998) exhortation about "working the hyphens" between insider and outsider status in any research study. Some of the images that I insert were found as I went along and seemed to reflect many of the messages in materials that I was compiling in a more purposeful way. They reminded me that, in any inquiry, there are always more data collected than analyzed and that no inquiry is ever entirely complete. They also function as reminders that there is always more to research than the data that undergo formal analysis and more to knowledge construction than formal learning. As I make clear in my analytical chapters, participants in this study have engaged repeatedly in informal research and learning.

Writing Up/Writing *as* the Inquiry

I have already cited Richardson's (2000) thoughts on writing as a form of inquiry. The final step in this inquiry is the writing of this text. This is not simply a matter of putting on paper the understanding that I have formulated in my head; it is a complex process of figuring out as I write. Richardson adopts a poststructural stance that emphasizes the importance of writing as experimenting with language to build knowledge. She writes:

> When we view writing as a *method*, we experience "language-in-use," how we "word the world" into existence (Rose, 1992). And then we "reword" the world, erase the computer screen, check the thesaurus, move a paragraph, again and again. This "worded world" never accurately, precisely, completely captures the studied world, yet we persist in trying. Writing as a method of inquiry honors and encourages the trying, recognizing it as emblematic of the significance of language. (2001, p. 35)

Throughout this study, the idea of writing as a method of inquiry resonated with me. As I wrote this text, much of my analytical points became more apparent and clearer. Perhaps this is a standard part of bricolage, in which analysis, like the rest of the research process, unfolds and assumes a purpose in a somewhat unpredicted and unpredictable way. I also discovered that there is much more than language at play here. My writing-as-inquiry involves images as well as worded texts, and it involves the aesthetics of the page as well as the words on the page. Richardson does not talk about these additional ways in which writing is not just a process of writing up an inquiry, but is an inquiry in itself.

However, this inquiry remains more than an unfolding word game that, in my view, poststructuralism seems most intrigued by. I do not abandon the critical purpose of an inquiry anchored by Gramscian concepts and concerns. At the same time as I appreciate the importance of language and other cultural objects, I try never to lose sight of the materiality of circumstances and relations.

Despite a degree of openness and flexibility, then, my inquiry is firmly anchored by theories, concepts, and values. Based largely on Gramsci's (1971) writings compiled in the *Prison Notebooks*, these also include feminist, critical race and postcolonial, and other critical scholarship on consumption, citizenship, globalization, resistance, and learning. Notable within the adult education scholarship is Griff Foley's (1999, 2001) writing on incidental learning, as well as writing on how emotion, sensuality, and spirituality complement intellect in adult learning (Dirkx, 2001; English, 2000; Hayes & Flannery, 2000; hooks, 2003; Tisdell, 1998, 2000). In Chapters 2 and 3, I review the analytical concepts that have been central in this inquiry, as well as the ontological, epistemological, and methodological principles—what Yvonna Lincoln and Egon Guba (2000) refer to as paradigmatic "axioms"—that underpin my research. In describing my methodology, I have settled on "case study bricolage," which I explain in Chapter 3. In short, the "case" here is shopping as a site of informal learning; the bricolage allowed me to look for evidence about the case in interesting and unusual ways and places, to include evidence found as I went along, and to employ a variety of analytical and theoretical approaches in interpreting it all.

Following these two chapters, I offer four chapters discussing my data analysis. I examine two qualitatively different forms of data: cultural texts and conversations with participants. I also introduce a distinct analytical tool in each chapter to examine the data in varied ways, in an attempt to reach a fuller understanding of the case under investigation. These analyses reflect the breadth of discourses, practices, and pedagogies that are routinely encountered and constructed by Canadian shoppers who are concerned about how their personal consumption implicates them in complex phenomena such as globalization, social relations, and citizenship. Chapter 4 offers a literary analysis of a selection of popular novels focused on shopping, consumption, and consumerism. In Chapters 5, 6, and 7, I discuss my analysis of the empirical data that I gathered with the help of participants.

I draw on Laurel Richardson's (2000) notion of *crystallization* as an expansive understanding of methodological and analytical validity. In contrast to the more common term *triangulation*, crystallization recognizes that there are more than three ways to explore and to interpret a phenomenon. These do not always yield consistency, but they produce fuller, deeper knowledge about complex phenomena. In each of the four analytical chapters, I make use of what I call a particular "analytical facet"—a theory-guided viewing of data. To retain a critical stance throughout this inquiry, I have limited my use of theories and concepts so that they are compatible with one another, even as they help me look at the data differently or to see different things within the data. Finally, Chapter 8 discusses some of the limitations, contributions, and implications of this study for adult educators, social policy advocates, and people who aspire to use shopping as part of an agenda for societal change.

The conceptual territory that I cover here ranges from consumer-citizenship (itself a conceptual amalgam) to globalization, identity to resistance and radicalism. Even methodology surfaces as an analytical concern. Such diversity and complexity are not superfluous pretensions; they are, rather, a reflection of the complexity of the case that I set out to examine. My focus on adult learning is the thread that stitches these topics together. Likewise, my departure from conventional dissertation-writing is not superfluous or, I hope, pretentious; it is, rather, the way that I developed to organize and to present the complications that became apparent as I read about and listened to and witnessed people's attempts to tie their consumption to citizenship and globalization, their shopping to their resistance, and all of this to continual learning.

INTERLUDE II

Images of Trouble
and Critique

Graffiti outside Central Train Station, Sydney, Australia, December 2006

Church sign, Dublin, Ireland, June 2007

Sign at the community market, Airlie Beach, Australia, December 2006

2

Under the Microscope: Conceptual Map

Research in the field of educational studies can be artistic, creative, and spontaneous, but, for the sake of ongoing usefulness, it also requires a purpose and a degree of rigour. The metaphor of the microscope that I use here recognizes that educational research has grown out of and challenges scientific traditions. Part of the rigour in research lies in developing and clarifying the concepts that anchor an inquiry and are used in making sense of phenomena under investigation. Borrowing from the physics of the optical microscope, I discuss the central concepts of my inquiry in this chapter. ☼ In many dissertations, this chapter would refer to "theoretical framework"; however, I avoid that phrase because I think that, as I discuss in the following chapter, the theories that are brought together to "frame" an inquiry are evident in the inquiry's ontology, epistemology, and methodology, as well as in its anchoring concepts and the analysis, which comes later. Over the course of my doctoral program, understanding and attending to the interrelated processes of conceptualization, methodology, and theorization in this way has helped me organize my thoughts and develop my inquiry.

The conceptual starting point for this inquiry is Gramsci's (1971) writings, especially those known as the *Prison Notebooks*. Returning to the metaphor of the optical microscope, I use his concepts to provide a "coarse focus" in my analysis of the "object on the stage"—shopping as a case of learning about the links between consumption, citizenship, globalization, and resistance. In using the *Prison Notebooks*, I am mindful of the fact that they were compiled during Gramsci's years of incarceration, a period when he had curtailed access to existing scholarship (especially Marxist work) and other individuals. He wrote largely to keep himself sane and did not have the regular advantages of cataloguing and publishing his writings, consulting a library of existing resources, or communicating with other theorists or activists. The *Prison Notebooks* is an unavoidably incomplete, ambiguous, inconsistent collection of thoughts. The "fine focus" is provided by more contemporary critical adult educators and critical scholars in related fields who help sharpen my view of shopping as a case of informal, political adult learning about

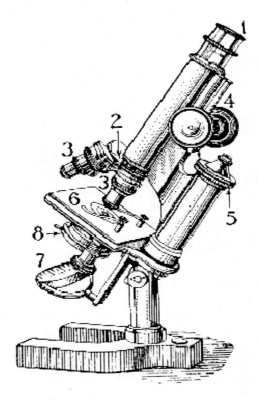

☼ Basic optical microscope elements:

1. ocular lens, or eyepiece   2. objective turret
3. objective lenses   4. coarse adjustment knob
5. fine adjustment knob   6. object holder or stage
7. mirror   8. diaphragm and condenser

Optical microscope, retrieved February 18, 2008 from Wikimedia Commons, http://en.wikipedia.org/wiki/Image:Mikroskop.png.

consumer-citizenship during contemporary globalization. Because they are central to experiences of consumer-citizenship and globalization, and to the guiding questions of this inquiry, conceptualizations of gender, class, and race are also included in this chapter. In relating these social categories to identity and status, I am then able to continue with a critical analysis of shopping, globalization, adult learning, and, perhaps most important, resistance. Together, these ideas constitute a conceptual map of my inquiry. ☼ This map is divided into topical sections, most of

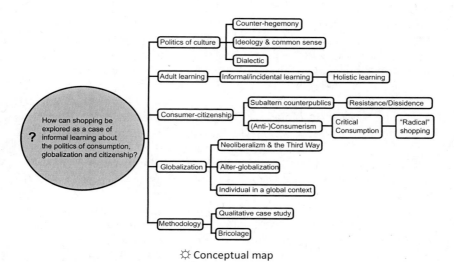

☼ Conceptual map

which I explain throughout the remainder of this chapter and explore in subsequent chapters.

Consumerism, anti-consumerism, and neoliberalism are all examples of ideologies active in contemporary Canadian culture. The ideas that I explore and develop in this chapter about holistic learning; critical, resistant, or possibly even "radical" shopping; and the individual in a global context are all examples of the dialectics of the individual and the collective, culture and social life. Even the methodology of case study bricolage, the explanation of which I leave for the next chapter, can be understood as an example of a dialectic within the culture of academe. Returning now to the metaphor of the microscope, I outline the central concepts in this inquiry and their mutual importance in addressing its underlying question.

Coarse Focus: Gramscian Theory and Concepts

The first step in bringing an item into view with a microscope is to use the coarse focus, which gives shape to what initially seems indiscernible. Gramsci's (1971) concepts provide this inquiry with that basic, preliminary focus. In trying to answer his own question—why the proletarian revolution predicted by Marxism did not spread beyond Russia in the early twentieth century—Gramsci assembled several conceptual pieces. The resulting theory combines culture, economics, and politics to explain how leaders in all democratic societies manifest a central paradox: Using a balance of persuasion and force, they achieve popular consent for the maintenance of power relations, even when those relations oppress the very citizens who are consenting to them. Gramsci's return to a Hegelian notion of the dialectic helps explain this paradox, and his use of the notion of "philosophy of praxis" and Marxist "historical materialism" sets the tone for his theoretical development.

While Gramsci's use of the phrase "philosophy of praxis" acted as a code in his writing for Marxism, a way to get his letters past the scrutiny of prison officials (see Crehan, 2002; Ives, 2004), it also recognizes the general role of theory and practice in understanding and changing socio-economic relations. Practice—the work of achieving societal change—is directed by theory, and theory is informed by practice. Because this back-and-forth relationship between theory and practice develops over time, historical analysis is central in understanding current society and moving toward change. Gramsci's primary contribution to Marxism is the assertion that a similar tension also exists between ideas and experience, politics and culture, and economic structures and ideologies. These are seen as irresolvable, necessary tensions of social life in which one side actually helps to define, rather than to contradict, the other side. (A famous visual illusion might be seen as a young woman or an old woman, depending on the viewer's perception; both images compose the picture at the same time, so that one cannot exist without the other.) ☼

From this notion of philosophy of praxis, Gramsci develops his ideas about the role of intellectuals and ideology in civil society, and of civil society in politics and the economy. For Gramsci, democratic society comprises three elements: the economy, the political (or state), and civil society. Civil society includes educational, religious, cultural, and media institutions, processes, and products. Unlike civil society, government has access to authorized force; like civil society, its institutions and discourses justify, reflect, and reinforce economic structure. In Gramsci's theory, civil society is important, because it is the sphere where ideologies and their associated common sense through which hegemony, the consent of sufficient groups of citizens, are constructed. Likewise, it is

---

☼ The true fundamental function and significance of the dialectic can only be grasped if the philosophy of praxis is conceived as an integral and original phase in the development of world thought. It does this to the extent that it goes beyond both traditional idealism and traditional materialism, philosophies which are expressions of past societies, while retaining their vital elements. If the philosophy of praxis is not considered except in subordination to another philosophy, then it is not possible to grasp the new dialectic, through which the transcending of old philosophies is effected and expressed.   —Antonio Gramsci (1971), *Selections from the Prison Notebooks*, pp. 435–436

Eric W. Weisstein, "Young Girl-Old Woman Illusion." Retrieved August 25, 2008 from MathWorld—A Wolfram web resource, http://mathworld.wolfram.com/YoungGirl-OldWomanIllusion.html.

in civil society where counter-hegemonic ideological discourses can germinate among marginalized groups—whom Gramsci refers to as "subaltern" classes—and where movements for societal change can emerge.

One of the criticisms levelled today against Marxists and other materialists is that, in their focus on socio-economic class, they overlook the role of culture and discourse in developing identity or subjectivity. Neo-Gramscians extend the original focus on class to other forms of inequalities and oppression and to sites of inquiry beyond formal workplaces. Roger Simon (1991), for example, notes that the family is a unique institution of civil society, because it is where women's unpaid and informal labour has traditionally occurred. Some scholars extend Gramsci's focus on class by arguing that "Gramsci was, in a sense, developing (in relation to social classes) a special case of a general theory" (Holford, 1995, p. 103). Civil society is a diverse constellation of social groups and "reflects the inequalities of class, race and gender which structure the society in which it is embedded" (Blakeley, 2002, p. 94).

Civil society, like its political counterpart, is shaped by ideology, defined by Gramsci as "a specific 'system of ideas' [that] needs to be examined historically" (1971, p. 376). Ideologies that are "historically

☼ One must therefore distinguish between historically organic ideologies, those, that is, which are necessary to a given structure, and ideologies that are arbitrary, rationalistic, or "willed". To the extent that ideologies are historically necessary they have a validity which is "psychological"; they "organise" human masses, and create the terrain on which men [sic] move, acquire consciousness of their position, struggle, etc. To the extent that they are arbitrary they only create individual "movements", polemics and so on (though even these are not completely useless, since they function like an error which by contrasting with truth, demonstrates it).   —Antonio Gramsci (1971), *Selections from the Prison Notebooks*, p. 376

organic" (p. 376) develop in conjunction with and support social and economic structures in particular societies. ☼ For example, the current ideology of consumerism accompanies and props up capitalist, patriarchal, and racist structures as they operate during globalization.

Gramsci discusses two types of intellectuals who lead the production and maintenance of ideology: traditional and organic. For Gramsci, "[a]ll men [*sic*] are intellectuals[;] one could therefore say: but not all men have in society the function of intellectuals" (p. 9). The purpose of intellectual activity is to build ideologies that operate through culture and politics. Hegemonic ideologies justify and bolster the status quo in economic and social structures that oppress certain groups of citizens; counter-hegemonic ideologies put forward an alternative vision of societal organization. Revolution, in the sense that most interested Gramsci, is a slow, educative process of fostering organic intellectuals to lead the adoption of alternative ideologies in order to generate a fairer society. Organic intellectuals are linked to a specific class (or, more broadly, social group) that develops in a particular society. Kenway explains that "Gramsci sees organic intellectuals as functioning to elaborate ideologies, to educate the people, to unify social forces, and to secure hegemony for the fundamental class to which they are organic" (2001, p. 52). In contrast, traditional intellectuals are unattached to any class and appear "as representatives of an historical continuity uninterrupted by the most complicated and radical changes in social and political forms" (Gramsci, 1957, p. 119 in Mayo, 1999, p. 41).

Some Gramscian scholars associate traditional intellectuals with the mainstream and organic intellectuals with the margins, in an apparent nod to Gramsci's interest in marginalized groups (see, for example, Strine, 1991); however, this is an example of how Gramsci's vagueness can come into play. I concur with Peter Mayo's understanding that "organic intellectuals can, if they are organic to the dominant class/group (for example, managers), serve to mediate the ideological unity of the existing hegemony" (1999, p. 41). It is also possible for traditional intellectuals to join the ranks of citizens who work for change. To align intellectuals with the types of social groups they lead, we can then distinguish between "conservative" and what Diana Coben (1998) calls "revolutionary" or "radical" or what Noam Chomsky (cited in hooks, 2003) calls "dissident" intellectuals.

It is through the work of the intellectuals that hegemony is produced, first in civil society and then politically. Although this concept did not originate in Gramsci's work, he developed it in a new, sophisticated way (Adamson, 1980; Coben, 1998; Ives, 2004; Kenway, 2001; Simon, 1991). Although, as Gramsci (1971) notes, democratic governments have access to force, what distinguishes them from totalitarian societies is hegemony, which requires and produces citizens' consent to accept existing power relations and structures. ☼ As Coben states, "Gramsci recognized that the state successfully maintains hegemony insofar as it succeeds in articulating dominant class interests as if they were universal" (1998, p. 15). Those in power make concessions to secure citizens' consent; if they cannot achieve consent with certain groups, they dominate through the exercise of force. Hegemony in this sense is fluid and constantly (re) negotiated between leaders and citizens, "a tool for understanding society so that we can change it" (Simon, 1991, p. 23). Gramsci's (1971) theory considers three ways in which change can be effected. Revolution can occur as a forceful, swift event (Gramsci's "war of position") or as a slow, intellectual process of recruiting citizens into a challenge of existing ideology and common sense (Gramsci's "war of movement"). Change can also be imposed from above, when a new force replaces an existing one by way of struggle between the two forces, rather than through mobilization of citizen consent (Gramsci's "passive revolution").

In the context of today's globalization, neo-Gramscian scholars argue that "acceptance of or acquiescence to globalization cannot be explained as merely the result of the domination of powerful economic and political forces without considering real improvements in people's lives" (Sassoon, 2001, p. 8). This argument recalls Coben's (1998) point that hegemony succeeds to the extent that it accommodates, rather than ignores, the interests of varied groups, in rhetoric if not always in practice. Although contemporary globalization is a distinct era and phenomenon, it bears similarity to Gramsci's time and many of the projects that he discussed,

---

☼ The methodological criterion on which our own study must be based is the following: that the supremacy of a social group manifests itself in two ways, as "domination" and as "intellectual and moral leadership". A social group dominates antagonistic groups, which it tends to "liquidate", or to subjugate perhaps even by armed force; it leads kindred and allied groups.   —Antonio Gramsci (1971), *Selections from the Prison Notebooks*, p. 57

including free trade and, perhaps most prophetically, Americanism (Gramsci, 1971; Sassoon, 2001). Gramsci's emphasis on culture, rather than the more orthodox Marxist emphasis on economy alone, is useful in an inquiry such as this one, which explores shopping as a site of learning. Shopping is clearly a process involving both the symbolic and the material; hence, it straddles the divide typically erected between materialist and poststructural perspectives. As Peter Ives states, "Culture is such an interesting concept because it travels on both sides of this distinction. My contention is that among other attractive features of Gramsci's writings is his refusal to accept the assumed opposition between the materiality of the economy and commodities versus the non-materiality of language, signification and communication" (2004, p. 127). ☼ Following a conceptualization of adult learning that draws largely on Gramsci's concepts and is used in this inquiry, I return to a discussion of how Gramscian concepts can help focus an exploration of the links between consumption, citizenship and resistance in contemporary times.

☼ [M]atter should be understood neither in the meaning that it has acquired in natural science . . . , nor in any of the meanings that one finds in the various materialistic metaphysics. The various physical . . . properties of matter which together constitute matter itself . . . should be considered, but only to the extent that they become a productive "economic element." Matter as such therefore is not our subject but how it is socially and historically organised for production.
—Antonio Gramsci (1971), *Selections from the Prison Notebooks*, p. 465

Fine Focus: Holistic Incidental Adult Learning

Gramsci's (1971) ideas about societal change contribute to the tradition of critical adult education (Brookfield, 2005; Coben, 1998; Foley, 1999, 2001; Mayo, 1999). Foley speaks of "a tradition which is in danger of being forgotten, at a time when it is sorely needed" (2001, p. 71). According to Gramsci (1971) and the critical adult educators who take up his ideas, both hegemony and revolution are processes of constant learning. Mayo clarifies further that, "The notion of critical appropriation of existing knowledge is central to the emergence of a new 'subaltern' and, in Gramsci's case, proletarian culture" (1999, p. 51). In the metaphor of the microscope, my conceptualization of education serves as the "fine focus" of this inquiry. Education, for Gramsci and for me here, is more than schooling; it is the development and popularization of understandings that reflect or challenge a social order. ☼

Gramsci's adult education project was exemplified by the Factory Councils of workers, which engaged workers in critical analysis of

☼ But the educational relationship should not be restricted to the field of the strictly "scholastic" relationships by means of which the new generation comes into contact with the old and absorbs its experiences and its historically necessary values and "matures" and develops a personality of its own which is historically and culturally superior. This form of relationship exists throughout society as a whole and for every individual relative to other individuals. . . . Every relationship of "hegemony" is necessarily an educational relationship. . . .   —Antonio Gramsci (1971), *Selections from the Prison Notebooks,* p. 350

mainstream ideologies and economic structures and the generation of new alternatives. In such a project, education involves "an analysis of common sense in order to retrieve and develop the elements of good sense inherent in it" (Coben, 1998, pp. 35–36). When adult educators discuss "critical," "emancipatory" (Foley, 1999), or "radical" (Foley, 2001) adult education, they invoke Gramsci's legacy and refer to the political nature of education and learning. ☼ Among feminist educational studies scholars, this work has been part of an agenda to move gender and other persistent social categories alongside class. In this way, feminist critical adult educators "consider the educational implications of ongoing and new forms of socioeconomic and symbolic injustice—how contemporary education is implicated in, and might yet challenge, economic exploitation, marginalization, deprivation, and cultural domination, nonrecognition, and disrespect" (Kenway, 2001, p. 62).

Although others have written about incidental learning as accidental and tacit (see Colley, Hodkinson & Malcolm, 2002; Marsick & Watkins, 2001), Foley's (1999, 2001) writing on adult education is especially helpful in this inquiry. He agrees that such learning is typically overlooked and "has to be uncovered . . . [because it is] informal,

☼ Domination originates in, and is constructed in, relationships of production and power, but it is also constructed in ideologies and discourses, i.e., in the ways in which people make meaning of situations and speak about them. So hegemony comes to be internalized, to be embedded in people's consciousness. But if domination is universal, it is also continually contested, so history may also be seen as a continual struggle by ordinary people to maintain or extend control over their lives. . . . The story of this struggle is one of gains and losses, of progress and retreat, and of a growing recognition of the continually contested, complex, ambiguous and contradictory nature of the struggle between domination and liberation. This struggle also has a learning and educational dimension which emerges when we examine concrete situations. I say "emerges" advisedly, because the learning is often embedded in other activities and has to be uncovered.
—Griff Foley (2001), "Radical Adult Education and Learning," p. 77

incidental and embedded in other activities" (2001, p. 77); however, his particular interest lies in the unintended, politically charged learning that occurs in the course of collective action. In his adult education research and practice, Foley expounds an expansive, Gramscian notion of learning (and teaching) which is ever-present. He explains that, "As people live and work they continually learn. Most of this learning is unplanned, and is often tacit, but it is very powerful" (p. 72). Attached to this concept is the understanding that educators are not always professional teachers. Community activists and "radical" (Coben, 1998) or "dissident" (Chomsky cited in hooks, 2003) intellectuals are types of progressive adult educators, while advertisers, journalists, and public relations professionals serve a similarly educational function, but more typically in support of the existing hegemony. In tracking incidental learning in settings ranging from a women's reproductive health clinic to a public school and from neighbourhood houses to an environmental action group, Foley (1999, 2001) returns to Gramsci's (1971) thoughts about the potential of all citizens to become intellectuals. Collective mobilization and action create opportunities for incidental, critical "learning in hegemonic struggle" (Foley, 2001, p. 76). ☼

☼ My definition of "adult educator" will also be expansive. Radical adult educators are those who work for emancipatory social change and whose work engages with the learning dimension of social life. Fewer and fewer people, even those whose primary work role involves the education of adults, see themselves as "adult educators" (rather they see themselves as "human resource developers" or "literacy teachers" or "nurse educators" and so forth). But social life requires learning, and a range of roles, from manager to activist, involve the facilitation of learning.   —Griff Foley (2001), "Radical Adult Education and Learning," p. 72

In addition to Foley's work, within adult education there is a body of work which focuses on social movements as sites of informal learning about societal transformation. Building further on Gramsci's (1971) thoughts on the role of intellectuals in culture and critical learning, Ron Eyerman and Andrew Jamison (1991) describe social movements as "epistemic communities" or sites of "cognitive praxis" whose work is guided by "movement intellectuals." Viewing knowledge as socially constructed, John Holford explains,

> This approach clearly holds possibilities for the study of adult education, by enabling us to move from the appreciation that social movements are important phenomena in the learning process of the individuals (and even collectively of the groups and organizations) which compose them, to a view that they are central to the production of human

knowledge itself. The forms of knowledge which exist in any society are, it is held, the products in part of the social movements which have emerged in, or had an impact on, that society. (1995, p. 101)

Shirley Walters (2005) adds the point that social movements function as sites of learning both for individuals heavily engaged in activism and for people who remain on the periphery.

Recently, the environmental movement has served as the basis for theorizing and research about adult learning. Exploring the "Clayoquot Summer" of 1993, when environmentalists converged in British Columbia's Clayoquot Sound to protest logging of old growth forests, Pierre Walter (2007) outlines the efforts of organizers, many of them women involved in the feminist movement. Their aims extended beyond building awareness of the devastation of the forests to developing non-violent resistance and consensual decision making. Consistent with the notion of holistic learning that I will develop, Walter's study indicates that social movement learning has intellectual, emotional, and spiritual dimensions. In my inquiry, I also establish that such learning is instru-mental and radical, formalized and informal, and content-based and process-based.

Critical learning within the arena of shopping is ironic, because it relies on a tool of globalization to oppose globalization. On the one hand, shopping and consumption are manifestations of hegemonic ideol-ogies. Marketers, economists, and politicians alike proclaim the benefits of these processes for individual consumer-citizens, local and national economies, and the advance of democracy itself. On the other hand, new social movements are heightening concerns about the environ-ment, social justice, personal health, and community well-being among consumer-citizens. Using tactics such as boycotts and buycotts, "the con-scious choice of goods for ethical and political rather than economic rea-sons because of their ethical convictions" (Micheletti, 2003, p. 4), these movements are fostering critical, incidental, holistic learning in the arena of shopping. In this way, it is possible to highlight some of the central dialectical tensions that infuse learning about the politics of globaliza-tion, consumption, and citizenship.

Although I begin with Foley's (1999, 2001) ideas on incidental learning, I back up from his starting point of the political learning that emerges in highly organized settings. My starting point is non-organized, apparently solitary activities, and my focus is on how individuals can, in the process of such activities, engage in incidental learning that con-tributes to their political analysis and social engagement. In this way, my inquiry highlights an under-studied type of incidental learning and extends the adult education field conceptually by using shopping as a case of such learning. The process of shopping, which is undertaken in the context of economic constraints, cultural affiliations, political regulations, histories of imperialism and national development, and advertising and media discourses that convey ideals of gender, race, class, and nationality, can spur incidental learning about many things: consumer rights and choices; the impact of globalization on understandings and experiences of citizenship and consumption; the role of gender, race, and class in determining social divisions; and the connection between the material and the cultural. As marino writes, the connection of Gramscian concepts, notably hegemony, to adult education provides a flexibility "to move between the individual and the social; it tells me that consent can be both personal and social" (1997, p. 20).

Working from a feminist critical race perspective, hooks (2003) offers a similar view of adult education as ongoing and ever-present, unbound by classroom walls, and focuses on its transformational purpose. Although she does not draw explicitly on Gramsci's work, her notion of "democratic" or "progressive" education focuses similarly on the aim of socially just transformation through adult education. She refers to "the world as classroom" (p. 1) and to "classrooms without boundaries" (p. 13). ☼ What she and other feminist scholars add to a critical conception of adult learning and to Foley's (1999, 2001) concept of incidental learning is an explanation of the role of affect or emotion, sensuality, and spirituality in learning, whether formal or informal (see also Barndt, 1999, 2002; English, 2000; Hayes & Flannery, 1998; Tisdell, 1998, 2000). ☼ Elizabeth Tisdell notes that these non-intellectual dimensions of learning are, generally, a contribution from feminist scholars to adult education. The work of John Dirkx (2001) is consistent with feminist scholars, as he argues that emotions affect motivation to learn and deepen intellectual understanding in the learning process. These dimensions of learning are seen as complements to, not replacements of, critical thinking. ☼ Tisdell's (2000) and hooks's (2003) writing on this matter is especially useful, because it consolidates ideas

---

☼ Rather than embodying the conventional false assumption that the university setting is not the "real world" and teaching accordingly, the democratic educator breaks through the false construction of the corporate university as set apart from real life and seeks to re-envision schooling as always a part of our real world experience, and our real life. Embracing the concept of a democratic education we see teaching and learning as taking place constantly. We share the knowledge gleaned in classrooms beyond those settings thereby working to challenge the construction of certain forms of knowledge as always and only available to the elite.   —bell hooks (2003), *Teaching Community*, p. 41

> ☼ Many of our students come to our classrooms believing that real brilliance is revealed by the will to disconnect and disassociate. They see this state as crucial to the maintenance of objectivism. They fear wholeness will lead them to be considered less "brilliant." Popular ideas of what constitutes academic brilliance continue to perpetuate that the critical thinker is unfeeling, is hardhearted. The assumption seems to be that, if the heart is closed, the mind will open even wider. In actuality, it is the failure to achieve harmony of mind, body and spirit that has furthered anti-intellectualism in our culture and made our schools mere factories.   —bell hooks (2003), *Teaching Community,* pp. 180–181

> ☼ I argue that personally significant and meaningful learning is fundamentally grounded in and is derived from the adult's emotional, imaginative connection with the self and with the broader social world. The meanings we attribute to emotions reflect the particular sociocultural and psychic contexts in which they arise. This process of meaning-making, however, is essentially imaginative and extrarational, rather than merely reflective and rational. Emotionally charged images, evoked through the contexts of adult learning, provide the opportunity for a more profound access to the world by inviting a deeper understanding of ourselves in relationship with it.   —John Dirkx (2001), "The Power of Feelings," p. 64

about spirituality and ideas about learning for societal change, rather than treating spirituality as a distinct, and largely individualistic, quality.

For an inquiry into shopping, which bridges material and cultural considerations, emotion seems especially important in coming to understand how people engage in critical or radical learning through their shopping. Today's mainstream Western consumer movements might emphasize availability of information and intellectual decision making based on considerations of value-for-money (Hilton, 2005; Zukin, 2005; Zukin & Maguire, 2004), but shopping and consumption are also emotion-laden and sensuous processes. For middle-class shoppers in the Global North, shopping creates myriad, often conflicting emotions and sensations, from temptation to stress, awareness to confusion, satisfaction to frustration. ☼ Shopping is often a hurried and stressful interruption in daily life, accompanied as much by learning moments when the "penny drops" as by deliberate reflection. Gramsci's (1971) connection of daily life in civil society to learning, politics, and economics is a starting point for understanding why shopping might be considered as a site and process of learning. Building on that central premise, Foley's (1999, 2001) notion of incidental learning helps me focus on unintended, politically charged learning, even though I use his concept in a qualitatively different kind of

---

☼ There is a perceived ideological fit between the self-managing, enterprising, choosing self and the model citizen of neoliberal societies who shoulders the responsibility for maintaining social order through his or her "good" choices (Cronin 2000, Entwistle 2000, Slater 1997). In addition, there is the troubling capacity of consumer industries to commodify—and disarm—dissenting voices, recruiting issues of women's empowerment, environmental sustainability, and racial equality into the service of product promotion, thus reducing social justice to the freedom to choose between products (Cohen 2003, Talbot 2000).   —Sharon Zukin and Jennifer Smith Maguire (2004), "Consumers and Consumption," pp. 182–183

---

setting and process. The recognition of emotions, senses, and spirituality in learning completes my working conceptualization of a form of adult learning that is incidental, critical, and holistic.

Having adopted this multidimensional understanding of learning, for the sake of consistency and clarity in this document, when I use the word *radical* I do so to discuss socially transformative learning or learning that is accompanied by a commitment to societal change. Consistent with adult educators interested in environmental education (Barndt, 2002; Clover & Hall, 2000; Walter, 2007), I include the "natural" environment and nonhuman life forms in my consideration of societal organization. Canada's West Coast has a history of environmentalist action and education (Walter, 2007), and environmental concerns such as global climate change, food security, and so-called peak oil have great currency within and beyond my local area. At the same time, I think that there is a social environment that is being overlooked by the environmental movement. Like Foley (1999, 2001) and a few of the participants in this inquiry, I use *radical* to infer a concern about the root or the basis of social problems. ☼ Such learning is also always grounded in lived

---

☼ Radical has the sense of fundamental or extreme, of the root, foundational, root and branch. Radical education is a fundamental departure from dominant practice or experience at one or more of the following levels: content, process, outcome, the relationship of education to other social processes. The word "dominant" directs our attention to the relative nature of radicalism. One's learning, or educational experience, is radical in relation to the way things are. This means, of course, that radical education and learning can take us as speedily in the direction of reaction as revolution. Neoliberal educational developments are testament to this, as are the hegemonic effects of the mass media. But in adult education radical education is generally taken to mean critical and emancipatory education, and it is this sense that I will work with in this paper.   —Griff Foley (2001), "Radical Adult Education and Learning," p. 72

experiences and social contexts. I am, however, aware that terminology is always tricky and that this word is accompanied by its own scholarly and popular traditions.

In Chapter 7, I further explore participants' understandings of radicalism and what they contribute to thinking about radical learning.

The Object on the Stage: Shopping as Learning in and about Contemporary Globalization

In this section, I introduce the site and process central to this investigation—what I might call shopping-as-learning, or learning-in-shopping. I draw heavily on scholarship in the field of cultural studies and critical consumer studies. I also note that shopping and consumption are not the same things; shopping is one element of consumption, but, increasingly, consumption involves shopping. Summarizing ideas explored in greater detail elsewhere (Jubas, 2007), I outline the historically developed links between consumption and citizenship in Western societies, contained by the conceptual term *consumer-citizenship*; the phenomenon that has become known as globalization; practices of resistance among consumer-citizens concerned about globalization; and the movement from the notion of consumer-citizenship to that of critical or radical shopping as part of a societal change agenda.

Consumer-Citizenship

In his now famous essay on citizenship, T. H. Marshall (1992) focused on the elements of citizens' rights, or status, and responsibilities. Keith Faulks (2002) expands Marshall's elements, delineating five elemental "Rs" that constitute democratic citizenship. His additions to rights and responsibilities are resources, recognition, and residence. Drawing on Nancy Fraser's (1992) notion of "subaltern counterpublics" and Holloway Sparks's (1997) concept of "dissidence," I add yet one more "R," that of resistance. As I outline below, these are six dimensions on which citizenship is contested, as issues of entitlement, obligation, and identity determine who qualifies for the status of citizen and who embodies and practices "good" citizenship.

Struggles over rights and responsibilities can seem abstract, but the struggle over limited material resources, Faulks's third "R," inserts a more concrete consideration into this mix. In the history of modern Western democratic citizenship, since at least the French Revolution (Riesenberg, 1992 cited in Faulks, 2002), democracy has developed in concert with capitalism, and economic resources have been centrally tied to debates about citizenship rights and responsibilities. In recent years, with the rise of postmodern thought about fluid, partial identity and neoliberal politics favouring the so-called free market and individualism, some theorists are concerned that recognition has gained ascendancy in academic, activist, and political discourse. For Fraser, this shift risks creating a "vulgar culturalism" (2003, p. 25) that displaces arguments in favour of social democracy and the redistribution of resources in the name of fairness and equity. However, Fraser acknowledges the post-structural concern that some strands of materialist analysis, including orthodox Marxism, risk creating the opposite problem: reducing social oppression to financial inequities and overlooking the reality that members of a single social group have multiple and varied affiliations and identities. I share Fraser's conclusion that a balance between redistribution of resources and recognition—what feminist scholars refer to as a "logic of encompassment" (Werbner & Yuval-Davis, 1999) or "differentiated universalism" (Lister, 2003)—is vital for social justice; for critical shoppers, as I explore later, achieving this balance is often the crux of the problem.

The fifth "R" in Faulks's (2002) framework is residence. This refers broadly to control of territory and is evident at local, national, and regional levels. Locally, struggles over residence are apparent in community planning, as political, commercial, and citizen groups press for policies and practices that promote their interests and priorities (Bender, 2003; Satterthwaite, 2001). From debates over building height restrictions to placement of public parks and recreational facilities to development of shopping centres, divergent arguments infuse municipal planning with politics. Nationally and regionally, such struggles appear in combination with rights and resources, as governments, corporations, and citizen groups battle over such things as rights to water, natural resources, and development (Shiva, 2005).

I add resistance as the sixth "R" to this framework. Consistent with Fraser's (1992) concept of subaltern counterpublics ☼ and Sparks's (1997) concept of dissidence, ☼ I limit myself to a consideration of non-violent resistance. Sparks does not include politically motivated boycotts in her list of possible tactics of dissidence, but such tactics can be associated with a collectivity, even if loosely organized, and often aim to educate and pressure others in the name of change. Social movements can be seen as sites in which subaltern counterpublics and their allies forge shared identities and assert themselves and their interests. They are the basis of the incidental learning outlined by Foley (1999, 2001). As Sparks (1997) establishes, using the example of American civil rights figure Rosa Parks, the resistance that they foster manifests the important quality of courage but is complicated, because it both opposes and

☼ I contend that in stratified societies, arrangements that accommodate contestation among a plurality of competing publics better promote the ideal of participatory parity than does a single, comprehensive, overarching public. . . . I propose to call these *subaltern counterpublics* in order to signal that they are parallel discursive arenas where members of subordinated social groups invent and circulate counterdiscourses to formulate oppositional interpretations of their identities, interests, and needs. . . . In general, the proliferation of subaltern counterpublics means a widening of discursive contestation, and that is a good thing in stratified societies.   —Nancy Fraser (1992), "Rethinking the Public Sphere," pp. 122, 123, and 124 (emphasis in original)

☼ I conceptualize dissident citizenship as the practices of marginalized citizens who publicly contest prevailing arrangements of power by means of oppositional democratic practices that augment of replace institutionalized channels of democratic opposition when these channels are inadequate or unavailable. Instead of voting, lobbying, or petitioning, dissident citizens constitute alternative public spaces through practices such as marches, protests, and picket lines; sit-ins, slow-downs, and cleanups; speeches, strikes, and street theatre. Dissident citizenship, in other words, encompasses the often creative oppositional practices of citizens who, either by choice or (much more commonly) by forced exclusion from the institutionalized means of opposition, contest current arrangements of power from the margins of the polity.   —Holloway Sparks (1997), "Dissident Citizenship," p. 75

reiterates elements of the status quo, in much the same way as hegemony accommodates and quashes change. ☼

Consumption is one plane on which these six "Rs" of citizenship are enacted. Like citizenship, consumption is a contested concept. Jean Baudrillard's theory of consumption argues that capitalism has turned consumption into a "system of needs" (1998, p. 75). This system bestows on objects and, presumably, services an importance that exceeds the

☼ Rosa Parks's performance of courageous dissent, however, relied on, invoked, and reinforced a number of gender, race, and class norms, even as it challenged others. Although Parks was, we have seen, a courageous dissident long before her arrest, she was a dissident who epitomized quiet, middle-class respectability. She was demure, feminine, heterosexual, married, family-oriented, hard-working, and churchgoing. Because of the risks she chose to face, she was indeed a "courageous heroine," but her dissidence was performed in a manner that did not conspicuously threaten traditional gender norms, sexuality norms, or class norms.   —Holloway Sparks (1997), "Dissident Citizenship," p. 99

enjoyment and satisfaction that they provide on their own. Consumables and consumption become the measure of happiness that, when combined with formal politics, function as common sense ingredients in the idealized recipe for equality. Consumerist culture and politics come together in constructing a pair of myths: that "growth means affluence" and that "affluence means happiness" (p. 51). ☼

> ☼ In fact, the consumer is sovereign in a jungle of ugliness where *freedom of choice has been forced upon him*. The revised sequence (that is to say, the *system* of consumption) thus ideologically complements and continues the work of the *electoral system*. The drugstore and the polling booth, the loci of individual freedom, are also the system's two mammary glands.   —Jean Baudrillard (1998), *The Consumer Society*, pp. 72–73 (emphasis in original)

Jeff Hearn and Sasha Roseneil (1999) offer the following definition of consumption, which is useful in my inquiry because of its comprehensiveness and clarity:

> Consumption is one of the basic ways in which society is structured and organised, usually unequally, sometimes incredibly so. Differential powers, resources and life chances are routinely produced and reproduced by and through consumption patterns. Consumption not only takes place within culture and thus within specific cultures; it also produces culture and cultures. . . . Furthermore, consumption also constructs, even consumes, the consumer. Just as production produces both products and the producer, the worker, so too consumption has a dialectical form. People do consumption, are "done to", constructed, consumed by that consumption. *Consumption is a structure, process and agency.* (p. 1, emphasis added)

Hearn and Roseneil further explain that consumption is itself productive—of meaning, personal and group identity, and culture. It exemplifies the constrained choices that individuals deliberate, enact, and embody daily. How individuals are identified in relation to others, how they are able to resist these identifications and construct alternatives, how they are included and excluded in society and community—these are all at play in one's consumption options and decisions, in addition to the immediate pleasure and satiety that consumption can provide.

It is the ideology of consumerism that helps create a culture emphasizing shopping and consumption as central to the embodiment of good citizenship. The common sense associated with this ideology advises that, in contemporary Western societies, shopping and consumption function alongside work and morality to accumulate and manifest one's social status. As several scholars point out, though, there have been different iterations of this ideology (Cohen, 2003; Hilton & Daunton, 2001; Jacobs, 2003; Mort, 2006; Nava, 1999). ☼ Each iteration has made sense within a particular social and economic context. Writing about the decades following the Second World War in Britain and the United States, Frank Mort makes the following concluding remarks about the coinciding changes in politics and consumer culture:

> This was not, of course, the first time that intellectuals and politicians had debated such a relationship and its consequences. The late-nineteenth and early-twentieth centuries witnessed related discussions about the connections between the new political subjects of mass democracy and the impact of popular leisure and entertainment across Europe and the USA. During the period after the Second World War projects dedicated to understanding this relationship were prioritized by a group of intellectuals who were central to both social democratic politics and commercial culture. (2006, p. 240)

☼ More specifically, I want to show how, during the 1950s and 1960s, both Marxists and conservative critics expressed their condemnation of mass consumption in similarly elitist terms, and how, partly in reaction, this produced during the 1970s and 1980s a very different body of work in which the consumer and consumption are defended and even celebrated.   —Mica Nava (1999), "Consumerism Reconsidered: Buying and Power," pp. 45–46

Lizbeth Cohen (2003) and Meg Jacobs (2003) outline the development of distinct discourses of consumer-citizenship throughout the twentieth century in the United States. In the early part of that century, consumers were regarded as individual customers. Government encouraged the development of consumer associations which argued that citizens' rights as both workers and consumers had to be ensured, and lobbied for both fair prices and wages. During the economic and social hardship of Depression years, the individualistic conceptualization of consumers was replaced by a nation of "citizen-consumers" (Cohen, 2003), who pressed for rights through price controls, agricultural subsidies, and similar protective policies and programs. Interestingly, Cohen (2003) also notes that oppressed groups in the United States, notably African Americans, used their consumer-citizenship to express their power as they organized boycotts and buycotts to protest racist business practices and support black-owned or black-friendly businesses. Here, then, is an example of a social movement that brought together a subaltern counterpublic (Fraser, 1992) and encouraged resistance through shopping.

Finally, in the post-Second World War decades, a "Consumers' Republic" (Cohen, 2003) developed, in which consumer-citizens were once again reconceptualized, this time as participants in a so-called free market. Their function in American society was deliberately invoked in the postwar years, when the image of the loyal American consumer-citizen—especially the idealized middle-class (and white) suburban housewife—was summoned in the service of anticommunist posturing (Spring, 2003). At the same time, the American civil rights movement of the 1960s, of which Rosa Parks herself became an integral part, continued to employ tactics of consumer-citizenship and additionally began to call for integration of minority groups into representations of the good consumer (Spring, 2003).

Writing about the version of consumerism that has come to characterize contemporary Western societies such as the United States, Britain, and Canada, Joel Spring (2003) points out that, "Inherent in consumerist ideology is the dictate that commercial leisure, such as movies, radio, and TV, should spur people to consume more, work harder, and live moral lives" (p. x). Contemporary consumerism in a Western society such as Canada combines materiality and cultural products and processes, and it instructs consumer-citizens that they are defined and recognized according to the work they do, the things they buy and use, and the values they hold.

Shopping, the arena that contained my focus throughout this inquiry, is one element of consumption. In Chapter 1, I summarized my understanding of and experiences with shopping, and how I tried to pay attention to other understandings and experiences that participants brought into the inquiry. ☼ Following most of the scholarship in this area, I alternate my use of the word *consumption* with the word *shopping* throughout this document.

☼ Understood as a process of looking for and deliberating options, acquiring goods, services and experiences, and, sometimes, deciding to forego a purchase, shopping for me typically involves going into a store. One exception, for me, is when I go to a seasonal farmers' market or a craft sale. On occasion, I go to garage or yard sales or speciality fairs. I have purchased books, airline tickets and vacation accommodation online. Having worked for some 15 years in the not-for-profit community service sector, often in revenue development, I have come to enjoy fundraising events, and have a collection of items that I bought at various auctions. Although I imagined that my conversations with participants would revolve centrally around shopping in stores, I was open to talking about these other types of shopping settings and experiences. Still other things that participants or other people mentioned to me during my inquiry include bartering, swaps, the free-cycle movement and even organized theft.   —"Chapter One: In the Beginning..." p. 39

During the hundred years from Marx until globalization was firmly underway in the late 1980s, shopping and consumption were dismissed as concerns secondary to production or paid labour (Hilton & Daunton, 2001; Mort, 1990; Rappaport, 2001; Zukin & Maguire, 2004). Today, as Aiwha Ong (2004) notes, citizens are "constructed in definitive and specific ways . . . —taxpayers, workers, consumers, and welfare dependants" (p. 157). Contemporary globalization moves the primary site of identity construction from production to consumption for several reasons. First, the stability of occupation, or the citizen's role in production, is being increasingly undermined by corporate global portability and technological developments (Bocock, 1993).

Second, groups other than the traditional classes, around which identity can be constructed, are asserting themselves. Characteristics such as gender and race, to which I pay particularly strong attention in this text, as well as age, sexual orientation, and (dis)ability, have become bases for social identification. Marketers are seizing these identities as new opportunities to advance their own brands and products (Bhachu, 2004; Bocock, 1993; Bowlby, 2001; Grewal, 2005; Hearn & Roseneil, 1999; hooks, 2001; Kenway & Bullen, 2001; Spring, 2003; Zukin, 2005).

Third, the mass production, retailing, and marketing that industrial capitalism first made possible has led to the increasing separation between production and consumption of goods, turning them into a "*harnessing of power*, rather than . . . products embodying work" (Baudrillard, 1998, p. 32, emphasis in original). If shopping and consumption become the measures of power, then citizenship must be either compromised or reconceptualized. Yiannis Gabriel and Tim Lang (2006) assert that, "Currently, political culture is poised between giving primacy to voting or shopping. Consumerism has encroached core citizenship terrain, including housing, healthcare and education" (p. 172). Variations in terminology, including "consumer citizenship" (Grewal, 2005; Hilton, 2003), "consumer-citizen" (Baudrillard, 1998; Bowlby, 2001; Zukin & Maguire, 2004), and "economic citizens" (Jacobs, 2003), reflect the growing attempts by scholars to articulate and explore the convergence of citizenship and consumption.

Democratic citizenship might promise equality, but its reality in the context of social structures is one of inevitable divisions and inequities. ☼ As a central ideology in contemporary Western hegemonies, consumerism exacerbates, rather than alleviates, these divisions and inequities. Even within a single society, discourses of consumer-citizenship are constructed, understood, and used in an array of ways, reflecting the diversity of interests and identities. For example, during the eighteenth and nineteenth centuries, the British abolitionist movement brought

> ☼ The system only sustains itself by producing wealth *and* poverty, by producing as many dissatisfactions as satisfactions, as much nuisance as "progress". Its only logic is to survive and its strategy in this regard is to keep human society out of kilter, in perpetual deficit.   —Jean Baudrillard (1998), *The Consumer Society*, p. 55 (emphasis in original)
>
> Consumption no more homogenizes the social body than the educational system homogenizes cultural opportunities. It even highlights the disparities within it. —Jean Baudrillard (1998), *The Consumer Society*, p. 58

together various interests in boycotts of slave-produced sugar. Members of religious sects opposed to slavery on moral grounds, and men trading in "freely" produced sugar from India who opposed slavery because it created competition with artificially lowered prices, joined women who used their responsibilities as shoppers to assert their power and agitate for formal political rights (Midgley, 1992; Sussman, 2000). Again, Gramsci's (1971) ideas are useful here: Hegemony, the constant balancing act between efforts at persuasion, the threat of force and citizens' consent, is an expression of the conflicting interests that emerge whenever all groups have some degree or form of power, but power is unequally distributed.

Ideologically based common sense, including the ideas that democracy produces equality and the "free" market increases choice, has become pervasive. Such discourses circulate throughout civil society, as well as political and economic institutions, and help to secure broad consent among citizens for social structures that inevitably maintain, more than challenge, unequal social relations. Specific discourses of consumerism and the consumer-citizen are used for economic and political ends and are brought into both marketing and election campaigns. ☼

As a sociologist of education interested in consumption, Spring (2003) ties shopping and consumption to both citizenship and learning, formal and informal. He talks about the use of censorship and the "purging of so-called *radical teachers*" (Spring, 2003, p. x, emphasis in original) during periods of conservatism, and the eventual development of a youth market, starting with preschool-aged children, which merged shopping, consumption, media, and learning. He mentions *Sesame Street*

> ☼ As generations of social historians have demonstrated, class and group identities are always subjective, constructed categories. They result not just from social construction, but they are also politically constructed. At key moments, politicians have sought to win elections and influence public policy by politicizing pocketbook issues and appealing to citizens, especially housewives, as consumers.   —Matthew Hilton and Martin Daunton (2001), "Material Politics: An Introduction," p. 251

and its spin-off toys, which, by the 1970s, were having a notable effect on young children's early learning about the subjects that they would soon encounter in school as well as their identities as media consumers and shoppers.

For adults, he goes back in history to the Chicago World Fair of 1893, where "fast food" was introduced through the exhibits of prepared foods. The accompanying narratives built a case for their use in school cafeterias and workplaces. He agrees that women had a special role in shopping and consumption, and discusses the emergence of home economics as a educational field aimed at women and offering a message for society-in-general: "Along with saving society, home economics was to liberate women from household drudgery and make them active participants in shaping society" (p. 33). This new, "scientific" field expanded women's role as coordinator of shopping and consumption by charging them with implementing a new discourse around diet and food management and the newly available commercial food products introduced into institutions such as schools and hospitals, as well as the home.

During the 1970s, the notion of choice, which has been instrumental in linking consumption to citizenship, entered the lexicon for children, youth, and adults. Children and youth had school textbooks that featured women working in a variety of occupations, and popular media portrayed women similarly. Girls were able to participate in new sports teams and vocational courses. Advertisers began to take notice of niche interests in the environment, feminism, and race relations, and they co-opted these issues into the service of marketing. By the 1980s, consumerism appeared more seamless with citizenship and the educational project, as corporations opened child care centres, high school academies, and after-school or summertime recreational programs. As Spring explains, "An important advance in consumerist ideology was the attempt to create a spontaneous association in the public mind among consumption, democracy, free enterprise, and Americanism" (2003, p. x).

In contemporary Western societies, directions for unbridled shopping to fulfil personal desires and support the economy play against cautions to use credit responsibly. Whether or not goods and services available in the free market are affordable brings resources to the forefront. Recognition, the fourth "R," has lain at the heart of status shopping since the development of department stores in the nineteenth century first offered growing numbers of citizens an opportunity "to enter and participate in an image of the aristocratic life" (Bowlby, 2001, p. 10). Today, a status-based consumerist culture plays on consumers' emotions and, combined with neoliberalism, encourages a form of status-based, competitive consumption recognized in the title and content of Sophie Kinsella's popular series of novels about "shopaholics." ☼

☼ "Hand-crafted applewood," he says. "Took a week to make."

Well, it was a waste of a week, if you ask me. It's shapeless and the wood's a nasty shade of brown.... But as I go to put it back down again, he looks so doleful I feel sorry for him and turn it over to look at the price, thinking if it's a fiver I'll buy it. But it's eighty quid! . . .

"That particular piece was featured in *Elle Decoration* last month," says the man mournfully, and produces a cutout page. And at his words, I freeze. *Elle Decoration*? Is he joking?

He's not joking. There on the page, in full color, is a picture of a room, completely empty except for a suede beanbag, a low table, and a wooden bowl. I stare at it incredulously.

"Was it this exact one?" I ask, trying not to sound too excited. "This exact bowl?" As he nods, my grasp tightens round the bowl. I can't believe it. I'm holding a piece of *Elle Decoration*. How cool is that? Now I feel incredibly stylish and trendy—and wish I were wearing white linen trousers and had my hair slicked back like Yasmin Le Bon to match.

It just shows I've got good taste. Didn't I pick out this bowl—sorry, this *piece*— all by myself? Didn't I spot its quality? Already I can see our sitting room redesigned entirely around it, all pale and minimalist. Eighty quid. That's nothing for a timeless piece of style like this.   —Sophie Kinsella (2001), *Confessions of a Shopaholic*, pp. 50–51 (emphasis in original)

Even as marketing pressures individuals to consume in certain ways, there are indications that consumers of all ages respond with their own ideas about consumption (Kenway & Bullen, 2001; Mort, 1990; Paterson, 2006). Resistance within civil society is evident in growing interest in critical shopping and in the social movements that feature discourses of critical shopping and consumption. For example, the fair trade and environmental movements indicate how resistance can be undertaken by consumers (Grimes, 2005). ☼ As the developing terminology that connects consumer and citizens suggests, consumption may be viewed as a marker of citizenship. Ultimately, though, the relationship between citizenship and consumption is itself one of a paradoxical tension, because citizenship and consumption have developed in tandem even as they undermine each other, particularly in the context of capitalist structures. ☼

Gender, Race, and Class: Consumer-Citizenship as a Social Construct

The previous discussion explicates how both consumption and citizenship can be described as "contested" on the grounds of the six "Rs" that I have laid out. The contests occur as hegemony structures relations between consumer-citizens and creates social categories. Struggles in

> ☼ Fair trade creates a bridge between the peoples of the developing nations and those of the developed ones. For consumers in First World countries, fair trade gives people the opportunity to not only purchase products that support their values of a more socially just and equitable world trade order, but to also learn about the producers' lives, their struggles, and our mutual interdependence.   —Kimberly M. Grimes (2005), "Changing the Rules of Trade with Global Partnerships," pp. 237–238

> ☼ Yet the essence of capitalism is that the basic means of production are not socially but privately owned, and that decisions about production are therefore in the hands of a group occupying a minority position in the society and in no direct way responsible to it.   —Raymond Williams (1980), *Culture and Materialism*, p. 186

the arena of shopping reflect the complications of consumer-citizenship. They are based on diverse social groups and interests, as well as political divisions between government and citizenry and material divisions between capitalist-producers and proletarian-consumers. Ideologies such as consumerism and neoliberalism have emerged historically, as capitalism and democracy have developed in concert with each other and now combine in nationally and locally particular ways.

Like all ideologically based structures in all democratic societies, patriarchy, racism, and capitalism have been both evolving and persistent. The result in Canada—one Western society in today's Global North—is an ideologically based presentation of the "good" consumer-citizen, who is idealized in terms of gender, race, and class. This individual is envisioned as white—the embodiment of a mythical Canadian heritage that identifies British and, to a lesser extent, French colonization as Canada's starting point. This idealized good consumer-citizen is also envisioned as middle class—the representative of the gainfully employed Canadian whose combination of work and consumption supports the national economy and a common sense understanding of this country's "way of life." The limits of consumer-citizenship are also apparent when discourses of citizenship and consumption are heard separately. While citizenship retains a certain masculinization, shopping and consumption retain a degree of feminization. When consumption and citizenship are brought together, gender often receives vague attention, especially in mainstream study and writing. ☼

In exploring social categories and inequities, feminist, critical race, and other critical scholars have been at the forefront of work arguing

> ☼ Ghosting both the projects of British sociologists and American liberal theorists [in the 1950s and 1960s] was an understated debate about gender and especially about how the core concepts of democracy, leisure and culture were differently inflected by masculine and feminine access to the structures of modern political and social power. . . . Gender was empirically present but structurally absent in much of the work. —Frank Mort (2006), "Competing Domains," p. 231

that gender, race, and class have real material effects in the lives of all consumer-citizens but are based in social, rather than natural or universal, determinations. Understandings of these categories might be fluid, but the categories themselves are persistent. This acknowledgement of the social construction of these categories in no way diminishes their cultural and social importance. As Ruth Frankenberg explains,

> Race, like gender, is "real" in the sense that it has real, though changing, effects in the world and real, tangible, and complex impact on individuals' sense of self, experiences, and life chances. In asserting that race and racial difference are socially constructed, I do not minimize their social and political reality, but rather insist that their reality is, precisely, social and political rather than inherent or static. (1993, p. 11)

Gender is the social categorization produced by and in response to patriarchy. Elisabeth Hayes and Danielle Flannery write that "gender [is] a type of social relation that is constantly changing, created and recreated in daily interactions as well as on a broader scale through such institutions as school, work and the family" (2000, p. 4). Patriarchy not only divides the social world into male and female, masculine and feminine; it also values the male and the masculine over the female and the feminine.

The increasingly evident connection between citizenship and consumption has benefits and drawbacks for marginalized groups, including women. Since the late nineteenth century, by which time industrial capitalism was well entrenched in Western societies, consumption and shopping have been seen as the purview of women. Capitalism, along with patriarchy and racism, developed in the context of earlier iterations of imperialism, including colonization, to separate the masculine from the feminine and the developed West from the primitive East. As men increasingly were understood as producers and women as consumers, a process of what Mies (1986) calls "housewifization" began to unfold in the eighteenth century among the upper classes. It was made possible by the convergence of colonial capitalism and patriarchy and was characterized by three tendencies: the domesticity produced by privatized wealth and luxury in the home; the expression of wealth through objects, rather than the number of loyal subjects; and the contraction of time apparent in the new availability of luxury items year-round. Wealthy women were encouraged to define themselves as good mothers, good wives, and—despite their lack of economic and political rights—good citizens by buying and consuming items produced by their husbands or in colonies.

Although consumerism has not arisen exclusively in capitalist societies, it has developed alongside technological innovations that made possible new manufacturing, transport, promotional, and retail options. Increasingly, consumption has become associated with shopping for goods rather than using goods that one has produced (Bocock, 1993). In a social world of dichotomies, shopping has been construed as a predominantly feminine activity disassociated from masculine labour in formal workplaces (Bocock, 1993; Bowlby, 2001; Mort, 1990; Rappaport, 2000). This does not mean that men have not shopped or enjoyed shopping, just as the masculinization of production does not mean that women have not worked within and, often, outside the home. The feminization of shopping builds on the attachment of femininity to family caregiving, and much of women's shopping and consumption has been seen as what they do on behalf of their husbands and families (Bowlby, 2001; Rappaport, 2000). Despite the idealized image of women as thoughtful caregivers, their portrayal as emotional rather than intellectual has had a demeaning effect on both women and shopping. Women have been characterized, alternately, as "purchaser consumers" (Cohen, 2003) for whom shopping expresses duty to family and the national economy, and as "flighty" (Bowlby, 2001, p. 119), impulsive shoppers.

As industrialization took hold, men's work and women's work were seen increasingly as separate realms. Over time, housewifization spread to other classes, establishing the nuclear family and gendered work as social norms (Mies, 1986). With the emergence of shopping areas in nineteenth-century Western cities, shopping became portrayed as a "'natural' feminine pastime" (Rappaport, 2000, p. 5). As feminist scholars explain, the attention being paid to consumption can be as a correction to the problem of omission of women's labour and experiences and as a challenge to the traditional academic emphasis on class as it introduces associated considerations of gender and race (Bowlby, 2001; Rappaport, 2000; Zukin & Maguire, 2004). In its discussion of social relations and revolution in binary terms, especially the realms of public labour in the industrialized workplace and private consumption in the home, Marxist theory can both challenge capitalism and reinforce social inequities made possible by patriarchy and racism. As I discuss later, this is an example of the complications of resistance, which itself exemplifies a dialectical relationship between radicalism and conservatism.

Since Mies's (1986) writing about housewifization, critical race, post-colonial, and other feminist scholarship has continued to link consumption and citizenship to social relations. For hooks (2001), racism divides the American society so that certain groups are constructed as rulers and consumers and others as the ruled and the consumed. ☼ Ong focuses on the socio-political basis of race in her exploration of how Asian immigrants to America are racialized on a "white-black continuum" (2004, p. 159), in part on the basis of their ability to shop and consume. In her research on British Indian culture, Parminder Bhachu notes that "consumption of 'orientalist' material culture was an integral part of the British Empire" (2004, p. 26). hooks (2001) makes a similar observation about the treatment of African American culture—regarded as exotic and desirable—in mainstream, white America.

> ☼ Currently, the commodification of difference promotes paradigms of consumption wherein whatever difference the Other inhabits is eradicated, via exchange, by a consumer cannibalism that not only displaces the Other but denies the significance of that Other's history through a process of decontextualization. —bell hooks (2001), "Eating the Other," p. 431

Frankenberg (1993) also describes how progressive individuals in the American racial centre think about race as a characteristic belonging only to those in minority or marginalized groups, rather than a type of relation that involves all community members and citizens. ☼ In the seventeen years since the release of Frankenberg's book, this tendency seems to have broadened. Liberal rhetoric of global citizenship emphasizes the humanity that unites all peoples and equalizes us all. Ultimately, though, whiteness remains the presumed norm in Western societies. Labels such as "ethnic foods" or "world music" are used to refer to cultural products and processes outside the centre, reducing difference to a matter of style and taste (Dhruvarajan, 2000). A paradox is created: There are claims that racism itself is being eliminated through the discursive elimination of whiteness. At the same time, members of racialized minority groups

> ☼ At this time in U.S. history, whiteness as a marked identity is explicitly articulated mainly in terms of the "white pride" of the far right. In a sense, this produces a discursive bind for that small subgroup of white women and men concerned to engage in anti-racist work: if whiteness is emptied of any content other than that which is associated with racism or capitalism, this leaves progressive whites apparently without a genealogy. This is partly a further effect of racist classification that notes or "marks" the race of nonwhite people but not whites.   —Ruth Frankenberg (1993), *White Women, Race Matters*, p. 232

are portrayed in reductionist, stereotypical terms, and centuries-old opposition of whiteness and Otherness is reiterated. Ann DuCille (1999)
refers to this paradox as "concurrent racing and erasing."

In response to these discursive tendencies, critical race scholars such
as Frankenberg (1993), Caroline Knowles (2003), France Winddance
Twine (2000), and Vanaja Dhruvarajan (2000) clarify that race, too, is
defined and lived out relationally. ☼ Like all social categories, it is a persistent construct *and* must be understood in terms of specific times and
places. Since the height of Canada's social welfare state in the 1970s, for
example, the idealized version of a white, middle-class consumer-citizen
has been juxtaposed with a policy discourse of tolerance and multiculturalism that, as Dhruvarajan writes, "has helped to manage diversity,
but it has not addressed the issue of inequality in power relations"
(2000, p. 169). If anything, she argues, Canada's multiculturalism policy
and the increase in ethno-racial diversity in this country serves European
ethnic groups (in addition to British or French) who are able to preserve
their cultural traditions; meanwhile, "this symbolic pluralism does not
help people of colour find jobs, housing or child care" (p. 170). This
social reality can be understood in terms of "discursive repertoires on
race" whose inherent contradiction between the human right to equality
and structures of racial inequality "can be exposed or obscured linguis-
tically, but not resolved. Thus, one reaches here . . . the limit point of
the value of a focus on discourse, and attention is drawn once again to

---

☼ The political landscapes of race are quite particular. This is not just a matter
of looking at national differences, although this is relevant. There are significant
microclimates in some places. There are important differences across Canada,
for example, in terms of migrant populations, individual and collective histories
or migration and settlement, and the relationship between migration and nation
building. Vancouver looks to the West and the Pacific rim for its arrivals and
historic exclusions. Its current migrants are wealthy. Toronto traditionally leans
towards the Caribbean and the less affluent, but now has a substantial Chinese
population in the suburb of Markham hedging its bets on the long-term effects of
government in Beijing on Hong Kong. Quebec with its own forms of nationalism
is quite different again. Often . . . I bring together material and examples from
Britain and the United States and so it is important to underscore the differences
between these *race*-political landscapes when they are wielded in this fragmented
form to make a point. Even though they are historically linked (as are Canada and
Australia) through empire and migration, Britain and America had quite different
relationships to empire business and to the (Black) Atlantic slave trade. Each made
and sustained whiteness by different routes: even if the migrants of one provided
nation building material for the other.   —Caroline Knowles (2003), *Race and
Social Analysis*, p. 16

the crucial interplay of discourse and material life" (Frankenberg, 1993, p. 190). Frankenberg's view resembles the outcome of policies and discourses that address gender-based discrimination without changing the structure of patriarchy. Norms of masculinity and femininity change, but the social world continues to be divided into men and women and to value the masculine over the feminine.

Like gender and race, class is a persistent social construct that is fluid across time and place and that has become a complicated consideration in contemporary scholarship. Unlike gender and race, though, class cannot be represented as a source of welcome diversity. As Walter Michaels states, "White is not better than black, but rich is definitely better than poor" (2006, p. 47). A discourse of multiculturalism, diversity, and tolerance might mask ongoing racism and patriarchy, but it ignores class entirely.

I find Bourdieu's ideas on class useful in this piece of my inquiry. Living as he did in the early twentieth century, Gramsci maintained an older Marxist understanding of class in terms of relations of production, although he did broaden his consideration beyond the proletariat to other subaltern classes, such as the peasantry. Several decades later, Bourdieu (1984) began to broaden the notion of class further, inserting an emphasis on the social, cultural, and symbolic to match the economic. The now-familiar term "socioeconomic class" reflects this expanded understanding, as Bourdieu's notions of social and cultural capital are added to economic capital in determining class. In Canada today, a doctor, a real estate agent, a plumber, and a lottery winner might have access to the same economic capital, but they do not necessarily share a class position. Gender is also implicated in class, as some historically feminized professions such as teaching might offer less income than historically masculinized trades such as plumbing. Although class structures have tended to value the professions above the trades, gender structures have tended to value the masculine above the feminine. Similarly, members of minority racial groups become associated with and are often slotted into occupations with relatively low social status and economic value. ☼ These

---

☼ The lowest positions are designated by the fact that they include a large—and growing—proportion of immigrants or women . . . or immigrant women. . . . Similarly, it is no accident that the occupations in personal services—the medical and social services, the personal-care trades, old ones like hairdressing, new ones like beauty care, and especially domestic service, which combine the two aspects of the traditional definition of female tasks, service and the home—are practically reserved for women.   —Pierre Bourdieu (1984), *Distinction: A Social Critique of the Judgement of Taste*, p. 108

examples illustrate how social categories intersect with and bisect one another. Another way in which class is intersected and bisected is through what Bourdieu (1984) refers to as "social trajectories," the means by which individuals develop their capital(s) from their socio-economic starting points. These trajectories distinguish factions of classes even when they have commonalities in their economic wealth.

Bourdieu was instrumental in ensuring that class was maintained as an important construct in social theory and research (Nesbit, 2006). Class is particularly relevant to this inquiry, which explores a society underpinned by consumerist and neoliberal ideologies and common sense promises of freedom of choice and individuals' ability to construct identity and status through shopping and consumption. In rebuttal to the argument made by scholars such as Beck that contemporary "individualization" diminishes the relevance of class, scholars such as Rosemary Crompton and Beverley Skeggs, both of whom adopt Bourdieu's perspective in their work, argue that individualization is a hegemonic discursive thread in neoliberal globalization. In that discourse, the image of the middle class (white man) is simply employed as a stand-in for the universal ideal of the good citizen. Like race, class relations might be increasingly complex, but they are presented in increasingly simplistic terms. Writing within Canada, Tom Nesbit begins to suggest the irony at play: "Especially in the United States, one commonly hears either that class has ceased to exist or, alternatively, that everyone is middle class" (2006, p. 175). Crompton cites Beck's characterization of class as "a 'zombie category' which is 'dead but still alive'" (2006, p. 663). At the same time, the lower, working, and middle classes are under concerted attacks through globalization's tactic of privatization, which transfers jobs from workplaces in the unionized public sector to workplaces in the non-unionized private sector. As Bourdieu states, "what the competitive struggle makes everlasting is not different conditions, but the difference between conditions" (1984, p. 164). Skeggs (2004) explores how studies in topics such as mobility dilute interest in and analysis of class; however, such conceptual framing of globalization studies overlooks the reality that different people have access to and enact mobility in different ways—a point that I raise again in my conceptualization of globalization. ☼

Crompton acknowledges that "although there has indeed been considerable and extensive social change, and individuals may indeed appear

---

☼ The mobility of choice of the affluent British middle-classes, conducted in relative ease, is quite different from the mobility of the international refugee or the unemployed migrant.   —Beverley Skeggs (2004), *Class, Self, Culture*, p. 49

to have more 'choices' to make than in the recent historical past, the concept of class is by no means redundant" (2006, p. 659). Her term "positive pluralism" encompasses a notion of class that is multifaceted and complicated, and includes "both economic resources and social behaviours (and even other axes of differentiation such as gender and race)" (pp. 659–660). Occupational categories remain useful in discussing class but "are better regarded as useful proxies for the economic dimension of class, rather than as encompassing the complex realities, material and cultural, of concrete classes" (p. 660). Although I think that Crompton's passage underestimates the extent to which occupational categories also operate as "useful proxies" for the cultural dimension of class, I take her point that there is more to its determination than occupation.

In a similar vein, Skeggs aims "to capture the ambiguity produced through struggle and fuzzy boundaries, rather than to fix it in place in order to measure and know it. Class formation is dynamic, produced through conflict and fought out at the level of the symbolic" (2004, p. 5). In an era when class struggles are ongoing, class boundaries are "fuzzy," and hegemonic discourse asserts a singularly valued and idealized middle class, it becomes more difficult for individuals to self-identify clearly and purposefully with class categories. Class identification is made even more difficult, Skeggs argues, by the growing tendency to affiliate with a middle class that, in its contemporary iteration, stresses individualization. In her conclusion, Skeggs makes the noteworthy point that

> [c]lass struggle is not just about collective action, for when are we aware of physically encountering a class? But it is also about the positioning, judgements and relations that are entered into on a daily and personal basis. Living class, which I'd argue is different from class-consciousness, is very much part of how class is made. (2004, p. 173)

These arguments follow Bourdieu's thinking and are largely consistent with a Gramscian framework. Skeggs explicitly notes her agreement with Gramsci's approach (see Skeggs, 2004, p. 45), as Bourdieu also does (see Bourdieu, 1984, p. 386). These are dialectical understandings of class. They retain the concept of class in order to avoid "vulgar culturalism" (Fraser, 2003, p. 25), or overlooking of material disparities in favour of struggles for cultural recognition; at the same time, they expand the concept in order to avoid simplistic economic determinism or the individualistic emphasis of some other sociologists. ☼

As this discussion establishes, gender, race, and class are constructs that are developed, adopted, and challenged in particular historical, geographic, and social contexts. They are both fluid and persistent, reiterating how social divisions are structured even as their precise meanings and

☼ For Beck, "the individual himself or herself becomes the reproduction unit for the social in the lifeworld" (Beck 1992:130). And, ". . . class loses its sub-cultural basis and is no longer experienced" (1992:98). Individuals, Beck maintains, although unable to escape structural forces in general, can decide on which ones to act and which to ignore. This, he argues, does not create a "free" individual; rather, it creates individuals who live out, biographically, the complexity and diversity of the social relations that surround them. This self, this biographical production, Beck calls "reflexive modernity". Central to this theory is an incredibly voluntarist individual who can choose which structural forces to take into account and which to act upon. However, as Savage (2000) points out, individuals still need to situate themselves socially in order for them to assess what kind of risks they are likely to encounter. They also need access to social resources, including forms of interpretation such as discourse, by which they can make sense of the "risks" that surround them and act upon them. In this sense they are always/already implicated in a process of positioning, cultural differentiation and resource access, that by necessity involves the making of social distinction. Thus individualization cannot be anything but a cultural process involving differentiation from others and differential access to resources.   —Beverley Skeggs (2004), *Class, Self, Culture,* pp. 52–53

roles are debated and changed throughout civil society. Because members of any one social category are also members of varied other social categories, it is impossible to speak definitively about the impact of one social construct on all its members. A more useful approach, then, is to regard genders, races, and classes as distinct but intersecting categories that every individual embodies. Barndt (2002), for example, describes "an interlocking analysis of power" (p. 62) to account for how individuals experience any given type of social relation in the context of other types of social relations and factors.

For over a century, entire industries and marketing campaigns have been built around idealized notions of feminine white beauty. Race and gender have been used to promote products by tempting consumer-citizens. Images of the primitive or exotic in early marketing materials and advertisements conveyed imperial conquest and connections, while images of wholesome white girls on soap packaging intimated ideas about the inherent cleanliness of white people (Bowlby, 2001; Paterson, 2006; Spring, 2003). In recent decades, age has become similarly exploited by advertisers (Bowlby, 2001; Kenway & Bullen, 2001; Martens, 2005; Paterson, 2006; Spring, 2003). ☼ Understanding the connection between identity and consumption in a consumerist society, as well as consumers' desire to be something other than part of the "mass," consumerism encourages the commodification, sale, and consumption of difference (hooks, 2001; Skeggs, 2004; Zukin, 2005). In tension with this impulse

☼ Whether explicitly named or not, the four categories of sex, class, age and race have retained their position as the primary advertising differentials throughout the twentieth century. As well as offering the possibility of infinite detailed variations and combinations, each of them leads itself to dualistic, hierarchical schemes—man/woman, higher/lower, older/younger, white/black (or western/colonial, indigenous/immigrant, and so on). It often happens that subordinate categories get lumped together as likely to share some particularly unsophisticated (which may also mean exploitable) predilections. —Rachel Bowlby (2001), *Carried Away*, p. 113

to consume difference, the structures of patriarchy, racism, and capitalism place limits on what is considered normal and desirable. From the commercialization of an initially political project such as hip hop to the popularity of bangra (Bhachu, 2004), consumerism churns acceptable difference through a marketing machine, stripping culture of its temporal and geographic roots and promising that every*thing* is available to every*one*. ☼

However, despite the "common sense"(Gramsci, 1971) emerging from neoliberalism and the associated capitalist ideology of consumerism that citizens' equality is best assured within a socio-economic system of competition and self-reliance, the "free" market system does not seek to and cannot eliminate social divisions. So-called consumer choice does not empower marginalized citizens. Like all hegemonic ideologies, neoliberalism and consumerism are designed to maintain existing ranks of

☼ Like rap music and professional basketball, certain designer labels have made a racial crossover. Identified as "black," they enjoy enormous commercial success among all shoppers, but especially among teenage males; their advertisements in fashion magazines play on the dubious dangers of the streets and the outward signs of criminal cultures; and, as their sales in department stores and speciality shops increase around the world, they attract the interest of Wall Street analysts and investors. No doubt about it, black is hot these days, but only if it sells.

The financial value of these fashions rests on the curious ability of mass-manufactured clothing to represent the cultural value of cool. Jeans and logoed sweats, baseball caps worn backwards, gold chains perhaps, and definitely athletic shoes: these have long since been elevated to their own fashion category of "urban wear" a business that is worth several billion dollars a year. That so much money is at stake signals a paradoxical triumph of both countercultural symbolic coding and corporate decision-making, which hangs, in turn, on creating a fragile balance between the changing body images of two volatile groups—teenagers and blacks. —Sharon Zukin (2005), *Point of Purchase: How Shopping Changed American Culture*, p. 146

status and privilege, rather than to alleviate power imbalances while appealing even to citizens on the social margins (Baudrillard, 1998).

What has become additionally problematic, as I have suggested above, is that mainstream discourse in Western democratic societies, which are able to exert force internationally because of their economic power, has begun to equate consumption with citizenship and consumer choice with democratic freedom. Consumerist ideology is being used to bolster a "myth of equality" (Baudrillard, 1998, p. 49), and a two-part example of common sense emerges: First, "growth means affluence," and, second, "affluence means democracy" (p. 51). This explains the statements made by President Bush and Mayor Giuliani cited in Chapter 1, as well as the contrary analysis of consumerism articulated throughout Douglas Coupland's novel, *Generation X*, whose main characters represent the first generation raised under the iterations of neoliberal consumerist ideologies in contemporary globalization. ☼ No longer the attempt to dismantle injustices or upset the existing balance of power, "revolution," according to these ideologies—and Canada's national airline—becomes the unending presentation of options for consumer-citizens-of-means.

☼ The car heads out on a long stretch that heads toward the highway and Claire hugs one of the dogs that has edged its face in between the two front seats. It is a face that now grovels politely but insistently for attention. She lectures into the dog's two obsidian eyes: "You, you cute little creature. You don't have to worry about having snowmobiles or cocaine or a third house in Orlando, *Flori*da. That's right. No you don't. You just want a nice little pat on the head."

The dog meanwhile wears the cheerful, helpful look of a bellboy in a foreign country who doesn't understand a word you're saying but who still wants a tip. "That's right. You wouldn't want to worry yourself with so many *things*. And do you know *why*?" (The dog raises its ears at the inflection, giving the illusion of understanding. Dag insists that all dogs secretly speak the English language and subscribe to the morals and beliefs of the Unitarian church, but Claire objected to this because she said she knew for a *fact*, that when she was in France, the dogs spoke French.) "Because all of those objects would only mutiny and slap you in the face. They'd only remind you that all you're doing with your life is collecting objects. And nothing else."   —Douglas Coupland (1991), *Generation X*, pp. 10–11 (emphasis in original)

Globalization

For critical, feminist, and other radical adult educators, contemporary globalization is a troubling phenomenon, because, among other outcomes, it encourages capitalism's "progressive colonization of new dimensions of human life" (Foley, 2001, p. 81). These educators hold that a strategic form of radical adult education is required to respond to this deliberately executed project. The concerns raised by these adult educators, other critical scholars, and activists outside academe imply that globalization, like citizenship and consumption, is an "essentially contested concept" (Lister, 2003, p. 14). William Carroll (2002) also characterizes globalization as a "problematic term." Regardless of how one understands it, there is a consensus that globalization has far-reaching political, economic, social, and cultural implications. In this section, I outline the historical development of what is now recognized as globalization, and some of the explanations of this phenomenon.

Many scholars trace the beginning of the period known as globalization to developments following the Second World War, notably the major international agreements that have become known as "the Washington Consensus" (Bello, 2002; Kiely, 2005). The stated objective of the Bretton-Woods agreement was to build stability after half a century of turbulence and violence. It linked the American dollar to the price of gold, set the dollar as the standard for all currency valuations, and established the International Monetary Fund (IMF) to regulate "[s]hort-term balance of payment problems" for trading states (Kiely, 2005, p. 51). For some twenty-five years, Bretton-Woods seemed to have been having the intended outcomes. Enjoying buoyant economies, governments in the Global North pre-empted radical shifts by funding social programs for marginalized citizens and compiled an international development agenda based on national currency and economic regulations, as well as investment in public services. In effect, these policies and programs helped solidify America-led Western hegemony internationally by ameliorating broad concerns about social welfare and marginalizing more radical voices.

Despite a discourse of fairness and democracy, the new institutions—including the IMF and the World Bank, as well as the United Nations (UN)—were weighted unevenly, so that certain states held more power than others. This imbalance was evident from the initiation of the Bretton-Woods agreement, which (corresponding to Gramsci's predictions) affirmed America's position as leader in a new, international hegemony (Kiely, 2005). ☼ From the end of the Second World War until the late 1970s, the underlying aim behind this hegemony was to secure the corporate interests of the Global North. A key strategy in fulfilling that aim was "the co-optation of Third World elites" (Bello, 2002, p. 40). When the American economy began to falter, experiencing a trade deficit and large military expenditures associated with the Vietnam War, the Nixon administration unlinked the American dollar from the price of gold. As debt, inflation, and unemployment climbed, the affordability

> ☼ Every relationship of "hegemony" is necessarily an educational relationship and occurs not only within a nation, between the various forces of which the nation is composed, but in the international and world-wide field, between complexes of national and continental civilisations.   —Antonio Gramsci (1971), *Selections from the Prison Notebooks*, p. 350

of social programs was questioned. In America and other industrialized countries, political change at the state and global levels in the late 1980s was led by the right-wing British Thatcher/Major governments and the American Reagan/Bush governments. These administrations introduced a neoliberal discourse of personal responsibility and potential coupled with a neoconservative social platform, and began the process of dismantling the post-Second World War social and so-called interventionist policies and programs (Kiely, 2005).

By the 1990s, New Labour emerged in Britain under Tony Blair's leadership and New Democrats in America under Bill Clinton's leadership; they brought a kinder, gentler Third Way discourse to electorates rocked by two decades of economic and social turbulence. In the Global South, the IMF and the World Bank replaced conventional loans with "structural adjustment loans . . . intended to push a programme of 'reform' that would cut across the whole economy or a whole sector of the economy" (Bello, 2002, p. 43). These reforms included reduced public spending and increased privatization; liberalized import, foreign investment and labour standards; and currency devaluations. Their explicit aims were to enhance the competitiveness of exports from the Global South and enable those countries to repay their World Bank loans, and to cut international development spending by countries in the Global North (Bello, 2002).

Although Gramsci's (1971) general focus is on the nation-state, his references to the international or global level suggest how his theory and concepts can be applied to a critical analysis of globalization. The hegemonic conception of globalization is well represented by British sociologist Giddens. He dismisses critics of globalization as "sceptics" and describes globalization as an unavoidable, new "runaway world" in which new technologies are combining with capitalism and democracy to create "a global order that no one understands fully, but is making its effects felt upon all of us" (1999a, p. 7). This has also been characterized as the "strong version of globalization" (Tabb, 1997 in Holst, 2007). According to Giddens (1998, 1999b), the combination of these new forces, traditional social values, and the evolution of institutions and discourses beyond twentieth-century "left and right" politics offers a "Third Way" of genuine progress. The assumptions hidden in Giddens's

Third Way discourse have become the mainstream "common sense" of globalization. ☼

☼ Appealing to such a wide constituency, the Third Way represents a new modernising movement of the centre. While accepting the central socialist value of social justice, it rejects class politics, seeking a cross-class base of support. It sets itself against authoritarianism and xenophobia. On the other hand, it is not libertarian. Individual freedom depends on collective resources and implies social justice. Government is not, as neoliberals say, the enemy of freedom; on the contrary, good government is essential for its development and expansion. —Anthony Giddens (1999a), "After the Left's Paralysis," p. 8

No rights without responsibilities, no authority without democracy: if these are the basic principles of the Third Way, they must apply to the business corporation as elsewhere.   —Anthony Giddens (1999a), "After the Left's Paralysis," p. 14

An emphasis on community seems to some critics out of line with the impact of globalisation. In fact it is consistent with it, since globalisation not only pulls away from the local arena but it "pushes down" on it, too, creating both new pressures towards and new opportunities for the restoration of community.   —Anthony Giddens (1999a), "After the Left's Paralysis," p. 17

The reformed welfare state will be a social investment state, establishing a new relationship between risk and security on the one hand and individual and collective responsibility on the other. . . . The main guideline of the social investment state can be simply stated: wherever possible *invest in human capital rather than the direct payment of benefits.*   —Anthony Giddens (1999a), "After the Left's Paralysis," p. 23

Despite his enthusiasm for a strong version of globalization, even Giddens has some concerns. He admits that, although globalization affects all regions, countries, and groups of citizens, often in unpredictable ways, "[i]t is led from the west, bears the strong imprint of American political and economic power, and is highly uneven in its consequences" (1999a, p. 4). He also recognizes that the global movement of capital and production threatens local economies, especially subsistence economies in the Global South. Still, he is convinced that globalization is both unstoppable and the source of new forces that, when combined with social values to create Third Way politics, provides an opportunity to move beyond previous economic, social, and political systems. For Giddens, the urgency for Third Way politics lies in the reality that older structures and allegiances have become irrelevant. Movement to his new political vision is necessary for the inclusion of social justice and economic well-being.

Critical adult educators who adopt a strong version of globalization tend to offer their critiques from what John Holst (2007) and others refer to as "civil societarian perspectives." They do not share Giddens's ultimate optimism about globalization and Third Way politics. They argue that, given globalization's erosion of both the power of national governments and the currency of class-based politics, people who are concerned about globalization must turn

> to non-governmental organizations (NGOs) and new social movements operating in what these adult educators call civil society (a sphere generally seen, to varying degrees, as relatively autonomous from the state and the market) as the agents best situated to protect and perhaps expand this social realm of civil society in the face of increasing "colonization" from new economy forces. . . . (Holst, 2007, p. 10)

I note that this understanding of civil society's relation to formal politics and economic structure is inconsistent with the Gramscian notion of dialectic. An understanding more consistent with Gramsci's thinking would avoid splitting civil society and culture from the state and the market.

In contrast to this strong version of globalization, other critics adopt what is referred to as a "long version of globalization" (Tabb, 1997 in Holst, 2007). Those who adopt this perspective on globalization see it as a phenomenon that encompasses new forms and uses of technology, but not one that is entirely new and unknown. Among those who work from this perspective, Marxist scholars argue that capitalism has always had a globalizing impetus and is prone to the turbulence that characterizes today's globalization (Callinicos, 2001; Harrison, 2002; Kiely, 2005). ☼ Furthermore, most foreign direct investment (FDI), which bolsters globalized corporate development and profit, comes from the Global North, and most of its pay-off flows to corporations and economies in the Global North. As Holst explains, "The fact that Northern economies still dominate FDI and invest it largely among themselves sheds light on the fact that the nation-states attached to these economies are still strong and in fact vital to the continuation of historical expansion of capitalist relations" (2007, p. 11).

☼ It is certainly worth bearing in mind that global economic structures are hardly novel. The late 1800s saw heavy international investment, buoyed by imperialist rivalries. World systems theorists date the origins of the modern world system to the mercantilist trade networks established in the fourteenth century.
—Graham Harrison (2002), "Globalisation," p. 17

Holst supports adult educators' attempts to incorporate critical analyses of and responses to globalization in their work, and, to that end, he compares the strong and the long versions of globalization. Although he agrees with much of the Marxist-initiated critique in the long version of globalization, he raises four limitations to it. First, he explains that "it misses the mark in understanding the dialectical process of change within capitalism. The fundamental contradictions within capitalism are not external relations (global/local), but contradictory relations internal to the process of capitalism itself" (p. 15). To be effective, opposition to globalization must understand and incorporate this aspect of capitalism, rather than portraying the tension between the global and the local as unique to contemporary globalization.

Second, he points to the lack of theorizing of the nation-state and formal politics, especially among adult educators in the Global North. He attributes much of the reluctance to undertake such theorizing to the tendency of adult educators to return to a civil societarian perspective on the diminished role of the state even if they reject the idea, also associated with civil societarianism, that globalization is inevitable. This is despite recent examples of strategies of resistance to hegemonic globalization in the Global South, including Venezuela and Bolivia, based on popular democracy and popular control.

Third, Marxist analyses might offer persuasive critiques of hegemonic globalization, the strong version of it, and the civil societarian response that they see as "a form of left-wing neoliberalism" (Holst, 2002 in Holst, 2007, p. 20); ironically though, given their conclusion that the nation-state retains an important role, Holst concludes that they have generated few viable alternatives for political organization. Fourth, and related to the previous point, with no new options for political organizing, Marxist analyses maintain their focus on traditional class-based structures of resistance, notably trade unions and labour-affiliated political parties. Writing from the United States, Holst (2007) points out that organized labour is in severe decline in that country, and traditional political alliances are being challenged. Here, he draws on Gramsci's political writings, which predate his incarceration and penning of *The Prison Notebooks*:

> The period of history we are passing through is a revolutionary period because the traditional institutions for the government of human masses, institutions which were linked to old modes of production and exchange, have lost any significance and useful function they might have had. . . . But it is not only bourgeois class institutions which have collapsed and fallen apart: working-class institutions too, which emerged while capitalism was developing and were formed as the response of the working class to this development, have entered

a period of crisis and can no longer successfully control the masses. (Gramsci, 1977, p. 175 in Holst, 2007, p. 21)

On the one hand, Holst (2007) rejects the strong version of globalization consistent with a civil societarian perspective and maintains that effective opposition to hegemonic globalization involves formal politics. On the other hand, he does not dismiss the importance of the new movements and organizations that are emerging in civil society, and the so-called globalization from below that they instigate. His critique reinstates a Gramscian appreciation for the dialectical relationship between civil society, the political, and the economic. Like Gramsci, he recognizes the ability to build new alliances in the struggle for societal transformation and the ability of such alliances to forge multiple sites of resistance. As he states: "While the civil societarian perspective has rightly identified qualitative changes at the level of the economic and the social, it has done so at the expense of the political" (Holst, 2007, p. 26), and the Marxist responses to the long version of globalization have largely neglected to consider the qualitative changes that globalization has brought to political and social institutions.

Outside the field of adult education, such scholars as James Petras and Henry Veltmeyer (2001) and Walden Bello (2002), who adopt an analysis of globalization as imperialism, argue that it is a project that continues to advance capitalism within a broader framework of imperialism, with the United States positioned as the new hegemonic imperial power. For that matter, there have been streams of Marxism—notably, the most radical stream supported by Rosa Luxemburg in the early twentieth century (see Scott, 2008)—that tie imperialism to capitalism, and both to a version of globalization. Today, scholars who take up elements of these analyses additionally argue that globalization reinforces socio-economic divisions between and within states, maintaining and even exacerbating, rather than ameliorating, inequalities and oppression (Barndt, 1999, 2002; Dhruvarajan, 2003; Hawthorne, 2004; Shiva, 2005). As they have in other historical periods, gender and race continue to act alongside class in constructing social divisions, and geographic location continues to reinforce the power of the already powerful. ✵

With no overall governance to demand and structure accountability, international bodies promoting free markets "are assumed to be objective and value-neutral, operating without human agency" (Dhruvarajan, 2003, p. 183). According to Graham Harrison, "Orthodox globalisation theorists portray globalisation as an economic process, relying on the standard liberal separation of the state and the economy to present globalisation as immanent, or embedded in an economic logic which states can only react to" (2002, p. 24). Other

> ☼ Globalization is a force that rides on the back of earlier waves of global exploitation, including European colonization spanning the previous 500 years. A new kind of globalization began to emerge in the years following World War II. The General Agreement on Tariffs and Trade (GATT), the International Monetary Fund (IMF), and the World Bank were created. As the process of decolonization moved across nations, capital became institutionalized in all but the remaining socialist and communist countries (Mies & Shiva, 1993, p. 298). Through colonization and decolonization, countries which had been previously oriented towards self-sustainability became, instead, export-oriented. —Susan Hawthorne (2004), "Wild Politics: Beyond Globalization," p. 244

scholars explore the changing meaning of the nation-state from another perspective, focusing on globalization as a producer of subjectivities that develop with transnational migration and ethnic, cultural, and racial hybridities (Bergeron, 2001; Bhachu, 2004; Grewal, 2005; Ong, 2004).

As scholars explore the movement of people, culture, goods, and capital across state borders, globalization proponents such as Giddens (1998, 1999a, 1999b) argue that the result of these processes is the declining authority of the nation-state. People who question that conclusion and the general "discourse of inevitability" (Giddens, 1999a, p. 182) are portrayed as "lacking in common sense. Such people are often called globophobes, Luddites, and protectionists" (p. 182). In response to these arguments, critical scholars point out that the state retains central authority over areas such as protection of property and deliberation over new multinational agreements; moreover, international bodies remain constellations of state-level representatives, without the accountability to citizens of any state (Bello, 2002; Harrison, 2002; Panitch, 2004).

Even feminist postcolonial scholars such as Inderpal Grewal (2005), who explore the transnational identities that are constructed as people and cultures move across state borders, acknowledge that the role of today's nation-states might be changing and complicated, but it persists. ☼ If identities are increasingly hybridized, they also remain tied to nationality, including its expression through the status of citizenship. Moreover, the transnational migration of people, often for the purposes

> ☼ In a transnational age, with millions of displaced and migrant subjects, questions of identity and citizenship became both crucial and vexed, since these subjects questioned the legitimacy of the nation-state while also reinforcing its ability to endow rights. —Inderpal Grewal (2005), Transnational America, p. 11

of paid work, has financial repercussions beyond individual workers and their families, as remittances from abroad offer an important source of capital to buoy national economies in developing countries (Parreñas, 2001). Sylvia Walby takes a somewhat different tack in disputing the demise of the nation-state during globalization, arguing that the very concept of nation-states is a historical fiction. Nation-states "may be widespread as imagined communities, or as aspirations, but their existence as social and political practice is much over-stated" (2003, pp. 529–530). Histories of colonization, warfare, and other reasons for human migration have resulted in states with multiple nations and nations that cross state borders.

This discussion confirms that globalization, like citizenship and consumption, is highly contested. It can be seen as a project, a process, a period, an outcome, or even a myth. It can be seen as directed purposefully by corporate and political powers, or constructed unpredictably through civil society activists and so-called ordinary citizens. Many scholars combine interpretations, acknowledging the multiple levels on which globalization is conducted and experienced. Scholars who pursue globalization as imperialism talk about the role of capitalism in globalization, and scholars who focus on globalization as producer of subjectivities might talk about capitalism and imperialism. Analyses of globalization do not always fit neatly under one label—it is a complicated, complex concept with analytical threads from multiple perspectives.

Given this multitude of perspectives and analyses, how do I conceptualize globalization in this inquiry? I outline four points central to my conception. First, like other critical scholars, I reject both the notions that globalization is undirected or apolitical and the idea shared by orthodox Marxists and globalization proponents that globalization is unfolding with no meaningful interjection by citizens. ✿ Invisibility doesn't reduce certain groups to victims; rather, these people "are also agents, courageously carving out their families' survival; while forced to work within a system that benefits but also exploits them, they constantly find ways, both individual and collective, to resist it" (Barndt, 2002, p. 57). Previous iterations of imperialism, such as colonization,

> ✿ From this alternative perspective, "globalization" is neither inevitable nor necessary. Like the projects of capitalist development that preceded it—modernization, industrialization, colonialism and development—the new imperialism is fraught with contradictions that generate forces of opposition and resistance and can, and under certain circumstances will, undermine the capital accumulation process as well as the system on which it depends.   —James Petras and Henry Veltmeyer (2001), *Globalisation Unmasked*, p. 12

constructed and depended on social divisions, such as gender, race, and class. Mies (1986) argues that the structures of patriarchy and capitalism actually are so intertwined that they are inseparable. Scholars from a range of disciplines establish that politics of gender and race, as well as class, continue to operate during and guide the development of contemporary globalization, within and across state borders. As even Giddens (1999a) recognizes, globalization is distinctly Western in its embrace of capitalist structures and neoliberal democratic ideology, which build on rather than overcome histories of imperialism.

Second, globalization, as both a project and an outcome, is replete with paradoxes, or, in Gramscian language, dialectical tensions. Among these paradoxes is that the ideological rhetoric of democratization—particularly in its neoliberal form—serves to extend the hegemony of globalization, even as it invites new opportunities for dissent. ☼ Accompanied by capitalist strategies such as the free market and privatization, this ideology produces a common sense which reinterprets democratic choice as consumer choice and gains broad—albeit far from unanimous—consent among citizens across states.

> ☼ As we crack open the globalization mystique, we begin to realize that globalization from above and globalization from below are, in fact, completely intertwined, like the tangled roots, each feeding and defining each other.   —Deborah Barndt (2002), *Tangled Routes*, p. 56

Third, I understand globalization as a worldwide phenomenon that is experienced with local variations. As Brendan Evans (2002) clarifies, globalized forces affect all nation-states, but nation-states continue to enact policies; moreover, globalization is reiterating, rather than eliminating, power differentials between nation-states. ☼ Set against a discourse of cosmopolitanism, local particularities are not dissolving into a singular culture, despite increases in privatization and transnational corporations that constrain citizens' and consumers' choices.

Cindi Katz (2001) focuses on the role of locality to illustrate how globalization affects people and places worldwide but yields effects that are evident in material experiences and practices that remain highly

> ☼ The more nuanced interpretation recognises the capacity of the state to act as an agent, and to adopt effective policies of its own choosing, despite the impact of structural forces from an internationalized economy. Nor should all states be seen as having an identical relationship with the world economy, as individual states are differently inserted into the global system depending upon their reliance upon exports.   —Brendan Evans (2002), "Globalisation," p. 157

> ☼ It is more interesting to me to examine the intersecting effects and material consequences of so-called globalization in a particular place, not to vaporize either experience of the local, but, quite the opposite, to reveal a local that is constitutively global but whose engagements with various global imperatives are the material forms and practices of *situated knowledge*. Examining these effects and practices as such is a means to develop a politics that works the ground of and between multiply situated social actors in a range of geographical locations who are at once bound and rent by the diverse forces of globalization.   —Cindy Katz (2001), "On the Grounds of Globalization," p. 1214 (emphasis in original)

localized. ☼ Reversing geographer David Harvey's notion of "time-space compression" (1989 cited in Katz, 2001), Katz speaks of "time-space expansion" that is evident in the increasing size and scope of the physical world encountered by people living in previously remote areas. For people who are prospering and succeeding, new opportunities for travel, communication, investment, production, and consumption might seem to make the world smaller; however, for many others, globalization is escalating the physical distance between their work and their home communities, and the social distance between them and globalization's "winners" (Hawthorne, 2004). In short, globalization maintains patterns of material inequality created by earlier phases of colonization, which were structured by capitalism, patriarchy, and racism. The point, as Skeggs says, "is not who moves or is fixed, but who has control—not only over their mobility and connectivity, but also over their capacity to withdraw and disconnect" (2004, p. 50).

Fourth, the importance of the local and the cultural complements, rather than displaces, the continued importance of the material in how individuals experience and respond to globalization. For Harrison, "against the arguments of orthodox globalisation, capital is not footloose; nor is it, against the liberal arguments of counter-globalisation, 'disembedded' (2002, p. 30). For all of the complex and unstable financial architecture created liberalisation in the early 1980s, capital relies on workers to produce surplus" (p. 30). Globalization is surely accompanied, and even made possible by, a production, trade, and currency deregulation, as well as a host of technological developments. These developments enable the instantaneous transfer of funds and the speedy transit of people and goods; however, they have not eliminated the material reality of human existence and social relations (Huws, 2004). ☼

Rather than eliminating materialist concerns, the technologies and regulations that ease the global movement of capital actually exacerbate the material divisions and problems associated with capitalism. These four points—(1) that globalization is a political, social, and economic project

> ☼ A few statistics on the consumption of . . . raw materials underline the point: in the UK, iron consumption has increased twenty-fold since 1990; the global production of aluminium has risen from 1.5 million tonnes in 1950 to 20 million tonnes today. In the decade 1984–1995 (during a period in which we should have seen the "weightless" effect becoming visible, if the theorists are to be believed) aluminium consumption rose from 497,000 tonnes to 636,000; steel consumption increased from 14,330,000 to 15,090,000 and wood and paper consumption more than doubled, from 41 million to 93 million tonnes.   —Ursula Huws (2004), "Material World," p. 226

that reiterates imperialist objectives and tactics; (2) that, like all hegemonies, it is supported by a set of ideologies (for example, consumerism and neoliberalism) and associated common sense (for example, a "free" market creates democratic choice) that help secure popular consent; (3) that it is a worldwide phenomenon with local, national, and regional variations; and (4) that it involves both materiality and culture—are central to my conceptualization of globalization. Positioning this discussion in the field of adult education, I return to the writing of Holst, and his conclusion that the potential for critical adult education exists in the realization that

> there is no solution to the day-to-day survival issues of a growing sector of humanity within the capitalist relation or working for a wage to buy what you need. This basic relation is breaking down and there is no resolution outside of cooperative socio-political economic relationships: the "big utopia" of socialism. . . . The dialectic of the objective and the subjective realization of big utopias resides quite mundanely in the day-to-day needs of the growing sector of the world's population increasingly on the margins of capitalism. Here is where a new radical adult education needs to and must reside. (2007, p. 26)

From Shopping and Consumption to Learning and Resistance

Having reviewed the conceptual pieces of this inquiry—the politics of culture, incidental and holistic adult learning, consumer-citizenship as a social and cultural phenomenon, and globalization—I can now return to the central question of this inquiry: How can shopping be seen as a site and process of learning about the politics of consumption, citizenship, and globalization? Following Gramsci's (1971) understanding of societal transformation as an inherently ideological and educational process, I attach the concept of consumer-citizenship and the site and process of shopping to my conceptualization of holistic, incidental learning. Sociologists of education establish ties between formal education and consumption. While Kenway and Bullen (2001) and Martens (2005), whose work I have already reviewed, concentrate on children, youth, schooling, media, and consumption, Spring (2003) discusses learning and consumption more broadly, dealing with both formal and informal learning as well as both children or youth and adults.

Until the final stage of writing, the working title of this text used the phrase "radical shopper" in an effort to be consistent with the language that I had decided to use around learning. Because I was going to investigate shopping-as-learning, radical shopping and radical learning suggested a similar interest in social analysis and transformation. I was interested in the extent to which radical shoppers shared discourses, purposes, and practices coordinated by shopping-related social movements. Like all social movements, critical shopping can then be seen as an example of Fraser's (1992) counterpublics, in which people are able to develop critical analyses and learn how to think about and enact resistance or dissidence (Sparks, 1997). As this inquiry proceeded, I faced questions from my committee members as well as from prospective and actual participants about the meaning of the word "radical" in the context of this inquiry. I explore these questions in greater detail in Chapter 7, but until then when I use the word "radical" I do so with the adult education writing of Foley (1999, 2001), Coben (1998), and Holst (2007) in mind. In the context of this inquiry, radical shopping infers a process of critical, incidental, holistic learning about the links between shopping, consumption, citizenship, identity, and globalization and using that knowledge in the name of transformation. It extends the concept of consumer-citizenship in the particular direction of social analysis, critique, and action.

As I have already illustrated, many theorists have separated production from consumption and producers from consumers; however, workers who worry about their livelihoods are also consumers who worry about financial limitations, personal health, and ecological threats (Aaronson, 2001). ☼ Attempting to narrow the gap between producer and consumer and between the Global North and the Global South, activist-educators who are troubled by the hegemonic version of globalization press for an alternative way forward, an "alter-globalization." Some of these activist-educators use the realm of shopping as a pivotal part of their radical strategies.

For marginalized citizens, consumer-based resistance to globalization is often manifest through collective action and projects. Because shopping is so frequently tied to women and poor women are especially marginalized, women play a central role as organizers of and participants in

☼ Although many Americans have a particular mind-set about trade, their multiple roles in society may make it difficult for them to be ideologically consistent. As an example, most Americans are simultaneously consumers and producers. From a consumer's perspective, freer trade can be good because it can yield a greater supply of good at lower prices. However, freer trade also may endanger consumer welfare. For example, the United States bans the use of certain pesticides at home but allows U.S. manufacturers to sell some of these pesticides abroad. These banned pesticides may eventually show up in imported food, creating a "circle of poison.". . . Finally, from a worker's perspective, trade may stimulate job creation. But foreign competition may reduce the market share of U.S. companies, and these companies may be forced to trim their staff or worker benefits to increase competitiveness.   —Susan Aaronson (2001), *Taking Trade to the Streets*, pp. 9–10

many of these projects. Locally, community kitchens and bulk buying or distribution projects help poor women get affordable, nutritious food for themselves and their families. These projects also bring these women together to learn not just about cooking and nutrition but also about how an apparently abstract phenomenon such as globalization is actually present in their lives (Moffatt & Morgan, 1999; Villagomez, 1999).

From Mexico, Maria Villagomez (1999) describes a community kitchen project in an urban community, as well as projects for women in rural communities that included savings clubs and credit and sewing cooperatives. From their participation in a local community kitchen, participants were encouraged to start a social enterprise and join women's organizations concerned with social and global issues. These projects have reinforced women's traditional roles, even as they have provided women with some material stability and "transformed their positions within the community, their relationships with other community members as well as with community authorities. Through this experience, the women of Valencianita are beginning to take part in the public sphere and to claim a political space" (Villagomez, 1999, pp. 202–203). Fostering both societal transformation and social conformity, the projects reiterate the dialectical nature of resistance that Sparks (1997) explicates so clearly.

From Canada, Deborah Moffatt and Marie Lou Morgan describe two projects initiated by the Toronto-based antihunger organization FoodShare that "bring to life examples of how women use food as a catalyst for personal and political change" (1999, p. 221). The Good Food Box is "a community-based non-profit fresh-fruit-and-vegetable distribution system" (p. 226), and Focus on Food was a one-year training program that provided life-skills training "as well as opportunities to learn about food through gardening, food preparation, cooking and catering, and nutrition education" (p. 230) to a group of women on social assistance. According to Moffatt and Morgan, "Each food project demonstrates how women have, in one way or another, taken back some control over the food supply from large corporate players and in the process have redefined who has access to healthy food and how it is accessed" (p. 222). Focus on Food utilized an especially strong popular education approach, building on participants' experiences and knowledge as immigrants, women, and people living in poverty. Like the Mexican projects discussed by Maria Dolores Villagomez (1999), these two projects illustrate how, through collective action and incidental, holistic learning, consumer-citizens can issue a radical challenge to assumptions about and practices of everyday shopping, consumption, and citizenship during contemporary globalization.

Among members of the middle or upper classes in the Global North, resistance to the hegemonic version of globalization seems more unorganized and solitary. Their resistance might also be based in shopping and consumption practices, and it might be heartfelt, but it does not seem to engage them in the tightly knit collectivities described above. ☆ A reflection of the neoliberal, consumerist ideologies that envision an idealized middle-class consuming citizen, this tendency also reflects the realities that, in capitalist societies, wealthier people have greater individual freedom and choice—in shopping as elsewhere—than do poorer people. It is precisely this more solitary, unorganized learning and resistance that has gone largely unnoticed, or at least unstudied, by scholars in the adult education field and is at the centre of this inquiry.

Still, there are attempts to bridge the solitary and the collective aspects of shopping and consumption by building global movements focused on shoppers and their shopping. They promote ideological alternatives to unfettered consumerism and practical alternatives to harmful consumption. The organic movement combines concerns about consumers' and farmers' health and ecology, while the local consumption movement, popularized by the original 100-Mile Dieters here in Vancouver, combines concerns about the local economy, food security, and the environmental impact of transport. The voluntary simplicity movement rejects rampant consumerism and aims to reorient consumers' priorities so that "our most authentic and alive self is brought into direct and conscious contact with the living" (Elgin, 1993, p. 25). The fair trade movement attracts consumers who want "to bring their values and beliefs into alignment with the way they live. And part of this transition includes changes in people's purchasing habits, switching to fairly traded goods, organic foods, items made from recycled materials; alternative health products; and spiritual goods" (Grimes, 2005, p. 241). Concerns typically raised in the fair trade movement include exploitive labour,

---

☼ **Shopping & Country of Or[i]gin Effect: Does it matter where your money goes?**
Comment posted by Jules, *Tue, 2006/05/09*

When you go shopping, does it matter to you where the item you are buying was made? Do you deliberately go out of your way to buy Australian/American/Canadian/your own country of origin items, over items made by another country? Even if they are more expensive? . . .

The "Buy Australian Made" campaign has been running in Australia for YEARS—I cannot remember when it started since I can't remember NOT seeing the triangular green & gold kangaroo tag on products. And even though I know that buying Australian made items means more money staying in Australia and more jobs for Australians, I don't find it enough of a reason to change my purchasing habits. . . .

So if the sweater or jeans that I like says Made in China, I'll buy them. . . . And I'll buy Kraft Peanut Butter (made in Australia, owned by an American company) because I like it better than the brand that is both Australian-owned and Australian-made.

But then I realised that there is a line that I draw with buying Australian made, and that is with fresh produce and meat, when I will always buy locally grown. Even if it is ridiculously expensive. . . .

So how far does your patriotism extend when shopping?

Patriotism isn't the only reason . . .
Comment by Pam *posted Wed, 2006/05/10*

I'm a million miles from a You-Ess-Ay screaming flag waver but I do think carefully about where my goods are made.

It's not about patriotism, however. It's about workers [*sic*] rights. USA made goods used to primarily come from union shops where the workers were treated fairly. With the unions weakened and nearly all of our manufacturing jobs moving overseas, it's nigh impossible to get US made underwear anymore—for example. So now, I look for union shops. Often, I just skip the shopping because I can't stand the moral conundrum and get my clothes second hand. (Okay I DO draw the line at second hand underwear and socks.)

I buy my produce from a CSA (Community Supported Agriculture) not because I think my strawberries should be American, but because the produce from close to home and from organic CSAs has a lower environmental impact than factory farm produce from somewhere across the planet. It's got nothing to do with my lettuce being American, it's to do with it being local.   —Postings on *BlogHer—Where the women bloggers are*, Retrieved June 14, 2006 from http://blogher.org/node/5200

---

environmental sustainability, social justice, and peace. Fair trade has had "rapid growth, even as the annual growth of world trade declines" (p. 242). Tracing the development of the fair trade movement from its beginnings in American Mennonite and Brethren shops in the 1940s to today's network of religious and secular associations, producers, and stores, Grimes links this movement to citizenship and consumption, explaining how it is "exemplary of participatory democracy":

> Fair trade creates a bridge between the peoples of the developing nations and those of the developed ones. For consumers in First World countries, fair trade gives people the opportunity to not only purchase products that support their values of a more socially just and equitable world trade order, but to also learn about the producers' lives, their struggles, and our mutual interdependence. (pp. 237–238)

Culture jamming (see, for example, Kenway & Bullen, 2001; Lasn, 1999; Sandlin, 2007) is another response that attempts to encourage consumer-citizens—both culture jammers and their audiences—to learn about and change their shopping and consumption. ☼ Moreover, it works by reclaiming space from corporate control for the benefit of public pedagogy and even enjoyment. By doing so, it challenges the infiltration of corporate-consumer ideology and a consumerist version of globalization, and demands a reconsideration of ideas such as the commons.

☼ Social activist groups often try to structure their organizations and activities to be models for, or to prefigure, the kind of ideal society they are striving to create. Culture jammers participate in the creation of culture and knowledge, enact politics, open transitional spaces, create community, and engage their whole selves—intellect, body, and emotions.   —Jennifer Sandlin (2007), "Popular Culture, Cultural Resistance, and Anticonsumption Activism," pp. 80–81

For some people, social justice extends beyond relations among human beings and incorporates animals of all sorts; part of the radical agenda of societal transformation for them is the promotion of vegetarianism and animal rights (see, for example, Connelly & Prothero, 2008). For others, adopting a vegetarian diet, like an organic diet, is a matter of personal health rather than societal transformation. This holds true for the burgeoning interest in environmentalism, manifest in the "100-Mile Diet." These can all be forms of resistance to some aspect of globalization; however, they do not necessarily challenge hegemonic gender, race, and class relations. Conceptually, they reiterate Sparks's (1997) caution that resistance to one social relational structure is likely to involve complicity in other structures. As scholars such as Roberta Sassatelli (2006), Deirdre Shaw (2007), and Connelly and Prothero (2008) point out, different consumers often do the same thing for different reasons or do different things for the same reason. This reality leaves consumption choices "fragmented and potentially conflicting" (Sassatelli, 2006, p. 224) and makes it difficult—if not impossible—to discern when consumers' decisions are politically motivated and exactly what politics are behind a shopping practice. However, this kind of confusion can also surface in the realm of formal politics. Citizens might vote a certain way because of long-standing affiliations with a political party; or they might cast so-called protest votes to ensure that the party in power is not returned to office; or, thinking that their first-choice candidate cannot win, they might cast defensive votes for their second choice in order to avoid what is for them an even worse outcome. Formal politics are, it seems, no less confusing and complicated than consumer politics, even if citizenship and consumption retain important distinctions.

In many Western societies, the historical and social connection between consumption and citizenship has been surpassed, and these two concepts are increasingly conflated. Various perspectives on and practices of conscientious consumption are seen "as a form of political activity . . . or as a new form of political participation" (Connelly & Prothero, 2008, p. 130). Additionally, a great deal of consumption in the Global North now takes place through processes of shopping, so that shopping provides an entrée into an exploration of understandings and experiences of consumption, citizenship, and globalization. According to Sassatelli, "People are increasingly and explicitly asked to think that to shop is to vote and that ethical daily purchases, product boycotts and consumer voice may be the only way that men and women around the world have to intervene in the workings of global markets" (2006, pp. 219–220).

In this inquiry, I combine a critical perspective on consumption and consumerism with a notion of holistic incidental learning (Dirkx, 2001; English, 2000; Foley, 1999, 2001; hooks 2003; Tisdell, 1998, 2000). At the same time, I reject a simplistic conflation between citizenship and consumption, or democracy and capitalism. Sassatelli issues the important reminder that, contrary to a discourse of the free choice provided to shoppers through capitalist globalization,

> the social sciences have shown that the *de gustibus non disputandum est* which seems to make of consumption a space where subjects can and must freely express themselves is more a wish than a social reality. In reality, tastes are anything but indisputable. Judgments are made on the basis of taste, and people are preferred and rewarded because of their own tastes and those of others. (2006, p. 220)

I also contextualize shopping and learning, as well as citizenship and globalization, in terms of the setting in which this study has been based: the area in and around the City of Vancouver, British Columbia. As I have already noted, my participants and I have enjoyed many social privileges. During this study, we were, overall, members of Canada's middle class, and many of us described ourselves as white. My use of shopping to frame an exploration of learning about globalization underscores the continual influence of gender, race, and class on this study.

Shopping is generally a topic of interest and concern to "middle Canadians"—those who self-identify as middle class and in the racial mainstream. The understandings and experiences of shopping discussed in this study reflect and are limited by the social locations of participants and me. It is the potential to tie them to the understandings and experiences of people in other social and geographic locations that makes them useful and important. All the participants in this inquiry described their engagement in politicized shopping practices, whether or not they also considered themselves and their practices to be radical. Trying not to presuppose anybody's understandings, motivations, or purposes, I welcomed individuals into my study as long as they identified with the terminology that I used in my call for participants. Ironically, although they had responded to my call for "radical shoppers," in their conversations with me most participants quickly rejected the word "radical" as a descriptor of them or their shopping practices.

As this inquiry has progressed, I have been encouraged to question the meaning of the word "radical" and the potential for radicalism in the arena of shopping and, for that matter, elsewhere in contemporary social life. Recognizing the limitations of shopping as a strategy of resistance, I nonetheless have attempted to move beyond cynicism about shopping and consumption. ✿ When all is said and done, this a study of learning. I view shopping as a first step, rather than an endpoint, in critical learning about globalization and citizenship, and how gender, race and class are implicated in these concepts and practices. Shoppers

---

✿ The counterculture has always protested against excessive consumerism, bemoaning the effects of excessive waste and greed on the environment. Riding on this discussion is the final, concluding and contentious observation: that the counterculture has now become consumer culture. Any alternative lifestyle or anti-consumerist ethic has become co-opted, been branded, marketed and sold back to us. This is the thesis of Heath and Potter (2005), and perhaps will leave a slightly nasty taste in the mouth in the last few pages. Although not a novel thesis, it is worth considering here since it revisits the contested "terrain of culture" that Gramsci (1971) and Hall (1989) describe. Thus the idea of the counterculture itself becomes oxymoronic, for no real countering is being achieved, only more consumption.   —Mark Paterson (2006), *Consumption and Everyday Life*, p. 225

cannot buy their way out of the margins, nor can they use shopping and consumption to fully realize all of the rights and status accorded in discourses of citizenship. What remains of interest to me in this inquiry is, first, how shopping can function as a site and process of informal learning, especially critical, holistic learning, and, second, how it can spur action for Canadian consumer-citizens concerned about contemporary globalization and its connections to ongoing social divisions and newer threats.

Interlude III

Shopping for a Dissertation

In talking to others about a doctoral program in my department, I heard the process outlined like this: First you take some courses; then you write the comprehensive examination; then you produce your research proposal and apply for ethics approval; then you conduct your research, analyze your data, and summarize it all in your dissertation. The dissertation is the purchase, both the product and the leverage, of the program.

I have come to understand the process a bit differently. Laurel Richardson (2000) outlines that writing is not just a way to share knowledge already developed; rather, it is also a process of inquiry and knowledge construction. The production of this text has been an extension of my research methods and learnings, not just a process of talking about them. All along the way, shopping and consumption, learning and globalization inserted themselves into the process, as I bought everything from a computer and printer to paper to dozens of books on consumption and anti-consumerism. (The irony that, in three years I spent more of my disposable income on anti-consumerist books than anything else has not escaped me!)

As I approached the analysis of my interview, shopping trip and focus group data, I was advised to use qualitative data analysis software. I considered two commercial packages, and attended educational sessions for those products. Thinking about my data and the context of my study, I got curious and conducted an online search for "open source qualitative analysis software." Open source software is, after all, an attempt by programmers to resist the corporatization of technology, which is so important to the globalization project, and to democratize its use and development. I found a program called Weft QDA and, after reading some reviews of it written by other researchers, decided that it was the best choice for me. It was affordable (that is, free of charge!), straightforward to learn, and helpful in highlighting and organizing patterns in my data. However, unlike the commercial products, it was unknown in my department, and I was on my own to figure it all out. Also, it soon became apparent that Weft QDA is more limited than the commercial programs; then again, I didn't think that I needed their bells and whistles. It's true that Weft QDA couldn't produce diagrams, but I found another open source package to generate a conceptual mind map. More than anything, using Weft QDA became a reminder of the constancy of consumption and learning, and the reality that even the most radical research is embedded in whatever project it tries to resist.

3

SNAPPING THE PICTURE: ENVISIONING THE RESEARCH PROJECT

Having laid out the analytical concepts that I will use in this inquiry, I move now to a discussion of what Lincoln and Guba (2000) outline as the axioms of any research paradigm: ontology, epistemology, and methodology. I also discuss analytical considerations that surfaced. Largely guided by what they call a critical theoretical paradigm, this inquiry also shares some of the elements of what Lincoln and Guba (2000) consider a constructivist paradigm, as the following discussion clarifies. Once again, I use a metaphor to structure the discussion in this chapter. This time, it is the technology of photography. ☼

Although the camera is often considered a technology that captures reality, the camera's mirror refracts light and flips images, and the presence of a viewfinder and a variable shutter speed clarify that any pictures it takes represent choices made by the photographer, just as any inquiry

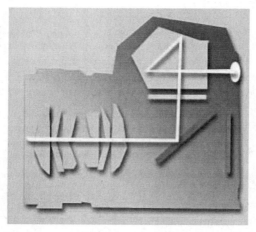

☼ Single-lens reflex camera. Retrieved and adapted February 18, 2008 from Wikimedia Commons, http://commons.wikimedia.org/wiki/Image:SLR_luz-visor.png.

111

represents choices or understandings of the researcher about the world, knowledge, and how to conduct research. This seems like an apt metaphor, a nod to my incorporation of visual and other unconventional forms of data into this proposal and my inquiry. As visual sociologists acknowledge, "the photographic image is 'true' in the sense (physical or electronic manipulation aside) that it holds a visual trace of a reality the camera was pointed at. But more fundamentally, all images, despite their relationship to the world, are socially and technically constructed" (Harper, 1998, p. 29).

Ontological Lens

My lens in this research is the *ontological stance,* or worldview, that I adopt. ☼ Whereas a wide-angle lens might be akin to quantitative research, both of which attempt to "see" the world in terms of breadth, a telephoto lens is more like the qualitative research that I undertook. The telephoto lens and the qualitative study both attempt to see details in pictures or hear details in individuals' life stories. This qualitative study conceptualizes human life and meaning as experienced and constructed within the context of both persistent social structures (for example, capitalism, patriarchy, racism) and variations in time, place, and personal circumstances. The combination of persistence and variability makes possible my understanding of hegemony, ideology, and common, which are being constantly adjusted but always retain traces of power relations from different times and places. As Williams states, "It would be in many ways preferable if we could begin from a proposition which originally was equally central, equally authentic: namely the proposition that social being determines consciousness" (1980, p. 31).

In their discussion of ontological paradigms, Lincoln and Guba (2000) discuss the emphasis on social structures as an element of the critical theory paradigm, while an emphasis on individuals' meaning-making is

---

☼ **ontology** . . . Any way of understanding the world, or some part of it, must make assumptions (which may be implicit or explicit) about what kinds of things do or can exist in that domain, and what might be their conditions of existence, relations of dependency, and so on. Such an inventory of kinds of being and their relations is an ontology. In this sense, each special science, including sociology, may be said to have its own ontology (for example, persons, institutions, relations, norms, practices, structures, roles, or whatever, depending on the particular sociological theory under consideration).   —John Scott and Gordon Marshall (Eds.) (2005), *Oxford Dictionary of Sociology,* p. 463

seen as consistent with the constructivist paradigm. They also acknowledge that, although paradigms are useful in outlining central features and purposes, paradigmatic boundaries are often breached in contemporary scholarship. Within their framework, my ontological stance combines critical theory and constructivism, as well as emerging feminist and critical race paradigms. This often uneasy combination of some elements typically regarded as structural and other elements typically regarded as poststructural reiterates Gramsci's (1971) understanding of dialectic and applies this concept to questions of the social and the cultural, structure and agency, materiality and discourse. ☼

> ☼ Thus, the Gramscian notion of struggle within popular culture not only emphasizes the agency of individual readers/viewers[/shoppers], but equate cultural consumption with the making of history. Everyday activities . . . are associated with the political rather than the private realm, elevating their status within academic inquiry.   —Dawn Currie (1999), *Girl Talk: Adolescent Magazines and Their Readers*, p. 66

Epistemological Prism

The understandings that I have about knowledge and learning—my epistemological stance—are analogous to the prism of a camera, through which information passes. ☼ (next page) As the researcher, I act as a sort of intellectual prism, turning information selectively into knowledge. Depending on the shape and angles of my prism, which informs the theoretical, conceptual, and methodological choices that I make (Harding, 1987b; Letherby, 2003; Morrow & Brown, 1994; Naples, 2003), information assumes meaning and usefulness. In returning to Gramsci, I concur with Killian Kehoe (2003) who notes that Gramsci's epistemology resonates with later poststructural and postmodern scholarship that disrupts traditional Western conceptions of knowledge. Gramsci's writing also resonates with Bent Flyvbjerg (2001) on the Aristotelian concepts of phronesis, or context-specific, experientially based knowledge—episteme, or universal knowledge developed through "analytic rationality," and techne, the "technical knowledge and skills . . . [derived from] pragmatic instrumental rationality" (p. 56).

Taking up Dreyfus's five-stage learning model, Flyvbjerg outlines how learners progress from novice to expert but reach the deepest levels of knowledge, evident in intuitive problem solving, only through phronesis. In adopting the sciences' insistence that epistemic knowledge is purest form, social scientists have largely abandoned the search for phronetic

☼ **epistemology** The philosophical theory of knowledge—of how we know what we know. Epistemology is generally characterized by a division between two competing schools of thought: rationalism and empiricism. Both traditions of thought received their most systematic philosophical expressions in the context of the scientific revolution of the 17th century. Both approaches were concerned with finding secure foundations for knowledge, and clearly distinguishing such well-grounded knowledge from mere prejudice, belief, or opinion. The model of certainty which impressed the rationalists (Descartes, Leibniz, and Spinoza) was that found in the formal demonstrations of logic and mathematics. They sought to reconstruct critically the total of human knowledge by the employment of such "pure" reasoning from indubitable axioms or foundations (hence Descartes' "I think therefore I am"). The empiricists (Locke, Berkeley, and Hume) took direct acquaintance with the "impressions" of sense-experience as their bedrock of infallible knowledge. Disputes between rationalists and empiricists centred especially on the possibility of innate knowledge acquired a priori, or independently of experience.

The 18th–century German philosopher Immanuel Kant is widely held to have achieved a transcendence of this conflict of ideas, insisting that a framework of basic organizing concepts (space, time, causality, and others) could not be acquired by experience alone, yet was necessary for us to be able to interpret the world of experience at all. These concepts were therefore prior to experience, but nevertheless (a nod in the direction of the empiricists) they could only be used to make objective judgements within the bound of possible experience. . . .
—John Scott and Gordon Marshall (Eds.) (2005), *Oxford Dictionary of Sociology*, pp. 193–194

knowledge. Such an approach to building knowledge is mistaken "in the study of human affairs, [where] there exists only context-dependent knowledge, which thus presently rules out the possibility of epistemic theoretical construction" (2001, p. 71).

What are the implications of Flyvbjerg's (2001) and Gramsci's (1971) methodological arguments for my inquiry? In investigating shopping-as-learning, I incorporate feminist, critical race, and critical cultural studies scholarship, and the assumptions associated with those bodies of scholarship must be incorporated into my methodological framework. Two important perspectives, which are often presented as incompatible rather than in tension with each other, are feminist materialism, often represented by feminist standpoint theory, and poststructuralism or postmodernism. In its later iterations, which I tend to draw on here, feminist standpoint theory contends that knowledge is subjective and multiple and that marginalized groups—such as women in a patriarchal society—yield especially deep knowledge. In her Marxist version of standpoint theory, Nancy Hartsock extends her analysis to class position, which, she explains, "not only structures but sets limits on the understanding of social relations . . . [so that] in systems of domination the vision available to the rulers will be both partial and perverse" (1987, p. 159). Feminist standpoint theorists, like other feminist materialists, challenge "authorized" knowledge (Letherby, 2003), by legitimating women's knowledge and validating experiential, disparate knowledges. ✵

> ✵ Once we undertake to use women's experience as a resource to generate scientific problems, hypotheses, and evidence, to design research for women, and to place the researcher in the same critical plane as the research subject, traditional epistemological assumptions can no longer be made.   —Sandra Harding (1987a), "Conclusion: Epistemological Questions," p. 181

Given the period when he lived and his affiliation with Marxist politics, Gramsci's writing predates poststructural and feminist writing about the social construction and mutability of identity and knowledge. Still, in his writing about the role of civil society, intellectuals, ideology, and common sense in producing hegemony, Gramsci (1971) moves away from the notion of power as residing in government, toward the notion of power relations, "so that power is diffused throughout civil society as well as being embodied in the coercive apparatuses of the state" (Simon, 1991, p. 28). His ideas can be seen as approaching later poststructural or postmodern theories of power relations. Moreover, Gramsci's initial education in linguistics and his break with the structuralist theories of language popular at the time indicate a seemingly poststructural sensibility (Ives, 2004). ✵

> ✵ The idea of "objective" in metaphysical materialism would appear to mean an objectivity that exists even apart from man [sic]; but when one affirms that a reality would exist even if man did not, one is either speaking metaphorically or one is falling into a form of mysticism.   —Antonio Gramsci (1971), *Selections from the Prison Notebooks*, p. 446
>
> Foreshadowing poststructuralism and other critiques of structuralism, Gramsci argues that history and the historical residues within language are fundamental in operations of power, prestige and hegemony. Gramsci emphasizes that meaning is created by language in its metaphorical development with respect to previous meanings. New meanings replace previous ones in a continual process of development.   —Peter Ives (2004), *Language and Hegemony in Gramsci*, p. 88

In contrast, many scholars poststructural or postmodern eschew an attachment to Gramsci and other theorists regarded as materialists (Kenway, 2001). ✵ One of their main objections to critical theory,

> ☼ Since the mid-1980s we have witnessed the rise of postmodern theorizing in much educational and feminist scholarship. Such scholarship has long been fascinated with Michel Foucault in particular, and Gramsci is no longer a fashionable theorist. This theoretical move has seen an eroded interest in the economy and social class, and intensified concern with discourse, difference and subjectivity and with consumption rather than production. Throughout this period there has been much more interest in mini-narratives rather than metanarratives, multiple identities rather than political identities, positioning rather than repositioning, discourse rather than the politics of discourse, performance rather than poverty, inscription rather than political mobilization, and deconstruction rather than reconstruction.
> —Jane Kenway (2001), "Remembering and Regenerating Gramsci," p. 60

including feminist standpoint theory, is that the notion of collectivity, suggested by gender- or class-based groupings, is inconsistent with the local and personal contexts in which identity is constructed (Hekman, 1997). Pointing to intragroup differences, they ask who is capable of understanding and speaking for whom. They also look to textual, rather than material, sources of meaning and difference. In response to this critique, feminist standpoint theorists contend that theirs—like Gramsci's—is a political project (Harding, 1997; Hartsock, 1997; Smith, 1997). "Knowledge," in the context of their work, is constructed on the basis of experiences of socio-economic privilege or marginalization and is valued for its potential to create "accounts of society that can be used to work for more satisfactory social relations" (Hartsock, 1997, p. 370). Unpredictable intragroup differences are present but do not eliminate structurally created divisions that have operated in social life and influenced socially constructed knowledge. Particularly in later iterations of their ideas, feminist standpoint theorists respond to challenges by and insights of poststructuralists and postmodernists, even as they insist that social groupings such as gender, race, and class remain present in society and that focusing research on marginalized groups can help produce knowledge that is useful in building socially just understanding and change. ☼ (next page)

Some of the feminist poststructural or postmodern scholars hold to the possibility of incorporating a political purpose within their research, in spite of the trouble that they see with social collectivities. Within that process, political resistance is newly "defined as challenging the hegemonic discourse that writes a particular script for a certain category of subjects. Resistance is effected by employing other discursive formations to oppose that script, not by appealing to universal subjectivity or absolute principles" (Hekman, 1997, p. 357). For Richardson, "a postmodern position does allow us to know 'something' without claiming

> ☼ Notice that it is "women's experiences" in the plural which provide the new resources for research. This formulation stresses several ways in which the best feminist analyses differ from traditional ones. For one thing, once we realized that there is no universal man, but only culturally different men and women, then "man's" eternal companion—"woman"—also disappeared. That is, women come only in different classes, races, and cultures: there is no "woman" and no "woman's experience." Masculine and feminine are always categories within gender, since women's and men's experiences, desires, and interests differ according to class, race, and culture.   —Sandra Harding (1987b), "Introduction: Is There a Feminist Method?" p. 7

to know everything. Having a partial, local, historical knowledge is still knowing" (2000, p. 928). Knowledge and resistance are possible, but only in a tentative manner, restricted by a limited understanding of both problems and solutions. She even uses the image of crystallization—similar to the metaphor of epistemology as prism—in discussing how ways of knowing and knowledges that can be produced by research are multiple. As researchers make even slight changes in how they gather and interpret information, a range of learnings become possible—just as looking through a moving prism or crystal produces changing views. ☼

> ☼ Crystallization, without losing structure, deconstructs the traditional idea of "validity" (we feel how there is no single truth, we see how texts validate themselves), and crystallization provides us with a deepened, complex thoroughly partial, understanding of the topic. Paradoxically, we know more and doubt what we know. Ingeniously, we know there is always more to know.   —Laurel Richardson (2000), "Writing: A Method of Inquiry," p. 934

So, how do I bring together strands of thought that are often presented in opposition with or, at least, contrast with each other? How does Gramsci (1971) continue to contribute to my project, which is both intellectual and political? In response to the first question, I find poststructural and postmodern writing often philosophical and abstract, yielding few concrete suggestions for research that aims to facilitate societal change. For example, poststructural discourse analysis offers the possibility of social critique, but how (and, indeed, whether) this methodology proposes to change social relations remains unclear (see Naples, 2003, p. 68). Like Nancy Naples, a self-described feminist materialist who draws on the work of the feminist standpoint theorists, I aim to maintain a dialectical relationship between materialist concerns with structures of gender, race, and class and poststructuralism's insistence that language and culture, and the localized contexts in which they are used, are important in the construction of identity. I have already noted that Gramsci's writings predate feminist standpoint theory and poststructuralism or postmodernism. How he might have stretched his ideas in response to these perspectives is an unanswerable question. What is evident is that, from his initial motivation to understand why Marx's prediction of proletariat revolution failed to materialize beyond Russia, he developed his theory of the role of ideology, civil society, and consent in maintaining and challenging social relations and knowledge that remain useful (Hall, 1991; Morton, 1999; Sassoon, 2001), and an epistemological perspective that seems, at times, amazingly contemporary. Writing in isolation and ill health as a political prisoner in Mussolini's Italy, Gramsci was undeniably rooted in particular partisan politics and personal circumstances. Still, as cultural studies scholars recognized after they began reading Gramsci's work when it was made available in English in the early 1970s, Gramsci's ideas on knowledge, as well as on culture and social relations, have a usefulness beyond their roots. As Stuart Hall advises, "I do not claim that, in any simple way, Gramsci 'has the answers' or 'holds the key' to our present troubles. I do believe that we must 'think' our problems in a Gramscian way—which is different" (1991, p. 114). ☼

> ☼ Certainly the philosophy of praxis is realised through the concrete study of past history and through present activity to construct new history. But a theory of history and politics can be made, for even if the facts are always unique and changeable in the flux of movement of history, the concepts can be theorised. Otherwise one would not even be able to tell what movement is, or the dialectic, and one would fall back into a new form of nominalism.   —Antonio Gramsci (1971), *Selections from the Prison Notebooks*, p. 427

Taking Hall's (1991) suggestion, I return to Gramsci's (1971) work in determining my epistemological stance, in "thinking" the problems central to this inquiry. Here, I find the work in critical cultural studies, as well as the feminist and critical race scholarship already reviewed above, helpful. Knowledge, in this perspective, is understood as emerging and constructed (by both participants and me) in the telling, hearing, seeing, reading, and sharing of various conversations, texts, and found objects or images. There are elements of phenomenology and subjectivism in the epistemological assumptions of this inquiry, as I emphasize people's lived experiences and their understandings of and feelings about them (Denzin & Lincoln, 2000; Saukko, 2003). At the same time, I remain convinced that social divisions continue to influence how individuals experience and understand cultural phenomena. This is the epistemological position of scholars such as Currie, who combines questions of the social and the cultural in her work and develops a critical cultural studies perspective that "aims to make visible and put into crisis the structural links between the disciplining of knowledge and larger social arrangements" (1999, p. 93). Although this current inquiry does not focus on marginalized groups, it retains the critical assumption of feminist standpoint theorists that gender, race, and class have epistemological effects. According to this perspective, social categories and relations "are produced and enacted in historically [and geographically] specific situations" (Denzin & Lincoln, 2000, p. 21). Finally, my concentration on discourses and practices of shopping inserts an element of cultural studies into this inquiry. As I discuss in later chapters, the dialectic between these perspectives creates constrained possibilities for knowing and acting during contemporary globalization in Vancouver, Canada.

Releasing the Shutter: Research Methodology

The last step in taking a photograph with an SLR camera is releasing the shutter, so that the image already viewed by the photographer and manipulated by other parts of the camera can be captured on film; this is like *methodology*, the third axiom of the research paradigm and the final consideration in designing a research project (Lincoln & Guba, 2000). ☼ As Gramsci (1971) again conveys, any understanding of social relations requires inquiries based in particular settings, because social relations are enacted in the context of particular historical processes and local situations. Two conclusions extend from this point: Social sciences require different methodologies from the natural or physical sciences, and no single methodological approach is desirable or possible across the social sciences. ☼ (next page)

☼ **methodology** . . . The principal concern of methodology is wider philosophy of science issues in social science, and the study of how, in practice, sociologists and others go about their work, how they conduct investigations and assess evidence, how they decide what is true and false. The topics addressed include whether the social sciences are in fact sciences; whether the social scientist needs to understand a sequence of social actions to explain it fully; whether there are laws in the social sciences which can predict as well as explain; whether research can be, or should be, value-free; causation and causal powers; inductive and deductive theory; verification and falsification; and other problems in the philosophy of knowledge and science (most of which are treated under separate headings in this dictionary).   —John Scott and Gordon Marshall (2005), *Oxford Dictionary of Sociology*, pp. 406–407

> ☼ It has to be established that every research has its own specific method and constructs its own specific science, and that the method has developed and been elaborated together with the development and elaboration of this specific research and science and forms with them a single whole. To think that one can advance the progress of a work of scientific research by applying to it a standard method, chosen because it has given good results in another field of research to which it was naturally suited, is a strange delusion which has little to do with science. There do however exist certain general criteria which could be held to constitute the critical consciousness of every man [sic] of science whatever his "specialization", criteria which should always be spontaneously vigilant in his work. Thus one can say someone is not a scientist if he displays a lack of sureness of the concepts he is using, if he has scant information on an understanding of the previous state of the problems he is dealing with, if he is not very cautious in his assertions, if he does not proceed in a necessary but in an arbitrary and disconnected fashion, if he cannot take account of the gaps that exist in knowledge acquired but covers them over and contents himself with purely verbal solutions and connections instead of stating that one is dealing with provisional positions which may have to be gone over again and developed, etc.   —Antonio Gramsci (1971), *Selections from the Prison Notebooks*, pp. 438–439

Within social science disciplines, case study methodology is often proposed as one sound option for researchers. Beyond the agreement that case study places real life context in the foreground of the inquiry, however, "there are virtually no specific requirements guiding case research" (Meyer, 2001, p. 329). Raymond Morrow and David Brown (1994) include within their understanding of this methodology the approaches of historical analysis, ethnography, participant action research, and discourse analysis. Andrew Sturman (1999) provides a similar list of research "styles," including ethnographic, action research, evaluative, and educational case studies. Alternatively, other scholars discuss case study, ethnography, and action research as distinct methodologies (Meyer, 2001). Characteristics that are regarded as common to case study research include use of multiple information-gathering techniques; a concern with relationships between elements of the case; the case's usefulness in investigating new or little understood phenomena; and its basis in the concrete (Meyer, 2001; Sturman, 1999). Critical research also values self-reflection or reflexivity, and is "not only distinctive in its concern with reflexive methods but also dialectical in its use of empirical techniques" (Morrow & Brown, 1994, p. 245).

Flyvbjerg's (2001) emphasis on phronetic, experiential learning leads to his endorsement of case study methodology (including ethnography) in the social sciences. He identifies and rebuts five "misunderstandings" about case study methodology: that it produces less valuable knowledge than positivist research; that its lack of generalizability means that it "cannot contribute to scientific development" (p. 66); that it is most useful for developing preliminary theories about new or under-studied phenomena; that its subjective nature makes it easy for researchers to verify their own assumptions; and that it is difficult to develop concise summaries and general theories from case studies. As I have already asserted, the social sciences are distinguished from the natural or physical sciences by the importance of context and the impossibility of timeless, formulaic generalizations; therefore, the first two objections to case study methodology demonstrate the mistaken preference for positivist, generalizable research models rather than faults with case study methodology.

In addressing the third objection, Flyvbjerg draws on the argument of Karl Popper to illustrate the value of case studies: "Popper himself used the now famous example of 'all swans are white,' and proposed that just one observation of a single black swan would falsify this proposition and in this way have general significance and stimulate further investigations and theory-building" (p. 77). The fourth misunderstanding is disputed with the explanation that all methods impose researchers' biases and assumptions, evident in the selection of variables and the construction of categories. Finally, Flyvbjerg sees the "irreducible quality of good case narratives" (p. 84) as a reflection of the complexity of the case studied, rather than a fault of the methodology. Summarizing the clash between qualitative and quantitative research, Flyvbjerg says, "The advantage of large samples is breadth, while their problem is one of depth. For the case study, the situation is the reverse. Both approaches are necessary for a sound development of social science" (p. 87). Here again, Flyvbjerg's argument is consistent with Gramsci's (1971) derision of scholars of the social who overlook qualitative research.

If Flyvbjerg (2001) shares Gramsci's (1971) support for qualitative research, feminist standpoint theorists share Gramsci's politically driven research agenda. Among the standpoint theorists, Dorothy Smith develops her approach of "institutional ethnography" (1987, 1999), which provides a notably complete "methodological guidepost for investigation" (Naples, 2003, p. 198). Although I did not conduct an institutional ethnography in this study, I note Smith's (1987) proviso that, to be of value, any case has to contribute to a larger project.

Attempting to integrate materialist and poststructural perspectives in her methodological work, Naples offers additional points for researchers interested in societal transformation. Just as study participants embody social locations, so, too, do researchers (a point discussed further in the following section). These positions "influence what questions we ask, whom we approach in the field, how we make sense of our fieldwork experience, and how we analyze and report our findings" (2003, p. 197). Naples also notes that, as agents, participants can be engaged in interpreting their own experiences and, especially in participant action research, can be involved in collaborative analysis and report writing. Finally, Naples draws on Patricia Hill Collins's (1997) thoughts—which recall the thoughts of hooks (2003)—about the value of emotions (for both researchers and participants) and empathy in producing and interpreting data (see Naples, 2003, p. 61), as well as the recognition of a distinct standpoint for black women.

Responding to standpoint theory, especially the notion of racial standpoint developed by Collins (1997), Twine (2000) raises several cautions. In practice, standpoint theory can lead to the conclusion that racial "insiders"—researchers who are also members of the group being investigated—are best able to understand and to elicit information from their participants. "Racial matching" is problematic, because, as Twine notes, "race is not the only relevant 'social signifier'" (2000, p. 9). Insider status can mislead researchers into bringing their own experientially based preconceptions and expectations into their inquiries and analyses or, conversely, can create expectations among participants that researchers will "conform to cultural norms that can restrict them as researchers" (p. 12). Although participants who share an identification with a researcher might feel more comfortable sharing information, they might also withhold information that they assume is already known by the researcher. Finally, as feminist standpoint theorists now readily acknowledge, a "standpoint is a project, not an inheritance; it is achieved, not given" (Weeks, 1996 in Hartsock, 1997, p. 372).

What is problematic is the simplistic expectation that "whites, as members of the dominant racial group, . . . [are not] knowledgeable about race and racism. In contrast, racial subalterns are assumed to possess a sophisticated understanding of racism" (Twine, 2000, p. 21). Even critically minded marginalized participants who share a racial identification do not necessarily attach the same meaning to that identification. Social divisions such as race (and gender and class and so on) are constructed differently in different societies; hence, geography is reinstalled as one determinant of social location. These issues complicate the determination of who is capable of representing which racial or social group and of "one's authority to make certain knowledge claims" (p. 22).

In attempting to cope with this particular methodological issue, Naples refers to the work of Collins and Smith, who talk about the importance of dialogue "to decenter dominant discourse, and to continually displace and rework it to determine how power organizes social life and what forms of resistance are generated outside the matrix of domination or relations of ruling" (Naples 2003, p. 53). From the former, she takes the idea of including participants of "diverse social locations" (p. 53); from the latter she takes the idea of engaging in dialogue between researcher and participants, in effect inserting the researcher into the inquiry in a self- reflective or reflexive way. Both of these strategies complicate the notion of "insider/outsider" status, at the same time as they recognize the reality and impact of differences. I attempt to use both of these tactics, albeit with limited success, throughout my inquiry.

Attempting to bring together these and other central points of different perspectives, Naples views hers as a "materialist feminist standpoint theory that incorporates important insights of postmodern analyses of power, subjectivity, and language as a powerful framework for exploring the intersection of race, class, gender, sexuality, region, and culture in different geographic and historical contexts" (2003, p. 5). Also working from a feminist materialist perspective, Currie asks questions central to cultural studies. Her feminist/critical cultural studies approach stresses the importance of "a materialist analysis [that] discovers ideology and its working in the everyday activities of actual people. Within this context, systems of representation and processes of meaning-making are material expressions of ideology which make available as preferred meaning a 'frame of intelligibility,' or way of knowing" (1999, p. 142).

Other methodologists have extended attempts to combine perspectives and insights in different ways. Joe Kincheloe (2001, 2005) builds on the writing of Denzin and Lincoln (2000) and outlines a new methodological direction that attempts to bridge critical purpose with poststructural thoughts about ontology, epistemology, and methodology: bricolage. ✿ Although the design technicalities and ramifications of bricolage remain unclear—Kincheloe (2005) himself recognizes that bricolage is still being conceptualized—his call to multidisciplinarity opens new possibilities for researchers interested in societal transformation. Well before bricolage was put forward as a

---

✿ The qualitative researcher as *bricoleur* or maker of quilts uses the aesthetic and material tools of his or her craft, deploying whatever strategies, methods, or empirical materials are at hand (Becker, 1998, p. 2). If new tools or techniques have to be invented, or pieced together, then the researcher will do this. The choices as to which interpretive practices to employ are not necessarily set in advance. The 'choice of research practices depends up on the questions that are asked, and the questions depend on their context' (Nelson et al., 1992, p. 2), what is available in the context, and what the researcher can do in that setting.   —Norman K. Denzin and Yvonna S. Lincoln (2000), "Introduction: The Discipline and Practice of Qualitative Research," p. 4

methodological option in the social sciences, Gramsci seemed to embrace its spirit of multidisciplinarity, drawing on his studies and knowledge of linguistics, philosophy, politics, sociology, history, drama, and literature (Ives, 2004). Even Kincheloe refers to "the dialectical relationship between knowledge and reality" (2005, p. 326), using language that recalls Gramsci's (1971) thoughts. Perhaps this is an example of how Gramsci's incarceration and isolation contributed to, rather than detracted from his scholarship: Although the harsh conditions of imprisonment doubtlessly took their tool on Gramsci's health and state of mind (Crehan, 2002), he was able to commit a great amount of time to contemplate his diverse interests. His inclusion of knowledge from several disciplines in developing his social concepts and arguments seems to correspond with the understanding of the bricoleur developed by Denzin and Lincoln (2000) as someone who uses whatever tools are available to address a problem.

Kincheloe (2001, 2005) expands Denzin and Lincoln's (2000) notion of the bricoleur and bricolage methodology in his subsequent articles. ☼ The requirement of researcher multidisciplinarity is stretched to include comprehensive knowledge of individual disciplinary research traditions and assumptions, a kind of "Foucauldian genealogy where scholars would study the social construction of the discipline's knowledge bases, epistemologies, and knowledge production methodologies" (Kincheloe, 2001, p. 683). As he also notes, such a bricolage is so time consuming and intellectually demanding that some scholars have questioned the potential for researchers—especially student researchers—to put it to meaningful use. Here I think that Kincheloe moves away from the sense of bricolage articulated by Denzin and Lincoln (2000), and, indeed, the usefulness of this concept initially brought to the fore by anthropologist Claude Lévi-Strauss in his descriptions of how members of one cultural group adopt and adapt tools from another cultural group in novel and unanticipated ways in dealing with their environments (see Kincheloe, 2001, p. 680).

☼ On one level, the bricolage can be described as the process of getting down to the nuts and bolts of multidisciplinary research. Ethnography, textual analysis, semiotics, hermeneutics, psychoanalysis, phenomenology, historiography, discourse analysis combined with philosophical analysis, literary analysis, aesthetic criticism, and theatrical and dramatic ways of observing and making meaning constitute the methodological bricolage. In this way, bricoleurs move beyond the blinds of particular disciplines and peer through a conceptual window to a new world of research and knowledge production.   —Joe Kincheloe (2005), "On to the Next Level" p. 323

In contrast to Lévi-Strauss's initial focus on the cross-cultural uses of tools in producing context-specific, practical knowledge, Kincheloe (2005) focuses on intended uses of intellectual tools in producing academic knowledge. This shift seems to keep research and knowledge construction situated as a traditional, academic, elite pursuit. Ironically, given Kincheloe's declared interests in opening up qualitative research to contemporary insights, especially from post-structuralist scholarship, his focus on academic work also seems to treat research and knowledge-construction as a pursuit which retains the limitations of specific disciplinary assumptions and more general academic privilege. In the name of complexity, Kincheloe's bricolage issues some important rebuttals, including one to "monological forms of knowledge" (2005, p. 326), as he portrays bricoleurs as researchers who "envision forms of research that transcend reductionism" (p. 327). ☼

☼ To account for their cognizance of such complexity bricoleurs seek a rigor that alerts them to new ontological insights. In this ontological context, they can no longer accept the status of an object of inquiry as a thing-in-itself.   —Joe Kincheloe (2001), "Describing the Bricolage," pp. 681–682

I agree with Kincheloe when he draws on Denzin and Lincoln's image of "the bricoleur as intellectually informed, widely read, and cognizant of diverse paradigms of interpretation" (p. 327) and open to using a range of research strategies; however, his increasing reliance on complexity and chaos theories and his proposal that bricolage assume the quality of a Foucauldian genealogy seems to move his notion of bricolage away from what he maintains is a critical purpose for two reasons. First, as Peter McLaren (2001) notes, the ideas that occupy Kincheloe's attention detract from, rather than contribute to, an agenda of societal transformation. A complex phenomenon is not necessarily best explained by complexity or chaos theory and, while I will not delve into either of these theories here, I will say that, in my limited exposure to them, I do not find them helpful in directing research with a political, transformational purpose. Second, the expectation that the bricoleur build expertise in the history and rationale of a wide variety of disciplinary methodologies and retain a political purpose seems overwhelming, unless the purpose of the research is to discern methodological traditions. In his conceptualization of bricolage, partly in response to accusations of superficiality and lack of rigour, Kincheloe (2001, 2005) burdens bricoleurs with untenable demands of knowledge and perhaps above all, time and energy. Kincheloe asserts that an object of inquiry must be seen as more than a "thing-in-itself" (2001, p. 682), that it must also always include a reflexive approach to ontological and epistemological assumptions and methodological processes. I concur with these assertions; however, I think that it is important for me, as a researcher, to be clear in my own mind and my writing about my political stance and purpose. There seems to be a certain irony in Kincheloe's poststructuralist-inspired advice that researchers avoid set conceptualizations, even though it is poststructuralists who argue that there is no such thing as neutrality.

Still, I think that bricolage makes a useful contribution to methodology in the social sciences. As Kincheloe (2005) notes, it requires a high degree of researcher reflexivity and conscious connection between the ontologies, epistemologies, methodologies, and analytical concepts informing inquiries. Bricolage also offers a way of dealing with the multiple ways of knowing which have been explored in postcolonial, critical race, feminist, and poststructural or postmodern scholarship. In mixing not just methods but methodologies, it supports new ways to combine concepts, and formulate both questions and at least tentative or partial answers to important contemporary research problems. Finally, it is designed to accommodate the numerous tensions and paradoxes which accompany today's globalization and, in keeping with my use of Gramsci's (1971) concepts and ideas, it understands human existence and issues as complex and dialectical in nature. Intrigued by the potential of bricolage, and understanding shopping as a case of informal learning, I use what I call "case study bricolage" methodology in this inquiry.

In addition to the traditional case study methods of interviewing and focus groups, I incorporate a form of participant observation, as I went on shopping trips with some participants. In the spirit of cultural studies, a field of study often associated with shopping and consumption, I also include popular culture, exemplified here by fiction, in my analysis. Finally, I have included visual images and texts that I have come across in the course of my inquiry. From graffiti in public spaces to blog entries, these items contribute to the evidence that I have gathered and helped construct. Their substantive differences invite different methodological approaches, from literary/narrative analysis to content analysis, or from semiotic analysis to intertextual analysis. I discuss these approaches and techniques in further in Chapter 4, as well as in the individual chapters detailing my analyses. Some of this material, particularly images and texts that I found in physical and virtual space, is never formally analyzed; its inclusion extends the analyses that I do conduct and suggests the breadth of data available to researchers.

Aperture, Speed, and Focus: The Final Adjustments

As I planned and prepared to undertake my study, several epistemological and methodological questions arose. Sometimes, these related to matters that are likely common to qualitative research processes. At other times, they seemed more unusual and particular to this study. They were concerned with me as a researcher and in relation to participants, to participants themselves, and to the nature of the case under study and its unit of analysis.

What Is a Case, and Where Is the Evidence?

In this inquiry, I use what I call a case study bricolage methodology to investigate shopping as a case of critical, incidental, holistic learning. Shopping has not been explored often in this way and, as case study advocates claim, that methodology is especially well suited for studying new or rarely explored phenomena (Flyvbjerg, 2001; Meyer, 2001; Sturman, 1999). As Michael Patton further explains, "Cases are units of analysis" (2002, p. 447). Although it is possible to view every participant in this inquiry as a distinct case, I do not tend to approach my data gathering and analysis in this way. I do not, for example, systematically contrast one participant's comments with the comments of other participants; rather, I use participants' comments about shopping, as well as other data sources such as my observations during shopping trips and my reading of works of fiction, to establish the breadth of messages and learning strategies present in the arena of shopping.

In using shopping as a unit of analysis, this inquiry presents a case in an unconventional way. Unlike most case studies, this one is not tied to a particular setting, although it ultimately has been bound by geography, my own linguistic limitations, and time. In this way, it has engaged in its own methodological dialectic, as it has both adopted and challenged mainstream rhetoric of case study methodology. My study's use of shopping, rather than a single shop or shopping area, illustrates the potential to stretch the understanding of what it means to define the boundaries of a case. Methodologically, this inquiry reflects and responds to a hegemonic conceptualization of globalization, which claims that a new status of global citizen has emerged as borders of the nation-state have become largely irrelevant. As my analytical discussion concludes, though, boundaries and their meanings might change but they have not disappeared.

I have already suggested that, as a bricoleur, I draw on Richardson's (2000) notion of crystallization and make use of ideas, methods, and resources from various disciplines in social sciences and humanities.

Bricolage demands a degree of "emergent design flexibility" (Patton, 2002, pp. 41–42). Investigating a complex question—How shopping can be a site and process of critical learning about the links between consumption, citizenship, social relations, and learning during contemporary globalization?—I looked for evidence where it seemed most likely to be found, chiefly among shoppers, but I also incorporate evidence found along the way.

These research practices give rise to questions of validity. In contrast to traditional, positivist emphases on objectivity, universality, and reliability, I borrow from poststructural and cultural studies scholarship in moving from "validity" to "validities." Paula Saukko outlines three approaches to validity, which overlap somewhat. "Dialogic validity" (2003, p. 20) emphasizes a version of truthfulness achieved through researcher-participant collaboration, researcher self-reflexivity, and inclusion of a broad range of possible stakeholders or participants. "Deconstructive validity" (p. 20) emphasizes the "postmodern excess" (p. 20) of possible truths about a phenomenon under study, the socio-historical basis of taken-for-granted "common sense" (Gramsci, 1971) and "deconstructive critique" (Saukko, 2003, p. 21), which aims to question and break down binaries of social organization. "Contextual validity" (p. 21) emphasizes "sensitivity to social context" (p. 22) and "awareness of historicity" (p. 22). Several elements of each approach are present in this inquiry. My incorporation of self-reflexivity is consistent with dialogic validity. My use of critical scholarship, my own critical reading of fiction, and my conversations with participants (and later analysis of them) suggest an attempt to dismantle hegemonic binaries, which is consistent with deconstructive validity. My conceptualization of globalization, consumer-citizenship and learning as socio-historical constructions is consistent with deconstructive and contextual validities. Finally, my continual positioning of myself and this inquiry within the context of a contemporary Canadian West Coast urban setting indicates contextual validity of my data and analysis.

Primary data largely emerged from and were constructed within interviews, accompanied shopping trips, and focus groups with participants who came forward in response to my call for individuals who had begun to connect their own shopping and consumption with an uneasiness about how they see globalization playing out. During this inquiry, I also picked up data that I happened to find. As I outline in the next chapter, I also draw on sources as diverse as popular scholarship, fictional narratives, postings to websites, and graffiti or other images in conducting this inquiry; for me, these are all sources of evidence, because they articulate contemporary hegemonic or resistant ideologies and confirm or challenge "common sense." They do not necessarily confirm one another but, with the aims of crystallization and bricolage in mind, they provide squares of fabric for my quilt.

Where Am I in This Picture? Researcher Reflexivity

Associated with questions of epistemology and methodology is the question of how researchers locate themselves in their research. Do they view themselves as inquisitive observers outside populations being studied or as value-laden actors who cannot help but enter into their studies? Decades before this question, and the related question of insiderness/ outsiderness was generally incorporated into social science research, Gramsci (1971), too, wondered about these issues. Like the intellect that, according to him, is evident in everyone, subjectivity develops organically. Gramsci's insistence that relations between people, and between people and the world, are "active and conscious" (1971, p. 361) suggests why reflexivity is regarded as so important. ☼ We are, all of us, socially embedded, and our experience and knowledge of life is possible only within the context of historically based social relations.

Reflexivity begins with an awareness that researchers are always involved in the outcomes of their own research. Not only did I write this

---

☼ I mean that one must conceive of man [*sic*] as a series of active relationships (a process) in which individuality, though perhaps the most important, is not, however, the only element to be taken into account. The humanity which is reflected in each individuality is composed of various elements: 1. the individual; 2. other men; 3. the natural world. But the latter two elements are not as simple as they might appear. The individual does not enter into relations with other men by juxtaposition, but organically, in as much, that is, as he belongs to organic entities which range from the simplest to the most complex. Thus Man does not enter into relations with the natural world just by being himself part of the natural world, but actively, by means of work and technique. Further: these relations are not mechanical. They are active and conscious. They correspond to the greater or lesser degree of understanding that each man has of them. So one could say that each one of us changes himself, modifies himself to the extent that he changes and modifies the complex relations of which he is the hub. . . . If one's own individuality is the *ensemble* of these relations, to create one's personality means to acquire consciousness of them to modify one's own personality means to modify the *ensemble* of these relations. . . . It is not enough to know the ensemble of relations as they exist at any given time as a given system. They must be known genetically, in the movement of their formation. For each individual is the synthesis not only of existing relations, but of the history of these relations. He is a précis of the past. —Antonio Gramsci (1971), *Selections from the Prison Notebooks*, pp. 351, 353 (emphasis in original)

text, I also had a hand in constructing data through conversations with participants. Although I developed a series of questions and exercises to guide interviews and focus groups, I was active in these interactions. When participants searched for words to complete their thoughts, I offered what I thought were good possibilities. I often tried to summarize participants' comments as we moved through a conversation, so that I was confident that I could represent their views. Sometimes participants asked questions of me and, although I tried to postpone my answers until we were close to the end of a meeting, I thought that it would be disrespectful to decline to answer their questions altogether. At other times, I repeatedly tried to engage participants in a discussion of a particular topic. I recognized participants in this inquiry as individuals who have thought carefully about the issues raised. Their responses to my call for radical shoppers implied that they were not easily intimidated. I assumed that they would stand up to me if I misunderstood them; indeed, there were several times when various participants corrected my understanding of their comments or pursuit of a line of thought that was inconsistent with their points of view.

This approach to conversation, text, and writing resonates with post-structural or postmodern advice "that writing is always partial, local, and situational, and that our Self is always present, no matter how much we try to suppress it—but only partially present, for in our writing we repress parts of ourselves, too" (Richardson, 2000, p. 930). Researchers join participants as subjects of study as they attempt, in part, to understand themselves/their Selves. Michelle Fine suggests "that researchers probe how we are in relation with the contexts we study and with our informants, understanding that we are all multiple in those relations" (1998, p. 135). By "working the hyphens" (Fine, 1998) between insiders and outsiders or Self and Other, researchers discard the positioning of the researcher as a neutral observer. Fine presents three possible strategies for working the hyphens: inserting "uppity voices" (p. 146) which challenge researchers' privilege and social anonymity; "probing the consciousness of dominant others" (p. 146); and engaging in research for with activists societal change.

Although I did not set out in this inquiry to investigate a particular social group, I recognize the presence and importance of social groups in cultural processes and products, such as shopping and the consumables that shoppers buy. How I understand myself, how participants understand themselves, and how we understand ourselves in relation to one another, this project, and our social world is part of my analysis. The extent to which I insert information about me and my background, and personal reflections about my experiences and understandings throughout this text, represents attempts to remember and remind my reader of my own active involvement in the construction of this project and its findings. Reflexivity, including the careful consideration of Self-Other and the disruption of "scientific neutrality, universal truths, and researcher dispassion" (Fine, 1998, p. 131), is an increasingly shared goal of feminist and critical scholars working from varied perspectives. ☼

In response to these points, I paused throughout this inquiry to consider my own social location. Starting with my reflections about my own background and experiences, acknowledging my active role in conversations with participants, and both recognizing and interrupting my interpretations are steps that I took as I moved through this inquiry. Like many participants in my study, I found it difficult at times to place myself categorically in a social spectrum. Gender seemed fairly straightforward, but race and class seemed trickier for me and, as I discuss more fully in a later section, for participants. I explore these issues in greater detail in later analytical chapters, as well as in Interlude V. For now, I step away from the role that participants had in this study and turn my attention to fictional characters and stories that convey messages about and portray practices of shopping, consumption, and consumerism.

☼ The best feminist analysis . . . insists that the inquirer her/himself be placed in the same critical plane as the overt subject matter, thereby recovering the entire research process for scrutiny in the results of research. That is, the class, race, culture, and gender assumptions, beliefs, and behaviors of the researcher her/himself must be placed within the frame of the picture that she/he attempts to paint. . . . This requirement is no ideal attempt to "do good" by the standards of imagined critics in classes, races, cultures (or of gender) other than that of the researcher. Instead, it is a response to the recognition that the cultural beliefs and behaviors of feminist researchers shape the results of their analyses no less than do those of sexist and androcentric researchers. We need to avoid the "objectivist" stance that attempts to make the researcher's cultural beliefs and practices invisible while simultaneously skewering the research objects beliefs and practices to the display board.   —Sandra Harding (1997), "Comment on Hekman's 'Truth and Method: Feminist Standpoint Theory Revisited': Whose Standpoint Needs the Regimes of Truth and Reality?" p. 9

4

Novel Consumption: Going Shopping and Learning with Fictional Characters

In this chapter, I begin to respond to my framing questions about learning-through-shopping: What do people learn to do? Who do people learn to be? How do people learn to make change? I have chosen to place this chapter at the beginning of my analysis for several reasons, some of which I have already noted in the previous chapter. In this chapter, I explore the characters and stories of four contemporary popular novels. By preceding the chapters that discuss my analysis of data from interviews, shopping trips, and focus groups, this chapter introduces evidence that culture is, as Gramsci (1971) argues, ideologically charged. It illustrates how individuals, including me and the participants who become the focus of my analysis in later chapters, encounter multiple understandings of and responses to hegemonic ideologies and, as consumer-citizens, negotiate our way through them in the context of our material circumstances.

My inclusion of fiction also confirms Gramsci's (1971) ideas on the role of intellectuals, such as novelists, in confirming or challenging ideologies and common sense and in spurring informal, potentially radical, learning in the course of everyday activities. As novelist and essay-writer Arundhati Roy (2001) understands, novelists may or may not self-identify as artists with a higher calling than producing works of fiction, but they always function as intellectuals with political importance. ☼ Later scholars influenced by Gramsci, such as Williams (1980), argue similarly that the analysis of literature plays an important role in understanding a particular society. ☼ In part, I use reading fiction as an analogy for shopping, because both are processes of consumption and "part of the construction of identity and identification" (Jarvis, 2003, p. 262). Furthermore, as Jarvis notes, reading of popular fiction is, like shopping, seen as a distinctly feminine pastime, "an indulgence, something women do . . . to escape the tedium of daily life" (p. 271).

> ☼ There's a very thin line that separates the strong, true, bright bird of the imagination from the synthetic, noisy bauble. Where is that line? How do you recognize it? How do you know you've crossed it? At the risk of sounding esoteric and arcane, I'm tempted to say that you just know. The fact is that nobody—no reader, no reviewer, agent, publisher, colleague, friend, or enemy—can tell for sure. A writer just has to ask herself that question and answer it as honestly as possible. The thing about this "line" is that once you learn to recognize it, once you see it, it's impossible to ignore. You have no choice but to live with it, to follow it through. You have to bear with all its complexities, contradictions, and demands. And that's not always easy. It doesn't always lead to compliments and standing ovations. . . . The trouble is that once you've seen it, you can't unsee it. And once you've seen it, keeping quiet, saying nothing, becomes as political an act as speaking out. There's no innocence. Either way, you're accountable.   —Arundhati Roy (2001), *Power Politics*, pp. 6–7

> ☼ I had become convinced in my own work that the most penetrating analysis would always be of forms, specifically literary forms, where changes of viewpoints, changes of known and knowable relationships, changes of possible and actual resolutions, could be directly demonstrated, as forms of literary organization, and then, just because they involved more than individual solutions, could be reasonably related to a real social history, itself considered analytically in terms of basic relationships and failures and limits of relationship.   —Raymond Williams (1980), *Culture and Materialism*, p. 26

In part, though, I also use the particular works of fiction discussed here as examples of how individuals learn about and through shopping. My assertion is that, for readers, getting to know and empathize with different characters, their stories, and their points of view can build awareness of social issues and encourage reflexivity in readers' daily lives. This is also Jarvis's (1998, 2000, 2003) point. Her question of how a reflective reading of literary fiction can facilitate critical learning is rarely researched among adult educators; however, she and a few other adult educators have begun to explore the more popular question of how media can be used in critical learning (Armstrong, 2000, 2005a, 2005b, 2005c; Jarvis, 2005; Sandlin, 2005b, 2007; Tisdell & Thompson, 2007; Wright, 2006, 2007). As the reader of these four novels who is also the writer of this chapter, I am exploring my own learning. Like Jarvis (2000, 2003), I am interested in combining literature and the humanities into a study of social life. ☼ This is consistent with Gramsci's (1971) stress on the dialect of the social and the cultural, as well as with my explanation of case study bricolage methodology. From the outset of my

☼ Students did indeed develop technical expertise in practical criticism, but also analysed texts in terms of their social and political agendas. These aspects of analysis were not separable. Their analytical skills meant that they were increasingly conscious of point of view and audience which led them to ask what kinds of interests or perspectives a text represented. They had developed an awareness of texts as constructed knowledge as opposed to text as image of reality. Many reported that they now tended to analyse texts, including social texts, in terms of their representation of women and to ask questions about gendered points-of-view. I found it interesting, however, that this shift in attitude towards knowledge appeared to be transferable across contexts. This was not a media studies course, we had not discussed news and information media, yet students reported a more critical approach to the news and a stronger interest in current affairs when asked how they had changed as a result of their course.   —Christine Jarvis (2000), "Reading and Knowing," p. 539

analytical account, then, I have positioned myself as both a researcher and a participant in this inquiry.

Aside from me, though, there are other learners in this analysis. They are the characters in the novels. Talking about the character Murphy Brown, from the television show of the same name, Elizabeth Tisdell and Patricia Thompson explain, "Sometimes fictional characters take on national significance, and even become part of public debate on social issues, which indicates the incredible power of the media to both construct and contribute to discussion and commentary on social issues" (2007, p. 653). Paul Armstrong (2000, 2005a, 2005b, 2005c) deals with the educational function of shows ranging from soap operas to the satirical *The Simpsons* and *The Office*. Robin Wright (2006, 2007) explores how Catherine Gale, a lead character in the version of the British show *The Avengers* which ran from 1962 to 1964, helped female viewers understand the British gender structures and develop a critique of them and an alternative sense of self. Even Jarvis (2005) turns her attention away from novels to explore lessons about lifelong learning in the television show *Buffy the Vampire Slayer*. Jarvis's analysis establishes that there is learning within the show that helps to develop the characters as the series progresses and helps them to fulfil their roles within the show, as well as learning among viewers about the nature of learning, human development, and the call to radical action. Moreover, Jarvis discusses the intellectual, emotional, intuitive, and sensual dimensions of learning in everyday life, a view that is consistent with my own conceptualization of holistic incidental learning.

Fiction, rather than media, interests me for several reasons. Media is the focus of study for a few leading scholars in the field of education;

however, as Tisdell and Thompson (2007) confirm, these studies often concern children and youth. I want my focus to remain squarely on adult learning, and literary fiction might be more useful than television or film in this study, which is concerned centrally with incidental (Foley, 1999, 2001) adult learning. Even if a television show or a film makes a critical or radical point, its viewers are continually confronted with commercial advertisements, challenging them to sustain a critical analysis of what they are consuming; fiction might be commercially produced and marketed, but it does not have the same direct attachment to advertising. Furthermore, the separation of the realm of literary fiction from the realm of advertising (that is, the advertisement of products other than the novel itself) suggests that authors of novels are less constrained than their colleagues in television or film. Film makers and television producers face direct pressure to reiterate hegemonic ideology and common sense because of their need for sponsors or advertisers.

Reading a novel also takes time, much more time than it takes to watch a television show or a film. Thompson notes that media technologies now commonly available to consumers in the Global North enable them "not only to be entertained by television shows and films but to stop and start them and thus to dissect, analyze, and learn from them" (2007, p. 84). Whether or not people actually consume media in this way remains an unanswered question, but most people do read novels in this way. (I certainly do.) Putting aside and returning to a novel, readers have an opportunity to think about what they have read and hold it up against their own daily experiences. This understanding of adult learning is consistent with a constructivist perspective. As Jarvis points out, "Narrative organization and point of view may lead readers to identify with characters whose values and actions are in opposition to their own. Reflection on this identification may challenge existing meaning perspectives at the personal or sociocultural level" (2003, p. 265). Finally, in my holistic conceptualization of learning, I combine critical thinking and reflection with emotion; my serious reading of and learning from this fiction has encompassed intellectual and emotional responses.

My purpose is not to conduct a comprehensive analysis of contemporary literature; rather, my intertextual analysis of fiction provides one way of exposing and examining the range of ideologies and common sense relating to shopping and consumption and circulating in Canadian society. Fictional texts are evidence of cultural and social reality. ☼ Intertextual analysis, a prime methodological tool of cultural studies, asks researchers to read texts "in relation to the wider cultural and social panorama, consisting of other texts" (Saukko, 2003, p. 103). "Texts" is used loosely in this sense, and includes media, political, and cultural writings as well as images and other forms of discursive representation.

> ☼ Knowledge and knowing are saturated with political purpose, intent, cultural and social values, and vested interests. And knowledge, as we have continued to create it in our discipline, has no greater claim to authenticity, to fidelity, to truth, to validity, or reliability than do the fictions we read, write, or tell ourselves daily in print or in conversations to get on with our lives. We tell ourselves stories in order to live, says Joan Didion. Well, we tell ourselves "truths" and "facts" for that reason as well.
>
> My first point, then, is this: knowing and knowledge are fictions as much as fiction is knowing and knowledge.   —Lorri Neilsen (2002), "Learning from the Liminal: Fiction as Knowledge," p. 208

As Currie (1999) clarifies, texts can also include research transcripts, ☼ and I occasionally intersperse my reading of novels with excerpts from transcripts of interviews, shopping trips, and focus groups that I conducted with participants in this inquiry. These excerpts relate works of fiction to experiences of everyday life, and reiterate my point that discourses are constructed and confronted in a range of forms and settings. Their inclusion marks a recognition that people interested in working for societal change are constantly engaged in processes of research and analysis, and it elevates participants' comments from raw data to a contribution to the analysis undertaken in this inquiry.

Juxtaposing the words of fictional characters and living participants, I use Richardson's (2000) tool of crystallization in this inquiry to acknowledge the breadth of possible data gathering strategies and analytical frameworks. As Currie (1999) cautions, though, this does not mean

> ☼ Here I am concerned with methodological issues surrounding the textual treatment of women's experiences as data. What I mean is that sociological research itself entails the creation of texts—written field notes, interview transcripts, questionnaire data, and so on—which become the basis of knowledge claims. Not too long ago, sociologists would not be willing to admit that they "read" rather than simply "measure" the social world. Such an admission draws attention to the subjective rather than objective activities of the social scientist. Nor would sociologists until recently consider in their wildest dreams that they actually "write" the social; in other words, that sociologists create rather than discover what we have come to think of as "the social" (see Game 1991). For better of for worse, anti-humanist critiques have forced us to think about these matters. Certainly, I could not evade them in a sociological study of the cultural realm. For this reason, Girl Talk can also be read for what it tells us about our own practices as researchers.   —Dawn Currie (1999), *Girl Talk: Adolescent Magazines and Their Readers*, p. 14

that cultural texts *become* social reality. The cultural is not the same as the social, and cultural products cannot simply replace social encounters as a source of data (Currie, 1999); however, as Gramsci (1971) clarified, each helps the other make sense dialectically. Methodologically, my reference to participants' comments in this way acknowledges the often deep reflection and analysis within them. Some of the points made by participants are the same analytical points made by scholars; sometimes, participants articulated them with great clarity, and, I think, their words have a legitimate place alongside the place where I often put scholars' words. Finally, I am also aware that this chapter is itself a text, which will be read in relation to the other chapters in this book, just as the book will be read in relation to other books. My insertion of this chapter in this text and at this point in it is an affirmation of intertextuality, inviting readers to consider how they bring their own wealth of experiences to the reading of any text. As well, it is consistent with my methodology of case study bricolage, which emphasizes the fitting together of disparate pieces in response to a problem.

The books that I discuss here all contain characters who understand, practice, and talk about shopping in particular ways. I begin with the novel *Confessions of a Shopaholic* (2001), written by Madeleine Wickham under her pen name of Sophie Kinsella, which reiterates the hegemonic consumerist discourse in contemporary Western cultures. I then explore what Williams (1980) might consider two different alternative responses, found in Gemma Townley's novel *Learning Curves* (2006) and Douglas Coupland's novel *Generation X* (1991), and oppositional responses exemplified by Ruth Ozeki's novel *My Year of Meats* (1998). Following Sandlin's (2005b) study of a lifestyle publication as a source of informal adult learning, the analysis in this chapter continues to use critical cultural studies, including Gramsci's (1971) anchoring concepts, to explore links between reading and popular culture, consumerist ideology, and adult learning. Finally, I relate this analysis to more formal adult education purposes, such as the critical consumer education discussed by Sandlin (2004, 2005a), as well as the contention of some adult educators that learning occurs throughout daily living and that a serious, engaged reading of fiction can spur critical exploration of social issues (Jarvis, 2000).

Narrative 1: Hegemonic Consumerism

> Don't get me wrong. I like museums. I really do. And I'm really interested in Korean art. It's just that the floors are really hard, and I'm wearing quite tight boots, and it's hot so I've taken off my jacket and

it's slithering around in my arms. And it's weird but I keep thinking I can hear the sound of a cash till. It must be in my imagination. . . .

I peer vaguely at a piece of tapestry, then stride off down a corridor lined with exhibits of old Indian tiles. I'm just thinking that maybe we should get the Fired Earth catalogue, when I glimpse something through a metal grille and stop dead with shock.

Am I dreaming? Is it a mirage? I can see a cash register, and a queue of people, and a display cabinet with price tag. . . .

Oh my God, I was right! It's a shop! There's a *shop*, right there in front of me! (Kinsella, 2001, p. 103)

Confessions of a Shopaholic (Kinsella, 2001) introduces Becky Bloomwood, a young, college-educated, white woman working in London for a small financial publication. As the novel's title suggests, Becky is "addicted" to shopping. The novel, part of a series about this character, follows Becky's daily experiences working in a boring job, shopping in fashionable neighbourhoods and stores. Living well beyond her means and unable to pay her credit card bills, Becky is overwhelmed by the inevitable pressure from her many creditors until she determines how to keep that pressure at bay:

As I'm about to leave, a pile of letters comes through the letterbox for me. Several of them look like bills, and one is yet another letter from Endwich Bank. But I have a clever solution to all these nasty letters: I just put them in my dressing table drawer and close it. It's the only way to stop getting stressed out about it. And it really does work. As I thrust the drawer shut and head out of the front door, I've already forgotten all about them. (p. 193)

In reading the novel, I followed Becky as she is first wooed by a wealthy and aristocratic (but unattractive and socially awkward) man, and then as she falls in love with Luke Brandon, a successful public relations professional (and a witty and handsome man). The story turns when Becky is drawn into the financial problems of her parents' neighbours who have been misled by an investment company and lost a substantial amount of their savings. To earn extra money, Becky writes a newspaper article about their predicament and, enjoying the resulting publicity, appears on a television show to talk about the problem of dishonesty among investment advisers. She brings the neighbours' case to the public eye and becomes, in the eye of her beloved Luke, a person of intelligence and integrity—as well as feminine beauty and style.

In many ways, this novel follows a conventional plot-line for romance novel. Women and men conform to traditional gender roles, and the heroes embody appropriately gendered, raced, and classed dispositions and habits. Becky corresponds to the Western hegemonic stereotype of the consumer-citizen as white and middle class. She represents the hegemonic stereotype of "woman" as an uncontrollable shopper who ultimately, means no harm and balances "man's" obsession with work (Bowlby, 2001; Rappaport, 2000). By the novel's end, even she recognizes that shopping and acquisition are insufficient; she comes to realize that what she is missing is a romantic relationship. Luckily, she discovers that her attraction to Luke is mutual. Her story embraces hegemony in several ways: It presents consumerism as a path to social identity and status; it reflects idealized notions of gender, race, and nationality; and its connection of consumption, gender, race, nationality, and class reiterates hegemonic cultural values.

What distinguishes this book and the rest of Kinsella's series from other romances is Becky's (and Kinsella's) knowledge of high-fashion brands. Becky is not just a shopper; she is a *connoisseur* of designer labels and up-to-the-minutes trends. Her consumption of fashion publications and other forms of popular media, as well as her shopping, enables her to invent the persona and, ultimately, the life of her dreams—dreams that mainstream media and advertising imply that are widely shared. ☼ Through shopping and consumption, she learns about who she is and, more important, who she can be. Shopping and consumption give her the confidence to socialize with wealthy men above her own

---

☼

ALICE: I find from billboards more and more they are, or advertisers in magazines as well, are telling us that we don't have enough or that we deserve it or that you should buy, like really bombarding with this message that you need to buy this. This will make your life complete. —Interview excerpt, February 17, 2007

JULIE: I think there's kind of two sets. The main message I get about shopping is do more. And that it will in some way make me happy. So I think there's quite a cynical message that almost feels to me as if it permeates the culture that says, if you are having any kind of problem, you can kind of buy your way out of it. And that, those messages I do think come primarily from the media. Magazines, TV, radio, even movies now. I mean you go to see a movie now and the first 15 or 20 minutes is ads for products. And the message within literature and movies and music that somehow having more things will make me happier, okay. The flip side of that is a message that I think really sort of denigrates women that is shopping is somehow frivolous. Women do it, women love it. Isn't that just typical of their gender? —Interview excerpt, March 14, 2007

middle-class position. At the same time, her shopping and consumption also remind me, the reader, of the common sense (per Gramsci, 1971) about the female consumer-citizen: She *must* shop! In response to this essentially female compulsion, Becky learns how to do several things: how to find and exploit credit well beyond her means, how to break her commitments to rein in her spending, and how to evade and lie to creditors. More than an intellectual process, Becky's learning involves an emotional investment in the construction of her identity as it is realized through shopping and consumption. This might not be the radical, incidental learning described by Foley (1999, 2001), hooks (2003), or Tisdell (1998), but it is an example of how emotion and sensuality are dimensions of learning (Dirkx, 2001; hooks, 2003; Tisdell, 1998).

Juxtaposing stores and brands that cater to the middle class, such as Marks and Spencer^PLC and The Body Shop™, with coveted designer boutiques and brands such as Agnès b.™, Kinsella (2001) suggests that she, like Becky, has the "cultural capital" (Bourdieu, 1984) necessary to sustain a desirable middle-class life in London and that middle-class readers can develop this cultural capital and use it to help build their own status through their shopping decisions. Kinsella established herself as such an expert on fashion and shopping that, after inventing a brand of scarves in her novel, she was contacted by readers inquiring about where they could find this brand. ☼ Shopping in a fashionable city's fashionable stores gives Becky what really matters for a woman: an enviable sense of style and an appropriately self-deprecating manner. As the reader of this novel, I become a student of Kinsella's and Becky's teachings. Presumably, my recognition and admiration of the particular shops and brands mentioned throughout the novel extend the possibility for me to become a real-life Becky or Kinsella, a success as a woman living in a Western society. In this way, this novel functions as a curriculum for contemporary consumer-citizen for the ideal white, middle-class Western, or at least British, woman.

> ☼ I also made up Denny and George scarves—which was a big mistake, as I then got loads of emails asking where can you buy one? So now I'm thinking I should go into scarf design on the side.   —Sophie Kinsella (n.d.), "Interview on *Shopaholic and Sister*"

What Sandlin refers to as "traditional consumer education" (2005a, p. 174) is aimed at shoppers such as Becky—people who understand the emotional and cultural appeal of shopping and just need to learn the art of self-restraint. "Traditional consumer education" has focused on instrumental learning, "which pertains to controlling or manipulating the environment or other people. It involves predictions about observable events which can be proven correct, determining cause-effect relation-ships and task-oriented problems solving" (Mezirow, 1995, p. 49 in Sandlin, 2005a, p. 168). Such consumer education encourages learners to become informed so that they can make careful, well-reasoned deci-sions in their shopping and consumption. The aim is to teach consumers how to choose wisely from among consumer options, rather than to upset consumerist ideology or the social and economic structures under-pinned by that ideology. In doing so, such education reiterates another part of hegemonic ideology, connected to learning rather than to shop-ping and consumption: Learning is an intellectual, rational process in which emotions, sensuality, and spirituality must be checked rather than followed. As for my final framing question—How do people learn to make change?—well, as far as Kinsella and Becky are concerned, why would anybody want to learn that?

Narrative 2: Reasonable Balance

> She caught a glimpse of herself in the mirror and recognized that perhaps she wasn't *that* fine. Passable, maybe, but she wasn't going to set the world on fire looking like this—an old baggy T-shirt and old jeans. . . .
>
> Jen hesitated, then, holding the suit several inches away from her as if it were a wet dog, she strode quickly into the cubicle. *I'm just going to try it on*, she told herself firmly. *There's nothing wrong with that.*
>
> "Wow!" Angel said appreciatively five minutes later as they both came out to take a little look at themselves. . . . "I've never seen you in a suit before. It looks great!"
>
> Jen shook her head bashfully, but she knew she wasn't convincing anyone. She did look great. Much better than she looked in her jeans, which had become so comfortable that they no longer held any shape, draping over her legs as if hungover and unable to think what else to do. (Townley, 2006, pp. 168–171, emphasis in original)

Townley's novel *Learning Curves* (2006) might not share the com-mercial and popular success of Kinsella's *Shopaholic* series, but there is a sisterly relationship between both the novelists and their novels. Like *Confessions of a Shopaholic* and the other titles in that series, *Learning Curves* is in the romance genre and treats shopping and consumption as central, contemporary concerns. It is likewise based in London, and its main characters share much with Kinsella's (2001) characters. There is one additional point of interest that has heightened attention to this novel: Townley and Kinsella are, in real life, sisters. However, the differences between the two novels introduce some of the variations in discourses of shopping and consumption, as well as their relationship to both social identity and globalization.

In *Learning Curves*, I met the main character, Jen. Like Becky, Jen is a white, middle-class, attractive, well-educated Londoner; in contrast to Becky, however, she is torn between the mainstream and calls for change. This intellectual and emotional split is represented by her divorced parents: her wealthy businessman father, George, and her environmentalist-social activist mother, Harriet. Working in Harriet's consulting firm, Jen agrees to enroll as a student in the business education program operated by George's corporation. Harriet suspects that George is involved in a corporate scandal, and Jen is sent into his corporation via the business program to spy on him. In the excerpt that opens this section, Jen's increasing confusion about what is right and wrong, as well as her own identity, is illustrated as she tries on a fashionable business suit in a clothing store. On a shopping expedition with her best friend, Angel, Jen is shocked to see that this suit actually does suit her well. This outfit is the icon of everything that is contrary to her life's work and her sense of self. By putting it on, her understanding of the world around her and her place in it is called into question.

Jen's uncertainty continues to surface and build throughout the novel. In a later scene, she has the following exchange with the tutor in the business program in which she has enrolled:

Bill stroked his beard. "Okay, then let me ask you something. Let's take a drug company. What do they do?"

Jen sat up straight. "Easy. They develop drugs which they then sell at a huge profit and convince governments to stop other companies producing these drugs cheaper, even if they could save lives all around the world. They're hideous companies. Really awful."

Bill smiled. "Okay, so you think that once they've developed a drug they should give it out for free?"

"They should sell it at the price it costs to make it. Not charge people an arm and a leg."

"But wouldn't the price include the research and development costs, which can mean years of scientists conducting expensive experiments?"

"Yes, but . . ."

"But?"

"But they still make huge profits."

"Which makes people want to invest in them, which means they have more money for research. . . . And if they didn't make a profit, do you think there would be the same level of investment?"

> Jen frowned. "I guess not . . ." she started, then stopped.
> "Business itself isn't bad," Bill said gently. "You need rules, codes of conduct. But making money isn't in itself a bad thing. . . ."
> "What about corruption?" Jen demanded. "Businesses are rife with it."
> "Not as rife as a lot of governments." (Townley, 2006, pp. 255–256)

This scene is interesting in the context of adult education research, because Townley presents the character of Bill the tutor, who teaches both the character of Jen and the reader of the novel. Whether or not Townley appreciates the insertion of this type of exchange, it functions as a reminder of the educational purpose of intellectuals—from teachers to authors.

This novel stops short of the whole-hearted and light-hearted portrayal of shopping or consumerism. By the end of the book, Jen and Harriet learn that George has done no wrong, and they actually reconcile and begin to work together in a new-found, common purpose. Their reconciliation is more than the healing of an interpersonal rift; it suggests the possibility of reconciling the general status quo with a measured commitment to alternatives. Finally, like Kinsella's (2001) Becky, Jen is rewarded with the man of her dreams, Daniel: a successful, handsome man who shares her racial and socioeconomic status.

While Kinsella's (2001) novel never wavers from its embrace of consumerist ideology—replete with overtones of gender, race, and class—and its central messages are consistent with the messages in mainstream advertising and popular culture, Townley's (2006) characters and plot are more tentative. Her regard for critics' caution regarding corporations and consumerism recognizes nuances that Kinsella's novel overlooks. Jen's "Mr. Right" is a highly placed publishing executive, rather than the so-called spin doctor of corporate communications who makes Becky swoon. Jen's parents and the array of other characters in the book portray two groups: those in power who attempt to build consent to social structures through the persuasive power of ideology and common sense, and other groups whose consent is sought. The challenge for Becky is to find a way to shop endlessly; the challenge for Jen is to negotiate a balanced position on consumerism and capitalism in a version that resembles Giddens's (1998, 1999b) caution about, but ultimate enthusiasm for, an unstoppable globalization.

This novel might not be intellectually challenging or seriously critical; it does, however, raise some of the substantive concerns of contemporary Western, middle-class consumers. In doing so, it exemplifies the second type of response discussed by Sandlin, which she characterizes as "individually questioning consumption" (2005a, p. 175). If Kinsella's novel reiterates hegemonic ideology and common sense in a simplistic way, Townley's novel suggests the possibility for other options even as it reiterates portions of hegemonic ideology and common sense. Williams expands on Gramsci's earlier thinking about hegemony by distinguishing between what he calls "alternative" and "oppositional" responses to hegemonic discourse: "There is a simple theoretical distinction between alternative and oppositional, that is to say between someone who simply finds a different way to live and wishes to be left alone with it, and someone who finds a different way to live and wants to change the society in its light" (1980, pp. 41–42).

I read the character of Jen and her story as an example of Williams's (1980) alternative response, and a candidate for Sandlin's (2005a) second reaction in consumer education. She and Harriet seem to be interested in working for widespread societal change and are motivated by emotional and spiritual understandings of ecology and fairness; however, plot turns such as Harriet's reconciliation with George and Jen's acceptance of Bill's lesson about the fairness of multinational industries such as pharmaceuticals imply that what is called for is not wholesale social or economic change, but more balanced individual choices.

Capitalism and class might be at the centre of the encounter between Jen and Bill, but gender and race also surface in the novel in ways that reinforce, rather than challenge, the hegemonic order. Jen meets and falls in love with Bill, and together they embody Western images of the perfect couple. One of the few characters from a racialized minority group, Jen's best friend Angel both reiterates and rejects stereotypes of her Indian identity. Angel is outspoken and spunky, and she adamantly rejects her parents' interest in an arranged marriage for her. When it comes to shopping, though, Angel reverts to stereotypes of gender and race. It is Angel who is with Jen when she tries on the fashionable suit, and, later in their shopping trip, they go to stores specializing in Indian women's wear:

> She [Angel] raised her eyebrow at the assistant who came wandering over to them. "I need to order five saris," she said firmly, putting on her mother's strong Indian accent. "None of your rubbish fabrics, I want pure silk only. And I don't have much time. Okay? Well, go on then!"
>
> As the assistant ran off obediently, Angel winked at Jen. "I'd make a great Indian matriarch, no?" (Townley, 2006, p. 166)

Kinsella relies on shopping and consumption—such as the time her white characters cook a curry meal—to acknowledge London's increasingly diverse composition; Townley takes an additional step and introduces racially, ethnically, and culturally diverse characters. As Angel's words indicate, many people relate gender, class, and race through shopping, albeit in the reductionist, superficial, stereotypical ways described by critical race scholars (Dhruvarajan, 2000; DuCille, 1999;

Frankenberg, 1993; Knowles, 2003; Twine, 2000)—and by at least one of the participants in this inquiry. ☼ In the excerpt cited above, the character of Angel recalls Mies's (1986) concept of "housewifization" as she asserts a stereotypically racialized and classed femininity in the context of shopping. There is no call in this book for societal change related to either these stereotypes or consumption practices; instead, the novel reiterates the understanding of learning, identity, and choice as individual, intellectual matters. The narrative suggests that individuals ought to become better informed so that they can make better consumption decisions. Articulating another contemporary Western ideology—neoliberalism—Bill the tutor offers one piece of advice to see Jen through the business education program and life in general: "You focus on your goals and align your life around them, and you'll get where you want to be" (Townley, 2006, p. 38).

☼

ELLEN: Well this is the biggest criticism of Canadian multiculturalism, is that cultures get reduced to their most popular identifiable obvious . . . salient component. Right? So Indian food gets reduced to samosas, Japanese food gets reduced to sushi, Mexican food gets reduced to enchiladas. And . . . we think of Japanese people as wearing kimonos. Well lemme tell you, you go to Japan, the vast majority of people ain't running around in a kimono. Right? Or, I mean, that's one of the things that's also really hard, is that cultures get marketed. Right? Like, bangra became really popular and like, you know, Britney Spears is sampling bangra in her music videos. I mean . . . has she ever dated a brown man or an Indian man? Would she ever, you know? Like, did she learn anything about the culture? Does she know anything about the history of bangra? No, it's just a cool beat that she brings in. Like, are we really supposed to see that as . . . cultural infusion [*chuckle*]? And you know, I'm sorry, she just found . . . some sampling and mixed it in. . . . And that is, I mean that's, that's one of my central critiques of multiculturalism. It's exactly what you said. It's like, Oh yeah, I know about . . . Eastern religions, I do yoga. No, you, like, go to the community centre and take yoga from a white woman. You know, you say, like, namaste at the start of every course [*chuckle*]. . . . That doesn't tell you anything about Eastern religions, you know. And there's no spiritual component to it. —Interview excerpt, April 24, 2007

Narrative 3: Cynicism

We live small lives on the periphery; we are marginalized and there's a great deal in which we choose not to participate. We wanted silence and we have that silence now. We arrived here speckled in sores and zits, our colons so tied in knots that we never thought we'd have a bowel movement again. Our systems had stopped working, jammed with the odor of copy machines, Wite-Out, the smell of bond paper, and the endless stress of pointless jobs done grudgingly to little applause. We had compulsions that made us confuse shopping with creativity, to take downers and assume that merely renting a video on a Saturday night was enough. But now that we live here in the desert, things are much, *much* better. (Coupland, 1991, p. 11, emphasis in original)

Although Coupland's novel is the oldest of the books that I discuss in this chapter, its cultural impact goes well beyond its date of publication or even its own readers. This novel popularized a lexicon, including the term "generation X." Reading this novel, I met narrator Andy, the other main characters, Dag and Claire, and an array of their friends, work acquaintances, and family members. Andy, Dag, and Claire have come from different places in North America, but, as Andy explains, "where you're from feels sort of irrelevant these days ('Since everyone has the same stores in their mini-malls,' according to my younger brother, Tyler)" (p. 4). Having left behind middle-class families and jobs, in favour of a "McJob ('Low pay, low prestige, low benefits, low future')" (p. 5), they live in the same housing complex in Palm Springs, California.

As the excerpts that I've already cited from this novel suggest, these three characters recognize the superficiality of their consumer culture. As the novel's title suggests, they are stand-ins for middle-Americans (and, by extension, Canadians) of their age (and, by implication, their white race). Coupland (1991) is not always explicit about this, but he gives me clues that he, a white man, is writing about white characters for a white reader. For example, he fills the margins of the book with his original graphic art, from comic-book-style portraits to graffiti to stylized definitions of the terms that he is constructing and using. Every portrait appears to be of a white person, making whiteness a parenthetical presumption, if not an overt mandate. Unlike Kinsella's (2001) novel, *Generation X* has a narrative that is critical of the aspiration toward middle class in a consumerist culture and of contemporary globalization more generally; however, critique, like resistance, can be partial (Sparks, 1997), and this narrative does not include a critical view of the social characteristics of gender and, especially, race. As critical race scholars— and one of the participants in this study ☼—clarify, a Canadian discourse of multiculturalism and diversity (and Coupland is a Canadian author) serves to diminish the apparent urgency of discussing race and race relations (Dhruvarajan, 2000) and suggests how, through culture, whiteness is constructed without being named (Frankenberg, 1993).

☼
AMITAH: . . . I mean with the age of the internet we've almost all become global citizens. People travelling, you know, businesses overseas and all these things. And it's much less, it's much less separate but a lot more separate. Do you know what I mean? [*chuckle*]
KAELA: So there's that paradox.
AMITAH: Yeah, there's definitely a paradox. And then of course we forget that here in Canada that we're actually living on stolen land . . . in the first place. . . . Nobody talks about that one. And the whole, this whole thing is really built on a lie. . . . The whole culture that we're all, you know, so proud of, this multicultural Canada, but how did we get here? Nobody wants to look at that because it would raise too many difficult questions.
—Interview excerpt, February 21, 2007

When it comes to the relationship between class, consumption, and globalization, *Generation X* has far more to say. Having reached adulthood in postmodern consumerist societies, Andy, Dag, and Claire recognize the false promise of post-Second World War consumerism, and the environmental and social problems that it has created. They articulate an unwillingness to embrace it. However, for almost the entire novel they do little more than belittle continued acceptance and enactment of consumerism, poking fun at the people around them and the society from which they have purposefully marginalized themselves. Moreover, like the previous two novels, *Generation X* continues to feature a cast of characters recruited largely from the middle class. This similarity among the three novels recalls Nesbit's suggestion that contemporary Western cultures are focused on either disputing class as a category altogether, or insisting that "everyone is middle class" (2006, p. 175). Finally, the characters in *Generation X* do not seem to share my concern that globalization is a project that is exacerbating class divisions. Having given up their middle-class, consumption-driven lives, choosing instead to live in a low-cost housing project and work in low-income "McJobs" (Coupland, 1991, p. 5), Andy, Dag, and Claire portray an understanding of class as an individually chosen characteristic rather than a matter of socially and materially structured relations. Just as whiteness is the default racial identity in these characters' social world, so, too, is middle class the default class position. One can choose to work and consume in a way that is consistent with that position, or one can—as Andy, Dag, and Claire have chosen to do—remove oneself from it in protest. ☼

In the case of these characters, though, this is as far as the protest goes. The response taken up by Andy, Dag, and Claire is, again, an example of what Williams (1980) refers to as an "alternative" response.

☼
KAELA: Do you think of yourself as middle class?
AMITAH: Well, I feel that I grew up that way. . . . Yeah. I think I've dropped out of
         the middle class . . . on purpose. . . . [*laughter*]
KAELA: As a, as a sort of a statement of what you want to be in your life.
AMITAH: Yeah, that's a good way to put it. I'll concur with that. [*laughter*]
         —Interview excerpt, February 21, 2007

These characters have no interest in educating or persuading others about their social analysis, and they issue no call to change society. They enact the cynicism about social institutions that Kenway and Bullen (2001) warn is developing among children and youth who are growing up within a "consumer-media culture." This is what distinguishes the alternative from an oppositional response (Williams, 1980) made by characters in other stories—whether fictional or, as I explore in later chapters, real-life.

It makes sense that Sandlin (2005a) does not identify a type of consumer education program that corresponds to the cynicism of *Generation X*. Consumer education programs aim to help individuals shop and consume better, according to the particular meaning of "better" constructed by the educator and the learners. Cynics neither embrace consumerism nor hold out the possibility to challenge it in meaningful ways. At points throughout his novel, Coupland adopts the tactics of culture jammers. He intersperses graffiti-like images and pieces of critical, colloquial jargon both in his texts and in his margins, resisting mainstream ideas about both consumerism and the cultural form of the novel. Contrary to the potential for culture jamming spelled out by Kenway and Bullen (2001) or Sandlin (2007), though, Coupland does not put his culture jamming to further transformational use. Ultimately, Coupland challenges elements of current North American hegemony and its cultural mainstream, without realizing the culture jammer's function as an intellectual who leads "learners [or, in this case, readers] to a moment of *détournement* (a turning around), in which they are no longer who they used to be but are caught off guard with the possibility of becoming someone different" (Sandlin, 2007, p. 79).

Cynicism has been taken up by a few scholars, such as Canadians Joseph Heath and Andrew Potter (2004), but it tends to be directed *against* the idea of a counter-culture that can resist consumerism. ☼ Although they have an educational purpose, cynics' basic message that people should be left alone to spend their money is not one that translates easily into the basis of a consumer education program. There is no possibility for counter-hegemony in this ontology.

> ☼ The idea of a counterculture is ultimately based on a mistake. At best, countercultural rebellion is pseudo-rebellion: a set of dramatic gestures that are devoid of any progressive political or economic consequences and that detract from the urgent task of building a more just society. In other words, it is rebellion that provides entertainment for the rebels, and nothing much else. At worst, countercultural rebellion actively promotes unhappiness, by undermining or discrediting social norms and institutions that actually serve a valuable function.
> —Joseph Heath and Andrew Potter (2004), *The Rebel Sell: Why the Culture Can't Be Jammed*, p. 59

The sarcasm of Coupland (1991) and his characters is witty, clever, and often insightful. As a reader, I frequently agreed with the characters about the senselessness of consumerism and the damage that overconsumption does to people's spiritual, emotional, intellectual, and physical well-being; however, the book's message that there are no preferable alternatives to the social status quo left me feeling anxious and frustrated. As the novel ends, Andy meets a group of "mentally retarded young teenagers" (p. 177) during a roadside stop. Feeling their warmth and nonjudgementalism, Andy has a form of spiritual awakening as he learns about a possibility for acceptance and connection that he has not been able to comprehend intellectually. Still, in this ending, I found only a momentary respite from the atomizing, alienating, wasteful consumerist society that Coupland presents.

Narrative 4: Committed Resistance

My American Wife!
Meat is the Message. Each weekly half-hour episode of *My American Wife!* must culminate in the celebration of a featured meat, climaxing in it glorious consumption. It's the meat (not the Mrs.) who's the star of our show! Of course, the "Wife of the Week" is important too. She must be attractive, appetizing, and all-American. She is the Meat Made Manifest: ample, robust, yet never tough. Through her, Japanese housewives will feel the hearty sense of warmth, of comfort, of hearth and home—the traditional family values symbolized by red meat in rural America. (Ozeki, 1998, p. 8, emphasis in original)

At the centre of Ozeki's novel is the character Jane Takagi-Little, a Japanese-American documentary film maker hired to produce *My American Wife!*, a television series promoting the American beef industry to Japanese consumers. The series uses "typical" American families in which women (who are also always wives and mothers) buy, cook, and serve meat-based dinners to men (who are also always husbands and fathers) and their children. Jane struggles to identify suitable families, even as she understands the impossibility of this task. Single and child-free, and an example of the racial and cultural hybridity held up as a model of postmodernity and globalization, Jane personifies the gap between the ideal American woman and the reality of contemporary American demographics. The novel's complex stories and characters include Jane's Japanese colleagues and the families she meets in the course of the series' production; her lover Sloan, a white, "dominant male" (p. 91) who plays saxophone in a jazz band; and the Japanese advertising representative handling this project, Joichi Ueno (who gives himself the nickname "John Wayno") and his unhappy wife, Akiko. Together, this ensemble and their stories both reflect and dispute hegemonic images of an America populated by white, middle-class, nuclear, heterosexually parented families who live according to clear gender roles.

In her travels across America, encounters with diverse families, correspondence with her supervisor in Japan, and eventual meeting with Akiko, Jane clarifies the extent to which cultural images of gender, race, class, nationality, and sexuality are socially constructed to meet certain ends. *My Year of Meats*, the fictional television series, has as its end the capitalist goal of commercial success for the American beef industry in Asia. *My Year of Meats*, the real work of fiction, is critical of that aim and the associated aims of cultural and racial imperialism. It exposes the damaging health and ecological consequences of cattle farming, beef production, and meat consumption, as well as the insidious penetration and acceptance of ideological constructions in individuals' lives and society in general. From the first couple in the series, who are coping with the husband's extramarital affair, to the last couple, who operate and live on a feed lot and whose prepubescent daughter has started to develop breasts, even the "perfect" families expose the falseness of the ideal American woman/wife/mother and man/husband/father. Ideals of gender, race, class, sexuality, and ability are also challenged, as Jane meets the parents whose beautiful, beloved teenage daughter is in a wheelchair, a poor black family for whom chicken is a luxury food item and meat is simply unaffordable, a white woman who has adopted children from several Asian countries, and a lesbian mixed-race couple with a biracial child. These assorted characters embody Martens's (2005) point that varied social characters and identities interact with the mass consumer-media culture that pervades society and helps individuals use and respond to consumer pressures and media representations in diverse ways.

As the image of the wholesome "all-American," "meat-and-potatoes" family is increasingly exposed as an ideologically based falsehood, Jane begins to sabotage the aim of the series so that she can showcase real people rather than imagined characters. As a documentary film maker, Jane has already come to accept that truth is in the eye, first, of the editor, and then of the beholder. ☼ This is the ontological and episte-mological reality that researchers in the social sciences must also accept. As a reader of the novel, I took note of Jane's/Ozeki's reminder and the range of settings in which individuals confront, research, and represent limits of the truth.

> ☼ I wanted to make programs with documentary integrity, and at first I believed in a truth that existed—singular, empirical, absolute. But slowly, as my skills improved and I learned about editing and camera angles and the effect that music can have on meaning, I realized that truth was like race and could be measured only in ever-diminishing approximations. Still, as a documentarian, you must strive for the truth and believe in it wholeheartedly.   —"Jane" in Ruth Ozeki (1998), *My Year of Meats*, p. 176

Accepting that there is no one truth does not mean dismissing the possibility of lies. Jane provides an example of how resistance and rad-icalism can still make sense for a documentary film maker, a community activist, a researcher, an adult educator, or a novelist, even if the poten-tial to achieve final, complete knowledge and emancipation is dismissed. Disturbed by what she is learning about the ecological and animal wel-fare issues in beef production, as well as the health and cultural implica-tions of its consumption, Jane chooses to disrupt the television series. Among the weekly wives, she includes the biracial lesbian couple, even though they are also vegetarian, and she delves into the hidden health problems of the girl growing up on the feed lot. Jane is eventually fired from the project but sends copies of her film footage to members of the families hurt by both the beef industry and how the television series presented them. The woman living on the feed lot explains what she wants Jane to do with the tape: "'Spread the word,' said Bunny. 'Give 'em your documentary. Nah, you ain't got no money. Sell it to them. Whatever you want. The main thing is, people gotta know!'" (Ozeki, 1998, pp. 357–358). By "people," Bunny is referring to shoppers who will buy and consume the meat that is not as wholesome and healthy as its image in beef marketing and, more generally, in culture.

Initially choosing an alternative response (Williams, 1980), Jane decides to stop buying and consuming meat. Eventually, though, she shifts to an oppositional response (Williams, 1980) and engages in a creative form of committed resistance that approaches Foley's (1999,

2001) notion of incidental learning with its radical ambition and potential. Consistent with the conclusions of other scholars who write about informal learning, her learning is based as much in her emotional response to what she sees and experiences as it is to her intellect (Dirkx, 2001; hooks, 2003; Tisdell, 1998), as well as her intellectual response to what she hears and reads. Twisting the original purpose of the footage, she edits it into a critical documentary that she sells to American and international media outlets. She creates a resource for the kind of holistic learning about the politics of consumption, as well as the politics of gender, race, class, sexuality, and dis/ability that I have described. That resource is most like the third form of consumer education discussed by Sandlin, "collectively politicizing and fighting consumption" (2005a, p. 176), typically delivered informally through community activist organizations or networks.

As Sparks (1997) suggests, though, dissidence, or what I call resistance, is complicated by the various social relations and economic structure in which people are enmeshed. They dwarf the individual consumer-citizen in the Global North and entire countries in the Global South. Hegemonic discourse proclaims that the world is shrinking and individuals have never-before realized decision-making power; however, institutions such as the World Bank and the World Trade Organization, which admittedly do not control every aspect of globalization but do direct its implementation, turn resistance against hegemony into a David-and-Goliath struggle. Jane recognizes the duplicity of consumer-citizens, even the would-be resistant ones, in this struggle:

> Coming at us like this—in waves, massed and unbreachable—knowledge becomes symbolic of our disempowerment—becomes bad knowledge—so we deny it, riding its crest until it subsides from consciousness. I have heard myself protesting, "*I didn't know!*" but this is not true. Of course I knew about toxicity in meat, the deforestation of the rain forests to make grazing land for hamburgers. Not a lot, perhaps, but I knew a little. I knew enough. But I needed a job. So when *My American Wife!* Was offered to me, I chose to ignore what I knew. "Ignorance." In this root sense, ignorance is an act of will, a choice that one makes over and over again, especially when information overwhelms and knowledge has become synonymous with impotence.

> I would like to think of my "ignorance" less as a personal failing and more as a massive cultural trend, an example of doubling, that characterizes the end of the millennium. . . . Fed on a media diet of really bad news, we live in a perpetual state of repressed panic. We are paralyzed by bad knowledge, from which the only escape is playing

dumb. Ignorance becomes empowering because it enables people to live. Stupidity becomes proactive, a political statement. Our collective norm. (Ozeki, 1998, p. 334, emphasis in original)

Still, Jane does what she perceives she can do to adopt a radical stance against rampant consumerism, as well as American cultural imperialism, by producing and releasing her documentary. In seeking exceptions to the idealized American family to feature in the television show, and in her own biracial make-up, she contravenes the preferred image of the middle-class, white, heterosexual, able-bodied American; however, by the novel's end, parts of her own story reiterate the image of the ideal man as strong and wilful, and the ideal woman as emotional and indecisive. Estranged from Sloan, Jane experiences a miscarriage. One night, she goes to see him at the bar where he and his band are performing, but it is not until she collapses on the ground in tears over the end of the (unplanned) pregnancy that he sweeps her up in his arms and agrees to reconcile. Although this novel does not otherwise fit into the romance genre, this plot twist, one of the final scenes in the novel, borrows just a bit from the traditions of that genre.

Summary

These novels offer four examples of the various narratives of and messages about consumerism, shopping, and consumption in contemporary Western societies. In works of fiction, characters might adopt one or another or these messages. More complex narratives and characters make a simplistic response to hegemonic messages less likely. Of these three novels, the most simplistic is *Confessions of a Shopaholic,* and the most complex is *My Year of Meats.* In the former, characters are recognizable, but, at the same time, they are superficial and stereotypical. The lives of the lead characters, as well as the assorted peripheral characters whom I met in this book, are consistent with hegemonic ideologies and common sense.

Read against discourses of neoliberalism, consumerism, multiculturalism, tolerance, and globalization, *Confessions of a Shopaholic* presents a society in which visible minority groups, regardless of the basis for their minority status, remain invisible, along with the problems that their existence poses to the social order. *Learning Curves* introduces a broader variety of characters and social relations, although it uses them to bolster, rather than challenge, hegemonic neoliberal visions of the individual and the corporation in society and in global affairs. This is most evident as the initially divergent cast of main characters move closer together intellectually, emotionally, and physically and develop a shared understanding that the status quo, with very limited, fixable exceptions, is just fine. *Learning Curves* might be more subtle and slightly more complicated than *Confessions of a Shopaholic*, but its female characters continue to construct their cultural and social identities largely in the context of shopping and, sometimes, in the shops. The main characters of *Generation X* understand that social structures, particularly class, exist but are simply resigned to living on the outskirts of the social order that they reject.

It is in *My Year of Meats* that characters represent the greatest range of circumstances and points of view. Jane learns something from all these characters, often unexpectedly, and her response to them conveys that learning does not necessarily involve adoption of one or another of the responses apparent in a narrative. What seems to interest Jane and what interests me is how individuals negotiate multiple narratives in their daily lives and how resistance and, perhaps, even radicalism become evident in people's lives, often in unexpected, unplanned ways. In addition to the lesbian vegetarians who offer a political analysis of production and consumption, this novel features Bunny, whose blonde, buxom appearance and light-hearted manner reiterate racialized gender stereotypes, but who is moved to action after becoming aware of the consumption-related problems that touch her family. Her learning involves intellect, as well as emotions and senses. She hears and understands Jane's explanation of the damage done by hormones used in farming; she sees that hormones are altering the physical development of her own daughter; it is her love for her daughter that compels her to act as a consumer-citizen—even if that action jeopardizes the livelihood of her family. While Williams's (1980) distinction among hegemonic, alternative, and oppositional responses might imply that individuals act consistently in one way or another, Sparks's (1997) elucidation of the complexity of dissidence clarifies how material circumstances and emotional needs combine with cultural ideals and personal histories to influence how people ultimately shop, consume, and otherwise behave. Seen in this light, the potential for radicalism is always limited, but not eliminated.

In this chapter I have presented examples of how a holistic form of incidental learning, which combines emotion, spirituality, and intellect, might occur in daily activities such as reading or shopping. Sometimes this learning reinforces hegemonic ideology and common sense; at other times, there is the potential for learning that disrupts hegemony. Still, the potential for an apparently mundane, often belittled activity such as shopping or a typically solitary activity such as reading to prompt radical learning remains largely unexplored. Sometimes, the line between incidental and more intentional learning becomes blurred. Learning about a topic can begin accidentally, as it does for Jane about the beef industry, and become purposeful, as it does for her as she seeks information and even undertakes research. The realization that adult learning occurs beyond educational institutions, in the diverse, unpredictable lives of individuals as they read and shop, suggests that adult educators consider the potential for the products of popular culture and the activities of daily life to deepen understandings of social connections, adult learning, and consumerism in the current era of globalization. After asserting the importance of fictional characters and their stories earlier in this chapter, I now acknowledge that fictional characters might be important, but they have the distinct disadvantage of not being able to respond to my guiding questions. In the following chapters, I turn to the conversations that I had with "real-life" participants during this inquiry to continue building an understanding of how, through shopping and consumption, people learn to do, learn to be, and learn how to make change.

INTERLUDE IV

A PhD Student, Her Books, and Her Search for a Bookcase

Doctoral students read a lot of books and journal articles and conference proceedings. Although I relied on online articles and the library as much as possible, I had acquired dozens of books to add to my five still-unpacked boxes of books and papers—in addition to what was unpacked and shelved. My progress, and the sanity of my partner, Karen and me, depended on our getting new bookcases. Except for my grandfather's towering bookcase, most of our bookcases used a simple modular system of pine planks. They were functional but gave our home the look of a student residence—temporary and inexpensive. We didn't want to extend that look any further.

Nor did we want to buy more bookcases like the one that we had bought a couple of years earlier. It looked fine in its spot in the hallway and was holding up well, but it didn't match the furnishings in the other rooms. Besides, since we had bought it, I had heard more about sustainable wood sourcing and was no longer comfortable buying furniture made from Asian wood, unless it came with a certification that I could trust.

Ikea, with its decent prices, aesthetics, functionality, and decent reputation for its sourcing of wood, had lots of bookcases; however, most of them were made of pressboard or fiberboard, both of which give off formaldehyde gas. Ikea had a couple of bookcases that matched our furniture, but they were either too small or too tall. Feeling like the fairytale Goldilocks without the benefit of Mama Bear's furnishings, I spent two years scouring local stores whose prices we could afford. I liked the idea of buying high-quality used furniture, and we turned to the many antiques and collectibles. China and curio cabinets abounded, but, except for the relatively small (and pricey) lawyer's bookcase with glass doors, bookcases were not to found.

With my book collection growing in size and diminishing in organization, I gave up on second-hand bookstores and turned to the few local stores we hadn't yet checked. How surprised we were to find bookcases made in the Lower Mainland from B.C. wood, available in different sizes and stains to hold our books and fit in our rooms, in the locally owned furniture store a fifteen-minute walk from home! We had avoided it because of its notoriously tacky television commercials; I had assumed that its inventory would match its marketing. The bookcases were reasonably priced and attractive, and we decided to put one in each of two rooms, chose stains, and placed our order. My search for a bookcase was over.

5

The Disciplines of Shopping: What Participants Learn to Do

In this chapter, I move from literary fiction to conversations with living people and begin to explore how participants in this inquiry talked about their encounters with and production of discourses, practices, and pedagogies of shopping. As my analysis illustrates, learning how to shop and what shopping means can happen incidentally as well as purpose-fully, and continually as well as sporadically. This learning is, moreover, a process that unfolds on multiple levels. As I outlined in Chapter 2, my conceptualization of learning combines critical adult education's em-phasis on intellect (Brookfield, 1998, 2005; Foley, 1999, 2001), as well an interest in emotion, sensuality, and spirituality more typically found in feminist scholarship (Dirkx, 2001; English, 2000; Hayes & Flannery, 2000; hooks, 2003; Tisdell, 1998, 2000). In my analysis here, I concen-trate on one of my framing questions—What do people learn to do?—as I apply this conceptualization to conversations and observations from interviews, shopping trips, and focus groups in order to extend the theo-rization of informal learning in the course of everyday life.

At least some of the learning involved in shopping can be regarded as "instrumental" (Mezirow, 1995 in Sandlin, 2005a) and relates to the control of one's resources and environment. Several interview questions asked participants about the skills and knowledge that they developed through shopping. ☼ Budgeting, making shopping lists, organizing time,

---

☼
- How did you learn about shopping and where to shop?
- What kind of information do you need or want when you go shopping? How do you go about finding that information? If you've ever encountered a barrier to getting the information that you feel you need, how have you dealt with the situation?
- Do you regularly shop in particular areas of the city or in particular stores? If so, which ones, and why do you prefer those places?   —selected interview schedule questions

learning how to decipher labels and logos, and learning how to navigate store aisles and procedures are all examples of the technical learning involved in shopping.

The traditional approaches to consumer education discussed by Sandlin might focus on a straightforward acquisition of information and decision-making skills, but the tensions of contemporary globalization, consumer-citizenship, and social identity can make shopping a much more complex process. In this inquiry, I was interested in talking to shoppers who have self-identified as individuals concerned about globalization and the role of their own consumption in this phenomenon. The focus of our conversations was their understanding and experience of this complexity. Some of my questions aimed to elicit participants' critical insights about shopping and consumption and their links to globalization and consumer-citizenship. ☼

After reviewing and coding the data, I identified five thematic understandings of how participants develop skills and knowledge through and about shopping. These resemble some of the skills and knowledge typically required in formal educational settings. First, I explore the ways in which participants have learned to learn. Second, I outline participants' ability to find useful, reliable information in a society made noisy with conflicting information and messages; in other words, they learn to do research. These first two areas of learning resemble areas of skill needed by all academics and students, regardless of their disciplines; however, participants' comments and practices also indicated that they were learning to do things that can be related to particular disciplines. Third, participants learned to identify and distinguish between value-(-for-money) and other sorts of values, tasks that might be associated with the discipline of philosophy. Fourth, they learned how to decipher text, symbols, and messages; in other words, they developed a specialized shopping literacy. Finally, they learned to think about sites and spaces of shopping and how local sites and spaces were linked to faraway places; in other words, they constructed a shopper's geography.

☼
- What kinds of messages do you regularly encounter about shopping, and where do you encounter them? How do you think they affect your shopping decisions?
- What, if any, other kinds of issues or considerations affect your shopping and consumption?
- Are there particular items that you try to buy or, conversely, items that you avoid buying? If so, what are they, and what kinds of considerations go into your decisions?　　—selected interview schedule questions

Learning to Learn

A central claim in this inquiry is that shopping itself is a site of critical learning about the politics of consumption and globalization and that it can contribute to an agenda of societal change. Indeed, my conversations with participants confirm that they do learn through their shopping. More specifically, they learn to learn in a way that is compatible with a social constructivist paradigm, which assumes "that human beings do not 'find' knowledge, but rather construct it" (Tisdell & Thompson, 2007, p. 656) through their experiences in social contexts.

Participants described a variety of strategies and dispositional qualities that helped them learn through and about shopping. Most were aware of the growing attention in news and other media to shopping, consumption, and consumerism. From the 100-Mile Diet and global climate change to safety-related questions about and recalls of products made in China, or from the loss of agricultural land and anxieties about food security to concerns about forced labour or unfair labour practices—most often in the Global South but sometimes here in Canada as well—various issues related to shopping crossed participants' "radar screens." Some of the main sources of their information were media reports, magazines, books, and documentaries.

SARAH: I don't usually read novels for fun. . . . I more read about the world or about, sometimes it's new-agey kind of stuff, like spiritual kind of stuff. And sometimes it's . . . like, I just pay attention to anything written in the newspapers or, like, magazines or, like, you know, like, what are those, the Canadian Geo–, the Canadian Geo–?

KAELA: Geographic?

SARAH: Yeah, like, magazines like that or newspapers and stuff. —interview excerpt, April 24, 2007

LINDA: And I try to buy organic produce because, not because I think it's good for my family but because I think it's important in terms of farming and the land that we have access to and not putting so many pollutants into the soil.

KAELA: So those are ecological reasons.

LINDA: Yeah, definitely, yeah.

KAELA: Are you hearing more about that now?

LINDA: Yeah, it definitely seems to be a, a more mainstream topic. I certainly don't feel like I'm a freak for being concerned about these things and I know that . . . [mainstream supermarkets], they're all coming out with more organic stuff. Some of it's a little bit frightening because I know Walmart's coming out with it . . . but they're putting pressure on companies and stuff for price point reasons, and that's, you know, that's not the point. . . . And I recently learned about how they're not necessarily treating the farm employees any better, and that kind of bugs me. You know I, the article that I read about, this was specifically talking about farmers in California. So now whenever something says that it comes from California I kind of go, huhhh, I don't know. But then at the same time I know we have migrant workers here, too, on our farms, and so you don't, you never know. But nobody really wants to pay what food is really worth when it comes to the work it takes to produce it. Myself among them, sadly.   —interview excerpt, April 29, 2007

We stepped away from the fridge, and Jody added, "I buy as much organic as possible, and really I do that since I saw the documentary . . . *The Corporation* . . ."   —shopping trip excerpt, Jody, February 12, 2007

Karen: I'll often read, like, *Mother Jones* . . . or the *New Internationalist*, which I haven't picked up in a long time, but just learn a lot from things like that.   —interview excerpt, February 2, 2007 ☼

Although the focus of many of these resources might not be shopping, learner-shoppers think about how they can extend the information and messages in these materials beyond their immediate focus and apply them in their shopping.

Another part of a constructivist understanding is that learners constantly adapt their existing knowledge as they encounter new situations and information. For critical learners, it is particularly important to

---

☼ Mother Jones is an independent nonprofit news organization whose roots lie in a commitment to social justice implemented through first-rate investigative reporting.   —August 17, 2008, www.motherjones.com/about/index.html

New Internationalist (NI) workers' co-operative exists to report on issues of world poverty and inequality; to focus attention on the unjust relationship between the powerful and the powerless worldwide; to debate and campaign for the radical changes necessary to meet the basic needs of all; and to bring to life the people, the ideas and the action in the fight for global justice.   —August 17, 2008, www.newint.org/

open up their existing knowledge to challenge. Many participants in this study described early exposure to the "common sense" (Gramsci, 1971) image in Western cultures of the female shopper. This was an image that several participants came to reject in their adult lives, even if their mothers had exemplified it:

> ALICE: It's ironic, because my mother's an avid shopper. She will spend hours shopping. I grew up with West Edmonton Mall being an essential part of life, because we had activities going on there as well as shopping, and family members would come in from out of town and we'd go there. So, yeah, I find it interesting that she really enjoys the experience, and I just can see her bringing all these things home, trying to decide on them, having to spend the time to return them, having to look for what she needs—I think maybe that's what has influenced me to realize that it's not a pleasurable activity, for me [*laughs*]. —interview excerpt, February 17, 2007

At the same time as they challenge and move beyond some early shopping lessons in adulthood, participants retain some of their early family-based learning in their shopping. Points that are valued and useful, even if they are not critical, are combined with the more politically charged learning that often comes later.

> KAELA: How did you learn about shopping and how to shop, and where do you think your ideas about shopping come from?
>
> EDDIE: My mom. And, and also just from hearing people, hearing activists talking about supporting this company and that company, buying Canadian, and that kind of thing. So I would have to say my, my mom as well as my, the overall community around me. . . .
>
> KAELA: Would you consider your mom an activist? . . . In terms of her own shopping habits or interests?
>
> EDDIE: No, not at all.
>
> KAELA: So what did she teach you about shopping that's different from what activists taught you?
>
> EDDIE: She taught me to buy at the lowest price, things like, wait for a sale, like walk to the store at the other end of the mall to see what's there.
>
> KAELA: So comparison shopping, value, those kinds of things.
>
> EDDIE: Yeah. And being content instead of always buying the latest trend. —interview excerpt, April 11, 2007

AMITAH: Okay, well where I did I learn about shopping? From my parents. . . . Usually from my mom. . . . She was the one, we went out food shopping with her, clothes shopping. And so my mom's sort of style was she's pretty picky about quality. When it came to food, she would always choose sort of fresh fruits and veggies. And she would cook a lot of things from scratch. We didn't buy packaged dinners. So that impacted the way I looked at food.   —interview excerpt, February 21, 2007

MARY: I mean how did I learn how to shop? My mother taught me first, for sure, and my ideas about shopping don't come from, well, some of them do, I mean the thing about frugality and not wasting, that's certainly from family of origin. So that remains. But, the rest of my ideas about shopping are very much embedded in political analysis that's supported by the rest of my lifestyle . . . and the rest of my life experience. —interview excerpt, March 14, 2007

These excerpts illustrate the relational nature of learning in everyday life. In contrast to the historically masculinized arenas of formal education and employment, processes such as shopping and child rearing remain largely feminized. Unlike employment, which is conceptualized as the basis of collective identity and action, these processes have also been perceived as solitary undertakings that provide little opportunity for learning; however, participants' recollections of their childhood shopping experiences offer examples of the early and long-lasting importance of relations and relational learning. Early lessons about how to recognize and evaluate quality and value-for-money remain important among participants' early learning even if, as I explore in the section below on Weighing Values, this learning confounds later learning and values.

Another thing that these excerpts make apparent is the extent to which family life in Canada continues to be gendered. This reality is despite recent decades of both counter-hegemonic feminist discourse and a hegemonic response of rights-based policies in arenas such as employment, housing, and access to public programs. Just like the multiculturalism policy, these policies signal a shift in hegemonic discourse and have made a difference in the lives of many individuals, without addressing the underlying structure of patriarchy. Patriarchy continues to exert an influence through cultural constructions of shopping as well as child rearing as predominantly feminine activities. The presence of patriarchy helps explain why, regardless of their ages, participants spoke about the importance of their mothers as early teachers about shopping and, by extension, the gendered division of labour within and beyond the home.

As they have grown beyond their early family-based teachings about and experiences of shopping, participants have relied on expanding family and social networks in their learning about the politics of shopping. Partners and friends who share concerns about consumerist ideology and rampant consumption prove to be helpful teachers. According to Jocelyn,

> how I shop now has certainly been affected by my husband. . . . [H]e's very socially aware. . . . He opened my eyes to a lot of those things because of his family I think, and his upbringing was much more to the left, whereas my family was way to the right.   —interview excerpt, January 22, 2007

Likewise, Linda described her husband's love of nonfiction books on topical issues, and Claire talked about her husband who is "nuts about reading things on the internet" (shopping trip excerpt, Claire, March 22, 2007). Both Linda and Claire tuned into the information that their husbands were able to find and incorporated it into their shopping and consumption. Most participants also talked about having friends, colleagues, and social networks who encouraged critical, holistic learning about shopping and consumption. Sarah mentioned "a friend who has been to, like, the garbage dump, and, I don't know, we'll all just really talk about something like that" (interview excerpt, Sarah, April 24, 2007). All these examples continue to reiterate the relationality of shopping and learning processes that, at first glance, might appear solitary.

In contrast to Foley's (1999, 2001) concept of incidental learning that, although unplanned, occurs in the context of collective action, my approach builds on participants' comments to suggest that incidental learning can be politically charged and appear solitary. Furthermore, the boundary between solitary and collective learning can become blurred, especially as learner-shoppers turn to globalization's information technologies such as the internet to engage with social movements. Along with an increasing number of popular books, documentaries, and magazines, the internet affords new ways for participants and other learner-shoppers to learn about and become involved with critical or radical movements and organizations connected to shopping and consumption. Unlike the traditional social action settings explored in Foley's (1999, 2001) writing, the use of these resources creates a paradox of individualization and collectivity in learning and action.

What complicates the incorporation of experts' and activists' teachings into shopping is the inconsistencies among experts as well as between experts' and participants' own knowledge and experiences. Part of participants' learning process is learning to trust their own judgements and feelings, even as they remain open to having their assumptions challenged and continuing to learn, and learning whom else they can trust. As critical media literacy scholars explain, a critical learner knows the importance of not accepting information at face value and carefully assesse the trustworthiness of an analysis and its conclusions (for example, see Jarvis, 2005; Sandlin, 2005b, 2007; Tisdell & Thompson, 2007).

During her shopping trip, Paula talked in depth about multiple sources of information and messages, and how she goes about determining what warrants her consideration:

> We proceeded to the end of that aisle, rounded the corner, and stopped in front of the soy beverages. She had been drinking them for health benefits but has more recently heard from one of her friends that you shouldn't drink too much of them. . . . I asked about how she decides which source of information to trust when making her shopping and consumption decisions, and she said, "I don't listen to the radio or the TV. I don't have cable." She said that some friends send e-mails about things that they have learned, but sometimes they are more radical than she is. . . . She also talked about how people, including her, will "pay a premium" to shop for products and brands that claim trustworthiness; however, ingredients such as cane sugar are often present in these products and, even if they are organic, can make these claims debatable. Paula thinks that people can be naïve and overly trusting, at the same time as they are judgemental. In the end, she thinks that you have to trust yourself, "my taste buds, my own decisions. I don't like to follow people blindly." She will go back and forth with friends about opinions and resources for information.   —shopping trip excerpt, Paula, August 14, 2007

Just as academics have rules to help them gauge trustworthiness of information, so, too, do participants have strategies to gauge the trustworthiness of products, producers, and retailers. As Paula explained, trust is often earned, in large part through personal contacts and experience.

The issue of trust arose again during a focus group exercise in which I asked participants to talk about something that they had brought with them. I was interested in hearing what they knew about those objects, how they had learned about them, and what those objects said about them. Jocelyn talked about the bag of fair trade coffee that she had brought with her:

JOCELYN: But, you see it says FT?
KAELA: Fair trade.

JOCELYN: Yeah.

KAELA: And, but they write that on themselves, do they?

JOCELYN: Well, I believe them.

KAELA: Right, because you know them.

JOCELYN: Oh, I've gone there lots, for years. I mean, partly because it's a local business that's owned by the two of them.

KAELA: Well they just don't preprint a lot of labels, I guess.

JOCELYN: No! No, he wrote that on there. And I said, I'd like you to write it just the way the sign is. But he told me something kind of interesting. They have a lot of trouble getting the fair traded [*sic*] coffee, because sometimes the people who could be selling to them sell directly to someone else, because they get more money 'cause they've cut out the middle man, so to speak, but you can't call it fair traded unless it comes through that system. . . . And the other thing he said was it's very dangerous—uh oh, I meant to find out where Sumatra was.

CARLA: Sumatra?

JOCELYN: Do you know where it is?

CARLA: Indonesia.

JOCELYN: Okay, well this isn't from Central [America], because we can't get the kind of coffee we want from Central America, because, you know, it isn't FT, fair traded, because, well, union organizers get murdered. That's what he said. Anyway . . . So I was in there for about 20 minutes, there weren't any other customers. . . .   —focus group excerpt, May 17, 2007

Jocelyn's comments reiterate the importance of personal relationships in learning, particularly in establishing trustworthiness. Jocelyn has concluded that she can learn from independent retailers who reliably provide the goods and services that she seeks and who take the time to talk to her and answer her questions. This realization does not mean that people and information judged trustworthy by participants was always correct, or that participants reached accurate understandings of their shopping options and choices. For example, some participants concluded that, by buying clothing produced or food grown in Canada, they were avoiding the problems of sweatshop labour and poor treatment of agricultural workers.

In contrast to sources of information and messages deemed trustworthy, advertising and popular culture, especially television, were considered suspect and were used judiciously. Five participants mentioned that they do not have a television set or that, if they have one, they use it to watch movies and do not subscribe to cable or satellite services. As the excerpts below illustrate, participants used a range of tactics to discriminate between valid, critical information or messages and invalid, hegemonic information or messages about shopping and consumerism:

JOCELYN: We don't have television, so . . . that's on purpose. . . . It fell off the table when our two youngest children were 3 and 4, and we just thought, hey, let's just not pick that up again [*laughs*]. So we haven't had it since then. They're 40 and 41 now.   —interview excerpt, January 22, 2007

KAREN: Well you know, what's interesting, we don't have a television. And when we go away on holiday and stay in a hotel and sit around and watch TV in the evening, we're always shocked by the commercials and can't believe that somebody would, you know, get sucked in by this. . . . Like, does this stuff really work? It seems so alien to us 'cause we're so unused to watching commercials. And . . . thinking about maybe in magazines, but generally the magazines I read don't have advertisements for, like, average consumer products.   —interview excerpt, February 2, 2007

SEAN: When I watch TV I keep the clicker going. The idea is to never see a commercial if I can avoid it. . . . I try not to see them when I read media. . . . Like, trying to avoid all advertising if at all possible. . . . I turn away from commercials on TV as much as possible. So I try and avoid messages as much as I can.   —interview excerpt, March 24, 2007

KAELA: So, if you, when the sales come, when you see ads about this great big huge sale, does that do anything to you, or—?

SARAH: No, usually I say, do I need that? . . . And then, if I need it, then I'm, like, Oh perfect! Maybe I should make a time to actually go look at it. . . . But if I don't need it I'm, like, Screw you, screw you, screw you [*chuckles*]. 'Cause . . . it's all, like, propaganda to me. . . . I don't know, just, capitalism is about control, right? We have to consume in order for capital to go around. And then I've been reading a lot lately about how, like [*sighs*], the only way to keep capitalism running is for everyone to be in debt, because then they have to work, you know. And then if they work then they consume, and, I don't know, it's this big vicious cycle, right? So, to me all those sales and stuff are, like, buy, buy, buy, buy, buy, buy more!!! Keep the capitalist system running!   —interview excerpt, April 24, 2007

Despite participants' frequent disdain for advertising and popular culture, some of them did acknowledge that, from time to time, cultural products offer a critical view. Ellen mentioned having seen an independently produced feature film that helped her expand her analysis and knowledge base:

> ELLEN: Like, I remember thinking after watching *Maria Full of Grace*, I could never buy flowers that are brought in from Latin America ever again. If they're not locally grown, and even if they're locally grown, God knows what conditions they're grown under, but that's, that's the ugly side of life that you won't normally, we wouldn't be interested in, we just want to see Diane Keaton and Jack Nicholson fall in love. You know [*chuckles*] . . . like, really fluffy stuff when you go to the movies. And these are things that are actually, like, whether it's a central theme in the movies or getting woven in as, like, a side story or a 2-minute aside, you're seeing more of it, and it's changing the way you go out into the world and shop and be and behave.   —interview excerpt, April 24, 2007

Likewise, corporate marketing materials, while suspect, can also provide new information:

> ALICE: There's a store in Edmonton called Earth General Store. . . . It's a little store, and does that guy ever put a lot of effort into researching the products that he sells and on his website! He will, he has this long diatribe about all these different products and why he carries these now and why he used to carry these and he doesn't carry them any more. He found that, for example, there was one, something, . . . and he said, There's just too much stuff in their, in their advertising, so I don't sell their stuff anymore. . . .
>
> KAELA: And did you just discover it on a trip back to Edmonton?
>
> ALICE: Yeah, yeah. He's really into community. He supports a lot of causes, environmental and otherwise. And he has things on his website.   —interview excerpt, February 17, 2007

This excerpt is helpful, because it indicates that, even within advertising and popular culture, there are multiple, often clashing, discourses that consumer-citizens can encounter.

On top of the critical information and resources that help them learn, participants also outlined some of the dispositional qualities that have helped them move toward critical learning through their shopping. These qualities—shared by academic researchers— include curiosity, caring, resourcefulness, intuition, scepticism, and determination.

> LINDA: I think I do waste a certain amount of time finding out about all these different things, just because I'm so interested in different ideas people have, and I think I'm just obsessed with reading or addicted to it or something. I mean I'll read shampoo bottles if they're sitting there and I have nothing else to read, but it, there's a certain, I guess, it's writing style. Some people are just really persuasive in the way they write. And I guess it's also kind of combining with other things I've read, like, if I've read a book that was, you know, well referenced and, and had arguments really well laid out, and then, you know, finding other things, people's opinions and blogs and what-not that sort of dovetail into that and give you other further things to think about.   —interview excerpt, April 29, 2007

While describing how she learns and makes decisions, she said that she doesn't need a long explanation "on why it's bad to have a whole stash of plastic bags; I know it's bad, but [my husband] would probably get all the facts and figures." She goes by "common sense" and described herself as "intuitive." Often, it's a matter of what comes across her radar screen (shopping trip excerpt, Claire, March 22, 2007).

> ELLEN: I just do research. On the internet, I talk to people, I read whatever I can. Read labels. Talk to, you know, talk to people who are better informed than I am. . . .   —interview excerpt, April 24, 2007
>
> MARY: How do you go about finding it? Well I'm a, I'm a voracious reader of popular media, some popular not so much, but you know the daily newspaper. But also a lot of independent media. And so I, I go about finding out the information by way of those things that come across my radar screen. My radar screen's pretty big.   —interview excerpt, March 14, 2007
>
> AMITAH: I think, then, it was generally accepted that ads tell you what's new and exciting, a very simplistic view of advertisements . . . which, now I'm a little more cynical around advertising [*chuckles*], and I tend to, I would say rebel against them, but definitely I have boundaries, psychological boundaries around advertisements.   —interview excerpt, February 21, 2007

These excerpts articulate the varied ways in which participants learn to learn through and about shopping. For the most part, they were discussing a form of learning that can be considered incidental, although in a slightly different way from Foley's (1999, 2001) discussions. While Foley focuses on the incidental learning that occurs in highly organized collective action, the participants in my study talked about incidental learning, which can also occur in the course of more unorganized activities of daily life. Like Foley's notion, though, the discussion in this section continues to illustrate how incidental learning is informal and unintended. In the following section, I also outline how incidental learning might become more formalized and purposeful as learner-shoppers become researcher-shoppers.

Conducting Research

> JAMES: Okay, if I'm looking at a particular item to buy, depending on the item, if it has a heftier price tag attached to it, I tend to do a little more research on, or a little more exploring, going from shop to shop. . . . You have to wade through a lot of information that may be out there or, even if it's conflicting reviews of the product, and then trying to assess a decision based on someone else's review, that's one set of difficulties.
> —interview excerpt, March 28, 2007

In the preceding section, I discussed how participants learn to learn through their shopping in an ongoing, often ad hoc way. Sometimes, though, questions might arise during the shopping process that cannot be answered immediately. When the question seems important enough, a more directed, purposeful approach to learning might be undertaken. Regardless of their disciplines or fields, all academics need to develop a contextually relevant and appropriate approach to conducting research. Academics learn how to do that in the formal setting of the university, and participants in this study described their learning in the informal setting of shopping. Having to wade through this volume of information certainly does prove to be "one set of difficulties," as James suggested. All shoppers in contemporary Western shopping settings have to learn how to cope with "musak," announcements, signs, and other distractions; critically minded shoppers who are interested in the links between consumption and globalization additionally learn how to sift through a constant hum of facts, opinions, warnings, and advice as they try to understand their shopping options and decisions. As they do this, they become a kind of researcher; indeed, they develop the skills of a bricoleur, who seeks information in new and novel places and incorporates it into knowledge construction.

The participants in this study talked about diverse research topics and questions, as well as sources of information and messages that have been brought into their research and analyses. Just as they used a range of resources for their ongoing incidental learning, participants also noted the many sources of information in their more deliberate research, including mainstream news and alternative media, education and advocacy organizations, and websites, documentaries, workshops, forums, and books.

> CARLA: I don't usually ask the company for any information, I go looking for it myself.
>
> KAELA: So how do you go—?
>
> CARLA: The internet. . . . Or I go to the library, and look up, there are, there are books out there. I had one, I can't remember, what was the name? I can't remember. That basically took lots of organizations throughout Canada and rated them on, based on labour, based on, you know, the expectations from workers. Things like that.   —interview excerpt, February 13, 2007
>
> AMY: I think for me when I don't understand the label or anything I won't buy it. And then I'll go home and do my own research.
>
> KAELA: Okay, so what kind of research? Online?
>
> AMY: Yeah, mostly it's online because there's so much information on the web nowadays.   —interview excerpt, February 7, 2007

Bonnie pointed to a bag of edamame and said, "I really like these edamame, but they'll all shipped from China." When I asked what the issue was with items from China, Bonnie explained that she had concerns about the levels of pollution there, especially for food items, as well as the environmental implications of shipping from so far away. She said that she had seen a documentary that showed Chinese agricultural workers putting little plastic bags over individual fruits to protect them from surrounding pollution. But she also noted that some food items that are certified organic are grown in China, and she likes to think that she can "trust" the certification. "I need to do more research," she concluded. I asked her how she goes about doing such research, and she explained that she does a lot online, searching for nongovernmental organizations, including Chinese NGOs that are pressuring the Chinese government on environmental issues.   —shopping trip excerpt, Bonnie, February 5, 2007

These excerpts suggest that participants can be motivated to research products and brands for various reasons. They might have had
a long-standing interest in and involvement with a certain issue, as
Bonnie has had with organics and vegetarianism; they might also find
new questions emerging while they are in a store, as Amy describes.
However, their findings and conclusions are always partial and influenced by their own experiences and biases as well as the constraints
of information. Bonnie noted the threat that pollution in China poses
to food grown there and the precautions that agricultural workers
take to protect the food, but she did not mention the threat that pollution poses to those workers or whether precautions are taken to
protect them. Perhaps her focus during that portion of our conversation was on recounting an image that she had seen in a particular
documentary film. Later in her shopping trip, I asked her about the
issue of labour standards and recorded the following exchange in
my notes: "She also mentioned labour standards as a concern in factory farming. I asked her, 'Are you concerned about labour standards
as well?' 'Oh yeah, that's why I won't buy non-organic bananas or
chocolate or coffee,' she answered" (shopping trip excerpt, Bonnie,
February 5, 2007).

Bonnie did have an awareness of some of the social justice issues related to agricultural workers, at least outside Canada in the countries
where bananas, chocolate, and coffee are grown; however, whether
this awareness carried over to agricultural production in Canada and
whether these social-justice issues were equal considerations to environmental degradation remains unclear from her comments.

Like those of any researcher, participants' conclusions are also always
tentative. There is always more to research and learn, as new information becomes available and participants are exposed to new experiences
and points of view. Using their skills as researcher-shoppers and learner-
shoppers, participants respond to the multiple demands and pressures
that become apparent in the arena of shopping. As I explore in the following sections, these generic skills help participants undertake learning
that might be related to three particular disciplines or fields: philosophy,
education, and geography.

Weighing Value(s)

For the most part, participants described themselves as middle class.
This class identification gives them a certain amount of choice in the
arena of shopping, but they are aware of the constraints to this choice.
Being able to assess value for the money that they are spending when

they shop is a primary value for participants, one learned early in life and typically from mothers. Recalling one side of the Western stereotype of the female shopper as the caretaker of middle-class family and home (Bowlby, 2001; Rappaport, 2000; Shor, 1980), participants' early shopping experiences were strongly gendered, as well as classed, from a young age.

Regardless of their class, age, or background, participants agreed that globalization seems to bring more shopping options to them. They also agreed that, because of a combination of new technologies and critiques of consumerism, they are in the paradoxical situation of having access to more information about individual products and consumption in general, even as information remains partial and suspect. On the one hand, media reports on diet and nutrition, as well as food labels with ingredients listings and nutritional information are helpful to many consumers. On the other hand, as participants noted, claims made on labels can be misleading, details can be confusing, and important information can remain obscured. This reality makes learning about shopping tricky and complicated, especially for shoppers who are concerned about globalization. Not all values respond directly to concerns about globalization; however, in the absence of reliable marketing and media reports, participants' personal values become important benchmarks for learning about and assessing the desirability, or value, of an item for sale.

Having a sense of the "going price" for items was helpful, and participants all described practices such as watching for sales or going to stores known for their competitive pricing. During her shopping trip, Kerri described herself as "a frugal shopper" (shopping trip excerpt, Kerri, April 29, 2007). The following excerpts, from both interviews and shopping trips, exemplify the role that value-for-money played in participants' shopping options and practices:

> ALICE: I don't shop all that much but when I do it's usually when all the sales are on.   —interview excerpt, February 17, 2007

> Paula returned to the issue of price as a factor in her shopping. "I look at flyers at home," she said and, if [they are] for a regularly purchased item, tries to time her purchase for the "next time it's on sale." For example, that's how she approaches buying something like toilet paper. —shopping trip excerpt, Paula, August 14, 2007

> Claire raised the issue of price again, commenting that she'll look at prices and, if an item she wants is expensive and not on sale, she'll come back on one of the customer appreciation days that Capers regularly has.   —shopping trip excerpt, Claire, March 22, 2007

Many participants talked about their early experiences of shopping with their parents, typically their mothers, who taught them about the importance of value-for-money and emphasized organization, restraint, and quality:

EDDIE: She taught me to buy at the lowest price, things like wait for a sale, like walk to the store at the other end of the mall to see what's there.

KAELA: So comparison shopping, value, those kinds of things.

EDDIE: Yeah. And being content instead of always buying the latest trend.   —interview excerpt, April 11, 2007

JOCELYN: So what I learned from her, for instance, she'd give me a list and some money. . . . And she would tell me how to pick out to be sure she gave us the best of the fresh vegetables. . . . I mean maybe some of the things I learned from her were good after all.   —interview excerpt, January 22, 2007

JULIE: And in that sense of not buying things on credit or buying what you can afford to buy, that I learned from my mother. Absolutely.   —interview excerpt, March 14, 2007

In these comments, participants confirmed Zukin's (2005) point that the immediate financial cost of an item is an important consideration, but it is only one sort of value that participants weigh in making their shopping decisions. ☼

Quality itself can be indicated in different ways. For participants, freshness, taste and appearance, brand name and reputation, personal experience with products, manufacturers and retail chains, and friends' recommendations have helped measure quality:

NICOLE: And to this day it still is somewhat, you know, if I see a two-for-one-sale I'm going to go for that. I'm not necessarily driven by, like, the name brand. Mind you, if I saw a no-name brand toothpaste I probably wouldn't buy it. So this is something that has probably been ingrained in me, is that if it's, if it's not flashy, if it doesn't have graphics, if it's not a household name, a trustworthy name, I'm not going to go for it.   —interview excerpt, February 17, 2007

> ☼ Learning to shop is more demanding than figuring out what things to buy. The most important part of shopping is learning to steer your way between what you desire and what you know is right.   —Sharon Zukin (2005), *Point of Purchase: How Shopping Changed American Culture*, p. 35

LINDA: And occasionally if I wanna go to Old Navy I go to Metrotown.

KAELA: So Old Navy you'll go to for, sort of, for price?

LINDA: For, yeah price is mostly it. T-shirts and pants because their pants do fit me. Although recently Reitman's has been the better choice for pants 'cause Old Navy pants always fall part.

KAELA: Okay, so quality's an issue.

LINDA: Yeah. I mean, I hate hemming so I don't want something that the hem's gonna fall apart. There are shops that I don't shop at all, because their hems fall apart within three weeks [*chuckles*]. —interview excerpt, April 29, 2007

Paula described having tried some of the packaged grain products, and finding them not as good as home made; so she doesn't buy these products. But she has used the organic broths and liked them. She finds them convenient, because making broth is so time-consuming, and very tasty and will buy them when they are on sale. —shopping trip excerpt, August 14, 2007

The considerations for Thérèse are taste, price, and family health. She pointed to the salad dressings that were opposite us, noting that she could get them for a much lower price elsewhere. We walked over to the bananas, priced at $1.18 per pound, and Thérèse commented that they were three and a half times as expensive as the conventional bananas for sale at the little neighbourhood Chinese grocer down the street from her. "But I'll get some 'cause I need them," she said. . . . —shopping trip excerpt, Thérèse, February 9, 2007

As these excerpts indicate, indications of quality can be both concrete and subjective. Tastiness, healthfulness, fit, and convenience might help participants evaluate quality and value-for-money.

Often, the search for quality and other values compete with finding good value-for-money and participants' own financial constraints. As Tamara asked: "How do you judge, how do you judge value? Do I want to spend that much on this product? Is that important to me, that I get a good quality product?" (interview excerpt, March 23, 2007).

This conundrum becomes especially apparent in participants' comments related to contemporary globalization. For example, almost all participants talked about balancing the need to spend money judiciously when shopping, with an awareness of the problems posed by production and shipping of items from different parts of the world. Products brought from the Global South to the Global North might carry relatively low financial costs, when compared to items produced in the Global North, but they are often perceived to carry greater ecological and human rights costs. Whether or not participants' understandings of these costs are accurate, the following excerpts exemplify how value-for-money and other types of values arise in and complicate the shopping processes of these shoppers:

> She thinks that "community spirit" is now exploited, because of the insistence on cheap labour to keep prices down. When I asked her more pointedly, she agreed that this was part of globalization. Globalization, in her opinion, is having an adverse ecological effect: "The plants, the fields—it's all suffering. . . . And money can't buy you out, because the fields can only sustain so much." She mentioned the destruction of the Amazon and suburban growth as examples of how globalization poses an ecological threat.   —shopping trip excerpt, Paula, August 14, 2007

SARAH: I try and stay away from the more expensive stores anyway, the ones that where I know where there's all that child labour crap going on.   —interview excerpt, April 24, 2007

AMITAH: And in terms of being one of the important qualities, now I would, where I am at in my life now, I would definitely say that considering sustainability and global impacts in shopping choices is important, too.   —interview excerpt, February 21, 2007

NICOLE: So I do selective buying, and I try my best to buy locally and educate myself on that.   —interview excerpt, February 17, 2007

Similarly, James talked about an item that he had purchased recently during the focus group that he attended. For the introductory focus group exercise, when I asked participants to discuss something that they had brought with them, James shared the following anecdote:

James: I just bought this today and, not thinking at all about the focus group tonight. . . . I wanted to get back into the habit of taking my lunch with me when I go [to work]. . . . And . . . to try and get away from using disposable plastics. And also the potential of plastics which leach whatever possible contaminant into food. But mostly to get away from the disposable nature of the plastics. . . . So . . . I headed down to Mountain Equipment Co-op, of course, and I was looking for, I had my thought originally set on a stainless steel set. And there was only one left and the little binder clip that was on it was not working properly, the spring on it was gone so it was hanging half open. And then I noticed these ones ☼ and I thought, Oh. Well, I looked at the weight, thinking, while the stainless steel set is nice there is this one. It is, these ones were twice the price, but being conscious that I would also want to use it for camping and backpacking and as we replaced items or acquired items for doing that activity, wanting light-weight materials because I know what it's like carrying around too much weight. So just to shave off a little bit here and there. So twice the price, half the weight. Of course they had the plastic resin ones which I was concerned about, the polycarbonate plastic, like, with Nalgene bottles leaching, bisphenol-A, I think it is, so the health matters, but also recognizing that they're a lot cheaper, and thinking, well, the plastics, they were made in Canada, whereas these were made in China. The metal is mined, so is that any better than having the plastic resin material which is being used? It, it just [*chuckles*], anyway, I, I settled on these more for the light-weight aspect of them then that they were reusable, and that's pretty much it.   —focus group excerpt, May 10, 2007

In this anecdote, James relayed the range of questions and considerations that can go into what initially seemed like a simple, straightforward shopping task. He also clarified some of the nuances of incidental learning. Its nature as partial and tentative can be frustrating when decisions have to be made; however, those elements also help shoppers with critical agendas develop the ability to continue asking questions

☼ James's anodized aluminum cutlery, focus group, May 10, 2007

and seeking solutions. This is, it seems to me, the meaning of lifelong learning, which is so often shunted aside in the hegemonic neoliberal discourse of lifelong learning as a never-ending formal education project.

Another value that was mentioned by all participants is convenience. Convenience can be manifest by participants' decision to get into their cars and drive to a setting where a range of items can be found during a single shopping trip. During her interview, Alice noted: "I often do go to a mall, I will admit, because it's all in one, convenient, it's a good variety" (interview excerpt, Alice, February 17, 2007).

Alternatively, convenience can be manifest in neighbourhood-level shopping. For her everyday shopping, Sharon dislikes the thought of "having to . . . travel long distances, especially driving a car just to . . . you know, shop. So I shop along Commercial Drive. . . . So, I tend to go into a lot of small little stores in that area" (interview excerpt, Sharon, December 19, 2006).

So far in this section, I have outlined value-based learning that stems largely from intellectual reflection about personal experience and material circumstance. Some adult educators have begun to explore the links between spirituality and learning (English, 2000; hooks, 2003; Tisdell, 2000). I incorporate spirituality, as well as emotion and sensuality, into my conceptualization of holistic learning and consider how it might influence learning about and through shopping. ✿

✿ "What would Jesus buy?" Graffiti on Fort Street, Victoria, March 16, 2008

Although I did not ask questions about spirituality, several participants raised this topic when discussing the values that figured in their
shopping and their attempts to become "good" shoppers. Most overtly
among participants, Eddie spoke about how he connected shopping to
spirituality and religious convictions: "And so then, like, I wouldn't go
and buy just any Bible. It has to be the right Bible. But yet, you know, so
I wouldn't want to support a certain Christian organization by buying
certain Bibles" (interview excerpt, April 11, 2007).

While Eddie attached shopping to spirituality in a particular, formalized way, for other participants, spirituality helped them develop
a broad critical analysis of hegemonic consumerism and motivated a
broader form of resistance to it and corporate globalization:

> CARLA: I know there are some [critical consumption organizations] . . .
> and actually I e-mailed one to some friends of mine who are
> Catholic, because . . . I thought, I mean, as someone who is
> Catholic, it's problematic to me that often it doesn't seem to
> come up in discussion. And I found this one group that did, and
> I thought, oh, I have Catholic friends who are also interested in
> this sort of thing, so I e-mailed it off to them.   —interview
> excerpt, February 13, 2007

> AMITAH: Probably in my teenage years, [I] went through the whole
> rebellion phase. I am an Aquarian [*laughs*], so I don't know
> if that has anything to do with it. But, I don't know. It just
> kind of, I can't say that there was one defining moment.
> The first sort of introduction to anything around that was
> making the switch to eating organic food.
>
> KAELA: And when did that happen?
>
> AMITAH: That happened probably in, when I was about 19. I got
> married fairly young and just interested in spirituality,
> interested in health, sort of exploring meditation and
> healing and food and nutrition.   —interview excerpt,
> February 21, 2007

Paula then shifted to a broader level again. "Why am I here?" is a
central question for her. She answered her own question, saying that
it's "a spiritual thing." She is "constantly on a search" and described a
kind of learning as a never-ending process (shopping trip excerpt, Paula,
August 14, 2007). During her interview, Mary also referred to the centrality of spirituality in her learning how to engage in shopping and
consumption:

KAELA: And how did you, how do you think you arrived at those criteria [for making shopping decisions]? . . .

MARY: Two primary things. One is, is the political analysis and, and economic analysis that I've had for 30 years, a little more than that. And the, so that's the one side, that's always been there. And the layering of the exceptions would be probably through my understanding of certain Buddhist and Hindu precepts.

KAELA: So it's a mix of political and economic analysis and spirituality.

MARY: Yeah.   —interview excerpt, March 14, 2007

Whether or not individuals manifest their spiritual affiliation within an organized religion, spirituality fosters an "imagined community" (Anderson, 1991), which I explore in the next chapter. For now, I will say that spirituality can bring certain values into the mix for critical shoppers and can help them respond to the often conflicting demands of different values.

There were still other types of personal experiences and feelings that helped some participants understand shopping differently. Paula described looking for natural cleaning products "because I've seen . . . [pollution] in the streams" (shopping trip excerpt, Paula, August 14, 2007) while on camping trips. Amitah thought that moving away from her native Britain to Canada and marrying while still fairly young encouraged her to distance herself from her family's mainstream attitude toward shopping and consumption and adopt a more emotionally and spiritually based perspective. Linda explained the importance of "having children and knowing that, you know, what I leave behind is up to them to deal with" (interview excerpt, Linda, April 29, 2007). Alice recalled having her own business helping clients clean out their clutter:

ALICE: And that was also a really good lesson for me in seeing how buying and buying and buying would not bring you happiness. I worked with some very wealthy people who were absolutely miserable. . . . And they had all this stuff around them. And I, you know, I would go in and think of all these people, I'd just recently returned from Guatemala, and I just thought of all these things that could have been used by people in developing countries that are just sitting there collecting dust. So what I started to do was offer to take those things to charity. . . . That really helped me and it helped them.

KAELA: It helped them as well?

ALICE: Yeah, they didn't feel guilty.

KAELA: So . . . you brought that into your business.

ALICE: Mm-hmmm. But I noticed that those clients had so many magazines in their homes and it was fuelling their, I feel it was helping them fuel this desire for more and more and more. And they had home décor magazines and beauty magazines and you name it.   —interview excerpt, February 17, 2007

Julie shared a poignant anecdote about an episode that followed her mother's death and helped put consumerism and consumption into a new perspective for her:

JULIE: Well, there's this little story. When my mother died, my sister and I went to help my father get organized. And we said, do you want us to deal with mom's personal stuff? And he said yes. And I, my mother was 77 years old, I took everything she owned that was a personal items in two Safeway grocery bags. And my mother would tell you she never did without. And I went home, and I looked in my closet and I thought, this is obscene! But, you know, there were more things in my closet that I could wear probably in a month. And it was, it was almost, it was, what's the word, it was an epiphany or something, you know.   —interview excerpt, March 14, 2007

Julie's excerpt is especially helpful in clarifying that not only can learning be incidental and holistic, it might become evident in an instant realization, just as it might over a protracted period of research and investigation.

One participant, Karen, spoke about *creating* value through consumption, rather than *finding* value through shopping. For her, value was connected to the amount of time that purchased items lasted and, in the case of clothing in particular, the amount of wear that they could withstand:

KAREN: I guess since I don't like shopping, if I find something I like I tend to wear it until I absolutely, it's falling apart and my husband says, you really can't be in public in that any more [*laughs*].

KAELA: So you really do sort of consume the things that you buy.

KAREN: Well I try to, yeah, definitely. I think because I try to spend a lot of time, you know, figuring out what it is that I need,

> and what is, what I feel most comfortable buying, that once I
> spend all that time buying it I don't want to get rid of it very
> quickly.   —interview excerpt, February 2, 2007

As Karen clarifies here, value is not just a quality apparent on a price
tag or a label; rather, it involves a process of projection of her future
use of an item and an ongoing decision to consume it fully before dis-
carding it.

Sometimes, values are not just multiple, they are competing and seem
to defy a happy compromise. During his interview, James outlined some
of these competing values:

> JAMES: There's the economic factor, the trying to be aware of where
> a product is produced or a food is produced and comparing
> that against personal values of . . . knowing that the workers
> are being paid justly or that it's produced locally or as near to
> local as possible. Sometimes they conflict. So there's something
> I think I saw last week. The organic food item which is coming
> all the way from California versus the locally produced but
> non-organic item. Which is better for you? Ultimately. Or
> which, I guess because it's comparing, it's trying to compare
> values. Personal health versus environmental impact.
> —interview excerpt, March 28, 2007

Fair conditions for workers who produce items, the environmental
costs of shipping, the personal health risks and benefits of consuming food products—these were all matters of concern to most of the
participants, and they complicate shopping decisions as learning about
them deepens.

For most participants, values lead them to particular shopping places
as well as items. Sixteen participants related how shopping at thrift
stores, buying second-hand, or participating in "swaps" helps them
weigh and balance value-for-money with other sorts of values, including
environmentalism. Participants used these tactics to acquire items from
clothing to sporting equipment to cars:

> AMITAH: I like to go to thrift stores for clothes . . . partly because, I
> don't know why. [*pause*] I think part of it is [*long pause*],
> because, hmm, I don't know why I like to go to thrift stores
> [*chuckles*]. I think it's not, I don't have a lot of disposable
> income. . . . That's part of it. The second part of it is, is I kind
> of feel like it's recycling.   —interview excerpt, February
> 21, 2007

ELLEN: If I need a pair of jeans or a sweater or I'd rather buy it used than off the rack or through a clothing exchange or something.   —interview excerpt, April 24, 2007

KAELA: Do you go to Craig's List for, what do you go to Craig's List for?

EDDIE: Free stuff, so that we don't have to put stuff in the landfill.   —interview excerpt, Eddie, April 11, 2007

KAREN: And for a long time I would only . . . shop at second-hand shops, because I felt at least that had lower impact and I was giving . . . to a charity that was maybe working locally.   —interview excerpt, February 2, 2007

SARAH: So I think that, and I also bought a used car, which is, like, a '91 [*chuckles*], right. I don't think I'll ever buy an expensive, like, a new car.   —interview excerpt, April 24, 2007

NICOLE: Well, my roommates and I and my friends realized that why would you go to Ikea when you're just, even though the prices are low, you're still buying a new product, you're still bringing that, whereas there's tons of things that are still out there. You can buy a shelf at Value Village, and it will act with the same function.   —interview excerpt, February 17, 2007

Although several participants appreciated finding ways to spend responsibly and efficiently, the mostly middle-class participants in this study were aware that they have many material and social privileges because of their class position. Still, they find that some options are foreclosed to them. The following excerpts provide some examples of how participants have encountered and learned to respond to this reality in the course of their shopping:

Opposite us was a stand with toilet paper. She pointed to the packages of . . . toilet paper made from recycled paper, priced at four rolls for $5.49. "That would last like a day in our house," she explained, as an example of why it would be too expensive to shop at [this store] all the time.   —shopping trip excerpt, Thérèse, February 9, 2007

At the sale boxes, I chatted with Annette. . . . We talked about food—buying organics especially. . . . She would like to buy more organics, but finds them cost-prohibitive. Considering her options, she suggested that she could buy and eat less so that she could choose organics more often, but that's not a trade-off that she's prepared to make. When it comes to clothes, size and finding things that are affordable and fit are other issues. Sometimes she will buy used or second-hand items. She explained, "If I want to buy cheap stuff, you have to go to SuperStore

and Walmart. And what does that say?"   —shopping trip excerpt,
mothers' network, May 19, 2007

A few participants approached this dilemma by arranging their values
into a hierarchy. Carla and Mary summarized how this helped them
weigh values and options and make decisions:

CARLA: So it's all sort of give and take and weighing these, balancing
          these. . . . There's no easy choices, and so if you can't, if you
          can't afford these organic foods, look closely at the label
          anyway, maybe you shouldn't be supporting that form of
          organic. If it's local and it's organic, then, you know, go, and
          if you can afford it, you know, power to you. But there's
          definitely a hierarchy for me when it comes to buying things.
          Like, for food, if it's organic and local it's first, if it's local
          but not organic it's next, and so on down the line. I do try
          to follow some rules that way.   —interview excerpt,
          February 13, 2007

MARY: So I guess what that means is that what shopping means to
          me is it becomes more and more a process of acting out my
          ethics. And you know, there are exceptions to that, one of
          which would be the buying of gifts for others. Okay, so my
          sister and niece, I went to visit not long ago, before Christmas,
          and I went into a mall and quite happily bought them each
          a nice coat. So the ethics of that in terms of consumption are
          not there. The ethics . . . around love and support of family,
          you know, supersede the political. But that doesn't happen
          very often.

KAELA: Okay, but, so there's something about ethics, but also
          sometimes conflicting ethics, conflicting ethical priorities.

MARY: No they don't conflict. . . . It's just that one is a higher, one
          is a higher order. . . . Love of family and need to support
          family is a higher-order ethic than an ethic of not consuming.
          —interview excerpt, March 14, 2007

Likewise, Vanessa recalled having heard advice to construct a hierarchy to guide food shopping. If a choice had to be made between local
and organic produce, the preference, according to the expert, whose name
she could not recall, was to buy locally rather than organically; however,
Vanessa had had cancer and felt strongly about the important personal
health benefits of organic produce. These processes illustrate "a kind
of juggling, conceding on one aspect and holding fast on other issues"
(Connelly & Prothero, 2008, p. 126) that surfaces as participants, like

the green consumers who participated in Connelly and Prothero's study, ask, "what practical concessions have to be made to one's cherished ideals, and how does all this play out" (p. 126).

In some instances, a happy resolution might be possible, but it can demand an inordinate commitment of time. As Jocelyn explained, values enter into shopping decisions: "[t]hey enter in, they don't always win" (interview excerpt, Jocelyn, January 22, 2007). Recalling a time when he and his partner were seeking a sustainable, healthy alternative to synthetic mattress covers, James had the following exchange with me during his interview:

> JAMES: So when we would go to other events, such as the Fibre Arts Festival on the Sunshine Coast, we happened to come across a vendor that sells all kinds of wool products, including mattress covers. So we were keeping it in mind, knowing the price, thinking, you know, you suffer a bit from sticker shock, but once you think about it and think about what goes into it, then you can kind of see how the value plays out. . . . But then there's concern about, okay, are these, we had also heard that some sheep on farms are, the way that they keep infections or pests under control is to actually expose the sheep itself to some, some other insect or pest repellent. . . . And so, because I don't know enough about it, and trying to find out some information but then there's also the matter of time. . . . The amount of time it takes to investigate.   —interview excerpt, March 28, 2007

Contemporary globalization, in which production and consumption are so heavily mediated by multinational corporations as well as local conditions and personal circumstances, might be heightening awareness of some values and exacerbating the clash between different values. One important lesson that participants have learned about weighing values, then, is that the scale is rigged to favour certain values, especially those connected to time and money, over others.

Developing Literacy

As the preceding analysis established, people bring a multitude of values to their shopping; however, shopping decisions are made on the basis of information as well as values. Shoppers are confronted with information throughout the shopping process. As shoppers increasingly attend to a range of issues and concerns, they seek and deal with additional types of information that they garner through various research and education strategies. In confronting information in their shopping practices, shoppers develop a form of literacy as part of their learning-through-shopping. For the participants in this study, this literacy is both technical and critical.

All shoppers encounter labels and ingredients lists. During their interviews and shopping trips, participants talked about reading these materials to help them weigh the values outlined above. For example, Violet talked about wanting to buy "cruelty free" and safe cosmetics: "Brand names, cosmetics, and beauty products, if they test on animals, and I'll also look for organic ingredients in beauty products as well" (interview excerpt, April 4, 2007). For Karen, organics and fair trade are important considerations, and she has learned to look for information about these things on labels and packages: "Right. It, definitely, like fair trade, I like to . . . look for that symbol because . . . it's not just marketing, it is reliable, yeah, from what I've seen" (interview excerpt, February 2, 2007).

Shoppers who take the time to read labels and lists encounter unique language and symbols. One example of these is the "best before" date stamp on food items:

> She then turned to the shelf of pies behind us and chose a boxed slice of pie. She checked the dates on it, and explained that she always does this. Whatever she buys has to be fresh, because it "has to be able to keep for a few days."   —shopping trip excerpt, Paula, August 14, 2007

When one is shopping for prepared or processed food items, there is even a possibility of encountering words that are unfamiliar. During several shopping trips, participants and I took note of labels and ingredients and wondered about what some of them really meant:

> We walked around the corner and stopped just after we entered the next aisle. Sandy looked at some packages of taco mixes. She looked first at a package . . . and noted that the first ingredient listed was maltodextrin. "What's maltodextrin?" I asked. "I don't know," she answered. Then she picked up another brand's package, this time labelled organic, and said, "Here's a package I can recognize the ingredients on but it's like five bucks! For five bucks I'll leave it."   —shopping trip excerpt, Sandy, February 5, 2007 ☼

This incident illustrates how shoppers might regularly encounter words that they have not learned in school. Nor do they see or hear them in everyday conversations, media accounts, or popular culture. Understanding a simple ingredients list can require an elementary

> ☼ Maltodextrin is a polysaccharide that is used as a food additive. It is produced from starch and is usually found as a creamy-white hygroscopic powder. Maltodextrin is easily digestible, being absorbed as rapidly as glucose. The CAS registry number of maltodextrin is 9050-36-6.
> Maltodextrin can be derived from any starch. In the U.S., this starch is usually rice, corn, or potato; elsewhere, such as in Europe, it is commonly wheat. This is important for celiacs, since the wheat-derived maltodextrin can contain traces of gluten. There have been recent reports of celiac reaction to maltodextrin in the United States. This might be a consequence of the shift of corn to ethanol production and its replacement with wheat in the formulation. . . .
> Foods containing maltodextrin may contain traces of amino acids, including glutamic acid as a manufacturing by-product. The amino acids traces would be too small to have any dietary significance.   —"Dextrin," retrieved May 12, 2008 from *Wikipedia*, http://en.wikipedia.org/wiki/Dextrin

technical literacy from fields such as chemistry and dietary science. Beyond ingredients, labels can contain other new information. Sometimes this information continues to test and expand shoppers' technical literacy, as it did during Kerri's shopping trip:

> Kerri stopped near the beginning to look at vinegar. She looked at a bottle of organic vinegar and read the explanation on the label about how non-organic vinegar can be sourced from wood chips. She and I commented that we had never heard this before and, in fact, had never really thought about what vinegar comes from.   —shopping trip excerpt, Kerri, April 29, 2007

In addition to technical literacy skills, critical literacy skills are developed, especially by shoppers who question the hegemonic status quo that advertising and other consumerist materials reiterate. Product packaging and other marketing materials that proclaim the benefits to consumers who buy that product are scrutinized. This relates to Linda's qualified admiration for Ikea® (and its self-promotion) as a responsible corporation that uses sustainably sourced wood, even as it continues to sell products with questionable environmental and personal health effects. Shopping trips were especially useful in providing examples of how participants both extract information about a product—from labels, packaging, and price tags—and treat such corporate communications as suspect:

> We then turned around and walked a few steps to the yoghurt section in the long dairy fridge. Bonnie reached for one single-serving berry

yoghurt . . . and put it in her basket. When I asked her about that choice, she pointed out that, as a vegan, she had only three choices from all the products in that large fridge. One she found "tastes like chalk," and she preferred the one that she got because it's locally produced. The third option is produced in Ontario.   —shopping trip excerpt, Bonnie, February 5, 2007

She first picked up a box of . . . toothpaste, read the packaging, and put it back on the shelf. "I have to deal with my price comparison issues," she said, and picked up a box of [another brand of] . . . toothpaste which was on sale for $3.99 and was less expensive. . . . She read the box, noting that its ingredients list include blue green algae. We wondered about the benefits of that, and I asked her if she thought that such things might be gimmicky. She acknowledged that marketing can be used that way in natural products, as it is in conventional products. She looked at the box again, and read the information about the advantages of blue green algae, which according to the information on the box, has antiseptic qualities. She chose the . . . toothpaste [that was on sale].   —shopping trip excerpt, Kerri, April 29, 2007

We had rounded the corner and were standing in the next aisle, looking at bread. Vanessa reiterated that you can't assume that an item labelled "multi-grain" is entirely whole grain, as she looked at one loaf of bread. "People get sucked in by that," she added. I had noticed that she spent a fair amount of time reviewing the information on labels and asked, "Do you normally read a lot of labels?" "Yes!" she answered. —shopping trip excerpt, Vanessa, May 4, 2007

In terms of her learning, she talked about reading labels carefully and the importance of understanding them. Often, though, it takes her time to learn about something. For example, she used to think that palm oil was an ingredient to avoid because of how people talked about it, but then she learned that "it's not really bad."   —shopping trip excerpt, Claire, March 22, 2007

Claire's learning about palm oil is instructive of how both technical and critical literacy must be developed by critical shoppers who hear conflicting messages. For several years, consumers have been advised that certain dietary fats are healthier that others. Palm oil was not considered a healthy option, although more recent thinking has refocused consumers' attention onto hydrogenated oils and advised that, as Claire suggested, palm oil is "not really bad" after all. However, as I have learned, ecologists are concerned that renewed acceptance of palm oil is now wreaking havoc as palm tree planting and harvesting heightens threats to already vulnerable environments and communities in the Global South. ☼

☼ Palm oil is used in a wide variety of foods including margarine, cooking oil, crisps, cakes, biscuits, and pastry. Vegetable oil production worldwide totals 95 million tonnes per year, and palm oil is the world's second largest after soy oil. Although being entirely GM free and having the highest yield per hectare of any oil or oilseed crop, it is recognized that there are environmental pressures on its expansion to eco-sensitive areas, particularly as oil palm can only be cultivated in tropical areas of Asia, Africa, and America. Palm oil sales are set to rise dramatically particularly in the growing economies of China and India. Sales in Europe have also grown recently due to palm oil being an effective substitute for partially hydrogenated soft oils such as soy oil, rapeseed, and sunflower, thereby eliminating trans-fatty acids from many products.   —Roundtable on Sustainable Palm Oil (2004), "New Global Initiative to Promote Sustainable Palm Oil," p. 2

Like any literacy, the literacy of shopping is socially contextualized, so that information's meaning and importance are constantly renegotiated. New information, as well as shifting considerations of health and well-being, mean that participants are developing their literacy skills continually. What is important, as Tamara pointed out, is questioning information and messages. Speaking about the disparity between multinational corporations' messages and practices, she made the following comments:

> Tamara: They have a good message, like, Gap was the first one to give, first sort of retail, to give benefits to same-sex marriages . . . to recognize them. You know, Starbucks is, you know all the . . . they do all this community stuff. And I mean they have shitloads of money, of course they can. But they treat the farmers like crap. And the same thing with Shell. Gets awards for environmentalism, they you know, they have positive employment things in their, in their stores. And, and we'll employ people with, with disabilities and barriers and so [on]. But, you know, go to Nigeria and see how they treat Nigerians and people that live around their wells. Starbucks, I mean watch Black Gold. It's fricken' amazing to see, you know they say we spend $2.00 a pound on our coffee. Well, who's getting paid that? Not the farmer, man. Because, like poverty, phenomenal poverty. Yet, you know, they have such a lovely message on our end. And that's what I don't like.
> —interview excerpt, March 23, 2007

One of the realizations that surfaced for some participants is that, even with a well-developed shopping literacy, they have a limited capacity to build their knowledge about products and brands. In part, this limitation results from corporate desires to withhold certain information and the development and use of confusing jargon to promote products. During Kerri's shopping trip, for example, we encountered rice labelled "nutra-farmed," as opposed to organic, and grapes labelled "certified transitional" (shopping trip, April 29, 2007). ☼ We chatted about the possible meanings of these phrases, which were outside our familiar lexicon.

Increasingly, this limitation to knowing and learning is also linked to the growing complexity of chains of production that make it difficult even for producers to know the minutiae of how the objects that ultimately bear their corporate monikers are actually made. A few participants, including Linda, noted this shopping dilemma:

LINDA: I guess at this point mostly I'm looking at the information that's already provided, usually with the packaging. So when I go to a store . . . for clothing, I'll look at washing instructions and sometimes I look at provenance, if it says made in wherever, although usually it's made in sweat shop central, so I've, it's just kind of, and you never know if it was made in a sweat shop or if it was made in a decent place.

KAELA: . . . So labels sometimes give you information and sometimes don't give you real information.

☼ Certified transitional grapes, shopping trip, April 29, 2007

LINDA: Yeah, I mean they give you . . . the basics, but you don't really know how much further into that you need to go.
—interview excerpt, April 29, 2007

For shoppers concerned about the links between their own consumption and globalization, being literate demands that they attend to and deal with technical claims and information critically, always anticipating answers to an existing question as well as the next set of questions.

Constructing a Shopper's Geography

In the preceding sections I have outlined participants' generic learning and research processes. Participants also discussed their more particular learning about the role of competing values around material well-being, social status, cultural norms, and personal ethics, as well as jargon and logos that carry meanings related to status, ethics, product quality, and price. In addition to this already complicated learning, shoppers also build a particular approach to and knowledge of geography. ☼

Consistent with the phenomenon of globalization, this knowledge relates to both local and global geography. On a local level, participants learn to map the city in terms of areas and stores where they like to shop, and areas and stores that they try to avoid:

> Claire mentioned that she has gone back to eating meat, but only poultry or lamb. She recalled that she always had liked turkey at Christmas. She still avoids conventionally farmed poultry though, and thinks that lamb is safer. She said, "I love places like Aphrodite's—you don't even have to worry" about what to order there because it's all organic/free range.
> —shopping trip excerpt, Claire, March 22, 2007

☼ **human geography** Geography is generally defined as the science which describes the earth's surface, its form and physical features, its natural and political divisions, climates, and productions. This broad-ranging discipline has numerous points of contact with the natural and the social sciences. In the case of the latter the sub-discipline of social or human geography is particularly pertinent.

Human geography was pioneered by the French geographer Paul Vidal de la Blache (*Human Geography*, 1918). A broadly similar development of social geography occurred in Germany, influenced by Friedrich Ratzel. Unlike physical geography, which is concerned principally with the description and analysis of the land, human geography focuses on the interaction between human populations and the territories in which they live. . . . —John Scott and Gordon Marshall (2005), *Oxford Dictionary of Sociology*, p. 280

Preferences for neighbourhoods or stores related to various considerations, including convenience of location, availability of products at attractive prices, and experiences of a shopping environment as pleasant. During her shopping trip, Claire noted that, if she is unable or unwilling to spend the money to buy specific items at natural products stores, she checks more mainstream drug or grocery chains to see if they are available at lower prices. A small number of participants mentioned Ikea® as a retail chain that helps them balance these values, or retail co-operatives, such as Mountain Equipment Co-op® (MEC), which specializes in outdoor gear and clothing:

CARLA: Another thing about MEC though, is they actually have organic products that are reasonably priced. So if I want an organic T-shirt, chances are I will find it there. If I want hemp pants, I got a really great pair of hemp pants there. I find clothes shopping at MEC not as painful as other places. So MEC and so I guess also Ikea sort of for the same reasons.
—interview excerpt, February 13, 2007

LINDA: We were going to buy a bed, too . . . and so my husband went .and bought us the cheapest bed at Ikea. So now we have a bed. But, yeah that's one place where I wish I didn't shop, but I know they are at least are making an effort at stewardship and so on.

KAELA: How do you know that about them?

LINDA: It's on their website and some of their advertising and catalogue. And in their store, like, they'll sort of highlight different issues, but I know that most of it is not very good.

KAELA: In terms of quality you mean or their—?

LINDA: Oh quality and provenance and things like that. . . . But I know that they are making an effort.

KAELA: Okay, so you say they're making an effort.

LINDA: But not on all their products. . . . So, you know, a lot of their inex–, their less-expensive stuff is particle board and stuff. So, you know, the fact that they're doing forest stewardship stuff is kind of irrelevant when you're buying particle board, but it's certainly, you know, better than some other places that are just, you know, putting together pine crap and, I don't know. It seems to be slightly better.

KAELA: So then why do you wish that you didn't buy there?

LINDA: Because I, well, partly I wish I had money to go elsewhere.
—interview excerpt, April 29, 2007

JULIE: So I have learned over the last couple of years by deciding to shop, where I can, through co-ops that are locally owned and locally controlled and have a whole set of principles that underlie them. And related to that, trying to support women-owned businesses and locally owned businesses and environmentally friendly businesses. So just being kind of mindful about not just how much something costs in a financial sense or an economic sense but how much of a contribution is that method of selling making to the rest of my life.   —interview excerpt, March 14, 2007

Many participants talked about avoiding large mainstream stores when doing grocery or clothes shopping. The following excerpts explain some of the participants' reasons for preferring or avoiding different places, and how they have established a sense of local shopping geography:

SHARON: I like to go to the local shops in my area, and if I've got time to do that I quite enjoy it. I take my little cart, you know, and I have my favourite little veggie store, and I have my, you know, bakery, and I have my other kind of places that I go to. And it's a bit of a, sort of, outing, and I, 'cause I like to do that rather than going to the big stores.   —interview excerpt, December 19, 2006

SARAH: So I, like, if I lived over on Commercial Drive I would never probably go to Capers or Choices, right? So, a lot of it is convenience, because these places are close to my house. If I do shop at a regular grocery store, for example I would go to IGA, though I don't like Safeway, I just don't like the layout of their food, and I don't like the selection, I think it's really poor for the stuff that I'm looking for. And I like to go to markets, too, and I will, like, drive to a market. Like, I . . . bike or whatever, like, I'll walk down to Granville Island. . . . And for clothes and stuff . . . I would just go to specific stores. Like, I'll go to, like, the hemp stores or the second-hand stores.   —interview excerpt, April 24, 2007

KAELA: Do you regularly shop in particular areas of the city or in particular stores and if so which ones and why do you prefer those places?

ALICE: I often do go to a mall, I will admit, because it's all in one, convenient, it's a good variety. But for a change I do like to support these local Chinese grocery stores.

KAELA: So the, so some sense of the importance of community-based businesses. . . . Small, local, locally owned, locally controlled.

ALICE: Yeah. However, what I've found though is when there was
a period of my life where I really wanted to support those
and just shun any kind of big business. And I found that
there was a huge price difference, and I just could not afford
[it]. . . . Those are tough decisions where you know you can
get it at Walmart or Staples, but, in the big picture, how am
I, what kind of a legacy am I leaving? And I do, I do shop
at Walmart but seldom. I really cut down on shopping there
because of all the stuff that I hear. But there are some things
that I need from there that I know I can get and I need them
quickly. I go there once maybe every three or four months, if
that.   —interview excerpt, February 17, 2007

As these excerpts indicate, convenience becomes a factor in a shopper's geography in complex ways, depending on neighbourhood, the
items sought during a shopping trip, and the availability of resources
such as time and money. A shopper's local geography takes into account multiple values, including one's material need to balance value-
for-money with other needs and wants.

Beyond a very local geographic knowledge, many, although not all,
participants also articulated an understanding of and concern about
global geopolitics and human geography:

ALICE: There are a lot of things to consider when you're buying
things. Is this environmentally, is this gonna have a negative
environmental impact? Who has made this? That's the first
thing that comes to my mind. When I see made in China,
I'm just, I, my heart kind of goes out. Should I really be
buying this? I have to admit I don't look at everything that
I'm buying to see where it's made, but if I happen to see
that it's made in China I wonder what kind of conditions
they were working under, how much they were being paid.
If I see something and I figure, oh this probably costs about
a dollar and it's 50 cents, I think, ahhh, what did this
person who made this, what did they make? And so when
somebody tells me, oh I got this great deal on something,
I really, that's the first thing I think of—that person, could
they feed their family that night?   —interview excerpt,
February 17, 2007

SARAH: I try and stay away from the more expensive stores anyway,
the ones that where I know where there's all that child labour
crap going on. So I, like, I don't mind, like, Lululemon is
expensive, but it's a Canadian-made clothing, right? So I don't

mind paying extra money for something that's Canadian made 'cause I know it's not the sweatshop stuff, right?
—interview excerpt, April 24, 2007

These excerpts suggest the extent to which awareness and concern relates to campaigns that have been garnering attention in media and popular culture. Notable among these is the discourse of Canada and other countries in the Global North as places where reasonable regulations and statutes foreclose the possibility of exploitive work conditions, such as sweatshops. Another discourse is that of fair trade, which often brings the conditions of production in the Global South to the attention of consumers in the Global North and combines a commitment to human rights and sustainability. One participant, Tamara, worked for an international development non-government organization with a particular interest in labour rights and the coffee industry. Violet was familiar with the Ten Thousand Villages® shops, which support fair trade and small-scale artisan projects in the Global South, and made a point of shopping there; Alice volunteered there.

However, even the most conscientious shoppers are not fully informed. Just as participants' literacy is limited, so, too, is the knowledge of the geography that they develop. Sarah implied that buying "Made in Canada" products avoids the encouragement of continued use of so-called sweatshop labour; however, there are certainly sweatshops here in Canada and other countries in the Global North, as well as in the Global South. As Jocelyn explained:

JOCELYN: You know, I don't understand totally what it means to buy something from Chile, for instance. . . . I know about some places, but I don't know about every place. I have much better, I mean, that'd be food. If I were buying clothing, time and again I'll look at these tags and they'll say, made in Sri Lanka, made in Turkey. And you wonder who did that. Now, as a Canadian, I can only say that when I see things and it says, made in Canada, I'm pleased. Now whether this makes any sense or not, I don't know. . . .

KAELA: Well do you think that? How easy do you think it is to know?

JOCELYN: I think it's not easy, or I would know! I mean, I'm not a totally uninterested and stupid person. But it seems to me that it's not easy to know. Or else I've blocked it out for some reason, there's that possibility. When you go shopping to buy clothes, for instance, you, I usually decide first whether I like it before I look and see where it was

> made. . . . And then, if it's made in India, I don't know
> if I have a hesitation, because I think about, you know,
> there's so many arguments on both sides. They say those
> people would be on the street starving if they weren't
> making these bedspreads or whatever it is. So I don't know.
> —interview excerpt, January 22, 2007

Part of a knowledge of global geography for shoppers, then, has to do with the early stages in the chain of production and consumption—where items are produced. The considerations for participants as they develop this sense of geography are both personal and political. While Jocelyn spoke about human rights concerns in the excerpt above, there was also talk about the link between geography, shopping, and personal health:

> NICOLE: So I question where it's come from. That's one of my most
> important, where it's come from. I'm also interested in
> the ingredients. I feel organic on specific things such as
> GMOs [genetically modified organisms], so corn, I'm not
> necessarily, wheat I know is not GMO as of now in Canada,
> so I'm not as wary about that. And if it's fruit and vegetables
> I'll take local over organic, because in some sense, like, . . .
> anything that's grown in Vancouver, I feel it's lower in price,
> but I know that it's also coming from the local [farms], so.
> —interview excerpt, February 17, 2007

On top of buying organics, she also mentioned her preference for buying locally grown/produced food, because she thinks it's better for the consumer, the people growing it, and the environment (shopping trip excerpt, Claire, March 22, 2007).

Turning to the left and standing in front of a refrigerated section, Jody picked up a cucumber and looked at the label, which indicated that it was grown in Mexico. "I was in Mexico," she said, "and you couldn't find one of these things to save your life." I asked her what she thought that was all about, and she said that they must be exporting their produce for more money. She added that she had found a similar thing with tomatoes—she could buy them in Mexico, but they looked to be of poor quality. She moved over a few steps and picked up a package of snap peas that were marked as having been imported from China. "This makes me crazy! They don't have clean irrigating water!" (shopping trip excerpt, Jody, February 12, 2007).

The excerpt from Jody's shopping trip establishes how shopping, globalization, and geography are remapping the world so that both the benefits and the problems of production and consumption are being redistributed across local, national, and regional borders. While the problems—from food shortages to sanitation and safety—remain concentrated in the Global South, the consumers in the Global North reap the benefits of new types and seemingly unlimited amounts of food and other items. This recalls Beck's (1992) conceptualization of the "risk society" that has developed in the Global North and demands that consumer-citizens self-reflexively deliberate the risks attendant to globalization. ☼

Still another part of this knowledge relates to later stages in the chain—where items are made available locally to the consumer. One distinct point about developing a shopper's geography was raised during Amy's interview. Born and raised in Singapore, Amy reflected on possible reasons for the lack of attention to provenance in this unique Asian country:

AMY: I don't think they, no one really thinks much about what you buy. Oh, okay, we do think about it when we buy it, but we have never thought about what's behind it. We just assume it

☼ The distribution of socially produced wealth and related conflicts occupy the foreground so long as obvious material need, the "dictatorship of scarcity", rules the thought and action of people (as today in large parts of the so-called Third World). Under these conditions of "scarcity society", the modernization process takes place with the claim of opening the gates to hidden sources of social wealth with the keys of techno-scientific development. These promises of emancipation from undeserved poverty and dependence underlie action, thought and research in the categories of social inequality, from the class through the stratified to the individualized society.

In the welfare states of the West a double process is taking place now. On the one hand, the struggle for one's "daily bread" has lost its urgency as a cardinal problem overshadowing everything else, compared to material subsistence in the first half of this century and to a Third World menaced by hunger. . . . Parallel to that, the knowledge is spreading that the sources of wealth are "polluted" by growing "hazardous side effects". This is not at all new, but it has remained unnoticed for a long time in the efforts to overcome poverty. This dark side is also gaining importance through the over-development of productive forces. In the modernization process, more and more destructive forces are also being unleashed, forces before which the human imagination stands in awe. Both sources feed a growing critique of modernization, which loudly and contentiously determines public discussions.

In systematic terms, sooner or later in the continuity of modernization the social positions and conflicts of a "wealth-distributing" society begin to be joined by those of a "risk-distributing" society.   —Ulrich Beck (1992), *Risk Society: Towards a New Modernity*, p. 20

> appears on the shelf already packaged and ready to go. . . . I
> mean, I never thought about who is making it and for what
> reason and who takes the money. . . .
>
> KAELA: But as you say, that's a, I mean, there's much more of a
> presence of things like organics and fair trade in, in Canada,
> or in Vancouver, let's say, than in Singapore.
>
> AMY: . . . I don't know, I think it's because we don't actually produce
> anything anyway. So it's like production doesn't really affect
> us. We're very used to being consumers and not producers.
> —interview excerpt, February 7, 2007

Having lived most of her life in an extreme example of a consumerist society, Amy learned about the importance that geography had in her practice of shopping and consumption.

Other participants who had spent most of their lives in North America recognized that globalization's multinational corporations are posing both opportunities and challenges for shoppers as they develop a sense of the local geography and its ties to global phenomena. The current interest in buying locally grown and produced food and other items can be contrasted with the ability to transport desirable goods across great distances efficiently or the increasing preponderance of multinational retail chains. As Barndt's (1999, 2002) Tomasita project also illustrates, understanding where and how things originate, why and how they arrive in local stores, and where retail profits go is all part of the geography lesson for critical shoppers. Karen summarized this point in her comments:

> KAELA: You . . . talked a lot about production. What about retail? So
> what about local stores, who owns the stores you shop in,
> stuff like that? Does that enter into your decisions?
>
> KAREN: Yeah, for sure, definitely, I mean that's one thing that does bother
> me about going to Capers. I mean they're an American company,
> but then there are other things that sort of, yeah, it's one of those
> trade-offs.   —interview excerpt, February 2, 2007

Even as globalization and multinational corporations make desirable products more accessible to shoppers, they violate some of participants' central values and priorities.

Two types of experiences seem especially important for fostering participants' learning in this regard: having travelled, worked, or lived abroad and having grown up on or around a farm.

> MARY: So, for example, I've spent a fair bit of time in India where,
> unless you're very very wealthy, and even then, people do not,

consumption is not the drug that it is here.   —interview excerpt, March 14, 2007

ALICE: Hmmm, what's the difference? I think I've lived in, I spent time in a developing country, and that set me on a different course, helping me appreciate what we have here. —interview excerpt, February 17, 2007

KAREN: When I graduated university, I worked, uh, I don't know if you've heard of Frontier College?

KAELA: Yup.

KAREN: I was a labourer-teacher. And . . . I've always thought about Frontier College and how it impacted my teaching practice and so many other aspects of my life. I don't think I ever thought about how it impacted how I feel about . . . shopping. . . . But definitely, working on a farm, I became more aware of, you know, issues around food production and how definitely our cheap produce is possible, because there are these impoverished people from Mexico who are willing to come and spend eight months a year doing totally back-breaking work. . . . And then also looking at, and also just being with the other people who were labourer-teachers with me. There were, like, eight of us together in, in a house, that tended to have more unconventional ideas about things like that. I did learn a lot from them and from, uh, I guess just working with these guys from Mexico as well, you know, people who had so little. And I went to Mexico afterwards and travelled around and, uh, went to visit the guys that we had worked with. And one of them, uh, borrowed his friend's truck and took us on a tour of some things he thought would be interesting. And one of them was a T-shirt-making factory. It wasn't really a factory, it was just like somebody's house. And they'd constructed this really ramshackle kind of area in the back, and there were these women who just, you know, sewing T-shirts. . . . And again that's something that I, you know, never had exposure to before. And it really made me think about, you know, the process of where it comes from. The people who are involved.   —interview excerpt, February 2, 2007

VIOLET: Well a couple of years ago I was an intern . . . for an . . . umbrella organization for all the agencies and NGOs working to, to fight child labour. And it's something that I really didn't take very seriously until I spent time with them and I did research for them.   —interview excerpt, April 4, 2007

In these excerpts, participants described how experiencing life in other societies changed their perspectives on life in Canada. In particular, spending time in a society in the Global South provided helped participants question a Western hegemonic ideology such as consumerism and all the common sense that accompanies it in Canadian society. This recalls Barndt's (2002) anecdote about a Canadian participant in her study who was able to spend some time with Mexican migrant workers on an Ontario farm. Even though she had not travelled to the Global South, her direct experience with citizens from Mexico who are living temporarily in Canada deepened her understanding of the politics of consumer-citizenship and globalization. ☼

Participants who had spent time on a farm also related that experience to their approach to shopping and consumption. Karen's experience enabled her to consider the ties between production and consumption, the Global South and the Global North, and structures and cultures of globalization and consumption. That experience became the basis for her continued learning when she travelled in the Global South and illustrates how learning occurs through and builds on lived experience. A couple of other participants talked about how having grown up around a farm became tied to their own consumption and helped them to appreciate issues such as food security.

> She then talked about going to the farmers' market and enjoying that experience of shopping. "I like to buy in-season as well, that's important to me as well," she explained. She added that buying locally grown produce is important, too, and that "I like to support farmers as well. . . . My dad's parents had a farm" where they grew produce and farmed animals. "I had that growing up," she explained. She helped her grandmother sell the produce, and, she added, "I know how hard they work." To her, buying directly from agricultural producers is

☼ While I would have loved to take Marissa to Mexico to meet some of the women at the other end of the tomato chain, that was not possible. But I was able to invite her along for a visit with Mexican migrant workers picking Ontario tomatoes two hours west of Toronto. . . . A few days after this visit, I received a nine-page letter from Marissa, filled with rich observations and analyses of what she had seen and felt: "The highlight for me was sharing this life experience with my 'sisters' from Mexico. . . . They all looked older than I had anticipated. . . . I was very interested in the relationship between the workers, government and 'patrons.' Such a powerful word relegated to a farmer who hires you as a picker."
—Deborah Barndt (2002), *Tangled Routes: Women, Work, and Globalization*, p. 238

a way of "giving back to people that I don't even know because I appreciate them." She then talked about having gone recently to a blueberry farm to buy berries. She had observed, "They have all these East Indian women working. . . . I see them, I know they work hard." By buying directly from the farms, she feels that she is supporting them. She also thinks that "It's more humane to be integrated with your food" and that seeing and engaging with producers helps her achieve that. She also spoke about other influences on her shopping and consumption, including travelling and a constant analysis that she undergoes in daily life and that gives her "an understanding of where people are coming from."   —shopping trip excerpt, Paula, August 14, 2007

When I asked about what first prompted her to pay attention to shopping and consumption in this way, she explained that her mother had grown up on a farm. Vanessa could see that the family farm was "becoming non-existent," and that encouraged her attention to local provenance and control.   —shopping trip excerpt, Vanessa, May 4, 2007

Although Vanessa and Paula had spent a lot of time in their youth on family farms, they developed different analyses of shopping and consumption, as well as globalization in general. Paula did not distinguish between her grandparents' family farm and the farms near Vancouver. Her statement that shopping at farms helps her understand "where people are coming from" seems like an ironic use of a colloquial expression rather than a literal recognition that most of these workers have come here from the Global South as immigrants or temporary migrants. ☆ In contrast, Vanessa acknowledged that corporate agribusiness was replacing "the family farm." Like Karen, Vanessa attached her personal experiences to social movements and organizations concerned with fair, sustainable production that does not compromise the health of producers or consumers. These two participants discussed buying shares in a co-operatively owned and operated farm, and Vanessa had served on the board of directors of another co-operative.

This section shows that all participants approached shopping with concerns and questions that connect their shopping to globalization. Some illustrated a more critical tendency to challenge the structures underpinning both Canadian society and globalization. Considerations of convenience, affordability, and consumers' health compete with human rights, community cohesion, and ecology as participants construct a knowledge of geography that encompasses the local and global landscapes, and the producers and consumers who inhabit them.

☼ Historically, BC has drawn on specific groups from poorer, non-white countries as a source of cheap labour, for dangerous occupations, with inferior employment and citizenship rights in Canada . As part of this history, early in the 20th century, BC farmers successfully petitioned the federal government to admit South Asians and Japanese to work in agriculture. . . .

BC farmers in the Fraser Valley rely largely on immigrants from the Punjab to replenish their labour force. Today, about 90 per cent of these farmworkers are Indo-Canadian; the majority are women, many in their 50s and 60s. Most immigrated to Canada as parents or grandparents under the federal family reunification program, sponsored by their Canadian children or grandchildren. . . .

While most BC farmworkers in the Fraser Valley are Indo-Canadian, Citizenship and Immigration Canada (CIC) began in 2004 to curtail this traditional source of labour by restricting the admission of parents and grandparents in its family reunification program. This policy shift contributed to the labour shortage that had been emerging in BC agriculture. Accustomed to paying seasonal harvest workers no more than the minimum wage (and sometimes less) and providing substandard working conditions, BC farm owners faced a labour shortage in the early 2000s. The provincial government did not raise minimum wages and standards in agriculture to attract workers to meet these shortages. Nor did the federal government seek to maintain or increase the number of immigrants that traditionally serviced this sector. Mechanization of farmwork proceeded slowly. Instead, the horticultural industry lobbied the federal and provincial governments to gain the right to hire temporary migrant workers. In 2004, BC joined the Seasonal Agriculture Workers Program (SAWP) by agreement with Canada and Mexico to give Mexican workers temporary employment visas in agriculture, with wages slightly above the provincial minimum.   —David Fairey, Christina Hanson, Glen MacInnes, Arlene Tiger McLaren, Gerardo Otero, Kerry Preibisch, and Mark Thompson (2008), *Cultivating Farmworker Rights*, pp. 13, 14

Summary

In this chapter, I have traced an analysis of what participants learn to do through their shopping processes. This analysis both consolidates and extends the concepts related to informal adult learning that have been central in this inquiry. In presenting how participants have learned to learn, to conduct research, to weigh values, to develop literacy, and to construct a geography, I have established that shopping is always a site of technical or "instrumental" learning (Mezirow, 1995 in Sandlin, 2005a) and is indeed also a site of incidental, politically charged learning for some people. Through my analysis, I have also illustrated why the activities of everyday life and the incidental learning that accompanies them deserve the serious attention of adult educators.

As well, I have demonstrated that such learning has multiple dimensions. Incidental learning is, as critical adult educators such as Foley (1999, 2001) and Stephen Brookfield (1998, 2005) imply, an intellectual process; however, as others argue, it is also an emotional, sensual, and spiritual process (Dirkx, 2001; English, 2000; Hayes & Flannery, 2000; hooks, 2003; Tisdell, 1998, 2000). Furthermore, it is a relational process that is both solitary and social, involving a wide range of "intellectuals" (Gramsci, 1971). Finally, learning-through-shopping is multidisciplinary, as critical shoppers attend to research, philosophy, language, and geography. Participants have learned about learning and the processes of research; they have learned about the tensions between material constraints and a wide range of values; they have learned how to read and use language and symbols; and they have learned about place and space.

This incidental, holistic learning about what to do in shopping is complex and limited. A comprehensive conceptualization of learning appreciates experiential knowledge, but Brookfield (1998) notes that it is naïve to think that personal experience always leads to more critical understanding. ☼ This concern resurfaces in Chapter 7, where I concentrate my analysis on learning about change. Although I have touched on issues of identity and making change in this chapter, I have yet to fully address the questions of who participants learn to be and how they learn to make change. It is to these questions that I turn my attention in the next two chapters, building on my presented analysis and introducing new theoretical facets in my remaining analyses.

☼ Simply having experiences does not mean that they are reflected on, understood or analysed critically. Neither are experiences inherently enriching. Experience can be construed in a way that confirms habits of bigotry, stereotyping and disregard for significant but inconvenient information. It can also be narrowing and constraining, causing us to evolve and transmit ideologies that skew irrevocably how we interpret the world. So a learner's experience can represent a barrier to, rather than an enhancement of, learning.   —Stephen Brookfield (1998), "Against Naïve Romanticism," p. 128

INTERLUDE V

My Dinner at Moyo's

In December 2007, I attended in a conference in Stellenbosch, South Africa. One night, delegates had dinner at Moyo's. Moyo's promotes itself as an African dining experience. The main dining tent also covers a stage at the centre and a stage at one end, and a couple of treetop dining platforms accommodate more intimate suppers. A pathway guides diners through the gift shop and into the dining area, where the buffet tables piled high with "African" dishes run alongside the length of the tent. The food was tasty (and I appreciated the variety of non-meat options), the service was pleasant, the entertainment—"African" drumming, dancing, and singing on the centre stage and Reggae music on the far stage—was lively, and the other delegates at my table were wonderful company. Still, I felt uncomfortable and confused throughout the evening.

Shortly after we were seated, we were greeted by a young woman who offered to paint diners' faces with geometric designs. I felt increasingly drawn into more than a dinner out; this was fast becoming a spectacle of consumption, and I didn't understand that spectacle or my role in it. Who were the musicians, dancers, and face painter, and which, if any, racial, ethnic, or cultural heritage were they representing? What was their role in this evening? How was I implicated in a commercial appropriation of culture, ethnicity, and race? What was "African" about all this? I declined the face-painter's offer.

During this inquiry, and especially since my dinner at Moyo's, I have thought often about what race, ethnicity, and culture mean for me. As a Jew, I understand myself as white/non-white/ never black. At some points in history, Jews have been engaged actively in Western cultural life and have been regarded as part of the social mainstream. At other points in history, efforts have been made to distinguish Jewish minorities. Nazism is the most notorious example, but the ghettos in European cities preceded Nazism by centuries. Back here in Canada, only two generations ago, universities had quotas restricting the number of Jewish students. My father grew up in Toronto, where signs in the Beach community advised "No Jews or dogs allowed." Today, in Canada as elsewhere in the Global North, Jews of European descent are racialized as white, and I live with the advantages afforded by whiteness. Still, the Medieval image of Shylock, the greedy Jew, continues to resonate culturally, and from time to time I've listened to other people relate with a measure of satisfaction how they managed to "Jew down" a contractor at home or a vendor at a vacation-spot marketplace.

6

Growing Up with, Growing Into, Growing Out of: Who Participants Learn to Be

KAELA: How did you learn about shopping and how to shop, and where do you think your ideas about shopping come from?

SARAH: Probably a lot from my mother [*chuckles*], to be honest. Probably a lot to do with when I moved out when I was really young, when I was 17, and I had to learn really early how to manage my money at a low-paying job before I went back to school. Right? So I think a lot of it had to do with my money management as well. Can I afford to buy clothing and pay for rent and buy my groceries and still be healthy and happy, right? And . . . also my mother also taught me a lot about food and being healthy, and I think that's probably why I don't feel bad about spending money on food.

KAELA: So was that, some people talk about growing up in households where they learned, where the real value around shopping was getting, getting good value. Getting a good deal. And other people talk about value in terms of quality.

SARAH: I think quality, yeah. Quality, not price. My parents spent a lot of money on food, and it was never a bad thing. It was always a good thing 'cause we knew it was healthy, good food for us. They did shop at markets a lot for fresh food, but I mean that's still part of healthy food, right? . . .

KAELA: Okay. And what about your, the way that you talked about being interested in the environment, for example? And, and the issue of over-consumption. Was that something that you grew up with or—?

SARAH: I think I grew into that. 'Cause my parents are definitely over-consumers. You know, when there was five of us at home we all had cars. When one car died we bought another one [*chuckles*].   —interview excerpt, April 25, 2007

207

The analysis in this chapter continues from the previous chapter, moving to the guiding questions related to who participants learn to be through their shopping. ☼ As the conversation cited above between Sarah and me hints, participants began learning what kind of shopper they ought to be at an early age. As children, they watched and listened to their parents and other adults, and they grew up with images of shoppers. As they matured, they grew into their own ideas of who they wanted to be as shoppers and grew out of some of their early shopping lessons in favour of new concerns, priorities, and commitments.

☼
- How do individuals living in Canada society, in which a postmodern sensibility and the phenomenon of globalization converge, understand and articulate the implications of their "location" (within cultural milieus, social structures and geographic places) for their shopping options, constraints, and preferences?
- How do they relate this learning and their consumption to citizenship in the nation-state and to "global" citizenship?
- What do participants learn to do, and who do they learn to be as social beings in through shopping?
- How do they learn to make change to their social identities and, more broadly, to structures of social relations?   —selected guiding questions

---

My analysis continues to draw on data from interviews, shopping trips, and focus groups. Concepts outlined in Chapter 2 remain central here. These include ideology, common sense, and the role of intellectuals in everyday learning (Gramsci, 1971); consumer-citizenship and identity; holistic learning, which is incidental (Foley, 1999, 2001), emotional (Dirkx, 2001; Hayes & Flannery, 2000; hooks, 2003; Tisdell, 1998), and, for some, spiritual (English, 2000; hooks, 2003; Tisdell, 2000); an understanding of globalization as an era and a project marked by global tensions and local particularities (Barndt, 1999, 2002; Evans, 2002; Harrison, 2002; Huws, 2004; Katz, 2001; Petras & Veltmeyer, 2001); and the complications of resistance or dissidence (Sparks, 1997). Additionally, I introduce a new theoretical facet through which I view these data as I attend to questions of who participants learn to be as shoppers: Benedict Anderson's (1991) concept of "imagined community."

By "imagined community," Anderson (1991) refers specifically to the nation-state as an imagined political community—and imagined as both inherently limited and sovereign. . . . It is *imagined* because the members of even the smallest nation will never know most of their fellow members, meet them, or even hear of them, yet in the minds of

each lives the image of their communion.   —p. 6, emphasis in the
original

Anderson concentrates on nation-building and discusses media as central to that project. If consumption, like citizenship, is a marker of national identity and part of nation-building, then applying Anderson's concept to shopping is consistent with his original intention. National cultures are constructed around a constellation of values and identities that bind populations together. These cultural values and identities are in turn expressed through discourses and practices of shopping and consumption. Tamara and James suggested these links between shopping and consumption and values and identities during their interviews:

> TAMARA: I think there's tradition there, there's culture. I think that
> has to be respected. You know, as cheesy and as stupid as it
> is . . . it has a sentimental value. And we need that. I mean
> we need those kinds of things. That's what creates society.
> —interview excerpt, March 23, 2007
>
> JAMES: I mean I suppose . . . that would go back to a personal feeling
> of the kinds of values or the way one likes to be envisioned
> or seen by others [*pause*]. I suppose for the most part people
> want to feel, or, I don't know, I'll just try and talk about
> myself. I like to feel that I am part of a community. . . . Because
> of the sense of belonging, the sense of having historical roots.
> At the same time [*pause*], I also do like the sense of, well,
> I like learning, I like discovery, I'm open to discussing, I
> recognize that there are issues with the community in terms
> of social, economic characteristics of it.   —interview
> excerpt, March 28, 2007

As well, emerging discourses associated with globalization, notably around global citizenship and cosmopolitanism, suggest that, while the nation-state retains central importance, it is only one of several possible scales of imagined community. Regardless of its divergent effects, globalization is loosening the weave of the social fabric of nation-states. New information and communication technologies are enabling individuals to connect with one another across borders. Whether they are hegemonic or counter-hegemonic, civil society organizations and social movements challenge Anderson's (1991) understanding of the centrality of the nation-state in structuring imagined community. For that matter, older examples of social organization, including religious institutions, can be seen as the basis of imagined community. As I discuss in my analysis here, spirituality, along with other bases of values and cultural practices, do indeed help structure the imagined communities apparent in the arena of shopping.

A Community of "Good" Shoppers

Thinking about colloquial phrases that are commonly used to characterize shoppers, I built on the varied meanings of the phrase "good shopper." I asked interview participants if they considered themselves good shoppers, and how they would define that phrase. This question, although not always asked verbatim during shopping trips, frequently arose, and data from those encounters are also included in this analysis. Does "good" measure skill and talent? Is it an ethical quality? Is it a sign of conformity? I am not alone in wondering about what the word "good" means in such a phrase as "good shoppers." Participants in this study, as well as cultural studies scholars, also ponder this question. ☼

The simultaneous availability of increasing consumer options and awareness of possible problems with those options gives rise to new questions for participants, even as they make it more difficult to answer questions. During their interviews, some participants, such as James, spoke about the frustration of living with this conundrum and trying to be a good shopper:

> JAMES: Okay, good shopper most of the time. And if it's just in the sense of getting good value then I would say yes. Or at least I do my best at it. The, I think some of the difficulties in evaluating that arise from the, your standards for judging it. . . . So in terms of getting the best value for money, as soon as issues of things like globalization and social justice and environmental damage, as soon as those enter the equation it becomes much more difficult.
>
> KAELA: Okay. So there's value, sort of financial, value for money. . . .
>
> JAMES: Financial value. You have a limited number of, limited amount of funds, and so you want to make it go the farthest. . . . And there's always something on the wish list. . . .

☼ "Good" has been drained of much of its meaning, in these circles, by the exclusion of its ethical content and emphasis on a purely technical standard; to do a good job is better than to be a do-gooder. But do we need reminding that any crook can, in his own terms, do a good job? The smooth reassurance of technical efficiency is no substitute for the whole positive human reference.   —Raymond Williams (1993), "Culture is Ordinary," p. 92

KAELA: Are there other factors that go through your mind or that, that you think go through the mind of a good shopper?

JAMES: Probably how the products will affect personal health.

KAELA: Is that something that you—?

JAMES: Yeah, it's, for the most part of I've been, it was a few years ago, some close friends who are a little farther along in terms of their commitment to buying . . . pesticide-free and organically grown food. Which I've been slowly progressing toward, but there's always the economic aspect of that as well, which makes it somewhat difficult to commit to. —interview excerpt, March 28, 2007

As I discussed in the previous chapter, participants have learned to weigh diverse values through shopping. Not surprisingly, participants mentioned various qualities summarized by the word "good." From "moral" or "ethical" to "sensible" or "reasonable," participants noted the qualities that they found most important in shopping. This variety in qualities corresponds to the variety of phrases used by scholars who write about social movements related to shopping and consumption. These include "demanding consumers" and "political consumers" (Micheletti, 2003) ☼, "consumer voters" and "ethical consumers" (Shaw, 2007), "green consumers" (Connelly & Prothero, 2008) and "critical consumers" (Sassatelli, 2006). ☼ (next page)

☼ "Demanding consumption" or *politisk konsumtion*, is the use of consumer choice for political purposes. This term is recent and Danish in origin. *Politisk forbrug* was coined by the Danish Institute for Future Studies to analyse the intensive involvement of Danes in the boycott of the Shell Oil Company in the mid-1990s for its decision to decommission the Brent Spar oil platform by dumping it into the North Sea. Although the British government granted Shell Oil permission to decommission the platform in this fashion, Shell Oil was the sole target of the boycott. Formally defined, political consumerism is choice among producers and products with the goal of changing objectionable institutional or market practices. These choices are informed by attitudes and values regarding issues of justice, fairness, or non-economic issues that concern personal and family well-being and ethical or political assessment of favorable and unfavorable business and government practice. Political consumers engage individually or collectively in such choice situations. Their market choices reflect an understanding of material products as embedded in a complex social and normative context.   —Michele Micheletti (2003), "Shopping as Political Activity," p. 6

The following excerpts illustrate the breadth of understandings and concerns that participants shared in their conversations with me about what it means to be a good shopper:

> ☼ Increasingly, we witness reports of consumers who actively seek a voice through their purchase "votes" in a similar way to which citizens register their voice through votes in political elections (e.g., Dickinson and Carsky, 2005; Dickinson and Hollander, 1991; Shaw et al., forthcoming). Consumers voting through practices such as boycotting and buycotting are not new but have been increasingly reported over recent decades and can occur with daily regularity (e.g., Friedman, 1996, 1999).   —Deirdre Shaw (2007), "Consumer Voters in Imagined Communities," p. 135

KAREN: I was gonna say, do I think of myself as a good shopper? I don't know, what is a *good* shopper? To my mother being a good shopper would be knowing what the bargains are and going for those things. And she's constantly giving me clothes that she has bought, but then she got home and realized that they didn't quite fit her right or she didn't really like but they were on sale so she had to get them. And if, in some ways I think I'm a good shopper. I tend to . . . think very carefully about what I'm going to buy. My husband and I, my husband more than me . . . does a lot of research on things. We both needed new shoes, and he spent a long time researching which companies were the, none of them were great, but, you know, which one had the best. . . .

KAELA: Like running shoes or—?

KAREN: Hikers, yeah, yeah. Which ones had the best, sort of, uh, reputation as far as sweatshop labour goes. Which ones had, had leather-free. We were, we're vegetarian and tried to, you know. . . .

KAELA: Oh, okay, you tried to find vegan shoes.

KAREN: Yeah, as much as possible. . . . Yeah, and not always easy, but as much as possible we try to do that.   —interview excerpt, February 2, 2007

ELLEN: I feel really good about a purchase when it was made in a responsible way or made locally, I should say. Or, I mean, I'm always looking for a good deal, because I don't have tons of extra money but what . . . [my mom] considers, quote, good shopping, is just a good deal. For me, there's far more, there's many more, like, factors that play into what I consider to be a good purchase or purchase that I feel good about. —interview transcript, April 24, 2007

EDDIE: Morally I think I'm a good shopper, because I try to think about where it's coming from, or at least who it benefits. I am not the good shopper in that I don't always find the good bargains. But I do try to support transit friendly locations and what have you, and I try to make sure I get, that it benefits the community as well instead of just my own, my own well-being. So, yes.   —interview excerpt, April 11, 2007

SEAN: I wouldn't say I'm a good shopper for food, I'd say I'm a *fantastic* shopper for food. So food I really delve into, I really think about where it comes from. Other stuff I'm probably a lousy shopper. Just 'cause I hate it so much I don't put the work into it.

KAELA: Okay. So being a good shopper means putting work into it?

SEAN: Well, really coming to an understanding of what you're buying, what the consequences of. . . . Yeah, here's, let me try and define what a good shopper is. . . . It's someone who knows all the inputs that went into the extraction of the resources, . . . the transportation of the resources, the manufacturing of whatever it is, the transport of the manufactured product, all the waste products that are produced, the packaging, and then the disposal. So to me that's a good shopper, is someone of the, of everything that goes into getting that product into my hand and what's going to happen afterwards.
—interview excerpt, March 24, 2007

These excerpts indicate how participants attempt to become good shoppers who make the "right" shopping choices. Like the excerpts cited in the previous chapter's section, Weighing Values, they clarify that choices involve multiple values and priorities around which participants develop a sense of imagined community (Anderson, 1991). Participants whose spirituality inspired them to shop in a certain way, for example, see themselves connected to other people who share their values and cultural practices, in shopping and in other arenas. If their expression of spirituality includes organized worship, the community of affiliation can be both real and imagined. Likewise, participants involved in secular civic organizations or social movements might think about the values and practices that bond them in common struggles, practices, and convictions to both their actual acquaintances and others whom they have never met.

At first glance, Anderson's (1991) notion of imagined community might not seem to resonate with shopping. While Anderson emphasizes the political authority inherent in the imagined community of the nation-state, hegemonic consumerism, especially when twinned with neoliberalism, treats shoppers as discrete, autonomous agents. This seems incongruent with the links that are necessary for a sense of community. Ironically, this incongruence can heighten when language around democracy and citizenship is appended to shopping. In her analysis of "ethical consumers," for example, Shaw invokes the metaphor of "shopping-as-voting." The counter-argument to her analysis, which Shaw lays out, is made that

> while voting in an election is a private action it is a public phenomenon and is publicly organised. Shopping . . . lacks this public dimension. As such the authors view political consumerism as an individualized act, highlighting that it is not restricted to any formalized design but rather exists as independent of time, space and choice because they are inherently individualistic. (2007, p. 136)

Shopping, according to this second point of view, remains an essentially private process. Inherently manipulative and encouraged in the service of hegemony, it is seen as silencing, rather than promoting, the development of a public sphere.

In contrast to that depiction, some emerging discourses convey an image of shoppers who are united by shared concerns and values. Shaw (2007) discusses ethical shopping as one such discourse and accompanying movement, which, she asserts, fosters a sense of shared identity among adherents. As Shaw further points out, rhetoric of consumer power—"the customer is always right"—constructs shoppers and consumers as sovereign. To the extent that shopping can be constructed as an exercise of sovereignty, Shaw argues, social movements formed around shopping and consumption are also examples of imagined communities. As my analysis in the previous chapter clarified, it is true that even critical shoppers are manipulated, if for no other reason than the unavailability of and, sometimes, deliberate withholding of information. It is, I think, also true that consumerism can serve the existing hegemony by distracting and dissuading consumer-citizens from engagement in formal politics. However, these shoppers are not merely duped into buying and consuming. They use a mix of learning sources and strategies to deepen their understandings of their own consumption and systems that draw them into global relations and processes. Nation-states might be constrained by the forces and structures of globalization, but they retain important powers; so, too, are critical shoppers constrained by social structures and material circumstances, even as they look for ways to exert their power. Ultimately, it is shopping's ability to function as both a conservative and a progressive force that makes it an ideal case for exploring the dialectical tensions and the resulting learning brought to the fore for today's consumer-citizens.

In the following sections, I continue to use Anderson's notion of imagined community and explore how participants have learned about who they are in the particular context of Canadian consumer-citizenship. In this analysis, I return to the concept of the consumer-citizen as a political and social construction. This concept both reinstates Anderson's (1991) interest in the nation-state as an organizing force for imagined community, and ultimately complicates the notion of a singularly ideal, "good" Canadian consumer-citizen.

From Good Shopper to Good Canadian Shopper: The Consumer as Citizen

Returning to the original context of Anderson's (1991) imagined community, I found that parts of some interview, shopping trip, and focus group conversations related more directly to living in Canada among Canadian consumer-citizens. This was not a topic readily pursued by most participants, even though I asked a question connecting shopping to citizenship in the interviews; however, a few participants were eager to discuss the association between shopping and citizenship and how hegemonic discourse portrays the good shopper as a good citizen.

> VIOLET: Yeah, designed in Canada, made in Canada, there's just a sense that you're supporting, I guess, the national economy, so it's better to provide something that's made in Canada as opposed to made in China, or something like that, 'cause you are then supporting, I guess, local, I guess you could say local labourers and companies. But then again you never know where they're being processed and manufactured, right? So —
>
> KAELA: . . . But that somehow, I mean to me that sort of links up with the idea of, that's an example of how consumption starts to link up with citizenship.
>
> VIOLET: National, like nationalism?
>
> KAELA: Yeah, the idea that somehow you're a good Canadian . . . if you buy Lululemon.
>
> VIOLET: Yeah yeah yeah. Yeah yeah yeah yeah, it's true. Yeah, it's true, that idea totally exists. Although there are, there's not many things made in Canada [*chuckle*].   —interview excerpt, April 4, 2007

During one focus group, there was a conversation that similarly recognized how the good shopper is characterized as consumer-citizen. As they were going through the first exercise—talking about an object that they had brought, what they knew about it, and what it "said" about them—Thérèse made these comments about a compact disc that she had brought:

> THÉRÈSE: This is a children's CD. . . . and I bought it because we have three kids and somebody I know is on one of the tracks. And it is made by . . . a Canadian company, although they are in the United States as well. And what was interesting is that it's children's songs but by Canadian artists who are very popular with adults also. And, for example, Sarah Harmer sings, Ron Sexsmith, Matthew Sweet, that kind of thing. . . . And a portion of the proceeds when you purchase this go to, uh, a nonprofit agency here in Canada. . . . And I guess you can separate what is, what is the content, which is culture. I mean, you know, what is, where is it being made? Well, Canadian artists creating Canadian art or recycled art. Then you can start thinking about, well, what was involved in paying certain copyright licences to recreate old songs? But the packaging and the plastic and the actual, I don't even know what CDs are made out of, you know, where was that made? Where does that come from? . . . So I would think that the content and production is Canadian. They're home grown and you can trace that, but all the other stuff, like the paper and the ink and who knows.
>
> KAELA: So the material things.
>
> THÉRÈSE: Those kinds of things, who knows? I mean, it's kind of an endless tracking of things.   —focus group excerpt, May 10, 2007

The Canadian-ness of this project is evident in the attachment of its performers and producers to this country, as well as to the sense of Canada as a country that cares about the less fortunate. Layers of Canadian culture are evident on this disc although, as Thérèse indicates, the materiality that is behind that culture remains more obscured. Both Violet and Thérèse articulated how buying Canadian-made or designed products is portrayed as an expression of national loyalty of Canadian consumer-citizens to an imagined community of fellow Canadians.

On an even more local level, some participants talked about shopping at farmers' markets and the sense of trust and well-being that these markets engendered:

> Kerri was talking about the confusion in shopping, even for natural products. The exception for her is the Farmer's Market—"I feel really safe there," she said.   —shopping trip excerpt, Kerri, April 29, 2007

SEAN: Like, I love, one of the reasons, I don't mind paying more to the farmer at the farmers' market . . . 'cause when I give him that 50 dollars, or her that 50 dollars . . . they get, they get all of it. Whereas if I bought the 50 dollars worth of stuff at the store, you know, they're getting, whatever, 5 dollars.   —interview excerpt, March 24, 2007

Mary: I'm kind of on the periphery of a bunch of the sustainable circles, okay, and that includes food. Uh, so yeah, most of my grocery money goes to Choices, um, and farmers' markets. —interview excerpt, March 14, 2007

Participants who enjoyed farmers' markets were insinuating a particular pleasure and comfort in that community setting. Kerri described a feeling of safety there. Mary talked about being on the periphery of "circles" of like-minded people who presumably shared her preference for a farmers' market. Several participants who did not shop regularly at a farmers' market, often because of distance, work schedules, or other logistical issues, had joined listservs promoting farmers' markets. Even though they did not shop at these markets, the internet gave them a way to join an imagined community of like-minded shoppers.

Born and raised in the United States, Ellen mentioned another way in which imagined community is evoked, this time in the hegemonic discourse of consumer-citizenship:

ELLEN: No, I will say that my mom grew up in tight times, economically. And so this is also the woman who will not throw away food, she washes plastic bags and, you know, aluminum foil, and I mean it's about saving money, it's about never having clothes as a kid, it's about being able to dress nicely and feeling really good about herself and doing it on a budget. . . . And I think that there is a sense from my parents who have both worked full-time for probably 40, 45 years. I mean they have worked so hard, to be able to go out and spend money for them is a real sense of accomplishment. Look, like, I'm not my parents. Right? I made it. I am the American dream [chuckles]. I have spending power [chuckles]. I have consumer [power], you know, I can consume [chuckles].   —interview excerpt, April 24, 2007

Ellen's comment returns to Anderson's (1991) emphasis on the role of imagined community in nation-building. In a society underpinned by consumerist ideology, one test of how well people are seen to enact citizenship is how willing and able they are to shop, buy, and consume. It is no overstatement to claim that, to the extent that they learn to enact a hegemonic version of shopping, consumer-citizens are participating in the hegemonic construction of the nation-state.

Several participants were Canadian raised but had lived abroad. Nicole and Karen spoke about how shopping and citizenship came together unexpectedly during these periods:

KAELA: In Canada today, shoppers can buy things from all over the world. What do you think this means for you . . . as a Canadian?

KAREN: Well, I mean, it's sad to see local producers of things maybe not be able to compete as well. I know that I was visiting my family . . . 'cause I was back for a visit and they were sitting around talking about how they thought it was really sad that Walmart in their little town had killed all these businesses. That . . . little shop was so nice! And I found it really frustrating listening to them, because I knew that all of them probably shop there weekly. I had kind of the opposite experience. My husband and I were in Taiwan for a while, and we were wandering around an open-air street market and . . . we saw some apples that were grown in BC so it was kind of . . . [nice] that—

KAELA: So you can sort of have a taste of home.

KAREN: Yeah, yeah.   —interview excerpt, February 2, 2007

NICOLE: Well, I had an interesting experience. When I was eight, I moved to Indonesia with my family for two years. We lived in Jakarta. And that I think in itself was an eye-opener and huge, different culture from Canadian culture. But in regards to shopping, I remember as a kid one of the first things I associated with living in Indonesia was that it was completely different from Western culture. And I felt that it was wrong. There was, I mean, this was from an eight-year-old perspective, . . . you know what you like in food, and it's weird, because here I am, like, I wanna eat organically, I'm very aware of what ingredients go into food, all this stuff, and yet as an eight-year-old kid I would want Kraft Dinner, hot dogs [laughs], you know, cheddar cheese that's orange, a very, I would assume, Canadian diet. Like, apples, ketchup, you know, all these really bright-coloured foods that are not necessarily food but that have been associated with my childhood. . . . So when you move to Indonesia, all this stuff doesn't exist unless you go shopping in the Westernized food markets, which are pretty much developed for the ex-pats. . . .

> And my parents would do a little bit of shopping there 'cause, you know, they have four kids and they're, they just can't change your life, this is a culture shock to begin with, just when you come to a new country, so they took us to these places, but they would never buy what we wanted. I mean, the one thing I remember was the fruits and vegetables. Here in Indonesia, a tropical country, they grow amazing fruits and vegetables and here I want a McIntosh apple and an orange orange from Florida. You know, where, Indonesian oranges are small and green. . . . Which is real, but because they're not orange, you want an orange and I wouldn't be able to eat those things.   —interview excerpt, February 17, 2007

For both Nicole and Karen, certain food meant a "taste of home." Nicole's comments are particularly interesting, because they suggest how shopping for and consumption of food become not only nationalized but also racialized. As a child, she saw goodness and rightness in a certain way of growing, preparing, and eating food, which was seen as distinctly Canadian. Juxtaposed with Indonesian culture and society, this Canadian way and Canadian society as a whole was also racialized as white. Nicole is in her mid-twenties and, although the prepared foods, hot dogs, and orange cheddar cheese that she recalled might be the culinary mainstays that many North Americans have grown up with, they do not reflect the diversity of consumption preferences and choices of Canadian consumer-citizens. In Chapter 4, I discussed the all-white, middle-class leading characters in Coupland's (1991) novel *Generation X* and their experiences as stand-ins for an imagined middle America (and Canada) that functions as the norm against which living people are measured. In much the same way, Nicole's favoured childhood foods reflect and contribute to the presumption of the all-Canadian consumer-citizen as white and middle class. Again, shopping and consumption are seen as active in the construction of the imagined national community comprised of good consumer-citizens.

At the same time as such idealizations help retain the importance of the nation-state in one's identity as a consumer-citizen, there is another discourse emerging in contemporary globalization that extends the concept of citizenship beyond the nation-state. "Global citizenship" is invoked as the ties between people who share not only a given society but also this entire planet. Often, this term is invoked to talk about the responsibility of countries in the Global North to come to the aid of governments and citizens in the Global South. What remains unarticulated in this developing discourse, though, is who sets the ground rules for citizenship on a global, let alone national, basis. A couple of participants commented, somewhat quizzically, about the prospect of global citizenship and its link to shopping and consumption:

> SARAH: So global, like, I guess, I guess it sounds, it sounds kinda nice, in a way you know, like, we're all equal, we're all just citizens of the world, but I don't really know how realistic that is. 'Cause people have their pride, their pride and they're attached to the things that are theirs, right. . . . I don't know, especially when you have a culture that's attached, you know, as well, and then you get the family and friends involved, 'cause they're part of the same culture and then it's just all, I don't know, I think it would be hard to say that we're all citizens of the world and not citizens of our country.   —interview excerpt, April 24, 2007

Here, Sarah seems to be evoking some of what Anderson (1991) attempts to convey in his concept of imagined community. The shared identity and patriotism that nation-states are able to foster among consumer-citizens through media and other institutions and processes can be seen as a call to a national culture. Even as the authority of the nation-state is disputed by proponents of globalization such as Giddens (1998, 1999a), it seems to have retained a central place in identity formation.

Finally, in the second focus group, there was a critical conversation about constructions of the good consumer-citizen. During the second exercise, when participants chose from a selection of media materials, Jocelyn chose a magazine advertisement for a popular automobile, and the following discussion ensued:

> JOCELYN: Mini Cooper, okay. . . . Okay, this one is really awful. It's got, it tries to diffuse any idea, here is, well what are these two symbols? What's the elephant?
>
> CARLA: Republicans and Democrats.
>
> JOCELYN: Yeah.
>
> CARLA: The donkey's the Democratic—
>
> JOCELYN: Is it a donkey?
>
> CARLA: Yeah, and the Republicans are the elephants. Yeah.
>
> JOCELYN: . . . Let's always be open, it says. Let's be law-abiding liberals on the gas pedal and ultraconservatives at the pump. What it's doing is ridiculing both sides of this discussion, I felt. . . . So what it's doing is ridiculing both sides of an issue, of a political feel, as well as the process. . . . I mean I just think this oughta be against the law. Let's skip all the mud slinging

and stick to the road ahead. Let's motor. I just thought that was awful. . . .

KAELA: Yeah, that's quite blatant. Just go buy the car and skip the politics.

JOCELYN: Yeah, that's what it says! . . .

KAELA: . . . There's a lot of talk about apathy, citizen apathy, and declining voting rates and things like that. And I wonder if—

JOCELYN: So this is playing right into it.

KAELA: Well is it playing on people's awareness of how that issue has been portrayed in media?

JOCELYN: Oh!

KAELA: I mean this, like, well, I guess that's a question that I have. Does this ad assume that people sort of have an awareness of these issues around cynicism and apathy and those kinds of things that are, especially around election time we see stories in the newspaper about how it's important to come out and vote and there's been a trend toward, you know . . . just this trend toward declining voter rates and that kind of thing. And I just wonder if that ad plays on people's awareness.

KAREN: Because it's a Mini ad, I would say absolutely, 'cause all of their ads seem so meant to play with, like, subtle double meanings and things like that, that I totally see them playing on awareness.

KAELA: So then is part of the message there not only that there is this cynicism and apathy but that savvy people know that and savvy people actually know, savvy people have moved beyond the political? And they're just buying the right car.

CARLA: Yeah. Buy your way out of these issues. . . .   —focus group excerpt, May 17, 2007

Paterson (2006) talks about the "savvy" consumer ☼, and, in this conversation, participants articulated an awareness of the layers of savvy that are required of a critical shopper. The advertisement under discussion pokes fun at formal politics and implies that driving a particular automotive brand and model is more important—personally and socially—than engaging in political debates. The participants' responses indicate that critical consumer-citizens must also be able to see through such manipulative attempts to define their identities as citizens who, are first and foremost, consumers.

In advising readers that freedom is found through shopping and consumption, the advertisement exemplifies the conflation between

> ☼ Being a "savvy" consumer is not about continually finding the best bargains, although that is a useful skill. Being a savvy consumer is to be aware of the contradictions between the marketing and advertising imposed on us, but still consuming items in intended and unintended ways in order to articulate something else—a sense of self-identity, of difference, or to express a social identity, that sense of belonging to a group based on shared tastes and values.   —Mark Paterson (2006), *Consumption and Everyday Life*, p. 152

democracy and consumption, and citizens' withdrawal from the arena of formal politics. ☼ This American advertisement seemed to reflect a Gramscian notion of common sense to the Canadian participants, as well as to Jocelyn, who was from the United States. The advertisers are conveying the message that Kinsella (2001) conveys through her character Becky in *Confessions of a Shopaholic*: They are advising to their readers that buying particular items signifies "cultural capital" (Bourdieu, 1984) and helps them to build not only freedom but also social status. Even though participants rejected this hegemonic portrayal of the good shopper as the good citizen, they recognized the link between citizenship and consumption; however, the portrayal of the good shopper consistent with neoliberal, consumerist ideology offers a vision of neither the consumer nor the citizen they want to be.

> ☼ Voter turnout in British and European elections, which was in steady decline for decades, has fallen rapidly for years, precipitating an atmosphere of crisis surrounding the structures of political representation. For Zygmunt Bauman, "Britain's exit from politics", manifested as apathy, a profound distrust of politicians and alienation from public institutions, has been fostered by successive governments that have encouraged the electorate to "buy oneself out of politics". According to Bauman, politics is now seen only as a nuisance, a barrier to real life, which lies elsewhere, in the world of personal freedoms, the market, human relationship and so on.   —Frank Mort (2006), "Competing Domains," pp. 225–226

An especially cogent rejection of the substitution of consumerism for liberal democracy and of the shopping as voting metaphor (see Shaw, 2007) was articulated by Tamara during her interview.

KAELA: Because consumerism and democracy are, or consumption and democracy are, conflated.

TAMARA: Yeah. And then that whole idea, it might be a bit off-topic, but that whole idea of vote with your dollars—it's such bullshit.

KAELA: But that's the citizenship. Everything is voting now.

TAMARA: But it's bullshit. . . . But I think my idea of, like, vote with
your dollar is that there've been so many decisions . . .
made for you before it's even put in front of you. That's not
democracy. . . . You don't know anything about it. You have
no education about what you're buying. . . . Yeah, and then
you think you're making your, your, you know, doing your
democratic thing by buying. . . . That's bullshit. It's really
bullshit. . . . I mean, education. You have to have a well-
educated society to have a good democracy, and we don't
have a well-educated society. We have, you know, what you
know about the product you buy is probably an ad you've
seen somewhere that promotes a lifestyle . . . but it's so much
a reflection of who you are. . . . And people get mad, you
know, when things become mainstreamed, right? Like, no,
because, like, I'm alternative, and I go against status quo,
and when, you know, sustainability is mainstreamed and you
see flashy stores that sell sustainable products, well then you
get cynical. Well! [laughs]   —interview excerpt, March
23, 2007

Tamara's analysis continues to illustrate the conflation of citizenship
and consumption. For her, the metaphor of shopping as voting props
up consumerist ideology and practices. Her comments also suggest how
the hegemonic discourse of shopping and consumption facilitate the
portrayal of Canada as a country whose citizens unite as one imagined
community through consumption. Ironically, I wonder whether this conflation might also illuminate the degree to which political voting is, for
many Canadian citizens, like the process of shopping for the candidate
with the most attractive "brand" image, rather than the most fair policy
platform. This flip side of the association between formal politics and
shopping was not discussed in our conversation, although it might have
yielded some interesting ideas. In thinking about everyday shopping sites
and processes as a politicized arena, I return to the understanding of
consumer-citizenship as contested territory whose divisions are social
as well as material (Cohen, 2003; Hearn & Roseneil, 1999; Hilton &
Daunton, 2001; Jacobs, 2003; Micheletti, 2003; Paterson, 2006).

The Shopper as a Social Character

The hegemonic ideologies of neoliberalism and consumerism construct the consumer-citizen as a freely choosing subject, unconstrained

by social structures and relations. Postmodernism's emphasis on partial, fluid identity or, more likely, identities, fits into these ideological refrains, creating a common sense notion of shopping and consumption as a series of choices that eliminate the meaning of social groups. One's affiliations and the trajectory of one's life are explained as choices made in a society that proclaims equality and personal responsibility. This is articulated, for example, in Beck's (1992) notion of individualization. ☼

☼ The tendency is towards the emergence of individualized forms and conditions of existence, which compel people—for the sake of their own material survival—to make themselves the center of their own planning and conduct of life. Increasingly, everyone has to choose between different options, including as to which group or subculture one wants to be identified with. In fact, one has to choose and change one's social identity as well and take the risks in doing so. In this sense, individualization means the variation and differentiation of lifestyles and forms of life, opposing the thinking behind the traditional categories of large-group societies—which is to say, classes, estates, and social stratification.   —Ulrich Beck (1992), *Risk Society: Towards a New Modernity*, p. 88

Indeed, several participants made comments that reiterated this hegemonic common sense:

ELLEN: Like, you know, you can actually, if you have the money, you can adopt an image, you can buy the clothes and the accessories and get the haircut and get the shoes, and you can, you can reinvent yourself every six months, every six years, however much you want to. That is a, if you want to consider it this way, a luxury that most people don't have. I mean, the vast majority of the world wears what they can wear.   —interview excerpt, Ellen, April 24, 2007

KAELA: Well, I just think, I just think that, . . . um, that fashion, . . . well, all consumption but particularly something like fashion, . . . part of what we're trying to do is convey something about ourselves. . . . And so . . . the idea of unlimited choice is I think a little, I don't think that our choices are unlimited, because, um, well, because we're trying to construct identities in a, you know, in a particular contextual way.

VIOLET: Mm-hmmm. But I think that anybody can claim any sort of identity just through clothes. I think that's a choice.

KAELA: That anybody can claim any identity through clothes. . . .

VIOLET: Yeah, yeah. . . . I think anyone can go into any store and, and decide that they want to look like a golfer one day and, or, like an athletic person, you know what I mean, because . . . there's a choice there.

KAELA: Do you think a black person would have that choice? . . .

VIOLET: I do, yeah.

KAELA: Do you think a First Nations person would have that choice?

VIOLET: Are you talking about money? Are you talking about financial constraints?

KAELA: Um, no, no.

VIOLET: No? If the money was unlimited, yeah. I think that absolutely they can claim any identity that they want.   —interview excerpt, April 4, 2007

Interestingly, Violet and Ellen were the participants who most clearly reiterated a postmodern, neoliberal view, and they were also the two participants with the most concentrated academic work in feminist and critical race studies. Both women seemed to recognize that material wealth, part of socioeconomic class, is a factor determining how much choice people actually have in their shopping; however, as the excerpts cited above indicate, they initially suggested that gender and race are much more malleable, controllable characteristics. Later in their interviews, both women offered quite different comments, and I outline some of those comments in the following discussion. I believe that such shifts in analytical perspective indicate the extent to which hegemonic ideologies and common sense are absorbed even by critical consumer-citizens and come to exist alongside their more critical ideas. For critical consumer-citizens, a steady, concerted effort to counter these ideas is required.

Despite these hegemonic ideologies and their resulting common sense, my analysis of conversations with participants recalls the conclusion of Kenway and Bullen (2001) that, especially in the Global North, consumer-citizens exercise choice creatively but always within the context and constraints of the social structures that remain evident. Consumer-citizens have multiple identities and social affiliations and often make choices that surprise and even contravene marketing pressures. At the same time, they cannot remove themselves from the relational categories that structure society, including gender, race, and class. ☼

One piece of long-standing hegemonic "common sense" (Gramsci, 1971) apportions the primary responsibility for shopping to women. Feminist scholarship on the history of shopping in Western societies establishes how, since the construction of the leisure shopper

---

☼ Consumer-media culture does have a "menu of meaning" but some have more choice to dine à la carte than others. Further, many "choices" are forced in the processes of production and consumption.   —Jane Kenway and Elizabeth Bullen (2001), *Consuming Children*, p. 153

drawn to Victoria-era malls and department stores, shopping has been seen as both a leisure activity and a task for women (Bowlby, 2000; Rappaport, 2001). Although shops for men also developed at that time (Breward, 1999), the idealized shopper was a woman and, more particularly, white and middle or upper class. This ideal shopper embodied contradictory qualities: She was responsible and caring as well as emotional, selfish, and easily persuaded. In fact, most of the participants in this study—29 of 32 people—were women. Most also described themselves as middle class or higher (18 of 32) or thought of themselves as temporarily inhabiting a lower-class position while they were full-time students or recent graduates. Whether or not they actually enjoy shopping, participants suggested a lasting association between being a middle-class woman and being (seen as) interested and engaged in shopping.

In response to my question about how they learned about shopping and how to shop, participants recalled childhood shopping trips with their parents, especially with their mothers. When Jocelyn, the oldest participant in the study, and I were talking about recruiting other participants, she mused that it might be difficult for me to find older individuals. I added that I anticipated a challenge in finding male participants, regardless of their age. I started to add that shopping continues to be feminized but, before I could finish my sentence, Jocelyn characterized shopping as "mother's work" (interview excerpt, Jocelyn, January 22, 2007). Mothers were generally seen as especially important influences in participants' early shopping experiences, often teaching their children about the importance of quality and good value in shopping, as well as the gendered construction of shopping.

During her interview, Julie moved from shopping-as-work to shopping-as-leisure. Although she acknowledged that many women, including her, are not avid shoppers, she recognized the cultural image of women for whom shopping is both a task and a hobby. As she said:

> I still know many, many women who would quite happily spend a Saturday afternoon shopping. Who view it as a social activity, who would even describe it as a mental health activity. Um, I know no men, at all, who, who . . . would just shop for pleasure.   —interview excerpt, March 14, 2007

A few participants described having grown up with mothers and even grandmothers whose love of shopping also reiterated the image of women as impulsive, compulsive shoppers. Their recollections suggest a mixture of confusion and resentment:

[M]y mother's an avid shopper. She will spend hours shopping. I grew up with West Edmonton Mall being an essential part of life, because we had activities going on there as well as shopping, and family members would come in from out of town and we'd go there. So, yeah, I find it interesting that she really enjoys the experience, and I just can see her bringing all these things home, trying to decide on them, having to spend the time to return them, having to look for what she needs, I think maybe that's what has influenced me to realize that it's not a pleasurable activity, for me [*laughs*].   —shopping trip excerpt, Alice, February 17, 2007

ELLEN: [*chuckles*] Well, as the daughter of a compulsive spender who also has this real, like, I'm a good shopper, I'm a smart shopper—everything my mother buys she comes home and says, This originally at the department store was $85. I got it . . . for $13. That's 75% off! You know, so, for my mom, particularly, it's always about finding the bargain. It doesn't matter if she's never going to wear it, if it's a white elephant, if it is cheap enough, if it's discounted enough [*chuckles*], she'll buy it. And when I say, I mean my mom in many ways sort of is a compulsive shopper, compulsive spender, she doesn't have a ton of money, so she's always going for these bargains. But she loves shopping. She always refers to, like, I need some retail therapy. And so she would pick us up from school, she'd get off work at like five and come pick us up . . . and literally take us to these, like, discount retailers [*laughs*]. And I think that's one of the reasons why I hate shopping so much, because, as a child, you want to go outside and play. You know, you want to go and be in the world, you don't want to be at . . . some bargain basement store, you know, sifting through department store rejects [*chuckles*] trying to find the best deal you can. So very vivid memories of my mom shopping for dresses, and my sister and I would crawl around on the floor of the department store picking up all the buttons and sequins that had fallen off. And we would have these boxes of buttons and sequins at home, then when we were doing art projects we would use to decorate [*chuckles*], probably sequins off some, like, Ralph Lauren evening dress [*chuckles*].   —interview excerpt, April 24, 2007

KAREN: And I know that my mother and my grandmother, you know, they go through the flyers together and . . . my grandmother doesn't, she's not as mobile as she used to be, so that's her big

> excursion of the week, is going through the flyers and going to find, you know, the cheapest things. My mom comes to visit, she asks if I get the flyers and if I know what's on sale and where. And I'm not interested in where I'm gonna get it cheapest. I'm interested in where I'm gonna get something that I feel comfortable buying.   —interview excerpt, February 2, 2007

Not surprisingly, given my appeal to individuals who were concerned about consumerism and globalization, these participants rejected the exuberance for shopping that they had seen in their mothers. Regardless of the critiques and alternative shopping practices they had developed and regardless of their ages, all participants acknowledged that their mothers had had a pivotal role in their early experiences with and learning about shopping. These individuals ranged in age from their early twenties to their early seventies and were raised in different communities across Canada and the United States. They grew up in cities, large and small, as well as towns. A few of them were raised in other countries: Amy came from Singapore, Paula came from Germany, and Amitah came from Britain. Regardless of their ethno-cultural affiliations and, for the female participants in particular, the distance that they had established between themselves and stereotypical portrayals of the female shopper, most participants identified the women in their early lives—mothers and, possibly, grandmothers—as their first teachers about shopping.

The specific lessons that participants learned from their mothers varied somewhat, depending on their ages and family circumstances. Nonetheless, some points remained central: the importance of value-for-money, for example. The meaning of gender has changed across time in any given place, and continues to vary across places; however, in many cultures, shopping remains part of the portfolio of tasks related to co-ordinating home and family life, which itself remains assigned to women in their idealized form.

In part, then, participants' early association of shopping with their mothers seems to reflect mothers' ongoing primary responsibility for care giving. It also reflects the reality that many shopping settings, especially in the Global North, have adapted so that children can join in adults' shopping. Shopping carts in which a parent can seat a toddler, child-sized shopping carts that can be pushed by children following their parents, play areas in some large suburban stores—these all illustrate how contemporary gender relations are enacted in family and broader social contexts.

As Rappaport (2000) and Bowlby (2001) explain, shopping has been associated with women's work and leisure since the Victorian era's development of shopping urban areas and malls and the evolution of department stores, but children's learning about shopping in those times would have been largely second-hand. More so than any other time, it is over the last fifty years or so that children have participated in shopping and have come to learn about it through their own experiences. An additional outcome of children's engagement in their parents', especially their mothers', shopping is that, as scholars note, children have been identified by marketers as a distinct and important group of consumers (Kenway & Bullen, 2001; Martens, 2005; Spring, 2003; Zukin, 2005). I see these outcomes in my own family, among my nieces and nephews. My oldest niece loves to go to the mall with her (girl)friends. My nephews love to go to that same place, but they talk about it differently: They go to the videogames store. This builds on my analytical conclusion from Chapter 6 that girls and women might accept or reject the association of shopping with their own aspirations for feminine identity, but they recognize that shopping is generally perceived as a feminine activity. The exception is shopping for masculine gadgets and gizmos. Gender relations undergo constant shifts in Canadian society, as they do elsewhere, but for the most part shopping remains an arena in which those relations remain evident.

In addition to gender, race is also a kind of social relation that is apparent in shopping. In Canada, neoliberalism works in concert with the political policy frameworks of equality between the sexes and of multiculturalism, which celebrates ethnic and cultural diversity without addressing structural barriers to the full inclusion of racial minority groups into Canadian society (Dhruvarajan, 2000). Although some participants, such as Jody, celebrated Canada's multiculturalism, others, such as Amitah, spoke in more critical terms about it:

> Jody chatted some more about living in Kensington Market. She had grown up in a suburban area and moved to the Market area when she could. She felt too sheltered in the suburbs and welcomed the diversity that the Market area offered. She described growing up, asking herself, "Who am I? The only difference between the boys and the girls was the colour of our shirts." —shopping trip excerpt, Jody, February 12, 2007

AMITAH: And then of course we forget that here in Canada we're actually living on stolen land . . . in the first place. . . . Nobody talks about that one. And the whole, this whole thing is really built on a lie.

KAELA: Right.

AMITAH: The whole culture that we're all, you know, so proud of, this multicultural Canada, um, but how did we get here? Um,

nobody wants to look at that, because it would raise too
many difficult questions.   —interview excerpt, February
21, 2007

Jody's memories about place and culture recall my earlier discussion
of how shoppers construct a geography as part of their learning. From
an entirely different perspective, Amitah's comments clarify how, despite
rhetoric of a free market and consumer sovereignty, the ultimate lesson
for consumer-citizens to learn from Canadian history and the history of
other colonized territories has more to do with force and theft rather
than freedom and fairness.

While completing his demographic form just before beginning his
interview, Sean retorted, "Race is a social construct and I refuse to participate in it!" Here, Sean reduces the social to matters of individual
choice, rather than structures with material and cultural pressures, constraints, and outcomes. The reality that one cannot simply choose to
withdraw from social structures such as race is contradicted by Sean's
determination to remove himself from an objectionable construct, even
as he, like all consumer-citizens, does continue to participate in it in the
course of his everyday life in Canadian society.

Policy frameworks of equality and multiculturalism instruct consumer-
citizens that to talk about race, with its obvious historical attachment
to colonization, slavery, and total social exclusion, is impolite, negative,
and outdated. Sarah's comments, which equate talk about race with
racism, reiterate Sean's view of race as an individualized choice and the
hesitation that he and most of the other participants felt in talking about
race:

SARAH: Racism? I think that, now it's hard for me, 'cause I, I don't
really like to talk about racism a lot considering that I am
white. . . . But I have a lot of friends that are from different
races, I don't really like to think of that, but I mean, you
know, Chinese or black or you know, whatever. And I, I
don't actually notice when I first meet someone what they
are and . . . like, where they've come from in terms of, like,
. . . what country their parents came from, I don't really
care, but I think that there is still racism that exists, I think
there's still prejudice that exists. . . . And also, I don't know
[*mutters*], people are scared. And it's pride, too, it's, like,
pride being in the way. I think it's people's pride and people's
fear getting in the way. . . . However, I think that we've also
come a long way with racism. Especially, like, Vancouver's a
really good example. Like, I think, from what I see, I know

> that I hear some stories here and there about racism. Like,
> my friend works, . . . a good girl friend of mine is a teacher,
> and she works in a private school, so she gets, she teaches
> kids from, you know, Russia, from Japan, from all over the
> world. And she says that every once in a while there'll still
> be racial acts in her classroom, and so I guess I think that
> it still exists. But I think that we've also progressed a lot as
> well.   —interview excerpt, April 25, 2007

Sarah's and Sean's comments echo Frankenberg's (1993) and Knowles's (2003) conclusion that race, including whiteness, has been constructed in the context and service of racism and that white people—especially those who consider themselves socially progressive—are reluctant to consider their own whiteness as part of a racial structure. For these participants, rhetoric of race is a reminder of the bad behaviour of white people from previous generations. Race and racism are psychological attributes of those who are fearful and proud, rather than social qualities of us all. Whiteness is eliminated from conversation so as not to (re)offend.

This rhetorical elimination of whiteness and race in general does not mean that race itself is eliminated as part of the social structure in Canada. Sometimes participants did speak about how relations of race and racial identity become apparent through shopping. Reesa is a white woman married to a man of Chinese descent. When she and I met for her shopping trip, she had already started shopping and was looking at packaged Asian-style soups. I recorded this passage in my notes: "'You found me looking at something I wouldn't normally buy,' she said, and explained that her husband likes them. He is of Chinese descent, she explained, 'and sometimes he tells me he's tired of Caucasian food'" (shopping trip excerpt, Reesa, May 2, 2007).

Linda, another white woman married to a man of Chinese descent, similarly shared her husband's racial identity with me while we talked about shopping and consumption:

LINDA: My husband shops at Metrotown a lot, partly because there's a train that he can take my kid on [*chuckles*]. The little one likes the train. And, I don't think he actually does any shopping while he's there.

KAELA: Oh, so it's an outing.

LINDA: Exactly. Maybe a little bit of grocery shopping at T&T supermarket. . . .

KAELA: And why T&T?

LINDA: Partly because it's right by where the train is and partly because it's an Asian speciality store, so they have a lot

of different things that you can't get at like Safeway.
Um—

KAELA: And is your husband Asian?

LINDA: Yeah, yes. . . . So, although he, he doesn't think of himself
as Asian. He was raised very Western. His mom didn't
even raise him in Chinese. He grew up speaking English.
—interview excerpt, May 30, 2007

A second anecdote that Linda shared with me during her interview
presented an example of how racism can be encountered in a shopping
setting. In this case, it was a matter of another shopper whose behaviour
was objectionable and even offensive to Linda:

KAELA: So do you think that racism has exited as a, as an issue?

LINDA: Oh no. It's still here. I mean, maybe not in the same way.
To a certain extent, where I am, I'm, in my life and the way
I've arranged my life I don't see racism. But occasionally it
rears its head in surprising ways. Like, I had a, somebody
who came to my pharmacy and phoned me back and said, I
wanna transfer all my prescriptions there because you don't
have any of those damned Chinese people. And I was just
like, um, my married name is [*Chinese*]. . . . I, do you get
this? I'm really not liking this, and I'm not going to transfer
your prescriptions here for that reason. I kind of was so
shocked.   —interview excerpt, April 29, 2007

This excerpt provides a marked contrast to Linda's earlier insinuation
and the generally postmodern insistence that shoppers can simply buy an
identity, as well as Sean's insistence that he can exit the social relations
of race and Sarah's impression that race and racism have diminished in
the Canadian social landscape. It illustrates that although Linda and her
husband tried to think of him as "Western" rather than Chinese, they
received constant and unpleasant reminders that they do not control
where they are located in relation to other Canadians.

Another participant, Amy, discussed race and nationality in the particular context of her home country of Singapore. Her comments recall
the writing of Arjun Appadurai (2000), which disputes that globalization
can be characterized by a singular, uniform threat of Americanization. ☼
Racialized as Chinese, she spoke about the importance of avoiding items
with a distinct association to traditional and Mainland Chinese culture:

AMY: I would say it's strange, but I try not to buy things that
encourage a cookie cutter image. . . . Like, you know, . . . I

> ☼ Most often, the homogenization argument subspeciates into either an argument about Americanization, or an argument about "commoditization", and very often the two arguments are closely linked. What these arguments fail to consider is that at least as rapidly as forces from various metropolises are brought into new societies they tend to become indigenized in one or other way. . . . But it is worthy noting that for the people of Irian Jaya, Indonesianization may be more worrisome than Americanization, as Japanization may be for Koreans, Indianization may be for Sri Lankans, Vietnamization for the Cambodians, Russianization for the people of Soviet Armenia and the Baltic Republics. Such a list of alternative fears to Americanization could be greatly expanded, but it is not a shapeless inventory: for polities of smaller scale, there is always a fear of cultural absorption by polities of larger scale, especially those that are near by. One man's imagined community (Anderson 1983) is another man's political prison.   —Arjun Appadurai (2000), "Disjuncture and Difference in the Global Cultural Economy," p. 230

> don't know, when you talk about Chinese, you tend to think of all the Chinese silks and, you know, all the really Chinese things with the silk . . . patterns . . . or something like that. I try not to buy that when I'm in Singapore, because it's, I mean, the thing about it is, like I said, it's identity, and, okay, we can't really establish who we are for now for Singaporeans anyway. I mean we are Chinese, but we don't want to be identified or associated with Mainland Chinese. . . . And so we try not to buy things that they buy.   —interview excerpt, February 7, 2007

I understand Amy's comments as a distinct attempt to tie shopping and consumption to the nation-building project. Amy was talking about her and her fellow Singaporeans' attempt to resist the regional imposition of an ancient Chinese culture on the relatively new nation-state of Singapore. To that end, she described a new notion of Chinese-ness.

When it came to discussing or referring to class, participants seemed to struggle with their self-identification and understanding in some distinct ways. As they were completing their demographics forms, some participants told me that they were unsure about how to define their class. Some participants described a sense of having been born into a working class but, with education and professional opportunities, began to identify with a middle or professional class. A few participants described the opposite experience: having been born into a middle-class family but thinking of themselves as temporary consigned to a lower class while they were full-time students or recent graduates. Descriptions on the demographic forms such as "Born working class unsure now" (Carla) or

"Upwardly mobile (I hope), poor with safety net" (Ellen) indicate participants' uncertainty about their class locations as their circumstances—both material and social—changed. As I noted during my shopping trip with Paula,

> She commented that she didn't know what socioeconomic status meant on the demographics form, and we discussed it. She said that it was difficult to locate herself, because she came from a lower-middle-class or working-class family but was now in university and, she hoped, headed upward in terms of her own class.   —shopping trip excerpt, Paula, August 14, 2007

Eventually, Paula described her class this way: "Poor student in debt and transitioning to upper middle class."

Bourdieu's (1984) ideas about class, which incorporates cultural capital and social status as well as economic capital, and his notion of "upclassing" are helpful here. By upclassing, Bourdieu refers to the illusion that, by mimicking the behaviours and practices of the elite class evident at one time, members of other, lower classes can raise their own class positions. ☼ Some people actually might achieve such a shift in their class positions; in Bourdieu's opinion, however, most are likely to experience confusion and frustration in their attempts.

Another participant, Ellen, had parents who had grown up poor but gained post-secondary credentials and done well for themselves professionally. Their class position shifted from lower class to professional/

☼ The dialectic of downclassing and upclassing which underlies a whole set of social processes presupposes and entails that all the groups concerned run in the same direction, toward the same objectives, the same properties, those which are designated by the leading group and which, by definition, are unavailable to the groups following, since, whatever these properties may be intrinsically, they are modified and qualified by their distinctive rarity and will no longer be what they are once they are multiplied and made available to groups lower down. Thus, by an apparent paradox, the maintenance of order, that is, of the whole set of gaps, differences, "differentials", ranks, precedences, priorities, exclusions, distinctions, ordinal properties, and thus of the relations of order which give a social formation its structure, is provided by an unceasing change in substantial (i.e., non-relational) properties. This implies that the social order, an "order of successions", . . . each group having as its past the group immediately below and for its future the group immediately above (one sees the attraction of evolutionist models). The competing groups are separated by differences which are essentially located in the order of time.   —Pierre Bourdieu (1984), *Distinction: A Social Critique of the Judgement of Taste*, p. 163

middle class; Ellen's comments, which I previously cited, are relevant here as they indicate how she continued to see remnants of her mother's lower-class identification:

ELLEN: No, I will say that my mom grew up in tight times, economically. And so this is also the woman who will not throw away
food, she washes plastic bags and, you know, aluminum foil,
and I mean it's, it's about saving money, it's about never having
clothes as a kid, it's about being able to dress nicely and feeling really good about herself and doing it on a budget. I mean
she always talks about the one cashmere sweater that her dad
gave her when she graduated from high school and how it
was, like, her prized possession, because she grew up without,
just without, right?   —interview excerpt, April 24, 2007

This stubborn, embodied memory of class refutes the postmodern portrayal of identity as continually, and often wilfully, reconstructed. Contrary to the postmodern vision of shoppers and consumers who change their identities, this anecdote clarifies that identity is never com-pletely shed; rather, traces of a prior class position are retained in one's memories and cultural habits.

Amitah was alone in her "choice" to shift her position from middle class to a lower class. On her demographics form, she provided this overview of her transition: "Grew up middle, dropped out," although she managed to avoid the cynicism evident in Coupland's (1991) lead characters, who describe themselves similarly. Other participants had also rejected the rampant consumerism that they grew up with in the context of their middle-class families; what set Amitah apart is her dras-tic separation from her family, their lifestyle, and their material circum-stances. Having moved from England to Canada and married at a young age, she made consumption and employment decisions that shifted her class position downward rather than upward. The shift in her class pos-ition was evident in more than her relatively low-income job. Among the participants in this study, Amitah had an extraordinarily sophisticated, comprehensive analysis; however, the fact that she did not complete high school distinguished her from other participants and the middle class in general. Despite the change in her material position, though, she con-tinued to relate on some level to the middle class:

KAELA: Would you still describe yourself as middle class?
AMITAH: Um, no. I don't think so. I don't know actually. Would I?
I don't think I'm in the income bracket for middle class
anymore [chuckles].

> KAELA: Do you think of yourself as middle class?
> AMITAH: Well I feel that I grew up that way.   —interview excerpt,
>   February 21, 2007

Again, a remnant of a former class position remained in Amitah's understanding of herself and class relations.

Although few participants attended a focus group, such groups do provide an interesting additional source of data. They encouraged reflection about the interrelatedness of gender, race, and class. Two conversations that occurred during the second exercise in each group seem especially helpful in this analysis. During this exercise, participants chose from among a series of media images that I had brought with me and discussed how these materials portray gender, race, and class and how they connect social characteristics to shopping and consumption. While conversations during interviews and shopping trips tended to cover the social categories of gender, race, and class separately, the materials discussed during the focus groups encouraged participants to think about how these categories intersect so that social relations become complicated. This again recalls Barndt's (2002) "interlocking analysis of power" (p. 62). I review two conversations that assumed this view of power.

The first image is an advertisement for a laptop computer taken from a Canadian business publication. The full-page, full-colour glossy advertisement features two men, one black and the other white, in a locker room. They both appear naked, except for the towels wrapped around their waists. The white man is sitting on a bench with the laptop open on his lap, facing the black man; the black man is staring down at the white man's lap(top), with an expression of amazement on his face. The following excerpts from the focus group conversation outline the understandings that participants and I had of this image:

> KAELA: So one of the things that jumped out at me when, the first
>   time that I saw that ad was the race of the men.
> NICOLE: I agree. That's the first thing that jumped out at me.
> KAELA: Okay, so can you, so what jumped out at you about that?
> NICOLE: Well just I, like, I mean I saw it from afar, but there was
>   two naked men, one black, one white. And, yeah, I mean I, I
>   mean sexuality, too, in what was being presented. . . .
> KAELA: Okay. Anything else about—? . . .
> JAMES: Yeah, there's a tension playing in there. Well, the stereotype
>   of the black man being more physically endowed than the
>   white man and here in his head sort of it's the white man

getting one up over, uh, over the black man. But, yeah the whole, part of it's I think also the competing gadgets, I mean that stereotype of men as well . . . sort of like, who has the best gadget? Because somehow that's, um, an indication of your, your intelligence, your style, um, as well as what you've got in your pocketbook. . . .

KAELA: So then the ad is playing with ironic possibilities in a few ways. It's playing with the, I mean, everybody knows that black men have what to look at in the locker room. And, you know, but actually, no, now it's the white guy's [laptop].

NICOLE: Right.

KAELA: So they're playing with that kind of racial stereotype.

NICOLE: Right.

KAELA: And they're, and they're playing with the, they're reversing the, the locker room stereotype about what gets noticed, which is the biggest, with the smallest gadget. . . . So technology makes the smallest more desirable. Okay, okay. . . .

SANDY: Well it's just interesting. I didn't pick up on the whole, like there are a lot of different interpretations of why they used a white man and a black man. . . . I just did not see any of that whatsoever. But I see it now as a lot of TV and ads do try to have a diversity of cultures, whereas ten or twenty years ago it was all . . . white people, mostly white males that you would see on TV or ads or stuff. So I think, I see it more as, as media making more of an effort to have a diversity in their . . . material.   —focus group excerpt, May 10, 2007

Nicole, James, and I conveyed an understanding of this advertisement as a play on several stereotypes connected to gender, race, and class. Sharing the same locker room, the two men presumably also share a class position. This overturns the stereotypical link between blackness and poverty. The image of the black man staring down at his friend's lap overturns a second stereotype that helps explain why this advertisement is placed in a locker room: that is, black men, not white men, have certain enviable assets. Moreover, the object of attention in this advertisement is noticeably compact, in contrast to the stereotypical male locker room contests over size. The three of us saw this advertisement as an attempt at humour that relies on an awareness of these stereotypes that it overturns but does not dismiss.

In contrast to that analysis, Sandy adopted a stance consistent with the contemporary Canadian discourse of multiculturalism. In her view, this advertisement is an affirmation that race is being reconstructed so that racism is eliminated. The new locker room accommodates people of all races; therefore, they must all be equal. As this conversation between me and several participants indicates, not everybody attracted to this study shared a social analysis, even if they shared a conviction that shopping and consuming in a more ecologically sensitive way was a necessary part of societal transformation.

The second image, chosen in the other focus group, is from an American women's fashion magazine. It features a bowl made by a well known crystalware company. During our discussion about it, hooks's (2001) concerns about the commodification of racialized cultural practices were echoed: ☼

CARLA: So in this case it's a wooden bowl surrounded by, what is there, . . . crystal, right? . . . I think they're making some sort of comment about art and that the . . . bowl is like art. You know, it, it's put in this room full of beautiful *objets d'arts*, you know, these beautiful objects. . . .

KAELA: The colours and—

CARLA: Yeah, the bright colours, the fact that it's, I mean . . . and this woman [in the painting pictured above the bowl] is clearly African, but it's the . . . sort of idea of, you know, the—

KAELA: The exotic.

CARLA: The exotic, the, the noble savage if you will. You know, here she is all, absolutely gorgeous in her sarong, pouring out the water. And I'm assuming it's supposed to go into the bowl. Um, so it, it's basically, the key audience is people who have expendable cash. . . . Yeah, I was making a joke about colonist envy, people who wish they, you know, who wish they lived in different times and could be colonists, you know.

KAELA: Colonizers?

JOCELYN: Colonizers.

CARLA: Yeah. Colonizers, imperialistic, because it is, you know, the African woman. Um, and, like I said, I really don't

---

☼ When race and ethnicity become commodified as resources for pleasure, the culture of specific groups, as well as the bodies of individuals, can be seen as constituting an alternative playground where members of dominating races, genders, sexual practices affirm their power-over in intimate relations with the Other.   —bell hooks (2001), "Eating the Other," p. 425

understand the message aside from . . . trying to relate [this brand] . . . with really beautiful art. . . .

KAELA: But it is, I mean you make an interesting point about, um, the colonist envy.

CARLA: Yeah [*chuckles*].

KAELA: And you pointed out that . . . it looks as if she's meant to portray an African woman.

CARLA: Yeah.

KAELA: And so is part of the, I mean is that actually part of the sort of unspoken message in that ad? That if you buy [this brand] . . . in some ways you are, you know, you do take on a kind of colonial status. Not power, not necessarily power, but part of that does become the ability to possess not just art, but I mean . . . that's not an abstract, it's not a still life. It's a very, you know, they've inserted something in a very purposeful way into that ad. And they've inserted the image of a black woman. . . . But so the idea that wealth and things like [this brand] . . . are actually even more than a sign of good taste. . . .

JOCELYN: You can buy yourself a black woman, basically.

CARLA: Yeah, it's a sign of status, yeah.

KAELA: And that status gets racialized.

CARLA: Yeah, yeah, that, you know. So, I mean, I don't know what the bowl is made of. Perhaps it's some sort of African wood and that's supposed to be the, the connection. . . . But certainly it does seem, I mean everything else in this room, too, like the, the walls, it all looks, it all looks like something that an English imperialist would have in his or her room, you know, in Nairobi or wherever.

KAELA: And, and that's also interesting in terms of globalization. . . . As much as we often hear that globalization is such a new kind of period and phenomenon that this ad sort of pulls us back into an earlier time.

JOCELYN: [*sighs*] Righhht.

CARLA: Hmmm, which was totally about globalization, yeah, I mean. . . . And I think what's interesting, too, is how, again how she is portrayed kind of as a, as this beautiful but sort of, but she's still primitive you know? . . .

JOCELYN: She doesn't have running water.

CARLA: She doesn't have running water, she has to carry it on her shoulder. And now she's pouring it into the beautiful bowl. Yeah, so it's highly exotic and you know. . . .   —focus group excerpt, May 17, 2007

By the end of the discussion, Jocelyn was convinced that this advertisement uses race in a way that is decidedly racist. Her statement that the image suggested that "[y]ou can buy a black woman, basically" indicates that she is troubled by its invocation of race. This image also attaches gender to race, presenting an exotic woman who enters and serves, and is available for possession. It also recalls Skeggs's (2004) point that qualities and dispositions are racialized so that, when they are embodied and enacted by different people, they assume different meanings. ☼ In the case of this advertisement, the painting of the black woman, although not the item offered for sale, suggests that purchase and ownership of the bowl attaches to an exotic aesthetic as well as a social organization that confines black women. This advertisement conveys a rather literal illustration of how some social groups and bodies are marked and restricted in social space, while other social groups and bodies retain a social and physical mobility.

This analysis adds a nuance to Anderson's (1991) concept of imagined community. Although the idea of a singular hegemonic discourse might suggest an idealized version of the Canadian consumer-citizen, the complexity of both citizenship and consumption that emerges from social and material divisions renders that version an unrealizable abstraction. Ultimately, there are multiple hegemonic discourses and images of the good Canadian consumer-citizens, all of which might emphasize the same qualities, but in different ways. For example, good working-class or poor consumer-citizens might be extolled as people who exercise responsibility by not overextending their credit; good middle-class and wealthy consumer-citizens might be extolled as people who demonstrate

---

☼ The interest here lies in how some forms of culture are condensed and inscribed onto social groups and bodies that then mark them and restrict their movement in social space, whilst others are not but are able to become mobile and flexible. —Beverley Skeggs (2004), *Class, Self, Culture*, pp. 1–2

To turn the intellectual gaze into a form of knowledge and competence for one's own enhancement is precisely how cosmopolitanism as a disposition is generated. This must involve access to the cultures of others, turning them into objects of distanced contemplation for oneself. The intellectual cosmopolitans learn to know themselves through travelling through the cultures of others. This then is the aesthetic/prosthetic self, shopping, sizing-up the value of what is available, participating in the art-culture system of otherness, where others become a resource—in the propertizing of the self. The property of this possessive individual is premised on access to valued cultural resources; on accruing cultural value through drawing to oneself the culture of others.   —Beverley Skeggs (2004), *Class, Self, Culture*, p. 158

their sense of responsibility by spending lavishly in support of the national economy. These differences exemplify how shoppers are marked as members of different imagined communities within Canadian society. Because people embody locations in more than one type of social relation at any given time, shoppers are also always marked as members of multiple imagined communities.

Summary

In this chapter, my analysis has focused on how shopping helps participants learn about and manifest who they are and who they want to be. Participants discussed various qualities that they strove to embody. These qualities helped guide them in their shopping deliberations. Participants talked about their notions of a "good" shopper, and, although they shared many concerns, conclusions and priorities, they did not necessarily imagine themselves in the same community. For some participants, spirituality and organized religion helped inform the approach to shopping of a few participants. For others, the ethics of community well-being, fair trade, environmentalism, or animal welfare had secular humanist roots, and some participants were involved in organizations connected to these movements. For example, Bonnie was involved in a vegetarian/environmental organization, and Alice volunteered at Ten Thousand Villages®.

Even participants who were not regularly engaged in organizations related to shopping and anti-consumerism found ways to connect with certain types of messages and shoppers. They read publications that aim to educate and engage readers in societal change, belonged to local retail cooperatives, surfed activist websites, and, on rare occasion, even participated in formal political activities. To the extent that imagined communities of like-minded consumer-citizens are constructed through organizational, media, cultural, and even marketing discourses and rhetoric, shopping becomes an arena in which individuals can translate imagined ties and the values that they bring forth into a concrete sense of themselves.

As I also explored in this chapter, part of who participants learn to be is shoppers within contemporary Canadian society. In Chapter 2, I conceptualized consumer-citizenship in terms of the social relations that constitute notions of gender, race, and class. Participants' comments help to establish how these relations are evident within the arena of shopping, even as efforts at their discursive erasure are made.

Finally, the analysis in this chapter suggests that a range of imagined communities are resisting some of the disturbing elements of globalization. These imagined communities exist within Canadian society and, thanks especially to new information and communication technologies, well beyond Canada's borders. Even if participants produce critical understandings of shopping, consumption, and consumerism, and affiliate with social movements that attempt to develop their own imagined communities, they remain constituents in the imagined community that is Canada. Images of the "good" Canadian consumer-citizen might celebrate diversity, equality, and choice, but they are silent on the topics of gender, race, and class. The extent to which participants backed away from these topics or talked around rather than about them, especially race and class and regardless of their own racial identifications, illustrates the talent of hegemony in absorbing initially counter-hegemonic points of view. This realization has implications for the capacity of shopping to serve as a site not only of critical learning but also of attempts to spur societal change. In the next chapter, I attend more closely to the movements and organizations that help frame these imagined communities and guide their members' efforts to change the direction of Canadian society in the early twenty-first century and globalization more broadly.

INTERLUDE VI

Radical Accidents

When I was a child, my father, Donny, loved to tell stories about his childhood. A favourite was about the time he and his friend, a black boy named Harry, went ice skating. The story is retold by Harry's father in his manuscript, A Black Man's Toronto:

There was one racial incident at that time-around 1945. . . . This was on a Saturday. [My son] Harry went to school with two Jewish boys, Danny [*sic*] and Sonny Jubas. Their father was a barber and the mother was a hairdresser. They came to my house, and Harry went to their house. One day I was ready to go out on a run to Ottawa. "Daddy," Harry said, "have you got any money?" "Yes sir, I have. How much you want?" And he says, "Just a dollar. Danny and I, we're going to the Icelandia to skate." That was a private skating rink. But I had read in the paper that they discriminated against Jews and Blacks at the Icelandia, and I says, "If they discriminate against Jews, you haven't got a chance, my boy." He says, "Daddy, Danny and I, we goes every place and we know how to behave ourselves." I said, "Be careful."

Now I didn't get back until Sunday night, and the wife had a nice supper for me. After she figured that my supper was digested, she sprung this on me: that Harry was refused admission to the Icelandia. He had paid his money, but when he entered the arena proper, the fellow stopped him at the door and said, "You can't go in." Harry said, "Why?" He says, "You're coloured." Well, Danny was already in, so Danny came back out and got his money refunded, which was very fine of Danny, and the boys came home. (Gairey, 1984, pp. 15, 16)

Despite the rink's discriminatory policy against Jews, my father's ability to pass as white afforded him privileges and opportunities that were denied to his friend Harry. Several years later, my mother Gilda accompanied her white Christian friend to the same ice rink. That time, my mother was recognized as a Jew and denied entry into the facility.

These stories clarify that race is socially constructed and suggest how intention and coincidence can combine in radicalism. What happened to my father was taken up as by activists, because it was recorded by Harry's father, a civil rights activist and union organizer. What happened to my mother was also recorded—in an article in the Toronto daily, where her friend's father happened to work; however, that article remained a one-off protest, unattached to social activists and their movements. Like Rosa Parks's famous incident on the bus, these incidents can be understood as matters related to consumer, as well as citizen, rights: Everybody who pays an entrance fee has the same right to partake in a service. The mythologized account of Rosa Parks often ignores her engagement with the NAACP and Highlander Education and Research Center. Again, it is in the meeting of the individual and the collective, of formal and informal, of experience and reflexivity that translates radical teaching, writing, and thought into learning and action.

7

AT THE ROOT OF IT ALL: HOW PARTICIPANTS LEARN TO MAKE CHANGE

> Demanding consumers need ways to assess political consumerism. We need to understand the importance of political consumerism as a force in global politics and evaluate its democratic potential. Scholarship on political consumerism has much to teach us. I use this research to compare the differences between political consumerism past and present and to evaluate boycotts and buycotts as political tools. (Micheletti, 2003, p. 17)

The analysis in this chapter carries on from previous chapter, moving to my third framing question of how participants learn to make change through their shopping. I continue to draw on the Gramscian concepts that I have already outlined as well as my conceptualizations of holistic learning, socially embedded consumer-citizenship, and the complications of resistance. In this analysis, I also return to the notion of radicalism and explore the meanings of "radical" and the potential for radicalism in the arena of shopping. Although, as Sparks (1997) establishes, all dissidence involves tension between creating change and maintaining the status quo, shopping-related resistance occupies an especially paradoxical place among social movements. Shopping fulfils the consumerist ideology, but critical shopping introduces protest into hegemonic discourse and practice. Shopping-based resistance is ironic, because it uses a tool of globalization to oppose globalization. ☼ In this way, such resistance is able to highlight some of the central dialectical tensions that infuse learning about the politics of globalization, consumption, citizenship, and societal transformation.

In framing much of my analysis in this chapter, I turn to an article by Jo Littler (2005) in which she introduces the concept of "relational reflexivity." Her theorizing suggests how different social movements and discourses encourage particular types of reflexivity and have differing potential to contribute to societal change. Within the arena of shopping,

> ☼ I shall go on to argue that these very distinct perspectives have in combination prevented us from recognizing the potential power of consumerism—and here I am talking about power in a quite orthodox pre-Foucauldian sense—a power which has been brought into focus latterly by the acceleration of Green activism, by South African boycotts and other instances of consumer sanction and support. Finally, I shall propose that consumer politics is able to mobilize and enfranchise a very broad spectrum of constituents, and moreover that it is productive of a kind of utopian collectivism lacking from other contemporary politics.   —Mica Nava (1999), "Consumerism Reconsidered," p. 46

different forms of reflexivity help shoppers learn how to understand and enact critical shopping and consumption, and how to carry their shopping-based analysis and resistance to other arenas.

Forms of Reflexivity

Littler develops her analysis "from a neo-Gramscian, post-Marxist premise in which wide-ranging coalitions, connected through commonalities, chains of equivalence and articulation are more politically fruitful than isolated avant-garde gestures" (2005, p. 229). Consistent with Beck (1992) and Connelly and Prothero (2008), Littler contends that anti-consumerist activism generally encourages reflexivity among consumers; however, she notes, reflexivity is often romanticized. She distinguishes between two forms of reflexivity that are apparent in the different approaches to anti-consumerism and that encourage different political and consumer responses among shoppers:

> I am interested in the possibility that two different types of reflexivity might be identified at work in anti-consumerist discourse, as well as in cultural theory: first, a relatively narcissistic form of reflexivity that acts to shore up a romantic anti-consumerist activist self, and second, an understanding of reflexivity as a more relational and dispersed process. (2005, p. 229)

Relational reflexivity is both affective and intellectual, and focuses "on the nature of the alliances through which the individual is constituted and situated" (p. 246), while narcissistic reflexivity maintains a neoliberal, individualistic focus that discourages collective action. These distinctions are not dissimilar from what Williams (1980) is trying to get at in his distinction between "alternative" and "oppositional" responses. Within the sphere of shopping and consumption, relational reflexivity extends to considerations of the ties between consumers and producers as well as the differences among consumers and the structures in which consumers live.

In making her argument and developing these concepts, Littler analyzes Anita Roddick's book, *Take It Personally*, Naomi Klein's hallmark book, *No Logo*, Bill Talen's persona of "Reverend Billy" and his Church of Stop Shopping, and Kalle Lasn's magazine *AdBusters*, as well as his Buy Nothing Day and Blackspot Sneakers projects. ☼ Roddick's approach is interpreted as the most narcissistic in its reflexivity. It encourages people to examine their own lives and make changes on an individual basis. Her book "predominantly interpellates the reader as a 'rational choice' consumer who, once equipped with enough information, will be able to challenge globalization from a personal perspective (Roddick 2001, pp. 42–43)" (Littler, 2005, p. 236).

> ☼ Blackspot campaign was born almost three years ago when we decided to stop merely criticizing the status quo and actually do something about it. It was born on the back of Nike, capturing the attention of the global media as a lively attack on the brand idolatry and sweatshop production methods of that multinational. Encouragingly, over 25,000 people are now wearing Blackspot shoes. Earth-friendly, anti-sweatshop, and cruelty-free, Blackspots are the only shoes designed to give Big Business what it needs the most: a swift kick in the brand. —Accessed June 17, 2008, www.adbusters.org/campaigns/blackspot/about.html

In contrast, Klein's book "interpellates its audience of youthful Generation X and Y consumers by gesturing emotively towards a shared habitus. It enacts a politics in which change is ultimately conceived of as happening through global laws, brought about through the movement-of-movements, and displays a somewhat contradictory attitude towards its own role as activist-text" (Littler, 2005, p. 242). Littler notes further that, despite Klein's critique of identity politics, which she thinks excludes material issues related to uneven distribution of wealth, she relies on her own analysis of identity politics and her (predominantly Western) readers' familiarity with those politics. In Littler's analysis, not only does *No Logo* itself become an object for consumption, its consumption can become the chief form of anti-consumerist activism for many readers. ☼ Littler complicates the function of *No Logo*, which both uses relational reflexivity in generating an analysis of consumerism and a resistant response to it and lacks reflexivity in considering who the book's audience is, how Klein relates to them, and her own position of authority in writing this book.

To Littler, Talen and Lasn use a combination of irony, performance, and culture jamming and work "less to advocate attempts to withdraw from corporate consumption as a continuous year-round general

☼ The text's implication is that readers have to find their own way to activism. Yet, for those outside activist circles, or uninvolved in the kind of educational spheres where such activism is examined, the act of reading *No Logo* is itself probably one of the most significant investments in "the movement-of-movements" that many people will make. This brings us to one of the most important, overlooked and problematic points about *No Logo*: the great issue—unspoken of in the text . . .—of the role for books like *No Logo* in putting such debates on the agenda and turning them into ideas that will seem to be popular and feasible. In short, the issues of mainstreaming, coalition building and creating broad-based counter-hegemonies. In effect, to discuss this is to discuss the role of the commodity of the book itself as a form of activism.   —Jo Littler, "Beyond the Boycott: Anti-consumerism, Cultural Change and the Limits of Reflexivity," p. 233

strategy and more as a promotional tactic to create discursive space for rethinking the relations of consumption" (2005, p. 239). Talen, who appears in character as Southern Baptist-style Reverend Billy with his choir at well-known retail outlets and who preaches the ills of consumerism, exemplifies "the politics of 'boycott culture' mixed prominently with a flamboyant advocacy of consumer abstinence" (p. 239). Lasn, largely through *AdBusters*, "energetically argues for large-scale social change by forming new principles of economic and environmental sustainability, and . . . imagines such change has the best chance of being brought about through ideological and discursive shifts" (p. 242). Seen as the best exemplar of relational reflexivity among these four examples, even Talen's Reverend Billy leaves his audience with "questions about not only what other types of change are imagined across the spectrum of contemporary anti-consumerist discourse as happening 'after the boycott' but also how these changes are imagined as emerging" (pp. 239–240).

Applying these ideas about reflexivity to the novels discussed in Chapter 4, I surmise that Kinsella's (2001) shopaholic Becky generally lacks reflexivity altogether. Townley's (2006) figure of Jen and Coupland's (1991) ensemble of main characters generally exemplify narcissistic reflexivity, although they engage in this process to different ends. Several of Ozeki's (1998) characters, and especially Jane, engage much more in relational reflexivity.

In her article, Littler (2005) clarifies that there is more nuance to reflexivity than I have suggested by this quick review of the four novels. She notes the limits of even the most relationally reflexive example of Talen's Reverend Billy and ascribes some degree of relational reflexivity to both Klein's book *No Logo* and Lasn's projects. It is only Roddick's book, *Take it Personally*, which, as its title suggests, remains essentially an example of narcissistic reflexivity. In the analysis summarized in the remainder of this chapter, I continue to employ Littler's ideas on reflexivity to explore how the comments and shopping practices of participants in this study relate to learning about making change and participating in a transformational or radical agenda. First, though, I take some time to discuss the concept of radicalism itself and the variety of views articulated by participants about this topic.

Radical: What's in a Name?

Throughout this inquiry, I have applied the word "radical" to both learning and shopping. As I explained in Chapter 2, my initial use of this word was meant to recall its meaning in critical adult education and denoted teaching, learning, and action directed toward socially just transformation; however, as I clarify in this chapter, "radical" does not mean the same thing to all people, and, even if a common meaning is assumed, the complications of social life complicate radicalism. After conducting only a few interviews, I began to ask participants how they understood the word "radical" and whether they considered themselves to be radical shoppers. I heard diverse opinions about radicalism as well as both the potential and the desirability of radicalism in the arena of shopping.

Etymologically, the word "radical" derives from the Latin word for "root." Further to its original English meaning of "fundamental" or "inherent," it has taken on additional meanings as "extreme" or "drastic." Colloquially, it is also used to mean "wonderful," in much the same way as such words as "cool" and "sweet" are used. ☼ In addition to these technical and colloquial meanings, "radical" has also been attached to certain bodies of scholarship. In its sense of "extreme" or "drastic," it has been applied to extreme or revolutionary movements, Marxism on the left of the political spectrum and conservatism on the right. ☼ Within the field of adult education, "radical" is often used by scholars and practitioners interested in critical pedagogy, which has grown out of Marxist as well as more recent epistemological and theoretical perspectives such as feminism and critical race studies. It can describe movements, individuals, or ideas. Foley (2001) cites the original meaning of the word and focuses on adult learning, which attempts to address the root of a social problem. He and other adult educators alternate the use of "radical" with other relevant words, including "emancipatory" (Foley, 1999), "revolutionary" (Coben, 1998), "dissident" (Chomsky in hooks, 2003), and the widely used "critical."

So, it seems that the word "radical" is loaded with assumed meanings and biases. It also seems that "radical" has different meanings. Somewhere

☼ **rad·i·cal**

adj.

1. Arising from or going to a root or source; basic: proposed a radical solution to the problem.
2. Departing markedly from the usual or customary; extreme: radical opinions on education.
3. Favoring or effecting fundamental or revolutionary changes in current practices, conditions, or institutions: radical political views.
4. Linguistics—Of or being a root: a radical form.
5. Botany—Arising from the root or its crown: radical leaves.
6. Slang—Excellent; wonderful.

n.

1. One who advocates fundamental or revolutionary changes in current practices, conditions, or institutions: radicals seeking to overthrow the social order.
2. Mathematics—The root of a quantity as indicated by the radical sign.
3. Symbol R—An atom or a group of atoms with at least one unpaired electron.
4. Linguistics—See root1.

[Middle English, of a root, from Late Latin rdclis, having roots, from Latin rdx, rdc-, root; see wrd- in Indo-European roots.]   —"radical" in *The American Heritage Dictionary of the English Language* (4th ed.)

along the line in this inquiry, I realized that the use of the word "radical" and the phrase "radical shopper" assumed a clear meaning on my part and a shared understanding among participants. I knew that I was using "radical" as a nod to the critical adult education scholarship of Foley (1999, 2001) and others, in the sense that I've already outlined: an attempt to identify, learn about, and respond to the root of a problem. I was not sure, though, that participants understood the word in the same way; so, I began to ask participants if they considered themselves radical shoppers and what the word "radical" meant to them. Participants' responses suggested that some adjustments were in order, including an amended subtitle for this text; however, the idea of radicalism cannot be removed completely from this project. It appropriately returns to my analytical discussion in this chapter, in which I respond to the question of how participants learn to make change through their shopping. Now, it is important to spend some time thinking about how participants and I talked about the challenges of coming to understand the meaning of, potential for, and desirability of radicalism during contemporary globalization, and how the arena of shopping might be helpful in or, on the contrary, a distraction from learning about radicalism and becoming radical.

In response to the assortment of meanings for the word "radical," some critical scholars and activists attempt to distinguish between radicalism

☼ **Radical** has been used as an adjective in English from C14, and as a noun from C17, from . . . rw *radix*, L–root. Its early uses were mostly physical, to express an inherent and fundamental quality, and this was extended to more general descriptions from C16. The important extension to political matters, always latent in this general use, belongs specifically to lC18, especially in the phrase **Radical Reform**. **Radical** as a noun to describe a proponent of **radical reform** was common from eC19. . . . **Radical**, especially with a capital letter, was by the second half of C19 almost as respectable as *liberal*, and **Radicalism** generally followed. . . .

C20 use has been complicated. **Radical**, with or without the capital, has continued to be used of the more vigorous elements of LIBERALISM (q.v.) and more generally to indicate relatively vigorous and far-reaching reforms. As such it has often been contrasted with "dogmatic" *socialism* or *revolutionary* programmes. It has also been widely used in its older general sense, as in "radical re-examination". Two further uses have complicated it. There is now common use in the phrase **Radical Right**, either to indicate extreme right-wing politics or more strictly to indicate active policies of change of a right-wing kind, as distinct from a more conventional CONSERVATISM (q.v.). On the other hand, **radical** was readopted, especially in the United States from the late 1950s, in a sense very close to the eC19 use; as such it is often virtually equivalent to socialist or revolutionary, and has gathered the same range of responses as in that earlier period. . . . **Radical** seemed to offer a way of avoiding dogmatic and factional associations while reasserting the need for vigorous and fundamental change. . . . It is interesting that the old phrase **radical reform** (q.v.) has been split into the contrasted **radical** and *reformist*, within the radical movement, while elsewhere radical (with *militant*) does service as a contrast with *moderate* (which in practice is often a euphemistic term for everyone, however insistent and committed, who is not a **radical**).
—Raymond Williams, *Keywords*, pp. 251–252 (emphasis in original)

and other sorts of changes that serve to reiterate and reinforce, rather than refute, the social status quo. A century ago, Marxist Rosa Luxemburg (2008 [1908]) warned against confusing revolutionary and reformist strategies in class struggles. ☼ (next page) A tactic such as unionization was seen as helpful in leveraging workers' limited power within capitalist structures. Although unionization could help improve the lives of workers, Luxemburg regarded such a tactic as strategically insufficient for ending capitalist relations and achieving true socioeconomic transformation. More recently, Audrey Lorde issued a similar caution about the limitations of using hegemonic tools to overturn that social order. ☼ Referring to inclusion of racialized minority women in the feminist movement, Lorde's well-known remarks about the impossibility of using the "master's tools" to "dismantle the master's house" (2002, p. 108) urge white feminists not to abandon a radical purpose by settling for a greater share of the privilege available to white men. In short, both Luxemburg and Lorde argue that efforts to reform hegemonic structures might improve the situation for oppressed

☼ Can the Social-Democracy be against reforms? Can we contrapose the social revolution, the transformation of the existing order, our final goal, to social reforms? Certainly not. The daily struggle for reforms, for the amelioration of the condition of the workers within the framework of the existing social order, and for democratic institutions, offers to the Social-Democracy an indissoluble tie. The struggle for reforms is its means; the social revolution, its aim.

It is in Eduard Bernstein's theory . . . that we find, for the first time, the opposition of the two factors of the labour movement. His theory tends to counsel us to renounce the social transformation, the final goal of Social-Democracy and, inversely, to make of social reforms, the means of the class struggle, its aim. Bernstein himself has very clearly and characteristically formulated this viewpoint when he wrote: "The Final goal, no matter what it is, is nothing; the movement is everything."   —Rosa Luxemburg (2008), *Reform or Revolution*, p. 41

What does the active participation of trade unions in fixing the scale and cost of production amount to? It amounts to a cartel of the workers and entrepreneurs in a common stand against the consumer and especially against rival entrepreneurs. In no way is the effect of this any different from that of ordinary employers' associations. In no way is the effect of this any different from that of ordinary employers' associations. Basically we no longer have here a struggle between labor and capital, but the solidarity of capital and labor against the total consumers. Considered for its social worth, it is seen to be a reactionary move that cannot be a stage in the struggle for the emancipation of the proletariat because it connotes the very opposite of the class struggle. . . . So that the scope of trade unions is limited essentially to a struggle for an increase of wages and the reduction of labor time, that is to say, to say, to efforts at regulating capitalist exploitation as they are made necessary by the momentary situation of the world market. But labor unions can in no way influence the process of production itself.   —Rosa Luxemburg (2008), *Reform or Revolution*, p. 57

☼ For the master's tools will never dismantle the master's house. They may allow us temporarily to beat him at his own game, but they will never enable us to bring about genuine change. And this fact is only threatening to those women who still define the master's house as their only source of support.   —Audrey Lorde (2002), "The Master's Tools will Never Dismantle the Master's House," p. 108

groups but do not eliminate the fact of oppression. Reforms that tinker rather than overhaul existing structures, in the way that Canada's multiculturalism responds to racism, mollify many critics, distract attention away from ongoing critical analysis, and marginalize radical positions.

Strongly based on Sparks's (1997) concept of dissidence, my conceptualization of resistance approaches the sense of radicalism offered by Luxemburg and Lorde, with the proviso that resisters, dissidents, and radicals avoid violent tactics. For Luxemburg, like Gramsci (1971), the solution involves a political party that can articulate a radical vision and work to implement a radical agenda; however, political activism was not a direction pursued by participants in our conversations. Although shopping is one arena in which consumer-citizens can develop and begin to implement resistance in concrete terms, its potential for true radicalism is uncertain. With his educational background in critical sociology, Sean actually thought of the phrase "radical shopper" as a *non sequitur*, because all shoppers participate in fundamentally oppressive capitalist relations.

> Sean: So, "radical," it's a bit of a [*pause*], in a sense it's radical but in a sense shopping makes the very, it's a bit of an oxymoron. A bit, not completely. . . . But a bit of an oxymoron. . . . 'Cause if you're shopping how can you be radical? . . . Because shopping is such an endemic part of the way that North American society is constructed.... Radical, if you think of radical as overthrowing that, that's where I more think of radical as overthrowing the whole structure. . . . But I come back, I go back to the sixties, when "radical" was overthrowing society and, and uh, you know, and institute the dictatorship of the proletariat. That to me, that's what radical is. . . . And so in a sense, I mean it's a cute phrase, and I kind of like it 'cause it, it does encapsulate some ideas, but it isn't really radical. I don't think the act of shopping can be radical.   —interview excerpt, March 24, 2007 ☼

☼ Is there such a thing as "ethical consumerism", or is this a oxymoron, like "huge dwarf" or "brave coward"?   —Mark Paterson (2006), *Consumption and Everyday Life*, p. 225

In the remainder of this section, I discuss how some participants discussed radicalism as not only a possibility within the arena of shopping but also an aspiration. I also discuss how, alternatively, some participants expressed discomfort with the moniker of radical and articulated their hopes in other terms. Finally, I explore the suggestion raised by several participants that radicalism, like other elements of identity, might be understood as a contextual, shifting concept rather than in a definitive way.

Radical Aspirations

Participants in this study held a range of views on what type and extent of change were important and worthy of their commitments. When I asked them to define their understanding of "radical" and whether they considered themselves to be radicals, participants articulated a similar range of meanings as those found in a dictionary. Although he drifted from the arena of shopping in his response, Eddie articulated an understanding of "radical" and, among all of the participants, most clearly characterized himself as someone with a generally radical purpose:

KAELA: So what does the word "radical" mean to you?

EDDIE: An extreme definition would be, or an extreme definition is of someone who absolutely is focused on making a specific outcome, a specific change and insists on roping everyone into the cause, sometimes nicely, sometimes not nicely. And just trying to get a certain goal done, really goal focused. And, but for me I would say, on a scale of 1 to 10, being, and 1 and 10 both being absolute extremes possible, that are possible for people, I would say I'm a, I'm an 8 out of a 10. So I'm, like, extremely, I'm 8. Like 10 being radical, and I'm an 8. I'm just guessing, though. —interview excerpt, April 11, 2007

Ironically, although my call for participants had reached out to people who identified as radical shoppers, Eddie was a notable exception; others were generally reluctant to associate themselves or their shopping to radicalism. Ellen, who comes from the United States, shared Eddie's enthusiasm for the idea of the radical shopper, although she aligned herself with a more recognizable image of the radical figure and purpose. Her comments were unique in another way, as they evoked a romanticized vision of the radical hero: "Right [pause]. Well . . . when [my husband] and I talk about our shopping practices and how we live in the world, we never say, we don't explicitly use the term 'radical,' but we always say, we're gonna Che it [giggle]. Like Che Guevara" (interview excerpt, April 24, 2007).

Although Ellen's comment might be construed as an attempt to bring some levity to the stress of choosing to think and act outside the social norm, the commodification of Che Guevara and other well-known radical figures, evident especially in the mass-produced items bearing their images, gives people a way of expressing radicalism as "cool" and fashionable. ☼ This construction of radicalism as trendy seems to create bonds of "imagined community" (Anderson, 1991) between individual consumer-citizens and famous figures who stand for something; however, it does not demand that individuals contemplate the kind of analysis, action, and sacrifice undertaken by those radical figures.

A couple of participants, Sean and Karen, had educational backgrounds that helped them understand the word "radical" in its original

☼ Handbag with image of Nelson Mandela, on display in Cape Town, December 2007

sense. During his interview, in response to my questions about radical shopping, Sean made this comment: "Well, of course the root of the word 'radical' is 'root.' No, there's my academic side coming out" (interview excerpt, March 24, 2007). Although, as I noted above, Sean was sceptical about the potential to find and manifest radicalism in the arena of shopping, both he and Karen were generally supportive of radical ideals and commitments, given that understanding of the word "radical."

Other participants shifted away from the idea of radicalism as learning about and responding to the very root of a problem. For them, radical shopping involved bucking convention. The idea of radical shopping was an intriguing, creative possibility, but one that requires great commitment and sacrifice. Violet, who was very fashion conscious, made this comment during her interview:

> Someone who's a radical shopper is someone who can think outside the box and think alternatively and not be affected by trends in society or not worry about the way that they look, etc. etc. So, that's my idea of a radical shopper. And I am not one.   —interview excerpt, April 4, 2007

Violet was clear in her opinion that she was not a radical shopper, but some other participants described an admiration for and aspiration to radicalism. Julie and Linda offered similar explanations of the radical shopper but were more interested in adopting the radical shopper's practices:

KAELA: And so I'm interested in how you, if you would describe yourself as a radical shopper and how you understand the word "radical."

JULIE: I understand the word to mean . . . at odds with convention. Swimming upstream [*pause*]. Would I describe myself as a radical shopper? I would describe myself as someone who tries to be a radical shopper. —interview excerpt, March 14, 2007

LINDA: Yeah, I think that "radical" means, you know, choosing really different choices than what's commonly available in the mainstream. And I know people who are radical shoppers, and I'd like to say that I'm one of them, but I'm not. I still shop at Safeway and I still shop at Metrotown and I still buy Reitman's clothes. But I know people who, they make a point of only buying organic clothing and only, you know, they just go so much farther than I have the time or energy to do. And I think they're like beta testers, people who buy the first edition of every piece of software that comes out. . . . But they pave the way. They provide a smaller market for companies to try things out. Um, and I think that's important. I'm not one of them. I'd like to be [*chuckles*]. I'm sort of the second wave. But there's definitely, those people are out there and I, and you, you see them. They walk down the street and they just look different. . . . And I wish I was one of them, whereas other people go, Oh! Crazy long-haired hippie [*chuckles*]! —interview excerpt, April 29, 2007

For Amitah, the idea of being a radical shopper was exciting if also puzzling:

[*laughs*] Am I a radical shopper? I don't know. Radical, hmmm. It's kind of exciting, the word [*laughs*]. I want to be radical [*laughs*]. It's a bit dangerous, you know . . . sounds dangerous. I would almost want to say yes, but I don't want to say yes, because I don't want those choices to be the radical choice. . . . I want it to be the normal choice. —interview excerpt, February 21, 2007

These comments indicate a level of uncertainty about what it means to adopt not only radical convictions and actions but also the identity of a radical. The participants cited above were generally accepting of the importance of real radicals, even if they were unsure about their own roles in radicalism. Many participants, though, were disinclined to consider the social function and importance of radicalism, in shopping as in other arenas of life. Often, they emphasized radicalism as extremism. Their comments resonated with Beck's (1992) writings on the "risk society," as they spoke about the dangers that radicalism posed to radicals themselves and, by implication, to others in society.

Radical Risks and Alternatives

Julie's, Linda's, and Amitah's comments recall Sparks's (1997) assertion that the quality of courage is essential to dissidence. Certainly, these three were not talking about the kind of courage demonstrated by Sparks's example of Rosa Parks or other well-known civil rights activists, but they were willing to take a certain amount of social risk inherent in stepping outside the middle-class mainstream. Social movement learning scholars recognize that people join or avoid organizations for a range of reasons beyond their commitment to a cause. Some people join social movements or activist organizations because of their existing social networks rather than their own deeply held convictions, although they are unlikely to become engaged deeply or for a long period (Kilgore, 1999). As Deborah Kilgore also notes, there are costs involved in participating in any social movement that agitates for societal change. These always include time and emotional commitment but can also include financial costs and threats to physical safety or social status. Assessing the risks involved in affiliating with any social movement, including those to social status or material wealth, is part of the decision about whether to get involved. In contrast to the individuals who engage with a social movement for reasons other than shared values, analysis, and identity, there are individuals who *do* share members' values, analysis and identity but remain absent because of the perceived costs of joining the movement. That is why courage is so important to dissidence. For her part, Amitah described attempts to "walk her talk," as the colloquialism goes.

KAELA: Do you think of yourself as middle class?
AMITAH: Well, I feel that I grew up that way. . . . Yeah. I think I've
           dropped out of the middle class . . . on purpose [*laughs*]. . . .
KAELA: As a, as a sort of a statement of what you want to be in your
           life.
AMITAH: Yeah, that's a good way to put it. I'll concur with that
           [*laughs*].   —interview excerpt, February 21, 2007

One of the interesting details about Amitah's understanding of radicalism in the arena of shopping is the implication that desirable but radical behaviour remains marginalized. Thinking of herself as radical meant realizing how much work was still to be done in helping others learn to change their "common sense" (Gramsci, 1971) and associated practices. Perhaps she, too, was hinting at the social costs of being radical, but, given her other comments and her willingness to step outside the social norm, it seems more likely that she found it disconcerting that important changes remain a long way away.

A few participants reversed Amitah's concern about labelling critical shopping as a radical activity. They argued that critical shopping cannot be considered radical precisely because it has become so accepted within the mainstream:

> KAREN: Yeah, I'd have to agree with you about not totally liking the word "radical." Because it seems like more and more it's starting, it's becoming in some ways more mainstream. . . . But, I mean, if you look at radical meaning, like, "root," there's a totally different meaning for it. But if you look at that word meaning "root" and you think about, that when I'm shopping I'm trying to uncover all kinds of things, get down to the root of things, . . . it does make sense, if you look at a different meaning of the word "radical." So, yeah, I'd say I probably try to be ethical . . . more than anything.   —focus group excerpt, May 17, 2007

> We left the produce section and, in the next aisle, I asked Claire about how she understood the word "radical," which I had used in my flyer. She defined it as "extreme" or "crazy." When I asked if she thought of herself as a radical shopper, she said no, that she was not extreme— "We're here on 4th Avenue! It's not extreme, especially on the West Coast."   —shopping trip excerpt, March 22, 2007

Still, the shopping and consumption practices of both Karen and Claire seem outside the ordinary, even for vegetarian-friendly Vancouver. Although she had resumed eating meat in limited amounts, Claire maintained a vegan diet for several years and, even after she resumed eating meat, she remained strict about buying and consuming only organic or free-range meat. Karen continued to maintain a vegetarian diet, had routinely shopped for vegan shoes and at second-hand stores, and chose to live in Vancouver's West End, where it is easier to avoid having a car. When we met for her interview, she happily displayed the jacket that she had recently bought, because it was stylish, made in Canada, and made with organically produced wool.

For the most part, remaining participants who expressed an opinion on radicalism in shopping or in other arenas offered a more negative view. Often, the word "radical" was associated with undesirable extremism, which, as I have already indicated, was seen as a threat to people's social standing and relations.

> KAELA: So I'll ask you how you understand the word "radical" and if you would describe yourself as a radical shopper.
>
> SARAH: I think a radical shopper would be an extreme shopper, and, no, I don't think I am.
>
> KAELA: Okay, so, radical, if you hear the word "radical" that's what it—
>
> SARAH: To me it's like an extreme shopper.
>
> KAELA: Okay. And that's negative?
>
> Sarah: Yeah.   —interview excerpt, April 27, 2007

> She was quite involved in [an environmental organization] for a few years, in 1990/1991 but was "turned off" by one active person who was very "intense." She thinks that sometimes "people who have an agenda and are very dominating" are looking for answers and drawn into an [an activist] organization . . . and a more radical lifestyle. She described their fervour as akin to being "born again." She said, "When I first learned these things I wanted to share," but she came to see that she had to be conscious of what she was saying to whom.   —shopping trip excerpt, Reesa, May 2, 2007

These participants embraced ethical or critical shopping as part of the demonstration of their values and concerns, but radicalism was rejected as a term to express those values and concerns.

Even some participants who were more supportive of people whom they characterized as radicals sometimes mentioned some unpleasant qualities and risks that they associated with radicalism. Linda described the tendency for radicals to come across as "holier than thou" (interview excerpt, April 29, 2007). In her mind, not only did such people risk social isolation, they also risked having their analyses dismissed by others: "And I, occasionally I find myself feeling that way, but then I go, No, you know what? Once upon a time I was like that, too. . . . And I didn't know any better. And if I'm gonna act like that nobody's gonna follow my example" (interview excerpt, April 29, 2007).

If "radical" was not an optimal word for most participants to describe their shopping-related ambitions, what were some of the more preferable alternatives, and how did participants connect them to change? Participants for whom radicalism had negative connotations of being extreme, authoritarian, and socially alienating were likely to seek more positive-sounding, palatable language and practices, as Reesa did during her shopping trip: "She also talked about being motivated more by a desire to 'support' rather than 'protest' and said that she thinks that she teaches by example" (shopping trip excerpt, May 2, 2007).

Reesa's sentiments raise a question in relation to critical shopping as a type of social movement learning. Scholars such as Connelly and Prothero (2008) assert that green or other types of critical shopping bring people together in social movements in which they learn to understand particular issues, the meaning and impact of their shopping and consumption, and their identities. In contrast, Donatella della Porta and Mario Diani (2006) express the generally accepted understanding that conflict and an oppositional stance are elements of a social movement. Many critical shopping movements, though, stress the possibility of resistance and change without overt protests against an identified enemy or opposition. For della Porta and Diani, movements that concentrate on solidarity and collectively generated and enacted solutions are more properly referred to as "consensus movements" (p. 22). ☼ This approach seems closer to the one that Reesa described in her comments. Perhaps most of the participants in this study were better aligned with the politics of consensus, rather than the oppositional politics that are a central element of social movements. At least some participants had seemingly embraced "personal and community empowerment" (della Porta & Diani, 2006, p. 23) rather than a radical transformation in social relations.

Still, several participants seemed comfortable apportioning blame, even if they were unwilling to adopt an overtly conflictual stance. Many

---

☼ In both social movement and consensus movement dynamics, actors share solidarity and an interpretation of the world, enabling them to link specific acts and events in a longer time perspective. However, in the latter, sustained collective action does not take a conflictual element. Collective goods are often produced through cooperative efforts that neither imply nor require the identification of specific adversaries, trying to reduce the assets and opportunities of one's group or preventing chances to expand them. Prospected solutions do not imply redistribution of power nor alterations in social structure, but focus instead on service delivery, self-help, personal and community empowerment. Likewise, the practice and promotion of alternative lifestyles does not require the presence of opponents defined in social and political terms. Collective actors may fight ethereal adversaries, ranging from bad or conventional taste, in the case of artistic and style-oriented movements, to "the inner enemy" in the case of some religious movements, without necessarily blaming any social actors for the state of things they intend to modify. —Donatella della Porta and Mario Diani, *Social Movements: An Introduction*, pp. 22–23

seemed interested in belonging to a movement that found a way to voice opposition and exercise resistance, without feeling as if they were in a constant state of conflict. The possibility that individuals and perhaps even an entire movement might alternate between a conflictual and a consensual stance, depending on the immediate circumstances and perceived urgency, is suggested by some participants' experiences and comments. Critical shoppers might, for example, alternate between tactics of boycotts and buycotts, depending on what they have learned and what their material and cultural options are. Moreover, boycotts can be expressed as buycotts: I do not boycott large multinational corporations, I just make a point of shopping at small, locally owned stores and for locally produced items. The tension between what della Porta and Diani distinguish as social movements and consensus movements bears further exploration among social movement learning scholars.

Putting aside the question of whether or not critical shopping can constitute a form of social movement, I return to the concerns raised by participants about assuming an identity as a radical. During the second focus group, the following discussion about the merits of and concerns about the word "radical" and the reasons for distancing oneself from radicalism ensued:

JOCELYN: I prefer the word "ethical" to "radical." For some reason, the word "radical" makes it seem far away. . . . "Radical," somehow it's too easy to knock it down. . . . My understanding of the word . . . [is] that when you buy anything, remember a certain number of values. One is, how does the production of this thing affect the earth? And that's, you know, you can think of that in lots of . . . subsets to that one. What are the conditions of the workers that produced it or farmed it or what all? . . . What are, what does the profit support? For instance, does it go either to military or pharmaceutical companies, two people that I'm particularly hoping that I wouldn't have to buy something [in support of']? Local is another one. . . .

CARLA: I don't know. I mean, I'm trying to think about what radical meant, and if I think about how it's used in education then "radical" usually refers to somebody like Freire and how Freire approached education. That concept of "radical," if we're using that concept of "radical" to describe a radical shopper, then I guess that's what I am, because I do try to find out more about what, what's happening in the world around me and to understand what the implications of each thing [are], which is sort of how I think Freire would,

would go about, um, so in that sense, yes, I, I guess I would call myself that, if used in that context. But radical's such a, radical's a really, whew, one of those words that have a lot of meanings associated with it.

KAELA: It's loaded.

CARLA: It's very, yeah, loaded. It's very loaded. . . . So I would probably go for "critical" or "ethical" or, I would try to think of, "conscientious" actually is one that I would, I try to be a conscientious shopper. . . . But there's . . . two reasons. Because . . . I mean there's altruistic reasons, which is the guilt thing. And also, the whole concept of someone, somewhere in the world getting paid a dime or less to make a pair of shoes that I'm gonna buy later on and pay over 100 dollars [for] pisses me off, right? [*laughs*] . . . So there's, there's another, I mean it's altruism, because I, I don't think someone should be working in poor conditions. They should, you know, they should get bathroom breaks, they shouldn't be locked into the factory. . . . But also it's, there's a level of selfishness, too. I get really angry that I have to pay this much when, when the company who, you know, made the product pays their employees so little. It just makes me really mad! But, and there's another sort of selfish reason. So, for example, if I'm buying house-cleaning products, shampoo or whatever, I try to get something that won't harm me, that doesn't, my own little environment. It's not just, I mean it's also the big environment. I don't want, I try to avoid pesticides, because overall it's bad for the environment, it's bad for the birds, it's bad for the fish or whatever. But my own micro-environment, I don't want it to be polluted either. So there's some selfishness there.

So what's possible to achieve? . . . I mean, I'm hoping for a fair, fairer global society and a cleaner environment, but obviously shopping's not going to be the only way you do that. So, for example, when I talk about the person who's getting the dime paid for every pair of shoes he or she makes, um, it's gonna take more than just me not buying the products. If anything, it's me not buying the product might be more damaging, so I have to think of other ways to, you know, to get on the company's back, to get on the government's back to try and, to . . . get other people around me to know what's going on so that way they too, hopefully, will feel the real power in, in the sort of . . . the real power of trying to change something. . . .

KAREN: Yeah, I'd have to agree with you about not totally liking the word "radical." Because it seems like more and more it's starting, it's becoming in some ways more mainstream. . . . But, I mean, if you look at "radical" meaning, like, "root," there's a totally different meaning for it. But if you look at that word meaning "root" and you think about, that when I'm shopping I'm trying to uncover all kinds of things, get down to the root of things . . . it does make sense, if you look at a different meaning of the word "radical." So, yeah, I'd say I probably try to be ethical . . . more than anything.
—focus group excerpt, May 17, 2007

In this conversation, Karen, Carla, and Jocelyn reiterated many of the reasons that participants were reluctant to assume an identity as a radical. They were concerned about being perceived as negative and having their analyses and responses marginalized, misunderstood, and dismissed.

Carla's comments sharpen some points that have arisen or been implied in this analysis. Critical shopping is important but is limited in its potential to help effect change. Her view of radical shopping is not the outright *non sequitur* that Sean had proposed but is instead a recognition of the need to engage in multiple tactics as part of a critical, or radical, commitment. Second, Carla's comments clarify that reflexivity is more than an intellectual process of thinking through an issue, as it is commonly understood to be. Her comments illustrate that other dimensions contribute to reflexivity. She talked about how, at times, she felt "really angry" and "really mad" about certain parts of shopping. These emotions gave her intellectual analysis a greater urgency and pressed her toward a more relationally reflexive understanding.

Third, whether or not it was considered radical, much of the impetus for participants' critical shopping emerged from relational reflexivity—thinking and caring about one's role in the global scale of social relations and the environment; however, some of it emerged from a narcissistic reflexivity that is consistent with neoliberal ideology and its individualistic orientation. On some occasions, participants' comments clarify Littler's (2005) distinction between narcissistic and relational reflexivity even further: Reflexivity involves consideration of the scope of a problem and the nature of a response. The narcissistic reflexivity in Roddick's book might lack a structural analysis and lead to individualized actions, but it calls for an appreciation of concern about and obligation for others. It is not an entirely self-involved reflexivity, in the way that some proponents of organics or local buying can be. For Carla, concerns about costs to personal health, safety, and finances remained present in Carla's mind, even though she conceded that, in some sense, she might be radical in her shopping after all.

What's Radical Is Relative

Poststructural and postmodern scholars assert that knowledge is always contextually constructed (Hekman, 1997; Richardson, 2000) and that "[r]esistance is effected by employing other discursive formations to oppose that script, not by appealing to universal subjectivity or absolute principles" (Hekman, 1997, p. 357). Another difficulty in ascertaining what and who is radical, according to participants, arises from their general understanding that radicalism, like gender, race, class, and even knowledge, is contextually determined. What is radical was defined in relation to what is happening within one's social and material world.

> ALICE: I wouldn't classify myself, I remember seeing that and thinking, I don't know if I really fit that description compared to some of my friends who are, I would classify as radical. . . . I think compared to a lot of people I know I would be considered radical, because there are conversations that come up where people will say, well, why don't we go to such and such a place, why don't we go to Walmart or Starbucks or whatever? And I found that just to avoid conflict I say okay, let's go. Because in the past when I've said, you know they're doing this or they're doing that, oh well, you know, what can I do? Who cares? It's cheap, let's go. So when I have my own personal choice I . . . tend not to go. —interview excerpt, February 17, 2007
>
> ELLEN: I mean . . . I think coming out of the States, which is so conservative, to me, like just not going to McDonald's would constitute radical shopping [*chuckle*] in the States, because radical is always going to be on a sliding scale, right. I mean it's radical in comparison to what?
>
> KAELA: So it's relative.
>
> ELLEN: Right, right, it's relative. It's, so I mean, honestly, I think "radical" means something very different in Canada, where, you know . . . there aren't guns on every street corner, and same-sex marriage has been allowed, you know, in many areas.   —interview excerpt, April 24, 2007
>
> NICOLE: It's very hard to step out, because you're just placing yourself in a Western idealism [or, ideology] kind of, how you've been brought up. . . . So, I mean you're not necessarily

taking yourself out of that box. . . . You may be questioning the box, but there's no way that you can pull yourself out, completely.

KAELA: So what does it mean to be radical? And is that, is that possible?

NICOLE: I guess challenging, challenging that idea, I guess actually, . . . questioning your surrounding . . . [*pause*] . . . I mean being, going against what is implemented, I guess. But it doesn't necessarily have to be, I mean I don't see, I mean, "radical" I think implies being extreme.

KAELA: Okay, so it has that kind of colloquial association. . . . Which actually isn't how I meant it.

NICOLE: Okay . . . I think it's just more about [*pause*], hmmm, yeah, it didn't necessarily mean extreme for me. I just think it means, it's just stepping out of context.   —interview excerpt, February 17, 2007

Searching for an example to help me clarify the difficulties in determining who and what is truly radical, I think about Fidel Castro. On the one hand, he radically transformed social and economic relations in Cuba, dismantling capitalism and racism in that country. On the other hand, patriarchy, as well as homophobia, is alive and well there, and Castro himself has not hidden his homophobic views. Mariela Castro's work to alleviate sexism and homophobia in Cuban politics and culture surely makes her a new "organic intellectual" (Gramsci, 1971), but, just as surely, it does not erase the radicalism of her uncle Fidel. Here, then, participants in this inquiry and this analysis contribute to the conceptualization of radicalism, seeing it as contextual, shifting, and, sometimes, unpredictable, rather than universal and static.

Having gone through these data, I am undecided about whether any of the participants were radicals, even if they engaged in relational reflexivity, and whether it makes sense to think about shopping as potentially radical. This inconclusive conclusion helps explain my decision to shift from the concept and language of radicalism in my analysis. There is, though, more to the question of how critical shopping is tied to change than whether or not it can be seen as radical. In the following discussion, I turn my attention to other ways of addressing this question.

Learning to Change Shopping, Shopping to Make Change

As I concluded in the previous section, one reason that participants might eschew an identity as a radical is that they are worried about possible social repercussions. Even people who are disturbed about the status quo might worry about not fitting into it. Facing the reality of materially and culturally defined constraints, needs, and desires, people might find overt shows of radicalism both admirable in others and unacceptable for themselves. Generally reluctant to identify as radicals for varied reasons, most participants nonetheless approached shopping with some form of reflexivity and desire to help bring about change. In this section, I explore how participants learned to understand the potential to make changes in their shopping practices and to ensure that their shopping contributes to an agenda of change.

During interviews, I invited participants to talk about movements and organizations that might have contributed to their learning about the politics of shopping, about changes in their shopping practices that they had made or were contemplating, and about how shopping is connected to formal politics. ☼ These questions helped me capture participants' thoughts and feelings about the links between their shopping and their interest in contributing to some sort of change. Amitah offered the following response to some of these questions:

KAELA: There's a saying that the personal is political. Do you think that your personal shopping practices can make a difference to local, national, or global politics, and if so, how? And on the flip side, what are the limitations that shopping and consumption can have?

AMITAH: So to the first question, yes, I think, uh, they can make a difference. Um, how? Because of the almighty dollar. . . . And on the flip side what are the limitations to that? Um, well, you're still playing in the same field. Um, even if I'm making a sustainable choice, I'm still consuming. . . . Things that I don't necessarily need. . . . So it's, you're still kind of in the same paradigm, although you're trying to take a, a higher road in a way. But somehow the basic foundation of that is still skewed.   —interview excerpt, February 21, 2007

☼
- Can you think of movements or organizations that seem connected to shopping and consumption? What kinds of statements do they make? Have you participated in any of them?
- How, if at all, would you say that your shopping practices have changed in recent months? Can you think of a particular time when you made or noticed these changes? Are there any changes that you've been thinking about making in your shopping practices?   —selected interview questions

Returning to Shaw's (2007) use of the shopping-as-voting metaphor, I have suggested some of the limits to the potential political impact of one's shopping practices. As I have already noted and as Amitah reiterated, critical shopping and the use of shopping to resist hegemony and participate in change is replete with the dialectic that characterizes all resistance, at least as I have conceptualized resistance in this inquiry. Even radicalism, for that matter, likely reiterates a portion of hegemony as it attempts to overturn other parts; it is difficult, if at all possible, to agitate for the overthrow of every structure that serves the hegemonic social order. As critical scholars now readily acknowledge and I have previously explained, individuals have complex identities and affiliations. Even social movements favouring some sort of radical change choose from among possible aims and priorities, and movement members might not share a common stance on issues beyond their established purpose. In the remainder of this section, I explore how this reality helps shape participants' understanding of the political potential and limitations of their shopping to an agenda of change, whether or not that change is considered radical.

It All Adds Up, but . . .

One of the common refrains that I heard while talking to participants is that what is important is that everybody undertakes some sort of critical analysis and response, through their shopping as well as through other processes and activities. Participants also concurred that, although people might not be willing or able to do *everything*, that does not mean that they should and can do *nothing*. Faced with the prospects of Kinsella's (2001) shopaholic Becky or the cynicism of Coupland's (1991) characters, participants did not necessarily endorse the conclusions reached by Luxemburg or Lorde; they thought that it was preferable to take some sort of action and that such action, including critical shopping practices, contributed to change in a meaningful way. Even apparently small actions and changes might make a difference.

ALICE: I think it's been a gradual process starting with simplifying my life to being, having friends who are . . . talking about not supporting Starbucks, then living in Guatemala. A lot of different pieces to the puzzle coming together to making me realize that I can make a difference through my shopping.
—interview excerpt, February 17, 2007

AMITAH: But I think change takes time and the movement's there.
—interview excerpt, February 21, 2007

NICOLE: Yeah, as . . . one person alone, there's limitations I suppose because you have to rely on a, um, you have to rely on others, I suppose. . . . But I think that changing your own way, you can make a difference.   —interview excerpt, February 17, 2007

After returning to Canada from Australia, concerned about animal welfare and ecology, Reesa "went into Greenpeace and said 'What can I do?'" The person told her that "how you live every day" really matters and can make a difference.   —shopping trip excerpt, May 2, 2007

CARLA: I think part of the problem, people think that, that to achieve this you all have to do the same thing. And that's not true. To achieve what you need to achieve you do different things. You do what you can in the space and in the time and the place that you're in. So . . . I understood that when . . . Joel Bakan came out to talk and someone asked, someone quite cynically asked, well what can I do? And, and he said, Well, I don't know. It's gonna be different for different people. For me it was the book and this movie. But for you it might be, it might be getting together with the parents, the parent council of your school and getting the Coke machines out of the school. And it was so funny, because there was this collective, Ohhhhh [*laughs*]. Like, it struck everyone at once, like, we don't all have to do the same thing. We don't all have to write a book. You know, we don't all have to make a movie. We all have to do something different with what we're given. And even a small thing like getting the Coke machines out of the school is, is enough. Well, it's a start anyway. It's a, a way to begin.   —focus group excerpt, May 17, 2007

The last excerpt, from the second focus group, reiterates a point made by Gramsci (1971) and also expressed by Ron Eyerman and Andrew Jamison (1991) that, although all people have the capacity to be intellectuals, not everybody functions as an intellectual in either maintaining or challenging hegemonic relations. In the previous chapter, I noted Walters's (2005) related point that social movements are sites and sources of learning for both individuals who are integrally involved in them and individuals who are not actively engaged in them but are affected by their discourses, campaigns, and actions. ☼ For that reason, the learning spurred by social movements is unpredictable.

There are, of course, different opinions about what it means to make a difference. Small actions might add up, but to what? In answering this question I can return to my previous discussions about radicalism and forms of reflexivity. From all of my conversations with participants,

> ☼ Social-movement learning includes both learning by people who participate in social movements and learning by people outside of social movements through the impact they make (Hall and Clover, 2005). Learning through a movement can occur informally through participation or through intentional educational interventions.
> —Shirley Walters (2005), "Social Movements, Class, and Adult Education," p. 55

there is one particularly clear example of narcissistic reflexivity and an understanding of change as reform, and it occurred during my shopping trip with Jody.

> At the check-out, the cashier asked, "Would you like paper or plastic?" "Paper, please," Jody replied. We chatted, and the cashier joined in, about packaging and how good the new recyclable, compostable packaging . . . is. Jody said, "Every little thing we can do, might seem little but it can change the world. Don't you think?" "Do you?" I asked. "I do!" she answered.   —shopping trip excerpt, February 12, 2007

This excerpt from Jody's shopping trip is particularly interesting as an illustration of a learning and perspective that can emerge from narcissistic reflexivity (Littler, 2005). Her opinion that choosing a paper bag over a plastic bag is not only a good habit but also a way to "help change the world" entirely overlooks the need to examine structures. It maintains that people can help change the world without making any real changes in their lives. Jody might have approached her food shopping carefully and inquisitively, but her questions focused on personal health and safety rather than social relations and politics. Her understanding that solutions to problems begin and end with better shopping options and choices recalls the narcissistic reflexivity that Littler (2005) sees in Anita Roddick's book. Her perspective is entirely consistent with neoliberal, consumerist ideologies that portray change as an individualized endeavour. It does not correspond to my conceptualization of resistance or Sparks's (1997) conceptualization of dissidence; it certainly is not radical.

There were, however, some participants who were somewhat doubtful about concluding that every small action necessarily contributes to meaningful change. One currently popular focus of resistance that plays out in the arena of shopping is environmentalism. Among participants, Bonnie had an especially long and strong affiliation with the environmental movement. Not only did she maintain a strict vegan diet and wear non-leather shoes, she was involved with an activist organization educating and advocating on the combined topics of animal welfare and the environment. She herself raised and connected several issues in a sophisticated way during her shopping trip, including the following point about the problem with the shopping-based resistance that often addresses animal rights and environmental concerns:

> She also talked . . . about the difference between antiracist or class-based activism and environmental activism. Because it's become easier for people to shop—especially for food—in an environmentally sensitive and animal-friendly way, replacing conventional products with vegetarian, organic, and fair trade products, the message is that you don't really need to make changes in your life. But activists focused on other issues "would never talk about race or class that way," Bonnie explained.　—shopping trip excerpt, February 5, 2007

In her comments, Bonnie was recognizing the shortcomings of critical shopping as a strategy of resistance, because it leaves inherently problematic structures in place in people's lives, in national policies and in global affairs. The central message in such resistance is that consumer-citizens can help effect societal change without making any great personal change. In contrast to Jody, who thought that choosing paper bags at the check-out counter helped change the world, Bonnie understood that the environmental movement in which she had situated herself often seems satisfied with responses that emerge from more narcissistic and limited reflexivity.

Like Bonnie, Karen and Carla raised some reservations about the full acceptance that small actions necessarily contribute to societal change. They discussed a trade show that offered a range of fair trade and environmentally friendly products for sale.

> KAREN: My husband and I went and it was interesting and it was, you know, we found some, some cool stuff. . . . But the whole time I was very conflicted about this whole idea of buying yourself out of the guilt. There's, here's these things you can do to buy your way out of feeling guilty for—
>
> CARLA: Did you see the ad in the bus for it?
>
> KAREN: No.
>
> CARLA: The catch phrase was, "Buy yourself a better future."
>
> KAREN: Oh yeah.
>
> CARLA: [laughs]
>
> KAREN: Oh yeah, I saw that. And that, that really drove me crazy.
>　—focus group excerpt, May 17, 2007

Again, these participants might have recognized the importance of doing even little things in the name of change, but they were not under the illusion that all little things add up to the same big change when they are combined. Carla suggested a move to a more relational form of reflexivity during her interview, when she noted the importance of always asking what more can be done and being willing to do more:

> CARLA: Do they make a difference? I think, me as an individual, no, I don't think they make a difference. I think, um, however, as a group of, me as an individual in one day, no. Me as an individual over my lifetime, yes. Me as an individual among all of my friends who have similar, you know, thinking, similar ways of thinking, yes. I think it's one of those things that, but again only to a point. And I'm thinking of *The Corporation* . . . and where Joel Bakan has said there's a point where, you know, this, this, this is effective but it's not, you need to go one step farther. You need to, you need to write to your government and tell them to be accountable and tell these organizations to be accountable.   —interview excerpt, February 13, 2007

I do not dismiss Luxemburg's (2008) and Gramsci's (1971) cautions against reformism and pragmatism, and the importance of connecting resistance in the cultural and material arenas to formal politics; however, I conclude that the incremental learning and changes discussed by participants are consistent with Gramsci's (1971) understanding of revolution as a slow process based in ideological transformation that mobilizes support for structural transformation. This conclusion is also reminiscent of marino's (1997) invitation to look for "cracks in consent" to begin a process of critical learning and transformation. It is precisely the unpredictability of learning and change that makes any sort of resistance worth paying attention to. Participants, like Anita Roddick, might stop at narcissistic reflexivity, individualized actions, and reform, but, then again, they might move on to more relational reflexivity, collective actions, and radical responses.

Each One Teach One

Originating in the field of literacy education, the slogan "each one teach one" expresses a widely held conviction in critical adult education that people share in their learning and, in turn, teaching others. Related to participants' general understanding that individual, small actions had a cumulative effect over time, there was a similar agreement among most— albeit not all—participants about the importance of sharing what one learned about shopping, consumption, and globalization with friends and family. They also knew that they had gained important information from others, both acquaintances and experts. This kind of very informal teaching and learning is one way that individuals on the periphery of a social movement can learn its message and tactics (see Walters, 2005). Such learning from the periphery suggests why it can be difficult to gauge how many people are actually aligned with a social movement.

A methodological extension of this claim contributes to my rationale for avoiding particular organizations in this study. As social movement learning scholars recognize, organizations are among the constituents of a movement, but they do not represent all of a movement's supporters (della Porta & Diani, 2006; Eyerman & Jamison, 1991; Walters, 2005). A movement's constituency grows and shrinks, often in ways that are not immediately observed or managed.

The following excerpts illustrate the different ways in which participants could have a hand in furthering anti-consumerist resistance by sharing their learning with others:

ELLEN: And so I, I personally don't think that I alone will bring Walmart down. But what if my friend . . . is really affected by what I said? And . . . she's an economics professor. And really starts thinking about these issues. And then what if she brings it up with her students, and what if her students then bring it up with their parents? I mean, I don't mean to be this, like, I am the pebble on the lake, I mean that's just too cheesy for words. . . . But I think that you can effectively engage in smear campaigns and protests and activities, and I don't think, I think at some point, we always want measurable outcomes. What was the outcome of this protest? What was the outcome of this letter-writing campaign? What was the outcome of not shopping there? And I think there's a danger in doing that, because we need to stop thinking of grand social movements and measurable outcomes and just say, you know, we really are human beings 24 hours a day and you educate yourself and you help educate other people and you open yourself up to being educated by others and you sort of live the best you can with what you've got, you know, and with what you can do. And, do I think that in the long run that'll really change? I actually think it will. I think if enough people, um, if we raise the consciousness of enough people, you know, myself included, I certainly don't know even a millionth of what I should know, I think eventually it will change.
—interview excerpt, April 24, 2007

[Paula] does not see herself as a front-line activist, but she supports such efforts by signing petitions for animal rights and organic foods. . . . And she doesn't just sign petitions; after signing them, she also tells her friends about them and the campaigns that they are associated with.
—shopping trip excerpt, August 14, 2007

ALICE: I read an article in a magazine about what to do in South Africa, and one of them was shop at this store, and these social-upliftment stores. So I started doing research and thought I would love to expose people, expose travellers to this.

KAELA: So is this something you do in your spare time, write?

ALICE: Yeah.

KAELA: Do you have a journalism education or—?

ALICE: No, no. I'm not a journalist [*laughs*], I don't have any stellar writing qualities, but my, I just have this desire to get the word out about where people can be shopping. . . . So I was in the Caribbean recently and I did, found a place where people who are, uh, disabled, where they're making items and tourists can go and buy things there.

KAELA: So getting the word out, there's something about getting the word out.

ALICE: Yeah.

KAELA: And that kind of education that you think is part of what you contribute . . . to this whole sort of shopping and consumption message. I mean you're sort of putting another message out there.

ALICE: Well, there are options.

KAELA: Okay. There are options, and it's important to think about the options.

ALICE: Yeah. Mostly places, they're doing good, but they don't have the money to market themselves.   —interview excerpt, February 17, 2007

At the cash register, Sandy used a canvas bag that she had brought with her and took a paper carry bag. She noted, "I did convince my husband to use reusable bags—I'm so happy."   —shopping trip excerpt, February 5, 2007

Although some participants were wary about how they shared information and concerned about being construed as self-righteous, on the whole participants were convinced that helping others learn about the politics of shopping and consumption could amplify the success of their resistance. Their teaching could range from small details such as persuading a partner to stop using disposable shopping bags to information about larger, more complex issues such as how the simple act of buying name-brand chocolate makes one complicit in the use of child slave labour (see Off, 2006). ☼

For several participants, one central site of mutual teaching and leaning was social enterprises or co-operatives. Karen and Vanessa had purchased shares in and volunteered at a co-operatively owned organic farm. Vanessa had also served on the board of directors of retail food co-operative that adds to its retail function public education about food security, the corporate agri-business, globalization, and the value of the co-operative movement in general. Alice volunteered at one of the Ten Thousand Villages® shops, and Tamara worked for a social venture marketing fair trade products. A few of the other participants were also involved actively in nongovernment activist and education organizations, where they both learned and shared information and analyses. Again, the perceived value of these volunteer activities in furthering societal transformation is in contrast to the thinking of both Luxemburg (2008) and Gramsci (1971), who cautioned against "volunteerism" and pragmatism in a radical agenda. Still, by sharing their knowledge, participants believed that they were expanding awareness about issues and the potential for resistance and societal change.

Further to Foley's (1999, 2001) important conceptualization of incidental learning that emerges through collective action and engagement in social movements, my analysis here suggests that it is also important to consider the learning that occurs among individuals who might appear to be disconnected from social movements or from one another in their learning, decision making, and practices. This learning might imply relational reflexivity or narcissistic reflexivity, but either way it encourages people to think about how they can change their shopping and, though their shopping, contribute to change.

☼ [Former Malian consul general in Bouaké, Côte d'Ivoire, Adboulaye] Macko tells me he eventually learned that the [cocoa] farmers had deals with an elaborate network of traffickers, and he began to understand that the real villains in the story were not the farmers but the crime rings who brought the children to the farms. The boys may have left their family farms voluntarily and even joined up with the smuggler of their own volition. "They were just kids who needed money for their families," says Macko. They didn't bargain for the kind of exploitation they experienced. He believes many of the cocoa farmers were also caught in an unbearable squeeze. Though some of the farmers were surely taking advantage of the desperation of the poor, most of those who were buying the children had been driven to do so by their dire economic straits. Preying on the hopelessness and needs of both groups, the middlemen were the ones making the profits.
—Carol Off (2006), *Bitter Chocolate*, pp. 129–130

Getting the Political Message to the Politicians

Participants were aware of clichés about the politics of shopping, including the shopping-as-voting metaphor taken up by Shaw (2007) and others. Even the participants who rejected consumer choice as democratic choice agreed that, by shopping selectively and purposefully, they were sending a politically charged message to manufacturers and retailers, as well as other shoppers. Whether that message reached politicians in Canada and in other countries, and, moreover, whether it is something that rightly concerns politicians were other matters. I tried to raise these issues in some of the questions that I've already noted, namely, those asking about the political impacts and limitations of critical shopping. ☼

Gramsci (1971) concurs with the Marxist argument that engagement in the arena of formal politics is necessary for societal transformation (see also Luxemburg, 2008), even though the necessary ideological challenge and reconstitution first occurs culturally in civil society. In their conversations with me, very few participants spoke about being active in an existing political party or about the prospect of any new parties being formed. Some of them, though, did say that it was important to become engaged in the process of formal politics and to convey what they had learned through and around shopping to politicians.

> ALICE: I'm thinking that with shopping practices what would need to happen is also sending out the word to government, because just by shopping at Caper's won't send a message to them. So coupling that with some sort of awareness programs or encouragement of contacting them to say that, that our importers should be going through more stringent, there should be more stringent laws of what we accept and what kind of conditions those products were made under, and certified. Again very idealistic, but, yeah, more pressure.
>
> KAELA: Okay, more pressure and more regulation. I mean you're talking about a kind of regulatory pressure.
>
> ALICE: Yeah, yeah.   —interview excerpt, February 17, 2007
>
> KAELA: Can you think of movements or organizations that seem connected to shopping and consumption? What statements do they make, and have you ever participated in any of them?

☼ There's a saying that the personal is political. Do you think that your personal shopping practices can make a difference to local, national or global politics? If so, how? On the flip side, what are the limitations to the impact that shopping and consumption can have?   —selected interview questions

SARAH: Yeah, there's this one thing, I don't know if you've heard of it, um, the Church of Pointless Consumerism.

KAELA: No.

SARAH: The Church of Pointless Consumerism. It's um, I think, it's a yearly kind of event. And it's actually put on, the Work Less Party puts on tons of events regarding this kind of stuff, and so the Work Less Party put on an event regarding this and they do it. And they pretty much make fun of consumption.

KAELA: Okay.

SARAH: And money money money money money! And they just go on about it. They do a play, and it's the most like obnoxious [*chuckle*] like, um, farce on, on consumption that I've ever seen. Um, and so I'll participate in stuff like that. And, like, the Work Less Party is always talking about consumerism, and I, I just really agree with them. So I'll go to events and stuff like that.   —interview excerpt, April 24, 2007

CARLA: So, yeah, I think . . . if I wanted to do something more . . . I would find groups that have campaigns about those sorts of things, or else write more letters.

KAELA: So who would you write letters to?

CARLA: I'd probably write to the government, get their act together, and this whole Mr. Harper thing we all know is just a splash of paint, and as soon as he takes a shower it'll be gone [*laughs*], he'll be blue all over again. . . .

KAELA: So you think there is still this continued connection between formal politics and, and consumption or, or sort of the corporate world? . . .

CARLA: I think, I still think there is. I realize that people can, that organizations can move from country to country. I'm trying to think of an example. Well, okay, how 'bout we take the European Union and the whole issue with uh, with uh genetically modified organisms. Um, the EU does not accept them. This is a formal governing body made up of democratically elected, um, members, and, uh, the people in the countries made it really clear that they didn't want this stuff on their soil. So, um, I think there is a process and I think that, um, to assume there is no process is to open yourself up to despair. Because then what are you supposed to do? Like, become an anarchist? [*laughs*] I don't . . . know what the answer would be. I think the problem is, is that people think that citizenship just means voting. But it's much more involved than that. And corporations are huge, and they move around, they do what they like, but at the same time we as a

society who have elected officials have to make it clear, this is
what we want, this is what we want for our country. . . . So the
world is all about, human life is all about finding solutions. It's
not about assuming horrible things will happen just because
you don't let the corporations do what they want, you know?
[*laughs*]

KAELA: Is shopping a kind of voting?

CARLA: I don't know if I would go as far as that. If it spurs you
to be more politically active, then yes. 'Cause I do think
it can be a political act but . . . [politics] can't just be that.
—interview excerpt, February 13, 2007

Hegemonic neoliberal political discourse argues against regulations
and in favour of the free market; however, participants understood the
continued importance of environmental and employment regulations
that could help protect them, as consumer-citizens, as well as ensure
that workers in Canada and in other countries had decent, safe work
conditions.

When participants did mention political parties that they supported,
they typically mentioned the New Democratic Party (NDP) or the Green
Party, which are already aligned with social movements and, in the case
of the NDP, a social group; Sarah was alone in mentioning the Work Less
Party, which is affiliated with other emerging social movements such as
voluntary simplicity. In general, though, participants seemed to reflect
the ennui, if not cynicism, around formal politics, most apparent—as
many of them noted—in declining voting rates. This suggests that, on
the whole, participants might have still been in what Gramsci (1971)
would consider an early phase in the process of change in Canadian
society, when ideological critique and education are of greatest importance. Aside from Amitah's view that she had "dropped out" of her
middle-class origin, participants did not talk about what it would mean
for them, as middle-class consumer-citizens, to dismantle Canada's capitalism, even if they did think it was unfair. Many of them thought that
great strides had already been made in dismantling racism and patriarchy, through a combination of formal politics (that is, human rights
legislation) and culture. Here, then, are examples of the seduction of
reformist strategies and the power of hegemony to absorb critiques and
neutralize them.

Answering Questions, Questioning Answers

During his interview, Sean offered a concise definition of the good
shopper. His version of that person is somebody who knows the full

environmental impact of every product bought and used. Unearthing that information is no small challenge. To add concerns about who made a product, what the working and living conditions of those individuals are, and how consumer options are connected with economic, gendered and raced structures operating within and between nation-states deepens the challenges. Although, as I discussed in the previous chapter, some participants were very adept, innovative, persistent researchers in their shopping processes, most of them surmised that basic questions can seem unanswerable. In their interviews, some participants described this reality:

JOCELYN: And they're, and they're much harder questions than the cut of this blouse or the colour or the fabric or, in terms of the food, the flavour. These other questions are much harder to understand.

KAELA: Why would you say they're harder?

JOCELYN: Because you don't, there's so many other factors.

KAELA: Okay, so they're harder to answer. They're complicated questions.

JOCELYN Yeah, they're too complicated. —interview excerpt, January 22, 2007

ELLEN: And I actually believe that most of us can't shop the way we want to shop because, well for starters, we can't, we can't know.

KAELA: We can't access the information, we can't—

ELLEN: We just can't know what it is we're really buying. —interview excerpt, April 24, 2007

SEAN: But to go back to your original question. Can you figure that stuff out? . . . It's really hard. . . . But if you work at it . . . you can get a really good sense of it, I think. And you can use it to guide as much, you can get enough information to usefully guide you choices. I mean the fact is, I just bought a laptop. . . . And it's almost impossible to know where parts and pieces came from. . . . And . . . [a computer manufacturer] is not going to tell me, 'cause it's gonna be a secret for, you know, for commercial reasons and stuff like that. . . . So with a lot of stuff it is impossible. And so my goal there is to just consume as little as possible. —interview excerpt, March 24, 2007

KAELA: Do you think that those questions are, um, well, I mean you said that there's a practicality in terms of time when it comes to answering those questions, but do you think that, um, those questions are always even answerable? Even if you had unlimited time.

JAMES: If I had unlimited time? I'm not convinced that they're all answerable.   —interview excerpt, March 28, 2007

VIOLET: Yeah, yeah. Yeah, getting the information. And it's not that cut and dry, either. You can't . . . completely avoid or boycott products made by child labour, because now I know that what happens is those things move underground now. . . . So it's, it's really tricky.

KAELA: Yeah. I also think it's tricky because there are so many stops in the chain of production.

VIOLET: That's right.

KAELA: And so things are so easy to hide.

VIOLET: Exactly.   —interview excerpt, April 4, 2007

I began this chapter with a discussion of the word "radical," which implies definitiveness; however, as the excerpts above indicate, the complexity of contemporary consumer-citizenship in a Western society such as Canada interferes with people's ability to discern the very root of a problem, let alone its resolution. The excerpts echo Connelly and Prothero's (2008) point that "individuals are left with a sense that *I should and can do something, but I don't know which is the right thing to do*" (p. 133, emphasis in original). They are also reminiscent of the reflections of Jane, in Ozeki's (1998) novel, about learning to be ignorant as a coping strategy in a world where messages and structures seem to overwhelm personal capacity to understand and make choices. On the whole, I had the impression that participants were trying to wade through a dizzying array of information, options, discourses, needs, desires, worries, and fears.

Most participants had not abandoned their commitment to societal change, even if they felt frustrated and ambivalent about the contributions that they could make through shopping as well as other types of activities. In this task, many participants found it important to retain a sense of hope and optimism and a positive outlook, whether or not these were linked to spiritual convictions. Some of the excerpts already discussed above, in which participants talked about preferring what they thought were more positive-sounding words, such as "ethical" or "critical," to the word "radical," reiterate this point. During his interview, Sean was explicit about the role that the emotion of hope assumed when intellectual conclusions pointed to defeat:

SEAN: Can I make a difference? I'll turn to Antonio Gramsci.

KAELA: My hero!

SEAN: Yeah, me too. Pessimism of the intellect, optimism of the will. . . . I'm gonna act as if they do, even if they don't, . . .

> 'cause that's what it takes for me to get through, from day
> to day. But I think, you know, they [that is, my decisions]
> can in some sense, but who knows? It's impossible for me
> to measure. So I'm going with Gramsci.   —interview
> excerpt, March 24, 2007

In a similar vein, Karen spoke about maintaining a sense of stubborn determination, if not hope:

> My husband and I were kind of discussing why is it that in some ways
> we're very nihilistic? Like, we really don't think that there is that much
> hope, so why do we bother? And we were sort of trying to weigh it out.
> Like, why are we vegetarians and don't own a car when really, we're
> going to hell in a handbasket and what can we, what can we do about
> it? And I think it kind of made it clear, I was, it was actually before Kurt
> Vonnegut died, but I remember reading something about him and how
> he had that, that same sort of, like, you know, there is no hope. We're all
> screwed. While we're here, be nice. And, and that was sort of the same
> thing [my husband] and I thought. That, I don't think that what I'm
> doing is gonna make much difference, but if it makes any difference then
> why not? Yeah, that's about it.   —focus group excerpt, May 17, 2007

If Gramsci (1971) is right and revolution occurs through a slow process of learning, alliance-building, and construction of new ideologies, then what might be most important is to encourage critical questioning and holistic learning, rather than to dismiss efforts at resistance as partial.

In discussing their learning about how to make change, participants were unanimous in their willingness to ask questions, even if answers were not easily forthcoming. A few participants added another point, about learning to respond to ambiguity with a sense of hope or sheer determination. Tying together the notion of asking questions with the belief that it was important to bring these issues to the attention of politicians, Karen explained why it is important to support nonprofit organizations that lobby for progressive regulatory and policy changes:

> It just seems that it is so hard to have any kind of political impact.
> Certainly, well, voter apathy is probably a good example of [how] most
> people don't look at the impact. It is, is does feel like an opportunity to,
> again, to say vote for that organization, however small a donation it is.
> That, you know, we do want to see that there's somebody questioning.
> —interview excerpt, February 2, 2007

All of this said, I appreciate Luxemburg's (2008) and Lorde's (2002) cautions against being lulled into a sense of success because some sort of change has occurred. Societal change, whether or not it is radical, is constant. This realization is integral to Gramsci's (1971) conceptualization of hegemony, even if most changes function to reiterate, rather than fundamentally alter, oppressive structures. Resistance enacted through shopping, as in other arenas, can be co-opted and absorbed into current hegemony. This point, again, is a reminder of Sparks's (1997) conclusion about dissidence, which both complies with and resists the status quo. The shift toward a "green" agenda by the current Premier of British Columbia follows years of activism by radical movements; however, the feminist consensus-based decision-making processes outlined by Walter (2007) are certainly not part of the Premier's agenda. In terms of Littler's (2005) analytical framework, the maintenance of hegemony seems to encourage the absorption of radical discourses and to neutralize them by replacing their initial relational reflexivity with an increasingly narcissistic reflexivity. Even shoppers who want to make change have to contend with the reality that, under consumerism and neoliberalism, "the personal is political" often is reinterpreted so that the personal becomes the full extent of the political. For the most critical shoppers, asking questions and questioning answers is a never-ending, cyclical process that accompanies, precedes, and guides continual change and learning.

If You Can't Join 'Em, Beat 'Em

A familiar cliché advises people to join forces with opposition that cannot be eliminated. In a reversal of that advice, most participants talked about their general discomfort with hegemonic consumerism. Some participants went further, rejecting a central premise of the contemporary iteration of Western consumerism: that shopping and consumption manifest the democratic values of choice and freedom. Drawing on his education in sociology and his admiration of Marxist analysis, Sean offered an especially cogent summary of the problems with consumerism:

KAELA: There's a saying that the personal is political. Do you think that your personal shopping practices can make a difference to local, national, or global politics, and if so how? And on the flip side, what do you see as the limitations to, um, the impact that your own shopping and consumption can have?

SEAN: I'm gonna start with the flip side. . . . Which is, the biggest limitation is, is all the structures. . . . The institutional structures that control the little quote-unquote . . . choices that I have. . . . Like what, what arrives in the places that I can shop. . . .

KAELA: Okay, so a lot of choices have been made for you before you
          enter the store.
SEAN: Yeah, yeah, exactly. Or, or that I even have to go into the store
          to get it.   —interview excerpt, March 24, 2007

At the same time as Sean identified a reality of shopping—that many decisions are made even for critical shoppers before they enter the store—some people are seeking ways around these apparent limitations and finding ways to express their agency and choice. This might be through a rejection of consumerist ideology, which I have already discussed somewhat in the preceding chapters, especially in sections in Chapter 5 on Learning to Learn and Weighing Values. As many excerpts that I have already cited suggest, most participants were uncomfortable with the idea of hegemonic consumerism and excessive consumption. Many did not enjoy shopping, or at least shopping for certain types of items, such as clothing, or feeling that they had to resort to shopping in certain types of settings, such as relatively affordable "big box" stores.

Some participants went further in their comments about consumerism and consumption. I did not ask participants questions about the voluntary simplicity movement in particular, and the phrase "voluntary simplicity" was not one invoked by participants in their conversations with me; however, a few participants articulated a perspective that resonated especially well with the central tenets of the voluntary simplicity movement. They described their commitments to slowing down their lives and their consumption, and learning to choose less rather than more.

AMITAH: It's always more, more, more. There's always something
          new. And you've gotta have it, you know?
KAELA: Yeah.
AMITAH: It's like you gotta keep up with, yeah, it's distraction and
          it just seems to be everywhere. . . . You know, where do
          encounter it? Not just on the television but on the radio and
          out, you know, when you're out and about, um, storefront
          windows, you know, wherever you are. Or if you're over
          at a friend's place and they've got this newest thing, you
          know. And what that does for me is that it makes me want
          to go more the other way. . . . And that's probably why I've
          dropped out of the middle class [chuckles] . . . 'cause I just
          don't believe in it. . . . It doesn't, you know, I'm, you know,
          I'll go to Value Village on a Saturday or something. Even
          though it's owned by Jimmy Pattison? Somebody told me
          that. And somebody else said, no it's not. But it's almost a
          big box store now, isn't it?

KAELA: Yes, yes.

AMITAH: I'll go there, and I'll spend three hours and spend, you know, $30 or $40 on four different sweaters and come back, but I'll still feel empty. . . . You know [*laughs softly*]. And I go, well, that was kind of fun, it wasted some time. Um, but at the same time it doesn't really fulfil anything. Um, there seems to be a general lack of fulfilment, and we're trying to fill that hole with things like shopping.   —interview excerpt, February 21, 2007

JULIE: I buy fewer, like significantly fewer clothes. Probably 20% of the clothes I might have bought 10 years ago. Not 20% less, 80% less . . . 80%, yeah. . . . [*pause*] I buy much less processed food. . . . So, we have a rule where . . . every time something new comes into the house, something existing has to go out. Well, it changes how badly you want something. —interview excerpt, March 14, 2007

SARAH: I don't like buying . . . all this technology drives me crazy. I think there's a place for it, but I also think that we're just wasting a lot.

KAELA: So the gizmo—

SARAH: Drive me crazy. . . . I mean, I have a cell phone, but I don't have any other phone, and it's just easier for people to get a hold of me, and I've kinda fallen into that, it's just kind of the way it works right now, right. But, I mean I never have the latest anything, and I have the, the free phone that came with my plan. You know, and if I need something electronic I'll just go with the basic standard. Just let me just, you know, I don't even care! If it works and gets me by that's all that matters. Um, and I think that we keep, we keep changing these annually so that everyone's throwing all their stuff out and using more stuff and it drives me crazy.   —interview excerpt, April 24, 2007

Another way that some participants talked about reducing their shopping as a way of resisting consumerism was to take up do-it-yourself practices. These include growing and preserving food, making clothing or gifts, and, in a couple of cases, joining an agricultural co-operative. In the following excerpts, participants discussed their use of these tactics:

"And I have my own garden and I grow stuff. I canned tomatoes and made jam," she also noted, as ways that she can control what she buys and consumes.   —shopping trip excerpt, Bonnie, February 5, 2007

CARLA: And, I make a lot of stuff for Christmas. I bake 'cause I don't like the idea of giving people things that they just collect. So oftentimes I give them things that they can consume. And I made a lot of gifts, too, like, uh, my neighbours, my parents, the neighbours to my parents, he's an old English gentleman, he loves the BBC, so I made a whole bunch of CDs for him on CBC plays.   —interview excerpt, February 13, 2007

JAMES: We've also taken to making our own preserves when the fruit is in season. Which also works well on the pocketbook because they turn into lots of Christmas gifts. So that's been . . . one of the benefits of staying locally and in season. . . . Because that gift-giving can really add up.   —interview excerpt, March 28, 2007

Linda went to bring him back into the store, and returned to the sale boxes. She picked up a T-shirt in size XL and said, "Maybe I could reconstruct this into something." I asked her about what she might do with it, and she explained that she had seen a book on things to do with old T-shirts.   —shopping trip excerpt, mothers' network, May 19, 2007

"I'm involved in an organic farm . . . ," she explained. This is a co-operative farm, and she owns a share in it.   —shopping trip excerpt, Vanessa, May 4, 2007

Certainly, there was more to participants' do-it-themselves than a commitment to anti-consumerist resistance. As James noted, shopping for prepared foods and ready-made goods becomes expensive, and for consumer-citizens with material constraints an interest and skill in cooking or crafts can be enviable for various reasons. Sometimes, these activities were also pleasurable hobbies and interesting challenges; sometimes, they offered a way for participants to express their heartfelt caring for recipients of gifts; and sometimes, they gave participants an alternative to going into a store and buying items that others had decided they wanted or needed. Like all shopping and consumption, learning about do-it-yourself and voluntary simplicity has multiple dimensions: intellectual, as well as psychological, emotional, and even spiritual.

These types of anti-consumerist resistance might help critical shoppers act on critical analyses of hegemonic consumerism and unrestrained consumption, as they engage consumer-citizens more directly in the process of production. Movements such as fair trade and local buying aim to narrow the gap between consumers and producers, but a movement such as do-it-yourself implies that this gap can be eliminated; however, the definition of consumption offered by Roseneil and Hearn (1999) that I have employed in this inquiry clarifies that consumption is always productive. On the flip side, I also note that production always involves consumption of energy and raw ingredients. In contemporary Western societies, moreover, production likely also involves shopping. From amateur "do-it-yourselfers" who grow their own food and people who farm for a living, producers of the most basic consumable items shop for seeds and soil, tools and equipment. Feminist scholars have argued that production and formal employment have been distinguished from consumption and home-based work largely for social purposes, namely, the privileging of masculinized spheres over feminized spheres. Even the historical academic focus on production has helped maintain a patriarchal social order. In blurring the sharp division between production and consumption, I contribute to the disruption of that social order and the ideological "common sense" (Gramsci, 1971) that underlies it.

Two Steps Forward, One Step Back: Patterns of Learning

One of the basic faults that poststructural or postmodern scholars find with critical scholarship is its tendency to speak about social development as a linear advance toward emancipation. Within the field of critical adult education, it is tempting to see learning as the process that enables people to participate in such an advance; however, changes in individuals' financial, health, or other personal circumstances contribute to learning and action. For a variety of reasons, some participants realized that they tended "to not mix with the crowd any more" (interview excerpt, Eddie, April 11, 2007) or were "not . . . joiner[s] in that stuff these days" (interview excerpt, Sean, March 24, 2007). For two participants, the change had to do with returning to Canada after doing volunteer work in the Global South:

> VIOLET: Well a couple of years ago I was an intern . . . in Bangkok, Thailand. And I worked for an . . . umbrella organization for all the agencies and NGOs working to, to fight child labour. And it's something that I really didn't take very seriously until I spent time with them and I did research for them. Yet I'm not really sure, I don't know, I'm just trying to reconcile that, because I know that I could make choices around child labour, like, [pause] that it's made by child labour, but I don't really know exactly which companies are doing it.   —interview excerpt, April 4, 2007

Thérèse clarified that she has come to understand—partly through her experience in Bangladesh—the layers of production and the

> impossibility of really knowing where something comes from. —shopping trip excerpt, February 9, 2007

> She also pointed out that her life has changed since she . . . [returned to Canada]. She is married and has children; she is in Canada, not Bangladesh.   —shopping trip excerpt, Thérèse, February 9, 2007

These stories illustrate how the constant construction of knowledge, priorities, options, and practices occurs as one's social circumstances and personal experiences mesh. Unlike Thérèse and Violet, Karen, Nicole, and Alice seemed to retain the lessons from their time abroad in their lives back in Canada. Perhaps there were differences in how dramatically their circumstances had changed since their return, or perhaps they were part of a social network or community—real or imagined—that helped them transfer a politics formed elsewhere to Canada. Why some people are able to hang onto certain pieces of radical learning or how they are able to transfer such learning into new contexts are important questions, and, although I am unable to answer them here, I note them, because they are worth exploring in future research.

Buying in or Selling Out: Concluding Thoughts

In contrast to the conclusions of Luxemburg (2008) and Lorde (2002), participants in this study did not summarily dismiss all hegemonic tools. Shopping is, after all, a primary tool of the consumerist ideology that underpins contemporary globalization, at least in Canada and throughout the Global North. According to the logic of Luxemburg and Lorde, shopping-based resistance likely distracts citizens from the aim of real structural change and reiterates, rather than transforms, societal structures. The question of whether and how shopping can move from a process that reiterates hegemonic ideology and common sense (Gramsci, 1971) to part of a transformative, rather than a conservative, social movement has no simple answer.

I began this chapter by outlining Littler's (2005) analysis of four examples of anti-consumerist activism. Her analysis points to the contributions made through anti-consumerist resistance such as the culture jamming of Kalle Lasn, even as she notes some of its limitations and complications. Undoubtedly, Lasn's critique of consumerism has helped build awareness of the problems with consumption and its driving ideology; however, this does not mean that his strategy and some of his tactics have gone without criticism. His critics argue that, by developing and marketing his brand of Blackspot Sneakers, he has become complicit with the neoliberal, consumerist ideology that he claims to oppose

(Haiven, 2007; Heath & Potter, 2004). Moreover, what is seen by some as *AdBusters'* lack of attention to structures of gender and race diminishes Lasn's credibility as a proponent of social justice. ☼

> ☼ It hardly seems worth analyzing the Black Spot campaign as it seems such an impoverished example of social critique that is neither especially socially minded nor particularly critical. But I would contend that this campaign, far from being discontinuous with *AdBusters'* prior and broader politics, represents only the latest crystallization of what I will call *AdBusters'* politics of [gestural] resistance, symptomatic of a broader tendency in many ostensibly resistant social texts. And this politics, which seems to be becoming remarkably fashionable in a variety of circles, must be critiqued as not only inadequate for confronting the contemporary global political and cultural hegemony of neoliberalism, but in many ways rehearsing key tenets of neoliberalism so as to make *AdBusters* a highly problematic political text, one made even more worrisome in that it smugly wears the mantle of radical resistance.   —Max Haiven, "Privatized Resistance: *AdBusters* and the Culture of Neoliberalism," p. 86

As Max Haiven writes,

> However, *AdBusters'* many myopias, notably its near total disregard for class (both as a "historic" and sociological category), its persistently simplistic, libertarian, and tacitly sexist approach to gender, its near complete indifference towards race, and its confusing (yet aggressive) ambivalence between revolutionary and reformist politics, all conspire to make the magazine an infuriatingly difficult text to approach. (2007, p. 87)

Such critiques, as well as the limitations that Littler (2005) spells out for the examples in her article, establish the complications of reflexivity and change. Although some discourses and responses, such as fully hegemonic books like Kinsella's (2001) novel *Confessions of a Shopaholic* or Roddick's book *Take it Personally* might not involve any reflexivity or might employ a narcissistic form of reflexivity, other projects, such as those initiated by Klein, Lasn, or Talen or Ozeki's (1998) novel *My Year of Meats*, can combine narcissistic and relational reflexivity. For their part, participants in this study often engaged in a complex of reflexive processes. Moreover, as Littler (2005) recognizes, relational reflexivity is not sufficient to persuade individuals to take radical action together with others in their communities—real or imagined (Anderson, 1991). People's emotional and material needs and priorities must also be recognized and accommodated within organizational and movement discourses. Littler offers these words:

"Anti-consumerism", then, and what it wishes for, is not a monolith. If an awareness of the role of popular discourse in shaping the citizen-consumer can be found, so to can romanticizations of activist enclaves that shore up its boundaries; if there are spaces where consumers are shaped as dupes, there are also sophisticated understandings of the affective investments and complex psychologies of consumer identities. Similarly, the type of consumer and anti-consumer being imagined, the role of activism to cultural and social change, and the scenarios imagined as happening after the boycott can all vary substantially. (2005, p. 242)

Who shoppers learn to be and how they learn to make change through and around their shopping varies in part, as Littler notes, by the type and level of their reflexivity. Building on Giddens's and Beck's ideas about the culture of reflexivity that is accompanying globalization in Western societies, scholars such as Connelly and Prothero (2008) use green shopping to exemplify how reflexivity has become a part of daily living. This understanding of reflexivity, considered an important aspect of learning, supports the assertion made throughout this study that learning occurs during the activities of daily life. What Littler clarifies is that reflexivity has nuances that help distinguish learning that is part of a societal change agenda from learning that is essentially reiterative of the societal status quo. Social and material differences between consumer-citizens increase the range of understandings about and practices in shopping, even if they all identify in some way as good or critical shoppers.

As Barndt (2002) further notes, over the past century or so, much highly organized, collective resistance has been carried out through labour unions in the arena of formal employment. Limiting the conceptualization of social action to such formalized strategies tends to masculinize resistance and overlooks much of women's historical and ongoing resistances, which can appear solitary and private. Sparks (1997) makes a similar point when she argues that dissidence is more likely considered a response for male citizens, because it requires the quality of courage that, according to hegemonic common sense, describes men, not women. Differences between individuals, and between the communities that critical consumer-citizens imagine and are imagined in, blur the difference between societal revolution and reform, between buying in and selling out.

INTERLUDE VII

Rumours and Queues

In 2005, Karen and I purchased a condominium in Victoria. A few weeks after we got the apartment, we were there for the weekend and out for a walk on Saturday morning. On our way to nowhere-in-particular, we noticed a short queue of people outside one of The Brick stores—a Canadian chain that sells home furnishings and electronics. Curious, we approached the queue and learned that this outlet was closing, and its inventory was deeply discounted. I persuaded Karen to join the queue and see what awaited us inside the store.

As we and the other shoppers-in-waiting stood patiently, the manager exited the store every so often to share some tantalizing news. One time, he announced that DVD players were on sale for $29! After he re-entered the store, I listened to the response of the woman in front of us. Turning to face her companion, she didn't seem excited by the manager's latest news. She seemed, rather, exasperated. "We have to stop buying these things for $29," she said. "$29. Who made these things for $29?"

Karen and I smiled at each other, struck once again, as we frequently were, by the tensions in shopping. What would bring someone into a queue outside a store if not the promise of low-low prices? And how could those low-low prices retain their appeal once someone recognized the cost behind the price tag?

Then we heard a woman behind us say something to a man in front of her. "Do you know if there's any truth to the rumour I heard that Thrifty's is coming in here," she asked him. He hadn't heard that rumour, although he didn't disagree with her as she shared her hope that, if a grocery store was coming into this location, it not be Safeway. With passion evident in her voice, she explained that a grocery store would be a wonderful addition to the neighbourhood retailers, but the last thing needed was another American supermarket.

Not long after that exchange, the doors to the store opened, and we were allowed to enter. I watched the others who rushed through the store and left empty-handed, as well as those who lingered and looked at everything slowly and carefully, and those who seemed determined to find something, anything. As we passed by the $29 DVD players, I heard the woman's words again, but only quietly against the constant announcements blaring through the overhead system and the din of shoppers eager to grab one of those bargains.

8

Somewhere around the Middle

As I start to draft this chapter, it is the middle of the Jewish holiday Passover. In my introductory chapter, I talked about growing up in a kosher household, but Passover makes the everyday rules of *kashrut* seem like a minimalist approach to dietary restrictions. In my family, we had special sets of dishes, cookware, and cutlery just for Passover. As children, my sisters and I would help my mother clean the house in the days before the week-long holiday. We would buy special foods—matzo and other items made with no leavening. Although we could have ordinary fruits and vegetables, many everyday staples such as rice, corn, beans, and lentils were off limits. Prepared foods had to be designated "kosher for Passover," because of the frequent use of additives that might violate the rules. For the most part, this special food was expensive, tasteless, and highly refined. One of the few food treats, for me, was chocolate (which I maintain should be accorded the status of a food group on its own). Chocolate was not a staple in our household, except for this one week when our cupboards were well stocked with kosher-for-Passover chocolate bars.

Again, I fast forward a few decades to 2006, when my doctoral research project was well under way. One morning, while listening to the radio show *The Current*, I heard an interview with journalist Carol Off, who had just had her book, *Bitter Chocolate* (2006), released. In that book, Off traces the development of chocolate as a favourite food item in Western culture for children and adults alike. She also traces the long-standing role of imperialism and slavery in cocoa production, and the legacy of both in today's cocoa-growing and harvesting areas, including the country of Côte d'Ivoire. As I shop for some traditional Passover foods in 2008, I wonder why none of the kosher-for-Passover chocolate available in Vancouver is not also certified fair trade. The irony of buying and consuming a treat that originates with the enslavement of children during a holiday that celebrates freedom from another long-ago enslavement is one example of the multiple, often clashing, discourses, practices, and pedagogies about shopping and consumption that I, like other shoppers, encounter and construct in everyday life. What I have learned about chocolate, globalization, and my own identity exemplifies the promise and desire as well as the trouble and critique of shopping.

Still later in the process of drafting this chapter, I find myself listening to accounts of the Democratic leadership race as it unfolds in the United States. Just as shopping and consumption can be seen as politically charged processes, formal politics in Western societies can also be seen as connected to the arenas of shopping and consumption. The hallmarks of consumer culture—market research, branding, advertising—have been extended to political parties and political candidates. Governing by policy is replaced by governing by polls, and positions are replaced by images. Just as shoppers can be said to vote with their dollars, so, too, can voters be said to shop for politicians. And, just as relations of gender, race, and class are evident in shopping and consumption, so, too, are they in the campaigns, operation, and media accounts of formal politics.

In this Democratic campaign, people insist that the campaign has nothing to do with social characteristics such as gender, race, and class. Barack Obama, the son of a white woman and a black man, who has lived in Hawaii and Asia, portrays himself as, alternately, an American and a citizen of the world. He appeals to a youthful generation of American citizens eager to put racism behind them. As Sarah suggested during her interview with me, racism and race are being discursively elided, so that the reluctance, particularly by individuals who consider themselves so-cially progressive, to be associated with racism becomes reluctance to speak about race. This point is in full agreement with the conclusions of critical race scholars such as Knowles (2003) and Frankenberg (1993).

Thinking back to conversations with other participants, I remember Ellen's frustration with the view that Obama and his steadfast supporter, Oprah Winfrey, are held up as fulfilments of the American Dream and the ability of all American citizens to shed the constraints of a racialized body. As the recent Democratic leadership contest confirmed, though, race remains very much alive in American society. Critical scholars con-clude that Canada's discourse of multiculturalism serves to deflect crit-ical attention away from ongoing racism (Dhruvarajan, 2000) and that social characteristics such as gender continue to function through a con-sumerist culture among other spheres of social life (Currie, 1999).

Likewise, gender relations are evoked during this political campaign, predominantly through the candidacy of Hillary Rodham Clinton. I also recalled another comment that Sarah made during her interview, when she suggested that women have achieved equality with men, at least in Canadian society. This claim, whether made in Canada or in the United States, seems inconsistent with both the disproportionately

high number of Clinton's female supporters, and the way in which mainstream American media continually takes aim at and lampoons Clinton
and the idea of a female president (Seelye & Bosman, 2008).

Class is also active in this Democratic campaign. Clinton is perceived
as the front runner among working-class voters, at least for members
of the white working class. The dilemma for Democratic citizens with
multiple social affiliations does not escape the attention of journalists.
One news article discusses the struggle between "loyalties" (Seelye,
2007) for female African-American Democrats. The participants in my
study might have found it difficult to talk about their class positions,
and Beck (2002 in Crompton, 2006) might describe class as a "zombie
category"; however, the Democratic campaign exemplifies the ongoing
operation of class, as well as gender and race, in Western societies.
These three social categories have unique histories in the social relations
of different countries, but, as the critical scholars cited throughout this
text and my analyses establish, they continue to shape material and cultural relations across the Global North, including in Canada. Despite
ideologies of neoliberalism and consumerism, consumer-citizens cannot
simply elect to extricate themselves from these relations, through either
voting or shopping. Globalization is altering the discourses, meanings,
and experiences of gender, race, and class, but, within Canada as in
other societies, these categories continue to structure social relations
among consumer-citizens.

If that conclusion is accepted, how might this exploration of shopping expand understandings of adults' informal learning about globalization, identity, and the politics of consumer-citizenship? Furthermore,
what does this inquiry contribute to the pursuit of research about globalization in this time of globalization? In Chapter 1, I posed a series
of questions that have guided the development and completion of this
inquiry. ☼ (next page) In the remainder of this chapter, I return to these
questions. Using the analyses discussed in the preceding chapters, I offer
some final reflections in response to these questions, outline some of the
limitations of my analyses and this study in general, and suggest some remaining questions and the potential for further research on these topics.

Conceptualizing Learning: Holistic Learning in Everyday Life

In Chapter 2, I conceptualized a type of learning that is incidental, as
well as holistic. Drawing on the writing of feminist and other critical
adult education scholars, I outlined a notion of learning that can be
based in emotion, sensuality, and spirituality (Dirkx, 2001; English,
2000; Hayes & Flannery, 2000; hooks, 2003; Tisdell, 1998, 2000), as

☼
- How do individuals understand and manifest the idea of "learning" and the potential to learn in the course of daily life?
- How do they learn to find and respond to complicated, obscured consumer information? How is this learning, and how are shopping and consumption practices more generally, integrated into other parts of their lives, including the possibility of social action in response to consumerist globalization?
- How do individuals living in Canadian society, in which a postmodern sensibility and the phenomenon of globalization converge, understand and articulate the implications of their "location" (within cultural milieus, social structures, and geographic places) for their shopping options, constraints, and preferences? Further to studies of the relationships between consumption and citizenship in earlier eras, how do individuals today relate this learning and their consumption to citizenship in the nation-state and "global" citizenship?
- How can "radical" be understood and acted out in the context of complicated identities and social relations, and a complicated phenomenon such as globalization?
- What new meaning might arise for case study methodology, which typically contains a study within a community setting or a specific site, in light of a phenomenon that claims to unbind social relations within and across nation-states? In an era that emphasizes multiple levels of experience—the individual, the local, the national, the regional, and the global—and gives rise to terms such as "glocalization" and "global citizenship," where and how is evidence to be found? How can critical research respond to postmodernism's dismantling of groups and categories?   —guiding questions

well as the intellect emphasized by Foley (1999, 2001) and other critical adult educators (see, for example, Brookfield, 2005). In the chapters that detailed my approaches to and outcomes of data analysis, I applied this conceptualization to illustrate how, indeed, everyday life is replete with sites and sources of such learning. Shopping, understood as the search for, learning about, comparison between, and acquisition of goods and services—typically through purchase but also through swaps or "freecycling"—can become one of these sites. In my analytical pursuit of this argument, I used empirical data from interviews, focus groups, and shopping trips with real-life participants, as well as stories of made-up characters from four popular novels that present discourses, understandings, and experiences of shopping, consumption, and consumerism in the Global North during contemporary globalization. That use of fiction not only provided data for analysis; it also suggests that the reading of fiction and the consumption of other forms of culture can be seen as additional sites of incidental learning apparent in everyday life.

Although I have talked about incidental, holistic learning throughout this text, I recognize that the line between incidental and more intentional learning can become blurred, just like the line between production and consumption. One of the findings that strikes me as noteworthy is that the appearance of a topic on a person's intellectual, emotional, or spiritual "radar screen," in combination with a curious disposition, might encourage a more deliberate learning process. In Ozeki's novel *My Year of Meats* (1998), Jane's initially incidental learning becomes more purposeful as she begins to seek information and conduct research into topics such as the use of growth hormones in cattle. Participants in my study provided several examples of how learning that begins as incidental can become more formalized when they recognize the importance and implications of what they have learned. These participants were aware of such learning, even if they were also becoming aware of its limitations.

Helen Colley, Phil Hodkinson, and Janice Malcolm suggest the possibility of thinking about elements of formality in informal learning and informality in formal learning; indeed, they argue that it might be more productive "to step outside the frames of this contest between formal and informal . . . learning, in which each set of protagonists exaggerates the weaknesses of the opposite case" (2002, p. 9). Academic developments such as community service learning move teaching and learning outside the confines of the classroom and beyond the authority of the teacher, increasing the informality of learning in formal settings.

In this era of contemporary globalization, a hegemonic discourse of lifelong learning has developed. It seems to conflate learning with education and to constrict the recognition of learning by imposing the logic of formality and credentialism on the learning that is most valued. As a site of learning, shopping is located outside the traditional, formal purview of the academy; however, there is a formality imparted into such a site by the social and economic structures and discourses that help shape people's lives and their learning. Still, I have not dispensed with rhetoric of informal learning. It is crucial that discussions of adult education respond to, without simply being guided by, a hegemonic script. If the way to talk about and bring recognition to the breadth and depth of learning that is not accompanied by a credential is to refer to it as informal, then for strategic reasons I am prepared to continue distinguishing between formal and informal learning, even as I note the limitations of that distinction.

My final note on adult learning theory relates to Foley's (1999, 2001) conceptualization of incidental learning, which has been so important to this inquiry. Although Foley emphasizes the incidental learning that emerges through organized, collective action, I have investigated an arena in which individuals seem to learn and act on a more solitary, unorganized basis. As I have uncovered the depth and breadth of learning that occurs in critical shopping, I have extended Foley's conceptualization. Through the use of Anderson's (1991) concept of imagined community, I have also extended the conceptualization of shopping. Shoppers might appear to learn and act in solitude, but they carry a multitude of contacts and affiliations with them into and out of the store. I am not suggesting that there is no distinction between the individual and the collective, only that the division between them—like the division between formal and informal learning, the global and the local, or production and consumption—can be blurred and that such blurring contributes to an enriched understanding of learning, globalization, and change.

Educating Critical Consumer-Citizens

On a general level, my conceptualization of holistic adult learning asserts that there are multiple dimensions of learning. Although I have focused in this inquiry on incidental learning, these dimensions are present in the classroom as well, and I think that this inquiry can contribute to critical adult learning in a formal arena of the classroom. Some of the thoughts that I raise in this section do not arise directly from my data; however, I think that they are important considerations in transferring the findings of this study of informal learning into more formal settings.

Formal education emphasizes the intellectual dimension of learning, but emotional, spiritual, sensual, and experiential ways of knowing do not disappear when learners—and teachers—move from everyday experience into the classroom. In fact, the classroom is itself a setting of everyday experience. Community service learning and other forms of practica, options for creative assignments, and encouraging reflexivity among students and in their own pedagogical practices might be helpful to adult educators seeking a more critical and holistic approach in their classrooms. The work of marino (1997) and Barndt (1999, 2002), both of whom incorporate visual art into their classroom-based and community-based education, offers interesting ideas and exercises.

Littler's (2005) concepts of narcissistic and relational reflexivity are useful to instructors in any course that encourages reflexivity among students. Although reflexivity is often regarded by adult educators as important and beneficial in a blanket way, Littler's concepts and my use of them help clarify that reflexivity can be taken up and put to work in different ways with very different purposes and ends. For feminist and other critical adult educators, it is important to teach about the distinctions between these two forms of reflexivity and encourage relational reflexivity in particular among their students.

The focus of many critical scholars interested in societal transformation is often on oppressed groups living in the margins of society. Fraser's (1992) concept of subaltern counterpublics emphasizes the role of oppressed groups in generating counter-hegemonic critiques and discourses, and Sparks's (1997) concept of dissidence is similarly focused on oppressed groups; however, resistance can emerge from the social middle ground, too. Many of the participants in this study, including me, described themselves as middle class and racially identified as white. On the whole, participants also had relatively high levels of education and career aspirations. In an inquiry into informal learning about the politics of consumption, citizenship, and globalization, these participants and I undoubtedly live with great social privilege. This lack of socio-economic diversity and, to a lesser extent, the lack of racial and gender diversity, point to a major limitation of this study. The best that I can hope to have yielded here is a partial understanding of part of a contemporary phenomenon that helps characterize social life in Canadian society.

Still, in this limitation there is also an opportunity. Chapter 2, in which I conceptualize consumer-citizenship, relates to both critical citizenship and consumer education. My discussion of resistance in that chapter, based on Fraser's (1992) notion of subaltern counterpublics and Sparks's (1997) notion of dissidence, and my application of it in the later analytical chapters might offer some interesting content for courses dealing with either of these topics, as well as the broader topic of globalization. Likewise, the analyses summarized in Chapters 5, 6, and 7 might contain relevant and useful points for courses exploring the workings of resistance, social movements, identity, and learning.

In general, I avoid introducing new concepts or literature in this concluding chapter. The work of Ann Curry-Stevens is the singular exception. My focus in this inquiry has been on informal adult learning, rather than on education, either formal or informal; however, I think that connecting my study to Curry-Stevens's work helps illustrate its implications for critical adult education. Like Gramsci (1971), Curry-Stevens understands that in a democracy with multiple "classes"—expanded to mean social groups—radical change is possible only when the oppressed and their privileged allies come together. Emerging from her empirical research with adult educators engaged in critical or transformative education with privileged learners, Curry-Stevens proposes a six-stage model "that intentionally seeks to engage privileged learners in workshops and classrooms and to assist in their transformation as allies in the struggle for social justice" (2007, p. 33). First echoing the Gramscian understanding about the importance of building alliances, she goes on to provide examples of noteworthy radicals who had enjoyed social privilege, from Mahatma Gandhi to Fidel Castro to Che Guevara to Paulo Freire. ☼

☼ Further support for the role of the privileged in social movements comes from a review of the leaders of revolutionary social and political movements: Fidel Castro with his roots as a student leader and lawyer; Che Guevara as a physician; Paulo Freire, educated in law and later a senior government official in education and culture; Martin Luther King, Jr., an ordained minister who also had earned a PhD; and Mahatma Gandhi, who was born into wealth, studied in Britain, and became a lawyer. The French revolution is understood to have been led by privileged students and the women's suffrage movement by many class-privileged women.
—Ann Curry-Stevens (2007), "New Forms of Transformative Education," pp. 35–36

Curry-Stevens develops the notion of "pedagogy of the privileged," in contrast to a Freirian pedagogy of the oppressed. She outlines the complications in determining who, exactly, is oppressed and who is privileged, given the reality of multiple identities for any individual. ☼ She carefully adopts a "'universal construction' of privilege" (p. 37), which conveys an understanding that both privilege and oppression are present in most people's lives.

☼ Participants in the study added complexity to this binary framework as they recognized that one's identity as privileged or oppressed fluctuates with the context in which one is situated. These educators advocate for a modified binary framework, where one's multiple identities serve to either moderate or exacerbate an experience of privilege, on one hand, and oppression, on the other. When trying to explain the patriarchal experience for a poor, White man, for example, it is helpful to describe his experience of patriarchy being moderated by being White and exacerbated by being poor. In this sense, supplemental identities that are privileged serve as protective devices that typically protect or buffer the individual from bearing the full brunt of that oppression. Similarly, bearing multiple oppressed identities serves to exacerbate or deepen one's experiences of discrimination, marginalization, and powerlessness. Understanding this construction of plural identities can be very helpful to the learner beginning to grapple with these issues.
—Ann Curry-Stevens (2007), "New Forms of Transformative Education," p. 37

However, this does not mean that everybody lives with privilege in equal measure and outcome. Nor is it sufficient to explore the particular oppression experienced by learners who live with relative privilege. According to Curry-Stevens, "Pedagogical applications of the universal construction of privilege will necessitate sufficient focus on each form of domination and, in so doing, decrease learners' tendencies to avoid the gaze that interrogates privilege" (p. 38). Using this approach, critical adult educators can avoid a simplistic "good guys/bad guys" binary and begin to draw even learners with a relatively high degree of privilege into a critical examination of how privilege and oppression are structured, talked about, and lived.

Curry-Stevens develops a preliminary pedagogical model for critical adult educators working with privileged learners. Her model involves a sequence of what she calls "confidence-shaking" and "confidence-building" (2007) among learners. As I have done in this inquiry, she recognizes the intellectual, emotional, and spiritual dimensions of learning. Using different language, she also agrees with Littler's (2005) conclusion that a shift from narcissistic to relational reflexivity, and individualism to collectivity, is necessary for meaningful change. Shifts on all of these dimensions, as well as in identity construction and behaviour, are all part of her educational project. Curry-Stevens's pedagogical model might help critical adult educators interested in consumption and citizenship develop courses and teaching strategies to work with learners, especially in the most privileged learning setting of the university classroom. The application of Curry-Stevens's model in an action research study set in a course exploring consumerism, citizenship, and/or globalization is an intriguing possibility to me.

Finally, I recall Foley's (2001) concern that critical pedagogy itself is being undermined, particularly in formal settings. ☼ Adult education has a long history of engagement in critical analysis and social justice, but this tradition is being increasingly marginalized within the educational sector as hegemonic neoliberalism encourages a human capital understanding of education. That view stresses education for credentialed rather than critical citizens and rewards profitable rather than critical education programs. In response to this shift, evident especially in universities, I call on the leaders of adult education programs and the leaders of educational institutions across Canada to strengthen their resistance to the increasing privatization, corporatization, and commodification of education and learning, and to reinstate critical studies across disciplines and departments to their previous and rightful place in public education at all levels. This can be achieved only by pressing governments at the provincial and federal levels to restore adequate funding for programs that might not be commercially lucrative but create knowledge of profound value for a society of learner-citizens as well as consumer-citizens.

> ☼ I write this paper as a contribution to a tradition which is in danger of being forgotten, at a time where it is sorely needed. A further question: How do we talk about radical adult education in these times, which seem to work only against it?
> —Griff Foley, "Radical Adult Education and Learning," p. 71

Walter (2007) describes the coming together of feminism and environmentalism in Clayoquot Sound during the early 1990s; however, many environmental organizations seem to have been absorbed into the mainstream and have lost sight of the reality that social relations are within, not outside, ecology. For example, Vancouver-based David Suzuki has become an iconographic Canadian spokesperson for the environment. His background has also included civil rights activism, which grew out of his family's internment during the Second World War; however, these concerns are absent in the work of the foundation that bears his name and much of what is recognized as Canada's environmental movement. The effects of poverty and wealth are as great an environmental issue as pollution, global climate change, and food security; in fact, these issues are inextricably linked. Several participants spoke fervently about the need for environmentally sensitive policies and practices but articulated no understanding of how environmental issues are also social issues. Even organizations and actions that still might be regarded as being outside the mainstream, such as Kalle Lasn's *AdBusters* and culture jamming, face criticism for neglecting important issues in their own analyses and critiques.

In his writing, Gramsci (1971) advocates alliance-building between the urban working class and the rural peasantry within the Italian society of his time. The potential for alliance-building has implications for the intellectuals who lead today's movements and organizations which aim to contribute to societal change, as well as the activists who enliven them. Neoliberal ideology discourages such alliances, as it does any kind of group identification and collective action. In my conversations with some participants, the emphasis was on narcissistic reflexivity (Littler, 2005). In conversations with other participants, there were indications of relational reflexivity, but these were accompanied by expressions of frustration with finding ways to put together disparate concerns and agendas, and to respond to dialectical tensions—between preferences and material constraints, between personal practices or circumstances and global conditions, between making change and reiterating the status quo. The presence of these types of reflexivity and frustrations implies that neoliberalism is affecting learning about change, confirming Gramsci's (1971) theory of the educational function of ideology and culture. Additional research investigating how particular organizations and movements encourage reflexive learning in the name of change would continue to build knowledge in this area.

Understanding and Enacting Change

Of all the themes explored in this inquiry, the issue of how to understand and enact radicalism and change remains the least conclusive. Conceptually, it is not difficult to distinguish between radicalism and reform, as Luxemburg (2008) does, but this distinction can seem more difficult to see in practice. There were examples of reformist, individualistic narcissistic reflexivity (Littler, 2005) evident in participants' comments, but these were outnumbered by comments with greater nuance and possibility. The most obvious example of narcissistic reflexivity is Jody's opinion that choosing paper bags rather than plastic bags is a little thing that can "help change the world." Among other things, Gramsci (1971) warns about the adoption of a strategy of pragmatism. Reformism elevates pragmatism to the level of strategy; what matters is seen as whatever seems doable and workable. The problems with this approach, in relation to a discussion of meaningful societal change, seem obvious, but the question of how to actually achieve and validate change is tricky to answer. Sparks's (1997) conceptualization of dissidence helps illustrate the tension between reformism and radicalism, status quo and change.

In her own terms, Lorde (2002) argues that the "tools" of the privileged cannot be used by the oppressed to upset power relations. Bricolage, the methodology employed in this inquiry, takes as its premise that tools do not have set applications. The bricoleur's view that nobody can claim ownership of "tools" has conceptual, as well as methodological, implications. My conversations with participants yielded no firm directives for change. Some participants seemed satisfied with narcissistic reflexivity and reformist ambitions, while others seemed interested in engaging in relational form of reflexivity and pursuing more substantive change. Faced with a combination of multiple ideological discourses and a sense that information is being obscured, participants live with the constant tension between knowing and not being able to know, in a society that also constantly pushes them to learn. As bricoleurs of sorts, participants and other critical shoppers look for ways to learn about the politics of their shopping and consumption and how to enact some form of resistance as they build knowledge and understanding. They understand the limitations of their knowledge, even if they find those limitations frustrating, and they make use of tools for knowledge construction in creative, often unanticipated ways.

The feminist critical scholarship by Barndt and marino extend Gramsci's ideas. marino's (1997) urge to look for "cracks in consent" and Barndt's (2002) ideas on the ordinariness of resistance acknowledge that apparently small actions might reflect great reflexivity and risk and relate to change in unpredictable ways. As Barndt (2002) further clarifies, the tendency to conceptualize resistance in terms of organized, collective action favours the masculinized arena of formal employment and overlooks less organized, more feminized forms of resistance.

Although most participants appreciated that their shopping and consumption had political importance, few spoke at length about the arena of formal politics. Gramsci (1971), Luxemburg (2008), and Holst (2007) explain that a party dedicated to radical purposes is necessary for societal transformation. Several participants spoke about the decline in voting rates and political engagement, although they did not know how to remedy that problem. Critical, holistic adult learning that incorporates critiques of hegemonic ideologies and their associated common sense is, as Gramsci (1971) realizes, a crucial first step in political participation and creation of a party dedicated to transforming society and its unjust social structures.

Protecting Consumer-Citizens

There are, as well, immediate and practical implications of this inquiry for consumer-citizens. In Chapter 5, I discussed the need for consumer literacy, and the confounding nature of information which is provided to shoppers. Labels can contain highly technical information and be difficult to read or understand. In the absence of evenly applied regulations across and beyond Canada, claims of organic production, fair trade and provenance have multiple meanings. Even shoppers who prefer to make certain decisions feel confused and ill informed. Recently proposed changes to regulations governing "Made in Canada" labelling are consistent with the clarity that several participants in this study are seeking and are, in my opinion, a welcome addition to consumer information and protection policies. Further clarification of organic and fair trade claims would similarly support consumer-citizens in their decision making, and should be driven by combined efforts of government and certifying bodies, as well as by organizations concerned with these issues and consumer rights more broadly. Similarly, concerns raised in this inquiry as well as recent stories in mainstream and alternative media about threats to personal health and safety posed by products ranging from plastics to paints, or from cosmetics to genetically modified food demand greater research, regulation (at the federal level in particular) and clarity.

Although they are appropriate and called for, the addition of such policies as well as improvements in consumer information would have a limited impact on the options available to consumer-citizens. As participants confirmed, affordability is still a major concern. Participants' largely middle-class status and urban residence might expand their shopping options, but they recognized their own financial constraints and the constraints on people with even fewer economic resources. Some participants attached these constraints to a broader analysis of globalization. They articulated an awareness of how policy directions such as "free trade" do not expand freedom for consumer-citizens, within and beyond Canada.

☼ Some participants talked about the insidiousness of a discourse of freedom at the World Trade Organization or the World Bank, which aids in the conflation between democracy and capitalism. No policy can protect consumer-citizens against this, but critical learning can provide a degree of inoculation.

☼

Kaela:	Right, okay. Today, shoppers can buy things produced all over the world. What do you think this means for you as a Canadian or as a citizen of another country living in Canada?
Amitah:	Hmmm, well, free trade isn't it? We're in the age of free trade.
Kaela:	Is it free?
Amitah:	Is it free, that's a good question [*chuckles*]. It's not free, is it? It's, well the world seems to be run by corporations these days. And we're told it's good for us, but is it really good for us? We don't see the impact. I think again we end up being disconnected from, um, from the things that we use or consume. We don't see the impact on people or on the planet, again. What does it mean for me here? Well, being in a wealthier country, I think it's our responsibility to use our, I mean the values of this society really are money. It's a money culture, and so that is, sort of, where the power lies. You know, talking about, of course, climate change and global warming and there's a lot people saying, you know, we need a carbon rationing system and we need to make people sort of pay for the carbon units that they use otherwise people will never, never change. Like, but if you have to pay for it . . . oh, you have to start having to make choices, because it's impacting you directly. . . . And it's measurable. So I think that all the cheap goods that are available to us, 99% of which are, is just stuff, we don't need it, it's just stuff to fill up our houses with and then throw out, what [goes into] the landfill . . . later, we need to, we need to really have more, we should be more educated, we should know better. Where am I going with this? What does it mean for me? I think we need to be more responsible, and change the way that we look at those things. And countries seem to be forced into this free trade global economy, and I think that in terms of the global economy it ends up making them dependent on us, and it's not a sustainable economy for other countries, you know, countries that are exporting so much food that they can't feed themselves. . . . But they have to keep exporting . . . to make money, you know. . . . It seems all backwards. So I think there needs to be that awareness, 'cause we're the ones that are buying it.
	—interview excerpt, February 21, 2007

Exploring Globalization

There are interrelated methodological and conceptual lessons emerging from this inquiry. Methodologically, this study confirms that bricolage is an intuitive, creative, cumulative, and practical process. Despite Kincheloe's (2001, 2005) cautions about using bricolage, this inquiry illustrates how case study bricolage and strategies of crystallization (Richardson, 2000) can contribute to the study of complex phenomena such as globalization and learning. Such an approach to research recognizes, works with, and disputes traditional boundaries around what constitute data and between insiderness and outsiderness of a study's researcher, participants, evidence, and disciplinary practice. The theory behind this methodological direction seems especially important to a phenomenon such as globalization in a period such as postmodernism, both of which are associated with a breakdown in borders, identities, *and* traditions.

Although I welcome many of Kincheloe's (2001, 2005) thoughts about bricolage, I am unconvinced that chaos and complexity theories can replace structural theories. For researchers concerned with social and environmental justice, conceptualizations developed from critical, feminist, or other structuralist traditions remain helpful. A central challenge is to incorporate poststructural and postmodern ideas about the fuzziness of boundaries and partiality of identity and truth, without feeding into neoliberal discourse by obviating structures. As critical race theorists such as Twine (2000) argue, race is constructed as people relate to one another in a society, but that does not mean that race is not structured in all societies. As Curry-Stevens (2007) further establishes, in the Global North it is possible to see both privilege and oppression in people's lives, but this does not mean that privilege and oppression no longer have any impact on them. Structures can be fluid and discursively constructed *and* be real and materially present.

Thinking through these ideas has helped me understand what it means to conduct bricolage with rigour. Rigour requires that I begin with ontological, epistemological, and methodological clarity, and I proceed with a commitment to the purpose and questions of the research project. I do not have to pursue a carefully planned and deliberately executed method and can be open to incorporating varied methods, sources of data, and analytical approaches that become apparent as I move through the inquiry. It also means that I am reflective, transparent, and consistent about my ontological, epistemological, and methodological stance.

I have already noted the limitation to this inquiry evident in participants' largely middle-class, white identity and related it to critical consumer and citizenship education. This can also be discussed as a methodological limitation. My framing of this study as centrally concerned with shopping seemed to appeal to participants with middle-class identity or aspirations. The scope of this study's appeal makes sense to me, given the hegemonic construction of shopping as a middle- and upper-class leisure activity. Although at least one of the Vancouver neighbourhoods where I tried to recruit participants—The Drive—is considered ethno-racially diverse, I did not achieve the diversity that I had hoped for. As I noted in Chapter 1, most participants came to the study through listservs or word of mouth, rather than by seeing in-store flyers. Other than the listserv from my department, I have no idea of the composition of the listservs that promoted my study. I am thankful for that promotional assistance, but I wonder if the members of these list-servs are, in the main, white, middle class, and well educated. A second limitation of this study is my decision to focus on shopping for goods. There is an expanding service sector in Western societies, and under-standings and experiences of shopping for services—including adult education itself—might yield interesting and important additions to scholarship in this area.

These methodological limitations point to an associated conceptual limitation. In studies of globalization, the tendency to construct binaries leads to the rhetorical division of the Global North and the Global South. Each side is then associated with other sets of binaries: wealth and pov-erty, privilege and oppression, developed and undeveloped. Participants' identification as middle class or aspiring-to middle class reiterates a problematic refrain of wealthy consumers in the Global North and poor producers in the Global South. It obscures the degree to which there are material and social divides within the Global North. A few participants, notably Amitah and Ellen, articulated an awareness of this fact, but it remained on the periphery of conversations. This fact also tended to remain unacknowledged in the novels that I analyzed, with the excep-tion of Ozeki's *My Year of Meats* (1998). It is something that needs to be intentionally inserted into conceptualization and teaching about glob-alization, as well as consumption and citizenship.

Closing Thoughts

Over the past few decades, the academic field known as cultural studies has developed. Although Raymond Williams, a pioneer in this field, iden-tified as an adult educator, cultural studies has drifted away from adult education. Strongly influenced by Gramsci's writing, Williams (1993) stresses the ordinariness of culture and its importance as a site of learn-ing. ☼ Although shopping and consumption have become popular topics

---

☼ Culture is ordinary: that is the first fact.   —Raymond Williams (1993), "Culture Is Ordinary," p. 90

for cultural studies scholars, the resulting scholarship often overlooks the role of the social in determining and understanding the cultural. This is the problem about which Currie (1999) cautions, and one that I have tried to avoid. In recalling a Gramscian understanding of the dialectical relationship between culture and social life, and the importance of that relationship for both adult learning and societal change, this inquiry represents a sort of reclamation of intellectual territory by adult education.

I titled my introductory chapter "In the Beginning," because it marked the start of this text and outlined the emergence of my interest in this project. Although this chapter marks the end of my study, I prefer to think of it as a mid- rather than an endpoint. As much as I have learned, my questions remain only partially answered. Participants' tendency to identify as middle class, white, and female, as well as my focus on in-store shopping, are two important limitations of this study. How can adult learning be more fully conceptualized and researched? How might other dimensions of learning, such as intuition, which I mention but do not focus on, contribute to such work? How can critical adult education about the dialectics of globalization, citizenship, and consumption be developed and put to use, from the classroom to the advocacy organization? What does change entail, and what is the potential for radicalism in everyday life? What methodological challenges and opportunities emerge in researching learning about and during globalization? This academic project might be done, but my exploration of the ties between adult learning, shopping, citizenship, and globalization is still very much in process.

REFERENCES

Aaronson, S. A. (2001). *Taking trade to the streets: The lost history of public efforts to shape globalization*. Ann Arbor: The University of Michigan Press.

Adamson, W. L. (1980). *Hegemony and revolution: A study of Antonio Gramsci's political and cultural theory*. Berkeley and Los Angeles: University of California Press.

Anderson, B. (1991). *Imagined communities: Reflections on the origin and spread of nationalism* (rev. ed.). London: Verso. (Original work published 1983.)

Appadurai, A. (2000). Disjuncture and difference in the global cultural economy. In D. Held and A. McGrew (Eds.), *The global transformations reader: An introduction to the globalization debate* (pp. 230–238). Cambridge, MA: Polity Press. (Original work published 1990.)

Armstrong, P. (2000). All things bold and beautiful: Researching adult learning through soaps. Paper presented at the 41st Annual Adult Education Research Conference, The University of British Columbia, Vancouver, BC. Available at www.adulterc.org/Proceedings/2000/armstrongp1-final.PDF

——— (2005a). Learning about work through popular culture: The case of office work. In V. Aarkrog and C. H. Jorgensen (Eds.), *Divergence and convergence in education and work*. Bern: Peter Lang. Available at www.education.leeds.ac.uk/research/uploads/70.pdf.

——— (2005b). "Managing" diversity in the workplace: Representation of difference in The Office. In P. Coare et al. (Eds.), *Diversity and difference in lifelong learning. Proceedings of the 35th Annual SCUTREA Conference*, University of Sussex, England, July 5–7, 2005. Available at www.leeds.ac.uk/educol/.

——— (2005c). Satire as critical pedagogy. Paper presented at What a Difference a Pedagogy Makes: Researching Lifelong Learning and Teaching Conference, University of Stirling, Scotland, June 24–26, 2005.Available at www.education.leeds.ac.uk/research/uploads/37.pdf.

At O'Hare, President says "Get on board." (2001, September 27). Remarks by the President to Airline Employees, O'Hare International Airport, Chicago, Illinois. Accessed August 25, 2008, www.whitehouse.gov/news/releases/2001/09/20010927-1.html.

Barndt, D. (1999). Introduction. In the belly of the beast: A moveable feast. In D. Barndt (Ed.), *Women working the NAFTA food chain: Women, food and globalization* (pp. 14–31). Toronto: Sumach Press.

———— (2002). *Tangled routes: Women, work, and globalization on the tomato trail*. Lanham, MD: Rowman & Littlefield Publishers, Inc.

Baudrillard, J. (1998). *The consumer society: Myths and structures*. London: Sage Publications. (Original work published 1970.)

Beck, U. (1992). *Risk society: Towards a new modernity*. London: Sage Publications.

Bello, W. (2002). *Deglobalization: Ideas for a new economy*. Dhaka: University Press Ltd.; Bangkok: White Lotus Co. Ltd.; Nova Scotia: Fernwood Publishing Ltd.; Bangalore: Books for Change; Cape Town: David Philip, London: Zed Books.

Bender, D. E. (2003). "A foreign method of working": Racial degeneration, gender disorder, and the sweatshop danger in America. In D. E. Bender and R. A. Greenwald (Eds.), *Sweatshop USA: The American sweatshop in historical and global perspective* (pp. 19–36). New York: Routledge.

Bergeron, S. (2001). Political economy discourses of globalization and feminist politics. *Signs: Journal of Women in Culture and Society*, 26(4), 983–1006.

Bhachu, P. (2004). *Dangerous designs: Asian women fashion the diaspora economies*. New York: Routledge.

Blakeley, G. (2002). Civil society. In G. Blakeley and V. Bryson (Eds.), *Contemporary political concepts: A critical introduction* (pp. 90–107). London: Pluto Press.

Bocock, R. (1993). *Consumption*. London: Routledge.

Bourdieu, P. (1984). *Distinction: A social critique of the judgement of taste*. Translated by R. Nice. Cambridge, MA: Harvard University Press.

Bowlby, R. (2001). *Carried away: The invention of modern shopping*. New York: Columbia University Press.

Breward, C. (1999). *The hidden consumer: Masculinities, fashion and city life 1860–1914*. Manchester: Manchester University Press.

Brodie, J. (2002). Citizenship and solidarity: Reflections on the Canadian way. *Citizenship Studies*, 4(6), 377–394.

Brookfield, S. (1998). Against naive romanticism: From celebration to the critical analysis of experience. *Studies in Continuing Education*, 29(2), 127–142.

———— (2005). *The power of critical thinking: Liberating adult learning and teaching*. San Francisco: Jossey-Bass.

Callincos, A. T. (2001). *Against the Third Way*. Cambridge: Polity Press; Malden, MA: Blackwell Publishers.

Carroll, W. K. (2003). Undoing the end of history: Canada-centred reflections on the challenge of globalization. In Y. Atasoy and W. K. Carroll (Eds.), *Global shaping and its alternatives* (pp. 33–56). Aurora, ON: Garammond Press Ltd.; Bloomfield, CT: Kumarian Press Inc.

Clover, D. E., and Hall, B. L. (2000). *In search of social movement learning: The growing jobs for living project.* NALL Working paper. Toronto, ON: Institute for Studies in Education, University of Toronto (New Approaches to Lifelong Learning).

Coben, D. (1998). *Radical heroes: Gramcsi, Freire and the politics of adult education.* New York: Garland Publishing, Inc.

Cohen, L. (2003). *A consumers' republic: The politics of mass consumption in postwar America.* New York: Alfred A. Knopf.

Colley, H., Hodkinson, P., and Malcolm, J. (2002). *Non-formal learning: Mapping the conceptual terrain. A consultation report.* Leeds: University of Leeds Lifelong Learning Institute. Available at www.infed.org/archives/etexts/colley_informal_learning.htm.

Collins, P. H. (1997). Comment on Hekman's "Truth and method: Feminist standpoint theory revisited": Where's the power? *Signs: Journal of Women in Culture and Society, 22*(2), 375–381.

Connelly, J., and Prothero, A. (2008). Green consumption: Life-politics, risks and contradictions. *Journal of Consumer Culture, 8*(1), 117–145.

Coupland, D. (1991). *Generation X: Tales for an accelerated culture.* New York: St. Martin's Press.

Crehan, K. (2002). *Gramsci, culture and anthropology.* Berkeley and Los Angeles: University of California Press.

Crompton, R. (2006). Class and family. *Sociological Review, 54*(4), 658–677.

Currie, D. H. (1999). *Girl talk: Adolescent magazines and their readers.* Toronto: University of Toronto Press.

Curry-Stevens, A. (2007). New forms of transformative education: Pedagogy for the privileged. *Journal of Transformative Education, 5*(1), 33–58.

della Porta, D., and Diani, M. (2006). *Social movements: An introduction* (2nd ed.). Malden, MA: Blackwell Publishing.

Denzin, N. K., and Lincoln, Y. S. (2000). Introduction: The discipline and practice of qualitative research. In N. K. Denzin and Y. S. Lincoln (Eds.), *Handbook of qualitative research* (2nd ed.) (pp. 1–29). Thousand Oaks, CA: Sage Publications.

Dhruvarajan, V. (2000). People of colour and national identity in Canada. *Journal of Canadian Studies, 35*(2), 166–175.

———— (2003). Feminism and resistance to globalization of capitalism. In Y. Atasoy and W. K. Carroll (Eds.), *Global shaping and its alternatives* (pp. 179–194). Aurora, ON: Garamond Press Ltd.; Bloomfield, CT: Kumarian Press Inc.

Dillabough, J., and Arnot, M. (2000). Feminist political frameworks: New approaches to the study of gender, citizenship and education. In M. Arnot and J. Dillabough (Eds.), *Challenging democracy: International perspectives on gender, education and citizenship* (pp. 21–40). London: Routledge Falmer.

Dirkx, J. M. (2001). The power of feelings: Emotion, imagination, and the construction of meaning in adult education. *New Directions for Adult and Continuing Education, 89,* 63–72.

DuCille, A. (1999). Black Barbie and the deep play of difference. In M. Shiach (Ed.), *Feminism and cultural studies* (pp. 106–132). Oxford: Oxford University Press.

Elgin, D. (1993). *Voluntary simplicity: Toward a way of life that is outwardly simple, inwardly rich* (rev. ed.). New York: William Morrow and Company Inc.

English, L. M. (2000). Spiritual dimensions of informal learning. *New Directions for Adult and Continuing Education, 85, 29–38.*

Evans, B. (2002). The Third Way. In G. Blakeley and V. Bryson (Eds.), *Contemporary political concepts: A critical introduction* (pp. 145–161). London: Pluto Press.

Eyerman, R., and Jamison, A. (1991). *Social movements: A cognitive approach.* University Park: Pennsylvania State University Press.

Fairey, D., Hanson, C., MacInnes, G., McLaren, A. T., Otero, G., Preibisch, K., and Thompson, M. (2008). *Cultivating farmworker rights: Ending the exploitation of immigrant and migrant farmworkers in BC.* Vancouver, BC: Co-published by the Canadian Centre for Policy Alternatives—BC Office, Justicia for Migrant Workers, Progressive Intercultural Community Services, and the BC Federation of Labour. Accessed September 10, 2008, www.policyalternatives.ca/sites/default/files/uploads/publications/BC_Office_Pubs/bc_2008/bc_farmworkers_full.pdf.

Faulks, K. (2002). Citizenship. In G. Blakeley and V. Bryson (Eds.), *Contemporary political concepts: A critical introduction* (pp. 73–89). London: Pluto Press.

Fine, M. (1998). Working the hyphens: Reinventing Self and Other in qualitative research. In N. K. Denzin and Y. S. Lincoln (Eds.), *The landscape of qualitative research* (pp. 130–155). Thousand Oaks, CA: Sage Publications.

Flyvbjerg, B. (2001). *Making social science matter: Why social inquiry fails and how it can succeed again.* Cambridge, UK: Cambridge University Press.

Foley, G. (1999). Ideology, discourse and learning. In G. Foley (Ed.), *Learning in social action: A contribution to understanding informal education* (pp. 14–26). London: Zed Books Ltd.

——— (2001). Radical adult education and learning. *International Journal of Lifelong Education, 20*(1/2), 71–88.

Frankenberg, R. (1993). *White women, race matters: The social construction of whiteness.* Minneapolis: Minnesota University Press.

Fraser, N. (1992). Rethinking the public sphere: A contribution to the critique of actually existing democracy. In C. Calhoun (Ed.), *Habermas and the public sphere* (pp. 109–142). Cambridge, MA: The MIT Press.

——— (2003). Rethinking recognition: Overcoming displacement and reification in cultural politics. In B. Hobson (Ed.), *Recognition struggles and social movements* (pp. 21–34). Cambridge: Cambridge University Press.

Fridell, G. (2007). *Fair trade coffee: The prospects and pitfalls of market-driven social justice.* Toronto: University of Toronto Press.

Gabriel, Y., and Lang, T. (2006). *The unmanageable consumer* (2nd ed.) London: Sage Publications.

Gairey, H. (1984). A black man's Toronto. *Polyphony* (a publication of the Multicultural History Society of Ontario), pp. 237–239. Accessed August 7, 2008, www.tgmag.ca/magic/mt70.html.

Giddens, A. (1998). After the left's paralysis. *New Statesman, 127*(4383), 18–21. Accessed March 5, 2006, Academic Search Premier.

——— (1999a). *Runaway world: How globalisation is reshaping our lives.* London: Profile Books Ltd.

——— (1999b). Why the old left is wrong on equality. *New Statesman,* October 25, 1999, 25–27.

Givhan, R. (2005, June 24). Oprah and the view from outside Paris' Hermes door. Accessed February 6, 2008, washingtonpost.com, www.washington post.com/wpdyn/content/article/2005/06/23/AR2005062302086.html.

Gramsci, A. (1971). *Selections from the Prison Notebooks* (Q. Hoare and G. Nowell Smith, Eds. and Trans.). New York: International Publishers.

Grewal, I. (2005). *Transnational America: Feminisms, diasporas, neoliberalisms.* Durham, NC: Duke University Press.

Grimes, K. (2005). Changing the rules of trade with global partnerships: The fair trade movement. In J. Nash (Ed.), *Social movements: An anthropological reader* (pp. 237–248). Malden, MA: Blackwell Publishers.

Haiven, M. (2007). Privatized resistance: *AdBusters* and the culture of neoliberalism. *The Review of Education, Pedagogy, and Cultural Studies, 29,* 85–110.

Hall, S. (1991). Postscript: Gramsci and us. In R. Simon, *Gramsci's political thought: An introduction* (rev. ed.) (pp. 114–130). London: Lawrence and Wishart.

Hao, R. (2006). And now a word from our sponsors: Feminism for sale. In L. Jervis and A. Zeisler (Eds.), *Bitchfest: Ten years of cultural criticism from the pages of Bitch magazine* (pp. 111–115). New York: Farrar, Straus and Giroux. (Original work published 1998.)

Harding, S. (1987a). Conclusion: Epistemological questions. In S. Harding (Ed.), *Feminism and methodology* (pp. 181–190). Bloomington: Indiana University Press; Milton Keynes, UK: Open University Press.

——— (1987b). Introduction: Is there a feminist method? In S. Harding (Ed.), *Feminism and methodology* (pp. 1–14). Bloomington: Indiana University Press; Milton Keynes, UK: Open University Press.

——— (1997). Comment on Hekman's "Truth and method: Feminist standpoint theory revisited": Whose standpoint needs the regimes of truth and reality? *Signs: Journal of Women in Culture and Society, 22*(2), 382–391.

Harper, D. (1998). An argument for visual sociology. In J. Prosser (Ed.), *Image-based research: A sourcebook for qualitative researchers* (pp. 22–41). London: RoutledgeFalmer.

Harrison, G. (2002). Globalisation. In G. Blakeley and V. Bryson (Eds.), *Contemporary political concepts: A critical introduction* (pp. 14–34). London: Pluto Press.

Hartsock, N. C. M. (1987). The feminist standpoint: Developing the ground for a specifically feminist historical materialism. In S. Harding (Ed.), *Feminism and methodology* (pp. 157–180). Bloomington: Indiana University Press; Milton Keynes, UK: Open University Press.

——— (1997). Comment on Hekman's "Truth and method: Feminist standpoint theory revisited": Truth or justice? *Signs: Journal of Culture and Society*, 22(21), 367–374.

Hawthorne, S. (2004). Wild politics: Beyond globalization. *Women's Studies International Forum*, 27(3), 245–259.

Hayes, E., and Flannery, D. (2000). *Women as learners: The significance of gender in adult learning*. San Francisco: Jossey-Bass.

Hearn, J., and Roseneil, S. (1999). Consuming cultures: Power and resistance. In J. Hearn and S. Roseneil (Eds.), *Consuming cultures: Power and resistance* (pp. 1–13). London: MacMillan Press Ltd., New York: St. Martin's Press, Inc.

Heath, J., and Potter, A. (2004). *The rebel sell: Why the culture can't be jammed*. Toronto: Harper Perennial.

Hekman, S. (1997). Truth and method: Feminist standpoint theory revisited. *Signs: Journal of Women in Culture and Society*, 22(2), 341–365.

Hilton, M. (2003). *Consumerism in twentieth-century Britain: The search for a historical movement*. Cambridge: Cambridge University Press.

——— (2005). The duties of citizens, the rights of consumers. *Consumer Policy Review*, 15(1), 6–12.

Hilton, M., and Daunton, M. (2001). Material politics: An introduction. In M. Daunton and M. Hilton (Eds.), *The politics of consumption: Material culture and citizenship in Europe and America* (pp. 1–32). Oxford: Berg.

Holford, J. (1995). Why social movements matter: Adult education theory, cognitive praxis, and the creation of knowledge. *Adult Education Quarterly*, 45(2), 95–111.

Holst, J. D. (2007). The politics and economics of globalization and social change in radical adult education: A critical review of recent literature. *Journal for Critical Education Policy Studies*, 5(1). Accessed March 25, 2008, www.jceps.com/?pageID=article&articleID=91.

hooks, b. (2001). Eating the other: Desire and resistance. In M. G. Durham and D. Kellner (Eds.), *Media and cultural studies: Key works* (pp. 424–438). Malden, MA: Blackwell Publishers Ltd. (Original work published 1992.)

——— (2003). *Teaching community: A pedagogy of hope*. New York: Routledge.

Huws, U. (2004). Material world: The myth of the "weightless economy." In A. Zuege, M. Konings, C. Leys, and L. Panitch (Eds.), *The globalization decade: A critical reader* (pp. 221–244). London: The Merlin Press; Canada: Fernwood Press.

Ives, P. (2004). *Language and hegemony in Gramsci*. London: Pluto Press; Winnipeg: Fernwood Publishing.

Jacobs, M. (2003). Pocketbook politics: Democracy and the market in twentieth-century America. In M. Jacobs, W. J. Novak, and J. E. Zelizer (Eds.), *The democratic experiment: New directions in American political history* (pp. 250–275). Princeton, NJ: Princeton University Press.

Janesick, V. J. (2000). The choreography of qualitative research design: Minuets, improvisations, and crystallization. In N. K. Denzin and Y. S. Lincoln (Eds.), Handbook of qualitative research (2nd ed.) (pp. 379–399). Thousand Oaks, CA: Sage Publications.

Jarvis, C. A. (1998). The contribution of teaching, textual interpretation and pedagogical research to understanding the development of critical consciousness. Paper presented at the 28th Annual Standing Committee on University Teaching and Research in the Education of Adults Conference, July 6–8, 1998, Exeter. Available at www.leeds.ac.uk/educol/.

———— (2000). Reading and knowing: How the study of literature affects adults' beliefs about knowledge. International Journal of Lifelong Education, 19(6), 535–547.

———— (2003). Desirable reading: The relationship between women students' lives and their reading practices. Adult Education Quarterly, 53(4), 261–276.

———— (2005). Real stakeholder education? Lifelong learning in the Buffyverse. Studies in the Education of Adults, 37(1), 31–47.

Jubas, K. (2007). Conceptual con/fusion in democratic societies: Understandings and limitations of consumer-citizenship. Journal of Consumer Culture, 7(2), 231–254.

Katz, C. (2001). On the grounds of globalization: A topography for feminist political engagement. Signs: Journal of Women in Culture and Society, 26(4), 1213–1234.

Kehoe, K. (2003). The praxis prism: The epistemology of Antonio Gramsci. Cork Online Law Review, 2. Published by the University College Cork, Ireland. Accessed February 1, 2006, http://colr.ucc.ie/2003ix.html.

Kenway, J. (2001). Remembering and regenerating Gramsci. In K. Weiler (Ed.), Feminist engagement: Reading, resisting and revisioning male theorists in education and cultural studies (pp. 47–65). New York: Routledge.

Kenway, J., and Bullen, E. (2001). Consuming children: Education, advertising, entertainment. Buckingham: Open University Press.

Kiely, R. (2005). The clash of globalisations: Neo-liberalism, the Third Way and anti-globalisation. Leiden, The Netherlands; Boston: Brill.

Kilgore, D. W. (1999). Understanding learning in social movements: A theory of collective learning. International Journal of Lifelong Education, 18(3), 191–202.

Kincheloe, J. L. (2001). Describing the bricolage: Conceptualizing a new rigor in qualitative research. Qualitative Inquiry, 7(6), 679–692.

———— (2005). On to the next level: Continuing the conceptualization of the bricolage. Qualitative Inquiry, 11(3), 323–350.

Kinsella, S. (n.d.). Interview on shopaholic & sister. Published on the Transworld Publishers website. Accessed May 28, 2008, www.booksattransworld.co.uk/catalog/interview.htm?command=search&db=twmain.txt&eqisbndata=0593052412.

———— (2001). Confessions of a shopaholic. New York: Dell.

Klein, N. (2000). *No logo: Taking aim at the brand bullies*. Toronto: Knopf Canada.

Knowles, C. (2003). *Race and social analysis*. London: Sage Publications.

Lasn, K. (1999). *Culture jam: How to reverse America's suicidal consumer bing—and why we must*. New York: Quill/Harper Collins Publishers.

Letherby, G. (2003). *Feminist research in theory and practice*. Buckingham: Open University Press.

Lincoln, Y. S., and Guba, E. (2000). Paradigmatic controversies, contradictions and emerging confluences. In N. K. Denzin and Y. S. Lincoln (Eds.), *Handbook of qualitative research* (2nd ed.) (pp. 163–188). Sage Publications.

Lister, R. (2003). *Citizenship: Feminist perspectives* (2nd ed.). New York: New York University Press.

Littler, J. (2005). Beyond the boycott: Anti-consumerism, cultural change and the limits of reflexivity. *Cultural Studies, 19*(2), 227–252.

Lorde, A. (2002). The master's tools will never dismantle the master's house. Comments at "The personal and the political" panel, Second Sex Conference, October 29, 1979. In C. L. Moraga and G. Anzaldúa (Eds.), *This bridge called my back: Writings by radical women of color* (3rd ed.) (pp. 106–109). Berkeley: Third Woman Press. (Original work published 1980.)

Luxemburg, R. (2008 [1908]). Reform or revolution. In H. Scott (Ed.), *The essential Rosa Luxemburg: Reform or revolution and the mass strike*. Chicago: Haymarket Books. (Original work published 1908.)

marino, d. (1997). *Wild garden: Art, education, and the culture of resistance*. Toronto: Between the Lines.

Marshall, T. H. (1992). Citizenship and social class. In T. H. Marshall and T. Bottomore, *Citizenship and social class* (pp. 3–51). London: Pluto Press. (Original work published 1950.)

Marsick, V. J., and Watkins, K. E. (2001). Informal and incidental learning. *New Directions for Adult and Continuing Education, 89*, 25–34.

Martens, L. (2005). Learning to consume—consuming to learn: Children at the interface between consumption and education. *British Journal of Sociology of Education, 26*(3), 343–357.

Marvasti, A., and Faircloth, C. (2002). Writing the exotic, the authentic, and the moral: Romanticism as discursive resource for the ethnographic text. *Qualitative Inquiry, 8*(6), 760–784.

Mayo, P. (1999). *Gramsci, Freire and adult education: Possibilities for transformative action*. London: Zed Books.

Mayor Giuliani announces details on further opening of Lower Manhattan for Monday, September 17, 2001. (2001, September 16). Release 315-01b. Accessed July 8, 2006, the *Archives of the Mayor's Press Office*, www.nyc.gov/html/om/html/2001b/pr315-01b.html.

McLaren, P. (2001). Bricklayers and bricoleurs: A Marxist addendum. *Qualitative Inquiry, 7*(6), 700–705.

Meyer, C. B. (2001). A case in case study methodology. *Field Methods, 13*(4), 329–352.

Michaels, W. B. (2006). *The trouble with diversity: How we learned to love identity and ignore inequality.* New York: Metropolitan Books.

Micheletti, M. (2003). Shopping as political activity. *Access, 9.* Accessed May 18, 2008, www.access.se/english/2003/09/theme_shopping.php.htm.

Midgley, C. (1992). *Women against slavery: The British campaigns, 1780–1870.* London: Routledge.

Mies, M. (1986). *Patriarchy and accumulation on a world scale: Women in the international division of labour.* London: Zed Books.

Moffatt, D., and Morgan, M. L. (1999). Women as organizers: Building confidence and community through food. In D. Barndt (Ed.), *Women working the NAFTA food chain: Women, food and globalization* (pp. 222–236). Toronto: Sumach Press.

Mohanty, C. T. (2002). "Under Western eyes" revisited: Feminist solidarities through anticapitalist struggles. *Signs: Journal of Women in Culture and Society, 28*(2), 499–535.

Morrow, R. A., and Brown, D. D. (1994). *Critical theory and methodology.* Thousand Oaks, CA: Sage Publications.

Mort, F. (1990). The politics of consumption. In S. Hall and M. Jacques (Eds.), *New times: The changing face of politics in the 1990s* (pp. 160–172). London: Verso.

———— (2006). Competing domains: Democratic subjects and consuming subjects in Britain and the United States since 1945. In F. Trentman (Ed.), *The making of the consumer: Knowledge, power and identity in the modern world.* Oxford: Berg.

Morton, A. D. (1999). On Gramsci. *Politics, 19*(1), 1–8.

Moving forward with courage. (2001, October 10). Accessed August 25, 2008, *Archives of the Mayor's Weekly Column,* www.nyc.gov/html/records/rwg/html/2001b/weekly/wkly1010.html.

Naples, N. A. (2003). *Feminism and method: Ethnography, discourse analysis, and activist research.* New York: Routledge.

Nava, M. (1999). Consumerism reconsidered: Buying and power. In M. Shiach (Ed.), *Feminism and cultural studies* (pp. 45–64). Oxford: Oxford University Press. (Original work published 1991.)

Neilsen, L. (2002). Learning from the liminal: Fiction as knowledge. *The Alberta Journal of Educational Research, XLVIII*(3), 206–214.

Nesbit, T. (2006). What's the matter with social class? *Adult Education Quarterly, 56*(3), 171–187.

Off, C. (2006). *Bitter chocolate: Investigating the dark side of the world's most seductive sweet.* Toronto: Random House Canada.

Ong, A. (2004). Cultural citizenship as subject-making: Immigrants negotiate racial and cultural boundaries in the United States. In L. D. Baker (Ed.), *Life in America: Identity and everyday experience* (pp. 156–178). Malden, MA: Blackwell Publishers.

Ontario Ministry of the Environment. (2002, Sept. 16). Municipal 3Rs in Ontario: 2001. Fact sheet. Accessed January 20, 2008, www.ene.gov.on.ca/programs/4148e01.pdf.

Ozeki, R. (1998). *My year of meats*. New York: Penguin Books.

Panitch, L. (2004). Globalization and the state. In A. Zuege, M. Konings, C. Leys, and L. Panitch (Eds.), *The globalization decade: A critical reader* (pp. 9–43). London: The Merlin Press; Black Point, Canada: Fernwood Publishing.

Parreñas, R. S. (2001). Transgressing the nation-state: The partial citizenship and "imagined (global) community" of migrant Filipina domestic workers. *Signs: Journal of Women in Culture and Society, 26*(4), 1129–1154.

Paterson, M. (2006). *Consumption and everyday life*. London: Routledge.

Patton, M. Q. (2002). *Qualitative research and evaluation methods* (3rd ed.). Thousand Oaks, CA: Sage Publications.

Penn, G. (2000). Semiotic analysis of still images. In M. W. Bauer and G. Gaskell (Eds.), *Qualitative researching with text, image, and sound: A practical handbook* (pp. 227–245). London: Sage Publications.

Peräkylä, A. (2006). Analyzing talk and text. In N. K. Denzin and Y. S. Lincoln (Eds.), *Handbook of qualitative research* (3rd ed.) (pp. 869–886). Thousand Oaks, CA: Sage Publications, Inc.

Petras, J., and Veltmeyer, H. (2001). *Globalization unmasked: Imperialism in the 21st century*. Black Point, Canada: Fernwood Publishing Ltd.; London: Zed Books Ltd.

Pollay, R. W. (1986). The distorted mirror: Reflections on the unintended consequences of advertising. *Journal of Marketing, 50*(2), 18–36.

Radical. (2000). *The American heritage dictionary of the English language* (4th ed.). Boston: Houghton Mifflin. Accessed May 21, 2008, www.thefreedictionary.com/radical.

Rappaport, E. D. (2000). *Shopping for pleasure: Women in the making of London's West End*. Princeton, NJ: Princeton University Press.

Recycling Council of Ontario. (1999, October). 3Rs terminology and symbols. Accessed January 20, 2008, www.p2pays.org/ref/20/19914.pdf.

Richardson, L. (2000). Writing: A method of inquiry. In N. K. Denzin and Y. S. Lincoln (Eds.), Handbook of qualitative research (2nd ed.) (pp. 923–948). Thousand Oaks, CA: Sage Publications.

———— (2001). Getting personal: Writing-stories. *Qualitative Studies in Education, 14*(1), 33–38.

Roundtable on Sustainable Palm Oil. (2004, May 8). New global initiative to promote sustainable palm oil. Press statement. Roundtable on Sustainable Palm Oil: Kuala Lampur. Accessed May 12, 2008, www.sustainable-palmoil.org.

Roy, A. (2001). *Power politics*. Cambridge, MA: South End Press.

Sandlin, J. A. (2000). The politics of consumer education materials used in adult literacy classrooms. *Adult Education Quarterly, 50*(4), 289–307.

———— (2004). Consumerism, consumption, and critical consumer education for adults. *New Directions for Adult and Continuing Education, 102*, 25–34.

———— (2005a). Culture, consumption, and critical consumer education for adults: Refashioning consumer education for adults as a political site using a cultural studies framework. *Adult Education Quarterly, 55*(3), 165–181. Available at http://aeq.sagepub.com/cgi/reprint/55/3/165.

Sandlin, J. A. (2005b). "Spend smart, live rich?": A critical analysis of the consumer education lifestyle magazine Budget Living and its readers' forums. Presentation at the 46th Annual Adult Education Research Conference, June 2–5, 2005, University of Georgia at Athens, GA. Accessed August 29, 2006, www.adulterc.org/Proceedings/2005/Proceedings/Sandlin.PDF.

———— (2007). Popular culture, cultural resistance, and anticonsumption activism: An exploration of culture jamming as critical adult education. *New Directions for Adult and Continuing Education*, 115, 73–82.

Sassatelli, R. (2006). Virtue, responsibility and consumer choice: Framing critical consumerism. In J. Brewer and F. Trentmann (Eds.), *Consuming cultures, global perspectives: Historical trajectories, transnational exchanges* (pp. 219–250). Oxford: Berg.

Sassoon, A. S. (2001). Globalisation, hegemony and passive revolution. *New Political Economy*, 6(1), 5–17.

Satterthwaite, A. (2001). *Going shopping: Consumer choice and community consequence*. New Haven, CT: Yale University Press.

Saukko, P. (2003). *Doing research in cultural studies: An introduction to classical and new methodological approaches*. London: Sage Publications.

Schensul, J. J., and LeCompte, M. D. (1999). *Enhanced ethnographic methods: Audiovisual techniques, focused group interviews, and elicitation techniques*. Walnut Creek, CA: AltaMira Press.

Scott, H. (2008). Introduction. In *The essential Rosa Luxemburg*. Chicago: Haymarket Books.

Scott, J., and Marshall, G. (Eds.) (2005). *Oxford dictionary of sociology* (3rd ed.) Oxford: Oxford University Press.

Seelye, K. Q. (2007, October 14). Clinton-Obama quandary for many black women. Accessed July 19, 2008, *The New York Times*, www.nytimes.com/2007/10/14/us/politics/14carolina.html?hp.

Seelye, K. Q., and Bosman, J. (2008, June 13). Media charged with sexism in Clinton coverage. Accessed July 19, 2008, *The New York Times*, www.nytimes.com/2008/06/13/us/politics/13women.html?_r=1&adxnnl=1&ref=media&adxnnlx=1216501442-ATz1N/QUHBrKko8LZnQ6mw&oref=slogin.

Shaw, D. (2007). Consumer voters in imagined communities. *International Journal of Sociology and Social Policy*, 27(3/4), 135–150.

Shiva, V. (2005). *Earth democracy: Justice, sustainability, and peace*. Cambridge, MA: South End Press.

Shor, I. (1980). *Critical teaching and everyday life*. Boston: South End Press.

Simon, R. (1991). *Gramsci's political thought: An introduction* (rev. ed.). London: Lawrence and Wishart.

Skeggs, B. (2004). *Class, self, culture*. London: Routledge.

Smith, D. E. (1987). *The everyday world as problematic: A feminist sociology*. Boston: Northeastern University Press.

———— (1997). Comment on Hekman's "Truth and method: Feminist standpoint theory revisited." *Signs: Journal of Women in Culture and Society*, 22(2), 392–398.

Smith, D. E. (1999). *Writing the social: Critique, theory, and investigations*. Toronto: University of Toronto Press.

Sparks, H. (1997). Dissident citizenship: Democratic theory, political courage, and activist women. *Hypatia, 12*(4), 74–110.

Spring, J. (2003). *Educating the consumercitizen: A history of the marriage of schools, advertising, and media*. Malwah, NJ: Lawrence Erlbaum Associates.

Strine, Mary S. (1991). Critical theory and "organic" intellectuals: Reframing the work of cultural critique. *Communication Monographs, 58*, 195–201.

Sturman, A. (1999). Case study methods. In J. P. Keeves and G. Lakomski (Eds.), *Issues in educational research*. Amsterdam: Pergamon.

Sussman, C. (2000). *Consuming anxieties: Consumer protest, gender, and British slavery, 1713–1833*. Stanford, CA: Stanford University Press.

Thompson, P. M. (2007). The influence of popular culture and entertainment media of adult education. *New Directions for Adult and Continuing Education, 115*, 83–90.

Tisdell, E. J. (1998). Poststructural feminist pedagogies: The possibilities and limitations of feminist emancipatory adult learning theory and practice. *Adult Education Quarterly, 48*(3), 139–156.

——— (2000). Spirituality and emancipatory adult education in women adult educators for social change. *Adult Education Quarterly, 50*(4), 308–335.

Tisdell, E. J., and Thompson, P. M. (2007). "Seeing from a different angle": The role of pop culture in teaching for diversity and critical media literacy in adult education. *International Journal of Lifelong Education, 26*(6), 651–673.

Townley, G. (2006). *Learning curves*. New York: Ballentine Books.

Twine, F. W. (2000). Racial ideologies and racial methodologies. In F. W. Twine and J. W. Warren (Eds.), *Racing research, researching race: Methodological dilemmas in critical race studies* (pp. 1–34). New York: New York University Press.

University of British Columbia. (2006). Policy number 89: Research and other studies involving human subjects. Accessed January 26, 2008, www.universitycounsel.ubc.ca/policies/policy89.pdf.

Villagomez, M. D. (1999). Grassroots responses to globalization: Mexican women's urban and rural collective alternatives. In D. Barndt (Ed.), *Women working the NAFTA food chain: Women, food and globalization* (pp. 209–220). Toronto: Sumach Press.

Walby, S. (2003). The myth of the nationstate: Theorizing society and polities in a global era. *Sociology, 37*(3), 529–546.

Walter, P. (2007). Adult learning in new social movements: Environmental protest and the struggle for the Clayoquot Sound rainforest. *Adult Education Quarterly, 57*(3), 248–263.

Walters, S. (2005). Social movements, class, and adult education. *New Directions for Adult and Continuing Education, 106*, Summer 2005, 53–62.

Werbner, P., and YuvalDavis, N. (1999). Introduction: Women and the new discourse of citizenship. In N. YuvalDavis and P. Werbner (Eds.), *Women, citizenship and difference* (pp. 1–38). London: Zed Books.

Williams, R. (1980). *Culture and materialism*. London: Verso.

—— (1993). Culture is ordinary. In J. McIlroy and S. Westwood (Eds.), *Border country: Raymond Williams in adult education* (pp. 89–102). Leicester: National Institute of Adult Continuing Education. (Original work published 1958.)

Wright, R. R. (2006). A different definition of "boobtube": What Dr. Catherine Gale, of *The Avengers*, taught women. In M. Hagen and E. Goff (Eds.), *Proceedings of the 47th Annual Adult Education Research Conference* (pp. 471–476), May 19–21, 2006, Minneapolis.

—— (2007). *The Avengers*, public pedagogy, and the development of British women's consciousness. *New Directions for Adult and Continuing Education, 115*, 63–72.

Zukin, S. (2005). *Point of purchase: How shopping changed American culture*. New York: Routledge.

Zukin, S., and Maguire, J. S. (2004). Consumers and consumption. *Annual Review of Sociology, 30*, 173–197.

ABOUT THE AUTHOR

Kaela Jubas is an Assistant Professor in the Faculty of Education at the University of Calgary, specializing in adult learning. She earned her PhD in educational studies from the University of British Columbia in 2009. Her research and teaching interests relate to consumption, popular culture, work, and other aspects of everyday life as sources of informal adult learning about the complications of identity and social change.